Literature and Religion
In the Later Middle Ages

Philological Studies in Honor of

SIEGFRIED WENZEL

Literature and Religion In the Later Middle Ages

Philological Studies in Honor of

SIEGFRIED WENZEL

Edited by

RICHARD G. NEWHAUSER

and

JOHN A. ALFORD

Medieval & Renaissance Texts & Studies
Binghamton, New York
1995

Library of Congress Cataloging-in-Publication Data

Literature and religion in the later Middle Ages : philological studies in honor of Siegfried Wenzel / edited by Richard Newhauser and John A. Alford.
    p. cm. — (Medieval & Renaissance texts & studies ; v. 118)
    Includes bibliographical references and index.
    ISBN 0-86698-172-1
    1. Christian literature, English (Middle)—History and criticism. 2. Christian literature, Latin (Medieval and modern)—History and criticism. 3. English philology—Middle English, 1100-1500. 4. Latin philology, Medieval and modern. 5. Religion and literature. I. Newhauser, Richard, 1947- . II. Alford, John A., 1938- . III. Wenzel, Siegfried. IV. Series.
PR275.R4L58 1994
820.9'382—dc20   94-9465
                                                          CIP

Printed in the United States of America

mediEval & RENAiSSANCE
TExTS & STUDiES

VOLUME 118

Tabula Gratulatoria

John A. Alford

David Anderson

Stephen A. Barney

Peter G. Beidler

Larry D. Benson

Robert G. Benson

Thomas H. Bestul

Charles Blyth

Joan Heiges Blythe

Marie E. Borroff

Betsy Bowden

David Lorenzo Boyd

Leonard E. Boyle, O.P.

George H. and
    Phyllis R. Brown

Ronald E. Buckalew

Martin J. Camargo

Lawrence M. Clopper

Thomas H. Connolly

Giles Constable

Stanley J. Damberger

Helen Damico

Ruth Dean

James A. Devereux, S.J.

A. I. Doyle

Hoyt N. Duggan

Patricia J. Eberle
    and John Leyerle

Kent Emery, Jr.

Eugene Falk

Joerg and Renate Fichte

John Hurt Fisher

Allen J. Frantzen

Delores Warwick Frese

Helmut Gneuss

Joseph Goering

Judah and Grace Goldin

Ralph Hanna, III

Albert E. Hartung

Thomas John Heffernan

Thomas D. Hill

John C. Hirsh

Henry Hoenigswald and
    Gabriele Hoenigswald

Patrick J. Horner

Anne Hudson

Edward B. Irving

James John

George Kane

Carol Kaske

Edward Donald Kennedy

Georg Knauer

Robert E. Lewis

Erica Lindemann

Albert Lloyd

E. Ann Matter

Paul and Ann Meyvaert

Anne Middleton

Walter Naumann

Richard G. Newhauser

James O'Donnell

Glending Olson

Kurt Olsson

Lee Patterson

Derek Pearsall

Richard Pfaff

Julian G. Plante

Dale B. J. Randall

Karl J. Reichl

Carter Revard

Florence H. Ridley

Wolfgang Riehle

George Rigg

Fred C. Robinson

William Elford Rogers

Mary A. Rouse
    and Richard H. Rouse

Howard H. Schless

Albrecht Strauss

Michael Twomey

University of Pennsylvania:
    Dean of the School of
        Arts and Sciences
    Department of English
    Department of Religious
        Studies

Linda Ehrsam Voigts

Christina von Nolcken

Luke Wenger

Edward Wilson

James I. Wimsatt

Joseph S. Wittig

Susan Yager

Table of Contents

Tabula Gratulatoria vi

Introduction 1

Chaucer

THEO STEMMLER *Chaucer's Ballade "To Rosemounde"*
—a Parody? 11

PIERO BOITANI *"My Tale is of a Cock," or The*
Problems of Literal Interpretation 25

EDWARD B. IRVING, JR. *Heroic Worlds: "The Knight's Tale"*
and "Beowulf" 43

ALBERT E. HARTUNG *"The Parson's Tale" and Chaucer's*
Penance 61

Piers Plowman

RALPH HANNA III *Robert the Ruyflare and His Companions* 81

JOHN A. ALFORD *Langland's Exegetical Drama: The Sources*
of the Banquet Scene in "Piers Plowman" 97

JOAN HEIGES BLYTHE *Sins of the Tongue and Rhetorical*
Prudence in "Piers Plowman" 119

Pastoral Literature

JOSEPH GOERING *The Summa "Qui bene presunt" and Its*
Author 143

A. G. RIGG *"De motu et pena peccandi": A Latin Poem*
on the Causes and Effects of Sin 161

A. I. DOYLE *"Lectulus noster floridus": An Allegory of the Penitent Soul* 179

CHRISTINA VON NOLCKEN *A "Certain Sameness" and Our Response to It in English Wycliffite Texts* 191

Scripture and Homiletics

A. J. MINNIS *Medium and Message: Henry of Ghent on Scriptural Style* 209

KENT EMERY, JR. *Monastic "Collectaria" from the Abbey of St. Trudo (Limburg) and the Reception of Writings by Denys the Carthusian* 237

D. L. D'AVRAY *Philosophy in Preaching: The Case of a Franciscan Based in Thirteenth-Century Florence (Servasanto da Faenza)* 263

DAVID ANDERSON *"Dominus Ludovicus" in the Sermons of Jacobus of Viterbo (Arch. S. Pietro D. 213)* 275

Lyric Poetry

KARL REICHL *"No more ne willi wiked be": Religious Poetry in a Franciscan Manuscript (Digby 2)* 297

RICHARD NEWHAUSER *"Strong it is to flitte"—A Middle English Poem on Death and Its Pastoral Context* 319

Siegfried Wenzel — List of Publications 337

Bibliographies

Manuscript References 347

Works Cited 351

Index 393

Literature and Religion
In the Later Middle Ages

Introduction

THE ESSAYS IN THIS VOLUME are presented to Siegfried Wenzel as our way of assessing and appreciating those concerns of philological scholarship in medieval studies of which he has been a leading practitioner for three decades. It is particularly important at this point in the development of medieval disciplines within the academy to recall that philology, in the terms in which Professor Wenzel himself has presented the case, will remain the foundation for all of our future insights into literary discourse (cf. "Reflections on [New] Philology," *Speculum* 65 [1990]: 11–18). Recently developed forms of elucidating literary texts as cultural, political, psychological, and gender-marked documents have proved to be valuable to the medieval community, but their starting point must be a philological analysis of the text if they hope to make a lasting contribution to the understanding of literature and its contexts. The approaches that have come after philology are perfectly valid and have a firm place in the history of literary and cultural studies, but they will not supersede philology. The essays in this volume not only represent a continuation of scholarship in the areas of Professor Wenzel's interests but also serve as a reminder of the vitality and continuity of the philological orientation at the heart of that scholarship.

The diversity of the areas touched on by philology understood in its most inclusive terms is indicated by the breadth of Professor Wenzel's published scholarship (see the bibliography of his works at the end of this volume): from the literary analysis of canonized texts (for example, Chaucer's *Troilus*) to an archaeology of the literary artifacts of popular culture (particularly lyrics embedded in sermons); from the broad reaches of intellectual history, as documented in his book on *accidia*, to detailed and focused editorial work on individual manuscripts, such as those containing copies of the *Fasciculus morum*; from the examination of historical concepts of aesthetics and literary structure, seen in his studies of the sermon as an art form and the pilgrimage of life as a verifiable medieval genre, to source criticism, as illustrated in his work on Chaucer's *Parson's Tale*; from the literary history of institutions (specifically, the development of penitential doctrine in medieval ecclesiastical history) to the documentation of ways in which literary texts negotiate their relationships to other significant systems of discourse (in particular, that of the seven deadly sins). Always at the center of Professor Wenzel's philological concerns is the text in its historical surroundings.

The directions in philology represented in Professor Wenzel's scholarship have served as the guidelines for the contributions to this volume. The literary analysis of Chaucer's poetry from a historical perspective was an early focus of his scholarship, and four contributions to this volume demonstrate the same concern with belles-lettres and the dominant author of Middle English literature. Historical delimitations on the interpretative process are at the center of Stemmler's essay, for his contribution to this volume is a historical-philological rejoinder both to the feeling of critical futility which maintains that ultimately we cannot reconstruct a medieval reading of *To Rosemounde* at all, and to the majority of modern responses to the ballade which interpret it as humorous or even as a parody of love lyrics. Stemmler's recovery of what was common (that is to say, unmarked) usage in the vocabulary and imagery of medieval expressions of love in Old French and Middle English is a corrective to many modern critics' recourse to the "ironic fallacy" when dealing with this poem. Boitani thematizes Chaucer's reflections on fictionality itself in *The Nun's Priest's Tale*, that is, on the possibility of unlimited (or any) significance in literary discourse beyond the literal level. He demonstrates the fallacy of a "Robertsonian" reading of the tale by showing how the context of allusions in the Nun's Priest's call to take the morality and leave the chaff aside is designed to deflect the reader from precisely such a pursuit. He notes that by the fourteenth century, Paul's dictum ("whatever was written was written for our instruction"), which Chaucer has the Nun's Priest employ as a hermeneutic guideline, implicated the chaff as well as the fruit. What underlies the priest's assertion that his story is as true as the fiction of Lancelot is neither biblical typology nor allegorical exegesis but rather, as Boitani shows, a free acceptance and justification of the letter by itself, without excluding the morality. Irving takes as his purpose the elucidation of the themes and images that place *The Knight's Tale* in the same "dark traditional dimension" of epic out of which *Beowulf* was written. Despite the differences that separate the two poems, Chaucer's work shows a single-minded focus on the heroic responses to mortality, the threat of entropy, and the forces of decay—a focus that demonstrates its affinity to the same epic point of view that produced the Old English work. Finally, Hartung proposes that Chaucer wrote *The Parson's Tale* (notoriously difficult to account for in the scheme of *The Canterbury Tales*), as a separate act of religious piety and individual penance. He hypothesizes that Chaucer's selective use of his sources (Raymund of Pennaforte, William Peraldus, and the *Summa virtutum de remediis anime*, as well as the *Quoniam/Primo* texts identified as Chaucer's sources by Professor Wenzel), especially in the passages concerning human sexuality, may have biographical significance.

The presence of two seemingly disparate worlds of discourse in the oeuvre of many important Middle English authors (poetic narrative and penitential doctrine) has presented a challenge to modern forms of textual interpretation. As Professor Wenzel has shown, this nexus is a fruitful source of new critical insights which philologists are in a unique position to exploit. Three essays in this volume demonstrate in different ways the innovative potential of this type of investigation as applied to one of the most complex of Middle English poems, *Piers Plowman*. Hanna argues that Langland's revisions of the portrait of "Robert the ruyflare," part of a larger series of alterations from the B to the C text, offer some insight into the poet's ambivalence toward the literature of hamartiology on which he drew but which he failed to endorse fully. The changes depend, in Hanna's view, on the structural principle of doubling: the personification of 3euan-3elde-a3eyn is added to the portrait of Robert, just as the figure of a priest is added to the friar taken over from the B text. In Hanna's analysis, the passage points to complications in Langland's view of the literature of institutionalized confession and the penitential situation in which this instruction was experienced, for the genuine acts of conversion in this section of *Piers Plowman*, those of Robert and 3euen, fall outside the description provided in the church's

penitential discourse. Alford discusses a later passage in which penitence is also a major theme, the banquet in B.13.21–214; but his evidence comes from biblical commentaries rather than from penitential
literature as such. The scene can be understood, he argues, as an
instance of "exegetical drama." That is, the banquet setting, much of
the table talk, and above all the central conflict between learning and
penitence (personified in the figures of Clergy and the gluttonous
friar on one hand, and Will and Patience on the other) can all be
found in the traditional exegesis of Proverbs 23. What distinguishes
Alford's argument from other examples of exegetical criticism is his
concern not with a single image or crux but with a pattern or sequence of events. The third essay on *Piers Plowman* ranges over the
entire poem. Blythe plots Langland's relationship to the literature of
vices and virtues by focusing not on one of the traditional seven
deadly sins, but rather on an innovation in moral theology of the
later Middle Ages: the sin(s) of the tongue. Drawing on the treatment
of the *peccatum linguae* in William Peraldus's *Summa de vitiis et
virtutibus*, the "ethical rhetoric" of Albertano da Brescia's *De arte
loquendi et tacendi*, and their scriptural foundation in the Epistle of
James (3.6) for a historical vocabulary to describe sinfulness and
virtue in the manipulation of language, Blythe argues that the progress of *Piers Plowman* demonstrates Langland's movement from
guilt-ridden verbal paranoia to the ideal of speaking *prudentissime*.
The opposition between the sin of the tongue and the cardinal virtue
of prudence apparent in Peraldus's *Summa* forms the background
against which Blythe charts the growth in Langland's confidence as
a speaker. Will's mandate to use rhetoric to chastise sin becomes the
verbal equivalent of what he "owes" in the penitential process: his
poem and his own confession.

   The intellectual, institutional, and textual history of treatises such
as *The Parson's Tale*, in which medieval penitential doctrines and the
pastoral concerns of moral theology were disseminated to a wide
variety of audiences, has formed the core of Professor Wenzel's
scholarship for many years. The primary focus of his attention has
always remained the development of such texts, and their influence,
in England. Four contributions to this volume are grounded in the
history of a discursive theological literature in England with broadly
pastoral interests. Goering investigates the content and authorship of
the *Summa "Qui bene presunt"* (ca. 1215–1220), one of the most

popular and influential pastoral manuals of English inspiration to circulate in the later Middle Ages. Written for priests in the spirit of the pastoral reforms that culminated in the canons of the Fourth Lateran Council (1215), the treatise is organized around a list of twelve basic catechetical items which were to serve as the foundation for sermons (that is, the creed, Paternoster, seven capital vices, Decalogue, etc.). Later English pastoral manuals develop a curriculum very much like the one found in the *Summa "Qui bene presunt."* The author of the text has long been known as Richard of Wetheringsett, but Goering further establishes that he is to be identified with "Richard of Leicester," the earliest known chancellor of Cambridge University, and probably also with "Richard Grant," as he was designated while chancellor of Lincoln Cathedral and briefly (1229–1231) archbishop of Canterbury. Rigg edits here for the first time a substantial part of a Latin poem, mainly in Leonine hexameters, which was also composed in the thirteenth century and has been preserved in a unique, though incomplete, copy in a manuscript from St. Albans: London, BL MS. Cotton Julius D.iii. *De motu et pena peccandi* describes in two sections, first, the process of sin (from suggestion to delight to consent), and then its consequences—the misery attendant on humanity's fallen nature, presented here both in its psychological dimensions and in terms of humanity's progressive physical decline through the "six ages of man." Part one is dependent principally on Augustine's *De sermone Domini in monte*; sections of part two closely resemble passages in Pope Innocent III's *De miseria humane conditionis*, while others were modeled on Isidore or Bede. Rigg's edition of the poem is accompanied by full notes elucidating the sources and analogues of the work.

A view of one direction taken by the vernacular literature of penitence in England is provided in Doyle's *editio princeps*, based on six manuscript copies (all carefully described here) of the *Lectus floridus*. This anonymous allegory of the penitent soul as a well-made bed which "oure lorde iesu crist < will haue > likynge to abide & reste inne" was composed in the late fourteenth or early fifteenth century in the southern half of England, and was intended for the instruction of both men and women without limitation on their status, whether clerical, religious, or lay. The basis for the allegory is provided by Song of Songs 1.15 ("Our bed is adorned"), but for the allegoresis of the significant parts of the bed, the author adopted some of the same

catechetical formulations that had been in circulation in pastoral
manuals in England since Wetheringsett's *Summa* (theological and
cardinal virtues, Decalogue, works of mercy, and so on) and interspersed them with other less numerically defined steps in the process
of penance (abstinence, good works, tears, etc.). Another genre of
English writing of the late Middle Ages, the instructional texts of the
Lollards, is the object of von Nolcken's study. Drawing on treatises
and sermons frequently composed in the vernacular, she identifies in
the unmistakable uniformity of Wycliffite productions not a gratu-
itous effect, but one that was actively sought by the authors. Von
Nolcken addresses in particular the rhetorical conception which these
texts have in common. Lollard authors, she argues, speak of themselves in the plural and view their opponents as a group, not only
because frequently enough Wycliffite works were written and studied
as communal productions, but also because this tendency to generalize closely approximated the perspective of philosophical realism
associated with Wyclif himself. As von Nolcken describes the intellectual environment in which these Lollard texts were produced,
their "sameness" becomes understandable as an expression of both
the group's desire to resolve itself into unity and its conviction that
its enemies were characterized by a dangerous diversity.

Professor Wenzel's scholarship has, of course, ranged far beyond
the borders of England to include the full extent of great Scholastic
Summae produced in university centers on the continent at a crucial
stage in the intellectual development of the medieval church. The
understanding of theology's task and, in particular, the direction of
scriptural hermeneutics are problems that bear directly on the formulation of philological approaches to the interpretation of medieval
literature. Minnis clarifies the view of sacred stylistics elucidated by
one of the most important, but insufficiently studied, late thirteenth-
century masters of theology: Henry of Ghent. Basing his study on
the prologue of the *Summa quaestionum ordinariarum*, which was
composed and later edited during the period in which Henry taught
in the faculty of theology at the University of Paris (ca. 1275–1292),
Minnis shows how Henry, like Augustine before him in *De doctrina
christiana*, brought the literary and rhetorical theory of antiquity
within the purview of scriptural exegesis. What was at stake here was
not only the question of whether Scripture could be seen as eloquent,
but also whether scriptural style could serve as a model for the

commentator, that is to say, for the theologian. Minnis shows, first, how Henry, following Augustine, privileges wisdom over eloquence in his analysis of theological speech, the language to be used in conveying the message of a divine science, and, next, how Henry develops his view of exegetical speech, the language to be used in expounding Scripture, in terms of the principle of individualizing discrimination (in both the teacher and his student). This principle justifies a diversity in interpretation while insisting on the unassailable unity of Scripture and its *auctor*. Emery focuses on some varieties of another type of expansive work frequent in the late Middle Ages, namely the *collectarium*, a volume containing collections of excerpted texts that evinces a unified rhetorical conception and physical presentation. Denys the Carthusian used the term *collectarium* to designate his commentary on Peter Lombard's *Sentences*. Denys's large work represents a flowering of earlier methods of compilation and collection, which he employs here to support not only memory but also dialectical argumentation. The topically arranged *Collectarium* composed from the 1530s to the 1570s by Trudo of Gembloux, monk at the Benedictine abbey of St. Trudo in Limburg, demonstrates the longevity of the form typically found in *florilegia* of classical authors. In all but one respect—Trudo's use of engravings from printed books as illustrative material—the *Collectarium* is a familiar type of late-medieval text. Emery carefully delineates three redactions of Trudo's work and draws attention to the extraordinarily large number of important medieval authorities excerpted there.

The means by which the pastoral concerns of moral theology were most widely disseminated, namely preaching, has been the object of much of Professor Wenzel's research. Two contributors here have adopted the same focus. D'Avray deals with an influence on homiletic literature which Professor Wenzel, among others, has termed "scholastic" in its more closely defined sense. He charts the penetration of philosophy, logical argument, and problem solving into preaching and locates this development in model sermon collections of the late thirteenth and early fourteenth centuries. He argues that philosophical influences are not limited to the Dominican order during this period, and he illustrates the use of metaphysical reflections in the work of Franciscan authors as well, for example in the sermons of Servasanto da Faenza. After a detailed examination of one

sermon on nature and grace (on the text of 1 Cor. 15.10: *Gratia dei
sum id quod sum*), D'Avray argues that Servasanto was in the vanguard of the late-medieval tendency to adopt philosophical argumentation for the needs of preaching. Anderson's essay also centers on an
Italian preacher, Jacobus of Viterbo, and the sermons he composed
year by year while archbishop of Naples (1302–1308). These are
preserved in an autograph manuscript now in the Vatican Library
(MS. Archivio di San Pietro D.213). The sequence of texts in the
codex allows Anderson to date two sermons to August of 1303 and
1304. Jacobus wrote them to memorialize the second son of Charles
II, that is, St. Louis (of Anjou; d. 1297, canonized 1317), who re-
nounced his projected inheritance of royal power to join the Franciscans. Pope John XXII canonized Louis during the period in which he
was combating the same radical Franciscan thinking on apostolic
poverty that some of the saint's close associates seem to have espoused. By emphasizing in his sermons Louis's tenure as bishop of
Toulouse, Jacobus perhaps influenced the attempt to reconcile Franciscan ideals of poverty with the traditional duties of secular office,
an attempt that became part of the new literature concerning the
saint after his canonization and suppressed any potentially unortho-
dox details in his biography.

As Professor Wenzel has shown in a number of important studies,
not only do homiletic materials provide a manuscript context for a
good deal of the surviving lyric poetry in Latin and the vernacular,
but they often supply us as well with philological evidence of the
medieval understanding of the lyrics they preserve. Although the
Franciscan Order is hardly responsible for all the religious lyrics of
the early Middle English period, its influence on Middle English
poetry was considerable; as Professor Wenzel has shown, for example, the *Fasciculus morum* itself is apparently of Franciscan authorship. Both Reichl and Newhauser base their essays on other manuscripts of probable Franciscan provenience that also present early
Middle English religious verse in the context of clerical and pastoral
treatises. Reichl examines the religious lyrics (a meditative passion
poem, a dialogue between Mary Magdalene and Jesus, penitential
pieces addressed to the Virgin, and a moral poem on abuses in the
Church) preserved in Oxford, Bodleian Library MS. Digby 2. The
volume contains computational writings and philosophical treatises
as well as poems in Latin, Old French, and Middle English, a few of

which are presented here for the first time in print. The computational works help date the codex to about 1280. Reichl argues that the inclusion in the volume of a number of Latin pieces by Franciscans associated with Oxford, along with the Middle English lyric "No more ne willi wiked be," in which the poetic speaker expresses his resolve to abandon a dissolute life and join the Franciscans, justifies the assumption that the manuscript was compiled in the Franciscan house of Oxford. He concludes that the codex was probably compiled by clerics whose scholarly interests are reflected in its computational, logical, and philosophical texts, as their spiritual concerns are documented by the religious lyrics. Newhauser's essay is centered on a brief Latin work contained in MS. Bodley 29, which includes a hitherto unknown variant of a short Middle English poem on death ("Strong it hijs to flitte / Fro worldes blisse to pitte"), edited here for the first time. Judging from the presence as well of Anglo-Norman in this text, the date of its composition was probably before the mid-fourteenth century. At least one part of the miscellany in which it is found may also probably be situated in the vicinity of the English Franciscans, for the treatise that contains the poem is a brief allegorical presentation of the physical characteristics and dress of what appears to be a gray friar as *pugil domini contra diabolum*. Each of the poem's three couplets is described in the Latin allegoresis as contained in one of the corners of the friar's shield (i.e., heart), and the shield allegory remained the permanent vehicle for the transmission of this *memoria mortis* poem. This allegory is also the same immediate context in which the only other known version of the poem was transmitted later in the fourteenth century. However, this poetic template allowed for re-interpretation and variation within the poem to suit different pastoral aims, for as Newhauser demonstrates, the later shield allegory with its Middle English verse is found in a sketch for a sermon that shows no obvious signs of Franciscan involvement.

The variety of the types of medieval literature examined in the essays here and the diverse philological approaches taken to elucidate these texts will be apparent to every reader. Such breadth and variety are in themselves a tribute to Professor Wenzel's creative influence in medieval scholarship during the last three decades, for the amount of information and the diversity of sources he can marshal to his arguments continue to set the highest standards. He has not simply succeeded in making himself a masterful practitioner of philology as another discipline in the modern academy's *artes liberales*; he also has helped shape the present and future of that discipline. For these reasons and as a tribute to the generosity that Siegfried Wenzel has always demonstrated in sharing ideas and information with those who care about medieval literature as he does, his friends and students have been moved to assemble this *Festschrift* in recognition of his achievements and influence:

> Das ist die ganze Wissenschaft,
> Das ist der Bücher tiefster Sinn.

R. N.
J. A. A.

THEO STEMMLER

Chaucer's Ballade "To Rosemounde" — a Parody?

A t the end of his short but perspicuous analysis of Chaucer's ballade *To Rosemounde*, C. S. Lewis gives vent to a well-known feeling of philological futility: "What effect Chaucer intended is just one of those things which ... we shall never know...."[1] I share only part of Lewis's pessimism. True, we can reconstruct the meaning of texts only approximately and we have considerable difficulty in verifying an author's intent. It is, however, often possible to find out what a text was not meant to mean. To falsify a hypothesis is easier than to verify it. This is what I am going to try: to reconstruct the meaning of Chaucer's text by falsifying most of the current comments on it.

Again and again, nearly all scholarly commentators pose one and the same overwhelming question: Is *To Rosemounde* a parody? Almost all have answered in the affirmative—though often in an oblique way. Two dozens of the altogether thirty or so critics were not in a position to concede a serious meaning to the poem. They described it as a "parody," "satire," "burlesque," "comedy," and/or called it a "humorous," "half-serious," "mock-serious," "mocking" text. Only three critics belong to the no-parody faction,[2] while two scholars abstain.[3] In the following debate with the majority, which is not at all silent but many-voiced, I shall concentrate on two

---

[1] Lewis, *Allegory of Love*, 171.

[2] Birney, *Essays*, 59; Blake, *The English Language*, 121–23; Mehl, "Weltliche Lyrik," 59.

[3] Davies, ed., *Medieval English Lyrics*, 328; Lewis, 170–71.

articles which contain all possible arguments for interpreting *To Rosemounde* as a parody.[4]

§

It all began a century ago when W. W. Skeat discovered the only extant version of the poem in Bodl. MS. Rawlinson Poet. 163 and published it in *The Athenaeum* (4 April 1891). He set the course for all future discussions of this text: he supplemented the title *To Rosemounde* and—more important—characterized it as a "humorous poem." He praised the "amusing touch" to be found in its last stanza. Three generations of scholars followed in Skeat's footsteps and elaborated on his assessment of the poem until they not only claimed to identify a tongue-in-cheek perspective, but discovered that the text was a full-blown parody of the courtly love-lyric. From Skeat's modest single shot, I immediately turn to the argumentative broadsides fired by some modern critics on readers and students of this text.

In Chaucer's ballade, as in countless other medieval love-lyrics, the beauty of the beloved lady and the pangs of her lover are described. The language used in these poems is always highly hyperbolic. *To Rosemounde* is written in this style which sometimes borders on hagiographical adulation and elevates the lady to the rank of a saint:

> Ma dame ye ben of al beaute shryne
> As far as cercled is the mapamonde.[5]

The hyperbole of the first line was not rare at the time when Chaucer wrote his poem. Little later it recurs in the *Tale of Beryn* and is applied to the beautiful wife of an emperor. She was

> so excellent of bewte þat she myȝt be shryne
> To all othir vymmen, þat wer tho lyvand.[6]

---

[4] Reiss, "Dusting Off the Cobwebs"; Fichte, "*Womanly Noblesse* and *To Rosemounde.*"

[5] I quote from Chaucer, *The Minor Poems*, ed. Pace and David, 167–69.

[6] *The Tale of Beryn*, ed. Furnivall and Stone, vv. 1114–15.

The serious meaning of lines 1 and 2 of Chaucer's poem has been disputed by Reiss. I quote his statement in full since it exemplifies the risks of where onomatopoetic speculation may lead:

> *Mapemounde* may not in itself be a comic word, but the sound *ounde* that appears twelve times as the *b* rhyme in the three stanzas of the poem brings in a touch of the ludicrous.... The sound is far too heavy—too mooing even—for the praise of the lady....[7]

I do not know how English cows of the fourteenth century made themselves heard, but it is unlikely that they made use of *ounde*. Why, moreover, this purportedly bovine sound *ounde* should produce a ludicrous effect remains a mystery to me.

It is instructive to cast a glance at Chaucer's *Sir Topas*, an indisputable parody. Here he does parody the poor meter of so many contemporary tail-rhyme romances by clearly recognizable devices: monotonous iambic rhythm and end-stopped lines.

True, the rhyme scheme of *Rosemounde* (with only three rhymes in 24 lines) is a tour-de-force, but it is employed as seriously as in its probable model, Machaut's ballade *Tout ensement com le monde enlumine*, where the same rhyme words in *-ounde* are used.[8]

Some critics make much of the "mapamonde" in line 2 and interpret it in connection with lines 3 and 4, which run:

> For as the Cristall Glorious ye shyne
> And lyke Ruby ben your chekys rounde.

Reiss claims, "The circle or circumference of the globe finds its microcosmic counterpart in the lady's cheeks, which ... suggests a largeness of her physical being."[9] Apart from the wrong use of the term "globe," this statement is untenable since it yokes two phrases which belong to different layers of the semantic hierarchy. Line 2 means, in Skeat's words: "As far as the map of the world extends."[10] Chaucer here offers a new variation on the old commonplace which praises

---

[7] Reiss, 63.
[8] See Wimsatt, "Machaut and Chaucer," 76–77.
[9] Reiss, 63.
[10] *The Works of Chaucer*, ed. Skeat, 1:549.

the lady as the most beautiful woman in the world. Middle English love-lyrics abound in hyperboles of this sort. Some authors are content to proclaim the beloved as Miss England:

> Bituene Lyncolne ant Lyndeseye,
> Norhamptoun ant Lounde,
> ne wot y non so fayr a may
> as y go fore ybounde.[11]

Others prefer a Miss World:

> Maiden murgest of mouþ;
> bi est, bi west, by norþ ant souþ. . . .[12]

So does Chaucer.

His initial statement is followed by several arguments which make clear why the speaker is so enthusiastic about his lady. "Globe" and cheeks are, therefore, not "counterparts": line 4 is logically subordinated to line 2.

Fichte puts it more cautiously: "The adjective *rounde*, though, connects lines 2 and 4. . . ."[13] Moreover, he claims a strong connection between lines 2 and 1: "In line 2 *cercled* implies an indirect comparison: the lady is as beautiful as a map is round, that is, her beauty is as perfect as a circle."[14] Again, the text does not bear out this interpretation: the lady is neither directly nor indirectly compared with a *mappa mundi* but her beauty is said to be peerless all over the world.

While Reiss takes the lady's "chekys rounde" to be a parodistic allusion to her plumpness, Fichte elaborates on this interpretation and claims, "The ruby-red cheeks in line 4 do not belong to the catalogue of female beauty. . . ."[15] This is simply not true. Countless medieval texts inform us about the lady's red and white complexion and her "ruddy" cheeks. W. C. Curry points out: "The cheeks of both men and women, to be beautiful must not be pale and wan, but

---

[11] Brook, ed., *Harley Lyrics*, no. 25, vv. 17–18.

[12] Ibid., no. 14, vv. 43–44.

[13] Fichte, 190.

[14] Ibid.

[15] Ibid.

fresh and well-coloured.... Such well-coloured, fresh cheeks or faces are sometimes said to be 'ruddy.'"[16] In the romance *Alisaunder* we read of "maidenes with rody face," in the *Destruction of Troy* of Briseis's "rede chekys,"[17] and in a Middle English love-lyric of the "roose red yn your chekes."[18] *Sir Gawain and the Green Knight* contains a double portrait of a beautiful young woman and of an ugly elderly lady which supports my view:

> Bot vnlyke on to loke þo ladyes were,
> For if þe ʒonge watz ʒep, ʒolʒe watz þat oþer;
> Riche red on þat on rayled ayquere,
> Rugh ronkled chekez þat oþer on rolled.[19]

The old lady is provided with a "yellow complexion" and "rough, wrinkled, loosely dangling cheeks," while the young beauty possesses a "fresh complexion" and (by implication) red, round cheeks.

So far Chaucer's description of the lady corresponds to the exigencies of the traditional canon and is not in the least parodistically-deflating. Fichte's following statement, therefore, seems to be debatable: "By virtue of this bathetic image in line 4 we have moved a distance from the ideal shrine of beauty in line 1." Referring to lines 5 and 6, he continues: "Rosemounde is not the ideal of womanly perfection, whose singularity is the source of virtuous action. Instead she is "mery and jocounde [*sic*], ..." which is more appropriate to a "revel" than to the shrine of all beauty.[20] Again, this view is not corroborated by the evidence of medieval texts. It is almost a truism to say that Rosemounde's jocundity belongs to the essential requirements of a courtly lady. It is not justified to interpret this feature and Rosemounde's participation in "revels" as detrimental to her perfection. Lines 5 to 7,

> Therwyth ye ben so mery and so iocunde

---

[16] Curry, *Middle English Ideal*, 91. See my dissertation: Stemmler, *Die englischen Liebesgedichte*, 185.

[17] For references, see Curry, 91–92.

[18] Robbins, ed., *Secular Lyrics*, no. 130, v. 16.

[19] *Sir Gawain*, ed. Tolkien, Gordon, and Davis, vv. 950–53.

[20] Fichte, 190.

> That at a Reuell whan that I se you dance
> It is an oynement vnto my wounde,

have parallels in many medieval texts where the activities of a courtly society are described. In the *Romaunt of the Rose* (vv. 759–60), to quote only one example,

> tho myghtist thou karoles sen,
> And folk daunce and mery ben. . . .

That the love-sick speaker in Chaucer's poem should subjectively be relieved by the sight of the dancing lady is understandable, though his suffering objectively worsens.

Stanza 2 begins with the controversial lines:

> For thogh I wepe of teres ful a tyne,
> yet may that wo myn herte not confounde.

Most critics interpret this excessive weeping as an exaggeration which serves a parodistic function. They concede a certain amount of weeping caused by love-sickness. But as soon as a certain point is reached, they do not take the lover's lachrymosity seriously any longer and declare him the victim of a parody. The problem is: where is the boundary between a serious and a ludicrous exaggeration? Many critics are apt to rely on their linguistic intuition without improving their competence by consulting the available contemporary evidence.

One of them, for instance, finds the tub full of tears a bit too hyperbolic. Would a bucket still be admissible? Sometimes this arbitrariness is combined with downright arrogance when the critic gives apodictic statements *ex cathedra*: "Each image undermines the credibility of the stanza it introduces and is only less fatal to his [i.e., the poet-lover's] aspirations than his lack of awareness that these images are inappropriate for plaints of refined love."[21] What entitles this critic to declare "that these images are inappropriate?" Only his own twentieth-century taste; medieval taste was different. Love-poetry especially was prone to exaggerations that were nothing else than seriously meant hyperboles. In one of the *Harley Lyrics* the author praises the beautiful lady's neck:

---

[21] Vasta, "To Rosemounde," 102.

> swannes swyre swyþe wel ysette,
> a sponne lengore þen y mette.[22]

Such an extremely long neck seems ludicrous to us but was meant seriously. The author—and many of his colleagues—thought long necks beautiful, and abnormally long necks exceedingly beautiful.[23] For these reasons I am doubtful that "the image of a tub full of tears" was really meant to be "amusing."[24] All the more since long ago Skeat unearthed a passage in a French romance where the same phrase is used seriously:

> Le jour i ot plore de larmes plaine tine.[25]

Besides these exaggerations, the weapons most frequently wielded by parody-hunters are incongruities. Lines 11 and 12 of Chaucer's poem deal with the lady's voice:

> your semy voys That ye so small out twyne
> Makyth my thoght in ioy and blys habounde.

The reference to the beloved's voice was an essential in a medieval *descriptio pulchritudinis*:

> The voices of women should be pleasant to hear, soft, flexible....[26]

Rosemounde's voice does not seem to comply with these high standards. One of the critics comments accordingly:

> It is the thin voice his beloved "twists out," i.e., brings forth laboriously.[27]

Middle English usage, however, tells a different story. In the *Tale of Beryn*, roughly contemporary with Chaucer's poem, the pilgrims leave Canterbury on a fine May morning; they are delighted by the birds' song:

---

[22] Brook, ed., *Harley Lyrics*, no. 7, vv. 43–44.
[23] See Stemmler, *Die englischen Liebesgedichte*, 186.
[24] Fichte, 192.
[25] *The Works of Chaucer*, ed. Skeat, 1:549.
[26] Curry, 71.
[27] Fichte, 191.

> The thrustelis & the thrusshis, in þis glad mornyng,
> The ruddok & the Goldfynch; but þe Ny3tyngale,
> His amerous notis, lo, how he twynyth smale![28]

The amazing similarity of the respective phrases leads us to the positive meaning intended by Chaucer: Rosemounde possesses a fine, delicate voice which enables her to sing pleasantly. This ability was praised in many medieval texts. In the *Romaunt of the Rose* (vv. 745–48) the courtly dancing is accompanied by a lady's songs:

> A lady karolede hem that hyghte
> Gladnesse, the blissful and the lighte;
> Wel coude she synge and lustyly,
> Noon half so wel and semely.

Some critics are of the opinion that Chaucer's ballade is addressed to a real person. Edith Rickert[29] was the first to plead for the French princess Isabelle, who, at the tender age of seven, came to England in 1396—as the future wife of Richard II. Others followed Rickert's lead; R. H. Robbins especially went out of his way to prove this assertion. He maintains:

> If Rosemounde had been fourteen, then the poet could have wooed her with the traditional language. But love demands are absent, and the implication must be that Rosemounde is too young to accede to such requests. She must be a sub-teenager.[30]

Such an argumentation is—with all due respect to this great scholar—preposterous. It draws an incorrect conclusion from a correct premise. "Love demands" are absent indeed—not because Chaucer addresses a child but because he makes the lover behave as countless others did before him: posing as meek, obedient lovers who patiently endured their lady's disdain. That this "sub-teenager" should be the seven-yearold Isabelle of France is pure speculation. Robbins's final conclusion is, therefore, not acceptable: "The humour in 'To Rosemounde' consists in the dramatic irony of the application of the

---

[28] *The Tale of Beryn*, ed. Furnivall and Stone, vv. 684–86.
[29] Rickert, "A Leaf."
[30] Robbins, "Chaucer's *To Rosemounde*," 78.

terminology of courtly love to a queen who was but a child...."[31]
Similarly untenable is his assumption that the pearl roses on one of
Isabelle's robes suggested to Chaucer the name Rosemounde. The
poet introduced this name in order to emphasize the lady's beauty:
the beauty of Rosamond Clifford (ca. 1140–1176), mistress of Henry
II, was proverbial, the epithet "Fair Rosamond" usual.[32] In one of
his poems, Lydgate praises a lady's "beaute surmounting with feyre
Rosamounde."[33] Similarly, Gower in his *Confessio Amantis* (1.2480–
83) associates the name "Rosemounde" with beauty:

> ... he Gurmondes dowhter fond,
> Which Maide Rosemounde hihte,
> And was in every mannes sihte
> A fair, a freissh, a lusti on.

Chaucer must have known this tradition and very probably made use
of it.

Lines 16 and 17 of Chaucer's poem contain a comparison which
has almost unanimously been interpreted as "ironical," "parodistic,"
etc. According to one critic, here "the parody reaches its climax."[34] In
my opinion this assessment is a typical case of what I once called "ironic
fallacy."[35] Again, a look at contemporary usage is indispensable.

First, we should realize that many critics get this ominous comparison wrong by confusing its primary and secondary meaning.
Most of them maintain that the lover is compared to a fish and thus
outrageously ridiculed. The primary meaning of the comparison is,
however, a different one: it is the movements of the sleepless lover
that the passage refers to. Chaucer himself uses this motif several
times in phrasings similar to, or even identical with, the lines in *To
Rosemounde*. In his *Legend of Good Women* (vv. 1165–67) the enam-
ored Dido betrays the typical symptoms:

---

[31] Ibid.

[32] See Heltzel, *Fair Rosamond*, 1; *Dictionary of National Biography*, 4:531 (s.v.
"Clifford, Rosamond").

[33] Lydgate, *Minor Poems*, ed. MacCracken, 2:380.

[34] Fichte, 193.

[35] Stemmler, review of Ransom, *Poets at Play*, 236. On the problem of parody
in Middle English literature, see Blake; Stemmler, "My Fair Lady"; Stemmler, "The
Problem of Parody."

> She siketh sore, and gan hyreself turmente;
> She waketh, walweth, maketh many a breyd,
> As don these lovers, as I have herd seyd.

After his separation from Criseyde, the unhappy Troilus (5.211) finds no sleep:

> To bedde he goth, and walwith ther and torneth.

In *The Wife of Bath's Tale* (v. 1102) the knight, who is reluctant to sleep with his ugly old wife, is nervously moving to and fro; he confesses:

> That litel wonder is though I walwe and wynde.

The phrase "walwe and wynde," therefore, may be used seriously or sarcastically—depending on the context. And so far, as we have seen, the arguments for a parodistic reading of Chaucer's ballade have proved unconvincing. The movements of the lover are thus compared to those of a pike rolled in a sauce.[36] Such a comparison is less ludicrous, if it is ludicrous at all, than the erroneously suggested direct comparison of a man with a fish. I have my doubts that even this indirect comparison is meant to be funny.

§

Many critics have discovered incongruities as a means of parody in medieval texts which actually were no such thing.[37] They apply their own subjective ideas about what is done and what is not done to texts which followed more catholic tastes. Thus, they find the combination of lover and pike in a comparison "out of place," "unlikely," etc. and read it as intended irony used for parodistic purposes. Why, by the way, is the pike in *To Rosemounde* ludicrous while the flea in John Donne's poem is not? One might interpret the

---

[36] "Galauntine" means "a sauce made of bread, broth or vinegar, and spices, usually served over fish, meat, or fowl" (*Middle English Dictionary*, s.v. "galauntine"). In his poem *The Former Age*, Chaucer (v. 16) mentions "sause of galantyne." The meaning "jelly" proposed by several critics does not make sense in a comparison whose *tertium comparationis* is a "to-and-fro movement."

[37] See my articles mentioned above (n. 36).

unusual comparison in Chaucer's poem as a sort of conceit *avant la lettre*. I give two examples which may corroborate my opinion.

In a totally serious *Harley Lyric* the love-life of women and worms is brought together:

> wormes woweþ vnder cloude,
> wymmen waxeþ wounder proude....[38]

This passage reminds us of Chaucer's proem to book 3 of *Troilus and Criseyde* (vv. 8–11) where the power of Venus is evoked:

> In hevene and helle, in erthe and salte see
> Is felt thi myght, if that I wel descerne,
> As man, brid, best, fissh, herbe, and grene tree
> Thee fele in tymes with vapour eterne.

Three stanzas later (vv. 34–35) Chaucer describes the fortuitousness of love and brings lovers and fish together; only love knows why

> she loveth hym, or whi he loveth here,
> As whi this fissh, and naught that, comth to were.

I owe my second example to D. Legge, who in one of her articles deals with a passage in the Old French *Lai de l'Ombre* (vv. 158–61) where the pains suffered by a courtly lover are compared to toothache.[39] She points out that Guillaume de Lorris in his *Roman de la Rose* (v. 2432) seriously uses the same comparison, and she rightly concludes: "[T]he Middle Ages saw far less incongruity than we do in the association of toothache and courtly love."[40]

The two remaining examples of alleged parodistic meaning are as inconclusive as the preceding ones. For no recognizable reason Reiss calls Chaucer's phrase "trew Tristam the secunde" (v. 20) "too extreme."[41] Middle English texts, however, abound with similar hyperbolic comparisons such as "Ector the secounde"[42] or "Semyrame the secounde."[43]

---

[38] Brook, ed., *Harley Lyrics*, no. 11, vv. 31–32.
[39] Legge, "Toothache and Courtly Love," 50–54.
[40] Ibid., 54.
[41] Reiss, 64.
[42] Chaucer, *Troilus and Criseyde*, 2:158.
[43] Chaucer, *The Man of Law's Tale*, v. 359.

Finally, the lover's offer to Rosemounde (v. 23):

> Do what you lyst I wyl your thral be founde

produces Fichte's peremptory statement:

> The traditional profession of service is made here, yet it is not the free service offered self-consciously by a loving knight but the abased servility of a "thral"—a fact further ridiculing the position of the speaker in the poem.[44]

Again, the allegation is refuted by the evidence of contemporary usage. In numerous Middle English texts the lover poses as Love's thrall:

> But unto Love I was so thrall....[45]

Or:

> Haf piete [*sic*] of me, cative bound & thrall....[46]

This extreme form of (rhetorical) servility is, of course, not confined to English texts. D. Rieger comments on the same phenomenon in Old Provençal lyrics:

> So erreicht die trobadoreske Unterwürfigkeit oft genug das Extrem einer ausgesprochenen Sklavenhaltung einer *domna* gegenüber....[47]

§

Thus, all odds are against interpreting *To Rosemounde* as a parody. Chaucer's ballade is, on the contrary, a seriously meant love-lyric. The author does not simply follow many well-known conventions of the genre, but also employs unusual phrases and comparisons which prevent his poem from being the umpteenth trite version of its kind.

---

[44] Fichte, 193–94.
[45] Chaucer, *The Romaunt of the Rose*, v. 5142.
[46] Robbins, ed., *Secular Lyrics*, no. 196: refrain.
[47] Rieger, "Die altprovenzalische Lyrik," 240.

In closing, I would emphasize that I have wanted to demonstrate paradigmatically that we should be more reluctant to interpret real or seeming exaggerations and incongruities as a means of irony or parody. Instead, we might enhance our linguistic, stylistic, and critical competence by taking the evidence of contemporary usage more seriously than we usually do.

Universität Mannheim

PIERO BOITANI

"My Tale is of a Cock"
or, The Problems of Literal Interpretation

y concern in this paper will be with the problems of
interpretation, particularly with those which arise out of
the conflict between the literal sense on the one hand
and the moral, allegorical, and anagogical ones on the other. These
problems surface not only when one looks at a specific text (which
often happens to be a medieval one not because the readers of this
essay are medievalists, but because the Middle Ages paid special,
systematic attention to the fourfold interpretation of scriptural and
other writings); they also have a theoretical and historical dimension.[1]

Reading has always produced exegesis, and once it goes beyond
the philological stage, exegesis cannot rest satisfied with the mere
letter. At its extreme, literal interpretation runs the risk of re-stating
the facts, the events recounted by a narrative text, or that of repeating word by word the lines of a book, as Borges' Pierre Menard does
when he rewrites *Don Quixote*.[2] How, for instance, can one read in
an exclusively literal fashion a poem by Keats? That question is
theoretical, but I shall try to answer it in an empirical manner by
going through the several layers of a piece of literature.

However, the problem of literal interpretation is also historical in
the more specific sense that people have worried about it, and
changed their attitudes towards it, throughout the ages. I will there-

---

[1] On the four levels of medieval textual interpretation, see de Lubac, *Exégèse Médiévale*, esp. 2:425ff.

[2] Borges, *Labyrinths*, 39.

fore provide some historical depth by using other texts, both theoretical and literary, from the medieval and the modern period. All these problems shall emerge as I go along, and more forcefully in the second part of this essay. But it is necessary to keep in mind that however serious the questions which will eventually be faced here, my tale is of a cock. Readers will already know it as Chaucer's *Nun's Priest's Tale*. It ultimately derives—the differences in genre and treatment between the sources are important for my reading—from the fable "Del cok e del gulpil" by Marie de France, from the corresponding episode by Pierre de Saint Cloud in Branch II of the *Roman de Renart*, and perhaps from the parallel in Branch VI of *Renart le Contrefait*.[3]

The narrative finale of the *Nun's Priest's Tale* finds the cock up on a tree, refusing to come down even when his enemy asks for forgiveness and promises to explain what he really meant by "trespas"— Chauntecleer has had enough of flattery. The reader (or listener) is then offered the appended moral: "Lo, swich it is for to be recchelees / And necligent, and truste on flaterye."[4] The ending is complete, or so it seems. *Littera gesta docet, Moralis quid agas*, the letter teaches what has happened, the moral sense what you should do: here, then, is the letter—a fairly straightforward narrative action throughout the tale—and a pretty simple morality in accordance with the tradition of animal fable. However, things are more complicated than may at first appear. In their long discussion about dreams, Chauntecleer and Pertelote quote *exempla* and authorities, and the cock, in particular, goes as far as to use a Latin proverb, linking it to the beginning of Genesis and John's Gospel:

> For al so siker as *In principio,*
> *Mulier est hominis confusio—*
> Madame, the sentence of this Latyn is,
> "Womman is mannes joye and al his blis."
> (VII, 3160–62)

Clearly, these are fairly special animals, with a spirit which Dryden

---

[3] Marie de France, *Fables*, ed. Ewert and Johnston, 41–42 (no. 32); *Roman de Renart*, ed. Dufournet, 177–95; *Renart le Contrefait*, ed. Raynaud and Lemaitre.

[4] Fragment VII, vv. 3436–37. All quotes from Chaucer's text are from *The Riverside Chaucer*.

seems to catch very well in his "translation" when he has his Chanticleer outdo Chaucer's in, for example, countering Partlet's quotation from Cato with a super-scholarly, post-Renaissance remark:

> Nor *Cato* said it: But some modern Fool,
> Impos'd in *Cato*'s Name on Boys in School.[5]

But of course Dryden's animals belong to a different age: "In the Days of Yore, the Birds of Parts / Were bred to Speak, and Sing, and learn the lib'ral Arts" (vv. 91–92).

From the very beginning of the second part of Chaucer's tale, one realizes that his narrator, the Priest, is going to run wild in the same vein. He announces that he will now tell of Chauntecleer's "aventure," and his overture is a mastery of solemnity:

> Whan that the month in which the world bigan,
> That highte March, whan God first maked man.
> (VII, 3187–88)

The chronographical technique, learnt from the classics, Dante and Boccaccio, is further refined: we go right back to the time of Genesis. But then we at once take in the full absurdity of this procedure: what the Priest really wants to indicate is not March, but May, the topical month for the beginning of an adventure. Thus he adds:

> Was compleet, and passed were also,
> Syn March [was gon], thritty dayes and two.
> (VII, 3189–90)

In other words it is the third day of May. To point this out, the Priest has had to use two subordinate clauses of time ("whan that . . . and passed were also"), plus no less than three further dependent clauses, of which two are again temporal ("whan God," "syn March," "that highte"). The reader/listener begins to suspect there is some parody in all this, and one brought off with a literary technique of rare refinement. But the Priest goes further. At last comes the main clause, and with it the subject:

---

[5] Found in Dryden, *Poems and Fables*, ed. Kinsley, 686 (vv. 203–4).

> Bifel that Chauntecleer in al his pryde,
> His seven wyves walkynge by his syde,
> Caste up his eyen to the brighte sonne.
>
> (VII, 3191–93)

Again the syntax is oblique, but the parody is finely balanced. The opening was the beginning of the world and the creation of man; now Chauntecleer, in all his Sultan-like pride, raises his eyes to the sun. Chauntecleer is a barnyard cock, as we know, but here he behaves and feels like the lord of all creation, addressing himself to the sun, the primeval light; the sun, as the author specifies in another parenthesis,

> That in the signe of Taurus hadde yronne
> Twenty degrees and oon, and somewhat more.
>
> (VII, 3194–95)

This really carries the technique of astronomical time-telling a bit too far. But as soon as one senses the exaggeration, one is brought back to Chauntecleer, now in his natural dress, as "commune astrologer," who "knew by kynde, and by noon oother loore, / That it was pryme" (VII, 3196–97). Chauntecleer, as we have already been told, is more reliable "than . . . a clokke or an abbey orlogge" (VII, 2845), for Nature herself has planted in him infallible knowledge of astronomy. Step by step, a two-sided irony is constructed, aimed on the one hand at the cock that thinks it is lord of creation, and on the other hand at man, who is called the lord of creation, but has to invent a complicated science ("loore") and sophisticated instruments ("orlogge") to work out what the cock knows by instinct:

> "The sonne," he seyde, "is clomben up on hevene
> Fourty degrees and oon, and moore ywis."
>
> (VII, 3198–99)

For four lines, in the meantime, the register and the sphere of reference remain the same, with the introduction of the new element, Edenic joy:

> Madame Pertelote, my worldes blis,

> Herkneth thise blisful briddes how they synge,
> And se the fresshe floures how they sprynge;
> Ful is myn herte of revel and solas!
>
> (VII, 3200–3203)

Chauntecleer, who refers to the other birds as "*thise* briddes," sounds
like a splendidly paternalistic Adam: "padre" and "padrone." Once
more, Dryden goes a step further. In surveying flowers and birds, his
Chanticleer feels that Nature herself has "adorn'd the Year" just for
him, and quite openly proclaims, "All these are ours"; then, with an
extraordinary leap, he adds: "and I with pleasure see / Man strutting
on two Legs, and aping me!" (vv. 459–60)—by which of course he
surpasses Adam to become some kind of God walking in the garden,
as it were, "in the cool of the day."

But to return to Chaucer's tale: at this point, by a process of
association which is part of what might be called a "stream of narrative consciousness," the Priest intervenes with the first of his comments, picking up the theme of joy and inserting it into the wider
pattern of Fortune:

> But sodeynly hym fil a sorweful cas,
> For evere the latter end of joye is wo.
> God woot that wordly joye is soone ago;
> And if a rhetor koude faire endite,
> He in a cronycle saufly myghte it write
> As for a sovereyn notabilitee.
> Now every man, lat him herkne me;
> This storie is also trewe, I undertake,
> As is the book of Launcelot de Lake,
> That wommen holde in ful greet reverence.
> Now wol I torne agayn to my sentence.
>
> (VII, 3204–14)

Here proverbial wisdom—indeed, priestly consideration of worldly
transience—suddenly turns to literary allusion and makes fun of
literature: a rhetorician might write a chronicle for his audience, that
is, a noble *historia* in the high style (perhaps a "tragedy" such as
those the Monk has just recounted "de casibus virorum illustrium"),
but the Priest's tale is a true "storie" like the story of Lancelot,
which women (witness Dante's Francesca da Rimini) esteem very

highly.[6] It is as "true," in other words, as a romance, which even by medieval standards is completely fictitious. I shall return to this problem; for the moment it should be noted that the Priest is playing with literature and with his audience—both women in general and the ladies on the pilgrimage to Canterbury in particular (Dryden, for instance, makes the connection with the Wife of Bath explicit at v. 570). But Chaucer's Priest is probably playing with the other pilgrims, too, because they have all just listened to the Monk's stories. Later on the Priest will find himself a rhetorician to make fun of—no less a figure than Geoffrey of Vinsauf—and he will continue his ironic remarks about women, who form the privileged audience of the man of letters, as in Chaucer's own *Troilus*. But now restraining himself, he switches back to his "sentence" (here with the meaning "subject"). At last, the fox appears (VII, 3215-25).

The narrator, however, cannot manage to stay outside his story: along with the fox he introduces the subject of predestination ("by heigh ymaginacioun forncast") and that of homicide, which was already mentioned by Chauntecleer himself in his speech on dreams (VII, 3050-57). The fox is full of iniquity, like the worst sinners of the Bible, the murderers. At this point, the Priest is carried away by his culture: he curses Judas, Ganelon and Sinon (thus bringing us back to somewhere between sacred and profane literature, to Scripture as well as classical epic and *chanson de geste*); he addresses his cock directly ("O Chauntecleer, acursed be that morwe / That thou into that yerd flaugh fro the bemes!"—VII, 3230-31); and, more briefly and prosaically than Troilus had done in Chaucer's poem, he launches into a discussion on predestination, free will and necessity (VII, 3230-50). This time, he takes in the world of the Schools—philosophy, "clerks," "altercacioun" and "disputisoun," Boethius, Augustine, and Chaucer's contemporary, Bradwardine. Chauntecleer's imminent tragedy seems now to acquire a cosmic dimension—it is placed on the level of universal destiny. But "that," as Lawrence Sterne would say, "is another story"—the story of Troilus, or of Arcite and Palamon. The Priest "wol nat han to do of swich mateere." "My tale," he firmly proclaims, "is of a cok," a cock who followed his "wife's advice in spite of the dream he had." And the

---

[6] See canto 5 in Dante, *Inferno*, ed. Sinclair, 72-79.

"conseils" of women, he continues, are often "fatal," witness that which "broghte us first to wo, / And made Adam fro Paradys to go" (VII, 3251–59).

Now this is a stupendous, abrupt *reductio*: "my tale" deals only with a cock. Yet its purport is not quite clear: is the Priest really talking about a cock, or rather about all mankind? The cock has taken the advice of his *wife*, not of the hen Pertelote, and this wife is immediately put on a par with all women, beginning with Eve. So, where exactly are we? We are back once again in Genesis, where both Chauntecleer with his *In principio* and the narrator had already taken us. In short, we are at the beginning of the world, in the Garden of Eden. Is this to be taken *litteraliter*? Obviously not. Can one then consider it a case of typology, Adam being the *figura* of Chauntecleer in the same way as he is the *antitypos* of Jesus, Pertelote being the fulfillment of Eve? While the cock in general does of course symbolically represent Christ in medieval iconography, the notion that *this* cock incarnates the Messiah and *this* hen (through Eve) the Virgin Mary is so preposterous *in the context* (thus the understanding of the "context" becomes fundamental for an interpretation of the "text" beyond a merely literal reading) that even the stoutest Robertsonian would—I hope—relinquish it at once.[7] Furthermore, our uncertainty is increased by two complementary statements. The first is Chauntecleer's Latin maxim, "Mulier est hominis confusio," which now seems to agree with what the Priest is saying about women. As the Priest quotes Eve to prove his opinion, so Chauntecleer authenticates his pronouncement by linking its certainty and truth to the first words of the greatest authorities, Genesis and John. But the cock then mistranslates his maxim with a version which means the opposite of the original: "Womman is mannes joye and al his blis." This, too, one must assume, is "al so siker as *In principio*," and in a sense of course it is perfectly true. Genesis does say that God thought it was not good for man to be alone, and woman was then created to be a "help meet for him."

Thus, the cock shows himself to be a fairly shrewd scriptural exegete. He seems to bring to extreme consequences the fourteenth-

---

[7] On the principles involved in Robertsonianism, see Robertson, *A Preface to Chaucer*, esp. 52ff.

century theory of "duplex sensus litteralis."[8] At one and the same
time he makes Genesis say the two apparently opposite things that
the *letter* of the biblical text predicates of woman. He does it by
using Latin first, and then an English mistranslation of the Latin.
The words of Genesis itself do not change: *In principio* is immutable.
But by turning the words that surround it from one language to
another, by offering an apparently innocent "sentence" or "plain,
literal meaning" of them, Chauntecleer interprets the biblical *littera*
twice over and makes fun of literal translation and interpretation as
such, casting, in addition, some doubt on the validating *In Principio*
as well. The point to note here is not so much what someone has—in
a different interpretative context, but, alas, not jocularly—called the
"de-cock-struction,"[9] but the fact that Chauntecleer is allowed to
offer as it were a triple reading of the letter, thus in a sense short-
circuiting it, *without* having to resort to allegory, morality, or anagogy. Is this part of the new "literalism" that, according to Beryl
Smalley, conquered scriptural exegesis with the advent of Aristotle
and the friars?[10]

I shall come back to this question presently. For the moment, I
will note that between the Latin *Mulier est hominis confusio* and its
English mistranslation there opens up a gap. The whole of the *Nun's
Priest's Tale*, as *ideological* message and as *cultural* statement (that is,
as a story provided with a "sense" and a historical dimension), is as
it were contained in that gap between the original and the translation
which Chauntecleer passes over in a sweeping leap of psychic suppression and wishful thinking.

This phenomenon looks particularly interesting when one views
it in the light of the English fourteenth century, a true age of translation that culminates with the Wycliffite version of Chauntecleer's
authorial text, the Bible itself, and with Chaucer's own "translations," from the *Roman* to *Boece*, from *Melibee* to the *Second Nun's
Tale*, from *Troilus* to the Knight's and the Clerk's *Tales*, down to the
Hugelyn version of *Inferno* XXXIII in the *Monk's Tale*. Indeed
Chaucer himself, Deschamps' "grand translateur," makes significant,

---

[8] Minnis and Scott, *Medieval Literary Theory*, 203–6.
[9] Pizzorno, "Chauntecleer's Bad Latin."
[10] Smalley, *The Study of the Bible*, 292–308.

and odd, remarks about his way of translating things. In the *Troilus*, for instance, he completely transforms one of Petrarch's sonnets, yet he declares that he is reporting not only the "sentence" (this elastic and often recurring word now meaning the "gist") of his *auctor*, Lollius (presumably Boccaccio), but also "pleinly" (fully), "save our tonges difference" (awareness of the "gap" is now explicit), every word contained in the source and pronounced by Troilus in his song.[11]

Translation and literalism share more than one problem. How does Chaucer's Priest respond to these? After quoting Eve with a negative connotation, he retracts:

> But for I noot to whom it myght displese,
> If I conseil of wommen wolde blame,
> Passe over, for I seyde it *in my game.*
>
> (VII, 3260–62)

So it was a joke. But was it really? With subtle malice, the Priest sends us back to the "authors": read them, he says, and you will see what they say of women (VII, 3263–64). Exactly! The only problem is that "authors," beginning with Genesis, say pretty contrasting things about women. Thus, Pilate-like, the Priest washes his hands of the whole business, and with a triple somersault attributes what he has just said to the subtle interpreter of Scripture, Chauntecleer:

> Thise been the *cokkes wordes, and nat myne.*
> I kan noon harm of no womman divyne.
>
> (VII, 3265–66)

A Priest leaving exegesis to a cock? We have not just lost the letter (which has gone up in smoke between Chauntecleer's Latin and his English), we are losing the very foundation of Roman Catholic doctrine, which affirms the authority of the magisterium over all interpretation, thus conditioning the "plain sense" or "sensus litteralis" itself. Where would society end up if everybody were allowed to interpret the Bible? Surely, if this were the fourteenth century, somewhere between Huss's Prague, Wyclif's Oxford and the abbey of Umberto Eco's *Name of the Rose*!

---

[11] See *Troilus*, 1:393ff.

As if this were not enough, from this moment on the tale is a succession of verbal fireworks and rapid changes of voice, from the characters to the narrator and vice versa. Texts and authors are invoked by all. The fox quotes Boethius' *De Musica* and "Daun Burnel the Asse," the beast tale by Nigel Wireker entitled *Burnellus*, or *Speculum stultorum*.[12] The Priest manages to bring in the *Physiologus*, "Ecclesiaste," the *Aeneid* and the destruction of Troy, Hasdrubal and the sack of Carthage, Nero and the burning of Rome (VII, 3355–73). In this melodramatic, apocalyptic atmosphere, Chauntecleer's tragedy unfolds: in a mock-epic crescendo the men, women and animals of the farm rush to the scene. The style throws an ironic light on the protagonists of the action and, indirectly, on the protagonists of the Peasants' Revolt of 1381, who are reduced by assimilation, as in Gower's *Vox Clamantis*, to beast-like figures: the noise made by the animals when the fox captures Chauntecleer is so "hydous" that not even Jack Straw and his mob shouted so much when they attacked the Flemings (VII, 3393–97). Historical, political reality bursts into the story with the seemingly urgent explosiveness of the present (forcing one to ask the question, where do the Priest and Chaucer stand on it, and at the same time giving no clue as to the answer). Yet the narrator promptly abandons this tricky ground and takes refuge in rhetoric. At one point, beginning with an appeal to destiny, with a closely linked series of tragicomic invocations, the Priest harangues Friday (Venus's day), then Venus herself, then Geoffrey of Vinsauf, who lamented the killing of Richard the Lionhearted, which took place on a Friday. Nothing is spared—neither dreams, nor courtly love ("servyce"), nor sexual pleasure and the commandment of Genesis ("moore for delit than world to multiplye"), nor the "sentence" and the "loore" of a "maister soverayn" of rhetoric (VII, 3338–51).

Meanwhile Chauntecleer, who once was Adam, becomes Richard the Lionhearted, Priam, Hasdrubal, and a Roman senator. The fires of Troy, Carthage and Rome burn the scene, envelop all, threaten to become infernal (VII, 3389). The world is about to come to an end, when suddenly Fortune turns (in a nice inversion of the Monk's pattern: VII, 3403–4), and Chauntecleer, once more a simple cock,

---

[12] Mann, "The *Speculum Stultorum*."

frees himself. Yet the Priest is not finished. He now adds the morality, and then concludes with another bit of dazzling profundity, a last flash of Scripture:

> But ye that holden this tale a folye,
> As of a fox, or of a cok and hen,
> Taketh the moralite, goode men.
> For Seint Paul seith that al that writen is,
> To oure doctrine it is ywrite, ywis;
> Taketh the fruyt, and lat the chaf be stille.
>
> (VII, 3438–43).

So, here is the audience's dilemma. This, the Priest now tells us, was *not* the silly, foolish tale of a cock. Leave the chaff aside, and take the morality. Very fine, and very appropriately medieval. A century later, in rewriting Chaucer's story for his *Morall Fabillis of Esope the Phrygian*, Robert Henryson picks up the "kirnill ... delectabill" which he says lies inside the "nuttis schell"—the "frute" under the "fenyeit fabil"—and expands the Priest's short *moralitas* into twenty-one lines about pride, vainglory and flattery.[13] And modern critics, particularly on the western shores of the Atlantic, have rushed beyond morality pure and simple, hunting for the *sensus allegoricus*, which is—it seems to me—quite a different thing: not "quid agas" (what you should do), but "quid credas" (what you should believe). Thus, the tale, they say, is an allegory of the Fall of Man: a sermon on alertness to moral obligation (with Chauntecleer representing the holy man and Russell the devil); an allegorical controversy between the secular clergy (the slothful Chauntecleer) and the friars (the fox); even a mock allegory, with Chauntecleer standing for the exegetical figure of the cock preacher.[14] Interpretation, as Pier Cesare Bori reminds us following John Scotus Eriugena, is infinite, and one could exercise one's imagination for a while, in particular trying to square the conflict between the two traditional genres of which the Tale is a combination, the moral fable and the amoral beast epic.[15]

---

[13] Henryson, *Poems*, ed. Elliott, 1 (vv. 15–21).

[14] Cf. the earlier allegorical readings of Dahlberg, "Chaucer's Cock and Fox," and Donovan, "The *moralite*," and see the criticism of these writers in Fichte, *Erläuterungen*, 1790–92.

[15] Bori, *L'interpretazione infinita.* On the genres involved, see Henderson,

Yet there is a preliminary move one *has* to make in any case—a choice between accepting or not accepting the Priest's invitation to take the morality and "lat the chaf be stille." Suppose, then, that one does grasp the fruit. In the Priest's version, this is fairly meager, but one might not be so hungry and be able to rest contented with it. However, there is still an awful lot of chaff left to dispose of. And furthermore, it should be remembered that St. Paul maintains that *all* that is written is written for our instruction. On the one hand, taken "literally" in the present context, this means the chaff as well. On the other, taken intertextually, it makes the *Nun's Priest's Tale* the equivalent of Scripture, for what Paul says in Romans 15.4 is that "quaecumque enim scripta sunt, ad nostram doctrinam scripta sunt, ut per patientiam et consolationem *Scripturarum* spem habeamus" (whatever has been written, has been written for our instruction, that by steadfastness and by the encouragement of the scriptures we might have hope), and this pronouncement comes after the quotation of a Psalm (68.10).

This is a bit unsettling, but one might decide to overlook the embarrassment at the apparent equation between chaff and Scripture, and go ahead, remembering that Alastair Minnis has proven that by the fourteenth century the "all" in Paul's sentence comes "to mean 'almost anything,' writings of all kinds."[16] At this point, one must ask what precisely the chaff is in the present case. And the answer is obvious: the tale of a cock, of course! This is as *true* a "story" as that of Lancelot, but not a *folye* ... as of a fox, or of a cock and hen. So, it is, and it is not, the tale of a cock; it is, and it is not, something else. One is neatly back at the beginning of the circle.

Thus, the reader/listener is forced to try the second course, refusing to take the morality alone because this is too cheap for such a story (Caxton, incidentally, makes it even cheaper by reading it as an *exemplum* of "ouer moche talkyng" and "to moche crowing"[17]) and because St. Paul and fourteenth-century "literary theory" apparently urge the interpreter to accept everything. With the fruit, one then eats up all the chaff. In other words, one chews—or, more precisely,

---

"Medieval Beasts and Modern Cages"; Manning, "The Nun's Priest's Morality."

[16] Minnis, *Medieval Theory of Authorship*, 205.

[17] *Caxton's Aesop*, ed. Lenaghan, 139.

"ruminates"—the letter. But what, again, is the letter? Clearly the whole *crust* made up of the various levels of fiction, culture and reality: the cock, the hen, the fox, Adam, Ganelon, Richard I, Nero, Bradwardine, Jack Straw. I repeat once more that there is no biblical typology here. Chauntecleer does not *fulfill* Adam or Priam as he would in Auerbach's *figura*—for a moment, he *is* Adam, and Priam.[18] And this single, climactic and very brief moment occurs when his narrator, the Priest (and behind him, Chaucer), decides to superimpose on top of each other, by allusion, two or more of those figures. In short, for the audience, who is listening to or reading the tale, and to whom it looks like a succession of those moments, a continuous explosion of names which are hurled out on the same level of speech, but which the audience knows belong to different levels of "being," the letter is letters—*littera* is *litterae, litteratura. All* of it is "true," like the story of Lancelot; all of it is written for our instruction, like the Bible, and like ... all literature.

For we have yet another complication. In the so-called "Retraction" which appears at the end of the last of the *Tales*, the Parson's (whenever this is complete in the manuscripts), "the makere of this book" takes his leave, asking his listeners and readers to thank Christ if they find in his work something they like, and to attribute anything they might dislike to the "defaute" of his "unkonnynge" and to his will. He would have said things better if he had been able to. "For oure book seith, 'Al that is writen is writen for oure doctrine,' and that is myn entente" (X, 1081–84). Whether this was actually composed by Chaucer does not really matter in the present context. But what does it mean? If "entente" stands for "intentio," one cannot forget that the generally accepted late-medieval view is, to put it with Thomas Aquinas, that "sensus litteralis est, quem auctor intendit": the letter is the "intentio auctoris."[19] And this leads us into another nice cul-de-sac. For, whether the "work" which is being spoken of in the Retraction is the *Canterbury Tales* or the "collected works" of Geoffrey Chaucer, the writer of the present sentence seems to say that the intention of the author is the literal sense, and

---

[18] Auerbach, "Figura." Cf. Allen, "The Ironic Fruyt."

[19] Aquinas, *Summa Theologica* 1a 1ae, q. 1. See also Minnis and Scott, *Medieval Literary Theory*, passim.

that this is, at least intentionally, all "doctrine." What, then, is "true" in these works? What, in particular, is "true" in the *Nun's Priest's Tale*?

In the twelfth century, Conrad of Hirsau had maintained in his *Dialogue on the Authors* that the "literal explanation is when one is told how the *nuda littera* is to be understood." He had then offered, in Isidore's tradition, an etymology of "fable"—*fabula*—from *fando* (speaking), and had added that "fable is fiction, not fact." "Aesopic" fables, according to Isidore and Conrad, "are made to relate to a moral end, and have been invented to give pleasure." "Their invent-ed stories about human events and characters correspond with the truth," says Conrad, "even though only in a certain sense"—and the crux lies precisely in this "certain sense," about which Conrad offers no explanation—"but the material Aesop invented never happened, nor could it have happened." As Isidore puts it, "ut ad rem, quae intenditur, ficta quidem narratione, sed veraci significatione veniatur" (so that one may come to the thing which is intended by means of fictional narrative but truthful meaning). Nor is this "fabulous" or "fabulistic" manner absent in Holy Writ. In Judges 9.7–15, Isidore and Conrad write, Jotham, the "only one to be saved when his brothers were killed by Abimelech, ascended Mount Gerizim and cursed the men of Shechem and the king chosen by them," saying that "the trees of the wood, the vine and the olive and the fig, had come together and sought to create a kingship over them from among their own number, but all to no avail, so that in the end they got the bramble as their king."[20]

The substance of this argument is picked up by Pierre Bersuire in the Prologue to his *Ovidius Moralizatus* and, even more interestingly, by Boccaccio in his so-called "Defense of Poetry" in the *Genealogie Deorum Gentilium*.[21] In book XIV, chapter ix, Boccaccio declares that "fabula est exemplaris seu demonstrativa sub figmento locutio, cuius amoto cortice, patet intentio fabulantis." Fable is a discourse which is exemplary and demonstrative under the veil of fiction (fig-ment); once you remove the cortex (the bark), the "intention" of the

---

[20] Minnis and Scott, *Medieval Literary Theory*, 48; Isidore of Seville, *Etymologia-rum . . . Libri*, ed. Lindsay, 1.40.1–7.

[21] Bersuire, *Ovidius Moralizatus* 1–4; Boccaccio, *Genealogie Deorum Gentilium*, ed. Romano 706–7, and see also *Boccaccio on Poetry*, ed. Osgood, 48–50.

fabulator, the narrator, appears evident (thus, the question of authorial intention, on which I have already touched, is clearly central for
both Isidore and Boccaccio). The writer of the *Genealogie* then
distinguishes four types of fables: the first type is Aesop's, which
"omnino veritate caret in cortice" (wholly lacks all appearance of
truth). Even this was not scorned by Aristotle, and one can find its
equivalent in the Book of Judges.

Were I to pursue this line of inquiry, my essay would never come
to a conclusion. But Boccaccio brings us to the second half of the
fourteenth century and to the emergence of a stronger "humanistic"
stance about the status of *litterae*. Is Chaucer's Priest, then, a "humanist?" Or is he merely repeating things already to be found in
Isidore and Conrad of Hirsau, i.e., central to medieval tradition?
Maybe in order to appreciate the distinction, in order to gain some
kind of historical, or even historicist, perspective, one needs to travel
further in time.

The prince of modern fable-telling, Jean de La Fontaine, has of
course quite a few things to say about the genre. The first is that as
far as Aesop's fables are concerned, "l'apparence en est puérile...:
mais ces puérilités servent d'enveloppe à des vérités importantes"
(their appearance is childish, but these childish things serve to envelop important truths). The second is his interpretation of Plato's
account in the *Phaedo* of how Socrates put Aesopian fables into verse
before dying. La Fontaine writes that suddenly it occurred to Socrates that perhaps the gods' advice that he should devote himself to
music meant that he should pay attention to poetry, for "there is no
good poetry without harmony." Yet, he adds, "there is no good
poetry without fiction, either": "et Socrate ne savoit que dire la
vérité. Enfin il avoit trouvé un tempérament: c'était de choisir des
Fables qui continssent quelque chose de véritable, telles que sont
celles d'Ésope" (and Socrates could only speak the truth: so he found
a compromise, that of choosing fables that would contain something
truthful such as those of Aesop). None of this syllogism is present in
Plato. But La Fontaine goes further. He argues—and this is the third
point—that what he is really talking about is the "Apologue," and
that this is exactly the same as a parable in the Gospels. Finally, he
distinguishes between the "body" and the "soul" of an apologue.

The former is the fable, the latter the morality.[22]

Where are we? In the Middle Ages or in the seventeenth century? Chaucer's Priest (and I emphasize this again, a *priest*) seems to be far less serious or "medieval" than La Fontaine—he only says the *story* is true. No more, but no less. By contrast, look at Dryden. He follows Chaucer in holding that "the Legend is as true I undertake / as *Tristram* is, and *Lancelot* of the Lake," but in his "Moral" concludes: "The Truth is moral, though the *Tale a Lie*." From his much expanded *moralitas* Dryden also eliminates St. Paul's *dictum*, though, like La Fontaine, he alludes to Christ's parables.

On the one hand, then, one has a medieval Priest who maintains his "story" is as true as fiction and who seems to liken it to Scripture, but in fact follows a "modern," contemporary fashion of justifying all writing by means of a sentence in St. Paul. On the other, one has two seventeenth-century writers who believe that the tale or fable is a lie, but liken it to a parable.

The two positions would seem to be similar, and indeed there is a "historical" way by which the latter would appear to have been "genealogically" prepared or even produced by the former. But the purpose of my paper is to show how subtly, and radically, different those positions really are. If I may put it boldly, Chaucer's stance is that of a man who seems to enjoy the pleasures, and to know the pains, of writing and reading in an ideological age.[23]

La Fontaine and Dryden smooth out both the joys and the sorrows. They make interpretation easy. Jesus, Dryden writes openly, knew perfectly well that a parable "was a pleasing way, / Sound Sense, by plain Example, to convey." Dryden had of course not read Frank Kermode's *Genesis of Secrecy*.[24] Chaucer, by contrast, seems to have had a look at "The Plain Sense of Things," an essay in which the same critic, beginning with a famous poem by Wallace Stevens, uses translation (another animal being involved this time: "the cat sat on the mat") to show that what the cock calls "sentence" ("the sentence of this Latyn") is impossible. Kermode then goes on to maintain that:

---

[22] Jean de La Fontaine, *Fables*, 1:43, 46, 48.
[23] See Alter, *The Pleasures of Reading*, esp. 206ff.
[24] Kermode, *The Genesis of Secrecy*, esp. 1ff.

The plain sense is not accessible to plain common sense. That is why it has been possible to say, "The plain sense is hidden." Luther believed that "the Holy Spirit is the plainest writer and speaker in heaven and earth," but we may well sympathize with Erasmus, who wanted to know "if it is all so plain, why have so many excellent men for so many centuries walked in darkness?"[25]

Chaucer, in sum, freely accepts the letter as literature, without excluding the morality. But in telling us to take the morality and leave the chaff aside, he justifies the letter by itself, and *forces* us to *stay* within it, so that we may have a taste of all the joys and the pains of the so-called "plain sense of things." The "fruyt," on the other hand, like that of the tree of knowledge, is forbidden, and the Priest makes us turn away from non-literal exegesis while inviting us to pursue it.

To stay with animal fables (and parables), I will conclude by noting that in reading Chaucer's Tale we find ourselves in the position of a certain Bucephalus and at the same time of those who look at him. Once, Bucephalus was Alexander of Macedonia's battle charger. Now, he is the new lawyer just admitted to the Bar. Though there is little in his present appearance to remind us of his former shape, "even a simple usher ... on the front steps of the Law Courts," "a man with the professional appraisal of the regular small bettor at a racecourse," can run "an admiring eye over the advocate" as he mounts "the marble steps with a high action" that makes them "ring beneath his feet." Bucephalus's position in modern society is a difficult one. There is no Alexander the Great, no blazing trail to India. "The gates have receded to remoter and loftier places." "So perhaps," Franz Kafka concludes, "it is really best to do as Bucephalus has done and absorb oneself in law books. In the quiet lamplight, his flanks unhampered by the thighs of a rider, free and far from the clamor of battle, he reads and turns the pages of our ancient tomes."[26] He is searching them—one may presume—for the letter, and maybe even for the allegory, the morality and the anagogy. But above all he is perplexed by his own strange metamorphosis. Who, or what, is Bucephalus? Does the new lawyer "fulfill" Alexander's horse? Neither

---

[25] Kermode, "The Plain Sense of Things," 176.
[26] Kafka, *Parables and Paradoxes*, 96–99.

he, nor we, are allowed to know anything for sure. In fact we, "the creatures outside," "look"—if I may be allowed to leap to another animal farm—"from pig to man, and from man to pig, and from pig to man again; but already it [is] impossible to say which [is] which."[27]

University of Rome

---

[27] Orwell, *Animal Farm*, 155.

EDWARD B. IRVING, JR.

Heroic Worlds:
"The Knight's Tale" and "Beowulf"

> Ther is ful many a man that crieth 'Werre, werre!'
> that woot ful litel what werre amounteth.
> —*The Tale of Melibee*

> For wyndowe on the wal ne was ther noon,
> Thurgh which men myghten any light discerne.
> The dore was al of adamant eterne,
> Yclenched overthwart and endelong
> With iren tough.—*The Knight's Tale*

Anyone about to offer a brief essay on the *Knight's Tale* as a tribute to an eminent medievalist ought really to begin with an ample *occupatio*, listing at length the topics he is not going to treat and the many critics he is not going to praise or argue with. Let these sentences serve as *occupatio occupationum*, with a general apology to those Chaucerians who have invested so much time in puzzling over this most opaque of the *Canterbury Tales*, scholars whose work I have neither time nor qualifications to discuss here. I will have nothing to say here, for instance, about courtly love or Boethius or the specific features of romances or Boccaccio and the early Italian Renaissance. I offer instead a limited point of view based on my own experience as an Anglo-Saxonist and student of epic.

I want to place the *Knight's Tale* within a broad context of epic atmosphere and epic themes, though well aware that that is not its only important context. Some idea of epic must have been in Chaucer's mind as he contemplated Boccaccio's *Teseida* and behind it the *Thebaid* of Statius, though it is difficult to guess what exactly such an idea consisted of, since he was unfamiliar with some basic works that go toward making up our modern definition of epic, such as *Gilga-*

mesh and the Homeric poems in their complete form. Even the nature of his acquaintance with and understanding of the *Aeneid* may be problematic.[1]

But Chaucer's creation of a recognizable heroic world does not depend solely on such intertextuality. His picture of such a world might have drawn much from his own experience as (briefly) soldier and prisoner of war in a campaign in France and (over a long period) court official well acquainted with the powerful. Perhaps he was familiar with such continuations of an earlier heroic tradition in his century as the alliterative *Morte Arthure* (the famous alliterative passage describing the fighting in the tournament would suggest some such familiarity: *Knight's Tale*, lines I. 2601–2616).[2]

From a different point of view, the fact that his major single work, *Troilus and Criseyde*, also shows a deep interest in a fictional pagan world seems to reveal his wish to study human behavior outside the constricting framework of Christianity (to the extent that that was possible for him). Epic and Christianity are not incompatible, but they are uneasy bedfellows. The pagan world is more readily seen as possessing certain heroic values.[3]

Let me first sketch out in overbold summary form some chief features of this heroic world, after which I want to suggest, by a more detailed comparison of the *Knight's Tale* with *Beowulf*, some ways in which these features work poetically. Despite many very obvious differences, the two poems are similar in both being composed by Christian poets examining, seriously and sympathetically, a pre-Christian heroic world. The *Beowulf*-poet is closer to actual paganism and views it with a warmth and understanding that Chaucer can hardly feel.[4]

The universe of the epic, though of course not the same in every

---

[1] David Anderson reminds us that the *Knight's Tale* was viewed as an epic rather than a romance up into the eighteenth century (*Before the Knight's Tale: Imitation of Classical Epic in Boccaccio's Teseid*, 192–94); his book as a whole and its documentation should be consulted. Edgar Finley Shannon, *Chaucer and the Roman Poets*, sees Virgil as a much less important influence on Chaucer than Ovid.

[2] References throughout are to *The Riverside Chaucer*.

[3] See A. J. Minnis, *Chaucer and Pagan Antiquity*, for a thorough discussion of Chaucer's pagan worlds, especially the pagan gods, and also John P. McCall, *Chaucer Among the Gods: The Poetics of Classical Myth*, especially 63–86.

[4] See my article, "The Nature of Christianity in *Beowulf*."

work, is more likely than not to seem bleak, forbidding, or hostile. Although in the *Iliad*, for example, supernatural beings exist in a higher and happier world, this world is not accessible to the heroes who live out their lives apart from the gods, or in spite of them. We are emotionally drawn into the affairs of the human beings who for all their mortality and weakness can be made to seem morally superior to celestial beings so alien to us and to our suffering, beings often viewed with contempt for their spite and capriciousness—and for their very immortality. For it is death that dominates epic: it may sometimes end the hero's life within the poem, but it is always a presence in every heroic exploit and every battle.

Death certainly plays a major role in the *Knight's Tale*, where an unforgettable and truly central image is the *taas*, the tangled heap of dead bodies that the *pilours* or plunderers paw their way through and from which they rip the nearly dead Palamon and Arcite (I. 1005-24). (The scene is reminiscent of the *pilours* who strip the corpses after the battle of Hastings, as depicted on the border of the Bayeux Tapestry.) In their complaint to Theseus at the poem's beginning, the Greek ladies tell how Creon has violated the bodies of their husbands by consigning them to a similar *taas*.

> He, for despit and for his tirannye,
> To do the dede bodyes vileynye
> Of alle oure lordes whiche that been yslawe,
> Hath alle the bodyes on an heep ydrawe,
> And wol nat suffren hem, by noon assent
> Neither to been yburyed nor ybrent,
> But maketh houndes ete hem in despit.[5]

The *taas* haunts the poem just as Matthew Brady's photographs of corpse-choked trenches haunt our concept of the American Civil War.

The hero's energies are usually directed toward staving off some form of chaos, disorder, sheer entropy—perhaps forms of societal death, often represented metaphorically in the form of monsters. Odysseus must move through fantastic monster-worlds (the Cyclops is a very Grendel-like figure) toward his firm-planted tree-rooted bed

---

[5] *Canterbury Tales*, I. 941-47.

in Ithaca. Roland and his rear guard of crusading knights must hold the pass against the monstrous hordes of pagans who would carry their Hell on into sweet France, and Earl Byrhtnoth in the Old English *Battle of Maldon* dies defending Essex against heathen Viking invaders.

The heroic effort not only takes this primary form of fighting but also of building and defending: strong images of walls, fortresses, cities abound in heroic poetry. The image of a wall or a barrier not only suggests this strenuous defensive effort, but it also implies a limit to the ordered space that can be cleared and held by heroic effort. This limit exists in time as well as in space: beyond and surrounding the cleared-out space of a human life lies the chaos of death and fate. What epics may be most concerned with is the way the hero comes to terms with such limits, or, to use the phrase Chaucer made famous, how he makes a virtue of necessity. Indeed no brief phrase better describes the way doom can seem to be transcended (though never conquered) by the hero's exhilarating confrontation with danger and death.

In *Beowulf* the image of limit is memorably expressed in the metaphor of the little clearing of light and warmth and love surrounded by a hostile world of monsters of the darkness.[6] The little fable Bede tells comparing human existence to that of a sparrow spending a brief moment in a warm lighted hall before going back into the dark has often been adduced to indicate that this may have been a habitual way of thinking for the Anglo-Saxons.[7] Chaos seems endemic, a chaos which begins in time almost immediately after God's creation of an ordered universe, when Cain is exiled for the fratricide that is the original sin of heroic society (*Beowulf* 86–114). The potential of humankind for destructive behavior is represented in one form by the semi-human figures of Cain's descendants, Grendel and his mother, externalized projections of our inner darkness, and in another form by the murderous and suicidal feuds within the

---

[6] John Halverson, "Aspects of Order in the *Knight's Tale*," refers to the lists in terms that apply equally well to Heorot—as "a *temenos*—an official or sacred precinct—the connotations of which include those of the settler's clearing in the forest and of the *tun* as well as of a sacred area: it represents the imposition of social order on the wildness of nature" (615).

[7] *Historia ecclesiastica gentis Anglorum*, 2:13.

lighted clearing, ineradicable upsurgings of violence typical of early Germanic literature. This is a world terribly threatened by violence and yet also upheld by violence, a world just barely surviving, supported above the abyss for an unknown but brief interval only by the most strenuous exertions of a noble hero—a world that can spare no energy, incidentally, for those years-long mopings and sufferings of noble lovers we find in the later romances and to some extent in the *Knight's Tale*.

The theme of mortality is expressed in *Beowulf* in the image of a single human life. The long curve of Beowulf's life first upward and then downward to darkness is preceded and foreshadowed by the small-scale curve of Scyld's career in the opening lines of the poem, which shows us how social chaos (lordlessness) can be temporarily remedied by a miraculous heroic saviour who comes in a boat from a far country, and whose inevitable death after a useful life must then be tenderly mourned by the abandoned survivors. As the main plot begins, the chaos brought upon the Danes by Grendel is explored and the hero Beowulf journeys to fight against it. He moves in the course of the poem from unpromising beginnings to an immensely powerful prime when he goes back to rule his own kingdom after exterminating the Danish monsters. We come to a final stage of chaos caused by the dragon's attacks, a chaos again temporarily remedied, but only at the price of the old hero's death and the dire prospect of future disorder and calamity, as the darkness closes in.

In the *Knight's Tale* the description of Arcite's dying and his final speech (I. 2742–97) are the most memorable instances of the mortality theme, but they are striking because of the shocking brevity of Arcite's truncated life-span. We do not have the same single life-cycle we have in *Beowulf*, though perhaps we see something like it in a static and staged-out form: Palamon, Arcite, and Emelye represent youth; Theseus maturity; Egeus senility. Death also pervades all three temple descriptions, in different ways. Venus is depicted as the goddess Fortuna, surrounded by her victims; Diana is a vengeful punisher; and of course Mars revels in a terrifying death-world. So heavy a stress on death in itself distances the *Knight's Tale* from the usual medieval romance.

I have noted that in *Beowulf* all the pressure of chaotic forces does not come from outside, even though that is the pressure most vividly represented in the poem's main action, the fights with monsters. The inner problem is one found in all heroic societies: the same violent energies required to defend and uphold this relatively primitive culture are also capable of becoming purely destructive. It is devotion, courage, and loyalty that lead inexorably to the disintegration of Malory's Round Table. We see the problem exemplified in *Beowulf* in the case of one individual, the former Danish king Heremod, who is gifted with all the requisite heroic talents but who becomes a morose killer of his own men rather than external enemies and is finally driven into exile (lines 898–915; 1709–22a).[8] Characters plainly have the freedom to choose their own behavior, and a nation's welfare hangs on these separate choices.

We are justified in blaming Heremod for his regression to violence; but more tragic, because it cannot be resolved by easy blame, is the situation at Finnsburg (1063–1159a), where a feud develops beyond control and we cannot in fairness find one of the sides more guilty than the other. What the poet focuses the audience's attention on is the impartial flame that blazes on the mutual pyre:

> Lig ealle forswealg,
> gæsta gifrost, Þara ðe þær guð fornam
> bega folces; wæs hire blæd scacen.
>
> (1122b–24)

(Fire, that greediest of spirits, devoured all of them, all those whom war destroyed, of both peoples; their power was gone.)

The "inside" form of chaos in the *Knight's Tale* is found chiefly in the bitter rivalry between Palamon and Arcite, but it is also to some degree externalized or reified in the terrible figures of Mars and Saturn (the latter added by Chaucer to his sources and given the crucial responsibility for Arcite's death). What "Mars" means is not to be controlled in any sense, however, merely by being given a name and locked away, safely catalogued, into a temple—"Mars" is simply what men do every day in this kind of heroic world, and "Saturn" is whatever bad happens to them.

In actuality disorder and violence are everywhere in the *Knight's Tale*, built into the very nature of things as in *Beowulf*, and combat-

---

[8] References will be to Klaeber's third edition of *Beowulf and the Fight at Finnsburg*.

ted at all points possible by the indomitable Theseus. Paradox
abounds. The passionate and unthinking violence of Palamon and
Arcite is necessary for their definition as virile knights; the merciless
war between Athens and Thebes defines the superb conqueror
Theseus. The opening of the poem, with its marvelous picture of
Theseus in terms of total power and conquest, leads us to expect
confidently that he will be able to control his world: a little later, we
see an unbroken run of victorious "ryding" (the image suggests that
his progress cannot be stopped) and the ruthless carrying out of
justice on Thebes to the point of devastation later to be described in
the temple of Mars: "the toun destroyed, ther was no thyng laft" (I.
2016).

Disorder not only permeates the Mars and Saturn descriptive
set-pieces, but spills over beyond them. War spreads from the *taas*,
the battlefield of horror, into the peasant's cottage where sows eat
babies; disaster extends through the Saturnian realm of calamity from
royal castles down to the lowly sappers who undermine them.
Here—as in the *Canterbury Tales* as a whole—Chaucer takes us well
beyond the narrow aristocratic world of dukes and knights and
ladies, that small area where Theseus struggles to keep the control he
has exerted in the past. When he cannot control even that area, chaos
is come again.

The ways that heroic resistance is applied to counter the on-
slaughts of these monsters differ in the two poems, but not as completely as one might think at first. Obviously *Beowulf* is dominated
by physical action, with a hero actually fighting and defeating monsters, but it also raises the problem of good administration and strong
kingship. Beowulf can boast on the verge of death that he held his
people well for fifty years as a strong protective king (2732b–2736a).
The first part of *Beowulf*, set in Denmark, stresses the painful disparity between an aggressive young warrior and a hollow shell of an old
king (Hrothgar), but the second part shows Beowulf as a strong old
king-warrior, with the two split parts now joined together in a single
individual.

Theseus, on the other hand, is depicted as a literal fighter only
briefly, though brilliantly, at the beginning of the *Knight's Tale*;
thereafter he appears very much as the Strong King—in fact, so
strong, strenuous, and dedicated a king that he ranks in the heroic
scale with any fighter. At the beginning of part IV, for example, we

see him not in active movement but seated in majesty, and yet still
powerfully imposing his desire on his submissive people.

> Duc Theseus was at a wyndow set,
> Arrayed right as he were a god in trone.
> The peple preesseth thiderward ful soone
> Hym for to seen, and doon heigh reverence,
> And eek to herkne his heste and his sentence.
> An heraud on a scaffold made an "Oo!"
> Til al the noyse of peple was ydo,
> And whan he saugh the peple of noyse al stille,
> Tho shewed he the myghty dukes wille.
>
> (I. 2528–36)

Fighting, or giving off such regal power as this, are active ways of
defending human society from the monstrous entropic forces, but
there is also a more passive defense in the form of what we can
simply call buildings. The image of the building (as I have suggested
at some length elsewhere[9]) is a massive central image in *Beowulf*.
Germanic heroic society lives in the incessant exchange of services
and wealth within the hall, a space cleared out of the center of the
chaotic world. Thus the chaos-monsters are instantly driven to
destroy such a building. Grendel was quiescent until Hrothgar (in a
Theseus-like act) commanded the building of the hall Heorot, but its
completion maddens him into his first attack, as he rips open its
mouth-like door and gobbles down its complement of feasting
thanes. The dragon later levels Beowulf's own hall with one blast of
avenging fire.

Buildings in the *Knight's Tale* are used in complex ways, chiefly
by Theseus, the hero as architect. In a sense Theseus initially
"builds" Athens through his successive conquests of Femenye and
Thebes, just as Hrothgar is enabled by his early conquests to attract
enough followers to make the erection of his new hall Heorot
appropriate. Theseus then builds (also figuratively) a prison to hold
the two young Thebans for eternity, extending his will for justice
(though we may see it less favorably as the vengeful violence of the
war) into the postwar world. But this prison cracks apart, it leaks, it

---

[9] Chapter 4, "The Hall as Image and Character," in *Rereading Beowulf*.

fails to work, when Palamon and Arcite leave it by different ways. Whereupon Theseus, after surveying the chaos presented by the two liberated rivals fighting ankle-deep in blood in the grove outside Athens, constructs the most elaborate building in the poem, the spectacular stadium of the lists with the three temples attached to it. As many have pointed out, this is an attempt to impose a new kind of order on the destructive rivalry of the two ex-prisoners.[10] Like the tower-prison, this building too fails in its purpose.

Theseus's obsessive passion for order and justice could be viewed indeed as a form of violence. The pathos of the two young men locked forever in the dungeon-tower, where they glimpse Emelye only "thurgh a wyndow, thikke of many a barre / Of iren greet and square as any sparre" (1075–76), makes us feel the weight of Theseus's equally iron will. As prisoners, what they may really fall in love with is Emelye's free "romyng to and fro" (mentioned five times in a few lines: 1052, 1069, 1099, 1113, 1119). Since Chaucer omits the explanation that Boccaccio offers for Theseus's motive in imprisoning the Thebans, he makes Theseus all the more absolute and arbitrary in his use of raw power, making him truly an iron man of whom we dare ask no questions. Some critics have interpreted lines 1663–72, which begin

> The destinee, ministre general,
> That executeth in the world over al
> The purveiaunce that God hath seyn biforn...
> This mene I now by myghty Theseus

as literally equating Theseus with "destinee," and the suggestion is tempting, because it is consistent with Chaucer's apparent purpose in characterizing Theseus as driven to hubristic harshness and cruelty by his rage for order.

In the lists, the monster-gods of disorder are given space in the

---

[10] William Frost, "An Interpretation of Chaucer's Knight's Tale," and Charles Muscatine, *Chaucer and the French Tradition*, have stated emphatically that Theseus's attempt to order a disorderly reality was at the core of the poem, and they have been followed in this view by Elizabeth Salter in her useful edition (*Chaucer: The Knight's Tale and the Clerk's Tale*) and most subsequent critics, at least until recently. Lois Roney presents an up-to-date review of previous interpretations in her *Chaucer's Knight's Tale and Theories of Scholastic Psychology*, 1–8.

temples, bound within the sacred circuit. Prayers which the characters address to the gods attempt to compel them to consent to human wishes, but the answers are always ambiguous. Significantly, it is the one god they forgot to build a temple for and pray to who decides the outcome of the battle and the poem. But then Saturn may deserve no temples; he is specifically the god of the ruin of buildings, of no buildings at all:

> Myn is the ruyne of the hye halles,
> The fallynge of the toures and of the walles
> Upon the mynour or the carpenter.
> I slow Sampsoun, shakynge the piler.
>
> (I. 2463–66)

The dragon in *Beowulf* makes a somewhat imperfect analogue to Saturn as God of the Shaft, of the sheer impersonal horror of disaster and accident. It has been the critical consensus that the dragon lacks the "personal" envy and malice that drive Grendel and his vengeful mother. Personal spite seems to motivate Saturn, however, and the dragon's blind rage at humanity is not quite the same thing. Saturn at a whim decides to kill one person; the dragon, in inexplicable alien fury at being intruded upon, kills as many human beings as he can, unselectively.

In addition to actual physical buildings, poets may also use verbal constructions to bind and contain the violence. Probably the very *naming* of structures is in itself thought to have power: Hrothgar creates the name for his great hall Heorot (="hart," perhaps a tribal totem-name with some pre-Christian significance), and Theseus dubs a grisly collection of horrors "Mars." One's personal name (=reputation) may be of the highest importance: the young hero Arcite when he is in disguise finds it a great hardship that "I dar noght biknowe myn owene name" (I. 1556). In *Beowulf*, the most striking example of this attempt to use words as binders is the language of the treaty that brings about a truce in the conflict between Frisians and Danes in the story Heorot's scop tells of the fight at Finnsburg. Circumstances force the two feuding tribes to share the same hall and serve the same king, Finn of the Frisians. Since this passage seems especially relevant to Chaucer's poem, I translate a few lines:

Then they concluded on both sides a firm peace-agreement.

Finn bound himself with oaths to Hengest, eagerly and without dispute, that he would hold the wretched surviving Danes
in honor, by his counsellors' judgement, so that there no man
might break the pact by words or deeds, nor ever mention in
spiteful malice that they were following the killer [Finn] of
their own dead king [Hnæf], as necessity required them to do;
if then any Frisian ever reminded them of that murderous
fight with his rash speech, then it would be *sword's edge* that
would settle the matter.[11]

A dramatic struggle to control a hopeless situation with words and
oaths precedes the sudden flashing out of *sweordes ecg* at the end of
the quoted passage, prefiguring the flashing of swords later in the
story when the feud breaks out again. A comparable passage from
the *Knight's Tale*, full of the same kind of tense negatives, contains
Theseus's rules for the tournament (the elaborate rules are again one
of Chaucer's notable additions):

> No man therfore, up peyne of los of lyf,
> No maner shot, ne polax, ne short knyf
> Into the lystes sende or thider brynge;
> Ne short swerd, for to stoke with poynt bitynge,
> No man ne drawe, ne bere it by his syde.
> Ne no man shal unto his felawe ryde
> But o cours with a sharpe ygrounde spere.
>
> (I. 2543-49)

A similar passage is the "forward" or agreement drawn up between
Theseus and the released Arcite: this is stated in such strict terms that
Arcite exclaims, "Now is my prisoun worse than biforn" (1224).
These passages strive passionately for a *rhetorical* control of violent
behavior; yet, by their very intensity of emotion and by the way the
massed negative phrases keep mentioning the weapons and the

---

[11] Da hie getruwedon   on twa healfa / fæste frioðuwære.   Fin Hengeste /
elne unflitme   aðum benemde, / þæt he þa wealafe   weotena dome / arum
heolde, þæt ðær ænig mon / wordum ne worcum   wære ne bræce, / ne þurh
inwitsearo   æfre gemænden, / ðeah hie hira beaggyfan   banan folgedon / ðeoden-
lease, þa him swa geþearfod wæs; / gyf þonne Frysna hwylc   frecnan spræce / ðæs
morþorhetes   myndgiend wære, / þonne hit sweordes ecg   seðan scolde (1095–
1106).

actions that might be unleashed, they tend to imply their own opposite: this rhetoric might fail. Actually, Theseus's rules do hold for the duration of the tournament. Finn's treaty holds for the stressful "slaughter-stained winter" that the two feuding parties are doomed to spend together in the same hall, but then spring brings vengeance and massacre when the pressures are released and the treaty is broken. In an analogous way, the blood-brother oath that ought to bind Palamon and Arcite together does not hold against the pressure of sexual desire.

The innate ferocity that resists such civilized constraints is expressed in animal images in both poems. The memorable and often discussed descriptions of the tournament's two champions, Lygurge and Emetrius, are full of such images. Lygurge is associated with a gryphon, bulls, a bear, a raven, hunting hounds, a steer: he is a Wild Man, a savage barbarically rich in heavy gold, a ferocious muzzled hound himself (I. 2128–54). Emetrius is a lion, carrying an eagle, with lions and leopards bounding alongside him; if less wild in appearance than Lygurge, he is equally barbaric and exotic (I. 2155–86). We have ferocity dolled up in both cases, and that is what the tournament itself is.

Animals also appear in different forms in *Beowulf*. Beowulf's own name (possibly his nickname) is thought by many to mean "bear" (i.e., an enemy to bees, a honey-eater), and his favored fighting-style is a crushing bear-hug rather than the use of crafted weapons. Violence reaches a climax at the end of the poem in the exciting account of the battle at *Hrefnawudu*, the ravens' wood, in which the Geatish warriors named Wulf and Eofor ('boar') have starring roles. The Messenger ends this account with a vision of a future in which exhausted warriors wield their morning-cold spears under the eager and ironic gaze of the carrion-eating creatures, wolf, eagle, and raven (3021b–27).

A third way to contain the violence is through converting it into relatively harmless game or play. This is of course what Theseus tries to do with his heavily rule-dominated tournament in which nobody is granted permission to die. The lists he builds are his prison/theater, where his suitor-gladiators are "free" to play the game within the limits of his strict rules. Theseus is reminiscent of another well-known fourteenth-century *magister ludi*, the Green Knight, who also provides a theater (a bed) in which Sir Gawain and the Lady can play their war-game. Probably the elaborate account of Arcite's funeral is to be viewed as a variety of "game" that dissipates grief through ritual activity, in the familiar manner of the ancient Greeks (though the athletic events seem to be viewed by the Knight/ Chaucer with some curiosity).

In *Beowulf*, there are several similar games. Warfare itself is conventionally referred to by words like *guðplega* 'war play'. Young Beowulf competes in a daring swimming contest with Breca, which would perhaps deserve Unferth's characterization of it as infantile and foolhardy if Beowulf had not gone on to play a larger and more serious game by clearing the channels of sea-monsters (*Bwf* 506–606). The verbal battle or flyting he has with Unferth over the Breca incident is a striking example of a popular early-Germanic game: the flyting dissipates through wit and harmless insult the real and possibly dangerous tensions that exist between Beowulf and the Danes he has come to rescue from their troubles. Sportsmanship is a necessary feature of such games. Beowulf is a good sport in not using a sword against Grendel, who does not know of such "good things" (*nat he þara goda* 681), just as Arcite will not kill the unarmed Palamon in the grove but sends him off to get some proper weapons for the duel (I. 1610–19). Of course Grendel, the dragon, and the pagan gods in the *Knight's Tale* altogether lack this human sense of fair play.

But it is not all playing games. The harshness and brutality of the heroic world elicit strong feelings of pathos, pain and loss. In the *Knight's Tale*, such feelings cluster around the life and death of Arcite, are found in the speeches of the young heroes, and are memorably focused in the descriptions of temples, particularly the temple of Mars. In actuality, Theseus's bold attempt to solve the problem of the lovers' rivalry through "game"—a kind of trial by combat—does not work. The ordeal or trial by battle dominates the Christian *Song of Roland*, but one may ask whether justice can be carried out in this way in a non-Christian universe where God does not supervise the play.

In *Beowulf*, painful and despairing feelings appear (in beautiful verse) in the so-called elegiac passages: one a speech by the "Last Survivor" who commits his nation's treasure to the earth before dying himself (2236b–70a); one an "epic simile" about an old father who must helplessly watch his son hanged unavenged (2444–59); one a vision of future slavery and suffering for the Geats after Beowulf's death (3010b–27). Here passive suffering, which is the opposite, and the result, of the strenuous activity that characterizes heroic literature, is given eloquent voice, as it is in the great laments of the Trojan women at the end of the *Iliad*. Some readers may feel that the laments by the various characters in the *Knight's Tale* contain its most moving poetry; we remember Palamon's conclusion that "wel I woot that in this world greet pyne is" (I. 1324), Arcite's "what is this world?"(I. 2777), and Theseus's statement of relief that Arcite has departed with honor "out of this foule prisoun of this lyf" (I. 3061).

It is often true that women are the most eloquent victims of all. No reader of *Beowulf* can forget the figure of Hildeburh, Hnæf's sister and Finn's wife, who is caught between the feuding male forces with no option but agony:

> Ne huru Hildeburh   herian þorfte
> Eotena treowe;   unsynnum weard
> beloren leofum   æt þam lindplegan
> bearnum ond broðrum;   hie on gebyrd hruron
> gare wunde;   þæt wæs geomuru ides!
>
> [lines 1071–75]

(Indeed Hildeburh had not the slightest reason to praise the good faith of the "Eotens" [=Jutes?]; innocent, she was bereft in the shield-playing of a dear son and dear brother; they fell by fate, wounded by the spear; that was a mournful woman!)

In its subtle way, alliteration stresses *unsynnum* 'innocent', and sets the tenderness of *beloren leofum* 'bereft of dear [ones]' against the macho joking embedded in *lindplegan* 'shield-play', and chiastically balances the brutal *gare wunde* against the emotion of *geomuru ides*, the mournful lady. Immediately after this we see another woman, Wealhtheow, Hrothgar's queen, who pleads in vain to anyone who will listen in behalf of the right of her young sons to accede to the throne we know they will never attain. They will apparently die in some future outbreak of fury only hinted at in the poem but probably well known to its original audience.

In the *Knight's Tale*, if Emelye is anything at all as a character (Chaucer systematically removes every individualizing trait Boccaccio had assigned her), it is as a passive sufferer, a woman who comes to life most vividly when she prays ardently to Diana that she might be given to neither one of her two impassioned suitors—in other words, that she might be allowed to get out of the story altogether. Surely we in our century may see irony in Chaucer's fine juxtaposition of Prison-tower with Garden, where the prisoners Palamon and Arcite look out at Emelye "roming" and gathering flowers: is she not as much a prisoner as they are? She is after all not only penned up like all women but a war captive and a trophy of conquest. It seems quite possible that the poet who could put such a powerful desire for freedom into the words of the Wife of Bath ("For evere yet I loved to be gay, / And for to walke in March, Averill, and May, / Fro hous to hous, to heere sondry talys" [III. 545–47]) might be aware of the paradox. Emelye has really no freedom to "rome" outside her garden or outside her assigned place in the men's plot. One recalls that the lais of Marie de France have several images of women literally imprisoned by men.

Women who are presented even more vividly as victims are the ladies in the beginning of the poem who petition Theseus for aid in recovering the bodies of their men. The scene shows them pathetically grasping his bridle and only slowly gaining his attention as he rides proudly back from stunning victories in love and war. He is high on his horse and high in his male pride; they lie low on the ground weeping. His descent, his *condescension*, his recognition of the claims of the miserable, is graphically rendered in purely physical terms: at last he dismounts, he walks to them, he stoops all the way down to the ground and picks them up in his arms—visually registering his "herte pitous" and his "gentilesse."

While I have been here drawing some parallels that some will consider forced, I know I have been ignoring very large areas of the *Knight's Tale*. I am arguing that the parallels help us better to see a dark traditional dimension in Chaucer, but other themes and tones are of course essential to the success of his great poem. The fresh descriptions of May mornings; the conventionally extravagant expressions of love; the quizzical joking of Theseus on the comic aspects of lovers; the gloriously hectic medieval bustle of squires, armorers and betting spectators on the morning of the tournament; the narrator's testy or anxious interjections; the Knight's character and the context of the *Tales* as a whole—there is no parallel whatever in *Beowulf* to any of these. Obviously they create a richness and variety that the older poem lacks, as it lacks Chaucer's illusion of an individual speaking voice (whether we want to hear it as his own or as one of his character's). *Beowulf* has only the communal voice of the oral-traditional poet, speaking the handed-down tribal truths in the ancient language of the scop.

This communal voice tells us of the divinely-sanctioned heroic energy that staves off the darkness for a pathetically short while: it speaks, in other words, in the tones of heroic tragedy, and provides a single, powerful emotional impact. The *Knight's Tale* too shows a deep awareness of heroic tragedy, but it is constantly distracting or diverting us from the glories and horrors of that heroic world. Perhaps it declares that we are all seeking that distraction, and perhaps that is what the much-discussed ending means.

The most famous of all speeches in the *Knight's Tale* is that of Theseus on the "Firste Moevere," a closing speech that, at least for those favoring a Boethian interpretation, makes its most important statement. The Firste Moevere is a very Theseus-like figure himself, setting up elaborate game-rules for the eternal universe, creating the "faire cheyne of love" (2955) to bind and keep its elements not only "in certeyn boundes, that they may not flee" but within limits of time ("over the whiche day they may nat pace"). Yet the earthly components of this stable and rule-bound universe are not themselves eternal. Chaucer brings in some venerable medieval *topoi* to make the point. Like the Wanderer in the Old English poem of that name, and in the same ancient *ubi sunt* tradition, Theseus thinks of crumbling walls and buildings: "the grete tounes se we wane and wende" (I. 3025). His meditation on the various ways men die—"som in his bed, som in the depe see" (I. 3031)—resembles another medieval commonplace exemplified by the Old English poem on *The Fortunes of Men*.

The word *grucchen* expresses the natural resentment—or, more seriously, anguish—human beings feel at their inexorable march into final defeat. Theseus uses the word three times (3045, 3058, 3062); he understands the full strength of this feeling because he shares it himself. It is against this *grucchyng* that he projects his appeal to all that they make the best of what is left to them. The courageous battle for order has been fought, and we have lost it, as we always will. For the pre-Christian hero, reputation (*dom* in *Beowulf*) is the only form immortality can take, and Arcite has that. The marriage of the two survivors will reward them for the values of *gentilesse* and *wommanly pitee* they have displayed.

At the end of *Beowulf*, there is only an anonymous collective of survivors, riding around a funeral mound, survivors who simultaneously confront their own terrifying future and honor the dead hero-king who has staved it off for so long. But the merry wedding that Theseus and the Knight so enthusiastically support is not a sentimental ending by contrast. What the characters have they have earned, within the harsh limits of this iron world—and neither poem envisions any other.

University of Pennsylvannia

ALBERT E. HARTUNG

"The Parson's Tale" and Chaucer's Penance[1]

The view that *The Parson's Tale* is a separately written work, composed outside the Canterbury scheme of things, has been with us for some time. But for the most part it has been something of a poor relation in comparison with the two main critical approaches to the tale of the last forty years or so. These approaches in various ways make the tale a crucial part of the whole Canterbury performance, in which it is considered as either the ultimate thematic religious statement which informs the whole work, or as a performance which must be considered dramatically as a statement about the Parson himself. Both of these views in various shadings have been persuasively argued, a fact that presents us with a problem that cannot easily be resolved. For they are basically irreconcilable, even though some attempts have been made to accommodate them to one another, and at the same time each makes a claim on us that has some validity.[2] And so since we cannot out-of-hand comfortably reject either one or the other of these views as completely unacceptable, we are left with the critical dilemma of

---

[1] An earlier and shorter version of this paper, now much modified, was read before the Medieval Club of New York, City University of New York, December 1, 1989.

[2] A convenient annotated listing up to the time of its publication (1978) of these divergent views, categorized as the moral absolute, the retrospective, the dramatic, and the biographical, may be found in Patterson, 333, n. 8. A more recent survey (1984) is Traugott Lawler's judicious treatment of Chaucer's prose works in *Middle English Prose*, ed. Edwards, 296–99, 306–7 (*Parson's Tale* and Retraction). Obligatory are Siegfried Wenzel's explanatory notes for Fragment X, *The Riverside Chaucer*, especially 954–57.

being persuaded by both, yet at the same time unable to give our critical allegiance confidently to either.

This dilemma is avoided by the view of various earlier critics that *The Parson's Tale* was a separate composition, perhaps not even by Chaucer, at least not originally part of the *Canterbury Tales*. It is given a typical, if somewhat uncertain, statement by Manly in *The Text of the Canterbury Tales*. After wavering on the subject of Chaucer's authorship, Manly notes the "undistinguished position" of the *Canterbury Tales* in the enumeration of Chaucer's works in the Retraction. They are neither first as most important nor last in a position of climax as one might expect if they indeed conclude the entire work. Possibly then both *The Parson's Tale* and the Retraction may have been by Chaucer and yet "have no legitimate claim to a place in [*The Canterbury Tales*]." Similarly Owen writes of *The Parson's Tale* as part of a "religious lacuna in the middle of the Canterbury period," adapted at an early stage as a conclusion to the collection, then rejected in this role.[3]

Even though the view that *The Parson's Tale* was composed outside the Canterbury framework is generally ignored in the criticism of the tale, it has never been entirely discredited because fitting the tale comfortably into the work poses a problem. The problem is caused by the Retraction. In violating the dramatic integrity of the work, it has the effect of taking the tale out of the work and making it a separate entity, a feature that modern criticism has responded to in a variety of ways.[4] For the earliest editors of Chaucer the Retraction possibly was also a problem, which Thynne (with Stow and Speght following him) solved by simply omitting it.[5] Perhaps

---

[3] See Manly and Rickert, 2:455, 471–72; 4:527. A more recent extension of Owen's views suggests that the retention of *The Parson's Tale* in the Canterbury framework is the result of the Ellesmere editor's desire to produce a "completed" work. See Owen, "Development," 459; "Alternative Reading," 243; also "Pre-1450 Manuscripts . . . Pt I," 23–24, on Longleat 29.

[4] For example, Howard, *Idea*, 387: "Sight, instantaneous vision, replaces time-bound utterance at the end of this most noisy book. So in his final words the author, grave and filled with hope, imposes silence on his feat of impersonation . . . and turns his eye upon the still center." Donaldson, *Speaking*, 11–12: "Chaucer the poet . . . operates in a realm which is above and subsumes those in which Chaucer the man and Chaucer the pilgrim have their being. . . . In this complex structure . . . I am not persuaded that in every case it is possible to determine which of them has the last word." See also Wurtele, 335–59.

[5] It is reasonable to suppose that Thynne knew of its existence at the end of *The*

Thynne, too, wished to avoid the implication of separateness the Retraction gives to *The Parson's Tale*. Of more significance, because it may help us to determine the nature of the ending of the tale when it left Chaucer's hand, is the response of the medieval editors and their scribes, who copied it. They were also faced with a problem. This is to be seen particularly in the variety of their attempts to impose an *ordinatio* on the ending of the work. Most typical is the rubric immediately preceding the Retraction at line 1081, which has found its way into all modern editions of the work—"Heere taketh the makere of this book his leve." This with variants is found in fifteen manuscripts, including Ellesmere. It occurs also in Latin. But there are other ways in which the *ordinatio* is handled: "Preces de Chaucer"; and also "Explicit tractatus Galfridi Chaucer de penitencia (*var.* de septem peccatis mortalibus) vt dicitur pro fabula Rectoris"— hence two ways of looking at the tale, as the Parson's but also as Chaucer's. And there are other manuscripts in which the text simply runs on from the concluding line of the "tale" to the beginning line of the Retraction without a break.[6]

For Tyrwhitt "the just inference from these variations in the Mss. is perhaps, that none of them are to be relied on; that different Copyists have given this passage the title that pleased them best," attributing it to Chaucer or the Parson as each felt most suitable. Doyle and Parkes convincingly support the same conclusion through a meticulous analysis of *ordinatio* in four early manuscripts of the *Canterbury Tales*. They all reflect attempts to impose an organization on the unfinished work. None has special authority. However, Ellesmere, the most spectacular example of the use of *ordinatio*, has most influenced modern editors.[7] It is an interesting meditation to

---

Parson's Tale. The consensus is that Thynne's base text was one of the earlier printed editions. The Retraction would have been included in them (with the exception of Pynson). See Blodgett, 46–47. The same would have inevitably also been true for at least some of the manuscripts which his son Francis tells us that his father either possessed or examined. For his father's acquaintance with Chaucer manuscripts, see Thynne, *Animadversions*, 6.

[6] See Manly and Rickert, 3:530–31 (Headings and Endings), which should be supplemented with the more detailed treatment in McCormick and Heseltine.

[7] Tyrwhitt, 2d edn., 1798, 2.513. A. I. Doyle and M. B. Parkes, "The Production of Copies of the *Canterbury Tales* . . . ," 194. See also M. B. Parkes, "The Influence of the Concepts of *Ordinatio* and *Compilatio*," 134.

consider what effect our being nurtured on the Ellesmere "Heere taketh the makere ..." rubric may have on our response to *The Parson's Tale* and the Retraction which follows it. But there is no evidence that it is Chaucer we are responding to, but simply the Ellesmere editor. What Chaucer gave us we do not know. The probability is that he did not give us anything. The very strong suggestion of a lack of authorial guidance lends at least some support to a view that is by no means a novelty in Chaucer criticism—that the Retraction is really the conclusion of "this lytel tretys" on penance, which we call *The Parson's Tale,* rather than of the *Canterbury Tales* as a whole, and that, considering the violation of dramatic integrity the Retraction presents, the two together might be considered as a unit separable from the *Canterbury Tales.*

In pursuing this view, one must of course reckon with the Parson's prologue with its clear and compelling connections with the beginning of the tale which follows. Nor is there any question that the prologue, tale, and Retraction belong together and are representative of Chaucer's intention to end the work on a moral and transcendent note. As Wenzel has pointed out ("Every Tales Strengthe"), the emphasis in the Parson's Prologue that this is to be the last tale (repeated in various ways), together with the image of "knitting up" which underlines its importance, is one such signal. Both the astronomical imagery which begins the prologue and the desire of the pilgrims transmitted to the Parson through the Host "to enden in some vertuous sentence" give further rhetorical weight to the prologue. Most significant and in keeping with the pattern of the *Divine Comedy* and the *Anticlaudianus*, as Wenzel points out, is the change of guide preparatory to being led into higher realms. The Host is now replaced by the Parson who will show the pilgrims the "wey in this viage."

But the fact is that the tale itself hardly lives up to its announced role. "Such an exalted function intended for *The Parson's Tale* is, unfortunately, not supported by its form."[8] Indeed, the fact that it is not so supported is a strong argument for the original separateness of the tale and Retraction from the prologue and thus from the whole work itself. The readiest solution to the problem of the

---

[8] Wenzel, "Every Tales Strengthe," 97.

incompatibility between prologue and tale is that the Parson's Prologue was composed for the already existing tale and Retraction with the task of complete adjustment left for the future.[9] The Retraction then goes with the tract on penance, an organic part of it, in structure and content not pointing at the Canterbury collection, but at the penitential work it is a conclusion to. This separate existence is, of course, not prior to the *Canterbury Tales*, but extra to it, and thus created outside it. The question then is for what purpose did it exist? Who needed the penance? The only answer left is Chaucer. The work then becomes a personal utterance in response to a personal need, and the dilemma of the incompatibility is resolved.

There is good reason for looking at *The Parson's Tale* in this way. If indeed it was at one time separate, this fact cannot be a matter of critical indifference. Yet the tale has suffered from a lack of criticism of it in its own right. Even those who do believe that originally it was a separate composition are most concerned with how it got *into* the *Canterbury Tales* and, once there, what role it plays, rather than with the possibilities for explication and critical insight it presents by itself, detached from any connection with the larger work. The expanded knowledge of the sources of the tale that we have, as a result of the work of Wenzel, shows that despite its occasional ambiguities and incoherences *The Parson's Tale* is a carefully meditated construction, drawing selectively on an extremely complex variety of sources together with matter that seems to be exclusively Chaucerian in origin. Far from being a word-for-word translation like *Melibeus*, it is better regarded as a work requiring a great deal of personal involvement, both intellectual and, as is clear, emotional. Finally, it is the nature of this involvement and the manner of its expression considered in relation to the sources that are most persuasive in linking it to Chaucer himself.[10]

---

[9] Such a situation would hardly be unprecedented in the *Canterbury Tales*, most obviously in the specially devised link for *Melibeus*, which had a prior existence as the "prose" the Man of Law was to have spoken. The striking and extensively developed prologue to the presumably early, even pre-Canterbury, *Monk's Tale* is another such example.

[10] Although Bestul in his illuminating study develops the formal characteristics of the *meditatio* tradition and its relevance to *The Parson's Tale* as a conclusion to the Canterbury collection, he comments also on the strategies of Chaucer's enhancement of the personal aspect of such meditations in the modifications Chaucer makes in the sources of the tale, 606.

To be sure, critics have long considered the tale, especially under the influence of the Retraction, as Chaucer's penitential statement, but there seems to be a reluctance to go beyond the view that this penitential response is based on more than the general position that we are all sinners and all in need of penance.[11] The problem here is that we tend to see only what Chaucer himself gives us in his poetry—a genial persona, sympathetic, ironic, amused, insightful, self-aware, understanding and tolerant, patient and resigned—the list can be extended. Perhaps a few venial sins here, a few there. But it is difficult to think of the man as a sinner of any substance. The intensity of opposition (at least by the older scholars) to imputations of irregular behavior (e.g., the suggestions about the parentage of Thomas Chaucer and what that implied) is instructive. How can such a person have been really that bad?

But it is possible to look at the "real" Chaucer in another way. The life records can be taken as showing that Chaucer may, from time to time, have had trouble with what are now called "interpersonal relationships." There was, of course, Cecily Chaumpaigne. There are other things possibly, less clear in their bearings. There was the Franciscan Friar and Chaucer's two-shilling fine for beating him up in Fleet Street. Was the younger Chaucer then something of a street thug? Is it possible to consider those debts that Chaucer incurred, and did not seem to pay, somewhat less charitably than they have been considered, perhaps as indicating a dimension of character other than that of merely an innocently impecunious poet trying to cope? In addition, is it not likely that there were things that we have no hints of at all? It is really not impossible for us to feel that Chaucer may have had reason to consider himself as more than a mere *pro forma* sinner.

So let us go further and assume that Chaucer needed penance, not merely on general terms, but because he had a conviction of sin arising out of some specific occurrence in his life that devastated him, appalled him—not simply a customary moral nervousness, but a real and present thing that he had to come to terms with in the only way

---

[11] Cf. Sayce, "Chaucer's 'Retractions,'" who by viewing the Retraction as literary convention implies a further detachment of penitential response from any specific personal significance.

that his culture made available to him. Seen in this way *The Parson's Tale,* with its strange varieties of intensity and response, and its amazingly complex web of literary and personal relationships, becomes not so much a key to the meaning of the *Canterbury Tales* as it does a personal document with decided implications for Chaucerian biography. If this view can be considered to have some validity, it should then be possible to find in the text of the tale indications of it.

There are problems here. The tale is a substantial and complex creation, consisting of a wealth of material and a variety of responses to it, so much so that it would seem to be really a matter of pick and choose to build whatever case one wanted to. But there are some guides available. There are the sources. And there is Chaucer himself. For Chaucer's use of his sources is eclectic and shifting, and even with considerable uncertainties at times may be an indication of what he has in mind. And the manner and intensity of what we may consider his personal utterance in response to his subject are similarly wide-ranging and an indication of what particularly engages him and what does not.

For example, the section on Gluttony together with its Remedy receives the briefest treatment of any of the sins. It is closely tied to its source. "[D]e remedio gule, idest de abstinencia" the *Postquam* tells us, and so does Chaucer, "Agayns Glotonye is the remedie abstinence." His close dependence on the *Postquam* here is beyond question, even though the 194 lines of the *Postquam* have only five as their counterpart in Chaucer.[12] This rather summary reduction in treatment is all too likely to remind us of what we suspect Chaucer's attitude on this subject to have been from the speech of the eagle in the *House of Fame,* soaring into the sky with a frightened Chaucer in his talons, who tells Geoffrey, "Thou art noyous for to carye," and later comments on Chaucer's compulsive reading habits which keep him indoors, "And lyvest thus as an heremyte, / Although thyn abstynence ys lite." It would be wrong to maintain that in *The Parson's Tale,* Chaucer could think of any sin lightly. Still one must feel that the treatment here, and in other sections of *The Parson's Tale* similar in tone, is programmatic rather than personal.

---

[12] Wenzel, *Summa Virtutum,* 267–77.

But there are other passages in which one must feel that the treatment is personal rather than programmatic. They seem to stand apart. They share a special response to their sources, showing a special intention. They share a common general area of concern. They share a common intensity of response. I feel they take us into the heart of the reason for *The Parson's Tale*'s existence.

I have selected five such passages to consider in specific detail. The first comes at the conclusion of Chaucer's treatment of the third of Pennaforte's six causes that move man to contrition.[13] Chaucer's treatment of all six causes is somewhat different from that in Pennaforte, especially in development (cf. Wenzel, *Riverside Chaucer*, note to 133). In his treatment of the third cause, "detestatio vilitatis ... peccati / desdeyn of synne" (142–57, actually treated second in Chaucer), this difference is particularly apparent. The basic image of the passage is that of sin as thralldom, variously supported by references to Peter, Seneca, Augustine (also in Pennaforte), and to Ezekiel and Augustine (not in Pennaforte). But as it continues, the passage develops a different emphasis and turns to the body and the special thralldom of the body to sin: "I am born to gretter thynges than to be thral to my body, or than for to maken my body a thrall" (145). To this passage, which in Pennaforte is attributed to "Philosophus" and in Chaucer to Seneca, Chaucer adds,

> Ne a fouler thral may no man ne womman maken of his body than for to yeven his body to synne./ Al were it the fouleste cherl or the fouleste womman that lyveth, and leest of value, yet is he thenne moore foul and moore in servitute. (146–47)

The passage continues with a development of the servitude that the body as erring servant can be guilty of, and then turning away suddenly and entirely from the pattern that Pennaforte has established bursts out against women: "O goode God, ye wommen that been of so greet beautee, remembreth yow of the proverbe of Salomon," referring to Proverbs 11.22: Circulus aureus in naribus suis, mulier pulchra et fatua [Douay: A golden ring in a swine's snout, a woman fair and foolish]. Chaucer renders it, "Likneth a fair wom-

---

[13] For the correspondences between *The Parson's Tale* and Pennaforte and Peraldus, see Petersen.

man that is a fool of hire body lyk to a ryng of gold that were in the groyn of a soughe." But he does not stop there. He turns to the *Primo* for the application:[14]

> Fatua mulier similis est porco qui faciem longam mergit in luto, et hoc sibi reputat pro convivio. Quamvis enim sus aureum annulum haberet in naribus, nichilominus grunnum ["groyn"] suum immergeretur turpibus. Hoc facit mulier fatua sollicite composita.

> (A foolish woman is like a pig which roots its long face in the mud and considers it a feast. For although a sow has a gold ring in her nostrils ["naribus"], nonetheless she would stick her snout ["grunnum suum"] in what is foul. Thus does a foolish woman elegantly arrayed.)

However, Chaucer's application of the scriptural passage, even though based on the *Primo*, is quite different: "For right as a sough wroteth in everich ordure, so wroteth she hire beautee in the stynkynge ordure of synne."

Let us consider the implications of Chaucer's handling of the passage. The earlier emphasis on the body as thrall to sin together with the adjuration to "wommen that been of so greet beautee" more emphatically establishes the target for the passage from Proverbs. In addition the "fair and foolish" of the scriptural passage is modified and becomes "a fair womman that is fool of hire body"—a modification, even though slight, that holds before us more emphatically the physical and sexual implications of what is being talked about. The mud ("luto") which the *Primo* pig considers a feast, becomes the excremental "ordure" reenforced by the repetition of "stynkyng ordure of synne," in which not the pig but the woman herself "roots" her beauty. As a result of Chaucer's treatment, the passage achieves an ugliness that seems to be intentional, in which beauty, body and sexuality, animality, and excrement are all brought together to evoke disgust and revulsion. It is worthy of note that to fulfill this intention, Chaucer left his basic source (Pennaforte) and turned to another source (Proverbs), then to still another (*Primo*)

---

[14] Wenzel, "Notes," 237–38.

because Proverbs did not give him enough, and finally perhaps to still another not yet identified.[15] The passage must be considered as showing a purposeful selectivity over a scattered group of sources. This together with the suddenness and unexpectedness of its appearance at the end of the section on disdain of sin strongly suggest that its motivation is a personal one.

It would, of course, be inaccurate to imply that Chaucer is unique in his heightened treatment of woman as sinful sexual object. There is no dearth of pulpit comment on the vices of women, particularly the foolish woman.[16] Most of it is expressed with uncompromising, superheated indignation. In this Chaucer is quite representative and in keeping with what the pulpit orators provide. But some of the most baffling characteristics of *The Parson's Tale* are the sudden changes and the variety that characterize its style and treatment of its subject.[17] If Chaucer matches, or even goes beyond, the intensity of utterance of the preachers in some parts of his work, he does not in other parts of it. The problem in critical analysis that this causes is considerably lessened if one considers the work as a separate, personal penitential statement in which Chaucer's variety of style and treatment are the result of his responding more powerfully to those parts of his subject which touch him most nearly. On the evidence of the passage above it is his disturbed response to sexuality and woman that is most striking and of particular interest in that it occurs together with a special configuration of his use of his sources.[18]

This disturbed response frequently occurs with another striking characteristic of Chaucer's treatment of the sexual in *The Parson's*

---

[15] Robert Rypon, a contemporary of Chaucer, compares a sow rolling its nostrils in the foulest dirt to foolish women rolling their beauty in the foulest dirt of lust (cited in Owst, 392). The closeness to Chaucer's diction suggests that the image may have had some currency.

[16] Owst, 385ff.

[17] A useful summary of critical opinion on this aspect of the tale may be found in Rowland, "Sermon and Penitential," 128–29, who feels that the work does not show homogeneity of style, that it is a "rhetorical collage" (132).

[18] Chaucer's response to sexuality has hardly been an untouched subject in Chaucer criticism. For a recent, feminist exploration of the subject, see Dinshaw's comprehensive treatment. The present study, confined to *The Parson's Tale,* is more limited in its scope.

Tale, his propensity toward the excremental. Although the preachers employ the various images of sin as filth and dirt, and inveigh against sexual temptation in these terms,[19] Chaucer goes beyond them in his characteristic use of the word "ordure" for this purpose. Ten of the thirteen occurrences in Chaucer's works of the word "ordure" are in *The Parson's Tale,* all but one in a sexual context,[20] perhaps most striking and repulsive in the reference to "thilke harlotes that haunten bordels of thise fool wommen, that mowe be likned to a commune gong, whereas men purgen hir ordure" (885), an image which approaches the pathological.

We find this emphasis on the excremental in the second passage to be singled out. Related in area of concern and in intensity to the gold-ring / sow's-snout passage above, it is the treatment of the superfluity and scantiness of clothing in the section on Pride (416–31). A lengthy passage, it has often been remarked both for its style and content, for its impassioned utterance and striking images. It is not very closely connected with Peraldus or *Quoniam/Primo,* but the existence of some of its images in a sermon by Robert Rypon suggests that Chaucer was not treading entirely new ground. Moreover, it clearly takes its departure from standard ways of treating the subject.[21] Still it would seem to be very much Chaucer's own creation and most certainly in intensity goes beyond what we find in the standard treatments. Women's "tails," gowns of inordinate length, are inveighed against elsewhere in the period.[22] Chaucer's treatment, although typical in many respects, nevertheless puts a greater emphasis on the excremental. He gives us gowns trailing in the dung and in the mire, and as a result of this trailing on the ground being "wasted, consumed, thredbare, and roten with donge."

---

[19] Cf. Owst, 184–85.

[20] Possibly nine, if one accepts "ardour" (on the basis of the source) for "ordure" (the reading of all manuscripts except one) in 916. See *Riverside Chaucer,* 135, note to line 916. In addition, "stinking" in the same sexual context is used more frequently in *The Parson's Tale* than elsewhere in Chaucer's works. See Tatlock and Kennedy, *Concordance.*

[21] Cf. Owst, 397–98 and 404, where he cites Rypon as preaching that men wear garments so short that they scarcely hide their private parts "et certe ut apparet ad ostendendum mulieribus membra sua ut sic ad luxuriam provocentur." See also Mark Liddell, *The Academy,* 1259 (June 20, 1896): 509.

[22] Owst, 397–99.

But it is in the treatment of the scantiness of clothing that one becomes aware of a special vehemence and a violence of imagery that seem to indicate a profound personal involvement. Man is the target here, specifically his sexual members and buttocks. Men arrange their hose to show "the boce of hir shap ... the horrible swollen membres" that are like the "maladie of hirnia." Their buttocks are like the hinder part of a she-ape in the full moon—i.e., "in heat." The white and red colors of their hose make their "wrecched swollen membres" seem flayed. Clad in other colors their privy members seem "corrupt" by the fire of St. Anthony, or by cancer. With pride they show the hinder part of their buttocks, horrible to see, where they purge their "stynkynge ordure." The striking intensity of the passage, the feeling one gets of Chaucer's obsessive involvement in his subject, taken together with the images of mutilation, pain, disease, and the repulsively grotesque make it stand out from its surroundings, a burst of appalled fury that is difficult to consider as merely a literary or a meditated penitential response, but rather as an intensely personal one.

The third passage that also seems to indicate a special personal involvement is that on contraception, abortion, and infanticide in the section on homicide (564–79) in Chaucer's treatment of the sin of Ire. It is worthy of note, for in this section Chaucer makes a striking change in his employment of source, turning from his general source, ill-defined at best, in Peraldus and returning to Pennaforte—but now to Liber II, Titulus 1, *De homicidio*, rather than Liber III, Titulus 34, from which he draws the bulk of his Pennaforte material. In keeping with Pennaforte's *De homicidio*, Chaucer defines and develops the distinction between spiritual and corporeal homicide. Spiritual homicide has six types (five in Pennaforte). Corporeal homicide has seven in Pennaforte, three by tongue, four in deed. Chaucer addresses three of these latter: by law, by necessity, and by accident. The fourth in Pennaforte, "voluntate," is not clearly treated by Chaucer, except perhaps by implication in what seems to be his chief concern with corporeal homicide in the passage under consideration (576–79): contraception, abortion, and infanticide. Pennaforte's treatment is, of course, canonical with a view to determining the nature of the penance to be required in the various kinds of homicide and making

distinctions between these kinds.[23] What, he asks (II.1.6), if someone strikes a pregnant woman, or gives her a potion or she herself
takes it so that she may abort or not conceive—is this to be judged
homicide and in breach of canon law? He answers, if the fetus is
formed or is moving and this occurs, it is homicide, but if it is not
moving it is not homicide in terms of canon law but subject to
penance. Later (II.1.12) after dealing with other material in five
intervening sections, Pennaforte considers overlaying, requiring grave
penance if intentional, but lesser penance if the result of unintention-
al negligence. It is notable that Chaucer does not use the intervening
material or the material which follows II.1.12 (e.g., homicide as the
result of argument or conflict, the outcome of medical or surgical
treatment, mutilation, exposure and starvation) but selects only those
passages which are on the subject of abortion, contraception, or
infanticide before he returns to Peraldus (and others?) for sins of the
tongue.[24]

In addition, Chaucer's special concern with the subject is further
shown in the fact that he does not stop with what Pennaforte provides, but with a heightened rhetoric adds to him. Thus, "unkyndly
synne, by which man or womman shedeth hire nature in manere or
in place ther as a child may nat be conceived" (sodomy and coitus
interruptus) finds no mention in Pennaforte's treatment, nor does "a
man approcheth to a womman by desir of lecherie, thurgh which the
child is perissed" (intercourse during pregnancy). More strikingly,
Chaucer also adds to Pennaforte both by his mention of contraceptive or abortifacient suppositories ("putteth certeine material thynges
in hire secree places to slee the child"), possibly original with him,
and by his mention of "wommen that mordren hir children for
drede of worldly shame," which is also without an equivalent in
Pennaforte.[25]

---

[23] Dudley R. Johnson was the first to note Chaucer's change of source. He, as
does Petersen, uses the Verona 1744 edition of Pennaforte, which according to the
modern editors at times contains extrinsic matter from elsewhere in Pennaforte.
The edition consulted here is that of 1976 of the *Universa Bibliotheca Iuris*, based
mainly on thirteenth-century manuscripts of the first and second redactions.

[24] Johnson, 54, "[Chaucer] picked out and pieced together certain ideas which
he found in Divisions IV and IX [i.e., 6 and 12] . . . to form the section on infanticide." Shaw, 299–300, suggests that vernacular treatments of the same subject
underlie Chaucer's treatment.

[25] Noonan, 215: "I have not encountered a single theological or canonical writer

The presumption here that Chaucer is dealing with something that concerns him nearly is given added support by a fourth passage, actually no more than a brief statement, in the section on the three species of penance (solemn, public, private) at the beginning of the tale (101–5): "Thilke penance that is solempne is in two maneres; as to be put out of hooly chirche in Lente for slaughtre of children, and swich maner thyng./ Another is, whan a man hath synned openly, of which synne the fame is openly spoken in the contree. . . ." Although Pennaforte writes of the imposition of solemn penance "pro crimine publico et vulgatissimo quod totam commoverit urbem" (III.34.6), he does not specify as a cause for solemn penance the "slaughtre of children," which Chaucer otherwise closely following Pennaforte departs from his source to mention. Indeed, there is not the slightest suggestion of it in this section of Liber III, which makes even more noticeable Chaucer's going out of his way to add it. The whole treatment of contraception, abortion, and infanticide in Chaucer is remarkable both for its unexpected shift of source and for the manner and content of treatment which go beyond the source, as if there is a special sense of compulsion on Chaucer's part, something that he has to speak about.

The final passage to be discussed must be considered as being more tentative. It occurs in Chaucer's treatment of lechery, which has a striking, and to some exasperating, bewildering wealth of material on man and woman, and husband and wife. The passage deals with the fourth of the five fingers of the devil to catch people to lechery, kissing:

> and trewely he were a greet fool that would kiss the mouth of a brennynge oven or of a fourneys./ And more fooles been they that kissen in vilenye, for that mouth is the mouth of hell; and namely thise olde dotardes holours, yet wole they kisse, though they may nat do, and smatre them./ Certes, they been lyk to houndes; for an hound, whan he comth by the roser or by other [bushes], though he may nat pisse, yet wole he heve up his leg and make a countenance to pisse. (856–58)

---

who refers so explicitly to contraceptive pessaries." Chaucer's treatment of "unkyndely synne" as a means of contraception is possibly derived from Peraldus; cf. Noonan, 226.

The passage is derived from a corresponding passage in the *Quoniam*:[26]

> Fugienda etiam sunt oscula mulierum.... Valde stultus esset qui fornaci ardenti os suum applicaret.... Beda super Parabolas: "Qui meretricem deosculatur, ibi pulsat inferni ianuas." Sed stulti leccatores sunt similes cani, qui transiens per rosetum vel virgultum, si maculare illud non potest, tibiam levat et signum facit. Sic etiam illi videntes pulchram mulierem, si maculare non possunt, signa turpitudinis sue relinquunt in osculis, contactibus, et huiusmodi.

> (To be shunned also are the kisses of women.... He may certainly be considered foolish who puts his mouth to a burning furnace.... Bede—*Super Parabolas* [*Salamonis*]: "He who kisses a whore, there he knocks on the gates of hell." But foolish lechers are like a dog, who passing through a rose garden or thicket, if he is not able to defile ["maculare"] it, lifts his leg and makes a sign. So also those seeing a beautiful woman, if they are not able to defile [her], leave signs of [their] dirtiness customarily in kissings, touchings, and the like.)

The chief difference is Chaucer's treatment of the lechers. In the source they are simply "leccatores," lechers—not specified as old or young. Their sexual insufficiency, as expressed in the dog comparison, is not assigned a cause, although to be sure the hint is there. Chaucer takes it out of the realm of suggestion and makes the cause for their ineptitude explicit. They are "olde dotard holours."

It is difficult not to feel that Chaucer here would also have been reminded of a passage in Boccaccio's *Ameto*, which is taken as the source providing the conception for *senex amans* central to the "Merchant's Tale." In that part of the *Ameto* relevant to the "Merchant's Tale," the young nymph Agapes complains of the unsuccessful attempts of her old husband in bed to become aroused—

> [E]gli ha molte volte con la fetida bocca, non baciata, ma scombavata la mia.   (XXXII.14)

---

[26] Wenzel, "The Source of Chaucer's Seven Deadly Sins," 372.

(He has many times with his fetid mouth, not kissed, but slavered on mine.)

Chaucer in the present passage from *The Parson's Tale*, which has other echoes in common with *The Merchant's Tale*, adds to his source, "yet wol they kisse, though they may nat do, and smatre hem," and thus develops and makes more explicit a different emphasis—the lechery of the old man. Indeed, although "smatre" is an exact translation of "maculare," it is possible to feel that Chaucer may possibly have connected it with the "scombavata" of the *Ameto*, both verbally and conceptually. The suggestiveness of the connection, even though tentative, again hints at a special Chaucerian preoccupation.

These then are the passages that seem to show a special Chaucerian presence in *The Parson's Tale*. The problem they present in the present study is, of course, that of justifying their being singled out exclusively as examples for the purposes to which they are here put. There is a wealth of material in *The Parson's Tale*, and these passages in terms of bulk constitute only a small part of it. Moreover, much of the rest of the material deals with the same area of response, such as, for example, the treatment of the "circumstances that agreggen muchel every synne" (959–80), which concerns itself almost exclusively with sexual sin. But this lengthy passage is closely tied to Pennaforte[27] and shows simply that Chaucer is for the most part following his source.[28] However, the passages under consideration here, in addition to the distinctiveness of their utterance, have also a distinctiveness when considered in relation to their source or, at times, absence of source. There may be other passages which should be included with them, but these are the only ones that can be identified as possessing this distinctiveness with some degree of assurance. Nor is it unreasonable to consider them in this way. Even though the whole tale must be considered as Chaucer's penitential exercise and statement, it is reasonable also to look for a specific

---

[27] III.34.31, *De interrogationibus*.

[28] Cf. Wenzel, *Riverside Chaucer*, note to 960—the rhetorical treatment is moderate and analytical in contrast to the passages considered in this study, although even here there are differences in emphasis, and language, for example in Chaucer's treatment of Pennaforte's "Ubi," which might also well repay close analysis.

cause, a single event, a compelling stimulus that brought Chaucer to compose it.[29] These passages offer the best evidence as to what that cause may have been.

What then can be said about these passages as a group? Their common denominator suggests materials for a case study. It embraces the following: a response to woman's sexual attraction in terms of a revulsion characteristically expressed in excremental terms; a violent response to male sexual display in terms of disease and mutilation; a concern with contraception, abortion, and infanticide, with implications for its connection with illicit sexual activity; and, finally, a disgust with senile lechery. Whatever the penitential need, it was, I believe, in response to some specific occurrence that occurred at some specific time in Chaucer's life in connection with these things. These are, I think, the materials with which we can begin to untie "the knotte why that [*The Parson's Tale*] is toold."

But there is a further problem beyond why the tale "is told," and that is its place in the Canterbury scheme. *The Parson's Tale* on the evidence of the Retraction as well as the Parson's Prologue belongs to the Canterbury period. The customary belief is that it came early in that period, because of Chaucer's mining of the tale for use in his other tales, although it has been argued that the process was the other way around.[30] I do not think that either position can be argued to an unassailable conclusion, although I find more persuasive the view that the prose tale preceded the poetry (another argument entirely). But for the relationship between *The Merchant's Tale* and *The Parson's Tale*, a few things can be said. Whichever came first, it did not, it would seem, come first by very much because both seem to be part of the same creative response to something deeply disturbing to Chaucer that we do not know. They share verbal echoes. In

---

[29] Here one almost inevitably thinks of the deed of release "de raptu meo" by Cecily Chaumpaigne, although no evidence can be advanced to connect it with whatever occasioned Chaucer's response in *The Parson's Tale*. Cannon's discovery of a new document in the case (the Memorandum) and his suggestions (and their implications) concerning the suppression of the word "raptus" in this later document persuade us that whatever did happen was not regarded in a casual way by those who were involved, to which one might add, perhaps least of all by Chaucer himself.

[30] Patterson, 356–70.

the lechery passage, even though it cannot be said that beyond a doubt they share a source (*Ameto*), the assumption that they do is a persuasive one. In their implications of a devastating sexual experience, they share a common subject and tone. Indeed, one can feel that *The Merchant's Tale* is the literary counterpart of the more discursive *The Parson's Tale,* and that it springs ultimately from the same origins.

Whatever it was that was so disturbing to Chaucer, he made his peace with it, as, for example, his Envoy to Scogan shows. This poem is generally dated 1393 because of its references to torrential rains, which are mentioned in the chronicles for that year. It would seem that dating anything on the basis of English weather is a rather risky business, and the poem may well be later. In it Chaucer replies to the imputed accusation that, now gray and "rounde of shappe," he still wishes to rime and "play."

> Nay, Scogan, say not so, for I m'excuse—
> God helpe me so!—in no rym, dowteles,
> Ne thynke I never of slep to wake my muse,
> That rusteth in my shethe stille in pees.
> While I was yong, I put hir forth in prees.
>
> (Scogan, 36–40)

It is generally agreed that Chaucer is here using *Anticlaudianus,* where in his prologue Alanus emphasizes the rejuvenating and exhilarating effect of literary creation and calls upon Apollo for aid.

> Auctoris mendico stylum, phalaresque poetae,
> Ne mea segnitiae Clio dejecta senescat:
> Ne jaceat calamus, scabra rubigine torpens....
> Fonte tuo sic, Phoebe, tuum perfunde poetam.
>
> (Migne, PL 210: 487–88)

(I beg the pen of the author and the ornaments of the poet, lest my Clio depressed by indolence wanes in strength, lest my pen lie sluggish with rust.... Steep, Phoebus, your poet in your fountain.)

Chaucer's witty reversal of Alanus (Chaucer will *not* awaken his muse) has been treated somewhat discreetly by the commentary, for it seems clear that his desire to leave his muse unawakened (i.e., to not write love poetry) is a *double entendre* with quite explicit sexual meanings. His muse (*stylus auctoris!*) rusts in its sheath. One thinks of the Reeve and his rusty blade, entirely appropriate for the response the Reeve makes to his sexual decline in his prologue, and also of the senile husband in the *Ameto*, who attempts in vain to till the gardens of Venus with an old poughshare rusted by age.[31] When Chaucer adds that when he was young, he "put hir forth in prees," it is difficult to be unaware of the amused and witty impropriety of what he is saying. And it is also difficult to think of the Envoy to Scogan, considering what it says and how, as having been written before *The Parson's Tale*. Coming after it, it suggests a remarkable recovery.

And if Chaucer made his peace with the personal tumult that *The Parson's Tale* seems to record, he made his peace too with the existence of *The Parson's Tale*. It has, of course, as critics claim, a considerable relevance to the rest of the *Canterbury Tales* and their tellers. But the relevance may well be not the result of authorial intention so much as it is the nature of the source *summae* themselves, which show a profound awareness of the nooks and crannies of all aspects of erring human nature (cf. Benson, *Riverside Chaucer*, 21–22). And so, recognizing this *sui generis* appropriateness of *The Parson's Tale*, Chaucer must have felt that the end of the collection was the inevitable place for it to be. For I feel that the arrangement of what are called the *a* manuscripts (as in Robinson's edition and the *Riverside Chaucer*) is what Chaucer wanted at the stage to which he had progressed, before he ceased work altogether.

To bring it into the tale framework (retaining the Retraction as something for future concern), he created the Parson's Prologue, and indeed it is this, as we have seen, that does most to give thematic meaning to the tale's relationship to the rest of the collection. But even here there are some loose ends. The Parson shows some characteristics that seem to clash with his role here as the speaker of the ultimate statement of the *Canterbury Tales*. The uncompromising line the Parson takes in his prologue on poetry, alliterative and rimed, and fables must certainly be a stance that shows a Chaucerian amusement. It suggests an interesting compatibility with the crustiness of the Parson in the Man of Law's Endlink. One suspects that the

---

[31] "... dalla antichità rosso," *Ameto*, XXXII.16.

almost universal, and mostly unsupportable, use of the word "cancelled" to refer to that passage (a better term would be "on-hold") has done much to obscure for us the fact that Chaucer must have had plans for the Parson, which he never lived to fulfill.

Even so, the tale itself is where it should be. And there is nothing untoward about Chaucer's concluding his great work with a religious statement resulting from the spiritual travail he himself had been through. Indeed, what better place could it have?

Lehigh University

RALPH HANNA III

Robert the Ruyflare and His Companions

his paper attempts to expand upon an especially constructive intervention by our honoree, Siegfried Wenzel. In *The Sin of Sloth* (135–47), he refuted the central contentions which had led Manly (1906, 1908, 1909) to propose the multiple authorship of *Piers Plowman*. Manly found grounds for his views in the A-text's failure to include a confession of Wrath and in what he took to be logical inconsequence in moving from the confession of Sloth to the unsorted appearance of "Robert þe robbour" (A.5.233, B.5.461): these problems he ascribed to a bifolium lost from the archetype of all A manuscripts. As a logical consequence, Manly could then declare that those revisions which created the other versions were the responses of persons other than the A poet, all of them attempting to make sense of what was senseless. In contrast, Wenzel demonstrated, first, that both the placement and the depiction of Robert the Robber in AB are not simply a misbegotten pendant to Sloth's confession but, on the basis of those parochial catechetical materials of which he is a master, form "a natural and logical sequel" (144)—although perhaps not a presentation logical or consistent when measured against other aspects of Langland's presentation of Sloth. And Wenzel, reiterating the ancient claims of Jusserand (287–92) and Chambers (3), reaffirmed (143, 146) that the C-version transfer of Robert (now "the ruyflare") into the confession of Couetyse (C.6.316) represents a thoroughly proper decision in terms of parochial instructional materials: the text "*reddite*" on which Robert looks commands one to restitute ill-got gains and is thus most directly appropriate to the sin of avarice.

Yet in spite of substantial differences in their local readings—

differences where Wenzel, through his deep knowledge of Langland's roots in instructional literature, has all the best of it—at a deep level, both he and Manly agree in what is at stake here. Both concur in seeing that Langland, although cognizant of and clearly drawing upon the literature of parochial instruction, fails to find in those materials the same clear map of the Christian life that other poets, for example Dante or de Deguileville, did. For Wenzel, this finding is explicit (135, 147; and cf. Muscatine). But Manly's effort to deconstruct single authorship presupposes a similar view—that no notion of the Seven Deadly Sins, whether schematic or organic, can account for Langland's behavior here: dismembering the poem among authors restores a coherence inherent in individual "selections" but not a property of the whole. And all commentators leave unresolved (as I will also) a related problem, the difficulties of rhetorical mapping at this point in AB: what structural principle does one believe at work in a passage which has climactic final position in the confession of the sins? Is Robert an eighth sin added to the conventional seven (as Peraldus added *peccata lingue*)? Is he a general pendant to all sins (cf. Wenzel, 145–46)? Or is he a specific pendant to Sloth (cf. Wenzel, 144)?

In this essay, I return to this site of contention, both between modern critics and between Langlandian creative impulses, to look again at the C rendition of this passage—"Robert the ruyflare," not "Robert þe robbour." Both in the authorship controversy and in Wenzel's reformulation of the difficulties, this piece of revision has somehow managed to remain *déjà lu*: Robert and his restitution have always seemed utterly appropriate, for commentators of every stripe, to the confession of Couetyse. Yet in asserting the obviousness of the association restitution/Couetyse, the commentators have assumed the problem under discussion to be a local one, a simple matter of transposition (cf. also Russell's misstatement, 64). They thus have neglected two ancillary problems in Langland's C-version reformulation of these materials: (a) that additional revisions occur in C both at that point where Langland deletes the AB "Robert þe robbour" and at that point where he inserts "Robert the ruyflare"; and (b) that the second of these two passages offers some interesting insights into Langland's sins and his attitudes to the context of parochial instruction which nominally underwrites their appearance in the poem.[1]

The C-text revision that creates "Robert the ruyflare" does not concern simply the movement forward in the text of the original "Robert þe robbour." Nor is it simply a question of Robert no longer being a pendant (whether to Sloth particularly or all sins generally) but now an integrated portion of a single (appropriate) sin-portrait, that of Couetyse. For Langland also truncates the portrait of Sloth as it appears in AB and advances in the poem, with Robert, what were originally Sloth's last six lines (A.5.227–32, B.5.455–60). And these lines are subjected to one minor yet revelatory revision: they cease to be the statement of a penitent Sloth and become that of a new speaking personification, "ȝeuan-ȝelde-aȝeyn" (C.6.309–15).

At the time of the authorship controversy, the force to be accorded this new personification was perfectly clear to all combatants, but Pearsall's noncommittal notes (309–30n, 330n) lead me to believe that the wisdom of Jusserand (293–95; cf. Manly 1909:110) has now been forgotten. In something like the same way in which personification proliferates and redoubles itself in B passus 2–4, Langland here doubles his personifications.[2] ȝeuan is supposed to be a second penitent thief (his sobriquet "ȝelde-aȝeyn" represents, of course, the anglicization of the command *Reddite* on which Robert looks in C.6.315).

Unpleasant as it may be to contemplate, Langland here counts on popular prejudice, on the propensity to voice satiric national stereotypes, for this identification. Welsh johns are robbers. Jusserand, in

---

[1] The revisions at the point of deletion (C.7.82) I address elsewhere, in the article "Will's Work," forthcoming in Kathryn Kerby-Fulton and Steven Justice, *New Historical Essays on Piers Plowman*. For this occasion, I would only note that the deletion, in a rather typically Langlandian move, removes from the confessions any sense of climactic closure (movement toward restitution and pilgrimage, traditional *opera satisfactionis*) which Robert's appearance might have provided. The new conclusion, materials now "frontloaded" from B.13.409–56, aligns the climax of the confessions with a major concern of the C Visio, the nature and status of Wille's poetic vocation.

[2] Consider the force to be given Meed's two parents (B.2.25–27a, 119–20), ultimately producing Conscience's "two manere of Medes" (3.231); or False's apparent role as both father and bridegroom (2.25, 41); or the two characters who appear as a team and exchange names, "waryn wisdom and witty his feere" or "Wisdom and sire waryn þe witty" (4:27, 67).

addition to materials from legal records, cites (294 n. 2) Gerald of
Wales, *Descriptio Cambriae* 2.2: "The Welsh consider it appropriate
to proceed in acts of plunder, indeed to live by ravine, theft, and
robbery, not simply against foreigners and hostile nations, but
among themselves" (6:207). And Gerald's comments, in spite of the
silence of standard modern proverb dictionaries on the subject of
Welsh thieves, can be extended through other medieval parallels, for
example the Marcher Walter Map's succinct "The glory of the Welsh
is in ravine and theft" (2.22, p. 196).[3]

Moreover, 3euan's Welshness may also give peculiar force to his
determination "thow me lyflode lakke ... as a lorel begge" (C.6.312,
314). At least if one believes Walter Map, among the things Welsh-
men take as common property, open to any kind of off-the-cuff
incursion, is their food: "anyone's food is anyone else's, and none of
them asks for bread at all, but seizes any bread he finds and whatever
foodstuffs he finds set out to be eaten—and without dispute in either
case" (2.20, 182).[4] Fundamentally, 3euan appears what Langland
elsewhere calls a "faitour," someone given to obtaining "lyflode"
under false pretenses and without labor. At this point in the text, he
resembles Robert in his professional antecedents (and in their mutual
desire at this moment to surrender them). The two figures do,

---

[3] "Ad hoc etiam rapinis insistere, raptoque vivere, furto et latrocinio, non
solum ad exteros et hostiles populos, verum etiam inter se proprium habent" and
"In rapina et furto gloria Walensium," respectively. Substantial parts of Map's
discussion at 2.9, 20–26 (144–46, 182–202) contain relevant detail, to some of which
I will return. For a further example, see our honoree's favorite, *Fasciculus morum*
340/65–68: "For it is said that in Ireland and in Wales one readily finds thieves that
steal their neighbors' cows, oxen, and other cattle, for which they are called ['open]
thieves.' But not in England, God be praised." ("Dicitur enim quod in Hibernia et
in Wallia bene inveniuntur latrones qui vaccas, boves, et alia pecora vicinorum
furantur, propter quod latrones apert[i] dicuntur. Set in Anglia—laudetur Deus—non
sic.") I adjust Wenzel's text and translation: the context suggests that the Irish and
Welsh should be called "open thieves" (in England, *Fasciculus* continues, people rob
covertly through embezzlement), not "thieves openly." This locution apparently
alludes to a distinction made in all Middle English *Somme le roi/Miroir du monde*
derivatives in discussing "theft" as a "part" of Avarice: "þer beþ opene þeues, and
preue þeues" (*Book of Vices and Virtues* 32/31–32; cf. *Jacob's Well* 128/3ff.; *Myrour*
133/19, with the locution "þefte aperte"; *Ayenbite* 37; *Disce mori*, fol. 53; and cf.
Chaucer, "Parson's Tale" I 799 "by force or by sleighte").

[4] "ut cuiusque alimenta cuiusque sint, et omnino nullus inter eos querat panem,
sed sine lite sumat inuentum, et quicquid uictualium ad esum presto repperit"; cf.
further 1.25 (100); Gerald, *Opera* 6:182; Higden, *Polychronicon* 1.38 (1:406–7).

however, enact a *distinctio* between two forms of penitent faitordom
/Roberdsmanship. 3euan is apparently capable of labor (since that is
the only way in which he can assure that "eche man ... shal haue
his" and can see the alternative as "in lysse to lyue," C.6.313, 315).
But Robert's more powerful example, of course, depends upon his
utter destitution—"[Y] neuere wene to wynne with craft þat Y
knowe" (C.6.323): his salvation depends totally upon God's mercy
which responds solely to his resolution, his good intent. To antici-
pate my developing argument, Robert's good intent frees him of the
actual psychology of sin which has created Couetyse/usury: "Usury
always rests upon such expectation or [corrupt] intention [of gain]."[5]

Yet, as I have indicated above, the transposition of Robert's
lament and the creation of his double 3euan do not form the only
revision which Langland effected in constructing this C-version
passage. Before moving on to survey the full extent of the quite
major expansions in preceding lines, it's worth pausing over a small,
but thematically relevant, detail which immediately precedes the
transposed 3euan and Robert. Repentance closes his speech before the
two robbers erupt on the scene:

> an hore of here ers-wynnynge may hardiloker tythe
> Then an errant vsurer, haue god my treuthe,
> And arste shal come to heuene, by Cryst that me made.
>
> (306–8)

Most immediately, Langland offers a devastating comparison between
the perquisites of the usurer Couetyse and the prostitute. And the
comparison evokes a fairly conventional distinction from the discourse of canon law. The topic of whether a whore can tithe (since
her income is tainted by the sin with which it was gained) is a
debatable issue, a subject of law-school disputation, one most canonical commentators seem in fact to answer affirmatively.[6] But the

---

[5] "Sola spes sive intencio [sc. corrupta] facit usuram" (*Fasciculus morum* 352/89–
90). Couetyse is directly connected with theft at several points in Langland's
portrait: C.6.236 (although in C without the locution of B.5.233 "a robberis þefte"),
265–71 (266 especially suggesting a connection with "lacchedraweres," a topic
related to those to which I turn in the next paragraph), and the climactic 349. Cf.
Jacob's Well 124/22–23: "A gouelere is a theef, for his gouyll is verryly thefte," with
a reference to *Decretum* 2.14.5.13 (*Corpus Iuris* 1:741).

[6] Three other references to the topic appear in C, at 3.299, 13.74, and 16.259–60.

prohibition of a usurer's tithe is in fact not moot at all, rather a matter of doctrine, settled by a general council at Lyons in 1274.[7]

Contextually, the whore intersects quite directly with that discourse Langland has developed with Robert and 3euan. For both spiritually and socially she is their ilk. The *memento*, the words of Dismas to Jesus on the cross, which Robert recalls (6.321), recalls also Jesus's answer, "*This day* thou shalt be with me in paradise" (Luke 23.43) and resonates with Repentance's promise that the whore "arste shal come to heuene." As one penitent enough to heed her religious responsibilities, she is a fit companion for Langland's repentant thieves.

Yet she is simultaneously also their social equal: all three figures are fundamentally *déclassée* when measured against the mercantile trader Couetyse. Although the most narrow attachment of the whore to Couetyse relies upon the learned language of canon law and its commentary, Langland implicitly fuses this with the vernacular of parochial literature. For Middle English *Somme/Miroir* derivatives include in their discussion of Avarice a most peculiar topic, what *Jacob's Well*, for example, calls "crafte of foly" (134/8), in the fullest accounts nine trades which can be construed as inherently dependant upon covetousness (see Owst, 370–74). The example cited universally in these works is the first trade of the fullest listings—prostitution; the extensive lists of *Jacob's Well* (134/8–34) and *A Myrour* (140/12–141/12) include as well "faitours" and "lacchedrawerys."[8] Such figures, in turn, are immediately associable with Robert and 3euan

---

Cf. Lyndwood's gloss at *Provinciale* 3.16 (195). Such volumes were the property of many parish churches (not just of their pastors), as shown by *Inventory*, a parish-by-parish register of church property in Norwich diocese, s. xiv med.

[7] See *Sext* 5.5.1–2, *Corpus Iuris* 2:1081–82, cited at *Fasciculus morum* 352/91–106. Note that the canon denies any validity to the will of a usurer who has not made restitution, an issue central to much of Langland's discussion. (Couetyse's hopes of *post mortem* benefactions, which will not inconvenience him, are thus dashed.) Other legislation on this subject includes Gratian's *Decretum* 2.1.1.27 (*Corpus Iuris* 1:369–70; cited *Fasciculus* 528/30–530/39); *Extra* 5.19.3 (Lateran III, 1175; ibid., 2:812; C.6.255 = X 5.19.9); *Clementines* 5.5.1 (Vienne, 1312; ibid., 2:1184).

[8] *A Myrour* calls these "crafte and office of vilanye" (131/34) or "office or crafte of foly" (140/12). Truncated discussions appear at *Vices and Virtues* 41/10–18 ("wikkede craftes," including the whore) and *Ayenbite* 45 ("kueade creaftes," also with the whore). *Disce mori*, fol. 54v ("fals worchers in fals crafftes") lacks any detail and may be describing other activities altogether.

through the discourse of English statutes, the only place outside these parochial texts and *Piers Plowman* where collocations like "Roberdesmen, Wastours, and Draghlacche" are known to occur (*Statutes* 1:268 [5 Edward III, c. 14]; cf. 1:96–98 [13 Edward I, the precedent legislation, without such specific language] and 2:32–33 [7 Richard II, c. 5]; see Chambers 3, Alford s.vv.). At this moment, the socially despicable serve to cut Couetyse down to size—in some sense his kinsmen, fellow thieves, and yet without any of his social eclat, they respond to religious propriety, as he will not.

But the tithing whore represents only a tiny bit of Langland's enormous revision at this point. The insertion of 3euan and Robert follows upon an immense C-version expansion. The first part of this new initiative, covering 6.258–85a (C.6.255 = B.5.263) simply represents Langland's routine C-version interest in narrative economy: it provides the material from the description of Hawkin's coat in B.13 (here 13.361–98a) which the poet regularly moves forward into the sin portraits of C.6–7. Such revision generally vitiates features of the confessions which readers have always appreciated, the relatively more unified dramatic sin figures of the earlier versions: Langland responds, at least momentarily, to a sense of appropriate parochial schemata, not of dramatic realism.

But the subsequent C.6.286–308, which run down to the moment when 3euan appears, equally represent an expansion. Here Langland develops extensively a brief B-version invention, Repentance's visualizing himself as a friar:

> For were I frere of þat hous þer good feiþ and charite is
> I nold cope vs wiþ þi catel ne oure kirk amende
> Ne haue a peny to my pitaunce, for pyne of my soule,
> For þe beste book in oure hous, þei3 brent gold were þe leues,
> And I wiste witterly þow were swich as þow tellest.
> *Seruus es alterius cum fercula pinguia queris;*
> *Pane tuo pocius vescere: liber eris.*
>
> (B 5.265–69b)

This friar is perhaps the best modern example of the breed who can be imagined—one, as C.6.288 rewrites it, "in good fayth." (The phrase is not, as Pearsall's punctuation would indicate, thoroughly parenthetical; cf. the similar mispointing of line 341 below.) But, as Langland has claimed since C.Prol.61–62, modern friars remain

thoroughly implicated in Couetyse's cash nexus; the accoutrements
this friar would reject from Couetyse—but apparently accept from
others with gratitude—are standard contested items from Franciscan
factional debates of the preceding century. The form of the habit (are
the copes of Prol.59 etc. really poor apostles' clothing?) and the
nature of fraternal buildings provided occasions for vehement debate
among Franciscans (Lambert, Leff passim). And the allusion to a
book with "brent gold ... leues" surely turns the account to satire:
Franciscan discussions of poverty often centered on whether any
book-ownership (even a psalter) could be construed as licit (cf. the
anecdotes about Francis reported at *Scripta Leonis*, chaps. 66, 70–74;
202, 208–16; see further Rouse 1987). Repentance implies—as Wille
will charge at C.12.15–22—that fraternal departures from their
original status, poverty, in fact depend solely upon abuse of the
penitential system.

The C-version extension of this passage whimsically develops
these ideas:

> Y ne wolde cope me with thy catel ne oure kyrke mende
> Ne take a meles mete of thyn: and myn herte hit wiste
> 3if thow were such as thow sayst, y sholde rather sterue.
> > *Melius est mori quam male viuere.*
> Y rede no faythful frere at thy feste to sytte.
> 3ut were me leuer, by oure lord, lyue al by welle-cresses
> Then haue my fode and my fyndynge of fals mennes
> > wynnynges.
> > *Seruus es alterius....*
>
> (6.288–94)

In Repentance's ironic imaginings, the very prevalence of worldly
Couetyse might contain the seeds of spiritual reformation, a return
to poor fraternal origins. To save their souls from sinful contamina-
tion, friars of good faith might well forsake rich men's "festes" (a
feasting friar will appear in C passus 15); instead, they might come to
prefer the humble veggies ("wellecresses") which should be staples in
their diets, as they were in those of the first friars (see, e.g., *Scripta
Leonis*, chaps. 39–40, 156–60 on not eating meat; cf. the peasant diet
described at 8.308–09, 321).

But if Langland further develops hints in B's friar, he also decent-
ers this portrayal through an expansion and recasting of B 5.270–78.

This passage returns to the canonical discussions which I have mentioned above in discussing the prostitute (who appears at the end of these lines). And such discussions, recall, deny to the usurer the ability even to tithe. But Repentance at this moment associates—as the parochial manuals do—sinful activity, not with the actually usurious financial wizard Couetyse, but with those technical "innocents" who profit by withholding for their own use the fruits of the usurer's transactions.[9] The C-text innovation, however, moves beyond assumptions that B.5.274–77 shares with parochial texts, that it's Couetyse's heirs who will be the culprits:

> 3e, þe prest þat thy tythe toek, trowe Y non other,
> Shal parte with the in purgatorye and helpe paye thy dette
> Yf he wiste thow were such when he resseyued thyn offrynge.
> And what lede leueth þat y lye, look in þe sauter glosed, on
>   *Ecce enim veritatem dilexisti,*
> And there shal he wite witterly what vsure is to mene,
> And what penaunce the prest shal haue þat proud is of his
> tithes.
>
>   (300–305)[10]

The gloss on Ps. 50.8 (Bennett 170, 283 n.; Pearsall 303a n.), in the B-version generalized in import, here is directed past Couetyse and his heirs directly to the parish priest. Easy penances, administered in hope of monetary contributions, here become, not just a problem of friars, but of religious persons in general. Repentance alleges that parish priests don't remember those canons which have been promulgated to govern their behavior: they must live on tithes, just as friars do on benefactions, and are not squeamish about their source.

This bit of revision ought to strike a familiar chord. For just as Langland has, in relation to the B version, doubled his penitent thieves, added 3euan to Robert, so he has also doubled his clerical

---

[9] See *Jacob's Well* 123/2–6: "þe thridde inche in þis gouyll is whan þou hast a thyng þat þi frend gat with gouyll, þe which is deed; be it fadyr or modyr, wyif or chyld, 3if þou wytte he gat it wyth gouyll, þou muste makyn asethe þerfore, and ellys þou art gylty as he þat dyde þe dede." Similar discussions appear at *Vices and Virtues* 31/7–11; *Myrour* 132/10–14; *Ayenbite* 35; *Disce mori*, fol. 53v.

[10] *proud is of* = "is elated by" (MED sense 2a, the same usage as with Piers at B.6.197).

figures, added the priest to the preexisting B friar. The two pieces of revision appear to be linked in their reliance on a similar logic of proliferation. And if Langland wants to draw a distinction here, it would appear analogous to that between 3euan and Robert: friars (like 3euan) can generate an extensive income and thus might well entertain the possibility of self-abnegation, while parish priests may through their "craft" only achieve a livelihood close to subsistence levels. Two similar figures, both scarcely penitent masters of the parochial penitential system, appear; and, of course, they are stock figures, contending adversaries in a legal controversy over the rights to hear lay confessions (cf. Fitzralph, 41–55). But where 3euan and Robert will surrender all to follow the command *Reddite*, these figures are engaged in a direct economic competition (*Reddite mihi*)— not surrender, but competitive multiplication of profits vis-à-vis one another.

Just like Wrath in his discussion (B.5.139–52), Repentance here advocates something like Wendy Scase's "new anticlericalism" (see esp. 28). He in effect says, "a plague on both your houses." Unlike Fitzralph or the Franciscan author of *Fasciculus morum* (468/58–66), both engaged in advocacy, each on behalf of a different side in this parochial controversy, for Repentance both religious groups are equally guilty in their grasping manipulation of the sacrament to personal advantage.

But simultaneously and more troublingly, both religious figures have proven themselves equally inefficacious at a central social function, helping Christians toward salvation through canonically appropriate penitential discipline. The conclusion of Couetyse's confession in the B version, broadly speaking, is doctrinal: it balances the strictures of canonical discourse with an appropriate devotional emphasis upon the power of God's merciful forgiveness. But in revising to form C, Langland problematizes this very insistence on the availability of mercy: in the social situation he describes, those who tell Christians how readily available mercy is damn themselves through their own avarice and compromise the very usefulness of their own counsel. Mercy can appear simply the name for that scam by which clerics seek to enrich themselves. In such a situation, any Christian might well doubt the divine promises friars and priests urge upon him, might well despair of the possibility of salvation. The bishop, who appears at the end of this confession (C.6.344–49 =

B 5.289–95), may provide one solution. But, through that act of revision I have already analyzed, the creation of 3euan (and the whore) and the moving forward of Robert, Langland also suggests another, more powerful model, a lay sorrow apart from any ecclesiastical direction: the two compromised species of clerics eventually appear less convincing teachers than the two lay figures who will shortly enter the poem.

The revision thus can be seen as part of Langland's typically powerful indictment of the contemporary church, can be constituted within a line of argument about the poem which goes back to its initial acceptance by sixteenth-century reformers. Yet I think that to do this would overlook a yet more powerful kind of doubling, in excess of proliferation of characters, which Langland executes here. For all the materials I have discussed, about eighty lines (C.6.258–338a) in all, are emphatically "insertions" into the confession of Couetyse. And, of course, I have managed to discuss this melange of various discourses (Langland chooses never to present that of parochial instruction thoroughly dissociated from other social languages) without making any protracted reference to the penitent Couetyse in description of whom (and in the service of whose salvation) these materials are ostensibly offered. If Langland's confession of the sins is to be appreciated for some variety of vibrant dramatism, as another prevalent form of critical recuperation would suggest, this revision severely challenges such a contention. All this material precisely interrupts drama—a true priest Repentance facing a potentially penitent sin. That conversation simply breaks off, and is not really restored, even at the very conclusion of the "confession."

Indeed, the entire revision through insertion which I have been describing itself forms a pronounced act of doubling—a substitution for or evasion of the scene one somehow expects, the conversion of a repentent sinner. Langland actually "dramatizes" what might be described as penitential deadlock: Robert and his companions—3euan, the tithing whore, grasping friar and priest—substitute for an action which cannot be written (or written, as I will suggest in a moment, to any effect), Couetyse's failure to repent.

If one tries to analyze the scene into which Langland inserts Robert and his companions in the C version, one can see it as characterized by a spiritual inertia which expresses itself as compulsive repetition or looping. In the lines which immediately precede the

revision, Repentance introduces the conception of restitution, which
we have seen is a major thread of the revision:

> Shal neuere seketoure wel bysette the syluer þat thow hem leuest
> Ne thyn heyres, as Y hope, haue ioye of þat thow wonne,
> For þe pope with alle his pentauncers power hem fayleth
> To assoyle the of this synne *sine restitucione.*
> *Numquam dimittitur peccatum, nisi restituatur ablatum.*
>   (6.254–57a; cf. B 5.260–64)

He returns to this theme at lines 296–308 and 342–49 (the very last
lines of the portrayal); and, of course, both 3euan and Robert address
the issue directly. But in spite of the extensive additions, the C-
version Couetyse shows absolutely no advance toward responsible
Christian activity. And Repentance's efforts become simply a (frus-
trated) attempt to dun his "penitent"—again and again and again.

That Repentance must do this testifies to a second blockage and
repetitiveness in the passage. When the priestly figure leaves off his
first demand for restitution, which I have just quoted, he expects that
he will receive in return what he has gotten from other sins, a
statement—however perfunctory—of contrition and a pledge of acts
appropriate to this sin which put contrition into some actual practice. If that is what he expects, Repentance will be sorely disappoint-
ed, for it is at just this point that Langland introduces his first insertion, Couetyse's reply.

This rather truncated version of materials from B.13 fails utterly
to address what Repentance has just said—that the sin must surrender
his ill-got goods. Instead, Couetyse seems to assume that he must
methodically confess more: having given what passes for a full
biography, he must, it seems, provide additional information as a
sign of contrite intent. But this act is, of course, not to advance, but
only to confess the same (if the biography of C.6.206–52 was adequate, nothing further is necessary), to repetitively add more detail
without changing the point at issue. Couetyse appears to hope that
if he just keeps his gums moving long enough, he'll somehow escape
this jam with absolution.

Perhaps most importantly, these newly advanced materials (esp.
6.272–83) do not describe Couetyse's willingness to accept Repentance's correction. They measure precisely his continuing resistance,
his insistence in repeating who he is (which is who he has been), his

utter distaste for ecclesiastical demands that he be sorry for his sin.[11] And these words form Couetyse's final contribution to the scene: he never speaks again. This treatment suggests that one might consider the primary doubling in the passage that very disparity between Couetyse's inaction, his repetitious concentration in his sinful past, and whatever mysterious force constructs conversion—makes 3euan and Robert (who have no discernible biographies) perform the actions which cannot be described in what constitutes the ostensible center of this passage, Couetyse's (over-)confession.

I think there are two different ways of responding to this penitential inertia, both of them Langlandian comments on the scene of parochial instruction and on that sacrament which is at its heart. On the one hand, one might construe Couetyse's response as in some sense legitimate, however stupid. In such a reading, Couetyse here responds only to what he can understand of lines 256–57—the English. (Having in the C version suppressed B.5.235–36 and 243, the lines contain the first non-English words in the confession.) The C-version Couetyse hears, not the Latinate commands to restitution, but the English "no one can assoil you, not even the pope," and simply assumes that he's not said enough—without ever realizing that, for sacramental purposes, he has already offered much too much. Such a reading, in a benign way, insists upon a distinction between the cluttered vernacular world of experience and the fundamentally Latinate frame in which such experience is measured for eternity.

But I remain equally struck by a phrase from the very end of Couetyse's (re)wandering in autobiography, nearly his last words:

> my muynde ... was more in my godes in a doute
> Then in the grace of god and in his grete myhte.
>
> (6.284–85)

"In a doute": does it modify "my godes" (when they were at risk) or "my muynde" (constantly in fear over loss)? For whatever it is that Couetyse understands when Repentance addresses him, one can at least read his response as stark terror—his eternal well-being, a set of goods he's always been loath to consider, is on the line. In these

---

[11] These lines "compensate for" the cancellation in the C version of B.5.105–12 which attribute such behavior to Envy.

terms, the vice's emotional state does not differ so radically from the over-explicit characterization of B.5.279 (which Langland cancelled in revision):[12] "Thanne weex þe sherewe in wanhope & wolde han hanged hymself."

In contrast to the traditional presumptions of penitential discourse and parochial literature, Repentance's activity produces in Couetyse neither serenity nor a return to spiritual health. A character whose biography depends totally upon "þe grace of Gyle" (C.6.213)[13] has been constructed in such a way that he must fail to see the power of merciful guile (cf. C.20 *in extenso*) inherent in "the grace of god" (285). Couetyse can perceive only fear—fear that that repetitious being whom he knows so well will be obliterated, either through the restitution which denies his very constructed personhood or through the infernal punishment which it has merited.

Thus, penitential inertia, as Langland describes it here, must always be endemic in the poem. The effect of parochial teaching proves exactly the opposite of its intent, insofar as the sinner Couetyse perceives only the gaping disparity between his very existence, what Repentance calls his wrongdoings, and his incapacity to be anyone different, what the sacrament identifies as atoning adequately, achieving that health which the penitential process terrifies the sinner into believing an utter necessity. Ironically, the more efficacious Repentance's penitential warning, the less efficacious the result may be: in its terrified sorrow, the sin/sinful self finds itself so repugnant as to be thoroughly rejectable, incapable of any power and so despicable as potentially to rebuff God himself. Couetyse's Wanhope here represents that paralyzing awareness of the gap between selfhood (wrongdoing) and the potential demands of divine justice, the sense that no restitution can be possible and, thus, that even the attempt to escape self is vain.[14] It is, once again, the inertial stance which re-

---

[12] Along with the following B.5.280, which may imply some constructive movement in the vice.

[13] "Gyle" in this line is presumptively the personification; cf. C.2.221-24.

[14] Cf. *Fasciculus morum*'s discussion of such despair (126/83–128/87): "This sin usually comes from three causes. First from faintheartedness, when a sinner thinks of the punishment that is due to his sins, such as doing seven years of penance for a mortal sin and the the the like; when he sees or hears that, the sinner loses heart, and in this torpor and despair does not take up his penance." ("istud peccatum ex tribus solet provenire: primo ex pusillanimitate, scilicet quando quis considerat penas pro

quires the doubling of Robert the ruyflare, who sees—at least within a professional, rather than personal, history—the possibility of divine mercy.

Langland's manipulation of "Robert the Ruyflare" thus involves considerably more complicated thematic adjustments than discussing the C-version movement of this passage as a "transposition" would suggest. Most particularly, all these revisions—beginning with the decision to create a second thief 3euan—involve doubling, repetition. And these, as I have argued, reveal some serious complications in the central "subject" of *Piers Plowman*, parochial instruction and the penitential situation in which such instruction is most normally experienced (cf. Lawton).

The revisions I have outlined certainly confirm Wenzel's findings in *The Sin of Sloth*. Langland's mapping of Couetyse's confession is precisely the sort of treatment which will later make even Contemplation complain: "þe way is full wikked, but ho-so hadde a gyde / That myhte folowe vs vch a fote" (C.7.307–8). The scene, obviously enough, depends upon the appropriation of parochial schemata, but such appropriation only occurs fitfully—and, in its fitfulness, is ceaselessly vitiated by the inclusion of other appropriated discourses—learned canon law, conversational stereotyping of national groups, arguments about Franciscan practice. Even in a portion of the poem narratively driven by penitential discourse, such discourse does not function as a "master-narrative."

Moreover, much of the revision I have outlined seems deliberately calculated to insure that no such "master-narrative" can emerge, that the poem cannot be assimilated to the most powerful single discursive strain on which it draws. For much of the revision addresses, almost as a test case, the very efficacy of that discourse on which it most firmly relies. Penance should conduce to (and, if necessary, coerce) amendment of life: that appropriate rigor, personified in Repentance, here can be perceived by (the consequently impenitent) Couetyse as grounds for inaction, or the repetitive action of remaining the same unregenerate person. On the other hand, as Repentance

---

peccatis debitas, puta vero pro mortali peccato septem annos penitere et huiusmodi, quod videns et audiens peccator fit pusillanimis, et sic lassus et desperans penitenciam non aggreditur. . . .")

tells at least Robert the Ruyflare (C.6.330–38a), penance sweetens its rigor with the promise of mercy: but mercy, at least in the social setting typified by friar and parish priest, may prove precisely anti-penitential by proliferating sin and suggesting to penitents an easy satisfaction which is not amendment.

Ultimately, the only efficacious penitential acts in the revision, those of Robert and 3euan, escape institutionalized penitential discourse altogether, come as shocking and undescribable acts of conversion. These changes one can understand, as one can understand that Robert's highwayman's "pyk-staff" (C.6.379) has ceased to be offensive weaponry and become a pilgrim's support; but they remain chameleonlike, magical, inexplicable. *Piers Plowman* never provides such a map as Dante's or de Deguileville's, at least in part, because Langland cannot suppress his wonder at that magic, what Christians call "grace," and because he remains so oppressively aware of the manner in which the worldly discourses and schemata which attempt to frame grace's advent are compromised by both the institutions and the individuals who seek to express them.[15] In *Piers Plowman*, where such magic appears an isolated, almost accidental emanation, a chance result inhering in but one situation arbitrarily chosen from among several analogues (Robert, but not Couetyse or the friar), repetition—not the linear advance instructional schemata always describe—becomes everything. If accidents can happen, perhaps the next try, the next scene or vision, will work. If not, there's always the next one after that.[16]

University of California, Riverside

---

[15] Including, among these individuals, the poet himself: the onset of Wille's despair, which terminates the A version (A.11:258–313), revolves around precisely the inability to comprehend the incursion of grace.

[16] I owe particular thanks to my four colleagues in the *Piers Plowman* annotation project, all of whom have contributed materially, either in conversation or direct commentary on various draft versions: John Alford, Steve Barney, Traugott Lawler, and Anne Middleton.

J O H N   A .   A L F O R D

Langland's Exegetical Drama:
The Sources of the Banquet Scene
in "Piers Plowman"

ne of the most memorable scenes in the B version of *Piers Plowman* is the dinner party given by Conscience (13.21– 214), at which the main topic of conversation is the meaning of "do well." Each guest has his own opinion—Clergy, Patience, the gluttonous friar, and of course Will the dreamer, who is always ready to take issue with anyone on any subject. Within the allegorical narrative of the poem the discussion is a pivotal moment. Up to now the dreamer's search for "do well" has been mainly intellectual, a fact reflected in the names of his guides: Thought, Wit, Study, Clergy, Scripture, Imaginatif. The banquet marks a shift toward a more active engagement of the will. In this scene, as R. W. Frank Jr. says, "the poet makes his first point about *doing* good— that knowing what is good is not enough. Knowledge must be transformed into action."[1]

The point is dramatized in the conflict between the learned guests who *know* the meaning of "do well" (the friar, Clergy) and those who are seeking to *live* it (Will, Patience). While the "maister" at the high table stuffs himself with expensive "mortrews and puddynges, wombe cloutes and wilde brawen and egges yfryed wiþ grece," Will and Patience, seated below at "a side borde," are served allegorical fare such as "a sour loof ... *Agite penitenciam*," a "drynke *Diu perseuerans*," "a dissh of derne shrifte, *Dixi & confitebor tibi*," and

---

[1] *Piers Plowman and the Scheme of Salvation*, 68. Frank's generalization is true mainly of the so-called *vita* section of the poem, passus 8–20, in which the dreamer's search for Do-well is dramatized; it does not apply to the poem as a whole, for "doing well" is, in fact, a central concern of the *visio*.

other penitential morsels from Scripture.[2] Patience could not be
happier. " 'Here is propre seruice,' quod Pacience, 'þer fareþ no
Prince bettre.' " But Will finds the service, especially in contrast to
that enjoyed by the friar, anything but proper. "It is noȝt foure
dayes þat þis freke," he complains, "Preched of penaunces þat Poul
þe Apostle suffrede" (13.65–66). If rich food is a form of suffering,
Will says sarcastically to the friar, "I wolde permute my penaunce
with youre, for I am in point to dowel" (13.111). Alarmed that one
of the guests is about to ruin his party, Conscience signals Patience
to quiet Will, and then he tries to turn the issue of "do well" into a
topic of polite dinner conversation. Conscience invites the learned
friar to go first, then Clergy, and finally Patience, who "haþ be in
many place, and paraunter knoweþ / That no clerk ne kan" (13.134–
35). But Conscience's efforts at diplomacy only make things worse.
For Patience's confident response—which seems to render learning
irrelevant—does not sit well with the clerks. The friar counsels that
Patience be sent on his way, "for pilgrymes konne wel lye" (13.178);
and Clergy offers to show Conscience a book and teach him "þe
leeste point to knowe / That Pacience þe pilgrym parfitly knew
neuere" (13.186–87). Now Conscience is forced to take sides. Explaining that the discussion "Haþ meued my mood to moorne for
my synnes," Conscience bids farewell to his learned dinner guests
and joins the pilgrimage of Patience. Will follows.

By any measure this is an extraordinary scene. Elizabeth Kirk
rightly observes that it is both "allegorical analysis at its most sophisticated" and "as fine an instance of social observation and the shrewd
exploitation of characteristic behavior as the poem has to offer."[3]
How this remarkable episode came into being is the subject of the
following pages. Scholarship has identified a scattering of sources on
which the poet might have drawn for individual details of the scene
(for example, the seating arrangement, the historical model for the
friar, the metaphor of food as Scripture).[4] But it has located no

---

[2] All quotations of the B version of *Piers* are from the edition by George Kane
and E. Talbot Donaldson.

[3] *The Dream Thought of Piers Plowman*, 146, 148.

[4] Robertson and Huppé (*Piers Plowman and Scriptural Tradition*) comment on
the seating arrangement: "The poet may have had in mind William of Saint-
Amour's sermon on the parable of the Pharisee" (who loved the first place at the

single source or scheme that might have served to pull these details together into a coherent whole. That scheme, I propose, can be found almost entirely in the traditional exegesis of Proverbs 23. This is to make a claim not only about Langland's source but also about his method of composition. Nothing influenced his craft more than the strategies of biblical commentary—the use of the *distinctio* to multiply meanings, of verbal concordance to support and connect them, of allegoresis to interpret them. The more familiar we become with the medieval interpretation of Prov. 23, the greater the impression that we are seeing the banquet scene of *Piers Plowman* in the making. That Langland often took his arguments from scriptural commentaries is well-known. In the banquet scene, I hope to show, he turns exegesis into drama.

§

An early precedent for Langland's "dramatic exegesis" of Prov. 23 can be found in St. Ambrose, whose writings are actually among the "sondry metes" placed before Will and Patience (13.39). In his *De Officiis ministrorum* (*On the Duties of the Clergy*), a treatise composed about AD 391 on the model of Cicero's *De Officiis*, Ambrose takes up the question of clerical conduct (particularly the obligation to "do well" and its relation to the will); and he illustrates his points by means of a social occasion, a banquet.[5]

Ambrose's little allegory of "the feast of Wisdom" is based on the conflation of Prov. 9.1 ("Wisdom hath built herself a house ... and

---

table) and "probably also had in mind Luke 14.7–11" ("When thou art invited to a wedding, sit not down in the first place. ... But when thou art invited, go, sit down in the lowest place") (160). Mildred Marcett sees in the dreamer's angry resolve to "Iangle to þis Iurdan" a punning reference to the Dominican William Jordan, a prominent figure in the antimendicant controversy, who, she argues, might have served as the historical model for Langland's gluttonous friar (*Uhtred de Boldon, Friar William Jordan, and Piers Plowman*). Other critics have traced the metaphorical equation of biblical verses and food to such texts as Matt. 4.4, "Not in bread alone doth man live, but in every word that proceedeth from the mouth of God," and John 4.34, "My meat is to do the will of him that sent me"—both of which figure explicitly in the "food" that Patience later offers to Haukyn the Active Man (see B.14.46a, 50).

[5] The Latin text appears in PL 16: 25–194. The translation used here is taken from *The Nicene and Post-Nicene Fathers of the Christian Church*.

set forth a table") and Prov. 23.1 ("When thou sittest to eat at the
table of a ruler consider diligently what is put before thee, and be
not desirous of his dainties, for they have but a deceptive life").[6]
Ambrose's commentary takes the form of an elaborate *distinctio* on
the word "food":

> But the feasting that Solomon speaks of has not to do with
> common food only, but it is to be understood as having to do
> with good works. For how can the soul be feasted in better
> wise than on good works; or what can so easily fill the mind
> of the just as the knowledge of a good work done? What
> pleasanter food is there than to do the will of God? The Lord
> has told us that He had this food alone in abundance, as it is
> written in the Gospel, saying, "My food is to do the will of
> My Father which is in heaven." ... Let us therefore eat the
> bread of wisdom, and let us be filled with the word of God.
> For the life of man made in the image of God consists not in
> bread alone, but in every word that cometh from God.... Set
> in the paradise of delight and placed at the feast of wisdom,
> think of what is put before thee! The divine Scriptures are the
> feast of wisdom, and the single books are the various dishes.
> Know, first, what dishes the banquet offers, then stretch forth
> thy hand, that those things which thou readest, or which thou
> receivest from the Lord thy God, thou mayest carry out in
> action, and so by thy duties mayest show forth the grace that
> was granted thee.   (28)

Here in embryo is the banquet scene in *Piers Plowman*. Ambrose's
distinctio on the meanings of "food" is realized dramatically in the
literal "mortrews and puddynges" of the friar, in the allegorical fare
of penitence set before Will and Patience, in the designation of the
various dishes as morsels of Scripture. Moreover, Ambrose's general
argument is summarized in the figure of Patience, who not only
personifies his definition of "do well" as conformity with the divine

---

[6] Ambrose alludes to Prov. 9.1 in the phrase *in convivio sapientiae* (XXXII.165);
he translates Prov. 23.1 from the Septuagint as follows: "Si sederis caenare ad
mensam potentis, sapienter intellige ea quae apponuntur tibi: et mitte manum tuam
sciens quod oportet talia praeparare. Si autem insatiabilis es, noli concupiscere escas
ejus; haec enim obtinent vitam fallacem" (XXXI.162).

will but later continues his imagery (drawing on the same scriptural authority) of spiritual food as *voluntas dei*:

'Lyue þoru3 leel beleue, as oure lord witnesseþ:
  Quodcumque pecieritis a patre in nomine meo &c; Et alibi,
  Non in solo pane viuit homo set in omni verbo quod procedit
  de ore dei.'
But I listnede and lokede what liflode it was
That pacience so preisede, and of his poke hente
A pece of þe Paternoster and profrede vs alle;
And þanne was it *fiat voluntas tua* sholde fynde vs alle.

(14.46a–50)

The immediate context of Ambrose's development of Prov. 23.1— a short essay on the virtue of kindness (I.30–34)—also contains significant parallels in the banquet scene. The two constituents of kindness are said to be good will (*benevolentia*) and liberality (*liberalitas*), that is, the desire to do well and its expression in actual works. Ambrose stresses their reciprocal relation. "It is not enough just to wish well," he says, "we must also do well [*bene facere*]. Nor, again, is it enough to do well, unless this springs from a good source, even from a good will" (25). These words are echoed in Conscience's declaration that no value can be placed on the "goode wil of a wight ... For þer is no tresour þerto to a trewe wille" (13.192–93) and virtually paraphrased later in Patience's insistence that all our efforts to do well are lost unless "oure spences and spendynge sprynge of a trewe welle" (14.198–99). Scriptural authority for the primacy of good will is found in the parable of the widow's mites. "The Lord preferred the two mites of the widow to all the gifts of the rich," Ambrose comments, "for she gave all that she had, but they only gave a small part out of all their abundance. It is the intention, therefore, that makes the gift valuable or poor, and gives to things their value" (25). Conscience draws the same conclusion:

Hadde no3t Marie Maudeleyne moore for a box of salue
Than 3acheus for he seide "*dimidium bonorum meorum do*
  pauperibus,"
And þe poore widewe purely for a peire of mytes
Than alle þo þat offrede into *Ga3ophilacium*?

(13.194–97)

The power of good will—it is "the parent as it were of all in common, uniting and binding friendships together" (chap. 32), "Goodwill expands in the body of the Church, by fellowship in faith, by the bond of baptism, by kinship through grace received, by communion in the mysteries" (chap. 33), "Good-will also is wont to remove the sword of anger ... [and] makes many to become one" (chap. 34)—such power is exactly the question at issue between Patience, who exemplifies it, and the gluttonous friar, who cynically denies it. The highest degree of "do well" is to love your enemies, *dilige inimicos*, says Patience.

> Thus lerede me ones a lemman, loue was hir name.
> "Wiþ wordes and werkes," quod she, "and wil of þyn herte
> Thow loue leelly þi soule al þis lif tyme.
> And so þow lere þe to louye, for þe lordes loue of heuene,
> Thyn enemy in alle wise eueneforþ wiþ þiselue."
>
> (13.139–43)

"It is but a dido," the friar retorts, "a disours tale. / Al þe wit of þis world and wiȝt mennes strengþe / Kan noȝt parfournen a pees bitwene þe pope and hise enemys" (13.172–74). Finally, in choosing to be guided by Patience, the embodiment of good will, rather than by the friar and Clergy, the embodiments of worldly wisdom, Conscience seems to be following the Ambrosian script to the very end. "Anyone," the saint concludes, "trusts himself to the counsels of a man of good-will rather than to those of a wise one" (28). Conscience puts the matter more bluntly. "Me were leuere," he says to Clergy, "Haue pacience parfitliche þan half þi pak of bokes" (13.200–201). Whether Langland knew Ambrose's *De Officiis ministrorum* directly or as part of the commentary tradition—or at all—is impossible to say. But to my knowledge it provides the earliest and certainly one of the closest analogues to the banquet scene in *Piers Plowman*.

What subsequent exegesis of Prov. 23 offered Langland was not only a wealth of additional detail, much of which seems to have found its way into the poem, but also a more coherent view of the chapter as a whole. Instead of remaining a miscellaneous collection of loosely related sayings, Prov. 23 gradually achieves over the course of centuries a dramatic unity based on the conflict of worldly wisdom and Christian penitence. The historical result is most clearly seen in a compilation like that of Hugh of St. Cher's *Opera omnia in univer-sum Vetus et Novum Testamentum* (mid-thirteenth century), one of the most popular commentaries of the later Middle Ages.[7] Judson B. Allen has even argued that it was the commentary used by Langland.[8] Whether this is so or not, it is difficult to read through Hugh's gloss on Prov. 23 without feeling that one is actually retracing the steps of the poet himself.

Let us start with the theme of learning or worldly wisdom. The influence of this theme begins with the interpretation of the first verse: *Quando sederis ut comedas cum principe, Diligenter attende quae apposita sunt ante faciem tuam* ("When thou shalt sit to eat with a prince, consider diligently what is set before thy face"). One would hardly guess that learning is the subject here. But Hugh glosses the phrase *in principe* as a reference to men of learning: "Quando sederis cum Principe, id est, cum Magistro vel Predicatore." What's more, medieval readers could easily have taken the gloss to be a reference in particular to *friars*.[9] Not only did friars constitute a large number of the *magistri* and *predicatores* of late medieval England, but they wore these designations as virtual titles. Learned members of both the Franciscan and Dominican orders were addressed as "masters," and the latter belonged, of course, to the *Ordo Predicatorum*. Langland himself calls friars "maistres" (e.g., B.Prol.62; B.8.18; B.10.67; B.15.70) and in one instance applies the word explicitly to the Franciscans or Minorites ("two freres I mette, Maistres of þe Menours" [B.8.8–9]). Thus the gloss on *cum principe* fits the friar perfectly. He is both a "maistre" (B.13.25, 33, 40) and a preacher (13.66, 76, 80, 85).

If "eating with a prince" is to mean conversation with or listening to a learned master, then the food itself is subject to interpretation as intellectual nourishment (words, speech, text). Like Ambrose, Hugh allegorizes the act of eating in Prov. 23.1 as the reading of Scripture. Of *ut comedas* he says, "that is, that you might refresh yourself with the bread of God's word, for man does not live by

---

[7] For its popularity, see R. E. Kaske, *Medieval Christian Literary Imagery: A Guide to Interpretation*, 20.

[8] "Langland's Reading and Writing: *Detractor* and the Pardon Passus."

[9] Whether Hugh intended such an inference is another matter, of course; he was himself a Dominican.

bread alone"; and the injunction *diligenter attende* he takes to mean "consider carefully the sense of the Scriptures set before you." Verse three, however, contains a caveat: *Ne desideres de cibis eius. In quo est panis mendacii* ("Be not desirous of his meats, in which is the bread of deceit"). Hugh's paraphrase of the literal meaning of this verse could have been written expressly as a warning to Will: When you dine with a great man, whose fare is likely to be "more splendid, more luxurious, more copious," Hugh says, be careful to exercise discipline not only over your appetite but also over your tongue; and consider your food diligently, that is, "not desiring something better, looking around at this or that person's servings, but considering only those things that are set before you." Still more suggestive is Hugh's allegorical interpretation. He sees in the verse a distinction between the bread of Scripture and the *panis mendacii* of certain "masters," that is, the bread of flattery, attractive lies, cloaked falsehoods, philosophical vanities.[10] This "bread of deceit" suggests both the fare of the gluttonous friar and his sophistical attempts to turn it into "fode for a penaunt":

> For now he haþ dronken so depe he wole deuyne soone
> And preuen it by hir Pocalips and passion of Seint Auereys
> That neiþer bacon ne braun, blancmanger ne mortrews,
> Is neiþer fissh ne flessh, but fode for a penaunt.
> And þanne shal he testifie of a Trinite, and take his felawe to
>   witnesse
> What he fond in a forel of a freres lyuyng,
> And but þe first leef be lesyng leue me neuere after.
>
> (13.90–96)

The friar's abuse of learning is prefigured also in Hugh's gloss on verses 6–7: *Ne comedas cum homine invido, Et ne desideres cibos eius; Quoniam in similitudinem arioli et conlectoris, Aestimat quod ignorat. Comede et bibe, dicet tibi; Et mens eius non est tecum* ("Eat not with an envious man, and desire not his meats. Because like a soothsayer, and diviner, he thinketh that which he knoweth not. Eat and drink,

---

[10] "Ne desideres de cibus eius, id est, ne desideres audire magistrum qui dulcedine mendacij, vel falsitate palliata, vel vanitate, Philosophica, vel adulatione auditores decipit" (3:50, col. 4).

will he say to thee: and his mind is not with thee"). Not to eat *cum homine invido* is taken to mean not to talk or dispute concerning Scripture with a heretic, who will interpret it as he pleases—a fault, Hugh laments, of many *Doctores & Discipuli* even within the Church. Such a man "thinketh that which he knoweth not." He is a hypocrite. "Eat and drink will he say to thee," that is, *"age, quod doceo"* ("do what I teach")—which is precisely what the hypocritical friar does say (" 'Dowel,' quod þis doctour, 'do as clerkes techeþ' " [13.116])—but "his mind is not with thee," that is, "in those things which he teaches, for he teaches many things he does not believe."

The critique of learning found in the exegesis of Prov. 23 applies as well to other figures than the pompous "doctour." Clergy, the very embodiment of institutionalized learning, is also a target of Langland's satire. This personification openly embraces the idea of personal gain as a legitimate motive for learning; he can hardly believe that Conscience might prefer the poverty of Patience to the lucrative career he represents:

> "What!" quod Clergie to Conscience, "ar ye coueitous nouþe
> After yeres3eues or 3iftes, or yernen to rede redels?"[11]

> (13.183–84)

Clergy's expectation of recompense for learning is in direct violation of Prov. 23.23, *Veritatem eme, et noli vendere sapientiam, et doctrinam, et intelligentiam* ("Buy truth, and do not sell wisdom, and instruction, and understanding"). As Hugh comments,

> And do not sell your wisdom, but freely give to the indigent: Matt. 10.8, "Freely you have received, freely give." For no one ought to appropriate knowledge for himself, but to share it with the entire body of the Church—just as the eye does not lay claim to sight for itself alone, nor the ear to hearing, nor the foot to walking, but rather on behalf of the whole body. No one can sell wisdom or instruction, because only the

---

[11] The ability "to rede redels" is evidently a hallmark of professional scholars, especially of those eager to gain from their knowledge. The friar has already been given an opportunity to solve Patience's riddle on Dowel. "Vndo it," says Patience (that is, both *unwrap* the packet, and *unfold* or explain the riddle); "lat þis doctour deme if dowel be þerInne" (13.157).

management of it is entrusted to him, in the same way that
bread is entrusted to a refectorer or wine to a steward. This
[i.e., verse 23] appears to be said against advocates and masters
of the arts and lawmakers, who sell their learning but claim
that they sell not their learning but only their labor. Against
which [verse], Prov. 11.26, "A blessing upon the head of them
that sell." I respond: It is good to buy and sell wisdom in a
spiritual sense but certainly it is bad to do so in a temporal or
carnal sense.[12]

Hugh's comment reflects the canonistic doctrine of *donum dei*:
learning, like justice or health or the air itself, is a "gift of God" and
is therefore not for sale. The doctrine is a recurring motif in the
poem. It is, in fact, the ground of Langland's running argument
against lawyers, judges, physicians, teachers and others who demand
"mede" for what the Creator intended to be the possession of all in
common.[13] Clergy is well aware of the doctrine. The significance of
his naming the rewards of learning as "yeres3iues or 3iftes" is that
these forms of recompense were common ploys for getting around
the prohibition.[14]

In the exegesis of Prov. 23, Langland would have found not only
a critique of prideful learning but also its antidote in humility and
penitence. The latter theme is hardly discernible, if at all, in the
biblical text alone. Yet Hugh discovers it as early as the second verse:
*Et statue cultrum in guttore tuo; Si tamen habes in potestate animam
tuam* ("And put a knife to thy throat, if it be so that thou have thy
soul in thy own power"):[15]

---

[12] "Et noli vendere sapientiam] tuam, sed gratis da indigenti, *Matth.* 10.b. Gratis
accepistis, gratis date. Nullus enim debet sibi appropriare scientiam, sed communicare toti corpori Ecclesiae, sicut oculus non vendicat sibi soli vsum, nec auris
auditum, nec pes gressum, sed toti corpori. Nemo potest vendere sapientiam, vel
doctrinam, quia sola administratio eius sibi credita est a Domino, sicut refectorio
panis, & cellario vinum. Hoc videtur esse contra aduocatos, & contra magistros
artium, & auctores legum, qui vendunt doctrinam suam; sed dicunt, quod vendunt
doctrinam suam, sed laborem. Contra *supr.* 11.d. Benedictio super caput venden-
tium. Respondeo: Bonum est spiritualiter emere, & vendere sapientiam, & doctri-
[n]am; temporaliter vero siue carnaliter malum" (3:52, col. 1).

[13] On Langland's knowledge of the doctrine, see Yunck, 146–47.

[14] See my *Piers Plowman: A Glossary of Legal Diction*, 170, for the meaning of
yeres3iues and for other examples.

[15] The meaning of this strange and difficult verse is as various as the number of

And put a knife] in penitence, by which means the "old man" is killed.[16] To your throat] by confessing your sins. If you have in power your soul] that is, if you have *in your soul the power* (as if this were the rhetorical figure *hypallage*) to shun and confess yours sins, it ought not to be undertaken in another manner.[17]

Only by an ingenious glossing of the words *put a knife to thy throat* and a wrenching of the grammar of *thy soul in thy own power* could Prov. 23.2 be forced to yield a penitential interpretation. The exegesis of verse 2 is consistent, however, with what Hugh and other commentators take to be a major theme of the chapter as a whole. The penitential motif is rediscovered in verse 8, "The meats which thou hadst eaten, thou shalt vomit up" (in penitence and confession), and continued through verses 16, "when thy lips shall speak what is right" (in the confessional); 26, "let thy eyes keep my ways" (the ways, that is, of innocence and penitence); and 31–32, "[T]he wine ... goeth in pleasantly, but in the end it will bite like a snake" (either through penitence in this life, or through punishment in the afterlife).

These exegetical associations of food and penitence are developed to great effect in the banquet scene. They account not only for a large block of the narrative (lines 37–93 or about a fourth of the total number) but also for some of the episode's most vivid imagery. The

---

translations itself. In his development of the banquet image in *De Officiis ministrorum*, Ambrose, reading from the Septuagint, takes it to mean "and put forth thine hand, knowing that it behoves thee to make such preparations." Modern translations from the Hebrew render it variously as "And put a knife to thy throat, if thou be a man given to appetite" (Authorized Version) and "And if you are a greedy man, cut your throat first" (New English Bible).

[16] To "put off the old man" (Eph. 4.23) is generally taken to be a reference to penitence.

[17] "Et statue cultrum,] poenitudine, quo iuguletur vetus homo. In gutture tuo,] confitendo peccata. Si tamen habes in potestate, etc.] id est, habes in anima tua potestatem vitandi peccata, & confitendi, ut sit hypallage, aliter non est accendendum." Hugh rationalizes his wrenching of the grammar (from "you have in power your soul" to "you have in your soul the power") by appeal to *hypallage*, which can be defined as follows: "A change in the relation of words by which a word, instead of agreeing with the case it logically qualifies, is made to agree grammatically with another case"—Smyth, *Greek Grammar*, 678, quoted by Richard Lanham, *A Handlist of Rhetorical Terms*, 56.

exegesis of verse 2 is elaborated in the description of the food served
to Will and Patience—the sour loaf of *Agite penitenciam*, the meat of
Miserere mei deus, the dish of *Dixi & confitebor tibi*. The exegesis of
verse 8—that the meats (of sin and false doctrine) shall be vomited up
(either now in the sacrament of confession, or *post mortem* in the
pains of hell)[18]—is echoed in Patience's ominous comment on the
friar's rich diet:

> Ac þis maister of þise men no maner flessh eet,
> Ac he eet mete of moore cost, mortrews and potages.
> Of þat men myswonne þei made hem wel at ese,
> Ac hir sauce was ouer sour and vnsauourly grounde
> In a morter, *Post mortem*, of many bitter peyne
> But if þei synge for þo soules and wepe salte teris:
> *Vos qui peccata hominum comeditis, nisi pro eis lacrimas &*
> *oraciones effuderitis, ea que in delicijs comeditis in tormentis*
> *euometis.*   (13.40–45a)

> (You who feast on the sins of men, unless you pour out tears
> and prayers for them, you shall vomit up amid torments the
> food you now feast on amid pleasures.)

Patience later gives his prediction a parodic twist: "He shal haue a
penaunce in his paunche and puff at ech a worde, / And þanne
shullen hise guttes goþele and he shal galpen after" (13.88–89).
"Penaunce" has become indigestion, and confession the rumblings of
a stomach.[19]

As the rift widens between learning (Clergy, the friar) and penitence (Patience and, though imperfect, Will), Conscience finds it
increasingly difficult to maintain the role of genial host. Finally he is
forced to choose. As noted already, his decision to be guided by

---

[18] Cf. Bede's comment: "*Cibos quos comederas evomes*, etc. Sensus perversos quos
ab haereticis didiceras, necesse est ut vel per poenitentiam corrigendus deseras, vel
post mortem pro his poenas luere cogaris, perdasque sermones confessionis, quibus
eis praedicantibus, humiliter favendum esse putaveras" (PL 91:1006). Bede's comment is repeated in the *Glossa ordinaria* (PL 113: 1106).

[19] Earlier Langland offers a more elaborate parody of confession along these
lines in the confession of the Sins in passus 5 (lines 331–60). See Nick Gray, "The
Clemency of Cobblers."

Patience rather than Clergy is foreshadowed in Ambrose's treatise *On the Duties of the Clergy*: "Anyone trusts himself to the counsels of a man of good-will rather than to those of a wise one." This is nearly, but not quite, the narrative formula used by Langland: Patience is identified explicitly with "goode wil" but the friar only seems (or thinks himself) to be "wise." Hugh's exegesis of Prov. 23, however, offers a formula that fits exactly the breakup of the banquet scene, particularly his exegesis of verses 19–21: *Audi, fili mi, et esto sapiens, Et dirige in via animum tuum. Noli esse in conviviis potatorum, Nec in comessationibus eorum qui carnes ad vescendum conferunt; Quia vacantes potibus et dantes symbola consumentur ...* ("Hear thou, my son, and be wise: and guide thy mind in the way. Be not in the feasts of great drinkers, nor in their revellings, who contribute flesh to eat: Because they that give themselves to drinking, and that club together shall be consumed ..."). Hugh's comment begins with an untranslatable play on the word *rectus* (straight, upright, correct, good, virtuous): "*Et in via*, and in the way of truth, *dirige animum tuum*, di-*rect* your mind, that is by a *rect* [straight, right] intention after the pattern of Christ. For where anything straight must be made, it must be placed against a straight rule. This straight rule is the conduct of Christ, the teaching of Christ, and Christ himself in that what he taught he also did."[20] Langland had a taste for this sort of moral geometry. He exploits it at length in the infamous grammatical metaphor of C.3.332–405 ("'Relacoun rect,' quod Consience, 'is a record of treuthe'" [3.343]). What is most striking in the context of the present argument, however, is the match between Hugh's tripartite rule for a Christ-like life and Langland's development of the concept of "do well." As Hugh defines it,

---

[20] "Et dirige in via] veritatis. Animum tuum,] per rectam intentionem per Christi imitationem. Quod enim debet rectum fieri, debet applicari regulae rectae, est Christi conuersatio, Christi eruditio, & est eadem regula, quia idem fecit, quod docuit" (3:51, col. 4). Hugh's verbal argument is based on the Vulgate's use of *dirigo* (past participle *directum*), "to direct, arrange, put in a straight line." The adjective *rectus* derives from the same root (*rego, rectum*). To direct one's mind in the way of truth, therefore, is to align it with the pattern of Christ, the "template," as it were, of Truth. This argument is central to the moral thinking of the Latin Middle Ages. For example, it forms the basis of Anselm of Canterbury's *De Veritate*. For my translation of *conversatio* as conduct or way of life, see Blaise, *Dictionnaire Latin-Français des auteurs chrétiens*, 219.

the *via recta* consists of three actions: to do, to teach, and to do what one teaches. This is precisely the friar's definition of "do well":

> "Dowel," quod þis doctour, "do as clerkes techeþ.
> That trauaileþ to teche oþere I holde it for a dobet.
> And dobest doþ hymself so as he seiþ and precheþ:
> *Qui facit & docuerit magnus vocabitur in regno celorum.*"
>   (13.116–18a)

Structurally this scheme of A + B + AB is replicated in Clergy's definition—"dowel and dobet arn two Infinites, / Whiche Infinites wiþ a feiþ fynden out dobest"[21]—but Clergy is unwilling to pour into this form any specific content, except to say that Piers Plowman has "set alle sciences at a sop saue loue one" in accordance with the biblical injunction *Dilige deum* (13.125-27). The definitions of "do well" offered by the friar and Clergy are conflated in that offered by Patience: "*Disce* and dowel, *doce* and dobet, *dilige* and dobest: / Thus lerede me ones a lemman, loue was hir name" (13.138-39). Virtually the whole of Patience's speech (13.136-71a) is devoted to a discussion of love. The progressive definition of "do well" (from friar to Clergy to Patience), giving greater and greater emphasis to love, reflects the movement within Hugh's commentary on verse 19. If we had to summarize the development of the dinner talk on "do well" as a product of rhetorical invention, we might say most simply that Langland found the friar's *argumentum* at the head of Hugh's gloss on verse 19 and then revised it (for Clergy) and re-revised it (for Patience) in the light of what followed.

What followed is this:

> Thinking of this rule [the *via recta*] as a straight line, the beginning is humility, by which, laying aside his glory and taking the form of a servant, Christ entered the world. The end is obedience, by which, obeying the Father even unto death, he exited the world. The middle is charity, by which he lived in the world. And thus humility brought him into the world, charity conducted him through it, obedience led him from it (Wisdom 10.10, "The Lord has conducted the just

---

[21] For a discussion of the meaning of "infinites" here, see Middleton, "Two Infinites."

through the right ways [*vias rectas*], and shown him the kingdom of God). This is the right way, the way of "the city of
habitation" [Ps. 106.4], the way of truth. Therefore direct
your mind in this way, imitating the humility of Christ, who
although he might have been rich and lord of all, was made
for your sake a pauper and the servant of all. To this way he
himself summons you: "Learn of me, for I am meek and
humble of heart" (Matt. 11.29). Next direct your mind in the
way by imitating the charity of Christ, so that just as he laid
down his life for you, so also be prepared to lay down your
life for him and your brothers (1 John [4.16]: in this: "we
have known the charity of God," seeing that he laid down his
life for us, and we ought to lay down our lives for our brothers). To this way he also summons you: "This is my commandment, that you love one another, as I have loved you"
(John 15.12). And in what manner? Behold, "Greater love
than this no man hath, that a man lay down his life for his
friends." Finally direct your mind in the way, by imitating the
obedience of Christ, that just as he obeyed his Father even
unto death, so you be obedient to God and to your prelate
even unto death. The first Adam withdrew from God through
disobedience; the second Adam returned to God through
obedience. And you, by imitating him, return with him and
after him. To this way he summons you: "Children obey
your parents in all things" (Colossians 3.20). Have, therefore,
humility, charity, and obedience, that is, the beginning, middle, and end of the way of Christ, and thus "direct your mind
in the way," turning aside neither to the right nor the left.[22]

---

[22] "Huius regulae quasi cuiusdam lineae rectae initium est humilitas, qua
seipsum exinaniuit formam serui accipiens, venit in mundum. Terminus ipsius est
obedientia, qua Patri obediens usque ad mortem exiuit de mundo. Medium est
charitas, qua vixit in mundo. Et sic humilitas induxit, charitas deduxit, obedientia
eduxit de mundo. *Sap. 10.b.* Iustum deduxit Dominus per vias rectas, & ostendit illi
regnum Dei. Haec est via recta, via ciuitatis habitaculi, via veritatis. Igitur (dirige
animum tuum) in hac via, imitando Christi humilitatem, qui cum esset diues, &
Dominus omnium factus est propter te pauper, & seruus omnium. Ad hoc te
inuitat ipsemet. *Mat. 11.d.* Discite a me, quia mitis sum, & humilis corde. Item
(dirige animum tuum in via) imitando Christi charitatem, ut sicut ipse animam
suam pro te posuit, & tu pro ipso, & fratribus ponere sis paratus, *1 Ioan. 5.c* In hoc

It would be hard to find a better description of the *via recta* represented by the pilgrim Patience. Hugh's gloss coincides exactly with Langland's development of the personification, as if it had served as a narrative blueprint. Humility is the first quality we see in Patience, who stood outside the palace "in pilgrymes cloþes / And preyde mete '*pur charite*, for a pouere heremyte' " (13.29–30), who delights in the confessional fare of *Miserere mei deus*, etc. (13.54), who takes comfort in the assurance *Cor contritum & humiliatum deus non despicies* (13.58a). Of such "propre seruice," the poet says ironically, "Pacience was proud" (13.59). Obedience is exemplified by Patience's efforts to instill a proper deference in Will ("Pacience parceyued what I þou3te and preynte on me to be stille.... And I sat stille as Pacience seide" [13.86, 99]); and after the resumption of the pilgrimage, by his calling attention to Haukyn's disobedience and offering him the "liflode" of *fiat voluntas tua* (14.50), which is the food of obedience even unto death ("Ne deeþ drede ... but deye as god likeþ" [14.58]). Charity, as we have seen already, holds the supreme place in Patience's speech on "do well" (13.136–71a): "*Disce* and dowel, *doce* and dobet, *dilige* and dobest: / Thus lerede me ones a lemman, loue was hir name" (13.138–39).

Just as Hugh's comment on verse 19 contains the words and deeds of Patience, so his comment on verses 20–21 describes the friar's reaction. Solomon's warning to "be not in the feasts of great drinkers" is interpreted both literally and figuratively. "*Ad literam*, for nothing so clouds a man's understanding as feasting and drunkenness. Hence Jerome, 'A bloated belly cannot think on anything subtle,' and Osee 4:11, 'Wine and drunkenness take away the understand-

---

cognouimus charitatem Dei, quoniam ille animam suam pro nobis posuit, & nos debemus animas pro fratribus ponere. Ad hoc te inuitat etiam ipse. *Ioan 15.b.* Hoc est praeceptum meum, vt diligatis inuicem, sicut dilexi vos. Et quomodo? Ecce, Maiorem hac dilectionem nemo habet, vt animam, &c. Item dirige animum tuum in via, imitando Christi obedientiam, vt sicut ille obediuit Patri vsque ad mortem; & tu similiter obedias Deo, & praelato tuo vsque ad mortem; Primus Adam recessit a Deo per inobedientiam; secundus Adam per obedientiam rediit ad Deum; & tu imitando eum redi cum eo, & post eum. Ad hoc te inuitat. *Apost. Col. 3.d.* Filij, obedite parentibus per omnia. Habe igitur humilitatem, charitatem, & obedientiam, id est, initium, medium & vltimum vie Christi, & sic diriges animum tuum in via, non declinans neque ad dexteram, vel ad sinistram" (3:51, col. 4).

ing.' " *Moraliter*, the verses are a warning against detraction. " 'Be
not [in the feasts of great drinkers],' that is, in the fellowship of those
who make themselves drunk on the reproaches of another life. 'Nor
in their revellings, [who contribute flesh to eat],' that is, they set
forth before their hearers the fleshly sins of others. 'Because they
that give themselves to drinking,' that is, delighting in detraction.
'And clubbing together,' that is, listening to detractions ... 'Shall be
consumed,' that is, they shall be consumed in the eternal fire, or in
detracting one another. Gal. 5.15, 'If you bite and devour one another; take heed you be not consumed one of another,' and also Job
31.31, 'If the men of my tabernacle have not said: Who will give us
of his flesh that we may be filled?' "[23] Hugh's comment fits the
friar not only as *potator*, whose drinking has clouded his understanding,[24] but also as *detractor*. The friar's reaction to Patience's
encomium on love is to dismiss it as "a disours tale" and then, in an
attempted confederacy with Clergy and Conscience, to discredit
Patience himself as "a liar."

"It is but a dido," quod þis doctour, "a disours tale.
Al þe wit of þis world and wiȝt mennes strengþe
Kan noȝt parfournen a pees bitwene þe pope and hise enemys,
Ne bitwene two cristene kynges kan no wiȝt pees make
Profitable to eiþer peple;" and putte þe table fro hym,

---

[23] "Noli esse in conuiuiis potatorum, &c.] Ad literam. Nihil enim adeo obcaecat
intelligentiam hominis, vt comestio, & ebrietas. Vnde *Ieron*. Venter pinguis nihil
tenue potest cogitare. *Osee 4.c*. Vinum, & ebrietas auferunt cor. Moraliter. Autem
detractoribus exponitur, qui carnes proximorum in huiusmodi conuiuiis conferunt
ad vescendum, facientes suctitium diabolicum, in quo, qui detrahit, apponit lin-
guam, & qui libenter audit, apponit aures; salsam dat, qui de hoc gaudet. Primo
dehortatur Salomon audire detractionem, Secundo monet non detrahere, vtrumque
enim peccatum est. Dicit ergo. Noli esse &c.] id est, in consortio eorum, qui
opprobriis alienae vitae se inebriant. Nec in commessationibus eorum, &c.] id est,
carnalia vitia aliorum referunt audientibus. Quia vacantes, &c.] id est, delectantes in
detractionibus. Et dantes symbola,] id est. audientes detractiones & partes suas ibi
ponentes. Consumentur,] id est, absumentur igne aeterno, vel adinuicem detra-
hendo. *Gal. 5.c*. Si inuicem mordetis, & comeditis, videte, ne ab inuicem consum-
mamini. Item *Iob 31.d*. Si non dixerunt viri tabernaculi mei, quis det de carnibus
eius, vt saturemur?" (3:52, col. 4).
[24] E.g., "For þis doctour on þe heiȝe dees drank wyn so faste: *Ve vobis qui
potentes estis ad bibendum vinum*" (13.61–61a); "For now he haþ dronken so depe
he wole deuyne soone ... " (13.90); " 'Dowel,' quod þis doctour and drank after"
(13.104).

And took Clergie and Conscience to conseil as it were
That Pacience þo most passe, "for pilgrymes konne wel lye."
(13.172–78)

Thus the doctor, like Patience, adheres to the exegetical script as
written by Hugh and his predecessors.

Similarly Conscience. Turning his back on the dinner party and
setting forth "to be Pilgrym wiþ pacience" (13.182), Conscience
plays out dramatically the precept of Prov. 23.19–21 to avoid "the
feasts of great drinkers" and to follow instead "the way" of humility, obedience, and charity.

§

The invention of the banquet scene is best explained, I have argued,
as the dramatic realization of the traditional exegesis of Prov. 23. The
use of exegetical materials to illuminate the poem is nothing new.[25]
What distinguishes my argument from most is this: I am not concerned with the meaning of a specific image or a few problematic
lines, a "crux," but rather with a long sequence of events, a pattern.
To prove the significance of coincidental patterns is always difficult
but especially in this case. So vast and comprehensive is the lexicon
of biblical exegesis that claiming to have found a biblically charged
poem like *Piers Plowman* in its pages can be like claiming to have
found a novel in the dictionary. Let me conclude, therefore, with a
few remarks on methodology.

The argument for an exegetical source should be subject to the
same criteria used in other kinds of source study. Besides verbal
correspondence, the securest proof, there are other tests that can be
applied. One is density. Are the correspondences few or many? Are

---

[25] For more than a half-century—since the publication of Dunning's *Piers
Plowman: An Interpretation of the A Text* (1937)—numerous scholars have claimed
to have discovered exegetical influences on this or that portion of the poem.
Robertson and Huppé's *Piers Plowman and Scriptural Tradition* (1951) is the most
ambitious example, followed in time and importance by Ben H. Smith's *Traditional
Imagery of Charity in Piers Plowman* (1966) and Margaret Goldsmith's *The Figure of
Piers Plowman* (1981). To single out any of the numerous articles that take an
exegetical approach to the poem would be difficult, but one can almost believe that
R. E. Kaske wrote half of them.

they scattered over a large area of the possible source or tightly concentrated? Do they account for a significant part of the later work? I do not know of any sources yet advanced for any extended passage of the poem that better meet this criterion than the exegesis of Prov. 23. All of the details discussed above can be found in a single commentary on this chapter. It is not necessary to roam like a modern *gyrovagus* from Hugh to Lombard to Bede and so forth, or even from one part of the commentary to another. If Langland composed the banquet scene under the inspiration of Hugh's commentary, he could have found all that he needed without turning a page.

Another criterion is uniqueness or rarity. Do the borrowings occur only in the presumed source, in a few other places, in relatively many? To be sure, some of the elements of the banquet scene are commonplace. The notion of Scripture as food is a *topos* (listed, in Curtius's inventory, under "the alimentary metaphor"[26]); and the gluttonous and hypocritical friar is a stock figure of anti-mendicant satire, including Chaucer's well-known *Summoner's Tale*. However, Hugh's gloss on Prov. 23 is the sole precedent not only for the particular *combination* of elements that make up the banquet scene but also for one of its most important parts, the identification of the three lives as "to do, to teach, and to do as one teaches."

There is also the criterion of context. Is the presumed borrowing contextualized in some way as to betray its origin? For example, many of Langland's quotations that occur both in the Vulgate and in the liturgy can be traced confidently to the latter because they have brought part of their liturgical setting into the poem. We can be fairly sure that Langland's citation of Ps. 111.9 as proof of the heavenly reward given "Laurence for his largenesse" (C.17.66a) was prompted by the use of this verse as the opening line of the Introit and Gradual for the Vigil-Mass of St. Lawrence.[27] Similarly Langland's dramatic expansion of Prov. 23 seems to have been prompted in part by the association of this text with the one he had just quoted

---

[26] E. R. Curtius, *European Literature and the Latin Middle Ages*, 134–36. As Curtius observes, "[T]he Bible is the principal source of alimentary metaphors" (134).

[27] See Tavormina, "*Piers Plowman* and the Liturgy of St. Lawrence." For other examples see my *Piers Plowman: A Guide to the Quotations*, 21.

at the end of the previous passus, namely, Psalm 22. The speaker is Imaginatif:

For *Deus dicitur quasi dans [eternam vitam] suis, hoc est fidelibus*;
Et alibi, si ambulauero in medio umbre mortis.
The glose graunteþ vpon þat vers a greet mede to truþe.

(12.293–94)

It is extremely helpful to know that Langland consulted a commentary on Psalm 22 just several lines before the opening of the banquet scene. There, immediately following the verse quoted, he would have found the words "Thou hast prepared a table before me, against them that afflict me"—a literal description of the impending meal with the friar—along with a gloss of the food (*mensa*) as "divine Scripture." If his "glose" was Hugh of St. Cher, he would have been led from the *mensa* of Ps. 22.5 to the *mensa* of Prov. 9.2 ("the feast of Wisdom"), which, as we have seen, is conflated by Ambrose with Prov. 23.1; or, using some other gloss, he might have been led directly to Prov. 23.1 (as in the thirteenth-century *Distinctiones monasticae*, which interprets Ps. 22.5 tropologically and then Prov. 23.1 allegorically[28]). Such cross-referencing is, of course, a fundamental strategy of biblical exegesis; and, as I have tried to show elsewhere, it is also a fundamental strategy in the composition of *Piers Plowman*.[29] The question of specific sources aside, Langland's quotation from Ps. 22 is virtually a prediction that he will turn next to "the bread of penitence," for this is the pattern established earlier in the poem (7.120–28a), where he quotes the same verse and comments almost immediately, "The prophete his payn eet in penaunce and in sorwe.... / *Fuerunt michi lacrime mee panes die ac nocte*" (Ps. 41.4). Langland thought in such clusters, and on such repetitive associations he built his poem.[30]

---

[28] J. B. Pitra, *Spicilegium Solesmense*, 3:214

[29] "The Role of the Quotations in *Piers Plowman*."

[30] The series or chain of parallels is actually much longer. In passus 13–14 Langland goes from Ps. 22.4 to the bread of penitence and false learning and detraction by a "diviner" and the theme of patience or *ne soliciti*; similarly, in 7.120–43a he takes us from Ps. 22.4, "Si ambulavero in medio umbre mortis," to Ps. 41.4, "Fuerunt michi lacrime mee panes die ac nocte," to Matt. 6.25, "Ne soliciti sitis," to Ps. 13.1, "As diuinour in diuinite, wiþ Dixit insipiens," to Prov. 22.10, "Ejice derisores & iurgia cum eis ne crescant."

Ultimately any source study will be judged by the criterion of usefulness. Does it add to our knowledge of the work or of its creation? I see the present argument as part of a growing body of evidence that the most important intertext of *Piers Plowman* is the glossed Bible, and that the poem must be read accordingly. If we cannot be sure about the exact lines of transmission, this much at least is clear. The banquet of Scripture, the tension between learning and penitence, the concept of "do well" and its three-fold definition, the "way" of patience, the combination of gluttony, learning, hypocrisy and detraction to form a single "character" like the friar—these were exegetical themes long before Langland took up the writing of poetry. He was not solely responsible for either their invention or their disposition. In the final analysis, the banquet scene in *Piers Plowman* is best understood as the product of a collaboration between Langland and, among others, Hugh of St. Cher, Ambrose, and the anonymous author of Proverbs.

Michigan State University

JOAN HEIGES BLYTHE

Sins of the Tongue
and Rhetorical Prudence
in "Piers Plowman"

I

ui loquitur turpiloquium is luciferes hyne" (Prol. 39), the
first of several hundred Latin quotations in *Piers Plowman*, signs the poem's focus on language.[1] From the
Prologue's indulgence-pandering Pardoner and idlers
singing "how trolly lolly," to the lingual penetration of Unity in the
last passus, Langland's quest for verbal truth is relentless. Yet many
critics have argued that Langland's skeptical critique of human speech
ultimately despairs over language's ability to convey any truth. This
critical position can be maintained only by ignoring Langland's debt
to an important theme in penitential tradition, the theme of *peccata
linguae* or "sins of the tongue." Understood with reference to such
works as Peraldus's *Summa de vitiis et virtutibus*[2] and Albertano da
Brescia's *De arte loquendi et tacendi*,[3] language-related failure in *Piers
Plowman* is not language's fault. The failure arises from ignorant,
willfully evil, or carelessly irresponsible individuals who do not
ground and shape their language in accordance with Christian truth
and Christian models.[4] Furthermore, from this point of view the

---

[1] All references to *Piers Plowman*, unless noted otherwise, are to Kane and
Donaldson, *Piers Plowman: The B Version*.

[2] All references to Peraldus are to the edition of 1668.

[3] Ed. Sundby, 1869.

[4] Other scholars have recognized the importance of the *peccatum linguae* theme
to the poesis of *Piers Plowman*. See, for example, Judson B. Allen's "Langland's
Reading and Writing: *Detractor* and the Pardon Passus." Although Langland's

vocational self-imaging of the poet at the end seems more positive and confident than negative or ambiguous: like Holy Church, Study, Scripture, and Love, all of whom teach the socially responsible use of linguistic power, he too in his sphere affirms the power of language that is inspired by "Spiritus prudencie."

"Tongues should be used for praying, repeating holy words, and taking the holy sacrament," Peraldus concludes in "De peccato linguae," the last section of his influential *Summa* (13th c.).[5] "The sin of the tongue must be spoken of last," Peraldus explains, "because ... many who may guard themselves from other sins are not safe from the sin of the tongue" (2.371). He supports this claim with the biblical *locus classicus* on tongue-evil, James 3.6–8, "And the tongue is a fire, a world of iniquity. The tongue is placed among our members, which defileth the whole body and inflameth the wheel of our nativity, being set on fire by hell. For every nature of beasts and of bird, and of serpents, and of the rest, is tamed, and hath been tamed, by the nature of man. But the tongue no man can tame." Arguably the most drawn-upon of the penitential handbooks written in response to the instructional mandate of the Fourth Lateran Council (1215),[6] Peraldus's *Summa de vitiis et virtutibus* from the first had secular readers as well as the clerics who used it to write

---

preoccupation with *turpiloquium* may have arisen from being "stung" by a Pelagianistically accusatory response to the Z text, as Allen contends (351–52), from the broader perspective of A and certainly of the completed B text, his concern with verbal evils encompasses far more than Detractor's whips and scorns. For a significant analysis from a different point of view of the tongue concept in *Piers*, see Barney. Bowers is closer to my own point of view, but he focuses more on faulty language than on the faulty speakers. Thus for him Langland has a "deep" "suspicion that language has the potential to corrupt mankind" (196). Although Bowers comes to similar conclusions about the poet and the language issue in his final chapter, he does not present them as I do from the perspective of the penitential handbook tradition. For a full investigation of the theme of "sins of the tongue" in the twelfth and thirteenth centuries, see Casagrande and Vecchio.

[5] Although I cannot prove that Langland knew first-hand Peraldus's *Summa de vitiis et virtutibus*, the work's influence on such major poets as Jean de Meung (Fleming, 172–73), Dante, and Chaucer (Wenzel, "The Sources" and *Summa Virtutum*; Patterson, "The Parson's Tale," 380), as well as its great importance for medieval studies generally (Dondaine, "Guillaume Peyrault," 162; Wenzel, *The Sin of Sloth*, 98; Newhauser, *The Treatise on Vices and Virtues*, 129–30), argue for using the work to gain insights into the moral landscape of *Piers Plowman*.

[6] Bloomfield, *The Seven Deadly Sins*, 124–25.

sermons and administer penance. The first part of Peraldus's tract, *De virtutibus*, covers the three theological virtues (faith, hope, charity) and the four cardinal virtues (prudence, fortitude, temperance, and justice), as well as the Gifts of the Holy Spirit, and the Beatitudes. The second part, *De vitiis*, takes up the usual seven deadly sins followed by an eighth, the *peccatum linguae.*[7]

Peraldus's "De peccato linguae" is important not only as part of a major penitential treatise, but also as a "para-rhetorical" manual. It circulated separately,[8] and many of its concepts reappear in later secular rhetorical tracts such as Albertano da Brescia's *De arte loquendi et tacendi* (1245) and parts of Brunetto Latini's *Li Livres dou Tresor* (ca. 1267).[9] Later works in the tradition of "De peccato linguae" include Johannes Geus's *Tractatus de viciis vocis* (1479), Erasmus's *Lingua* (1525, in his *Opera omnia*, 4), and Jeremias Drexel's *Orbis Phaethon: De universis viciis linguae* (1621).

In the first part of "De peccato linguae" (2.371–76), Peraldus declares that since God distinguished humans by endowing their tongue with the potential for speech, he judges them primarily by how they use it. A wicked tongue combusts the speaker, the audience, and the subject. What should be the best—the word—becomes the worst. On the other hand, those who guard the tongue are perfect. In the much longer second part of "De peccato linguae" (2.377–418), Peraldus explains *lingua*'s twenty-four evil progeny: *blasphemia*, *murmur* (complaining), *peccati defensio* (excusing sin), *periurium* (wrongful swearing, false oaths), *mendacium* (lying), *detractio*, *adulatio* (flattery), *maledictio* (slander), *convicium* (wrangling, violent censure), *contentio* (strife, controversy), *derisio* (scorn), *prauum consilium* (false counsel), *peccatum seminantium discordias*, *peccatum bilinguium* (hypocrisy), *amantium rumores, iactantia* (boasting), *secreti revelatio*, *indiscreta comminatio* (indiscriminate threaten-

---

[7] Peraldus probably completed *De vitiis* by 1236 and then wrote *De virtutibus*. According to Dondaine, by 1250 the two parts were circulating usually as one text. In accounting for the primacy given texts on the vices, Wenzel comments: "The primary object of moral theology ... was sinful man.... Attention to ... 'vices,' must and did come first. ... [T]he literary genre of the *summa* on the virtues came into being only as a companion and sequel to the *summa* on the vices" (*Summa*, 7).

[8] Cf. Vat. Palat. Lat. 252.

[9] Latini, xxix.

ing), *indiscreta promissio* (false promising), *verbum otiosum* (idle word), *multiloquium* (too much talking), *turpiloquium* (foul talk), *scurrilitas/iocularitas* (vulgar joking/inappropriate laughter), and *taciturnitas indiscreta* (remaining silent when you should speak). All of these sins of the tongue have specific remedies, such as thinking on the God-given nobility of the tongue and the dangers in speaking; clapping a hand over one's mouth when tempted to misspeak; speaking rarely and slowly; using few words; making God custodian of the tongue through prayer; and silence. The general remedy, however, is prudence.

Although Peraldus extols the remedial qualities of prudence in "De peccato linguae,"[10] his principal discussion occurs earlier in part 1, *De virtutibus*, under the heading of "De prudentia." In describing prudence—the first and, for its rational direction of the human will, the preeminent of the four cardinal virtues (1.198)[11]— Peraldus includes many rhetorical concepts. Conforming to a tradition that goes back to Aristotle, and one that would underlie the new vitality in Renaissance attitudes toward reading and writing,[12] Peraldus deems moral discourse the chief manifestation of this virtue in works (as opposed to mere theory). Citing Seneca, he declares, "Prudentia dicitur scientia operandorum" (1.190). This knowledge of what must be done depends on prudence's ability to distinguish between good and evil. Peraldus links Augustine's definition, "Prudentia est amor ... sagaciter eligens," with Cicero's, "Prudentia est rerum bonarum & malarum & utrarumque scientia" (*Rhetorica*, 1.191). Since the prudential ability to differentiate between good and evil depends on proper instruction, the discussion of pedagogical principles makes up the heart of "De prudentia." These positive,

---

[10] In a gloss on Ecclesiasticus 21, Peraldus distinguishes three degrees of the virtue: "The prudent person knows when to speak; the more prudent person speaks what ought to be said and is free from falseness and harming neighbor and God; the most prudent person speaks sweetly without clamor and sharpness" (2.375).

[11] According to Lottin, Prudence had accrued even greater importance in the twelfth century: "On sait que, d'apres Pierre Abelard, la prudence est, non point une vertue, mais le reine mère des vertus" ("La Traite," 21). That Prudence (Phronesis) is "the heroine" of Alain de Lille's *Anticlaudianus*, stealing the limelight from Nature, Reason, Concord, and the other illustrious allegorical figures, as well as from humankind (see Sheridan, 35) is but one example of this.

[12] See Kahn, *Rhetoric, Prudence, and Skepticism in the Renaissance*.

hopeful attitudes toward language (derived primarily from Augustine's *De doctrina christiana*) are in stark contrast to the dire warnings
of "De peccato linguae." Nevertheless, despite the differences in
tone, many of the verbal principles in "De prudentia"—such as, do
not lie, talk too much, boast of one's own suave eloquence, or
indulge in over-zealous correction; do be brief, know when to be
silent and listen, and use the tongue for promoting love of God and
neighbor—parallel those in "De peccato linguae."

Albertano da Brescia's *De arte loquendi et tacendi* features similar
rhetorical guidelines. This treatise often circulated with and reflected
aspects of his *Liber consolationis et consilii*.[13] In this latter work
Prudentia (whom A. Checchini calls one of the most influential
female characterizations in medieval literature [57]) uses the qualities
of *ratio, intellectus, providentia, circumspectio, cautio*, and *docilitas* to
persuade her husband to change his negative rhetorical posture to a
positive one. Unlike other popular thirteenth- and fourteenth-
century rhetorical treatises, but like the language position of Peraldus's "De peccato linguae," *De arte loquendi et tacendi* opens with
the premise "in dicendo multi errant."[14] Since Albertano then
quotes from James 3, the "erring" he is referring to is moral not
technical. With Peraldian zeal he eschews overly ingenious organization and preoccupation with the colors of rhetoric. He focuses
instead on basic rhetorical precepts, principally what would be
considered under *inventio*: the character of the speaker, the character
of the audience, and the subject matter of discourse. The virtuous
speaker, guided by prudence and reason, promotes truth and justice,
implements words in deeds, and values patience, restrained speech,
and silence. The evil speaker loves worldly status more than truth,
drinks too much, indulges in uncontrolled verbosity, lasciviousness,
obscurity, and contorts his face and body. Although Albertano
clearly knows the classical rhetoricians, notably Cicero and Seneca,
his treatise is ideologically closer to penitential writers like Peraldus.

---

[13] Ed. Thor Sundby, repr. 1983,

[14] In contrast is Cicero's *De oratore*, which begins with the positive glories of
eloquence.

II

The approach to *peccatum linguae* found in Peraldus and Albertanus, both the analysis of the various species of the sin and their universal remedy in prudence, is repeated in *Piers Plowman*. The Latin quotations in the poem offer an important clue to Langland's purpose. As Alford has demonstrated, they are an organic part of the poem's meaning and artistry.[15] The first quotation occurs in the macaronic line "*Qui loquitur turpiloquium* is Lucifer's hyne" (Prol. 39);[16] the last (and its variants), recurrent in passus 19 and 20, is *redde quod debes*. The first lays out the rhetorical moral orientation of *Piers* where God's servants and Lucifer's are known by their languages (which according to Peraldus are as distinctively discernible as German speakers to French). The last signals that the poet has learned what best to do with his own sin-prone tongue: expose and berate the verbal degeneracy of others and teach God's story and human responsibility. A survey of tongue lore in *Piers Plowman* suggests that Langland shares Peraldus's and Albertano's fear of the pathologically errant human tongue as well as their hopeful views about the good that could come—in "Spiritus Prudencie"—from Christian tongues well-reined, bridled, and curbed.

The many sins of the tongue that throng the carnivalesque midway of the Prologue provide a precis of verbal abuses which Langland's allegory will later explore in more complexity. Anticipating the prevalence of sloth in *Piers*,[17] images of *verbum otiosum* and *iocularitas* abound, including the minstrels who make "murþes" and "geten gold with hire glee" (33–34) and the "Iaperes and Iangeleres" who "Fonden hem fantasies and fooles hem makeþ" (35–36). *Mendacium* rules the pilgrims bound for St. James, who have tongues "tempred to lye / Moore þan to seye sooþ" (51–52), the friars who preach only for profit (59–61), and the pardoner who brokers false penance (68–75). *Multiloquium* typifies the "Goliardeis, a gloton of

---

[15] "The Role of the Quotations."

[16] In *The Ethical Poetic*, Allen argues that the source of Langland's *turpiloquium* is Col. 3.8 (276), but the fact that Peraldus's discussion of *turpiloquium* opens with Ephes. 5.3–5 would tend to support critics who argue that this passage lies behind the first *Piers* Latin quotation.

[17] Wenzel, *The Sin of Sloth*, 135–47.

wordes" (139); *pravum consilium*, the rat who advises the impossible belling of the cat; wicked refusal to speak the truth (*indescreta taciturnitas*), religious professionals who seek London riches instead of preaching and administering penance (87–96), and lawyers who are mum unless "moneie be shewed" (216). Although the dreamer's timid "for I ne dar" (to speak aloud his dream) of line 210 seems a response to the just-told political fable of the rats, it also suggests his own reluctance to tell the truth he sees in all the Prologue images of verbal abuse, an anxiety that will surface more obviously in passus 11.

Holy Church who opens passus 1 with kindly advice on how to distinguish good from evil is the first and most memorable of a series of figures in *Piers* infused with the "*Spiritus prudencie.*" Her mandate, that Truth "wolde þat ye wrouȝte as his word techeþ" (13), has a particular meaning for Will, who as a Christian poet must render up finally a non-blasphemous similitude of divine truth. The main challenge to doing so, she says, comes from the logos-undermining trinity of the world, flesh, and devil. Repeatedly, Holy Church connects vocation, truth-telling tongue work, and divine similitude: "For who is trewe of his tonge ... [and] Dooþ þe werkes þerwiþ. ... He is a god by þe gospel.... The clerks þat knowen it sholde kennen it aboute" (88–92). "Werkes" here anticipates the quotation of James 2.26 in line 188, "*Fides sine operibus mortua est.*" Like other Latin quotations in *Piers*, this ideological touchstone of the whole poem (from "Iames the gentil") should be interpreted in relation to its source context.[18] James 1 ends with a tongue warning, and James 3 is preoccupied with dramatic images of the evil tongue. The pattern is repeated in passus 2–4.

Since the sin of avarice is writ so large in the Lady Meed episode, the extent to which these passus continue Holy Church's theme of the true versus the wicked tongue may be missed. In his discussion of *mendacium* Peraldus says that the liar is like one who mints false money. This mendacious essence of Meed is affirmed in 2.25–27: "For Fals was hire fader þat haþ a fikel tonge / And neuere sooþ seide siþen he com to erþe, / And Mede is manered after hym." We then learn that Liar has set up Meed's nuptial scheme (43). Expelled by the king, Liar first is "nowher welcome for his manye tales"

---

[18] See Alford, "The Role of the Quotations," 87; Allen, *The Ethical Poetic*, 343.

(220), an image recalling the tale-telling, lying pilgrims of the Prologue. Similarly echoic of the Prologue is the association of Liar with
Pardoners (2.222–25), "leches" (2.226–27), grocers (2.228–29), "Myns-
trales and Messagers" (2.230), and friars (2.232–35), who like Liar and
Favel are known for "fair speche" (the name of Favel's horse). For
Peraldus, all "suave eloquence" done for its own sake or for financial
gain is a form of *mendacium* (2.393). That Liar has leave of the friars
"to lepen out as ofte as hym likeþ" (234) anticipates his friarly
insinuation into the Barn of Unity at the end of the poem.

The liar-friar connection also leads into the false confession of
Meed by the honey-tongued, money-for-windows-Friar in passus 3.
This outright scam and the fact that Meed is essentially "fikel of hire
speche" (3.122) and "talewis of tonge" (3.131) obscure the deeper
level of language perversion. The difficulty of distinguishing prudent-
ly between true and false speakers and among ideologically different
semantic systems provides a strong bond between the seemingly
disparate elements of the Visio and Vita. Holy Church has specified
that language is valid only if grounded in Christian love. But Meed
seeks to devalue language by substituting herself for the validating
principle, as evidenced in her solipsistic use of the word "amend"
discussed below. In the ideal state, Conscience says, Meed would be
banished and the judge would be "Trewe-tonge" (3.321).

This true-tongue concept is figured in passus 4 by dense image
clusters of prudential speech precepts. Thus Reason enters accompanied by his knave, Cato, "curteis of speche" (17) and Tom "Trewe-
tonge-tel-me-no-tales-Ne-lesynge-to-lauȝen-of-for-I-loued-hem-neuere"
(18–19).[19] Once more alluding to the horse and bridle images of the
sinful tongue in James 3, Langland gives Reason a horse called
"suffre-til-I-se-my-tyme" (20), who has a "witful" girth, and requires
a "heuy brydel to holde his heed lowe" (22). With this kind of
iconographic referent,[20] we expect Reason's verbal victory over
Wrong and the lawyers suborned by Meed. As in passus 3, the
conflict in passus 4 centers on Meed's and Reason's understanding of
the concept "amend": for Meed it means fixing the problem with

---

[19] For the most comprehensive treatment of Reason, see Alford, "The Idea of
Reason."

[20] Blythe, "The Influence of Latin Manuals," 280–81.

money (cf. 4.96, 103) instead of amending one's life. This semantic shift illustrates the evil tongue species *peccati defensio*. Peraldus's treatment of this sub-sin focuses on the primary necessity of eradicating it through penance. Accordingly, Reason interprets "amend" as getting one's life in order with respect to God's word. In his apocalyptic prophecy Reason says he will not have pity until "Seint Iames be souʒt þere I shal assigne" (126). Because of his deep concern for virtuous speech, Reason surely alludes here to the book of James in a direct challenge to all that Meed represents and to the attitudes of those in the Prologue on their way to the shrine of St. James of Compostella.

Reason's verbal victory in passus 4 leads to his sermon on the godly meaning of amendment in passus 5. The dreamer muses, "Of þis matere I myʒte mamelen wel longe" (21)—which shows progress from the Prologue when he did not dare to comment on his dream—but the word *mamelen* ("mumble") suggests his continued lack of confidence. Reason's sermon-closing admonition to seek St. Truth (5.58) reiterates the language values taught by Holy Church and ties in with his concluding arguments in passus 4. Unlike the clamorous and falsely fair words of Meed and her crew, the words of Truth, Piers says, are "louelich" (553), and he specifies the first landscape marker on the way to Truth as the brook, "beþ-buxom-of-speche" (566).

The main way to use "buxom speche," Peraldus says, is by confessing sin, an act dramatized in the next major sequence. As in the handbooks, which do not treat the subject separately, the *peccata linguae* appear most numerously in association with envy and wrath in the confession of the seven deadly sins. Envy's words, for example, are "of a Neddres tonge" (5.86), and his chief livelihood "chidynge," "chalangynge," "bakbitynge," "bismere," and "berynge of fals witnesse" (5.87–88). Wrath, like the earlier manifestations of Liar, is a friar known for lies, low speech, and easy penance; he provokes "Ianglynge" (*amor rumoris* in this case), "wykkede wordes" (*maledictio* and *seminatio discordiae*), "flux of a foul mouth" (*turpiloquium* and *multiloquium*), and *revelatio secretorum* (5.158–81). Sins of the tongue are prominently confessed by other sins as well. Glutton who broadly confesses to having "trespased with my tonge" (5.368) is guilty of "grete othes" and needless and habitual swearing (aspects of *blasphemia*), idle words, too much laughing (*iocularitas*), and love of rumor. Sloth admits to similar sins of the tongue: idle tales, lies, needless swearing, false promises, inappropriate laughter, *peccatum bilinguium* ("That I telle wiþ my tonge is two myle fro myn herte" [5.401]), and, most typically (and most relevant to Will), *taciturnitas indiscreta*—failure to speak when he should. Avarice's evil, like Meed's, arises from his failure to understand a Christian orientation of language; just as Meed perverts Reason's "amends" into handing out bribes, so Avarice misinterprets Repentance's "restitucioun" as "ryflynge" (235).[21]

The perils of trying to communicate with those who base their language and lives on different value systems are also illustrated in Piers's efforts at social reform in passus 6 and 7—reminiscent of Peraldus's (in "De prudentia") and Albertano's admonition that one should not attempt to address fools, drunks, or those sleeping. Although Piers banishes the obviously sinful tongue-users "frere faitour" and "Robyn þe Ribaudour for hise rusty wordes" (6.72), he does not at first see into a more serious tongue malaise: the would-be Truth seekers value only language of the body. Like those at the end of the Prologue calling "go we dyne, go we" and those in our time whose most pressing daily question is "where shall we eat?" the half-acre folk (with the exception of the knight who does respond to Piers's urging to "be trewe of þi tonge" [6.50]) have a much more lively interest in their bellies than in speaking and acting on the basis of Christian charity. For them food is the validator of life and language. Guilty of the sin of *murmur*, Peraldus says, such worship the stomach, not God: "Ecce homo plenus querela, ventris sui cultor. Tales enim non Domino Iesu Christo, sed ventri suo seruiunt" (2.385).

Piers's exasperation over the priest's response to the pardon at the end of passus 7 is a rejection of this view for himself ("I shal cessen of my sowyng ... / Ne aboute my bely ioye[22] so bisy be na moore" [7.122–23]), for he vows to live by the principle of loyal love of God (7.128). The Priest's scorn for both the pardon and for Piers

---

[21] A more obvious example of the serious confusion of "nomen" and "res" or disjunction between the sign and what it ought to stand for is imaged in the man who wears many "signes" (5.519, 524, 529) of his pilgrimages to seek "gode seyntes," but hasn't a clue when asked the whereabouts of Truth.

[22] Skeat's reading "bely ioye" is adopted here rather than Kane and Donaldson's "bilyue."

indicates that he does not ground his language in God as Piers does. Piers checkmates the priest's *derisio* with a favorite sins-of-the-tongue biblical citation, Prov. 22.10 (7.43a), translated in the A text as "Slynge awey these scorners ... with here shrewid fliting" (Skeat, 8.125). When this sin of the tongue wakes the dreamer, his earlier verbal reluctance has altered dramatically: instead of "mamelen" about whether he dare speak, he passionately admonishes his audience to Do-Well.[23]

That Will in passus 8 challenges the friars who claim that Do-Well dwells with them shows that his prudential judgments between good and evil have improved since the Prologue. By speaking out against the friars' *peccatum bilinguium* the Dreamer himself participates in the Do-schema: Thought's catalogue of Do-well's virtues begins with "Whoso is meke of his mouþ, milde of his speche, / Trewe of his tunge" (80–81); Do-Bet's with "He is as lowe as a lomb, louelich of speche" [like Truth in passus 5] (8.86).

In passus 9 Wit powerfully reinforces the positive potential of language and Langland's identity as creator-poet. Wit first explains God's will, word and workmanship in terms of a "lord" who needs parchment and pen to "make lettres" (39–40). This idea recalls the commonplace in Peraldus that the tongue ought to be the pen of the Holy Spirit ("Lingua calamus est Spiritus S[ancti]" [2.412]; cf. Psalm 44). Particularly significant for *Piers* is that this metaphor occurs in Peraldus's "De verbo otioso," which also includes a stern warning against using the tongue for jests and fiction: "Labia sacerdotum custodiunt scientiam, & legem requirent ex ore eius, non nugas vel fabulas" (2.412). Later in passus 9 Wit figures God's will and poetic responsibility even more vividly in a description of doing best:

He dooþ best þat wiþdraweþ hym by daye and by ny3te
To spille any speche. . . .
And siþþe to spille speche þat spire is of grace
And goddes gleman and a game of heuene.

---

[23] Similar to the sins of the tongue, faith and works, and catechetical aspects of the Visio, the Do-Well emphasis may have come from James: "If then you fulfill the royal law, according to the scriptures, *Thou shalt love thy neighbour as thyself*; you do well" (2.8).

Wolde neuere þe feiþful fader his fiþele were vntempred
Ne his gleman a gedelyng, a goere to tauernes.   (9.99–106)

Wit's injunction not to waste speech mirrors the ideal of guarded
speech mandated in Peraldus and Albertano; the well-tempered
tongue (poet, fiddle) should show restraint, not prostitute talents on
an unfit audience. The metaphor of speech as God's poet affirms
Will's growing understanding that through godly poetry he lives
more in accord with Christian vocation than many religious.[24]

Dame Study in passus 10 also teaches Will about audience awareness and the value of responsible and restrained speech. Her characterization, like that of Lady Holy Church, reflects the *prudentia*
tradition. Study says, for example, why speak to fools who care more
for land than for Solomon's proverbs (frequently cited in tongue
treatises). Such fools prefer the sinful "Iaperis and Iogelours and
Iangleris of gestes" to the true man "þat haþ holy writ ay in his
mouþe" (10.31–32). Study criticizes those who spit, speak foul words
(*turpiloquium*), drink, drivel, and gnaw God in the gorge when their
guts are full. Such "grete maistres ... carpen of god faste" but are
"meene men in herte" (10.67–71) and neglect the audiences who need
good instruction. These habitual tongue abusers also commit great
evil when they employ "crabbed words" in heated doctrinal dinner
disputes (an example of Peraldus's *convicium*). Peraldus and Albertano both warn that overeating leads to bad speech, that the drunk are
neither good speakers nor good audiences, and that the good speaker
will always abstain from impudence and scurrility. Will, on the other
hand, shows his potential for godly language: Dame Study praises
him for his "mild speech" and directs his route to Clergy by a court,
"Kepe-wel-þi-tunge-Fro-lesyngs-and-liþer-speche-and-likerouse-drynkes"
till he sees "Sobretee and Sympletee-of-speche" (10.168–70).

In passus 11 Scripture (another *prudentia* figure) and Reason
further promote Will's language-growth. Scripture begins by blaming

---

[24] This sense of personal poetic prophetic vocation as being equally justified in
the eyes of God as the vocation of religious professionals is another bond between
Langland and Milton. It is significant that Milton's only reference to *Piers* is in his
Apology Upon a Pamphlet. There also Milton says that "he who would not be
frustrate of his hope to write well ... ought himself to be a true poem" (*Complete
Poems and Major Prose*, 694). Both Langland and Milton moved from satire related
to their own quest for vocation to being "true poems" in their epic voices.

Will for lack of self knowledge: *"Multi multa sciunt et seipsos nesci-unt"* (11.3). In Christian *peccatum linguae / prudentia* texts, having "self knowledge" means living and speaking like a child of God. Albertano, for example, says you cannot speak well until you know who you are, an image of God. Scripture also is in the spirit of Peraldus and Albertano when she tells Will that the just person is silent about what must be kept silent and speaks about what should be spoken. Reason similarly urges restrained speech: Will must patiently learn to rule his tongue better; he must correct himself before speaking and not meddle in things that don't concern him.[25] In the same vein as Reason (and of Peraldus and Albertano, who assert that the accomplished speakers who know when to be silent are next to God), Ymaginatif rebukes Will for not listening more. *"Philosophus esses si tacuisses,"* he says, and observes that Adam "whiles he spak noȝt hadde paradis at wille" (11.417–18).

Passus 11, like passus 10, affirms Will's poetic voice. Will desires to write but hesitates for fear of being one of the evil speakers. This dilemma defines his narrational personality. As the poem searches for theological answers, Will ever questions his own role as rhetor. Although Dame Study in 10 does speak of the seven liberal arts, and although they and the terms "grammar" and "logic" are mentioned several times elsewhere, the actual term "rhetoric" occurs only once and basically at the center of the poem. When Will, replying to Loyalty's "Wherfore lourestow?" says he wishes he could dare to tell his dream "amonges men" (11.86), Loyalty answers, "wherfore sholdestow spare / To reden it in Retorik to arate dedly synne?" (11.101–2). The "reden" of 11.102 links by verbal echo if not etymo-logically to the "redde" of the final passus's *redde quod debes*. Will's carrying out Loyalty's mandate to use rhetoric "to arate dedly synne" becomes "what he owes," his poem, and his own patient penance. Unlike the references to "logic" in *Piers*, which from the Prologue on are mostly pejorative (as in 11.222–25 when Trajan says that all Christians who don't love to lie should not cleave so much to law and logic), "Retorik" here has a positive meaning—persuasion of the will to right action—rather than the common, negative one of misleading speech or mere ornamentation.

---

[25] Ecclus. 11.9; quoted by Albertano under what you should speak about.

In passus 12 Ymaginatif continues to challenge Will's tongue use. He begins by asking him to justify his writing. This, the first time we are actually told he is writing, occurs only after Study encourages Will to tell his dream. His retort to Ymaginatif that if he could meet an expert on Dowel, Dobet and Dobest, he would not need to write shows Will's growth as writer. As part of his instruction Ymaginatif recounts Moses' writing "to wisse þe peple" (12.72) and Christ's writing "caractes" that both save the woman taken in adultery and damn those who would stone her (12.72–82). Christ's letters here, which either save or damn, are compared to his body, which either saves or damns depending on whether it is worthily taken (lines 85–89). This comparison may be related to Peraldus's statement in "De peccato linguae" that tongues should be used for praying, repeating holy words, and taking the eucharist. Will's participation in this triad will be realized by the poem's end. Ymaginatif reminds Will that God writes true books through the Holy Spirit who "seide what men sholde write" (12.102). As mentioned above, Peraldus's image in "De verbo otioso" of the tongue as the pen of the Holy Spirit has particular relevance for *Piers*. *Otiosa verba* is usually translated in English writings on sins of the tongue as "ydle words," as in Chaucer's "Parson's Tale" (line 647). But *otiosum* can also be read as "unemployed," "disengaged"—a description of Will's status through most of the poem's first half. Except for the peroration at the end of the Visio he is largely a disengaged observer. In the Vita, however, he becomes increasingly more involved both as a participant in the poem and as a writer. *Otiosa verba* can also mean words used just for personal pleasure. This is the spirit of Will's telling Ymaginatif he writes for solace (12.22). That six lines later he says he is working on the Do's suggests he is more employed as a True Tongue at this point than he seems to know. Besides the positive images of writing associated with God and Christ, passus 12 justifies Will as poet when Ymaginatif says that on the night of Jesus's birth the angel "to pastours and to poetes appered" (12.148), and in later instruction uses the expressions "as telleþ þise poetes" (237) and "Thus þe Poete preueþ" (262).

Passus 13's verbose and repulsive Master of Theology seems to leap forth from Dame Study's anatomy of the evil speaker in passus 10. The Master's gluttonous word use matches his literal gluttony: he gorges on mincemeat, boar's flesh, and fried eggs washed down with flagons of wine. The florid Master, who as he starts to deliver a speech on Do-Well, rubs his "great cheeks," coughs, and keeps on drinking, makes a strong visual impression, whereas Patience and the Pilgrim, relegated to a side table, make virtually none at all. We do recall, however, their words, although at first they say little. The Master-Friar's lavish dinner which has no relation to bodily nourishment parallels his famed verbal skills which have no relation to spiritual nourishment: he exemplifies Albertano's dictum that the mind confused in words surpasses every evil.

In contrast, Patience's fare—a sour loaf of Do Penance and drink of Persevere Daily—correlates directly with his "symple" language. The virtue of patience lies at the heart of James 3, of Peraldus's remedies for the *peccatum linguae*, of Albertano's precepts about speaking well. Patience's later speech (framed by *pacientes vincunt*) and that of Love emphasize the transformative power of the language of love, which should generate all speech.[26] The rhetorical philosophy infusing this contrast between the drunk, overfed, proud, angry, deceitful, blasphemous, unjust, but acclaimed speaker and the humble, plain, proverbial, truthful, slow to speak, or often silent one has more to do with the Christian rhetoric of the penitential "*peccatum linguae-prudentia*" tradition than with the Christianized versions of classical rhetoric.

Langland's portrait of the friar, the epitome of *peccata linguae*, prepares us for Hawkyn's confession of the sinful "plots" on his coat. As in the confession of the seven deadly sins in passus 5, here sins of the tongue such as "unboxom speche" and "bolde oþes" pervade. Sins-of-the-tongue consciousness also informs the shift in voice from Hawkyn to (apparently) the narrator himself in 13.409. His question, "whiche ben þe braunches þat bryngen a man to sleuþe?" betrays Will's own fear that he is only an unemployed wanderer dealing with idle words. It also facilitates the directional shift in focus from the immediate subject of *acedia* to the basic theme of the whole passus, the difference between true and false speakers. Here, in keeping with the voice of the poet and earlier references to

---

[26] This concept is centered on line 13.151 "Wiþ half a laumpe lyne in latyn, *ex vi transicionis*." For explications of this line's vital importance to the poem, see Kaske, "'Ex vi transicionis' . . ."; and Blythe, "*Transitio* and Psychoallegoresis."

language as "goddes gleman" and "fiþele," the distinction between godly and satanic language is imaged by true and false minstrels.

On the one hand, "flatereris" and "lieris" who make people laugh with their "foule wordes" "Leden þo þat liþed hem to Luciferis fest / Wiþ *turpiloquio*, a lay of sorwe, and luciferis fiþele" (13.454–56). This *turpiloquium* bonds with the "*Qui loquitur turpiloquium*" of the Prologue and reinforces a broad meaning of *turpiloquium* in both instances as not just foul words but all kinds of wicked speech. The "Mynstralles" of the Prologue who get gold with their singing are not "giltless" as the dreamer there surmises. By the standards of 13 they are also "luciferis hyne." In contrast are three kinds of "goddes minstrales" (13.439), one of which, the "lered man," teaches "what our lord suffred / For to saue þi soule from sathan þyn enemy, / And fiþele þee wiþoute flaterynge of good friday þe geste" (13.444–46). By implication this extended metaphor commands Will as poet-minstrel to "sing" to save souls by teaching the kerygma and the path to penance.

The transformation of Will's tongue from one speaking *otiosa verba* to the active life of being God's minstrel continues in passus 14. When Hawkyn finds his coat soiled with "som ydel speche" (14.13), Conscience declares that if he would wash it through confession, "Shal noon heraud ne harpour haue a fairer garnement / Than Haukyn þe actyf man ... / Ne no Mynstrall be moore worþ" (14.25–27). Patience keeps repeating that becoming an ideal speaker requires above all being "sobre of siȝte and of tonge" (14.55) and living in accord with the doctrine of *pacientes vincunt* (14.54–55). As the categories of minstrels in passus 13 include the poor as well as the teachers of God's word, so in 14 the crucial concept of patient poverty is bound up with the virtuous tongue. Thus Charity, as Patience explains to Hawkyn, dwells where "parfit truþe and poore herte is, and pacience of tonge" (14.100). Hawkyn responds to Patience's patient-poverty lectures by using his tongue properly, that is, by praying for forgiveness of sin.

Also in an apparent response to the lecture on patient poverty, the dreamer at the start of passus 15 becomes totally consumed by the search for Do-Well and thoroughly uninterested in worldly regard. Langland's quotation of James 2.1, "*Ne sitis personarum acceptores,*" at line 88 announces a major subtext of the passus. According to James, those who get the "respect of persons" by oppressing the poor and honoring the rich are guilty of blasphemy: "Nonne ipsi blasphemant bonum nomen, quod invocatum est super vos" (2.7). Hugh of St. Cher's gloss of "bonum nomen" as "Iesu Christi scilicet qui est salus vestra" heightens the seriousness of this form of *blasphemia* which, as Hugh says, denies what God is by "trahendo fideles pauperes ad iudicia cum deberent eos iuuare" (7:315r). Passus 15's demand that tongues be used to aid the *fideles pauperes* by means of responsible teaching covers both the subject matter and the style of godly communication. The passus begins with an allusion to the *blasphemia* that denies what God is; it concludes with the affirming-what-God-is *sententiae* of the Apostles' Creed. Along the way, as in earlier passus, the presence or absence of sins of the tongue distinguishes the good from the wicked. But the positive movement in passus 15 toward the closing credal affirmation of charity (instead of toward contrition and confession) accords more with the "spiritus prudencie" (which emphasizes that good can be achieved by the well-governed tongue) than with the pessimism of "De peccato linguae" that the tongue will probably commit deadly sin if let loose from its dental stockades (2.414; 2.417).

These particular Peraldian passages and others that likewise regard the tongue as an unruly beast liable to crash through teeth walls are in stark contrast to the description of Anima as "Oon wiþouten tonge and teeþ" (15.13). The absence of those very language-defining, sin-tending elements of creatureliness causes Will to ask "If he were cristes creature" (15). Anima replies, "I am." At least one step away from humanly understood creatureliness, however, Anima argues for control of the tongue as crucial to true speech. Anima's tonguelessness, an image driven by Will's would-be-free-from-guilt tongue, suggests the value of a tongue-less state. Learning how to be silent and to listen is a foundation for good teaching. This recalls Ymaginatif's telling Will that if he learned to be silent, he would be a philosopher. This essence of Anima coordinates as well with the interior assumption of charity, the realization of Christ within: "Therfore by colour ne by clergie knowe shaltow hym [i.e. Charity] neuere, / Neiþer þoru3 wordes ne werkes, but þoru3 wil oone" (15.209–10). This "oone" harks back to the earlier "oon wiþouten tonge" and ties in with Will's saying he never saw Charity except in a mirror as one such as himself (15.162).

Interpreted from the perspective of the *peccatum linguae* species of

iocularitas, Will's jesting response ("al bourdynge þat tyme" [15.40])
to Anima's explanation of his names and modes of existence provides
a bridge to the subsequent themes of the passus and the *spiritus
prudencie* that infuses their presentation. The word "tyme" in this
context may be read with reference to Peraldus's declaration that
inappropriate humor steals that most precious of all possessions, time
(2.415). Right before this Peraldus quotes from 2 Thess. 3.11, "Audi-
vimus enim inter vos quosdam ambulare inquiete, nihil operantes,
sed curiose agentes. Iis autem, qui eiusmodi sunt, denuntiamus." The
image of one walking around anxiously preoccupied with curious
matters well suits Will. It also accounts for Anima's testy response to
Will's joking remark since Anima accuses him of hankering after
what is in effect "curious knowledge"—that is, knowledge that is not
germane to Christian instruction and living. For Will's seeking to
know "Alle þe sciences vnder sonne" Anima calls him "oon of
prides kny3tes" (15.47–50) and condemns all masters and friars who
live badly and preoccupy themselves with "materes vnmesurable"
(15.71) instead of preaching to the uneducated about the ten commandments and seven sins.

   In Peraldus's "De prudentia" the first of twelve concept-clusters
for those who teach includes living a worthy life, listening carefully,
and informing oneself in doctrine before teaching others—all repeated
themes in passus 15 (for example, 94–95; 105; 110ff.; 307–8; 391–92).
Peraldus then refers readers to "De appetitu magisterii" in his "De
superbia." There he condemns "Studium curiosorum" as "occupatio
mala, peior, & pessima" (2.250). The first biblical citation of the
section is James 3.1, "Nolite plures magistri fieri fratres mei" (2.248).
Commenting on this verse, Hugh says, "In hoc tertio capitulo
dehortatur dilationem nominis, vel appetitum famae popularis. Et
quia per magisterium saepe solet nomen dilatari, propter hoc tam
peritos, quam imperitos dehortatur hic ab appetitu magisterii"
(7:316v). One sense of "dilatio nominis"—as the expansion of a
name—is indeed conveyed by Will's citing "an heep" of names for
"bishop." Furthermore, this literal "dilation" upon a name is closely
allied with magisterial appetite both in Will and in the wicked
preachers and teachers Anima condemns.

   Anima's censure is not aimed at getting the preachers or Will to
confess sin, but to indicate (albeit mostly by negative examples) that
one is *"Beatus"* who *"verba vertit in opera"* (15.60–61); or, in the

words of James, "perfectus" who "in verbo non offendit" (3:2); or, in the words of Peraldus, "prudentissimus" who "modum seruat in verbis" and "dulciter loquitur absque clamore & asperitate" (2.375). This last may serve as key to the relevance of Peraldus's "De prudentia" instructional dicta on the necessity of teaching useful things— ones based in charity and moving others to charitable action. Charity as the subject matter, stylistic determiner, and result of good preaching (teaching) becomes from line 148 on the main focus of Anima's discourse. Thus Charity, who commits no sins of the tongue, does not curse (15.171), lie, or "laughe men to scorne" (15.172), avoids "braulynge and bakbitynge and berynge of fals witnesse" (15.238), and dwells with hermits who "selde speken togideres" (15.275). In keeping with the positive practice of prudence which insists on a pleasant pedagogical manner to encourage love of what is taught, Charity is "murieste of mouþ" (15.217) and, on account of "The loue þat liþ in his herte," "liȝt of speche" and "compaignable and confortatif" (15.218–19).

In contrast are the wicked teachers and preachers who mask non-concern for doctrine and their audience with *"bele paroles"* (15.115). In the fourth species of prudence Peraldus says those who hide vacuity of thought with ornate and carefully arranged words are guilty of *peccatum bilinguium* (1.207). Because the validating principle of their language is avarice, not charity, they are as far from divine similitude as Satan. The audience-traducing, ignorant clerks and preachers reviled at the end of passus 15 fail the first species of prudence because they do not learn what they should teach, the third in their indifference to their students or parishioners, and the twelfth in their refusal to sow seed. But Anima uses hopeful prudential language in closing the passus as she anticipates a time (echoing words of Holy Church in passus 1) when prelates "kouþe speke and spelle," "Recorden ... and rendren" the essential doctrine of the Apostle's creed (15.611–12).

The fact that at the beginning of passus 16 Will asks the right question—for instruction on charity, not about how to gain all knowledge (as at the start of 15)—shows an advance in his prudential rhetoric. The positive, kindly language stressed in chapter V of "De prudentia" and illustrated by Charity in passus 15 is figured first off in 16 as leaves of "lele wordes" and blossoms of "buxom speche and benigne lokynge" on the charity-bearing tree of Patience (16.6–7).

However, Piers tells Will in the inner dream, these flowers have difficulty developing into the fruit of charity because the devil attacks them with "Bakbiteris brewecheste, brawleris and chideris" and steals them via a ladder whose rungs are "lesynges" (16.43–44). The oppositional pairing of charity and *peccatum linguae* recurs about midway in the passus when Jesus accuses Judas: "Falsnesse I fynde in þi faire speche / And gile in þi glad chere and galle is in þi laughyng. / Thow shalt be myrour to many men to deceyue" (154–55). The riposte to Judas-embodied verbal evils is not only Jesus's jousting in Jerusalem (163), but also the prudential rhetor, Abraham, who establishes his verbal truthfulness at the outset: "I am feiþ . . . it falleþ no3t to lye" (176).

Abraham's words, which fill Will with "wonder" (253), cover biblical history and Christian doctrine on engendering. On the literal level the line "*Maledictus homo qui non reliquit semen in Israel*" refers to the trinity of man, woman, and child, but on a tropological level it bespeaks the commonplace mandate to spread the verbal seed: "Iactamus semina, spargimus semina" ("De prudentia," *De virtutibus*, 1.209). Will's human seed has borne fruit in his daughter. The acceptance and validation of his role as verbal seed sower is achieved in the next four passus.

Moses (*Spes*) embodies the concept of godly writing at the beginning of passus 18. His saying he is a "spire" who carries "the writ" recalls the tongue-use passage in 9.103, where speech is referred to as a "spire" of grace. Will is eager to "se þi [Moses'] lettres" and is impressed that the gloss on "love God and your neighbor" was "gloriously writen wiþ a gilt penne" (17.15). Though Moses' writing has saved thousands, his efficacy, as Abraham's, falls short without the Christian sacramental salvation lived and espoused by the Good Samaritan. At the beginning of "De peccato linguae" Peraldus says that tongues should be used for praying, repeating holy words, and taking the sacrament. Abraham and Moses do the first two; it is the Samaritan who insists on the third: "ac stalworþ worþ he neuere / Til he haue eten al þe barn and his blood ydronke" (17.99–100).[27] Right after this the Good Samaritan in effect squares the triadic circle

---

[27] The "he" refers to the man found in the ditch but also, by extension, every person.

of faith, hope and charity by adding Will as one who does "oure werkes" (17.104). As I have argued elsewhere, this inclusiveness confirms Will's sense of worth as a poet.[28]

Passus 18 contains some of the most compelling poetry in all of *Piers Plowman*. Coming after Will's vocational confirmation in 17, it is notable that this is the first passus whose contents Will actually says that he wrote down: "Thus I awaked and wroot what I hadde ydremed" (19.1). As the dream within the dream in passus 16 focuses on the deep subconsciousness of Will, so here the Book episode, interjected in the midst of the harrowing of hell, signifies a movement into deeper consciousness. Like Aeneas's experience in the underworld, Will's narrational descent propels him into completing his epic mission: Book's function is comparable to Anchises'. At first blush Book seems to stand for the gospel. But on a personal level Book stands for *Piers Plowman*. When Book says that he will be burnt if Jesus is not resurrected (18.255–59), he is reiterating the validating principle for all language. The meaning of the lines is similar to that expressed in 1 Cor. 15.14, "Si autem Christus non resurrexit, inanis est ergo praedicatio nostra." Book is also in brief the essence of the rest of the passus. Although the harrowing of hell dominates, the passus on the whole is an expansion of credal tenets, and as such, along with passus 19, can be seen as Will's poetic and Christianly prudential response to Anima's mandate for prelates to keep studying the creed until they can "speke and spelle," "Recorden" and "rendren" it.

"Rendren" is what Will is about at the start of 19, a passus about inspiration, vocational responsibility, and penitential satisfaction for sin. The first three lines describe Will using his tongue in a proper manner: he is repeating holy words (writing down the dream of the harrowing of hell), praying (implied since he is at mass), and about to take the sacrament. That his dream starts at the beginning of the offering anticipates the *redde quod debes* call recurrent throughout the passus (187; 193; 259; 390). The central event of the passus, the coming of the *spiritus paraclitus*, demands the dreamer's response. Thus Conscience says, "if þow kanst synge / Welcome hym and worshipe hym wiþ *Veni creator Spiritus*," and Will responds,

---

[28] Blythe, "*Transitio* and Psychoallegoresis," 144.

"Thanne song I þat song; so dide manye hundred" (209–11). What counts here is not the mob enthusiasm (which the poem repeatedly shows is unreliable), but the faithful response of the individual. For Will to *reddere quod debet*, to fulfill the call and inspiration of his muse—the *creator Spiritus*—is to "sing" his poem.

That sinful tongue users are the first phenomenon Conscience describes as heralding the coming of Antichrist ("And false prophetes fele, flatereris and gloseris / Shullen come" [19.221–22]) affirms Langland's intense preoccupation with the *peccata linguae* throughout *Piers Plowman*. This further is borne out in the many sins of the tongue that characterize the deadly sins captaining Antichrist's troops and the final subversion of the Barn of Unity. Therefore it is fitting that the first group of faithful workers to whom Conscience gives weapons to fight the onslaught of Antichrist are those who use "wit with wordes" to bear witness to truth and thus faithfully to live "by labour of tonge" (19.229–32). Will's faithful "singing" of a religiously instructive song places him in this vanguard group.

The primacy of faithful language workers against Antichrist also correlates with the first cardinal virtue that Grace sows—the seed of *Spiritus prudencie*—since, as discussed above, penitential presentations of *prudentia* included rhetorical guidelines aimed ultimately at the salvation of souls by promoting love of God and neighbor. This is the language lesson at the heart of Prudence's assurance that "whoso ete þat ymagynen he sholde, / Er he dide any dede deuyse wel þe ende" (19.277–78). When the end is not love of God and neighbor, but "wynnyng" (19.453), the *Spiritus prudencie* becomes usurped by the *peccatum linguae*, well illustrated in lines 454–62. As before, it is not language itself that is at fault but people.

A more subtle linguistic undermining is explored at the beginning of passus 20 in the Need sequence, one of the most perplexing in the poem. In spite of Robert Adams's persuasive reading of this passage from the perspective of medieval theology,[29] it is hard to feel positive about Need. That Fals (*mendacium*), working at the behest of Antichrist, facilitates "mennes nedes" (20.55) seems a grotesque parody of Need's justification of lawlessness to meet bodily necessities. Like Milton's Satan, Need appears at noontime, the time the

---

[29] Adams, "The Nature of Need," 34.

devil is known to walk. Also like Satan, Need mixes true-seeming discourse—such as here on Jesus's accepting a needy role—with hard-to-detect speciousness. Unlike the good speakers in *Piers,* who seem modeled on the language ideal of *prudentia,* Need does not use kindly buxom words but accosts Will "foule" and calls him a false maker ("faitour" [20.5]). Need's chiding "Couldestow noȝt excuse þee as dide þe kyng and oþere" (20.6) sounds like *peccati defensio,* which, along with *blasphemia, murmur,* and *periurium,* Peraldus considers the worst sins of the tongue since they are primarily directed against God (2.377). He gives the first two kinds of excusing wrong as that blamed on the body and based on the pretext of "everybody's doing it": "Alii propter infirmitatem carnis ... Alii multitudine peccantium" (2.389). These are exactly the bases upon which Need argues that theft of needed food and clothing is excusable and that devaluation of the cardinal virtues is understandable since their ideals are often abused. The opposite of and remedy for *peccati defensio* is the act of penance. This pairing functions in a main way in the downfall of Unity.

Fulfilling Conscience's prediction, sins of the tongue become a major factor in the attack on the apocalyptic Barn of Unity. For example, Lechery flaunts "pryue speche," inappropriate laughter, "peyntede wordes," false oaths, lies, and "vntidy tales"; Avarice, "glosynges" and "gabbynges"; Sloth, perjury and double tongue; Envy, idle tales, joking, lying, wicked silence, and hypocrisy. It is significant that both Sloth and Envy make use of *peccatum bilinguium* since it is the main cause of the barn's collapse (20.333). Although the friar who insinuates himself into Unity is called Flattery, the "Hende speche" (352) he uses is more a function of *peccatum bilinguium* and *mendacium* than simple *adulatio.* "Hende-speche" here in conjunction with the friar's "groping" of Contrition conveys the sense of "grasping-speech" or "speech that seizes you," not just the clever speech typified by Chaucer's "hende" Nicholas. By facilitating *peccati defensio* the friar undermines the foundational act of penance, which is contrition. Langland's dramatic image of one loose tongue savaging what seems to be the best efforts of humankind to save their souls makes Peraldus's statement that one loose tongue can destroy a whole country (2.374) seem an understatement. The frightening aspect of passus 20 is not just that the *peccatum linguae* suborns Unity, but that it does so finally by duping "good" characters who ought to know better, characters who fail in the exercise of prudence and cannot discern "bona a malis, & bona ab inuicem, ostendendo quid sit melius: & mala ab inuicem, ostendendo quod sit maius malum" (1.191), especially when it comes to verbal evil. That the poet-dreamer of *Piers Plowman* is not one of these toward the end of the poem becomes increasingly evident.

In "De peccato linguae" Peraldus says that the Holy Spirit came in a fire to the tongue rather than to other bodily members because since the tongue itself is such a great fire of evil it needs a great heavenly fire to counter it (2.373). In passus 19 Grace is an intrinsic part of the gift of the *spiritus paraclitus,* which is there portrayed as an inspiring principle for the dreamer's "song." Conscience's cry "after grace" in the last line is also the poet's. Whereas other epic writers invoke their muse at the start, Langland invokes his, the Holy Spirit, at the end, and, since he has said he woke to write down the previous three passus, we are left at the end of passus 20 imagining him writing after he "gan awake." It is especially in the last passus when he has found his most successful poetic voice, that Langland indicates he is by no means one of Lucifer's servants guilty of *turpiloquium*. Much rather Langland should be deemed "prudentissimus" since, by Peraldus's standards, he "est ille qui modum servat in verbis: qui scilicet dulciter loquitur absque clamore & asperitate" (2.375).

University of Kentucky

JOSEPH   GOERING

The Summa "Qui bene presunt" and Its Author

A treatise familiar to the readers of Siegfried Wenzel's works is the "Summa brevis" or, as it will be called here, the Summa "Qui bene presunt" (Qbp).[1] Written by Richard of Wetheringsett (of Leicester) in the early years of the thirteenth century, this summa became one of the most popular and influential pastoral manuals of English inspiration in the later Middle Ages. As late as the fifteenth century, scholars were seeking to obtain copies in the Oxford book market.[2] Along with the so-called Summa confessorum ("Cum miserationes Domini") of the Salisbury sub-dean, Thomas of Chobham, the Qbp established a new type of didactic religious literature that would flourish for centuries on English soil.[3] Richard begins his summa with a verse from 1 Timothy 5.17: "Qui bene presunt presbyteri duplici honore digni habeantur, maxime qui laborant in uerbo et doctrina" ("Let the priests who rule well be esteemed worthy of double honor, especially those who labor in the word and doctrine"). He explains that the priest labors in "the

---

[1] See especially Wenzel, Sin of Sloth; idem, "Vices, Virtues"; idem, Verses in Sermons. See also Richard W. Hunt, "English Learning"; Kellogg, "St. Augustine"; Kemmler, "Exempla" in Context, 46–59; Goering, William de Montibus, 86–95.

[2] See the note on fol. iii of MS. 328/715 in Gonville and Caius college library, Cambridge: "Fiat scrutamen in foro nuncupato Jaudewyn Market de libris subscriptis si poterint ibi venales reperiri, videlicet: Qui bene presunt, Legenda sanctorum, Speculum ecclesie, Abstinentia, Gemma sacerdotalis," quoted by James, Descriptive Catalogue of Gonville and Caius College, 1:371.

[3] See Thomae de Chobham Summa confessorum, ed. Broomfield. On the place of these two works in the development of a literature of pastoral care, see Goering, William de Montibus, chap. 3.

word" by exhorting the learned, and in "doctrine" by instructing the uneducated; he exhorts and instructs these audiences concerning "faith and morals." The essence (*summa*) of the Apostle's teaching, Richard concludes, is that the priest, once himself instructed, should instruct the people in faith and morals.[4] Richard conceives his summa as a treatise on the priestly office.[5] He writes in the spirit of the pastoral reforms of the later-twelfth and early-thirteenth century which sought to instill in every priest, even the simple curate of a parish, a zeal for the highest forms of soul care.[6] The *Qbp* is designed to instruct priests and candidates for the priesthood in everything they need to know to perform their pastoral office. Because this office entails the subsequent instruction of the laity through preaching, Richard organizes his summa as a preaching manual. In this way he fulfills the Apostle's mandate: by studying this summa, priests will themselves be instructed in faith and morals, and by using it as a guide to preaching, they will instruct others.

Richard identifies in his prologue twelve topics that "belong most basically to faith and morals, and that must be preached very frequently":

    1. The creed, with its twelve articles of faith;
    2. The Lord's Prayer, with its seven petitions;
    3. God's gifts, especially the seven gifts of the Holy Spirit;
    4. The four cardinal and the three theological virtues;
    5. The seven capital vices;
    6. The seven sacraments;
    7. The two evangelical precepts (love of God and neighbor);
    8. The ten commandments of the Law;
    9. The rewards of the just and the pains of the wicked;

---

[4] "Et notandum est quod sequitur: 'maxime qui laborant in uerbo et doctrina.' In uerbo, id est in exhortatione scientium, in doctrina, id est in instructione nescientium; in uerbo quo ad mores, in doctrina quo ad fidem. . . . Et est summa ut ipsi instructi populum instruant in fide et moribus" (London, BL MS. Royal 9.A.XIV, fol. 18va). All transcriptions are from this manuscript (designated *L*) unless otherwise specified.

[5] "Hiis igitur circa ministerium sacerdotum tractatis, finem libet facere sermonis" (*L*, fol. 112va).

[6] See, for example, Boyle, "Summae Confessorum"; idem, "The Fourth Lateran Council"; idem, "The Inter-Conciliar Period"; Maccarrone, " 'Cura animarum.' "

10. The things in which many people are misled;
11. The things to be avoided (i.e., sin, assent to sin, and whatever is prohibited by one's superiors);
12. The things to be done (i.e., that which is proper to each person's office and status, and especially that which is commanded by God or by one's superiors).[7]

These topics he summarizes in six lines of verse:

> Hec sunt precipue sermonibus insinuanda,
> Bis sex articuli fidei septemque petenda,
> Donaque uirtutes,[8] presertim crimina septem,
> Septem sacra, duo Domini mandata decemque[9]
> Legis, iustorum merces peneque malorum,
> In quibus erratur, quid uitandum, quid agendum.
>
> (*L*, fol. 18vb)

Although each of these twelve topics has a history that begins in the twelfth century or earlier, Richard created something new by bringing them together in the *Qbp*. By selecting these twelve topics from the mass of pastoral and religious themes available to him, he helped to establish them as the proper and sufficient content of pastoral and "catechetical" instruction.[10] The list of topics struck a responsive chord, especially in English writers. Robert Grosseteste was perhaps inspired by the *Qbp* in composing his very popular treatise for educating priests, *Templum Dei*.[11] Edmund of Abingdon's *Speculum* also rings the changes on the topics put forward in the *Qbp*.[12]

---

[7] *L*, fol. 18va–vb. The text is quoted in Goering, *William de Montibus*, 89–90, and from another manuscript in Kemmler, 48–49 (transl. 209).

[8] MS. *L* reads "Virtutes, uitia." The reading "Donaque uirtutes" found, for example, on fol. 115va of MS. HM 19914 in the Huntington Library, San Marino (CA), corresponds better to the actual contents of the *Qbp*. The original form of these verses can only be reconstructed from a thorough collation of the manuscript copies.

[9] MS. *L* agrees with many other copies in adding "precepta" after "decemque," but this addition is unnecessary, and will not scan; "mandata" in line four can be read with both "duo" and "decemque."

[10] Wenzel calls these "catechetical matters," see "Vices, Virtues," 29. On the originality of Richard's list, see Goering, *William de Montibus*, 86–95.

[11] Robert Grosseteste, *Templum Dei*, ed. Goering and Mantello.

[12] Edmund of Abingdon, *Speculum religiosorum and Speculum ecclesie*, ed. Forshaw.

Wetheringsett's suggestion that these matters should be preached frequently also is echoed in English synodal legislation. Robert Grosseteste required, probably in 1239, that the clergy of Lincoln diocese should know and preach about the Decalogue, the seven criminal sins, the seven sacraments, and the faith as contained in the Creeds.[13] This requirement was repeated in the statutes for the dioceses of Worcester, Norwich, Winchester, Durham, Ely, Wells, Carlisle, York, and Exeter during the next fifty years.[14] Many bishops supplemented their statutes with practical treatises designed to help priests in understanding and in explaining these matters to the laity. Perhaps the first was Alexander of Stavensby, bishop of Coventry (1224–1237), who ordered that all parish priests instruct their parishioners on Sundays or other feasts about the seven criminal sins.[15] Walter of Cantilupe, bishop of Worcester, published in 1240 a pastoral treatise teaching his clergy to explicate the Ten Commandments, the seven deadly sins, the sins of thought, word, and deed, and the articles of faith; this *summula* was reissued in 1287 by Bishop Peter Quinel for the diocese of Exeter.[16] Roger of Weseham, bishop of Coventry, listed the seven sacraments, the seven gifts of the Holy Spirit, the seven virtues, the seven petitions of the Lord's Prayer, the eight beatitudes, the ten commandments, the seven deadly sins, and the twelve articles of faith as the things that must be taught frequently to the parishioners in their own language.[17] The most famous of such provisions, of course, is in Canon 9 ("Ignorantia sacerdotum") of the Lambeth Constitutions, issued for the entire province of Canterbury in 1281 by Archbishop John Pecham.[18] Each of these pastoral initiatives can be seen as carrying out a programme very like that which Richard recommends in the *Qbp*.

The first section of the *Qbp*, "On faith" (*De fide*) reveals Richard's technique. He begins with definitions of faith, and insists

---

[13] *Councils & Synods*, ed. Powicke and Cheney, 1:268; cf. Wenzel, "Vices, Virtues," 29.

[14] Wenzel, ibid.

[15] *Councils & Synods*, 1:214; cf. Wenzel, ibid., 28.

[16] Printed in *Councils & Synods*, 2:1062–77. See Goering and Taylor, "The Summulae."

[17] Printed in Cheney, *English Synodalia*, 149–52.

[18] *Councils & Synods*, 1:900–905; cf. Wenzel, "Vices, Virtues," 29–30.

that all Christians are required to believe the "articles" of the Apostle's creed: the clergy explicitly, and the laity implicitly by believing "what the Church believes and by not disbelieving any article of the creed."[19] He then discusses the qualities of faith required in believers and the testimonies to the truth of the faith to be found in miracles, in arguments, and in "similitudes" or correspondences in the created world. He sums up, characteristically, with a few lines of verse:

> Integra, firma, fides sit et inuiolata, fidelis;
> Scripta fidem monstrant, firmant miracula, testes,
> Roborat exemplum, ratio, sermo manifestat.
>
> (*L*, fol. 19vb)

Richard refers the reader to William de Montibus's *Numerale* for a fuller discussion of the articles of faith and of the authorities and similitudes by which they can be taught to the uneducated.[20] He then proceeds to explicate each of the twelve "articles," following closely the exposition of his Master, William de Montibus.

The identification of discrete "articles" of faith is a novelty of the twelfth-century schools,[21] and the division proposed by William and Richard is one of the earliest to have survived. The twelve articles follow closely the order of the Apostles' Creed: 1) the Trinity of God, 2) the incarnation, 3) the virgin birth, 4) the passion and death of Jesus, 5) His burial, 6) descent to the dead, 7) resurrection, 8) ascension, 9) and second coming as judge, 10) the resurrection of the body, 11) the rewards of the just and punishments of the wicked, and 12) the seven sacraments of the Church. Richard summarizes these twelve articles in verse:

---

[19] "Nam singuli apostoli singulos bolos apposuerunt, hoc est singulos articulos, ad quos firmiter credendos tenentur omnes fideles explicite uel implicite: explicite quo ad clericos, implicite adminus quo ad laycos minus peritos, ut firmiter scilicet credant quod credit ecclesia et maxime ut nullum articulum discredant" (*L*, fol. 19ra).

[20] "Hos articulos et eorum auctoritates et similitudines quibus facilius possunt mentibus rudibus persuaderi predictus Magister Willelmus de Montibus, in fine libelli sui quem Numerale appellauit, sic composuit" (*L*, fol. 19vb). William devoted a long section of Book Twelve of his *Numerale* to the twelve articles of faith; see Goering, *William de Montibus*, 227–60.

[21] Hödl, "Articulus fidei."

Hii sunt articuli: Quod sit trinus Deus unus,
Christus homo factus, natus, passusque sepultus,
Descendens, surgens, scandens, iudexque futurus,
Premia det, surgant omnes, quod sacra sacrum dent
(L, fol. 19vb).

The twelfth article, a belief in the seven sacraments of the Church, is not part of the Apostles' Creed, but it is increasingly emphasized in popular enumerations of the articles during the thirteenth century. Robert Grosseteste condensed the first eleven articles above into five, so that each of the Church's seven sacraments could be assigned a separate article in his list of twelve.[22] Grosseteste's list was even more popular than Wetheringsett's, and was rivalled in England only at the end of the thirteenth century by Archbishop Pecham's list of fourteen articles of faith.[23]

Richard concludes his discussion of the Faith by choosing three of the articles for special consideration: the incarnation or nativity of Jesus, His passion on the cross, and His dreadful second-coming to judge the living and the dead. These three, he tells us, should be taught assiduously.[24] Such practical advice to the priest is characteristic of Richard's summa, and it illustrates his purpose in composing the *Qbp*. Having first learned a good deal about the Faith and its "articles," the priest should then preach to the people the essentials of that faith in a way that is suitable to them. The accuracy of Richard's view that the Nativity, the Passion, and the Last Judgement should receive special attention is borne out by the popularity of these themes in the art and literature of the subsequent centuries.

In the second part of the *Qbp* Richard explicates the Lord's Prayer (Mt. 6.9–17). He explains that the first phrase, "Our Father who art in heaven," is a *captatio benevolentie*, and that each of the seven phrases that follow ("hallowed be thy name," "thy kingdom

---

[22] Grosseteste, *Templum Dei*, ed. Goering and Mantello, 32–33; cf. Wenzel, "Grosseteste's Treatise on Confession," 233–34, 244–47.

[23] Pecham's list of fourteen articles is found in the famous chapter "Ignorantia sacerdotum" (c. 9) of his provincial council held at Lambeth in 1281, printed in *Councils & Synods*, 2:901.

[24] "Item inter cetera premissa inculcandum est de tribus articulis fidei premissis: primo de benigna incarnatione Iesu Christi uel de eius natiuitate, secundo de uili et humili eius passione, tertio de terribili eius aduentu ad iudicium" (L, fol. 21va).

come," etc.) is a petition or request with special significance. He discusses the literal, allegorical and moral implications of the petitions, illustrating his points with apposite proverbs, similitudes, and distinctions. He stresses that each of the seven petitions can be understood as remedies for one of the seven deadly sins, and he recommends that they be taught as such for the "benefit of listeners" (*utilitate audientium*). For the "curiosity of readers" (*curiositatem legentium*), one might wish to align the seven petitions with the seven gifts of the Holy Spirit, the seven virtues, and the seven beatitudes as well.[25]

In the sections that follow, Richard discusses the seven gifts of the Holy Spirit, the seven virtues, the seven vices, the seven sacraments, the two evangelical precepts, the ten commandments, and the Last Things. He explicates each of the Holy Spirit's gifts by means of "similitudes" derived from a comparison of the Holy Spirit to fire and to water. He explains that the cardinal virtues are so called because they give access to God in the same way that the Roman cardinals give access to the pope.[26] He explicates the vices by explaining the many ways that they can be classified. For example, all sins can be comprised under the numbers one to seven:

One = "Pride is the beginning of all sin" (Ecclus. 10.15), or:
      "Cupidity is the root of all evils" (1 Tim. 6.10);

---

[25] "Ad similitudinem iam dictorum, salua integritate fidei et doctrine catholice, pro utilitate audientium licet singulas petitiones singulis peccatis opponere. Si quis curiositatem legentium uoluerit petitiones septem in dominica oratione contentas donis et uirtutibus et beatitudinibus et uitiis adaptare, modum per subiectos uersiculos retineat; et petitiones intelligat per earum principia, et tunc cetera adaptanda uideat quid in eis expressum sit:

> Sanc<tificetur>, timet, est pauper, regnat, perit inde superbus;
> Ad<ueniat>, pius et mitis, terram tenet, ira recedit;
> Fiat, scit, plorat, solatur, et inuidus exit;
> Pan, fortis, sitiens satiatus, tristia pellit;
> Di<mitte>, dat consilium, miseris miserans, flet auarus;
> Temp<tationem>, intellectum, mundat, uidet, et gula transit;
> Li<bera>, sapit, est pacis, est filius, et uenus exit" (*L*, fol. 30ra).

For similar associations suggested by Wetheringsett's contemporaries, see Thomas of Chobham, *Summa confessorum*, 37–39, 574–75, and Grosseteste, *Templum Dei*, 36–38.

[26] "Item quedam uirtutes appellantur cardinales propter istam rationem, quia sicut per cardinales habemus accessum ad dominum papam, ita per istas uirtutes ad Deum" (*L*, fol. 37va).

Two = "All sins are either sins of omission or of commis-
    sion," or: "All sins are either carnal or spiritual";
Three = "All sins are sins of thought, word, or deed" (*cordis,
    oris, operis*);
Four, etc.[27]

Richard recommends that the preacher should concentrate on the
seven "capital" sins and on the "threefold vice" of John's canonical
epistle (1 John 2.16: "For all that is in the world is the concupiscence
of the flesh, and the concupiscence of the eyes, and the pride of
life").[28] This latter paradigm, however, receives only a brief treatment in the *Qbp*; Richard, like contemporary and subsequent writers,
concentrates primarily on the seven deadly sins.

In treating of the seven sacraments, Richard again provides a
wide-ranging compendium of the knowledge necessary for the priest,
and intersperses this with specific advice for instructing the laity.
Concerning baptism, he emphasises that the laity must be taught to
baptise their own children if there is danger that one might die: "that
they must pronounce clearly and distinctly, in their own language,
the words 'Ego baptizo te in nomine Patris et Filii et Spiritus Sancti,
Amen,' and that they immerse the child three times, or once, or at
least sprinkle the child with water."[29] In the discussion of the eucharist, Richard urges that "the laity be taught firmly to believe that
the body and blood of Christ are transubstantiated from bread and
wine when the priest utters, in the form of the Church, the transub-
stantiating words, 'Hoc est corpus meum' and 'Hic est calix.' "[30]

---

[27] Cf. *L*, fols. 49rb–va.

[28] "Et notandum quod inter omnia uitia frequenter in sermonibus sunt inculcan-
da septem uitia capitalia, et triplex uitium canonicum, de quo 1 Ioh. ii: 'Omne quod
est in mundo et est concupiscentia carnis, et concupiscentia oculorum, et superbia
uite' " (*L*, fol. 49va–vb).

[29] "Item diligenter instruendi sunt layci quod in necessitatis articulo paruulos
baptizent antequam moriantur, et quod uerba in ydiomate suo sibi magis noto
proferent plene et aperte: Ego baptizo te in nomine Patris et Filii et Spiritus sancti,
amen; puerum autem immergant ter, uel semel, uel saltem aspergant aqua si tanta
fuerit necessitas et aque penuria" (*L*, fol. 65rb–va).

[30] "De hoc sacramento simpliciter instruendi sunt layci quod firmiter credant
corpus Christi et sanguinem de pane et uino transubstantiari cum a sacerdote in
forma ecclesie proferuntur uerba transsubstantialia, Hoc est corpus meum, et Hic
est calix etc." (*L*, fol. 68va).

Similarly, after explaining the complexities of penance and confession, Richard advises that the requirements of a good confession should be fully explained to the simpler folk, and that the requirements can be reduced to those things which are expressed in a general confession, namely sins of thought, word, deed, consent, and omission."[31]

The tenth section of the *Qbp* is rather unusual in the literature of pastoral care. Richard describes it as concerning "the errors of the laity, from which they must be restrained."[32] The idea for this comes from Richard's mentor, William de Montibus, chancellor of Lincoln Cathedral and head of the cathedral school. William composed a treatise called *Errorum eliminatio* in which he discussed the various errors committed by clergy and laity in the Church.[33] Richard focuses on the errors of the laity. The basis for his discussion is four lines of verse:

> In quibus erratur sunt hostia, gleba, repertum,
> Nupta, timor, decime, sal dans malus et male partum,
> Omen et augurium, periuria, sompnia, fatum,
> Finis et exemplum, differre, retentio rerum.

> (*L*, fol. 105ra)

In the exposition that follows, Richard describes dangerous practices and erroneous beliefs concerning the eucharist (*hostia, gleba*);[34] marriage (*nupta*); baptism (*sal*);[35] relations with neighbors and between lords and servants (*repertum, timor, periuria, retentio rerum*); tithes

---

[31] "Item aliquantulum plenius et planius simplicioribus possunt annotari ea que requirenda sunt in confessione et reduci ad ea que exprimuntur in confessione generali, scilicet ad peccata cordis, oris, operis, consensus et omissionis" (*L*, fol. 77rb).

[32] "Sequitur de erroribus laycorum a quibus sunt cohibendi" (*L*, fols. 104vb–105ra).

[33] Printed in Goering, *William de Montibus*, 139–57.

[34] "Item errant sacerdotes plerique imponentes glebam ori hominis suspendentis uel alterius in periculo mortis constituti cum non possit uel non meruerit in forma ecclesie communicari. Nichil enim cedit in loco eucharistie preter hostiam consecratam, nihil in corpus Christi transubstantiatur preter panem triticeum et uinum. Sufficit si firmiter credat in predicto periculo constitutus, quia dicitur 'crede et manducasti'" (*L*, fol. 105rb).

[35] "Item in sale errant muliercule obstetricantes, que cum plene tenentur baptizare puerum in periculo mortis constitutum ... solum sal in ore ponuntur paruuli, quod nichil est nec expedit eis nec competit, et sola necessaria dimittunt, scilicet in aquam immergere et plene uerba proferre cum intentione faciendi circa puerum quod facit ecclesia" (*L*, fol. 106va).

(*decime*); omens, divinations and fortune telling (*omen, augurium, sompnia, fatum*); moral behavior (*finis, exemplum*); and penance (*differre*).

Unlike the first nine sections, the "errors of the laity" never became a standard element in catechetical teaching and preaching. Nevertheless, the content of this section was found useful by many readers, and it reappears in some of the most influential pastoral texts of the English Middle Ages.[36]

The final sections of the *Qbp* concern those things that should be avoided (*Quid sit vitandum*) and that should be done (*Quid sit agendum*). Among the things most to be avoided are the three enemies of humankind—the world, the flesh, and the devil.[37] One should also flee every mortal sin, the opportunities for sinning, and the various ways of consenting to sin.

Richard divides the things to be done into works of grace and works of nature, corresponding to a person's right and left hand. Works of nature include the mechanical arts, and Richard has little to say about them. Works of grace are those things that are done for the sake of an eternal reward, and it is with a discussion of these that Richard concludes his summa. It is the priest, above all, who performs works of grace, and the final pages of the *Qbp* constitute a kind of *speculum sacerdotis*. He insists that priests and beneficed clergy fulfill their special responsibilities, above and beyond those of the laity, in a fitting and proper manner. He reminds priests (and their teachers) that the souls of the people depend on them, and that if they wish to receive the two-fold honor promised in the first line of the summa ("Qui bene presunt presbyteri"), they must perform their proper work diligently.[38]

---

[36] See Kemmler, 56–59.

[37] See Wenzel, "Three Enemies of Man." Richard illustrates one of the dangers posed by worldly riches with the macaronic verse: "Mundus clamat aue, set aue conuertit in haue" (*L*, fol. 108va).

[38] "Igitur uos magistri et presbiteri, ex quibus pendet anima populi ut legitur Iudith viii (8.6): 'qui bene presunt presbiteri dupplici honore digni sunt,' uel 'digni habeantur,' ut premissum est in principio huius summe. Operemini igitur sic opus ut uobis reddatur merces" (*L*, fol. 112rb–va).

§

Richard composed his summa shortly after 1215. The *terminus post quem* is established by an unambiguous allusion to chapter 21 of the Fourth Lateran Council of 1215: "ex institutione ecclesie tenetur quilibet Christianus adultus et discretus saltem semel in anno communicare sacramentaliter, et peccat qui non communicat nisi forte in penitentia susceperit abstinere a communione."[39] No firm *terminus ante quem* has been established, but neither internal nor external evidence would suggest a date after ca. 1220.[40]

About the author himself there has been much speculation.[41] The manuscript copies of *Qbp* are extraordinarily helpful in that many carry full and explicit ascriptions of authorship.[42] Nearly all of the texts that bear contemporary or near-contemporary ascriptions

---

[39] *L*, fol. 69rb. Cf.: "Omnis utriusque sexus fidelis, postquam ad annos discretionis pervenerit, omnia sua solus peccata confiteatur fideliter, saltem semel in anno proprio sacerdoti . . . suscipiens reverenter ad minus in pascha eucharistiae sacramentum, nisi forte de consilio proprii sacerdotis ob aliquam rationabilem causam ad tempus ab eius perceptione duxerit abstinendum," *Conciliorum oecumenicorum decreta*, ed. Alberigo et al., 245.

[40] A critical edition will be necessary before we can speak confidently about the sources used by Richard. None of the sources identified so far is later than the Fourth Lateran Council of 1215. One significant textual reading would seem to confirm that the text was composed shortly after that Council. In discussing penance, Richard alludes a second time to c. 21 of the Council (see previous note): "Item, ut *in euuangelio* institutum est semel in anno saltem communicare, sic et saltem semel in anno generaliter confiteri" (*L*, fol. 75ra). The words "in euuangelio" may be a scribal error for something like "in nouo concilio" (no Gospel text requires annual communion or confession!), but all the manuscripts consulted so far read "in euuangelio." This implies that the error crept into the manuscript tradition at a very early date, before this ecclesiastical provision had become a commonplace in the literature.

[41] See Russell, *Dictionary*, 124–25; Glorieux, *Répertoire*, 1:280–81; Emden, *Biographical Register of Cambridge*, 367, 679.

[42] The most recent list of manuscript copies is in *Incipits*, ed. Bloomfield et al., no. 4583. Bloomfield lists 64 copies, but the following manuscripts noted there do not contain the *Qbp*: Cambridge, Jesus College MS. 34; Paris, Mazarine MS. 985; Oxford, Bodleian Library MS. Laud misc. 345, MS. Rawlinson A.345. Two copies said to be in Cambridge, Magdalene College MSS. 118 and 258 are actually in Pembroke College. Two further copies should be added to the list: Gloucester, Cathedral Library MS. 14, fols. 28ra–29rb (extracts); San Marino (Calif.), Huntington Library, MS. HM 19914, fols. 115ra–158rb.

agree that a Master Richard is the author.[43] Many copies add the cognomen "de Wetheringsett" (Wedringletus, Wethersett, Weressete, Wetheringesset, Wetrhigsete, etc.) to Richard's name, and others designate him as "of Leicester." A copy of the text now at Shrewsbury School (MS. 7), written in the mid-thirteenth century, neatly reconciles these two surnames by describing the author as "Master Richard of Leicester, rector of the church of Wetheringsett" ("summa magistri Ricardi de Laycestria, rectoris ecclesie de Wetrhigsete, de hiis que pertinent ad eos qui presunt").

But there is more. At least ten copies claim that Richard was chancellor of Cambridge University. Several of these ascriptions are from the fourteenth and fifteenth century, and might be thought to have been influenced by another Richard of Wetheringsett who was chancellor of Cambridge University in the fourteenth century.[44] But two of the ascribed copies are from the middle years of the thirteenth century and thus bear witness to an early tradition that the author of *Qbp* was one of the first chancellors of the University.[45]

External evidence confirms these early ascriptions. A Richard of Leicester is the earliest known chancellor of Cambridge University.[46] He attested a charter of Maurice Ruffus or le Rus, a prominent Cambridge citizen, along with Laurence of Stansfield, prior of the Augustinian house at Barnwell.[47] Laurence became prior in 1215,

---

[43] The exceptions are those that ascribe it to William de Montibus, chancellor of Lincoln Cathedral, who is cited frequently by name in the *Qbp*. This confusion came full circle in the 16th century when John Bale, no doubt influenced by copies of the *Qbp* that he had seen with ascriptions to Richard of Leicester, began referring to William de Montibus as "of Leicester," an erroneous identification that has lasted into the present century; see Goering, *William de Montibus*, 5 n. 9.

[44] See Emden, *Biographical Register of Cambridge*, 632.

[45] The two earliest ascriptions to Richard as chancellor of Cambridge are in San Marino (Calif.), Huntington Library MS. HM 19914: "Incipit speculum sacerdotum secundum magistrum Richardum de Leycestria cancellarium Cantebrigensem," and in Cambridge, University Library MS. Add. 3471: "Incipit summa magistri R. Cancellarii de Kantebrug'." The latter inscription is included on the frontispiece of Emden's *Biographical Register of Cambridge* with the explanation: "Mag. Richard of Leicester *alias* Wethringsette, the earliest known Chancellor of the University (probably by 1222), portrayed lecturing in the illuminated initial letter 'Q' of a 13th-century copy of his *Summa* 'Qui bene presunt presbiteri', in Cambridge Univ. Libr. Add. MS. 3471."

[46] Hackett, *Original Statutes*, 48–51.

[47] "Notum sit omnibus sancte matris ecclesie filiis quod Rector hospit' sancti

and Maurice Ruffus died ca. 1232, so Richard must have been chancellor sometime between these dates.[48]

That this Richard of Leicester is the same as the author of *Qbp* is made even more probable by the latter's association with the church of Wetheringsett. The parish of Wetheringsett in Suffolk was a wealthy benefice in the gift of the bishop of Ely in whose diocese Cambridge University was located.[49] We can well imagine that the benefice was bestowed on a prominent scholar who would, in turn, serve as chancellor to the fledgling university at Cambridge. It seems quite likely that the author of the *Qbp* was Master Richard of Leicester, rector of the church of Wetheringsett, and one of the first chancellors of Cambridge University.

Another tradition would identify the author of the *Qbp* with Master Richard le Grant *alias* Weathershed, chancellor of Lincoln Cathedral from ca. 1220 to 1229, and archbishop of Canterbury from 1229 until his premature death in 1231.[50] This tradition has no solid basis in the manuscript ascriptions of the Summa—none refers to the author as archbishop of Canterbury[51]—but it has an inherent plausi-

---

Johannis Cantebr' et fratres eiusdem loci communi assensu concesserunt Maur' ruffo et heredibus suis cantariam in capella sua sitam in parrochia Sancti Petri extra Portam Trumpetun' ... Predictus Rector et fratres predicti et Mauritius predictus huic scripto sigilla sua apposuerunt. Et in testimonio huius rei una cum sigillis virorum predictorum Dominus Laur' Prior Bernewell et Magister Ric' de Leycestr' Cancellar' Cantebr' signa sua apposuerunt. Renunciavit autem predictus Maur' se et pro suis omni foro exceptioni et apellationi" (Cambridge, St. John's College Archives, C 7.1, fol. 19r). I thank Malcolm Underwood, St. John's Archivist, for a description of the charter, and Norman Zacour for transcribing the relevant portions.

[48] On Laurence see Knowles, Brooke, and London, eds., *The Heads of Religious Houses*, 151. On Maurice Ruffus see Hackett, *Original Statutes*, 49 n. 1.

[49] See *Taxatio ecclesiastica Angliae*, ed. Astle, Ayscough and Caley, 123. The church was valued at more than £33 in 1291, one of the highest parochial valuations in the diocese.

[50] For a brief survey of current opinions on Richard Grant's authorship of the *Qbp*, see Kemmler, 47. The most influential authority identifying Richard as the author is the learned catalogue of Royal manuscripts in the British Library, London. The description of MS. Royal 4.B.VIII is typical: " 'Qui bene presunt presbiteri.' Without title or author's name, but styled elsewhere 'Summa brevis' and attributed to William of Leicester or de Monte (Bale, *Scriptorum*, 258), and, with more reason, to Richard Wethershed, *al.* Grant, *al.* of Leicester, Chancellor of Lincoln (1221–1227) and Archbishop of Canterbury (1229–1231)," *Catalogue of the ... Royal and King's Collections*, ed. Warner and Gilson, 1:84–85.

[51] Several copies ascribe the work to a chancellor of Lincoln Cathedral, but

bility. It seems, however, that the evidence for and against Richard Grant's authorship has never been carefully evaluated.

There appear to be two reasons for ascribing the *Qbp* to Richard Grant. The first is that he was one of the early successors of William de Montibus as chancellor of Lincoln Cathedral. The author of the *Qbp*, also named Richard, was a student of William de Montibus at Lincoln. It would seem fitting that this talented student should be rewarded with the chancellorship, and be expected to carry on the scholastic tradition that William de Montibus had begun in the Lincoln schools.

The second argument for identifying Richard Grant with the author of the *Qbp* is that both seem to share a common surname, "de Wetheringsett." As we have seen, the author of the *Qbp* is often called Richard of Wetheringsett. Richard Grant is assigned the *alias* "de Wethershed" by all modern authorities.[52] "Wethershed" is not an attested English placename, and William Hunt suggests that it is the "Wetheringsett in Sussex or in Suffolk."[53] If both Richards are to be connected with the rather uncommon placename "Wetheringsett," this is strong *prima facie* evidence for equating the two.

A closer look at the documents surrounding Richard Grant as chancellor of Lincoln and as Archbishop of Canterbury reveals a good deal of uncertainty about his surname. In the diocesan and royal records he is referred to simply as "Master Richard," "Richard the chancellor," "Richard the Archbishop," etc., without surname. The earliest written document that I have found to connect Richard Grant with Wetheringsett is an entry in some of the manuscripts of

---

these ascriptions arise from an understandable confusion with William de Montibus, chancellor of Lincoln, whose name and title appear frequently in the summa itself (see above, n. 42); e.g., Oxford, New College MS. 94: "Hic incipit summa magistri Ricardi de Montibus Lincolniensis Cancellarii."

[52] See H[unt], "Grant, Richard," 401; Emden, *Biographical Register of Oxford*, 3:2188; John le Neve, *Fasti*, 17, etc.

[53] H[unt], 401. This information seems to derive from Hook, who writes in his *Lives of the Archbishops*, 104: "He is so called by Godwin [*De praesulibus Angliae commentarius*] i. 89. 'Hunc Ranulfus Polychronici author, Richardum appellat de Wethershed ... quem plerique Richardum Magnum nuncupatum contendunt.' ... But where is Wethershed? There is a Wetheringsett in the union and hundred of Hurstemonceaux, in the county of Sussex. It has been conjectured that this may have been formerly written Wethershed. There is a Wetheringsett, also, near Eye, in Suffolk."

Ralph Higden's *Polychronicon*: "Cui [Stephen Langton] successerit magnus ecclesiae Lincolniensis decanus(!) magister Ricardus *de Wethirsheved*."[54] This would seem to be rather weak evidence were it not for the chance survival of Richard's official seal on a document in the Lincoln archives. The seal confirms that Richard used the surname "de Wetheringsett," or something similar, during his years as chancellor at Lincoln. The seal, now damaged, reads: SIGILL MAGRI RIC : DE : W.... CANCELL : LINCOLNIE.[55]

Upon Richard's elevation to the see of Canterbury, at least one chronicler referred to him as "Richard II," to distinguish him from the twelfth-century Archbishop Richard of Dover.[56] Others used the cognomen "le Grant" or "de Graunt," perhaps because of Richard's imposing physical and spiritual presence.[57] None called him Richard of Wetheringsett. There may be many reasons why Archbishop Richard was not called "of W[etheringsett]" by his contemporaries, but one intriguing explanation is that the cognomen ceased to be appropriate upon Richard's elevation to the see of Canterbury. If Richard had been rector of the church of Wetheringsett, he would have been required to resign the benefice upon his elevation.[58] That this is precisely what happened may be confirmed by a reference in the Patent Rolls of Henry III. A letter dated 2 May 1229 announces that the King has presented Philip of Eye, a cleric of Hubert de Burgh, justiciar of England, to the church of Wetheringsett.[59] Richard Grant was presented to the see of Canterbury by

---

[54] Higden, *Polychronicon*, 8:204.

[55] Printed in *Registrum antiquissimum of Lincoln*, ed. Foster and Major, 8:10 (Add. charter no. 2194). Nicholas Bennett, the Cathedral Librarian, graciously examined the seal, attached to a deed (ref. D&C Dij/77/2/6). In a personal communication he notes that "the edge of the seal is unfortunately damaged between 'RIC DE W...' and 'CANCELL.' There would only be room in this space for about three characters. It is just possible to make out that the character immediately after the 'W' begins with a downstroke, that is, it might be an 'T' or an 'E'; further than this, however, it is not possible to go."

[56] "Notandum sane quod omnes Archiepiscopi Cantuarienses, qui istum praecesserunt, diversa habuere vocabula, nec quisquam illorum hoc vocabulo nuncupatus est, praeter unum duntaxat, qui huius vocabuli exstitit primus; iste vero huius nominis dignoscitur esse secundus." "Annales monasterii de Waverleia," 2:307. Cf. Hook, *Lives of the Archbishops*, 102–3.

[57] Cf. Hook, *Lives of the Archbishops*, 105; H[unt], 401.

[58] See Benson, *The Bishop-Elect*, 112.

[59] "Philippus de Eya, clericus H. de Burgo comitis Kancie, justiciarii Anglie,

Pope Honorius III on 16 or 19 January 1229, he received the tempo-
ralities on 24 March and was consecrated on 10 June.[60] This coinci-
dence of dates would suggest that the rich benefice of Wetheringsett,
resigned by Richard upon his elevation, was part of the political
settlement (or at least part of King Henry's consolation) around the
disputed election to the see of Canterbury in 1229.[61]

Richard Grant's short career as archbishop of Canterbury, 1229 to
1231, has received little attention from historians. He has been described
as "a distinguished scholar, well known to the members of the [papal]
curia" and "far from a nonentity ... but rather an independent compe-
tent prelate; for the history of both church and state in England might
have been different if he had not died at the very beginning of his
strenuous campaign against the secularity of some of his fellow bishops
and the abuses of non-residents and pluralists."[62] Such a prelate might
well be thought to be the author of the Summa "Qui bene presunt."

The reasons for confusion regarding Richard of Leicester, Richard
of Wetheringsett, and Richard Grant are now manifest; nevertheless,
a plausible case can be made that these three names refer to a single
person. I would suggest the following as a working hypothesis:

Richard of Leicester was a student of William de Montibus at
Lincoln at the beginning of the thirteenth century.[63] He was subsequently appointed rector of Wetheringsett, and, after 1215, wrote the
summa "Qui bene presunt." Richard may have used the income of
his benefice to finance a sojourn in the Paris schools, where he was
known as "Ricardus Anglicus" or "Ricardus Magnus."[64] He was
appointed chancellor of Cambridge University, probably before

---

habet litteras de presentatione ad ecclesiam de Wetheringesete, vacantem et ad
donationem domini regis spectantem ratione episcopatus Elyensis [vacantis] et in
manu domini regis existentis. Littere ille directe sunt episcopo Norwicensi, Teste
rege, apud Westmonasterium, ij die Maii," 13 Hen. III, m. 8; Calendar of Patent
Rolls of Henry III, 247.

[60] John le Neve, Fasti, 17ff.

[61] On the election see, H[unt], 401; Gibbs and Lang, Bishops and Reform, 79.

[62] Gibbs and Lang, Bishops and Reform, 32, 34; cf. idem, 193.

[63] A document was witnessed at Lincoln by "Ricardo clerico cancellarii" [i.e.,
William de Montibus] in the late 12th century (Registrum Antiquissimum, 9:106), and
another by "Magistro Ricardo de Leicestr'" between 1206 and 1219 (ibid., 10:178).

[64] Emden, Biographical Register of Oxford, 3:2188; Glorieux, Répertoire, 1:281;
Catalogue of the Royal and King's Collections, 1:232 (Royal MS. 8.C.V); Chartularium
Universitatis Parisiensis, ed. Denifle and Chatelain, 1:85 (no. 27).

1221, where he was still known as Richard of Leicester. By 1221 he had returned to Lincoln as chancellor of the Cathedral. He retained his benefice at Wetheringsett, and, perhaps because of the frequency of "Leicester" surnames in Lincoln diocese, he styled himself "Richard of W..." on his official seal. When he was presented by the pope to the see of Canterbury in 1229, Richard resigned his church at Wetheringsett, and was finally designated by his English contemporaries as Richard Magnus or "le Grant."

It seems impossible at present to prove or disprove this hypothesis. Further research in the diocesan and other records may help to confirm or deny it.[65] At present, however, there is nothing implausible or indefensible in asserting that the author of the *Qbp* was Richard of Leicester, rector of Wetheringsett, chancellor of Cambridge University and Lincoln Cathedral, and, briefly, archbishop of Canterbury.

University of Toronto

---

[65] I am grateful to Dr. Dorothy Owen for her patient and learned responses to my queries about the church at Wetheringsett, and about the records that might shed light on Richard's identity. Her painstaking research on these records continues.

A . G . R I G G

"De motu et pena peccandi": A Latin Poem on the Causes and Effects of Sin

he poem described here consists—in its extant, incomplete form—of 946 lines, mainly hexameters, variously rhymed.[1] It is of interest for both its contents and its combination of sources. The first part (1–323) describes the process of sin, through suggestion, delight and consent, with biblical parallels; this part is based primarily on Augustine. The second part (324–946) describes the consequences of sin, especially those arising from man's fallen nature and evident in his physical decline. The poem is too long to edit here in its entirety, but I hope to quote enough of it to make its meaning and flavor evident.

The Manuscript

The unique copy of the poem is found in London, British Library, MS Cotton, Julius D. iii.[2] This St. Albans manuscript consists of two distinct parts:[3] fols. 1–124, a cartulary of the Sacrist of St. Al-

---

[1] I am grateful to the British Library for permission to quote extracts from the poem. It is not recorded in Walther, *Initia carminum* (cited as WIC); this may be because it is acephalous, but I have checked all entries under *de peccatis* without seeing a sign of it. The title is my own, conflated from two separate rubrics in the manuscript. I owe considerable thanks to Joseph Goering for help in searching for the sources and to Lawrin Armstrong, who suggested the Breviary as a source.

[2] The account in the catalogue of Cotton manuscripts is seriously deficient: for example, it lists an item "Angelicos cetus" as a separate poem, whereas it is in fact a sermon in the middle of the life of St. Alban.

[3] See Ker, *Medieval Libraries*, and Watson, *Supplement*, 59.

bans (s. xiv/xv, after 1393);[4] fols. 125–196 (s. xiii), a poetic anthology
containing the following poems:

fol. 125r	Verse life of St. Alban by Ralph of Dunstable, inc. "Albani celebrem celo terrisque triumphum."[5]
fol. 159r	"Quasi coruus crocito": sixteen Goliardic stanzas lamenting the state of the church; not in WIC.
fol. 159v	The present item, inc. "Exposito iam proposito."
fol. 171v	"Est nemus unde loquar": a debate in elegiac couplets between the four seasons; unedited; not in WIC.
fol. 181r	*De virtutibus imitandis*, inc. "Hic exempla satis uobis scribam nouitatis"; unedited; not in WIC. Possibly unfinished, as the only virtue described is Justice. Followed by short pieces, possibly separate.
fol. 184r	Verse life of Becket, inc. "Mens in parte cupit"; unedited.[6]
fol. 191r	*Biblical Epigrams* of Hildebert of Le Mans.[7]
fol. 196v	"Hic ardent seraphim" (WIC 7854), incomplete.

The manuscript ends abruptly at the foot of folio 196v.

State of the poem

In the introductory lines (below) the poet implies that he has already
set out a plan ("exposito iam proposito") and described the working
of the seven deadly sins; this suggests that something is lacking at the
beginning. The end also appears to be incomplete: he promises (524–
30 below) to describe the human miseries arising from self-will and
the devil. He gives only two full examples of self-willed misery
(courtier and soldier), with only two lines on peasants, and does not
mention the devil's work at all. The ending is too abrupt to suggest
that he merely tired of the subject. The rubrics (which are quite full

---

[4] Davies, *Medieval Cartularies*, 95.

[5] Extracts printed by McLeod, 407–30.

[6] WIC 10906b; recorded in *Bibliotheca Hagiographica Latina*, no. 7227.

[7] A. B. Scott, Deirdre Baker, A. G. Rigg, "The Biblical Epigrams of Hildebert
of Le Mans: a critical edition," 272–316; for an account of the version in this
manuscript, see A. B. Scott in *Sacris Erudiri* 16 (1965): 404–24.

in the earlier parts) are sometimes inappropriate or misplaced, suggesting that they have been copied from a margin (where some still remain).[8]

Metre

Nearly ninety per cent of the lines are simple Leonine hexameters, with rhyme between the strong caesura and the end of the line. There are thirteen single-sound couplets, one triplet (e.g., 281–82, 327–28, 336–38, 339–40). There are fifteen couplets (one triplet) with collateral rhyme (e.g., 137–38, 611–12). There are nineteen couplets of trinini salientes (e.g., 1–2, 475–76, 573–74, 750–51, 752–53). There are three lines of tripertiti, in which the hexameter is divided into three blocks of two feet each (e.g., 3). There are three pentameters (e.g., 769). There are five lines in which the rhyme is monosyllabic or entirely lacking, possibly corrupt.

Sources

The principal source for the first part of the poem (13–323)—the triple motion of sin, its analogue in the Fall of Man, the three degrees of sin, and their parallels in Christ's three raisings from the dead—is Augustine's *De sermone Domini in monte*, where he is explicating the passage on adultery in the heart.[9] Augustine's discussion was widely known in the Middle Ages.[10] It was used by Innocent III in his sermon on Ash Wednesday;[11] the three raisings were the topic of Hildebert's *Epigram* 68 and mentioned by Peter Lom-

---

[8] *De suggestione* (after 47) should precede 21; *De memoria rerum prius habitarum* (before 37) would be better before 31; of the promptings to sin through the five senses, only one (*De motu peccandi per auditum* before 68) is given a heading; the section 227–38 is about malice in speech but is headed *De hiis qui peccant pro natorum utilitate*, a title more suited to 221–26 (which is headed *De hiis qui peccant causa utilitatis proprie*); before 879 is the heading *De lumbricis significacio*, but this refers only to 879–80 and the new section beginning at 881 has no heading.

[9] *Sancti Aurelii Augustini de sermone Domini in monte*, I.12, ed. Almut Mutzenbecker, 35–39; see below notes 24, 25, 26, 27, 30, 31 for extracts.

[10] Its diffusion is not discussed, however, in the thorough survey by Lottin, "La doctrine morale," 49–173. This particular passage is not discussed by Guindon, "Le 'De Sermone Domini in monte' de S. Augustin," *57–*85.

[11] *Sermo XI in die cinerum*, PL 217: 360–61.

bard.[12] The passage was used by Raymund de Pennaforte, also quoting Hildebert,[13] whence it passed to Chaucer's *Parson's Tale*.[14] The *De sermone* was readily available,[15] but the frequent use of I.12 suggests that this section may have enjoyed separate circulation. In the modern (Pius V) Breviary, there are twelve readings for III Nocturns from the *De sermone* (though not this section of it); medieval breviaries (Sarum, Hyde, Hereford) do not have the relevant passage either, but I suspect that others (which remain unedited and unindexed) may have included it.[16]

The debt to Augustine is somewhat confused by the mention of the "fourth dead" (319-21), which comes not from Augustine but Gregory's *Moralia in Job*,[17] in a passage which itself was known elsewhere.[18] Gregory cannot, however, be the sole source for the poem, as he has four *motus* of sin, not three.[19] Clearly some combination of Augustine and Gregory was used.

The account of the physical consequences of Original Sin (536-791) closely resembles Innocent III, *De miseria humane conditionis* I,

---

[12] On Hildebert, see note 7 above. Lombard, *Sententiae* lib. 4, dist. 16, pp. 336-37, is too brief as a source for the poem.

[13] Quoted by Germaine Dempster, "The Parson's Tale," in *Sources and analogues of Chaucer's Canterbury Tales*, 732. For the present purpose this is more useful than Petersen, *The sources of the Parson's Tale*. In general, see Robertson, *A Preface to Chaucer*, 72-75.

[14] *Parson's Tale* 330-31 (without the raisings).

[15] See Römer, *Die handschriftliche Überlieferung der Werke des heiligen Augustinus*, Bd. II.1 *Grossbritannien und Irland: werkverzeichnis*, 168-69, who records 27 English manuscripts, of which fourteen are 13th-century or earlier.

[16] For another use of Augustine, see note 34 below.

[17] *Moralia in Job*, 193-97; for a list of manuscripts, many English, some early, see pp. xiv-xxix. The passage is quoted in note 32 below.

[18] It appears very abruptly in Alexander Neckam's *De naturis rerum*, chap. 180, p. 318, with no explanation of why he is the fourth; Neckam also interprets it as a case of flattery; he also used it in his *Corrogationes Novi Promethei*, ed. L. S. Cropp, lines 1047-50:

> palponis typus est quem tangere dextera patris
> noluit, et subdens uerba salutis ait:
> defunctos sine defunctos sepelire; sepultos
> palponem et quos fraus decipit ore uocat

[19] See nn. 31-32 below. The four *motus* form the topic of *Biblical Epigram* No. 2 by Hildebert (see above, nn. 7, 12), who thus follows Augustine in *Epigram* 68 but Gregory in *Epigram* 2.

chapters iii–x,[20] in its account of conception, birth, and old age. Innocent does not, however, deal with the Six Ages as such (599–791), for which the poet's scheme resembles Isidore or Bede.[21] There is an extended account of man's six ages in Alexander Neckam's *Corrogationes novi Promethei*, but Neckam stresses the games appropriate to each age.[22] The poet's account of the occupations of man (887–946, cf. 348–463) may have been inspired by Innocent, *De miseria*, I, chapters xi–xiv (placed immediately after the section *De incommodo senectutis*), but there is no direct influence; similarly, Neckam's accounts of specific occupations (*De naturis rerum*) could only have been indirectly influential.

POEM: SUMMARY WITH EXTRACTS

Introductory (1–12). The poet has stated his plan, has distinguished the sins numerically, has set out the three causes of sin (will, speech, action), and has shown how sin's three offspring spread through the seven limbs and bind the soul with seven chains (presumably the seven deadly sins). Next he will proceed to discuss sin under this outline.

> Exposito iam proposito cause patuere
> Tres scelerum, que per numerum distincta fuere:
> Culpa uolendi, noxa loquendi, crimen agendi.
> Tres scelerum partus septem fudere per artus,
> 5   Que scelerum cause proserpere lacius ause
> Tres in septenis animam pressere catenis.
> Prima nocens anime, preponderat altera prime,
> Vltima de trina grauior solet esse ruina.
> Micius hec penam, plus exigit illa cathenam,
> 10   Tercia ter nectit, quem pena grauissima plectit.
> Fiat. Item quo plus agitem? De crimine cedam

---

[20] *Lotharii Cardinalis (Innocentii III) De miseria humane conditionis.*

[21] Isidore of Seville, *Etymologiae*, XI.2; Bede, *De temporum ratione*, chap. LXVI, in *Chronica minora*, 247–48, and in *Bedae Venerabilis Opera*, 463–64. Se notes 36 and 38 below. In general, see Sears, *The Ages of Man*; Burrow, *The Ages of Man*, especially pp. 82–90 and 200–201 (quoting Isidore).

[22] See the edition by Cropp, cited in note 18 above.

Sub tali racione: mali distinctio quedam.[23]

Part One: De motu peccandi (13–323)

Introductory (13–20). There are three motions of sin, in mind, speech, and deed: namely, suggestion, delight and consent.[24]

> Tres sunt in mente, tres in sermone nocente
> Motus peccandi, tres sunt ad facta notandi.
> 15   Prima subest animo suggestio fomite primo;
> Delectacio se mediam confert operose;
> Consensus demum se contulit esse supremum.

They are the root, growth, and crop:

> Hinc radix, inde culmus, seges aucta deinde;
> In prima seritur, medie quasi flos aperitur,
> 20   Tercius in reliquum fructum maturat iniquum.

I. *Suggestio* (21–106) operates through the mind, either (a) from the inside, or (b) from the outside:[25]

> 21   Prima fit in mente suggestio mota repente
> Quolibet auctore uel ab intro uel exteriore

(a) from the inside it operates through the memory (e.g., recalling old feuds):

> 33   Quando recordaris lites cum rebus amaris
> Quas animo tristi socio ledente tulisti,
> Iurgia cum dampnis recolens a pluribus annis,
> Hinc ad opus sceleris, ira stimulante, moueris.

(b) from the outside it operates through the senses, and is then passed on to the interior mind:

> 52   A foris elicitur quod suggerit interiori:
> Intus suggeritur quod prodit ab exteriori.

The senses are sight (58–67), hearing (68–70), smell (80–85), taste (86–91), and touch (92–96), e.g.:

---

[23] The punctuation (and meaning) of 11–12 are uncertain.

[24] Augustine, *De sermone*: "Nam tria sunt quibus impletur peccatum: suggestione delectatione consensione." See note 26 below.

[25] Augustine, *De sermone*: "Suggestio siue per memoriam fit siue per corporis sensus, cum aliquid videmus uel audimus vel olfacimus uel gustamus uel tangimus."

58 Forte uides coram mulierem stare decoram:
    Non deerit ueneris suggestus ad os mulieris . . .
70 Audis inflictum dampnum tibi uel maledictum:
    Mentem punire suggestio pellicit ire.
    Femina te teste forme laudatur honeste:
    Motus laciuos facit hec fieri rediuiuos . . .
84 Hinc fit odoratis ut carnibus esuriatis
    Et gula subridet, ubi laucior esca renidet . . .
90 In sapidis escis uentris moderamina nescis,
    Et potus grati seruit sapor ebrietati . . .
92 Nec minus ad tactum peccati suggerit actum;
    Sunt pro peste satis quante fuerint bonitatis.

II (a) *Delectatio* (107–46) is the stage of delight in what has been suggested but not yet put into action.[26]

107 Quod si suggestis accesserit intima pestis
     Ipsaque proficiat ut delectacio fiat,
     Hoc uideas tandem quantum uigeant ad eandem
110 Motus suggesti . . .

But it is not yet a sin:

117 Nondum tota tamen affectio gestit ad actum,
     Nondum conamen iniit cum crimine pactum.

Finally, however, delight entices the mind to consent:

135 Hinc secum tacite deliberat omnia rite
     Tempora, signa, status seriemque modumque reatus.
     Sic, cor ut inflectat, tria tela decent inimicum:
     Suggerit, oblectat, consensum format iniquum.

II (b) *The Fall of Man* (147–74). The triple motion (suggestion, delight, consent) is paralleled by the events in the garden of Eden.[27]

---

[26] Augustine, *De sermone*: "Quod si frui delectauerit, delectatio inlicita refrenanda est. Velut cum ieiunamus et uisis cibis palati appetitus adsurgit, non fit nisi delectatione: sed huic tamen consentimus, et eam non dominantis rationis iure cohibemus. Si autem consensio facta fuerit, plenum peccatum erit, notum deo in corde nostro, etiamsi non innotescat hominibus." Section II(b), on the Fall of Man, really applies to all three *motus*. Section II(c), on Sins of Speech, is classified under "Delectatio" because of the poet's desire for symmetry: the second stage corresponds to "noxa loquendi" (3), and "tres in sermone nocente / Motus peccandi" (13–14). Despite the implication of 13–14, it would have been impossible to assign three *motus* each to will, speech, and action.

[27] Augustine, *De sermone*: "Tria ergo haec, ut dicere coeperam, similia sunt illi

Adam would never have consented to eat the apple, if it had not
been offered by Eve; Eve would never have delighted in the apple, if
it had not first been suggested by the serpent:

147 Nunquam primus Adam dampnasset in arbore quadam
Hunc mundum totum cum posteritate nepctum,
Nunquam primus homo dampnasset postera pomo
150 Spernens certa mali gustu presagia tali,
Ni porrexisset uetitum tangique petisset
Femina de costis data, non collega sed hostis!
Immo nec ad uetitum poterat flexisse maritum
Femina feralis, auidis exercita malis,
155 Decipiens ore blando pomique sapore
(Primo carpendi uia, post exemplar edendi),
Ni prius affatu serpens, ni uipera flatu
Suggessisset ei primordia perniciei.
Denique suggestu colubrum nocuisse uides tu,
160 Pomum morderi quod suggessit mulieri?
Femina serpentis nimium fidens documentis
Est delectata specie, gustu saciata.
Vir male traductum uitali stipite fructum
Dante comedit Eua, nobis, socio, sibi leua.
165 Serpens suggessit, fallenti femina cessit,
Adam consensit, ut ab omni parte nocens sit.
Sic nos instigat demon monituque fatigat:
Delectata caro monitori cedit amaro.

II (c) *Sins of speech* (175–238) are discussed here because of the poet's
desire for symmetry,[28] and occur in three ways:
175 Transeat inde manus ad eos quos sermo prophanus
Motus dictauit, sicut distinctio cauit.
Dicitur ergo fore triplici distincta tenore
Omnis uerborum series et summa malorum
(i) *Surrepcio* "cheating" (183–206) arises from three causes:

---

gestae rei quae in Genesi scripta est, ut quasi a serpente fiat suggestio et quaedam
suasio, in appetitu carnali tamquam in Eua delectatio, in ratione uero tamquam in
uiro consensio. Quibus peractis tamquam de paradiso, hoc est de beatissima luce
iustitiae, in mortem homo expellitur."
[28] See note 26 above. I have not found a source for this section.

183   In causa triplici poterit surrepcio dici,
      Que sunt, ni fallor, incuria, mos malus, error

The poet shows, by the image of a ship, how disaster can arise from carelessness, bad habits, and error, when we neglect the truth and favor the wicked:

203   Nescimus uerum meritis ascribere rerum,
      Optima carpentes, reprobis errore fauentes

(ii) Sins of speech committed out of necessity (207–26) fall into two groups: those committed under torture, when a Christian is forced into infidelity (210–20):

212   Cedit tortori, cruciatibus atque dolori,
      Vt neget ore Deum: Phebum uocet atque Lieum,

and those committed for some advantage (221–26), which may not be entirely bad:

225   Hos pulsant aliqui motus nec prorsus iniqui,
      Nec tamen ad tales causas prorsus ueniales

(iii) The third sin of speech (227–38) is very bad and arises from malicious rage:

229   Non hanc spes, terror, incuria, mos malus, error
      Sed furor extorsit, quo pernicies grauior sit ...[29]

238   Nunc in presentes, nunc inuehit in procul entes.

III. *Consensus* leads to the deed of sin (239–323): A. This is committed in one of three ways, secretly, openly, or habitually:[30]

241   Omne quod illicite fit in huius tempore uite
      Clam, coram, solito—tribus hiis distinguere scito

(a) secret sin (243–48) is least culpable, as no one follows its precedent:

243   Que clam proueniunt sine teste uel indice fiunt,
      Non diuulgantur ut plures illa sequantur

(b) sins committed openly (249–60) set a bad example:

259   Condicio talis multo minus est uenialis,

---

[29] quo ... sit: que ... fit MS.

[30] Augustine, *De sermone*: "ita ipsius peccati tres sunt differentiae: in corde in facto in consuetudine, tamquam tres mortes [*see next note*]: una quasi in domo, id est cum in corde consentitur libidini, altera iam prolata quasi extra portam, cum in factum procedit adsensio, tertia, cum ui consuetudinis malae tamquam mole terrena premitur animus, quasi in sepulchro iam putens."

Multa censura scelus expositum luitura

(c) habitual sin (261–70) is the worst, and arises from a lack of *timor* and *pudor*.

B. These three ways of sinning are paralleled by three miraculous raisings from the dead performed by Christ (271–318):[31]

(a) of Jair's daughter (Matt. 9.23–26), which was performed inside the house (281–88):

281   Prima Jair nata clam patris in ede locata

Intus curata, facili sermone leuata,

Illum designans, qui nullo teste malignans

Clam leuiterque satis redit ad formam pietatis

(b) of the widow's son (Luke 7.12–16), which took place before a crowd (289–300):

296   Turba presente, mundo peccata uidente,

Ad tumulum latus, ad criminis ima dicatus

(c) of Lazarus (John 11.1–44), who had been dead for three days (301–12):

306   Mortuus inclusus tumuloque diucius usus

Quisque per excessus longo iam crimine pressus

(d) to the redeemable sins, however, the poet adds a fourth case (319–21), which comes ultimately not from Augustine but Gregory;[32] this is the occasion (Luke 9.59–60) when Christ did not raise the

---

[31] Augustine, *De sermone*: "Quae tria genera mortuorum [*see last note*] dominum resuscitasse quisquis euangelium legit agnoscit. Et fortasse considerat, quas differentias habeat etiam uox resuscitantis, cum alibi dicit: 'Puella surge!', alibi 'Iuuenis, tibi dico, surge!', alibi 'infremuit spiritu' et 'fleuit' et 'rursus fremuit' et post deinde 'uoce magna clamauit: Lazare, ueni foras!'" Augustine's stress on the three different levels of command needed to perform the miracle is reflected in the poet's "facili sermone leuata" (282), a detail not in Gregory (below).

[32] Gregory's account (*Moralia* 4.27.49) cannot entirely be the poet's source, as to the three *modi* of sin (suggestion, delight, consent) he adds "audacia defensionis" (illustrated by Adam's attempt to excuse himself). On the other hand, he interprets the scene of the second miracle as a symbol of the public (imitable) nature of the sin: "Iam quasi extra portam educitur cuius iniquitas usque in inuerecundiam publicae perpetrationis aperitur." Gregory is also the source for the "fourth dead": "Quartum uero mortuum Redemptor noster nuntiante discipulo agnoscit, nec tamen suscitat quia ualde difficile est ut is quem post usum malae consuetudinis etiam adulantium linguae excipiunt, a mentis suae morte reuocetur. De quo et bene dicitur: 'Sine mortuos sepeliant mortuos suos.' Mortui enim mortuos sepeliunt cum peccatores peccatorem fauoribus premunt." This fourth case is also in Neckam, but in a form too brief to have been used by our poet.

father of his disciple but said "let the dead bury their dead":

319 Quartus desperat: non est ut surgere querat.
"Quartum defunctum defunctus habet sepelire,
Spe nulla functum."

Part Two: De pena peccati (324–946)

Introductory (324–29). The consequence of sin, human misery, is either internal or external:

326 Prima sub internis animi confota cauernis
Bellum languoris denominat interioris;
Altera uero foris causam fouet exterioris
Ex hiis que misere possunt per membra nocere

I. *Internus languor* (330–516) arises from three causes, (a) love of having, (b) fear of losing, (c) sorrow at losing or failing to gain:

336 Primi tortoris primum genus: estus amoris.
Inde suis loris premit intima pena timoris;
Tercia non minor hiis urget pressura doloris.
In perquirendis amor est et rebus habendis,
340 Inque reponendis timor est et uix retinendis;
De non inuentis dolor est frustraque retentis

(a) *Amor habendi* (348–93) seeks bodily advantages, and is illustrated by the various pursuits of men: sailor (354–57), soldier (358–61), merchant (362–63), farmer (364–67), husband (368–72), philosopher (373–75), mechanic (376–77). All have constant toils and worries that lead to fear.

(b) *Timor perdendi* (394–463): where once one labored in acquiring possessions, one now suffers from fear of losing them:

398 Inde laborauit procurando quod amauit;
Hinc studium mentis furor anxius urget habentis

This is illustrated by the fears of the soldier (404–5), student (406–7), farmer (408–9), who fears for his beasts and crops:

408 Rusticus arctatur ne bos ruat aut moriatur,
Ne uicium terre ualeat sata queque referre,

husband, wife and parent (412–23), and child, who fears that it will lose its father and be reduced to poverty (424–27):

425 Scitque timore pari puer in patre sollicitari,
Ne patre sublato, re uel uita spoliato,
Fatum pupilli fortuna subingerat illi

All ways of life are accompanied by fear:

456   Hinc uarie cure uarios actus pariture
      Vanis fomentis agitarunt corda timentis

(c) *Dolor* (464–516) arises from love of having and fear of losing:

468   Quando querentis amor aut cautela timentis
      In perquirendis frustratur uel retinendis,
      Summum tormenti genus imminet inde dolenti

The victim is sorry that he was ever born; he plans suicide and various methods are described:

475   Natalis sed fatalis maledicitur hora
      Que nati male fatati non clauserit ora . . .

485   Gracius esse rati mala funeris accelerati
      Quam multis horis dispendia ferre doloris . . .

499   Hic iugulum cultro, latus hic transuerberat ultro,
      Huic miserum pectus concidit mucro retectus,
      Hunc rogus inuoluit, hunc fluctus sponte resoluit,
      Hic pre merore suffocato perit ore,
      Hic a fomentis et corporeis alimentis
      Abstinet omnino sompno, dape, nectare, uino

II. *Exterior sorrows* (517–946) are the muse's next topic:

517   Exterior pene pars est tractanda camene,
      Vt patuit plene pars interioris habene

There are three species, arising from (1) the father (i.e., Adam) alone, that is Original Sin, (2) the father and our own madness, (3) the father, our own madness, and the devil's incitement:

524   Quedam non minima, que sunt ab origine prima,
      Fiunt auctore primo tantum genitore,
      Multaque summa mali procedit origine tali.
      Multa quibus miserum presens quatit orbita rerum
      Carnis ab auctore ueniunt proprioque furore.
      Multa diabolico fieri de fomite dico
530   Et de figmentis propriis meritoque parentis

(1) Original Sin (536–880): its effects can be divided into three sections: (a) conception and birth, (b) the six ages of man, (c) man's unsettled nature.

(a) the account of conception and birth (537–98) resembles Innocent III:

537   Causa noue gentis blandis utriusque parentis

Edita fomentis et sompni conuenientis
In the womb the foetus is surrounded by poisonous matter:[33]
554 Sanguis et humorum sanies et massa ciborum
Et digestiua uirtus fetore nociua
Quoddam tormenti genus est in uentre iacenti
An escape from this might be thought welcome, but weeping is almost universal:
567 Quippe sue pestis factus querulus sibi testis
Et flendi cura uates de sorte futura
Only one person, Zoroaster, laughed on being born:[34]
573 Nullius nisi solius risum Zoroastis
Inuenies, quamuis decies lectis tibi fastis
At birth other creatures are better equipped than man, who is supposed to be their superior:[35]
591 Ad primum partus momentum subrigit artus
Omne pecus, stando simul et cum matre uagando.
A se cuncta fere possunt solamen habere,
Tanquam nature natiuo predita iure:
595 Hispida iam pellis menbris aptata nouellis,
Vngula dura pedi facit ut nequeant cito ledi.
Rector homo pecorum nature cedit eorum
(b) the scheme of the Six Ages is basically from Isidore or Bede:[36]
infantia (to 7), *pueritia* (to 14), *adolescentia* (to 28), *iuventus* (to 49), *senectus* (to 70), *aetas decrepita* (70+). The poet's stress is on each

---

[33] Innocent, *De miseria*: "Qui fertur esse tam detestabilis et immundus, ut ex eius contactu fruges non germinent, arescant arbusta, moriantur herbe, amittant arbores fetus, et si canes inde comederint in rabiem efferantur."

[34] Augustine, *De civitate Dei* 21.14: "Quae (infantia) quidem quod non a risu sed a fletu orditur hanc lucem, quid malorum ingressa sit nesciens prophetat quodam modo. Solum quando natus est ferunt risisse Zoroastrem, nec ei boni aliquid monstrosus risus ille portendit." This is quoted by Vincent of Beauvais, *Speculum Historiale* I, ch. 101. Augustine took it from Pliny, *Naturalis Historia* VII.16.72 or Solinus, *Collectanea*, 1.72.

[35] Innocent, *De miseria*: "Flebiles, debiles, imbecilles, parum a brutis distantes, immo minus in multis habentes: nam illa statim ut exorta sunt gradiuntur, nos autem non solum erecti pedibus non incedimus, verum etiam curvati manibus reptamus."

[36] Isidore, *Etymologiae*, XI.2; Bede, *De temporum ratione*, ed. Mommsen, 247–48, ed. Jones, 463–64. It is Bede that has *senectus* and *aetas decrepita* (Isidore *gravitas*, *senectus*).

age's vulnerability to disease and death.

First Age (603–52). The infant constantly needs help; at first it crawls on four feet, then, with a staff, it manages on three, and at two years it is a toddler;[37] its life is constantly in danger:

611   Infans semper eget ope sollicite uariata,
          Quam si quisque neget, mors imminet indubitata …
615   Quadrupes in primis numquam se tollit ab imis,
          Cernuus ad limum tam uertice quam pede primum …
625   Discit paxillo niti modicoque bacillo
          Et miserum tripedem se circumferre per edem …
635   Sepius ergo cadit, dum sic tremulo pede uadit,
          Et uicio casus modo bucca perit, modo nasus …
641   Quem pede precipiti cupidum per lubrica niti
          Estus flammarum, rabies inuoluit aquarum

Second Age (653–75): *pueritia* is the "pure age":[38]

653   Etatem mundam nos dicimus esse secundam,
          Puraque signatur puericia quando uocatur
but it brings with it the miseries of school:

667   Ad ferulam dextra callis riget, intus et extra
          Tota rubet pellis, grauibus detrita flagellis

Third Age (676–705); this takes up the sum of the first two ages:

676   Post quas expletas sibi tercia uendicat etas
          Annos hec totidem summe quos addit eidem,
          Equans illarum mensuram sola duarum
It is the age of pleasure:

686   Mos adolescentis baccari more furentis
          Et circumferre luxum per publica terre
but it brings danger on itself by offending others:

694   Cum sibi uel reliquis nocuissent rebus iniquis
          Hos irritantes, se deliciis onerantes,
          Mors morbis horum subit ex dampnis aliorum

Fourth Age (706–33); this extends to the forty-ninth year; increased strength brings more work and worry:

---

[37] See below, p. 175 and note 39.
[38] Isidore, XI.2.11: "Puer a puritate vocatus, quia purus est."

710　Hec ter septenis uite quos adicit annis
　　　Efficit ut pleni sint quadraginta noueni.
　　　Tanto maiori nos mancipat illa labori,
　　　Quanto maiorem dedit ex etate uigorem ...
732　Hinc pro mensura tibi nec labor est neque cura,
　　　Vt nimis affligant animum que menbra fatigant

Fifth Age (734–53). This is an age of physical decline, with the humiliation of returning to walking on three feet, with a cane:

744　Marcent cincinni, deturpant ora cachinni,
　　　Flauescunt dentes, solita paritate carentes,
　　　Rictus horrescunt, pallet gena, labra rigescunt,
　　　Visus caligat, gressum torpedo fatigat,
　　　Et uigor exclusus et frustratus pedis usus,
　　　Et senio partus torpor per quoslibet artus.
750　Hec racio pedis officio male scit uegetari,
　　　Et uetulum facit ad baculum gressum moderari.
　　　Hec racio solet in senio curuare staturam,
　　　Et bipedem facit in tripedem mutare figuram

Sixth Age (754–91). This is the age of decrepitude and runs to the end:

754　Euum decrepiti sextum dixere periti:
　　　Tempus decrepite durat cum tempore uite,
　　　Quod nobis demum uoluit Deus esse supremum

Life becomes a burden. The sufferings of the *senex* are nothing compared to those of the *decrepitus*:

768　Tantaque decrepiti sunt per discrimina triti
　　　　　Quanta senectutem non habuisse putem ...
772　In sene curuatur grauitas ut fuste regatur;
　　　Hic frustra uires eciam cum fuste requires.
　　　Illum spectamus tripedem baculoque leuamus;
　　　Hunc quasi quadrupedem querimur reptare per edem

Finally, the poet makes explicit the riddle of the Sphinx:[39]

782　Hoc est quod retegi paucis possibile legi
　　　Fallaci lingua solitam proponere Spinga:

---

[39] Maximian, *Elegiae*, I.219–20: "Fitque tripes, prorsus quadrupes, ut parvulus infans,/ Et per sordentem (flebile) repit humum." Also used in Neckam's *Corrogationes Novi Promethei* (see note 18).

"Quid sit quod primo quasi quadrupes incubat imo,
Inde tripes factum bipedis mutatur ad actum,
Hinc tripes est iterum, fit quadrupes ordine rerum?"

(c) Man's moods are constantly fluctuating (792–880): now hungry, now overfull; now thirsty, now hung over; sometimes eager to go visiting, then worn out, then restless again:

809   Visitat absentes procul a regione parentes;
       Nunc idem fessus multa uertigine gressus
       Dum male lassescit captata sede quiescit.
       Nunc quia torperet si iugiter ipse sederet,
       Sedem fastidit et plus in itinere fidit

Sometimes he is wakeful, sometimes craves sleep. He turns to religion but backslides, now full of life, now fearing death. He is always vulnerable to something: enemies, serpents, drowning, poisons, flies. Even if he avoids these, his own nature will get him:

868   Et licet ex aliqua se possint parte tueri[40]
       Semper erit sua cui poterit natura noceri

Sweat produces worms that eat the flesh, and the stomach produces its own worms:

879   Quid de lumbricis quos gingnunt intima dicis?
       In stomachi uillis pressura redundat ab illis.

(2) *Self-willed misfortunes* (881–946). From Original Sin, the poet turns to the miseries that we bring on ourselves:

881   Hic reticere uolo mala que sunt a patre solo;
       Proxima que subeunt a nobis et patre fiunt.
       A nobis quando? Minus affectum moderando
       Spe uacua lusi sumus in discrimina trusi.
885   A patre quando bonis diuine condicionis
       In patre priuati sumus ad mala multa dicati

Three examples are given, a courtier, a soldier and a peasant (of which the last is incomplete).

(a) Ambition at court (887–920). Someone seeks fame and fortune at the king's court:

891   Hic ut honoretur et diuiciis oneretur
       Regia tecta terit; regi se iungere querit

---

[40] parte: parce MS.

He is driven off by the servants; he returns but is imprisoned, beaten, and finally led to execution:

916 Et laqueo furum pudet appendi moriturum,

Et rogus in nichilum redigit uel culleus illum,

Et cruciante rota sero dampnat sua uota

(b) Some take up arms as a soldier (921–44):

921 Pugnant inmites abrupta pace quirites

Et terit armorum grauitudo corpus eorum

They fear nothing as long as they achieve their ambition:

925 Dum modo summopere querant quod proposuere,

Et nomen clarum uel aceruum diuiciarum

They endure heat and cold, and have to spend nights outdoors; both attackers and defenders often suffer death without achieving their reward:

941 Sepe uidemus in hiis tot milia facta ruinis,

Quot leto strata, tot uulnere debilitata.

Hinc equites duri uexantur amore futuri,

Antea detriti quam sint mercede potiti

(c) There are just two lines on peasants:

945 Rusticus exercet sua iura bouesque choercet

Nexibus et loris ad opus solempne laboris

§

The poem ends here. Clearly there should be more on the peasant and his woes, and the misfortunes inflicted by the Devil ("multa diabolico fieri de fomite dico," 529) would need a section to itself. Assuming that there was some kind of general conclusion to the poem, I would estimate that at least a hundred lines are lacking.

University of Toronto

A . I . D O Y L E

"*Lectulus noster floridus*": An Allegory of the Penitent Soul

he Middle English prose piece edited here may have had a single source in another language but I have not traced it. There is no relation, for instance, to a sermon on the same words from the Song of Songs (1.15) attributed to Heinrich Suso.[1] Wolfgang Riehle has mentioned the interpretation of the soul as a bed in Hugh of St. Victor, the *Ormulum*, and Richard Rolle, and as a "chambre secrete" in *The Mirror of Simple Souls* (translated from Margarete Porete, d. 1310).[2] The elaboration of the allegory combines the mystical with moral applications, as had been done in the vernacular as well as Latin since the thirteenth century at least. In the Summa "Postquam," the knowledge of which we owe to Siegfried Wenzel, we have "Meekness is the soft pillow on the bed of conscience, on which our soul rests in safety," and he notes that the image of the pillow also occurs in Hugh of St. Cher's gloss on Matthew 5.4 (*Beati mites . . .*).[3] In the *Somme le Roi* of Frère Laurent and its English versions there are the soul as the garden of God, with Dread as the door-keeper, and Shrift as the chamberlain sweeping the house,[4] or the lady Dread as porter of the cloister in the *Abbey of the Holy Ghost*, likewise from a French original of the thirteenth century.[5] In the *Pilgrimage of the Lyf of the Manhode*, the English

---

[1] *Altdeutsche Predigten*, ed. Wackernagel, 552–61.
[2] Riehle, *Middle English Mystics*, 38.
[3] Wenzel, ed., *Summa virtutum*, 154–55, 345.
[4] Michael of Northgate, *Ayenbite of Inwyt*, ed. Morris, 1:94, 121; *The Book of Vices and Virtues*, ed. Francis, 172.
[5] *Yorkshire Writers*, ed. Horstman, 1:329.

prose version from Deguileville (d. ca. 1360), we find Penitence as chamberer to God the Father.[6] And in the fifteenth-century English "letter sent to a religious woman of the twelve fruits of the holy gost" we read "so suche a Joyful soule restith more swetly in such a bedde of clennes: þan in a bedde of synnes. of þis swete bedde of flouris spekith salomon in þe boke of loue. in þe persone of all mery soules in clennes. lectulus noster floridus. Oure bedde he seith of oure consciens. smellith swete with flouris of vertu. where in we rest with oute torment. of remorse."[7]

The present piece employs these figures together with a selection of catechetical formulations: the three theological virtues, ten commandments, seven works of mercy, four ages, four cardinal virtues, the four daughters of God, and the five wits, interspersed with a number of less tabulated concepts; amendment and prayer, sorrow and meditation, abstinence and chastity, pity and patience, good works, free will and free choice, right and reason, understanding and wisdom, silence, perseverance, compassion, conscience, dread, tears. The instruction is better than rudimentary. It is addressed (in every copy) to a man or a woman, without limitation of status, clerical, religious or lay. The language and style of the piece are compatible with a late fourteenth- or early fifteenth-century origin in the southern half of England.[8] I know of four separate copies in manuscripts ranging from perhaps the first decade of the fifteenth century to the second decade of the sixteenth, two copies incorporated in the large mid-fifteenth-century Middle English compilation entitled *Disce mori* and one in the related English work referred to (from its starting text) as *Ignorancia sacerdotum* (after 1442 or 1446).[9] In view of the demonstrated number of other derivative passages in the last two works[10] and of the apparently earlier dates of two or

---

[6] Deguileville, *Pilgrimage*, ed. Henry, 1:27–32.

[7] *A Devout Treatyse*, ed. Vaissier, 52, lines 15–19.

[8] The interesting vocabulary is all well attested by this period in the *Middle English Dictionary* or the *Oxford English Dictionary*. The first scriptural quotation coincides with the Later Version of the Lollard Bible and one other with both Early and Late Versions, but the others are independent.

[9] Cf. Jolliffe, *A Checklist*, 113–14, (I.35); Raymo, "Works of Instruction," 2334–35, 2542.

[10] Raymo, 2263–64, and see note 25 below.

three of the separate copies, there is no reason to think that the piece is an extract from the former, but rather that it is an independent composition.

The copy on which the text below is based is on fols. 74v–75v of University College, Oxford, MS. 123,[11] by the same minute, neat anglicana formata of early fifteenth-century character as the rest of the volume. It follows the *Mirror of the Life of Christ* of Nicholas Love, without his name or either of the Latin notes found in many copies, of which one records its approbation about 1410 by Archbishop Arundel, so it is conceivable that this copy may have been made previously, or else be taken from a copy which was.[12] After the *Lectus* comes another short treatise, a unique copy so far as I know, on fols. 76–77v, justifying the seven sacraments from the New Testament against heretical diminution. This echoes the express purpose of the *Mirror*, and its appended short treatise on the Eucharist, against the Lollards. The book is in a London binding of ca. 1520, and from the quality of its membrane and writing could be a professional product there of a hundred years or so before. Its language is assigned to Buckinghamshire.[13]

Bodleian Library, Oxford, MS. Douce 302 is the collection of poems, with a couple of prose pieces, made by John Audelay, a blind chantry priest at the Augustinian Haghmond Abbey, Shropshire, in and possibly after 1426.[14] The two prose pieces occur in the second half of the collection, by the main hand, under one original item number (36) but are divided by four blank lines; the first, fol. 32r–v, is an extract from Rolle's *Form of Living*, chapter 6, on sins of heart, mouth, deed and omission, unascribed, and inserted into the last at the appropriate point one finds an alliterative thirteen-line rhyming stanza on "ouerhippers and skippers" of divine service, related to verses in the *Fasciculus Morum*.[15] The words "Quicumque inspexe-

---

[11] Coxe, *Catalogus Codicum Manuscriptorum*, 1:36–37.

[12] Doyle, "Reflections."

[13] Oldham, *English Blind-stamped Bindings*, AN.k.(1); McIntosh et al., *A Linguistic Atlas*, 1:154, 3:18.

[14] *The Poems of John Audelay*, ed. Whiting; *Summary Catalogue*, 4:585–86, no. 21876. The colophon giving the date is on fol. 22v and may be only that of the composition of the preceding poems (calling them a book entitled *Concilium Consciencie*, *Scala Dei* and *Vita Salutis Eterni*) or of a previous copy, since the rest of this manuscript is uniform.

[15] Rolle, *English Writings*, ed. Allen, 97–99, lines 10–100; the insertion occurs at

rit" before the blank show that this piece was meant for the examination of conscience and confession, to which the piece on the bed,
fols. 32v–33v, would be the sequel. Like a number of the poems of
the collection, there is no reason to think it Audelay's own composition, and his poem on St. Brigit of Sweden, with its reference to the
foundation of Syon Abbey (written after 1422 and before 1431),
shows that he was not out of touch with regions other than the West
Midlands. It has been suggested that corruptions in the texts of the
poems are owing to dictation, but that is less likely with the prose
pieces. The book later passed through the hands of a Coventry
minstral to an Austin canon of Launde, Leicestershire.[16]

Another copy of the *Lectus*, or *Bed*, is on fols. 49v–52 of St.
John's College, Cambridge, MS. G.8, by the second hand of the
volume, an anglicana formata probably of the second rather than first
quarter of the fifteenth century.[17] It immediately follows a copy of
the *Speculum Christiani*, with the only known ascription of that
work to Philip de Spencer, a person unfortunately not yet identified.[18] The other contents are wholly in Latin, the next piece in the
same hand being on the obligation of priests and other clerics to the
divine office, and a third collaborator is responsible for the *Scala
claustralium* of Guigo II, prior of the Grande Chartreuse, anonymous
here.[19] This volume, in a medieval wrapper, looks like the product

---

the middle of line 87; cf. Wenzel, *Verses in Sermons*, 184–86; Wenzel, ed., *Fasciculus
morum*, 418. All but the last four lines are written as prose and were recognized as
making up the stanza by Susanna Fein. The second hand observed by Whiting, viii,
was responsible for corrections, as of this passage, and also headings throughout the
volume, besides the last poem; what she took as a third hand for *Cur mundus
militat* on fol. 34v is probably a more formal mode (bastard anglicana) of the
second; cf. "Quicumque inspexerit" on fol. 32v.

[16] The language of both hands is of Staffordshire, where the town of Audley
lies, and the last two poems in the manuscript, thought not to be John Audelay's
own compositions but earlier, one in each hand, have more northerly features than
Shropshire: McIntosh et al., *Atlas*, 1:148, 3:454–55; McIntosh, "Some Notes."
Versions of other poems are found in the Vernon manuscript, from north Worcestershire: Doyle, "Shaping," 9 n. 31.

[17] James, *Descriptive Catalogue of St. John's College*, 210–11.

[18] *Speculum Christiani*, ed. Holmstedt; for its Carthusian connections see
Gillespie, "Cura Pastoralis in Deserto."

[19] Guigo II, *Lettre sur la vie contemplative, Douze méditations*, ed. Colledge and
Walsh, 10–12, 45–46: the St. John's copy appears to belong to group IV(e).

of a clerical community, and the language of the *Speculum Christiani* is assigned to Nottinghamshire.[20]

The fourth separate copy is in Bodleian Library, Oxford, MS. Laud misc. 19, fols. 22v–30v, an octavo paper booklet with a laced glove and star watermark of the 1520s or 1530s[21] of devotional pieces in English, starting with an instruction to a "Brother," based on and including extracts from Hilton's *Scale of Perfection*. After the *Bed* follows an indulgence for saying the Hundred Pater Nosters and some well-known verses on the name and passion of Jesus coupled with a prose account of what are elsewhere identifiable as the Syon prayer beads, here said to be "regestred" (i.e., displayed?) in St. Paul's Cathedral on the south side—all this "written by the hande of your humble servant and daley Bedman Giles Brewse" (fol. 33v).[22] He was with little doubt of an East Anglian family, the second son of Jane, née Scrope (addressee of Skelton's *Philip Sparowe*) and so nephew of Elizabeth de Vere, Countess of Oxford (d. 1537), in whose will he is mentioned. She was a devout widow and book-owner who made bequests to many religious houses, led by Barking and Syon abbeys and the London and Sheen Charterhouses.[23] Was Giles, thus, writing for a lay or clerical recipient?

The remaining copies of the *Bed* are more closely related, being embodied in three manuscripts of two allied works. The first of these is the *Disce mori*, a large compilation of much more general scope on Christian life and devotion than its title suggests, in English prose with a prefatory poem addressing it to a sister Alice, in seclusion from the world, the flesh and the devil. She was presumably a nun, but possibly an anchoress or vowess.[24] The work is best known for

---

[20] McIntosh et al., *Atlas*, 1:64.

[21] Heawood, "Sources," 440, no. 138; idem, *Watermarks*, no. 2492 etc.

[22] Bodleian Library, *Catalogus Codicum Manuscriptorum*, 2:col. 63, 543; Kirchberger, "The Homely Presence"; Rhodes, "Sixteenth-Century Bed-Making," 6–8, with a modernization of the text; for the Syon or (mistakenly) Sheen beads, about which I am indebted to Dr. Rhodes, cf. Hirsh, "Fifteenth-Century Commentary."

[23] Jane had close relations with the Benedictine nuns of Carrow, Norwich: Edwards, *Skelton*, 292–98; Skelton, *Complete English Poems*, ed. Scattergood, 405–6; Doyle, "Books Connected with the Vere Family." Giles's name also occurs on Rosenbach Foundation, Philadelphia MS. 1083/80, a mid-fifteenth-century manuscript of Hoccleve's *Regiment of Princes* and Walton's Boethius.

[24] Raymo, 2263; *Book of Vices and Virtues*, ed. Francis, xxxix.

its quotation from Chaucer's *Troilus and Criseyde* and its incorporation of passages of Walter Hilton's writings, *Chastising of God's Children*, and other ascetical and contemplative treatises of the later fourteenth or early fifteenth century.[25] In chapter 3 of the final Exhortation, on p. 559 of Jesus College, Oxford, MS. 39, we find "oo þing I counsaile þat þou neuere forgete þis name Jesus ... and maketh for it a bed. and a restyng place. in wise þat foloweth," and on pp. 560–62 the text "Whanne þe chambre. . . ." This is the earlier of two known copies of the work, by a fine secretary hand of the middle of the fifteenth century and with delicately flourished initials.[26] It bears the name of "Dorothe Slyght," who was a nun of Syon at its suppression in 1539, from which it has been supposed that the manuscript (and also the work) originated there. This hypothesis is not unlikely, but she was a widow with property and connections in St. Albans, a related center of monastic and anchoritic spirituality in the first half of the fifteenth century, offering alternative candidates for Dame Alice.[27]

The second copy of *Disce mori* is Bodleian Library MS. Laud misc. 99, where the *Bed* is on fols. 123–24, of the very late fifteenth or early sixteenth century, generally inferior but apparently independently from the same source as the Jesus College manuscript in the extracts from the *Chastising of God's Children*.[28] Its medieval provenance is unknown, but it was probably in the southeast of England in the second half of the sixteenth century.[29]

The allied work is one for priests on fulfilling the pastoral prescriptions of Archbishop Pecham's constitution of 1281, *Ignorancia*

---

[25] Wager, " 'Fleshly Love' "; *Chastising*, ed. Colledge and Bazire, 6, 25–29; Hudson, "A Chapter"; Patterson, "Ambiguity and Interpretation."

[26] Coxe, *Catalogus*, 2:14–15. The beveled boards of the repaired binding appear to be medieval.

[27] In *Chastising*, ed. Colledge and Bazire, 6 n. 1, I am quoted as saying that there were two nuns of the name: this mistake arose from her having made a will, 20 January 1533, while she intended to enter Syon. The will was probated on 10 March 1535, but only after her profession, not death (Public Record Office, London, Prerogative Court of Canterbury, register Hogen 30).

[28] Bodleian Library, *Catalogus Codicum Manuscriptorum*, 2:104, 546; *The Chastising*, 28–29.

[29] It has a note of birth of William Hordern at Putney, 1561, with one godmother from Merton Abbey (Surrey), though such notes were often retrospective.

sacerdotum, but going much further than previous treatments of the subject and in fact largely derived from *Disce mori*.[30] The author says he was a priest and graduate in canon law, aged 59, and as he writes of "my lord seynt Austin," he was probably an Austin canon or friar, or possibly a Dominican or Brigittine, since these two orders also followed the Augustinian rule. It may be that he was also the author of *Disce mori*, from his intimate handling of its contents and the personal style of both. Its reference to William Lyndewode indicates that it was composed after 1442 or 1446.[31] The only known copy of the work, Bodleian Library MS. Eng. th. c. 57, is by two distinct hands of the middle of the fifteenth century with delicate flourishing of initials, and the "Bed" occurs on fols. 131v–32v, following four blank lines after a form of confession, without introduction but with an original side-note "De Lecto. Rubrica" and in a minute form of the same hand in the top outside corner of fol. 132 "De lecto preparato ad inhospitandum sponsum nostrum Jesum Cristum." The textual correspondence here and elsewhere points to this manuscript being directly dependent on Jesus 39, which has many neat contemporaneous marginal directives for copying and omission of passages, corresponding with the content of Eng. th. c. 57 and similar directives there.[32]

My text is based on U(niversity College Oxford MS. 123), with some corrections and augmentation in angle brackets from S(t. John's College Cambridge MS. G.8) and MS. D(ouce 302). Selective evidence is also adduced from M (MS. Laud misc. 19), E (Bodl. MS. Eng. theol. c. 57), and J(esus College Oxford MS. 39). MS. Laud misc. 99 follows Jesus MS. 39. A colon has been used for the punctus elevatus; a double virgule is the usual indicator for a paraph, not filled in U. I have coupled separated elements of prepositions.

---

[30] Hodgson, "*Ignorancia Sacerdotum*"; *Chastising*, 26–27; Raymo, 2264.

[31] He not only refers to Lyndewode as Bishop of St. David's, but to the gloss he "made," which may imply his death.

[32] On fols. 81 and 82 there are tiny marginal notes exactly as in Jesus MS. 39, pp. 158, 161, against the same passage. The first copyist writes fols. 1–55v, the second fols. 56–151, with the *Ignorancia* discourse ending on fol. 141, followed by the *Liber Prophecie Johannis de Rupescissa qui vocatur Vademecum in tribulacione*; a third hand writes fols. 154–56 (with 152 a reject of the top of 154), extracts from three sermons attributed to St. Augustine. The binding is of medieval boards (stripped of the original covering).

The most significant variants imply that none of the separate copies
(U, S, D, M) is derived from any of the others, and there are changes
and corruptions suggestive of longer and wider circulation. U and S are
most frequently paired, then SD and DM. J, E (and L) form a distinct
group, with deliberate variations, but agreeing sometimes with D alone,
pointing to a common parentage nearer the original. Two mistakes in U
("unclene" for "encline," and "who seer" for "ussher") possibly come
from scribal voicing rather than oral transmission, and one in D ("enolyne" or "euolyue" for "enclyne") must be from a written exemplar;
"ri3t" (UJE) for "reuth" is ambiguous.

Bonum lectum

Take here hede and lerne howe3 þou schalt make an honest
bede and a good plesinge vnto god profitabel and worschipful
vnto þi soule.[a]

5   When þe chambour of þi soule þorowe veri confescion[b] is
clensed from alle synne: þen þou schalt araie a bede þere in þis
wise in þe wiche oure lorde iesu crist wille haue likinge[c] to
reste inne. But first þou must make þe a liter. þat schal be made
of mynde of[d] alle þe synnes þat euer þou dedest. and geder
10   hem togeder as into a liter of strey ‖ þane loke þou schake ou3t
of þis liter þat is mynde alle þe duste of synne and of foule
þou3tis wiþ þe schacforke of kyndenes[e] þe wiche schal haue
tuo greynes. þe ton is wille to amende þee: þe toþer is bisy and
deuou3te praier to god in herte 3euenge wiþou3t cessinge þat it
15   so þorowe his grace may be. For poule seiþ. *sine intermissione
orate*. [1 Thess. 5.17] þat is wiþou3t cessinge praie 3e. & crist
seiþ in þe gospel. *Qui perseuerauerit vsque in finem hic saluus
erit*. [Matt. 10.22 or 24.13] þat is who so euer endureþ in to þe
ende in vertue he þis [*sic*] schal be safe.[f] ‖ þe canuas nexte þe

---

[a] Bonum lectum. Take ... soule] *U only*; Lerne I rede þe: howe thy
bedde. made sall be *S*; Here folowyth a short tretyse of making of oure
bedde *M*; De Lecto *E*

[b] confescion] contrition and satisfaction *add. M*

[c] likinge] his plesaunce *JE*

[d] mynde of] *om. M*

[e] kyndenes] hoope of mercie *JE*

[f] is bisy ... be safe] *U*; pray god þat it so be *S*; it may be so *M*; is to pray

20   stree must be bittur^g sorowe for þi synne þe wiche wille if þou
consider welle to þi consciens make þee to water þe litter of þi
bede wiþ þe teres of þine iȝen. < as Dauid says. *Lacrimis meis*
stratum meum rigabo. [Ps. 6.7] with my terys my bed stree y
schall watter. > ^h ‖ þe materas of þe bede schal be holyⁱ medi-
25   tacions þei wille putte ouȝt of þi soule alle foule þouȝttis þat
defoule or <encline >^j hit to synne. and þerfore seiþ þe wise
man. *Peruerse cogitaciones separant animam a deo.* [Sap. 1.3] þat
is unclene þouȝttis departen þe soule fro god.^k ‖ þe two blan-
ketis of þi beed schul be abstinens aȝene glotonye and chastite
30   aȝene lecherie & lust of fleischely likingis and þerfore seiþ
poule. *ab omni specie mala abstinete vos. quia si secundum car-*
nem vixeritis moriemini. si autem facta carnis mortificaueritis
viuetis^l [1 Thess. 5.22]. ‖ þe neþer schete schal be a siker beleue
wiþouȝt any douȝte in any poynte þerof for beleue is grounde
35   of criston religioun.^m ‖ þe ouer schete schal be a siker hope to
be saued þoroweⁿ gode werkes & þorowe þe grete mercy of
oure lorde iesu crist.^o ‖ þe couerlet of þis bede schal be charite
þat is þat þou haue loue^p to god ouer alle þinge and to þi
neiȝtbore as þi self. forþi poule [*sic*] seiþ^q < *Quia caritas operit*
40   *multitudinem peccatorum* >^r [1 Pet. 4.8] þat < is to say > charite coueriþ þe multitude of synnes. ‖ þe pilowe<s>^s þat þe
hede schal be onne schulde be pite and paciens. þat is þou haue

---

god of grace þat hit mow so be *D*; is prayer to god for grace that it so be *JE*

  ^g bittur] enterele *D*; entier *JE*

  ^h as Dauid . . . watter] *om. U*

  ⁱ holy] mody *add. D*; deuoute *JE*

  ^j encline] *SMJE*; unclene *U*; enolyne *or* euolyue *D*

  ^k and þerfore seiþ þe wise man . . . fro god] *om. SDMJE*

  ^l and þerfore seiþ poule . . . viuetis] *om. SDMJE*

  ^m is grownde . . . religioun] is growndytt *D*; it is impossible to plese god
JE

  ⁿ þorowe] by þe passion of Crist and by the mene of *add. JE*

  ^o iesu crist] without whiche þe beleeue is dede *add. JE*

  ^p þat þou haue loue] a trew lofe *SDM*; whiche is a trewe perseuerant loue
JE

  ^q as þi self . . . seiþ] þis may wele be called oportorium *JE*

  ^r Quia caritas . . . peccatorum] *SDJE*; Quia *om. S*

  ^s pilowes] *sing. U, pl. SDM*, ij pelowes *JE*

pite one þe pore[t] and be pacient in aduersite. ‖ þe bolster þat
þe pilowes schul be onne schal be bisines[u] in gode werkes
worchinge lest heuynes wolde make þee to falle into dispere or
to slepe to longe in synne. ‖ þe tester at þe heede schal be <li-
berum arbitrium þat es[v]> fre wille & fre choise. so þat þou
chese no þinge aȝene þe comandement of god. nor helþe of
þine oune soule. ‖ þe courteyne one þe riȝt side schal be riȝt
and resoun. ‖ þe curteyne onne þe left side schal be vndurstandinge & wisdome.[w] lat þes tuo courteynes renne one tene
ringgis of þe tene comandementis and loke no rynge be broken.
for if þei be broken þe curteynes wille sagge downe.[x] and
þanne þe enmy þe fende may loke ouer into þi bede of iesu. ‖
þe curteyne at þe feet schal be þine owne wille. lat it renne one
vij ringgis of þe vij werkis of mercy. so þat alle þi bisines be as
ferforþe as þou maist euer more to plese god. and if þi free
chois wolde perauenture chese any þing at þ<e>[y] counselle
of þi wille loke þou do it neuer but if resoun and vnderstand-
inge be cheffe of þi councel and acorde welle þerto. ‖ þe sil-
loure ouer þi bede schal be silens. þat is kepinge þi tounge so
þat þou sclander no man ne þe name of god in ydelnes. and in
gret oþes sweringe <Kepe the fro bakbityng>[z] and foule
wordes speikinge. ‖ Lat þe corde þat þe siller schal be tied vp
wiþ to þee rydels be made of dowbel silke or twyne of perse-
uerance þat is wille to abide stille in þi gode lyuynge al þi life
into þe last endynge. ‖ þe hokes þat þe rydelis schul be tyed vp
with is a siker purpos neuer to turne aȝene into synne. ‖ þou
must haue ane hamour þat þei must be smyten in wiþ into þe
foure wallis of þi chambour. þes wallis ben þe foure ages wiche
ben þes. childe-hode. ȝougþe. and perfiȝte age. and þi last age as
when þou art an olde man or an olde woman. ‖ þis hamour
schal be compascioun of þe gret payne þat oure lorde iesu crist

[t] pore] pepill *add. SDM*
[u] bisines] and wakyng *add. DJE*
[v] liberum arbitrium þat es] *om. U*
[w] vndurstandinge & wisdome] u. *om. JE;* w. *om. S*
[x] downe] *om. SJE*
[y] þe] þi *U*
[z] Kepe the fro bakbityng] *om. UJE*

suffered one þe rode tree for þee. þe hede of þine hamour schal
be made of þe harde nayles of iren þat nailed þe handes and þe
feet of oure lorde iesu crist to þe cros. ‖ þe schaft þerof schal
be made of þe cros þat oure lorde iesu died vpon. take þis
hamour heed wiþ þe shaft < with þe scharpe poynte of þe spere
hede þat smote iesu to þe hert >[a] and þe scharpe þornes þat
þrilleden his brane panne. þis beed ȝut[b] must be borded lest þe
streye wille falle ouȝt. þes foure bordes of þis bede must be þe
foure cardenal vertues. and þou must be stronge in beleue[c]
< of > aȝeyne temptacions of þe fende. þou must be prudent
sly ware and wise. aȝene alle þes worldely sleiȝttis and sotel-
tes.[d] þou must haue temperance aȝene fleiscly likinge.[e] and
þou must be riȝtful in alle maner lyuynge & þanne naile togeder þes bordes at þe foure corneris. wiþ pes, treuþe. mekenes.
& < reuth >.[f] and loke þanne þat alle þ<e>[g] cloþes of þi
beede be white in token of clennes. and powder þerinne þo
rede roses portrede[h] wiþ þe reede blode þat oure lorde iesu
crist schade in his passioun. þis is þe bede þat oure lorde iesu
crist speikeþ of in his < boke >[i] of loue.[j] and seiþ < Canticorum primo [15] Lectulus noster iam floridus est >[k] oure bede
is ful of floures. ‖ þi chamburleyne schal be þi consciens.[l] for
he can aspie defauȝttis. and lat hym liȝt vp a lampe of loue þat
he may see abowȝte hym. < Make > drede < usshyer >[m] at þe
dore of þi chambour for he wille noþinge latt in at þe dore ne

75
80
85
90
95

---

[a] with … hert] *om. USM*
[b] þis beed ȝut] Bot this bed *S*; Bot ȝet þis bede *D*
[c] beleue] of *add. U*
[d] soteltes] couetise *JE*
[e] likinge] lustis *D*; desires *JE*
[f] reuth] riȝt *UJE*; pity *M*
[g] þe] þi *U*
[h] portrede] pouder *DMJE*
[i] boke] *om. U*
[j] loue] lawe *D*
[k] Canticorum … est] *DJE*; Lectus *JE*; iam *om. JE*
[l] þi chamburleyne shal be þi consciens] Make concyence þi chaumbyr-
leyn *SDM*; Lete goode conscience wele ruled be þi chamberleyn *JE*
[m] Make drede usshyer] in drede who seer be *U*; *JE diverge widely from
others here up to the end of the text*

at þe ȝate[n] ne at þe wyndowes of þi v wittis þat schulde
<raise>[o] oure lorde iesu crist from his rest ne defoule his
100   chambour ne disaray his bede. In þis bede[p] oure lorde iesu crist
<will haue>[q] likinge to abide & reste inne. Deuouȝte pray-
our and swete teres of deuociun schal brynge þe gode lorde þe
louely spouse iesu to þis likinge bede of þi cely soule. & wiþ
hym many heuenly consolaciouns and make þis bede al whote
105   þorow verfure of deuoscioun. þane maist þou tast somdel
þorow grace howe swete þi spouse is in his loueris.[r] & whane
he is þus in þi bed angelis wille synge abouȝte hym þis songe of
þe prophecie. <*Exulta & lauda habitacio syon. quia magnus in
medio tuo sanctus israel*>[s] [Is. 12.6] þow syon mannes soule þe
110   duellinge place of iesu: be þou ioyful and glade for þe grete
holy god of israel is nowe wiþinne wiþ þee. þe wiche is iesu so
mut it be. Amen.

Explicit lectus Floridus.[t]

University of Durham

---

[n] ne at þe ȝate] *om. SDMJE*
[o] raise] *om. U*
[p] In þis bede] Thys es þe bed þat *SDM*
[q] will haue] haue wille and *U*
[r] Deuouȝte ... loueris] *om. DJE*
[s] Exulta ... israel] *D*
[t] Explicit lectus floridus] *U only*

CHRISTINA VON NOLCKEN

A "Certain Sameness"
and Our Response to It
in English Wycliffite Texts

he texts with which Wycliffite (or Lollard) teachers and
preachers sustained their flocks offer an obvious test case
regarding the extent to which it is possible for us successfully
to "negotiate" the past.[1] As has been remarked more than once, they
were written as if for initiates.[2] Their authors also assumed that
whether or not a person was an initiate depended on his moral rather
than his intellectual disposition. Admittedly, they convey their views
on such matters mainly in relation to the Bible, the text they did no
more than translate:

> He that redith scriptures of God and wole fynde God, and his
> good lyuynge is maad as the legt of lampe bifore hise iyen of
> his herte, and openeth the wai of treuthe. Treuli he that hastith
> not to leue worthili to God and redith of God, sekith not God
> to his helthe, but onli the kunnynge of God to ven glorie.
> Therfore thoug he rede euere he schal neuere fynde; as neithir
> philosophiris founden, wiche sougten for the same cause.
> (*The Holi Prophete Dauid seith*, ed. Deanesly, 450)

But they would certainly have considered such views relevant to what
they wrote themselves. When William Thorpe describes a properly

---

[1] On the terms "Wycliffite" and "Lollard," see Hudson, *Premature Reformation*,
2-4. "Negotiate" is, of course, the term Patterson, *Negotiating the Past*, uses of the
activity that issues in historical understanding.

[2] By, for example, Hudson, "A Neglected Wycliffite Text," in *Lollards and Their
Books*, 62; eadem, "Wycliffite Prose," 249; Spencer, "Fortunes of a Lollard Sermon-
Cycle," 390.

disposed sermon audience, for example, it consists of "all the faithful lovers and followers of Christ [who] have all their delight to hear God's Word, and to understand it truly, and to work thereafter faithfully and continually"; when he describes an improperly disposed one it consists of "lusty men and worldly lovers [who] delight and covet and travail to have all their wits quickened and sharpened with divers sensible solace" (Pollard, ed., "The Examination," 142).[3] It would seem that any merely intellectual attempt we might make to reach what the original users of these texts would have considered their meaning must be doomed to failure.

It is hardly surprising, therefore, that modern readers seem not on the whole to have made such an attempt. The writers of recent scholarly literature have undoubtedly made great advances in identifying Wycliffite texts and in providing them with their historical and social contexts.[4] But when responding to the texts these scholars have all too often simply echoed a remark Matthew made as long ago as 1880: "It cannot be denied that there is a certain sameness which makes these tracts rather tiresome to read continuously" (*The English Works*—henceforth M—, xlviii).[5]

It is true that if anyone could respond with justice to the Wycliffites' texts, Matthew could, for when he made this remark he had just edited some twenty-eight of their tracts and was about to become co-founder of the Wyclif Society. Here, however, he is very obviously responding to the texts from the perspective of his own culture, one that placed a premium on the difference that comes with individual achievement and one whose criteria for assessing the texts were primarily aesthetic. Under the circumstances, "a certain sameness" could only be "rather tiresome" for him, as it has evidently remained for others since.[6]

---

[3] Hudson is preparing a new edition of this text for the Early English Text Society. For discussion of medieval theories underlying such a concept of audience, see Minnis, "Authorial Intention"; Jeffrey, "Chaucer and Wyclif," especially 115–16.

[4] As, for example, Aston in her collected essays on Wycliffite matters, *Lollards and Reformers*, or Hudson in hers, *Lollards and Their Books*.

[5] See, for example, Hudson's comment on their "repetitiousness" ("Contributions to a History of Wycliffite Writings" in *Lollards and Their Books*, 1), or Bennett and Gray's on their "monotony and wearisome iteration" (*Middle English Literature*, 335). Matthew was not in fact the first to make such dismissive remarks: see, for example, Wyclif, *Last Age*, ed. Todd, ix.

[6] As made clear by some of the publications accompanying the quincentenary of

There does remain room for negotiation between the modern reader and the Wycliffites, however, even as regards this sameness. For in responding to this effect Matthew does not seem to have been responding to one the Wycliffites themselves would have considered irrelevant or without significance. It seems, rather, to have been one they cultivated, and not only in the written texts that have reached us. As Hudson has documented, for example, several of their contemporaries were struck by the predictability with which they deployed certain lexical items.[7] And what the monastic chronicler, Henry Knighton, had to say in the late 1380s or early 1390s about how "amazingly" alike the followers of Wyclif could sound is by now well known; his comments nevertheless deserve quoting in full:

> Similiter et caeteri de secta illa frequenter et absque taciturnitate in suis sermonibus et sermocinationibus inexquisite clamitaverunt, *Trewe Prechoures*, *False Prechoures*, opinionesque mutuas et communes sicut unus ita et omnes. Et ita connexae erant atque concatenatae opiniones eorum, quod qui istas [*sic*] habuit, habuit et alterius; et qui alterius opiniones habuit, habuit et opiniones istius. (*Chronicon*, ed. Lumby, 2:179)

> Et licet de novo conversi, vel subito et recenter hanc sectam imitantes, unum modum statim loquelae et formam concordem suae doctrinae mirabiliter habuerunt; et doctores Evangelicae doctrinae tam viri quam mulieres materno idiomate subito mutato effecti sunt. Et hoc acsi essent de uno gignasio educati et doctrinati ac etiam de unius magistri schola simul referti et nutriti. Quod credibile haberi potest, nam credi absque ambiguitate potest, quod qui eos sibi in servos et malorum dolorum initiatores et invidiarum inter Christicolas propinatores adoptavit, idem ipse eos eadem identitate spiritus sui simul aptavit, et

---

Wyclif's death, there remain some evangelical readers who in certain ways read these texts much as many Wycliffites must have done: see further von Nolcken, "Wyclif in our Times," especially 149–52.

[7] In "A Lollard Sect Vocabulary?" in *Lollards and Their Books*, 165–80. In addition to Knighton's remarks cited below, which she quotes (165–66), she notes those by the Carmelite polemicist, Thomas Netter of Walden, on the Lollards' use of the term *fideles* (167), and by Reginald Pecock on their use of the term *knowun men* (ibid.) and perhaps *Bible men* (168).

conformitate unius loquelae cum fervore desiderii in suum
obsequium inspiravit.   (Ibid., 186–87)[8]

When considering the extent to which it is possible for us to reach the
meaning of the Wycliffites' texts, therefore, we could probably not do
better than to start with their sameness.

We could, doubtless, examine this sameness in relation to various
kinds of features in the Wycliffites' texts. Knighton points the way by
roughly isolating three—the opinions the Wycliffites express, their
vocabulary and phraseology, and (following his "unum modum ...
loquelae") what we might term their overall mode. Of these, the third
is the one we know least about. We already know something of the
sameness of the particular opinions expressed in Wycliffite writings, as
we have traditionally looked to just these opinions when trying to
decide whether or not a text is Wycliffite in the first place.[9] We also
know something of the sameness of their particular lexical choices
thanks largely to Hudson.[10] But their mode we have hardly considered at all.[11] Is is with a feature associable with this, therefore, that
I shall largely concern myself here.

---

[8] On the date of the section containing these extracts, which Knighton enters
under 1382, see Galbraith, "Chronicle."

[9] When identifying texts as Wycliffite, we have tended to rely on the opinions
they express, using for our criteria what we know of Wyclif's own opinions, of those
in texts we have external evidence for accepting as Wycliffite, and those defined by
opponents of the Wycliffites as erroneous or heretical. A useful guide to these
writings is provided by Talbert and Thomson, "Wyclyf and his Followers," 521–33,
supplemented by Hudson, "Contributions to a History of Wycliffite Writings," in
Lollards and Their Books, 1–12, 249–52. For examples of commentators using such
criteria when establishing whether a text is Wycliffite and, if so, how extreme its
Lollardy is, see, for example, Hudson, "A Lollard Quaternion," in *Lollards and Their
Books*, 195; eadem, "The Expurgation of a Lollard Sermon-Cycle," ibid., 201–15; von
Nolcken, "Unremarked Group," 239–41; eadem, *"Piers Plowman,"* 78–82.

[10] See further Hudson's references to such seemingly distinctive items of vocabulary in, for example, "A Neglected Wycliffite Text," in *Lollards and Their Books*, 52–
53. See also Knapp, *Chaucer and the Social Contest*, 68–69; note that Knapp's reference
(150 n. 18) to Hudson's "A Lollard Sect Vocabulary?" in *Lollards and Their Books*
misrepresents both its title and its location.

[11] Those who have attempted to discuss Wycliffite style include Hargreaves,
"Wyclif's Prose," and Knapp, *Style*—note that few today take the sermons here
discussed to be by Wyclif himself. For suggestive discussions of Wyclif's own style,
see Mallard, "Clarity and Dilemma," and Auksi, "Wyclif's Sermons." I have
discussed something of what I take to be the mode of the writing in *"Piers Plowman."* For a rather different approach see Kendall, *Drama of Dissent*, 14–89.

Despite advances made by recent scholarship, we have a lot left to learn both about the Wycliffites' own texts and about some of those adjacent to theirs. We are not yet in a position to discuss what might characterize the mode of Wycliffite writing with much assurance, therefore. Even so, it does seem safe to say that a modal feature shared by very many of the texts we would class polemically as Wycliffite, and one that by its very nature would contribute to any sameness of effect these texts might have, is a tendency to generalize. Wycliffite authors do treat the Gospel narrative in all its historical particularity, whether in translation, paraphrase, or within their exegesis.[12] But the narrative of their own times they tend to generalize, and with a striking moral confidence. As always, when one makes such sweeping claims obvious exceptions immediately spring to mind: texts like "A Lollard Chronicle of the Papacy" (ed. Talbert) that treat the particulars of post-biblical history, for example, or Wyche's account of his particular dealings with Bishop Skirlawe ("The Trial," ed. Matthew) and Thorpe's of his with Archbishop Arundel ("The Examination," ed. Pollard). But in this respect at least these latter texts seem marked; they demand special explanations.[13]

Such a tendency to generalize reveals itself very obviously in how Wycliffite authors treat those they oppose. Very seldom do they do this in terms of particularizing singulars—only occasionally do they give room to such specific figures as the bishop of Norwich (M, 152), Pope Urban (Hudson and Gradon, eds., *English Wycliffite Sermons*—henceforth *EWS*—, 1:609/50, 617/81; 3:278/30), Pope Clement (*EWS*, 1:238/48, 3:278/29), or Archbishop Arundel (*Tractatus de oblacione*

---

[12] We see this especially in their sermons. See, for example, those of the principal vernacular sermon cycle at present being re-edited by Hudson and Gradon (*English Wycliffite Sermons*). These often provide translations of the relevant readings, sometimes in large sections at the beginning of the sermon, more often by spreading the translation in short sections throughout; sometimes by various degrees of paraphrase (see further *English Wycliffite Sermons* 3:lxxvi); the writer then comments on their particulars. In the Latin sermons in Oxford, Bodleian Library MS. Laud misc 200, by contrast, the writer allegorizes the particulars of the biblical text (on these sermons, see further, von Nolcken, "Unremarked Group"); the same is largely true of the sermons in London, British Library, Additional MS. 41321 and related manuscripts (Cigman, ed., *Lollard Sermons*). The tracts tend to refer only less frequently to the Bible and to proceed in a consistently more generalizing way.

[13] I am at present preparing a study of some of these more marked texts, especially Wyche's.

iugis sacrificii, in London, British Library MS. Cotton Titus D. v, fol. 13v).[14] Rather, these authors treat those they oppose in terms of generalizing plurals, and often ones they confidently provide with morally loaded modifiers. As Knighton indicates, for example, they often make these opponents *false prechoures*: (*false prechouris—Select English Works*, ed. Arnold—henceforth A—, 3:274; *falsos predicatores*—Oxford, Bodl. MS. Laud misc. 200—henceforth L—, fol. 6); they likewise make them *false prestis* (*EWS*, 1:231/103–4); *falsi sacerdotes* (L, fol. 26); *falsi seculares sacerdotes simoniaci* (L, fol. 121v); *falsi fratres* (L, fol. 187), *fals prophetes* (*Glossed Gospels*, quoted by Forshall and Madden, eds., *The Holy Bible*—henceforth FM—, 1:x); *religiosi falsi* (L, fol. 140); *falsi Christiani* (L, fol. 67v).[15] Taking a hint from Christ (see *EWS*, 2:340/317–20), they make them *pseudo-clerkys* (*EWS*, 2:52/103, 90/53); *phseudo-frerys* (*EWS*, 2:17/36; M, 296); *pseudopristis* (*EWS*, 3:252/40); even plain *pseudoes* (M, 319, 479). They make them *feyned religious* (A, 3:302); *veyn religious* (M, 273); *owre newe religiowse* (*EWS*, 2:373/196); *worldly clerkis* (A, 3:302); *sacerdotes mali* (L, fol. 66). And they often make them *anticristis clerkis* (M, 273; *EWS*, 2:334/157—this is probably the term they use most often of them); also *anticristis worldly clerkis* (M, 140); *anticristis prechouris* (M, 175); *anticristus preestis* (*EWS*, 2:17/42); *Anticristis proctours* (A, 3:361); *Anticristis sophistris* (A, 3:227); *anticristis truauntis* (*EWS*, 1:652/44); even *Luciferis heretikis* (A, 3:303). Examples could be multiplied, for these authors show themselves quite inventive within their prescribed patterns; what is important is that by using these plurals they generalize those they oppose into the relative sameness of a group. It is a group that still contains some multiplicity, however:

> And in archebischopis & bischopis is þe bodi of anticrist. But in þise cloutid sectis, as mounkis chanouns & freris is þe venymous taile of anticrist.
> (*Lanterne of Liȝt*, ed. Swinburn, 16/13–15—henceforth *Lanterne*)

For the grand generalization that could subsume all its members,

---

[14] Anne Hudson is preparing an edition of this text for EETS; I am grateful to her for letting me see her typescript.

[15] Such diction tends to be ubiquitous; I have, therefore, normally contented myself in this and the following sections with one or two examples of each usage, usually selected at random. The forms of the examples are of the first cited.

usually Antichrist, sometimes Satan, the Fiend, or Lucifer, has only done so intermittently.[16]

Hardly surprisingly, this tendency also reveals itself in how these Wycliffite authors treat those they support. For again, they do this in terms of generalizing plurals, and again, they often provide these with morally loaded modifiers. We find Knighton's *trewe prechoures*, thus, (as *trewe prechours—Lanterne*, 101/2, cited by Hudson in *Lollards and Their Books*, 166; *ueros predicatores—L*, fol. 18v); *veros prophetas & predicatores* (L, fol. 19); we also find *trewe men* (*EWS*, 1:637/48, 639/19); *trewe cristen men* (in *Selections*, ed. Hudson—henceforth *SEWW—*, 20/50, cited in Hudson, *Lollards and Their Books*, 167); *trewe men in Crist* (*EWS*, 2:329/32), *trewe preestis* (*EWS*, 2:17/27–28; M, 79), *trewe clerkis* (M, 236), *trewe techeris of cristis mekenesse* (M, 119), *trewe techeris of cristis lif & goddis hestis* (M, 134). We find *fideles predicatores* (L, fol. 18v); *pore men* (M, 87); *pore cristen men* (*Glossed Gospels*, quoted FM, 1:ix), *pore prestis* (M, 79); *pore clerkis* (M, 237); *symple men* (*EWS*, 2:58/105) *symple preestis* (*EWS*, 2:16/3); *simplices sacerdotes* (L, fol. 187); and *Cristys prechowres* (*EWS*, 1:242/59).[17] Sometimes we find simply *men* (*EWS*, 1:599/40, 600/66—the identification of the sermon writer with these is particularly marked here); *many men* (*EWS*, 1:635/43; 2:19/87, 91); also *sum men* (*EWS*, 1:616/71, 2:328/4); and *summen* (M, 421). Almost always we find the relative sameness of a group, however, although again, the grand

---

[16] See, for example, fluctuations such as "& ʒit anticristis clerkis tellen false lesyngis. . . . And so anticrist wolde. . . ," (Matthew, *English Works of Wyclif*, 273), or between "þese frerys" and "antecrist" (*English Wycliffite Sermons* 2:17/29, 32).

[17] As Hudson, *Lollards and Their Books*, 167, has noted, the term *trewe men* probably traces to 2 Cor. 6.8; Matth. 5.3 could similarly be the source for the modifier *poor* (see further *English Wycliffite Sermons* 2:72/36, for the translation "pore men" here); Matth. 10.16 could perhaps account for the liking for *simplices*. It may be, however, that we should look to the patristic quotations so much favored by the Wycliffites for sources for some of these usages: see, for example, von Nolcken, ed., *Middle English Translation*, 91/28–31 for a passage from Gregory that could have helped establish "pore symple men and ydiotis" (Lat., following Cambridge, Gonville and Caius MS. 217/232, fol. 162v, "pauperes simplices & ydiotas"); 92/40–41 for a passage from Augustine cited in Canon Law that could have helped establish "trew men or untrew" (Lat. "fidelis siue infidelis"—fol. 163r); and 93/18–24 for a passage from the *Opus imperfectum in Matthaeum* that could have helped establish the idea of a *trew* versus a *false Cristen man* (Lat. *verus* versus *falsus christianus—*fol. 214r). For terms Wyclif uses of those he supports, see, for example, Cannon's chart in "Poor Priests," 463; Workman, *John Wyclif*, 2:201 n. 2.

generalization that could subsume all its members, this time Christ, has done so only intermittently.[18]

Just how much these authors liked to generalize probably reveals itself best in how they present their particular selves. As has often been remarked, they do not surround themselves with any of the particularizing details that would help us identify them.[19] They do sometimes refer to themselves in the singular. But when they do, they use highly conventionalized terms, ones also often accompanied by modifiers very similar to the ones they use of those they support: "a symple creature" claims responsibility for the Wyclif Bible translation (FM, 1:57), for example; "quidam ruralis simplex discipulus" for a tract on images in Prague Univ. MS. X. E. 9, fols. 210ff. (Loserth, *Shirley's Catalogue*, 8, no. 27); "a synful caytif" (FM, 1:viii), "a pore caityf" (FM, 1:ix), "a symple creature of God" (FM, 1:ix) for various of the *Glossed Gospels* (also "this coward synful caitiff," "this poor scribbler," "this scribbler," "a simple creature").[20] It has been suggested that these terms could inform an initiated audience about the identities of particular authors.[21] This is unlikely, however, given that what these authors really seem to have liked to do is refer to themselves in the plural. Sometimes they merge their singular selves into the group: the author of the "General Prologue" wavers between presenting himself in the singular or as one of a group, for example,[22]

---

[18] See, for example, fluctuations such as "Clerkis possessioners pursuen crist to deþ (. . .) & pursuen falsely to deþ trewe techeris of cristis lif & goddis hestis" (Matthew, *English Works of Wyclif*, 134).

[19] On the anonymity and datelessness of Wycliffite texts, see especially Hudson, *Premature Reformation*, 9–18: she comments (17) on how "infuriatingly vague" topical references in these texts tend to be. On how rare such details are in Wyclif's own texts, see, for example, Workman, *John Wyclif*, 1:52; Thomson, *Latin Writings of John Wyclyf*, 9.

[20] For a list of these terms, see Deanesly, *Lollard Bible*, 276–77. On the use of such terminology by the author of *The Pore Caitif*, see Brady, "Lollard Sources," 406–7. Brady argues convincingly (391–409) that the *Glossed Gospels* constitute one of the sources of *The Pore Caitif*.

[21] As by Deanesly when trying to assign material to Purvey (*Lollard Bible*, 275–77). See, however, Hudson, "John Purvey: A Reconsideration of the Evidence for his Life and Writings," in *Lollards and Their Books*, especially 106.

[22] He uses "I" when discussing how he rendered particular Latin constructions into English (Forshall and Madden, eds., *Holy Bible*, 1:57), but says "diuerse felawis and helperis" helped him establish a good text of the Latin Bible (ibid.); when he refers to the finished English product as "the trewe and hool translacioun of symple

and in *Five Questions on Love* the "men" trying to answer the questions in English merge the "mek prest in God" who was originally asked the questions into their own group (A, 3:183–85).[23] Perhaps more often, they present themselves as a group from the start: "pauperes sacerdotes" and "inbecilles" in the case of the *Floretum* (von Nolcken, "Notes on Lollard Citation," 432–33/8, 12), for example; "pauperculi sacerdotes" in the case of a complaining letter probably to Archbishop Arundel (*Snappe's Formulary*, ed. Salter, 131); "we pore men, tresoreris of Cryst and his apostlis" in the case of the *Twelve Conclusions* (*SEWW*, 24/1).[24] *We* is a pronoun these writers favor.[25]

It is possible, of course, that these authors generalize themselves rhetorically in these ways because they actually worked on their texts in groups. We have good reason to believe that they did this in the case of the Wyclif Bible translation, and it is likely that they also did in the case of some of their other larger efforts.[26] Hudson has argued convincingly for the collaborative nature of the *Glossed Gospels* (*Premature Reformation*, 248–56), thus, and has also noted that the same is probably true of the Wycliffite Psalter commentaries (ibid., 259–64). It is also likely that these authors worked together on some of their sermon collections.[27] Although that anti-Lollard polemicist, Thomas

---

men" (Forshall and Madden, eds., *Holy Bible*, 1:58), he seems to be mainly thinking of the "symple men" as its translators rather than as its possessors, though the ambiguity is telling. This section has also been edited by Hudson (*Selections from English Wycliffite Writings*, 67–72, 173–77); she suggests elsewhere (*Premature Reformation*, 243) that the author's use of the singular is "only for ease of expression."

[23] This tract follows Wyclif's *De amore sive ad Quinque quaestiones* (ed. Loserth, *Opera minora*, 8–10), where the "men" do not appear; instead the constructions used, *patet* (8/11), for example, are impersonal. The sermons in L are similarly impersonal; that on fols. 202v–207r, which is obviously unlike the other sermons of the group in that it explicitly follows Grosseteste's Dictum 119 throughout, is also exceptional in its "declarabo" (fol. 202v).

[24] A usage also recorded in a bull from Boniface IX to King Richard, which considers the Lollards pseudo-Christians "qui se pauperes homines thesauri Cristi et eius discipulorum nuncupant" (Capes, ed., *Registrum*, 406).

[25] Knapp (*Style*, 46), for example, observes of the sermons in the main vernacular cycle that "I" occurs only ten times, and then almost exclusively in constructions such as "I wot" or "I ween"; her point is valid, although her figure is too low.

[26] On the Wycliffite Bible translation: Hudson, *Premature Reformation*, 238–47.

[27] Under 1382 the author of the *Continuatio eulogii* indicates that they did this (Haydon, ed., *Eulogium historiarum*, 3:355), and this may well be what happened, though in a very controlled way, in the case of the vernacular sermon cycle (see further *English Wycliffite Sermons* 3:xcviii).

Netter of Walden, refers to a single "author Floreti" too, we should probably believe its Prologue that a group was responsible for it, as the work is very long and follows a format that invites group endeavor.[28] The Wycliffites' habit of taking over and adapting existing texts or parts of texts also means that even if the communal activity didn't take place at a particular time, it did over a longer one.[29] Nevertheless, the similarity of the diction these authors use of themselves with the diction they use of those they support suggests that there is more conceptually to these generalizing plurals than we can explain so literally. We are dealing with authors who want to present themselves as writing both as and from a group.

They also present themselves as writing for this group—this is one of the features, indeed, that makes their texts seem written as if for initiates. Again, those they address are sometimes singular persons.[30] But when they are, it is very seldom that they are anything other than unparticularized *thous*—Wyche is highly exceptional in addressing a particular person—one with a wife and a mother-in-law ("The Trial," ed. Matthew, 543)—in a specific community.[31] Again, it is possible that these authors refer to their audience in the plural because this audience actually was a group. Obviously it would have been in the case of the sermons, and we have far more evidence that the Wycliffites heard and studied their texts in groups than that they did these things as individuals.[32] But in a period when vernacular texts of reli-

---

[28] Netter's references to the *Floretum* (*Doctrinale*, ed. Blanciotti, 2:cols. 793, 834, 837) were first noted by Hudson, "A Lollard Compilation in England and Bohemia," in *Lollards and Their Books*, 41. As Netter was probably writing this section in the 1420s, well after the *Floretum* was compiled (before 1396, as established by an *explicit* in London, British Library MS. Harley 401), it is likely that he did not know anything about the actual processes of compilation.

[29] On this habit, see further Hudson, *Premature Reformation*, 27–29. It may be that some such process will account for the variety noted by Cigman of the group of vernacular sermons she has edited; as she puts it, "(T)he variety of style, structure and content indicate that this collection may have been the work of several writers" ("Preacher as Reformer," 70; see further *Lollard Sermons*, li, lii, lxvii). See also above, n. 23, on an earlier sermon obviously inserted into the collection in L.

[30] See, for example, Cigman's note (*Lollard Sermons*, xliv).

[31] Although Wyche does not name the friend he primarily addresses, he sends messages and greetings to others whom he does name, *Laudens* and *Greme* (*sic*), for example (Matthew, ed., "The Trial," 543).

[32] On Lollard schools and "underground reading parties," see Aston, "Lollardy and Literacy," in *Lollards and Reformers*, especially 198–206. On the centrality of the

gious instruction were very often written for single persons—even for single persons whose existence scholars have questioned—,[33] we cannot but be struck by the extent to which Wycliffite authors write instead for a plural audience. The compiler of the "Short Gloss" on Luke writes, thus, for "the pore men of his nacioun" (FM, 1:ix), that of the gloss on John for "pore symple men" (ibid.), that of the "Short Gloss" on Matthew for "lewid men & symple lettrid prestis" (Brady, "Lollard Sources," 407); the compiler(s) of the *Floretum* "pro fidei domesticis" ... "ad simplicium Christicolarum illuminacionem" (von Nolcken, "Notes on Lollard Citation," 432-33/14, 24-25).

Despite the prominence in the Wycliffites' texts of this tendency to generalize, where commentators have considered it they have done so only partially and they have explained it inadequately. They have normally pointed only to the reluctance of Wycliffite authors to provide any particulars about themselves and their immediate audience, and they have then tried to explain this reluctance in terms of a persecuted community's need for secrecy.[34] Such an explanation undoubtedly has some validity. It is true that as time went on the Wycliffites increasingly risked loss of career, later of life, for holding their opinions. It is also true that our ignorance of the particular circumstances surrounding the composition of particular texts does sometimes stem from the erasure of relevant information.[35] But in itself this explanation tells us little about the texts' larger liking for generalization, or the moral confidence that accompanies it.[36] For a more adequate explanation of these features we clearly need to look elsewhere.[37]

---

group during the later years of Lollard history, see Hudson, *Premature Reformation*, 449-51.

[33] As in *Chastising of God's Children*, ed. Colledge and Bazire, 41.

[34] See, for example, Forshall and Madden, eds., *Holy Bible* 1:xiii; McFarlane, *Wycliffe and English Nonconformity*, 125; Brady, "Lollard Sources," 407.

[35] On the erasure of ascriptions to Wyclif: von Nolcken, "Lollard Citation," 422.

[36] It is telling here that Hudson has begun associating the anonymity of most Wycliffite texts with features more of the kind we have been considering: see, for example, her passing comments in "Wyclif and his followers," 40; *Lollards and Their Books*, 10; and *Premature Reformation*, 10-11.

[37] In the following section I am heavily indebted to Robson, *Wyclif and the Oxford Schools*; Leff, *Heresy*; Kenny, *Wyclif*.

There has been a good deal of debate recently about Wyclif's realism.[38] Whatever the precise nature of this realism, however, it would have enabled those espousing a version of it to find a real continuity between temporal being as we perceive it through particulars here and the increasingly generalized extra-temporal forms of being we can deduce from these. It would also have encouraged them to try to favor the latter in their thinking. For as is well known, in the face of those he termed "Ockham et multos alios doctores signorum,"[39] Wyclif argued that the universal terms towards which our reason enables us to resolve the particulars that surround us here have real existence as archetypes, ultimately in the mind of God. Unlike those espousing a version of the thinking we usually term nominalist, therefore, he refused to admit the possibility of a real disjunction between the nature of archetypal being as God knows it and that of temporal being here. And as he held that it is God's knowledge of the archetype that ultimately enables us to know it in its particulars, he tended, as Leff has pointed out, to favor higher over lower being:

> There was therefore a chain of being from the archetype in God to the individual in the material world; so that ultimately, as Wyclif himself was wont to say, the individual's existence was merely accidental to its being which inhered eternally in God.   (*Heresy*, 2:502–3)

If the vernacular sermon cycle is to be believed, Wyclif's followers were happy enough to leave such thinking to the scholars, or better still, to the Holy Spirit:

> And certis, siþ þat God wyste, ȝe, byforn he made þis world þat Abraham schulde be, þanne hit was soþ. And herfore seyn clerkys þat euerich creature haþ beyng in his sawmple þat is wiþowten eende.
>
> [...] And so to blaberyng in þis speche mennys voises be not

---

[38] In addition to the discussions listed above, n. 37, see, for example, Paul Vincent Spade's introduction (2:vii–l) to Wyclif, *Tractatus de universalibus*, ed. and trans. Mueller and Kenny; Kenny, "Realism of *De Universalibus*"; Kenny, "Realism and Determinism."

[39] See further Courtenay, *Schools and Scholars*, 350 and n. 60.

sufficient, but som glymeryng we han in owre sowle of þis
trewþe, and bettur knowen hit in owre herte þan we kan speke
hit in voys. And blessud be þe Hooly Goost þat sette syche
wordis in his lawe, þat alle men here in erþe kan vnneþe vndir-
stande hem.   (*EWS*, 1:422/101–4, 107–12)[40]

We cannot doubt, however, that these followers did allow this thinking to inform various of their particular opinions. We see this perhaps
most clearly in their discussion of the Church.[41] Like Wyclif and
unlike their opponents (who seem in this to have been the intellectual
descendants of those *doctores signorum* Wyclif set out to counter), they
were not content to define this in the purely contingent terms appropriate to our perception of particulars here. Instead, they looked
towards it in its higher being and devised a definition appropriate to
this. For them, the church became less a temporal institution populat-
ed both with those who would finally be saved and with those who
would not, than the congregation of those eternally predestined to
salvation.[42] The question "an mali sint pars ecclesie catholice" would
be one that would help define their heresy.[43]

---

[40] We occasionally find some exposition of theory, especially in discussions of the
Eucharist; the Wycliffites are here anxious to counter any belief that after the words
of consecration the accidents of the bread and wine can stand unsupported by substance. See, for example, Arnold, ed., *Select English Works*, 3:352–53, 378–79, 430–31.

[41] We also see it demonstrated in their discussion of the Eucharist: see further
above, n. 40. On the relation of Wyclif's own views with those of his immediate
predecessors and contemporaries see, for example, Leff, "Ockham and Wyclif";
Catto, "John Wyclif and the Cult of the Eucharist"; Keen, "Wyclif, the Bible, and
Transubstantiation."

[42] For examples of such Wycliffite definitions of the Church as "þe congregacion
of juste men for whom Jesus Crist schedde his blood" (Arnold, ed., *Select English
Works*, 3:273), or as "alle þylke þat schulleþ be in blysse after þe dome" (ibid., 3:101);
see further von Nolcken, *Middle English Translation*, 111–12. What is at issue between
the Wycliffites and their opponents is clearly conveyed by Thorpe, when he has
Arundel seek the contingent definition of current orthodoxy while he has himself
insist on one appropriate to its higher as well as to its temporal being (Pollard, ed.,
"Examination of Thorpe," 128–29).

[43] See no. 40 of the jurist's list of questions for use in heresy trials preserved in
the *Register* of Thomas Polton, bishop of Worcester 1426–33 (ed. Hudson, "The
Examination of Lollards," in *Lollards and Their Books*, 134); the answer of a suspect
in 1449 that they are not is recorded in the *Register* of Thomas Bekynton, bishop of
Bath and Wells 1443–65 (ed. Maxwell-Lyte and Dawes, *Register of Bekynton*, 1:124).

In itself, realist thinking like Wyclif's will not explain the confidence with which he and his followers generalize the group they oppose specifically toward Antichrist and the one they support and identify with specifically toward Christ. But as is also well-known, Wyclif further held that the Bible, although composed of books written at particular times by men and about men, is in its essence the Word whereby God reveals to those able to understand something of the nature of the archetypes stored in his mind.[44] Its temporal account of Christ and the members of the apostolic church provided information, therefore, about the qualities of members of the archetypal Church of Christ. And its temporal account of those who opposed Christ and the apostolic church similarly provided information about the qualities of members of the archetypal Church of Antichrist. If Wyclif and his followers confidently generalize those they temporally opposed toward the Church of Antichrist or even toward Antichrist, it is because they can point first to the resemblances between these opponents and Christ's temporal opponents. If they then generalize themselves toward the Church of Christ or even toward Christ, it is because they can see themselves rather than those they oppose as resembling Christ and the members of the apostolic church on earth.[45]

Wycliffite authors do express their awareness that they themselves remained in this temporal being where appearances can still confuse: both Wyclif and the Wycliffites observe repeatedly that we cannot know while here who belongs to which Church.[46] But in their writings at least they do not let this awareness deter them from viewing this being as if from a perspective where these appearances are already beginning to resolve themselves toward essence. They may not always describe what they see in the generalizing terms appropriate to such a

---

[44] Wyclif expounded his view of the Bible mainly in his *De veritate sacre scripture* (ca. 1377–78; ed. Buddensieg). On his view, see Robson, *Wyclif and the Oxford Schools*, 163–64; Smalley, "Bible and Eternity"; Leff, *Heresy*, 2:511–16; Kenny, *Wyclif*, 56–67.

[45] For Wyclif's own confident deployment of a rhetoric of generalization together with many of the specific usages that we have been observing in the texts of the followers, see his *De ve octuplici* (*Opera minora*, ed. Loserth, 313–53), for example, or the works Buddensieg (Wyclif, *Polemical Works*) classed as polemical.

[46] See, for example, Wyclif, *Tractatus de ecclesia*, ed. Loserth, 5/24–27, 77/9–13; *English Wycliffite Sermons* 1:463/112–14, 2:2/39–42.

higher perspective. But even when they don't, they tend to interpret what they see with the moral confidence appropriate to some higher perspective. For them, the relation between higher and lower, inner and outer, is already relatively transparent: hypocrisy need hold little mystery for the narrator of *Pierce the Plowman's Crede*, for example,[47] and Thorpe can easily relate the outer *words* and *works* of those he encounters with their inner *wills*:

> For as their words sound and their works shew to man's judgement, dreading and loving faithfully God; their will, their desire, their love, and their business, are most set to dread to offend God and to love for to please Him in true and faithful keeping of His commandments. And again, they that are said to be in the faith of Holy Church at Shrewsbury and in other places, by open evidence of their proud, envious, malicious, covetous, lecherous, and other foul words and works, neither know nor have will to know nor to occupy their wits truly and effectuously in the right faith of Holy Church.
>
> ("The Examination," ed. Pollard, 122)[48]

The kind of thinking we associate with Wyclif, therefore, can explain a good deal both about Wycliffite texts' liking for generalization and about the moral confidence that accompanies it. It can also tell us something about the texts' sameness. As the authors of these texts generalized toward the higher perspective that made their confidence possible, so the potential scope for their discussion became narrower. Increasingly they had to eschew the variety and multiplicity that belong with particulars here: the many "I"s had to become "we," the "we" ultimately "I" again. Again, these authors may not finally have managed to reach any level very much above the purely temporal: as we have seen, the groups towards which they generalize still contain multiplicity. It remains possible to claim, too, that they do finally manage to discuss a good deal in a variety of ways.[49] Even so,

---

[47] On this poem, see further von Nolcken, *"Piers Plowman,"* 90–96.

[48] On the significance of the words, works and will triad, see Burrow, "Words, Works and Will."

[49] As, for example, does Coleman, who claims that Lollard texts dating from ca. 1384–1425, in the wide spectrum of their interests and the variety of their types, "can be taken as a literary microcosm of the wider literary trends of the period" (*English Literature in History*, 211–12).

that there should be a certain sameness about their texts is inevitable, at least by comparison with texts in the highly particularized style recent commentators have associated with nominalism.[50]

The sameness of Wycliffite texts does not derive only from the overall mode in which the texts were written, however. As we have seen, recent discussion has tended to confirm that it derives also from their authors' common deployment of more particular features, like the terms "trewe prechoures" and "false prechoures" remarked on by Knighton. Space precludes even a cursory examination of such features here. What is important for us to note, however, is that to a far greater extent than the features we have so far been concerned with these are often ones that an individual author must have deployed relatively consciously. They bear witness that sameness was not an effect Wycliffite authors simply accepted as inevitable, but one they also actively sought to achieve. And as we have also seen, they seem to have done this not only as they wrote their texts but also as they lived their lives.

It is only to be expected that the Wycliffites should have developed various means, linguistic and other, to establish a group solidarity, especially given that they were increasingly liable to persecution.[51] It would be easy, therefore, to go some way in explaining why they sought to achieve an effect of sameness by referring to the purely practical. But that they also aimed at a special kind of solidarity, again one informed by their realist vision, is indicated by a further contrast they establish between those they support and those they oppose. Those they support they regularly associate with the impulse toward resolution.[52] And those they oppose they associate with a resistance to this. Where Christ worked in his temporal life for unity, for example, members of the new orders are characterized by diversity:

And þus þei han monye mowþus to preye and to preche wiþ,
for somme preyon for þer breþren, and accepton þer persone

---

[50] For a recent commentator who has made this association, see, for example, Collette, "Critical Approaches," 100.

[51] For brief discussion of what is involved in the development of suitable forms to mark solidarity within the group, see Enkvist, *Linguistic Stylistics*, 64–65.

[52] See, for example, what they have to say about the disciples (as *English Wycliffite Sermons* 2:16/6–8, 247/18–248/37).

byfore God; somme prechen for money, and somme for oþur worldis good. And so onheed of mouþ shulde make acord in holy chyrche; but now dyuersite of mowþus makiþ discord among men. But þis dowblenesse was not in Crist, siþ he traueylude for onhede. (*EWS*, 1:483/69–75)

Where meek priests have one right view of what the rival popes ought to do, "clerkys and lewyde men" are content with many wrong ones:

[R]aþur schulde boþe þes popis go mekely to þe emperour, and renounse al þe lordschipe þat þei han of secleris; and siþ lyue a pore lif as Petur and Poule dydon, and algatis meue no men, ne counseyle hem, to fiȝte þus. And in þis opynyon reston manye meke preestis. In oþer poyntus of þis matere ben an hundret opynyones among clerkys and lewyde men, and alle ben of bataylus. (*EWS*, 2:112/25–31)

Examples could be multiplied. When Wycliffite authors sought to sound alike, it was because they were trying to find the impulse toward resolution in themselves. They wanted to demonstrate in this as well as other more obvious ways that where they really belonged was with the group of those resolving themselves towards the One.[53]

When with Matthew we respond to the sameness of the Wycliffites' texts as "rather tiresome," therefore, we are doing just what their authors would have expected an uninitiated audience to do. We are proclaiming how little moved we are by any impulse toward resolution. We are revealing ourselves just like Thorpe's badly disposed audience, interested only in "divers sensible solace." Our culture is not yet so far removed from that of the Wycliffites that we have to leave things at this, however: we can do both ourselves and the texts better justice than this. We will surely never be able to accept that the greater the sameness of the texts the greater their probable value—to this extent the gap between the kind of criteria we apply when responding to the texts and those the users of these texts would have applied remains absolute. But we can carry our negotiations far enough to realize that if we finally dismiss the texts, it should not be

---

[53] As Wilks, "*Reformatio Regni*," 119, put it, the band of poor priests Wyclif sought to create, "would endeavour in their own lives to emulate the righteousness of their ideal identities."

for an effect that bears witness to what must have been their users' highest aspiration.

University of Chicago

A . J . M I N N I S

Medium and Message:
Henry of Ghent on Scriptural Style

enry of Ghent, a Parisian secular master and one of the key figures in the doctrinal controversies current at the end of the thirteenth century,[1] has been seen, rather simplistically, as an interestingly eclectic thinker who did not subscribe to the tenets of any single school, the evidence consisting of his attempt to effect a reconciliation between certain strands of Neoplatonism and Aristotelianism. Recent research, however, is revealing him as one of the truly great ideological synthesizers of his day, the creator of a system which in its scope and depth rivals those of the Dominican master Thomas Aquinas and the Franciscan master Bonaventure.[2] This paper will attempt to isolate one aspect of Henry's thinking which is particularly germane to the research interests of the distinguished scholar whom we are here meeting in print to honor— no easy task, for the strands of Henry's thought are often so inextricably intertwined that they present the appearance of

---

[1] Between 1278 and 1280 Henry was principal archdeacon of Tournai. From 1270 onwards his main sphere of activity was Paris, where he taught first of all in the university's faculty of arts and subsequently (from ca. 1275 until 1292) in its faculty of theology.

[2] In large measure this changing awareness is due to the work of Dr. Raymond Macken, the co-ordinator of the *Henrici de Gandavo Opera omnia*. See especially his articles "La temporalité radicale," "La théorie de l'illumination," "La volonté humaine," "Les sources," and of course *Bibliotheca manuscripta*. On the earlier volumes of Henry's *quodlibeta* published in the *Opera omnia*, see the notice in *Scriptorium* 39 (1985): 142*–44*; an edition of the *Summa* has been projected. See further Marrone, *Truth and Scientific Knowledge*, and Tachau, *Vision and Certitude*, 28–39.

a seamless web, which cannot be divided without doing violence to the entire fabric.

Our subject is Henry's contribution to what might be termed "sacred stylistics," viz., some of his views on the literary and didactic styles (or *modūs* as they were called at the time) as used by the inspired biblical writers, and indeed by the exegetes who followed in their footsteps. Should theological discourse be obscure, or ornamental, or just plain and simple? And how and in what ways should such language or languages be seen as suiting the capacities of the *auditores* ("listeners," "students," "audience") of the supreme science of theology? In a famous passage in *De doctrina Christiana*, St. Augustine had declared that the Christian teacher has a duty to bring the truth, "no matter how difficult it may be to comprehend or how much labor may be involved, to the understanding of others."[3] Here a principle of classical rhetoric—that one should adapt one's speech to one's audience—is being assimilated to Christian doctrine. Augustine's problem is also Henry's; indeed, this paper may be read, to some extent, as an essay in the "reception history" of *De doctrina Christiana*. Both thinkers grappled with the problem of how the methods of scriptural exegesis could accommodate ancient literary and rhetorical theory. Did the scriptural *auctores* care for eloquence, or was it sufficient for them to be wise? Moreover, to what extent, if at all, should the commentator take the stylistic practices of the *auctores* as models for his own?

Here we will be considering passages from the Prologue to Henry's *Summa quaestionum ordinariarum*, first written ca. 1275–76 and subsequently edited towards the end of his career, in 1289.[4] This long *Introductio ad theologiam*—an exceptionally elaborate amplification of the traditional theological *accessus* or "Aristotelian Prologue"—contains Henry's opinions on those topics which usually occupied the initial position in a *Summa* or *Sentences* commentary:[5]

---

[3] Augustine, *De doctrina Christiana*, 4.9.23 (CCL 32:132).

[4] I am grateful to Dr. Macken for valuable discussion of this dating. On Henry's process of revision, see Macken, "Les corrections d'Henri de Gand à sa Somme"; cf. idem, "Les corrections d'Henri de Gand à ses Quodlibets."

[5] On the development of such introductions in the thirteenth century, see Köpf, *Die Anfänge*; Théry, "An Unedited Text"; Long, "The Science of Theology"; Nash, "Giles of Rome"; Chenu, *La Théologie*; Prassel, *Das Theologieverständnis*. Cf.

"science" or knowledge (*scientia*) and the knowable in general, the manner of knowing and what can be known by man, the human desire and appetite for knowledge, the attainment of knowledge, theology considered as a science in itself, and theology in comparison with the other sciences (these being the subjects of Articles 1–7). Articles 8–20 consider the four causes of theology. After this, Henry proceeds to discuss God in terms of His existence, *quidditas*, unity, nature, essence and knowability, and so forth.

His consideration of the four causes of theology is one of the most sophisticated and thoroughgoing to have survived. Article 8, "Concerning the final cause of theology," discusses the usefulness (*utilitas*) of theology, its necessity for mankind, whether it is a theoretical or practical discipline, and the significance of its having been written down. Articles 9–13 examine what might be called the chain of efficient causality characteristic of theology, beginning with the unmoved mover (God), proceeding to the moved and moving (the teachers and preachers of the science), and then to the moved (its students or audiences).[6] Articles 14–18 concern the formal cause of theology in all its ramifications: the various scientific and didactic *formae* or methods (*modūs tradendi*) used in the Bible; its various "senses" or types of meaning (principally the literal, allegorical, tropological and anagogical senses) and the concomitant methods of textual exposition or *modūs exponendi*; the people to whom and by whom it should be expounded. The next part of the prologue provides an account of the material cause of theology, followed by an excursus on the kinds of speech or style through which the subject-matter of Scripture is communicated. Here Henry discusses the way in which language concerning God and divine matters is used in theology, and how this discourse is to be expounded.

From Henry's impressive array of interrelated topics we may attempt to single out those which relate most immediately to "sacred stylistics." The relevant *quaestiones* occur within Articles XVI, XVII, XVIII and XX which may be outlined according to Henry's scheme as follows:[7]

---

the summary accounts in Minnis, *Medieval Theory of Authorship*, 28–32, 75–84, 118–30; and Minnis and Scott, *Medieval Literary Theory*, 198ff.

[6] This section of Henry's Prologue is discussed in Minnis, "The *Accessus* Extended."

[7] Not all the specific topics here outlined will be discussed below, this being

Article XVI, Concerning the mode of expounding this science in respect of its exposition:

1. Whether a profound exposition is to be sought.
2. Whether a manifold exposition is to be sought in this science.
3. Whether solely a fourfold exposition is to be sought in this science.
4. Whether a multiple exposition is to be sought everywhere in this science.
5. Whether truth is inherent in every exposition and sense.
6. Whether every true exposition is to be accepted, without discrimination, in this science.
7. Whether it is to be expounded by the investigation of reason.
8. Whether exposition by the investigation of reason is more efficacious than by authority.
9. Whether the investigated exposition is to be propounded in plain speech (clarus sermo).

Article XVII, Concerning the mode of expounding this science, namely theology, in respect of the person to whom it is expounded:

1. Whether theology is to be expounded indiscriminately to everyone.
2. Whether any exposition whatever is to be propounded indiscriminately to anyone.

Article XVIII, Concerning the mode of expounding this science in respect of the person who has to expound it:

1. Whether this science is to be expounded by man.
2. Whether it is to be expounded by any man, indiscriminately.
3. Whether a man can expound it without special divine illumination.

---

beyond the scope of a single paper. This full outline may be useful, however, as a means of locating such *quaestiones* as are considered within the larger scheme of Henry's Prologue. Article 19, here omitted, "Concerning the material cause of theology," contains questions on whether the science's subject "is God or something else" or whether it "is something knowable in general."

Article XX, In what manner speech concerning God and divine matters is used in theology, and in what manner what is understood about such things is to be expounded:

1. Whether human speech should be used in theology concerning God and things divine.
2. Whether the signification thereof by things and by words should be spoken of without distinction [i.e., without applying the distinction between significative words and significative things].
3. Whether this science ought to speak of divine matters in a style which uses words that retain their proper meaning and is clear, or one that is figurative and [deliberately] obscure.
4. Whether this science ought to talk about divine matters in a simple or ornate style.

In order that Henry's argument may be made as clear as possible in a small space, however, we must start at the end of this sequence, with the discourse of theology itself. Should it be clear or obscure, simple or ornate? Which stylistic media, as used by biblical authors, are best for the conveyance of the supreme message of the highest and best of all the sciences? Having reviewed Henry's answers, we may proceed to hear what he has to say on the discourse of exegesis, the ways in which Scripture should be expounded. This will involve an investigation of the kinds of audience to which the different kinds of exposition are supposed to be appropriate.[8]

I. Obscurity, Ornament—and Clarity

Should theology speak of divine matters in a style which uses words that retain their "proper" or normal meaning, or one that is figurative and deliberately obscure (Article 20, qu. 3)?[9] Henry begins with two arguments in favor of the proposition that Holy Scripture ought to use a style (*sermo*) which is clear rather than obscure. First, it is an accepted principle that the teaching of a wise man is easy to follow.

---

[8] For the following discussion of Henry's prologue, I used two early printed editions, *Summae quaestionum ordinariarum* (Paris), and *Magistri Henrici Goethals a Gandavo (...) Summa* (Ferrara).

[9] Paris ed., fol. 121r–v; Ferrara ed., 304–5.

But when teaching comes from the wisest *auctor* of all, God, "at whose command holy men of God wrote it down,"[10] then it ought to be very easy to follow, and this simplicity is surely best achieved by writing it in a straightforward manner (*modus clarus*) and avoiding words which are figurative and obscure (*figurativus et obscurus*). Second, since all men should have a knowledge of this science, it should be described in such a way that it can be understood by all. This argument would seem to gell with the statement with which Article 17, qu. 2 ends, that, in the case of a mixed-ability audience, difficult matters should be tempered so that everyone should get something out of the exposition. But there, as we shall see, Henry is more concerned to develop the idea that that "something" will not be the same for everyone, a principle of discrimination which permeates his treatment of the medium and message of Scripture. But here his emphasis is on the mixed and composite nature of Scriptural style itself, rather than on distinctions which exist within its audience.

Henry cites St. John Chrysostom (one of his favorite authorities) as being in favor of the opposite view concerning the issue of scriptural obscurity. Commenting on Matthew 23.13, "Woe to you who close up the kingdom of heaven," Chrysostom had declared that the Scriptures are not closed up, but obscure, so that some effort is required to discover their meaning.[11] But Henry's own view, recorded (as is usual in this scholastic genre) in the *responsio* or *solutio* of the *quaestio* form, is that, because Holy Scripture is absolutely essential and has been written to bring all men salvation, it must be made to suit all men and provide for all the nurture which is necessary for that purpose. Those who investigate any kind of knowledge

---

[10] "As we proved above," Henry adds, a reference back to Article 9, qu. 2: "Whether God is the author of Holy Scripture." Paris ed., fols. 71r–72r; Ferrara ed., 176–78. Here Henry declares that God alone may rightly be called the *auctor* of the science of theology; His human scribes, the recorders of His message in sacred Scripture, were its "secondary authors." They are not, therefore, to be compared with the manual workers as described by Aristotle, who act in an incomprehending way under the direction of a superior artificer who knows the reasons and rules of which they themselves are ignorant (cf. *Metaphysica* 981a–b). The Bible was inscribed by ministers who in effect co-wrote the Scriptures and contemplated His wisdom inasmuch as it is possible for human hearts to do so. Thus, they perfectly understood the rules of the art—in terms of human perfection, that is. For a fuller account of this discussion, see Minnis, "The *Accessus* Extended."

[11] Pseudo-Chrysostom, *In Evan. Matth. hom.*, 44 (PG 56:881).

can be divided into the elementary students (*simplices*) and the more advanced (*provectos*). Holy Scripture, therefore, must be written in such a way as to suit both groups. It suits the elementary students if it is written in a clear style and in words which retain their own meaning: otherwise they cannot understand it. On the other hand, it suits the advanced students whichever of the two styles (*modūs*) it employs.

Three reasons are then given for this. First of all, the obscure style may hold the attention of advanced students, while the straight-forward one instructs them. Citations from Augustine are offered in support of this view. For instance, in *De vera religione* he says that the method of imparting any kind of teaching is in part extremely straightforward, and in part done through similitudes, in words, deeds and sacraments, adapted to suit every level of instruction and exercise of the soul.[12] Henry adds that if only straightforward texts existed, texts which were readily understood, one would not pursue the truth with any great eagerness, nor would its discovery be such a sweet experience (*nec suaviter inveniretur veritas*).

The second reason is that truth should not be undervalued by appearing too self-evident, and should be all the sweeter (*dulcior*) for being discovered in an obscure style. This is what Augustine says in the second book of *De doctrina Christiana*. Divine providence, declares the saint, devised this style to counter intellectual pride, which tends to despise that which is readily understood.[13] More-over, he continues, "it gives one far greater pleasure to find the answer to a question of which the solution has been difficult." The Holy Spirit ordained Scripture in such a way that it should directly satisfy the hunger for knowledge with its more straightforward passages, while it banishes boredom with the more obscure ones.[14] Similarly, in his *Contra mendacium* Augustine argues that the sayings

---

[12] Augustine, *De vera religione*, 17.33 (CCL 32:207). Here Henry also cites Augustine's *De diversis quaestionibus*, 53.2 (CCL 44A:88/lines 66–70), and *Contra Adimantum*, 17.5 and 28.2 (PL 42:161, 172).

[13] *De doctrina*, 2.6.7 (CCL 32:35–36). However, here Henry does not cite Augustine's famous interpretation of the Song of Songs 4.2 ("Thy teeth are like flocks of sheep . . ."): that appears in his discussion of the question of whether Holy Scripture should be expounded in an obscure style (Art. 16, qu. 9), on which see below, 223–24.

[14] *De doctrina*, 2.6.8 (CCL 32:36).

and actions of the prophets are clothed in figures, which serve as veils (*amictūs*), simply in order "to exercise the mind of the sincere seeker after truth, and lest they should be little valued if they were presented unadorned and in a form readily understood." This obscurity ensures that the student will think "all the more highly of them, with the result that if they are removed from his reach, he misses them all the more, and when the longed-for truths are discovered, his joy is all the greater."[15]

Moreover, because a passage provides nourishment more effectively when the one text offers several meanings, therefore the first reason for obscurity is this particularly: that Scripture should be obscure in order that it may give a richer yield of knowledge. As Augustine says in *De civitate Dei*, "an obscure style is useful because it gives rise to several meanings, and brings them out into the light of knowledge when different people interpret it in different ways."[16] The second reason for its obscurity is that it may remain hidden from those who are unworthy, and who cannot be bothered to study it, as is made clear by Chrysostom's commentary on Matthew 23.13. The main point of this passage is that scriptural truth "is not kept obscure in order that those who seek it may not find it, but rather that those who do not really want to seek it may not see it; so that the reputation of those who find it may be enhanced, because they have longed for it, and sought it out and found it," and conversely, so that those who have not longed for it, nor sought it, nor found it, may be condemned.[17] Furthermore, (Pseudo-)Dionysius states that it is most fitting for mystical discourses to cloak the divine mysteries in such a way that they cannot be understood by the majority. For not everyone is holy, and not everyone is privileged to speak of holy things.[18]

The third reason for this obscurity, according to Chrysostom in that same commentary on Matthew 23.13, is because God wanted some to be teachers and others to be students. For if everyone knew

---

[15] *Contra mendacium*, 10.24 (CSEL 41:500–501). Henry also cites here Augustine's *Enarr. in Ps. 140*, 1 (CCL 40:2026).

[16] *De civitate Dei*, 11.19 (CCL 48:337–38).

[17] Pseudo-Chrysostom, *In Evan. Matth. hom.*, 44 (PG 56:881–82).

[18] *De coelesti hierarchia*, 2 (PG 3:139). Henry proceeds to cite *De divinis nominibus*, 13 (PG 3:995), and *De ecclesiastica hierarchia*, 1.1 (PG 3:371A).

everything, there would be no need for any teacher, and the natural order of things would be turned upside down.

Henry then proceeds to argue on a different tack. One should seek the difference of style in Holy Scripture (as between the obscure and the straightforward) not only in different passages but also in one and the same passage. For a passage of Scripture may have one straightforward sense on the surface, but conceal an obscure sense in its essential kernel.[19]

Finally, Henry returns to his two initial statements. The proposition that the teaching of a wise man is easy is true inasmuch as the better the understanding a man has of something, the more clearly he can express and explain it. However, it does not follow from this that the wiser a teacher is, the more straightforwardly he should present his knowledge. For he must set it out in the way in which he knows it will be more profitable to his readers and hearers, and this is the reason why the science of theology has obscure passages mixed in with passages that are straightforward. The second proposition, that knowledge which is necessary for all ought to be understood by all, and therefore should be written in a plain style, must also be acknowledged as true—in respect of those beliefs which are necessary for our salvation. But with regard to other beliefs, which do not relate to our full attainment of salvation, such knowledge is not necessary because it is not expedient: that is, we can be saved without it, in contrast with the knowledge which is essential for our salvation.

Thus Henry explains his belief that Holy Scripture is designed to suit all men, both the *simplices* and the *provectos*; obscurity stimulates the latter while the straightforward passages ensure that everyone gets what he needs in order to attain salvation. So much for obscurity; what about literary artifice and eloquence? Should the supreme science of theology talk about God and divine matters in an ornate and complex *modus* (Article 20, qu. 4)?[20]

Two arguments are offered in favor of this proposition. First there is the statemement of "the Philosopher" in the second book of

---

[19] Here Henry quotes St. Gregory, *Moralia in Job*, Prol.4 (CCL 143:6), and Augustine, *Confessiones*, 6.5.8 (CCL 27:78–79), in support of this viewpoint.

[20] Paris ed., fol. 122r-v; Ferrara ed., 306–8.

the *Ethics* that one should seek out styles (*sermones*) which suit the subject matter (*materia*).[21] Therefore, where the subject matter is more refined, the style in which it is presented ought to be more refined. But that subject matter which deals with God and divine matters is the most elegant of all, and so the most elegant style is the one most suitable. Since the most elegant style may be understood as the one which is most ornate and complex, the proposition is therefore proved. Second, Holy Scripture ought to speak in the way in which it may more effectively convince men of the truth, for this is of course why it was written. This end is achieved when the ornate style of speech is used. Against the proposition, however, seems to be the opinion that all divine words are rustic and artless (*incomposita*).

Henry begins his *responsio* by citing the *Timaeus*: "the faculty of voice and hearing have been bestowed on man for the full instruction of human life, if indeed there is an exchange of speech according to agreed rules, so that men may readily learn each others' wishes."[22] Therefore, science ought to use the style whereby it can most effectively give instruction and set out the intention (*intentio*) of its subject matter (*materia*). But Henry is anxious to emphasize that in writing which relates to divine matters attention should be paid to what is being said, and that in all subjects generally the nature of the style must serve the needs of the essential subject of the material (*quidditas rei*) which has to be expounded.

Thus, a distinction must be made concerning stylistic composition and ornamentation. For either this serves the needs of instruction, so that teaching is imparted more effectively and the author's intention (*intentum*) expressed more clearly, or alternatively it can have the opposite effect, by obstructing that same instruction and expression. Such obstruction can be the fault of either the speaker or the listener or the author himself, according to Henry's analysis. First, it can be the fault of the speaker, the one conveying the message (*ex parte proferentis*), because too much concern about pronunciation often leads him to forget the substance of what he is conveying. As Augustine says in *De doctrina Christiana*, "we should be careful lest the

---

[21] *Nicomachean Ethics*, 2.2 (1104a). Here as elsewhere Henry uses Robert Grosseteste's translation of this work.

[22] *Timaeus* 47C; following the Calcidius version, *Timaeus a Calcidio translatus*, 44.

message we are supposed to convey escapes us while we are concentrating on expressing that message artistically."[23] Second, it can be the fault of the listener (*ex parte audientis*), for the pleasure he gets from the style may lull his ears, concentrating his attention on himself and preventing him from paying attention to the substance of the passage. St. Augustine speaks against this in *De doctrina Christiana*, declaring that it is the truth in the words which great intellects love, and not the words themselves.[24] Third and last of all, it can be the fault of the author who is putting his idea forward (*ex parte ipsius sententiae proferendae*), for often this is hidden by elaborate stylistic composition (*compositio*) or ornament, while a plain style puts it clearly.

The priorities of theology are therefore manifest. In reaction against the three kinds of obstruction here identified, Henry is concerned to affirm that this science does not value an elaborate and carefully structured style if it hinders clear teaching. Thus, it takes no account of harmonious sound or word order in a passage, preferring to incur the fault of barbarism or solecism than in any way to diminish the integrity and full expression of the meaning (*sententia*). Christian teachers must be aware of this, as Augustine says. What is the advantage of having correct diction if the hearer does not understand the message?[25] There is no point at all in speaking if those whose enlightenment we seek do not understand: clarity is far more important than elegance. Correct diction, explains Augustine, is simply the retention of the custom of others confirmed by the authority of former speakers.[26] But men are offended by violations of such custom according as their belief is weaker, and they are weaker in their belief according as they desire more eagerly to become more learned, not in terms of real learning (*res*), which may build up their faith, but of outward signs (*signa*), knowledge of which cannot help but make them arrogant, since even the knowledge of the real truth (*scientia rerum*) makes a man raise his neck in pride,

---

[23] *De doctrina*, 4.3.4 (CCL 32:118).

[24] *De doctrina*, 4.11.26 (CCL 32:134–35).

[25] *De doctrina*, 4.10.24 (CCL 32:132–33). Here Henry rearranges passages from the ninth and tenth chapters of the fourth book of this work by Augustine.

[26] *De doctrina*, 2.13.19 (CCL 32:45).

unless it is repressed by the yoke of submission to the Lord.[27]

Having warned against putting style before substance, with the formidable support of Augustine, Henry apparently feels that he can then proceed to make a measured defence of literary elegance. If a carefully structured style with fully correct grammatical agreement does not prove a stumbling-block to the expression of the truth in any of the above-mentioned ways, then it is altogether useful and is to be cultivated. And once again Augustine's De doctrina Christiana has a powerful argument to offer.[28] The man who is at once wise and eloquent, it now seems, is the more able: whoever "is willing to speak not only wisely but also eloquently will certainly be more helpful for having both gifts." But he should not overdo it. The avoidance of stylistic blemishes is desirable, but excessive ornament should be eschewed, lest the reader be confused.

In defining the correct combination of elegance and wisdom, Henry launches into yet another long quotation from the fourth book of De doctrina Christiana. Since the art of rhetoric is used to urge the claims of truth and falsehood alike, truth should not stand unarmed in its defence against lies. It would be stupid to fail to see that good men should cultivate eloquence, "so that it may do service for the truth, if wicked men take it over for their perverted and vain goals, to further error and wickedness." Anything which "is sweet but harmful" should be avoided. "But what is better than something which is sweet but also beneficial, or something which is beneficial but also pleasant?"[29]

The canonical books of the Bible were written with both wisdom and eloquence, of superlative kinds, as Augustine also proves. He could not "imagine anything written with greater wisdom or eloquence" and ventured to say that "all who understand correctly what they have to say, immediately perceive that their authors could not properly have spoken in any other way."[30] But worldly eloquence was and is inappropriate to the science of theology, for theology does not rely on the "wisdom of mere words" (cf. 1 Corinthians 1.17).

---

[27] De doctrina, 2.13.20 (CCL 32:45).
[28] De doctrina, 4.5.8 (CCL 32:121).
[29] De doctrina, 4.2.3 (CCL 32:117).
[30] De doctrina, 4.6.9 (CCL 32:122).

Just as "there is a particular kind of eloquence which is more suitable for the young to employ, and another more suitable for the old, and that cannot be called eloquence which does not suit the person of the speaker," similarly "there is a kind of eloquence suited to men who, by reason of the very high authority which they possess, are held in the very highest esteem and regarded as truly divine." This exceptional style suits them alone, and "the more it seems humbler than that of others, the more it transcends them, not by means of bombastic eloquence but because of its solidity."[31] It "has not been created by human skills, but is welded together wisely and eloquently with a wisdom that is not directed to achieving mere eloquence but rather manifests eloquence which never parts company with wisdom." Hence, Augustine can write of a rhetoric which is found in Scripture alone, asserting that "the authors of the biblical canon were eloquent as well as wise, and that our teachers used such eloquence as was proper for persons of that kind."[32]

Finally, Henry returns to his initial propositions. Is not the most ornate and complex style the one appropriate for the most refined subject matter, the doctrine of theology? This may be accepted as true, with the proviso that such ornament must be in keeping with the serious nature of this science. The second point, that eloquent style is more effective in persuasion, is also true, but nevertheless the ornament should not overstep the bounds of propriety, and this would be the case if it were decked out with the sort of rhetorical "coloring" which is described in the art of rhetoric. This should not, of course, be read as some sort of scholastic attack on rhetoric, but rather as yet another affirmation of the priorities of the Christian teacher. Henry is simply saying what Augustine had said at the beginning of the fourth book of *De doctrina Christiana*, where he set out to "thwart the expectation of those readers who think that I shall give the rules of rhetoric here...." "I admonish them," continued the saint, "not to expect such rules from me, not that they have no utility, but because, if they have any, it should be sought elsewhere if perhaps some good man has the opportunity to learn

---

[31] Ibid.; Henry also draws on *De doctrina*, 4.6.10 (CCL 32:122–23).
[32] *De doctrina*, 4.7.21 (CCL 32:131).

them."[33] His main objective is a different one: the privileging of wisdom over eloquence, which yet accommodates the principle that eloquent wisdom is, in many cases, highly efficacious and quite desirable. And Henry of Ghent utterly agrees with that.

II. Capacity and Receptivity: In Defense of Discrimination

Now we are in a position to consider Henry's views on how scriptural style—by turns obscure and straightforward, combining clear expression with appropriate and unostentatious ornament in a way which is unprecedented and unique—affects and appeals to its intended audience, along with his sense of the role which the scriptural exegete plays in helping to convey the sacred message.

Given that Holy Scripture often employs an obscure style, should an obscure style be used in expounding it? That is the question Henry poses in Article 16, qu. 9, and he begins by offering two arguments in favor of the proposition that an obscure style should indeed be used in exegesis.[34] First, the Bible is to be expounded in such a way that it should remain unknown to the impious, whereby what is holy should not be given to dogs (cf. Matthew 7.6). Therefore, the exposition should be in an obscure style, so that the impious cannot understand it. Second, Scripture should not be expounded in such a way that it is cheapened and devalued. That is why it was not transmitted by the authors of Scripture in a clear style. Therefore, neither should the expositors of Scripture use a clear style. On the other hand, since Scripture is expounded principally in order that it should be understood, maximum understanding entails maximum exposition, which can be achieved only if the exposition is in a clear style.

Henry's own position is that, since the expositors of a given science do not labor for themselves alone but also for others, other people must therefore be able to understand and remember their explanations, past explanations being handed down so that the task of present scholars is the easier. Biblical exegesis, therefore, should not be in an obscure style. Augustine's *De doctrina Christiana* is cited as stating that the writings of expositors should themselves not

---

[33] *De doctrina*, 4.1.2 (CCL 32:116–17). Here I cite the translation by Robertson, *On Christian Doctrine*, 118.

[34] Paris ed., fols. 90v–91r; Ferrara ed., 276–77.

become the objects of exegesis; rather, "in all their utterances they should first of all seek to speak so that they may be understood."[35]

To the argument that what is holy should not be given to dogs, it can be replied that the exposition of Scripture is for those people who are pious and learned. For this special audience the exposition should be couched in the clearest style possible—according to our human capacities, of course, but the more obscure passages which exceed the capacities of the exegetes should be indicated clearly. However, the argument that the exposition of what is obscure actually devalues it is simply untrue, Henry declares. On the contrary, such exposition makes it all the more attractive, when it is seen how under the obscure style is hidden a most profound meaning. Besides, in Scripture obscure passages are interspersed with clear ones, by which the more obscure passages may be elucidated.[36]

Because the Scriptures were first transmitted in an obscure style, they were not vilified. Subsequently, however, they have been most clearly expounded so that they can delight to the highest degree, as is witnessed by the pleasure which St. Augustine took in the exposition of the Song of Songs. To be told that there are certain men whose lives and customs are an exemplar whereby the Church is able to destroy the superstitions of those who come to it and assimilitate them into itself as men of good faith, is not so delightful as hearing the Song of Songs 4.2 ("Thy teeth are as flocks of sheep, that are shorn, which come up from the washing, all with twins, and there is none barren among them") making the very same point. For the saints can be contemplated more pleasantly when they are envisaged as "the teeth of the Church cutting off men from their errors and transferring them to her body after their hardness has been softened as if by being bitten and chewed."[37] No one doubts, Augustine concludes from this example, that "things are perceived more readily through likenesses and that what is sought with difficulty is discovered with more pleasure." Such obscurity in the text of Scripture induces a hunger to know in those who really want the truth; clarity

---

[35] *De doctrina*, 4.8.22 (CCL 32:131–32); trans. Robertson, *On Christian Doctrine*, 132–33.

[36] Cf. Henry's later citation of *De doctrina*, 2.6.8 (CCL 32:36), discussed below, and our subsequent discussion on 233–34.

[37] *De doctrina*, 2.6.7 (CCL 32:35–36).

might induce a disdainful attitude, because what is being sought is found too easily. But the obvious implication is that clarity of expression is the stock-in-trade of the exegete, who can expound the obscure places of Scripture with the aid of the more open places, there being "hardly anything ... found in these obscure places which is not found plainly said elsewhere" (to return to Henry's citation of Augustine).[38] Here Henry indicates his belief in the essential importance of the *sensus litteralis* of Scripture. Allegorical exposition, while it still has a place in Henry's exegetical theory and practice, is certainly not as fundamental as it was in monastic *lectio divina*. Scholastic exegesis had very different methods and required language which could provide the raw materials for syllogistic argument, and from the literal sense alone can an argument be drawn, as Augustine said elsewhere—to the general approval of thirteenth-century schoolmen.[39] Henry's "literalism"[40] is a feature of several of his other *quaestiones* on the abilities, intellectual and moral, of the *auditores* of theology, as we shall see.

Exegesis, it would seem, should not be obscure. But should it be profound (Article 16, qu. 1)?[41] Henry's answer is that since each and every exposition of Holy Scripture is conducted in order that biblical truth may shine forth to its learners, two things must be attended to: evidence of the truth, and the capacity of the learner. Concerning the first, it may be said that the exegete should not stop until he reaches secure and certain truth. When "the letter" offers this, he should stop there, at the literal understanding; when "the letter" hides the truth, however, then a more profound exposition should be sought, this being the spiritual sense of the passage in question. But the exposition should always be prepared with the capacity of the learner in mind, and since many learners are coarse (*grossus*) and stupid, in their case a broad (*grossus*) and common exposition is, in the main, to be offered. The notion of "gross" and

---

[38] *De doctrina*, 2.6.8 (CCL 32:36).

[39] *Epistulae*, 93.8.24 (CSEL 44:469–70); cited, for example, by St. Thomas Aquinas, *Summa theologica*, 1a 1ae, Article 10; trans. Minnis and Scott, 242.

[40] On this late-medieval movement in general, see Minnis, *Medieval Theory of Authorship*, 73–74, 84–93. On Henry's unease with a certain kind of allegorical interpretation, see 106–7.

[41] Paris ed., fol. 104r–v; Ferrara ed., 259–61.

uneducated listeners who require a general, untechnical exposition owes something to Aristotle's account of the scope and status of the science of ethics, in the *Nicomachean Ethics*, 1.3 (1094b19–21), as understood by thirteenth-century thinkers. For example, Giles of Rome—an arch-opponent of Henry's in some areas—had this passage in mind when he declared that "in the whole field of moral teaching the mode of procedure, according to the Philosopher, is figurative and broad (*grossus*)."[42] Similarly, in his *Rhetorica*, 3.18 (1419a), Aristotle had warned against asking questions which uneducated listeners would not understand. Giles of Rome, commenting on this passage, explains that the audience of rhetorical orations is supposed to be *grossus*, and so the enthymemes must be suited to the capacity of the minds of such "gross" people.[43] To return to Henry's discussion: St. Paul is supposed to have had "gross" people in mind when he said "I could not address you as spiritual men, but as men of the flesh" (1 Corinthians 3.1). However, to more able learners a proportionately more profound exposition should be offered, with the proviso that profound inquiry must always be governed by the rules of faith, lest the investigators fall into heresy. St. Paul warned that men should not try to be more wise than is befitting to mankind, but rather be sober in this endeavor (Romans 12.3), which passage the *Glossa ordinaria* explains as meaning that one should investigate the divine mysteries temperately and without presumption, a precept which all heretics transgress.[44] Whence, profound investigation of Holy Scripture should be left to spiritual and perfect men, for to others it is perilous.

The dangers of intellectual pride on the part of the expositor are fully appreciated by Henry, and the importance of the virtues of moderation and humility for those persons who have the prerogative of opening up the sacred text. The problems caused by personal wilfulness are also considered in the context of another of Henry's *quaestiones*, namely "Whether every true exposition is acceptable,

---

[42] *D. Aegidii Romani (...) de regimine principum*, fol. 1v; trans. Minnis and Scott, 248.

[43] *Rhetorica Aristotelis cum Egidii de Roma commentariis*, fol. 117r.

[44] *Glossa ordinaria interlinearis*, In Rom. 12.3, in *Textus Biblie*, 6.27r. I have used this rather than Migne's "edition," since he does not include the interlinear component of the *Glossa*.

indiscriminately, in this science" (Article 16, qu. 6).[45] Generally speaking, the exposition of Scripture should tend to the building up of faith or behavior. Since this is "the intention of the letter" (*intentio litterae*), expositions which support this objective may be accepted, even though they may be deemed irrelevant to the specific "circumstances of the letter" (*circumstantiae litterae*), i.e., the total literal context of the given passage which fixes its actual meaning.[46] But to move away from the "circumstances of the letter" is to take risks, Henry continues, proceeding yet again into a citation from Augustine's *De doctrina Christiana*.[47] Whoever finds a lesson in Scripture which is conducive to charity, even though he has not said what the author may be shown to have meant in that passage, has not been deceived nor is he lying in any way. Such an exegete, Augustine says, is like the man who leaves a road by mistake but passes through a field to the same place toward which the road itself will lead. But this is not to say that all charitable expositions are on a par: discrimination is necessary. Thus, such a person should be put right and shown that it is better not to leave the road, lest he form bad habits and his deviation become deviousness. It is clear, then, that one should avoid the risk of perverse interpretation by ensuring that one's exposition of a given passage is consistent with what others are known to mean. This is the basic principle behind Henry's recommended method of validating the senses of Scripture, both literal and mystical, which expositors offer. When many congruous meanings are possible in a given passage, there is a sort of scale of acceptability, an exposition which can be confirmed by "the letter" of other passages always being preferable. Where such checks are lacking, the exegete can have recourse to his own powers of reasoning, even in cases where a meaning is being posited which was not intended by the scriptural *auctor*. But, as Augustine says in *De doctrina Christiana*,[48] "this is a dangerous pursuit; we shall walk much more safely with the aid of the Scriptures themselves. When we wish to examine passages offered by figurative words, we should

---

[45] Paris ed., fol. 121r–v.

[46] For brief discussions of this notion, see Chenu, *Towards Understanding St. Thomas*, 144; Minnis, "Chaucer and Comparative Literary Theory," 63.

[47] *De doctrina*, 1.36.40–41 (CCL 32:29–30).

[48] *De doctrina*, 3.28.39 (CCL 32:100).

either begin with a passage which is not controversial, or, if it is controversial, we should conclude with testimonies applied from places wherever they are found in the same Scriptures."

The well-prepared exegete has to discriminate not only between different expositions, but also between different types of *auditor*. This issue is addressed directly in *quaestiones* which consider the intellectual and moral capabilities of the receivers of exposition. Article 17, "concerning the method of expounding this science, in respect of the person to whom it is expounded," comprises two relevant discussions, the first of which asks if theology should be expounded to everyone, without discrimination.[49] On the face of it, it would seem that this is indeed the case, for at the end of Matthew's gospel (28.19–20) Christ orders His disciples to go and make disciples of all nations, baptizing them and teaching them all He had commanded them. This must necessarily involve exposition, since correct understanding of Scripture is impossible without it. Henry further cites Matthew 13.47, where Christ likens the kingdom of heaven to a net which was thrown into the sea to gather fish of every kind. The *Glossa ordinaria* on this passage compares the net to evangelical preaching, which calls all types of men. But these men cannot be called unless Scripture is expounded, so that they can grasp it, whence the *Glossa* says that Peter and Andrew, Jacob and John made their net from the Old and New Testaments and cast it into the secular sea.[50] This involved exposition, the one Testament being expounded by reference to the other. However, against the proposition is the injunction of Matthew 7.6 not to give what is holy to dogs, or cast pearls before swine, which the *Glossa* explains as meaning that to such people the mysteries of Scripture are not to be opened up.[51]

Henry turns once again to patristic authority for his solution—not Augustine this time, but Chrysostom; specifically, to what Henry calls the "second edition" of Chrysostom's exposition of Matthew 7.6. Since divine mercy allows the sun to rise on both the

---

[49] Paris ed., fols. 111r–12r; Ferrara ed., 278–80.

[50] *Glossa ordinaria marginalis*, in Matt. 13.47, in *Textus Biblie*, 5.46v.

[51] *Glossa ordinaria marginalis*, in Matt. 7.6, in *Textus Biblie*, 5.28r. Cf. the treatment of this scriptural passage in an earlier discussion, art. 16, qu. 9, discussed on 222–23 above.

evil and the good and sends rain to fall on the just and the unjust
alike (Matthew 5.45), it would seem that exposition is not only for
the few but for all. However, as Chrysostom says, there is an error
in this reasoning, for God does not indiscriminately dispense all his
benefits to the good and bad alike, but only carnal things, the spiritual benefits being reserved for the good.[52] Therefore, it must absolutely be said that sacred Scripture is not expounded to all indiscriminately, let alone propounded in simple fashion, but only to those
who are receptive to it and who find it useful, as are the faithful and
obedient. To such people it should be expounded, whether by lecture
or by preaching. (Here Henry refers back to Article 12, on the
auditor of theology, wherein those who are entitled to hear public
lectures in schools of theology are carefully delimited. For example,
no women are to be afforded this level of education.) Different
people require different methods of exposition, he continues, promising to treat this more fully in the following question. From the
exposition of Scripture are to be expelled "dogs," i.e., heretics and
gentiles living in impiety, and also "swine," i.e., carnal and animal-
like Christians living in the mire of luxury and perpetually dwelling
in filth. The teaching of the faith is indeed recommended and thus
expounded to all—*before* obstinacy sets in. Pride renders the listener
unworthy of, and unfit for, it. What, then, about that universal net
of preaching as described in Matthew 13.47? That, again, was true at
the beginning, but afterwards certain people rendered themselves
obstinate, and from them the exposition of Holy Scripture is to be
removed.

Henry then proceeds to inquire, in the second *quaestio* of Article
17, if each and every scriptural exposition should be offered to
everyone indiscriminately.[53] The hearer who is in need of education
would seem to be in a position to benefit from any exposition
whatever. Besides, if a particular exposition is not offered on the
grounds that certain people in the audience cannot understand it, this
is surely unfair to those who *are* able to understand it.[54] On the
other hand, a person who is given an exposition he does not under-

---

[52] Pseudo-Chrysostom, *In Evan. Matth. hom.*, 17 (PG 56:728).
[53] Paris ed., fols. 112r–13r; Ferrara ed., 280–82.
[54] Drawing on Augustine, *In Ioan. evan. tract.*, 1 (CCL 36:1).

stand will not be nourished thereby. Henry finds some truth in all of these views. A particular exposition should not be offered to someone whose abilities are inadequate to cope with it. The exegete must consider, when preaching or simply speaking, the composition of his audience. If he is addressing a mixed audience of those who are capable and spiritual on the one hand and carnal and incapable on the other, then no subtle question should be omitted on account of the incapacity of some, because he should seek to benefit those who are able to comprehend it. It is not that different things are said to the different classes of people—rather that one and the same thing is understood spiritually by those who are spiritual and carnally by those who are carnal. Conversely, "gross" (*grossus*) or broad expositions are not to be omitted for fear of "talking down" to capable people, because such people can cope with both the major and the minor, for what is minor is conducive to what is major, and what is major enables one to comprehend what is minor. Henry proceeds to argue that those who are capable are not to be given a profound exposition individually: individuality relates rather to the different capacities of the capable, some being more capable than others.

Although an exposition may offer subtle and profound doctrine, Henry continues, it should be offered only to those who are able to comprehend it, for to others it may be useless and dangerous. As far as lesser mortals are concerned, exposition should limit itself to what is sufficient for salvation. The desire to avoid piecemeal exposition (as Henry would see it) cannot lead one to the conclusion that everyone should get everything in terms of exposition. To the second argument in favor, viz., that no exposition should be omitted on account of the *rudes*, it must be said that this is indeed true, in the case in which the audience is mixed in the manner described above. But the exposition should be suitably tempered so that each listener can grasp it in accordance with his capacity. It is up to the expositor, then, to ensure that everyone will get *something* out of a given passage of Scripture— but not, of course, necessarily the *same* thing.

These arguments are utterly consistent with those found in an earlier *quaestio* in Henry's *Summa* (Article 12, qu. 8):[55] should every faithful man, without discrimination, be admitted to hearing the

---

[55] Paris ed., fols. 89v–90v; Ferrara ed., 223–24.

science of theology? Are certain aspects of theological teaching to be
reserved for spiritual men only, and passed over in silence when
carnal men are being addressed (as John 16.12 would seem to suggest)? Henry points out that Augustine, in *De doctrina Christiana*,
states that there are some things which are not understood or are
hardly understood with their full implications, no matter how
eloquently they are declared, or how often, or how plainly. And
these things should never, or only rarely on account of some necessity, be set before a popular audience.[56] Henry replies by distinguishing between a *statement* of what must be believed and the *understanding* of what must be believed. Taking the first sense, there is nothing
in sacred Scripture which should be spoken to spiritual men and
hidden from carnal men. For there is nothing in the whole of Scripture which cannot be taught to a child—at least, if the superficial
letter be followed. In public, Scripture nourishes the young; in
private, however, subtle minds are raised up in admiration by the
divine mysteries which lie behind the surface. In this first sense,
then, there is nothing in Scripture which should not be propounded
to every faithful man indiscriminately, whether in preaching or in
lecturing. Taking the second sense, relating to the *understanding* of
what is to be believed, of course not everyone has the capacity for
that, and so there are indeed certain things which can be given to
spiritual men by profound exposition, and hidden from carnal men.
This, Henry believes, is what Augustine was talking about in the
passage from *De doctrina Christiana* which he quoted earlier in this
discussion.[57]

In these *quaestiones* Henry is explaining the diversity of biblical
interpretation in terms of the differences between human capacities
and capabilities (whether in the expositor or the auditor), rather than
something inherent in sacred Scripture itself. The consistency with

---

[56] *De doctrina*, 4.9.23 (CCL 32:132). Similar thinking is found in Henry's
Quodlibet X, qu. 16, "Utrum doctor sive magister determinans quaestiones vel
exponens scripturas publice peccet mortaliter non explicando veritatem quam
novit" (ed. Macken, 304–7). It is a matter of the capacity of one's audience: if a
doctor fails to convey doctrine which would be "useful, fruitful and necessary" to
a given audience, then he indeed sins mortally; on the other hand, he is perfectly
justified in censoring material which he knows would be harmful.

[57] I.e., *De doctrina*, 4.9.23 (CCL 32:132).

what he says elsewhere in the Prologue to his *Summa* is marked—
particularly in his disagreement with the method of analysing the
"multiple mode" (*multiplex modus*) of biblical discourse which had
firmly been established by the *Summa theologiae* attributed to Alexander of Hales, a work which actually had been completed by
Alexander's pupils after their master's death in 1245. Here *modus*
refers to the diverse *modūs agendi* or *modūs tractandi* of Scripture,
the idea being that the Bible proceeds by way of precept, example,
exhortation, revelation, prayer, and so forth, because these modes
assist the formation of a pious disposition, which is the objective of
the science of theology.[58] Defending this position, the *Summa Alexandri* declares that there are three reasons why the *modus tractandi* of
Holy Scripture must be manifold.[59] First, the holy Spirit is "single
yet manifold" (Wisdom 7.22), and this fact must be reflected in
theology. Second, the subject of theology is divine Wisdom, which is
manifold, and so "in order that the mode may match the subject, it
too must take many forms." Third, the objective of theology is
instruction in those matters which pertain to salvation. And the
conditions (*statūs*) of men are manifold. Some lived in the time of the
Law and some after; some in the time of prophecy, some in the time
of grace. "Even within these periods," the argument runs in the
Summa Alexandri, "the conditions of men are manifold. For some
are sluggish in matters relating to faith, some are rebellious in matters relating to good morality, and [fall short] in different ways.
Some pass their lives in prosperity, some in adversity, some in good
works, some in sin." The conclusion is then drawn that the teaching
of Holy Scripture, which has been ordained for the salvation of men,
must employ a multiple mode, so that the mode matches this objective.

Henry attacks this in Article 14, qu. 1 of the Prologue to his
Summa.[60] The diversity in question (giving commands, issuing
prohibitions, and so forth) does not consist, he claims, "in the mode
of treating or handing down this subject-matter, but rather in the

---

[58] *Tractatus introductorius*, qu. 1, chap. 4: De modo traditionis sacrae Scripturae,
art. 1, ad ob. 2, in *Alexandri de Hales Summa theologica*, 1.8.

[59] *Tract. int.*, Qu. 1, chap. 4, Art. 3, responsio, in *Alexandri (. . .) Summa*, 1.10.

[60] Paris ed., fols. 99r–100v; Ferrara ed., 247–49.

subject matter which is being treated."[61] The *modus* of this science
should not be called *multiplex* just because its *materia* comprises
many different things. Turning to the points made by the *Summa
Alexandri* concerning the manifold wisdom of God, Henry declares
that, while this is certainly true of God, it does not entail a manifold
mode for theology. It is incorrect to say that one piece of the manifold science of God is taught in one passage of Scripture and another
in another; rather, it is true that in each discourse (*sermo*) a manifold
knowledge of God is gained in accordance with the multiplicity of
textual meaning (*sensus*) and of exposition. What, then, of the idea
that diverse *modūs tractandi* are appropriate to diverse human conditions? Henry says that the logical conclusion of this argument would
be the unacceptable proposition that theology "would have to be
passed on to one sort of men in one place, and to another sort in a
different place, and not in its totality in all places. Thus, it would not
be offered in its totality everywhere to every condition of men."
This is quite false, he declares, for theology "is offered for consideration in its totality everywhere to every condition of men," there
being no grounds for the belief that the different conditions of men
require different modes of treatment. He proceeds to attack the
notion that all the individual things relating to theology "should be
treated separately, and receive different treatment as is best suited to
various people, and in so far as [the teachers] can impart information
in different ways about different aspects of Christian belief." The
truth of the matter, Henry argues, is that "the mode used ought to
be such that disparate teachings (*sententiae*) concerning different
subjects and different tenets of belief should be contained in one and
the same discourse." Different men may understand this discourse
according to their individual capacities, some being content with the
literal surface while others look under it for the spiritual understanding. But, considered in itself, the *modus tradendi* of Scripture is
"characterized by the utmost simplicity and oneness of form."[62]
Behind these statements seems to lie Henry's conviction that there
are no divine ideas of individuals, but only of species.

---

[61] Trans. Minnis and Scott, 252.
[62] Minnis and Scott, 252–53, 255.

Clearly, this is very much of a piece with the teaching of the *quaestiones* which we have considered above. As has been demonstrated, Henry is in fundamental agreement with St. Augustine's appropriation of the essential principles of rhetoric in exegesis, including the ideas that eloquence is by no means antithetical to wisdom and that the teacher of theology, no less than the secular orator, should suit his style to his audience. The Bible caters to both *simplices* and more advanced learners: the faithful are given what is sufficient for their salvation by its simpler passages, while the learned are attracted and stimulated by its obscurities. Obscurity gives rise to polysemy; the more obscure a passage is, the more meanings it will yield as different people interpret it in different ways. Such interpretative diversity is fully discussed in his impressive array of *quaestiones* which consider the capacities of exegetes and their several audiences for understanding the stylistic media of Scripture. Scriptural exposition should always be prepared with one's specific audience in mind. For the *simplices* a "broad" (*grossus*) and common exposition is, in the main, appropriate, while a proportionately more profound exposition should be offered to more able listeners, and to such people alone, for to others it may be useless and even dangerous. As far as lesser mortals are concerned, exposition should limit itself to what is sufficient for salvation. The desire to avoid piecemeal exposition (as Henry would see it) cannot lead one to the conclusion that everyone should get everything in terms of exposition. The exposition should be suitably tempered so that each listener can grasp it in accordance with his capacity. It is up to the expositor, then, to ensure that everyone will get something out of a given passage of Scripture—but not necessarily the same thing.

In sum, Henry explains the need for diversity of interpretation in respect of the differences between human capacities and capabilities (whether in the expositor or the auditor), rather than something inherent in Scripture itself. And so the unity of Scripture is saved. The consistency with what he said when investigating the notion of the *multiplex modus* of Scripture is obvious. "All Scripture is offered on a common basis to all men for consideration, and it adapts itself to each man according to his capacity to understand"; the same teaching is "presented to all, but, because of their different capacities, for some it serves as the milk of faith only, while to others it is solid food."[63] The *modus* of Holy Scripture is singular, but the needs of human beings are diverse—and hence stylistic diversity and pluralism in the Bible, and exegetical diversity and pluralism on the part of Bible commentators, is fully justified.

What we are confronted with in Henry's *quaestio* on the *modus tradendi* of theology are the consequences of his conviction that theology is not primarily affective (an idea found in the *Summa Alexandri* and elaborated by, for instance, Giles of Rome)[64] but speculative. Those who believed the science was fundamentally affective quite naturally tended to see the diverse biblical styles as having marked similarities with the various styles and strategies of Ciceronian rhetoric, which were designed to affect and move the audience, different types of listeners requiring different methods of persuasion and information. The assimilation and development of the secular *accessus* by theologians had, from the twelfth-century "Renaissance" onwards, indubitably encouraged this attitude.[65] But Henry seems to have felt that this trend tended to conceal the essential differences between secular and sacred letters, secular works having mere men as their authors but the Holy Scriptures being uniquely possessed of divine authorship and authority. It is somewhat ironic that Henry, who produced one of the most sophisticated amplifications of the theological *accessus* to date from the thirteenth century, seems to have been suspicious of the assumptions which it had encouraged in some of his predecessors and contemporaries. As we have shown, he does not wish to dismiss rhetorical principles or

---

[63] Art. 14, qu. 1; trans. Minnis and Scott, 255. Henry takes the metaphors of milk and solid food from Augustine, *Tract. in Ioh.*, 98.3 (CCL 36:577–78).

[64] See *Alexandri (. . .) Summa*, 1.8. Giles's views are made very clear in his commentaries on the *Sentences* and the Song of Songs. For the former, see *In Lib. sent.*, prol., qu. 3, art. 4, resolutio, in *Comment. b. Aegidii Romani in primum lib. sent.*, 31. For the latter, which is found among the works of Thomas Aquinas in several early prints, see *Comment. in Cant.*, in *Thomae Aquinatis opera*, 14.387–89, and the translation in Minnis and Scott, 243–47.

[65] For a summary account of the movement of the *accessus* from the *artes* into theology, see Minnis, *Medieval Theory of Authorship*, 15–39. See also Richard W. Hunt, "The Introductions to the Artes." Regarding the late-medieval *accessus* or "Aristotelian Prologue" in particular, Robert Kilwardby's early use of this paradigm is discussed at length in Osmund Lewry's splendid dissertation, "Robert Kilwardby's Writings."

"artificial" analysis, but rather, in the manner of Augustine, to keep them in their place. And that is precisely because Henry was determined to keep the divine *auctor* of Scripture firmly in *His* place; he seized every opportunity of affirming the supernatural and superhuman origins of theology.[66] This sets him somewhat apart from some of his thirteenth-century contemporaries who seem to posit for the inspired human authors of Scripture a degree of autonomy as "instrumental efficient causes" working under the primary and initiating cause, God.[67] Henry drew on the Aristotelian theory of causality in his own thinking on this matter (as on so many others), but alongside his recognition of the high status of Scripture's "secondary authors" is placed an emphasis on their fundamental subservience. Clearly, Henry was anxious to avoid statements which could be taken as implying a devolution of authority from the divine author to the human authors of the Bible.

These convictions permeate the above discussions of the mixed discourse of Scripture (by turns obscure and straightforward, profound and simple, ornamented and plain) and the didactic procedures of the body of exegesis which seeks to explain it—of the various stylistic media, in other words, of both *auctores* and commentators. As a theologian, Henry of Ghent would have been shocked by the modern suggestion that "the medium is the message" (to use Marshall McLuhan's classic formulation). For him the divine message is paramount, and therefore the rich range of scriptural styles must be treated in a way which keeps the power and the responsibility for the entire process of mediation firmly at the top.

University of York

---

[66] Hence, he argues that its *modus tradendi* is narrative rather than argumentative or ratiocinative, i.e., that it is beyond the processes of normal human inquiry. Art. 14, qu. 2: Paris ed., fol. 104r–v; Ferrara ed., 259–61.

[67] On the development of this doctrine, see Minnis, *Medieval Theory of Authorship*, 73–84.

KENT EMERY, JR.

Monastic "Collectaria" from the Abbey of St. Trudo (Limburg) and the Reception of Writings by Denys the Carthusian

n my studies of manuscripts containing writings by Denys the Carthusian (Dionysius Cartusiensis, 1402–1471), I have examined several hundred workaday monastic manuscripts, for the most part from the fifteenth and sixteenth centuries.[1] Many of these contain collections of texts that evince a unified rhetorical conception in their assembly and arrangement and a unified manuscript presentation and execution.[2] Among other things, my research also confirms that medieval conceptions of the organization of books and medieval practices of producing manuscripts continued well into the sixteenth century, at least in northern Europe. In this paper I treat a group of manuscripts, called *Collectaria* by their compiler and copyists, which were produced in the mid-sixteenth century but which in almost every respect are "medieval books."

From the early Middle Ages onward, the term *Collectarium* (or *Collectarius*) referred to one of the liturgical books constituting the recitation of the Office of the Hours. Usually, the *Collectarium* "brought together" in one volume the antiphons, prayers, chapters, versicles and responses and blessings used in the liturgical hours of the day *per circulum anni*, but it sometimes also included a liturgical calendar, litanies and other assorted prayers: "Modus dicendi capitula, Preces, Modus terminandi horas, Benedictiones, Capitula, Modus

---

[1] Emery, *Dionysii Cartusiensis ... Bibliotheca manuscripta*, CCM 121–121a, henceforward cited according to the CCM volume numbers.

[2] See my discussions and descriptions of manuscripts in CCM 121a and a forthcoming essay, "Copyists, Text-Collectors and Authors."

dicendi Pretiosa [chapters at Prime], Principia Antiphonar um, Modus dicendi Versiculos.''[3]

In the late Middle Ages, the word *Collectarium* came to signify a collocation of excerpted texts—quoted verbatim, paraphrased or abbreviated—disposed according to some unified rhetorical conception. As early as the ninth century one finds the term used in this sense. Rabanus Maurus wrote a work called a *Collectarium*, which gathers together comments by the Holy Fathers on the Epistles of Paul. A chronicler speaks of Rabanus's work in terms that define well its later usage: "He also made a *Collectarium* over the Epistles of Paul, collecting (*colligens*) sentences from diverse writings of the Holy Fathers and disposing them in order.''[4]

As this quotation suggests, the term *Collectarium* is related to a series of other medieval terms that name what modern scholars call *florilegia*: *Alphabetum, Compilatio, Compendium, Dicta, Excerpta, Exceptiones, Flores, Manipulus, Manuale, Rapiarium, Repertorium, Sententiae*, etc.[5] It is inseparably linked with the nouns *collectio* and *collectaneum*, the verb *colligere*, and the past participles—sometimes used substantively—*collectum, collecta*. The term *Collectarium* in this usage equivocates rhetorical methods of memory, invention, and disposition; the title of a composition; and the name of what is found in a manuscript book.

Throughout his many writings, Denys employs the terms *collectio, collecta, colligere, compilatio, compilare, componere* to signify the

---

[3] Fiala and Irtenkauf, "Versuch," 118. For the early formation of liturgical Collectars and variant names, see Corrêa, ed., *The Durham Collectar*, 3–138.

[4] For Rabanus Maurus's *Collectarium de sanctorum patrum opusculis in epistolas Pauli*, see Stegmüller, *Rep. bibl.* 5: 32 n°s 7063–77. The text quoted comes from Rudolphus (monachus), *Miracula sanctorum in Fuldenses ecclesias*, in *MGH* (folio series) 15 (1887): 340: "In epistolas quoque Pauli . . . Collectarium fecit, colligens de diversis opusculis sanctorum patrum sententias eorum et in ordinem disponens." There exists a small treatise, attributed to Priscillianus Abilensis (4th c.), entitled *Collectario de diversis sententiis*, printed in *Patrologiae Latinae Suppl.* 2: 1508–10. Petrus de Herenthals (de Floreffia), O.Cist., wrote a work entitled *Collectarius super librum Psalmorum* in the fourteenth century. Jean Gerson wrote a work entitled *Collectorium super Magnificat* (*Oeuvres complètes*, ed. Glorieux, 8: 163–534). The term here designates a complex literary organization. Into the *sportas* ("baskets") of the canticle (that is, under each verse), Gerson stuffs various materials, subdivided into *notulas*.

[5] Hamesse, "Le vocabulaire." See also the classic study by Paul Lehmann, *Mittelalterliche Büchertitel*, and Rouse and Rouse, "Florilegia."

procedures of memory, invention and disposition whereby he produced his enormous corpus. In modern but exactly fitting terms, his body of writings reveals a systematic method of "storing, retrieving, and recycling" materials originally located or memorialized in one place and then transferred, as occasion requires, from one work or treatise to another. Thus, for example, the texts of Scholastic doctors stored in his huge commentaries on Peter Lombard's *Sentences*, prepared privately in the monastery over several decades and then abbreviated in outline texts that serve as finding guides, locate and supply material for individual treatises on specific topics. Likewise, the materials compiled in his commentaries on every book in the Bible find their way into his sermon sequences and other treatises. His *Summa de vitiis et virtutibus* is a storehouse for *moralia* useful in sermons and special treatises. The materials are abbreviated or expanded from one place to another, as appropriate.[6]

Moreover, to a great extent Denys's writings are collected and excerpted from the works of others, indeed, from almost the whole library of medieval religious literature. When he could find them, Denys drew his extracts from *originalia*, or complete texts. Other times he plundered compilations, such as the great moral/preaching *Summas* and encyclopedias as well as philosophical compilations.[7] His technique varied from verbatim quotation to abbreviation to broad paraphrase, as in his "translation" of the works of John Cassian "ad stilum facillimum."[8] Denys's writings represent an abundant late-medieval flowering of collecting and compiling methods of composition that were devised and employed at least two centuries earlier, especially in the production of materials to aid preaching.[9]

---

[6] See Emery in CCM 121: 15–38, 47–50, and a forthcoming essay, "Denys the Carthusian and the Invention of Preaching Materials."

[7] Emery, "Denys ... and the Invention" and "Did Denys the Carthusian."

[8] I cite Denys' texts from the edition, *Doctoris ecstatici D. Dionysii Cartusiani opera omnia*, henceforward cited *Op. om.* Denys' paraphrases of the works of John Cassian are printed in *Op. om.* 27.

[9] Emery, "Denys ... and the Invention" In composing his encyclopedias and other writings, closely related to preaching, Vincent of Beauvais, like Denys after him, compiled and wove together texts of authoritative writers and texts from other compilations and "recycled" his own writings from one text to another. See Schneider, "Vincent of Beauvais' "; Paulmier-Foucart, "La compilation" and "Ordre encyclopédique."

In the preface to his commentary on the *Sentences*, Denys calls his large work a *collectio*, and in one of his epitomes or digests of this work, he refers to his commentaries as *collecta* and *collectum*.[10] A fifteenth-century register of Denys's titles properly describes the work: "Super quatuor libros sentenciarum scripta doctorum scholasticorum reducendo in unum," and his sixteenth-century editor calls the work a *collectaneum*.[11] In his commentary on pseudo-Dionysius's *De coelesti hierarchia*, Denys calls his commentary on Peter Lombard's *Sentences* a *collectarium* (or *collectarius*).[12] This *collectarium*, as he calls it, serves more than the memory; it rises to the levels of *ratio* and *intellectus*. Denys arranges his extracts on each question authoritatively and dialectically. First, on one side of the question, he recites the arguments of the more famous doctors and then those of their prominent followers; next, in the same fashion, he recites the opinions of doctors on the other side of the question. In passing, Denys inserts his own comments, and at the end offers his own resolutions to the issues raised in the collected materials. His bringing together of all this material and reducing it to order serves an important intellectual purpose. Denys says that it is a great mistake to cling pertinaciously or incautiously to the opinion of just one doctor, as so many do, and that one will find many "beautiful" and "useful" things in the writings of one doctor that he will not find in the writings of another.[13]

One of Denys's more widely circulated writings exposes the skeleton of his collecting method. Denys dedicated and sent his *Monopanton, seu Redactio omnium Epistolarum beati Pauli in unam ad materias* to Cardinal Nicholas of Cusa in 1451. The writing, which is essentially a research tool, attained the status of a "work" probably because of its dedicatory letter.[14] In this writing, Denys links

---

[10] *Op. om.* 19: 36; 33: 92C'.

[11] Emery in CCM 121: 65, 104.

[12] *Op. om.* 15: 60D': "De quibus etiam in collectario super primum Sententiarum, diligenter pro viribus est tractatum."

[13] Emery, "Denys the Carthusian and the Doxography," 332–33.

[14] The *Monopanton* is printed in *Op. om.* 14: 465–537. For book names with -*pan*, see Lehmann, 28. One wonders whether Denys' work was in any way inspired by Jean Gerson's concordance of the Gospels, *Monotesseron tetramonum sive unum ex quatuor* (Lehmann, 59). Denys wrote an *enarratio* on the Passion "ex quatuor Evangelistis sumpta et collecta" (*Op. om.* 31: 425–546). For more on the

together the verses of Paul's diverse Epistles into one, continuous text, "mixing together" and "moderating those words and places which seem to sound alike, accord well and coincide." He divides and arranges the verses under thematic and topical headings. By means of alphabetical signs in the body of the text, corresponding to marginal annotations, he indexes the sentences of Paul's Epistles that he redisposes. This apparatus is found in the exant autograph manuscript, and is usually reproduced faithfully in copies.[15]

In a manuscript owned in the Middle Ages by the Augustinian Canons Regular of the Windeshcim Congregation in Gaesdonck, made ca. 1460, a copy of Denys's "redaction of all of the Epistles of Paul into one" is accompanied by five others of the same kind (all anonymous), which link together under thematic headings key verses culled from the canonical Epistles, Acts, the four Gospels, the Apocalypse and the Wisdom books. The text collections were probably intended as private research tools "useful to preachers." Two of the items are called *Collectarii*. Here the term signifies texts collocated *ad verbum*.[16]

§

In an extraordinary cache of manuscript books produced in the sixteenth century at the Benedictine abbey of St. Trudo in Sint-Truiden in Limburg, the term *Collectarium* is used as a book title, designating collections of generous extracts drawn from many works, disposed topically and reduced to a comprehensive rhetorical order. The *Collectaria* contain many excerpts from the writings of Denys the Carthusian, which increase greatly in number from redaction to redaction. This may reflect the abbey's acquisition of volumes of the printed edition of Denys's writings, produced by Dirk Loër and the

---

Monopanton, see Emery, "Denys . . . and the Invention." Most of the medieval lists of Denys' writings cite the text as an *Epistola ad Cardinalem Nicolaum de Cusa*.

[15] Emery in CCM 121: 226 n° 39.

[16] Gaesdonck, Bibliothek des Collegium Augustinianum, MS. 5. See Hövelmann, "Gaesdonck MS 5," and Emery, "Copyists, Text-Collectors and Authors." I examined the manuscript in Gaesdonck (1982), but a microfilm in Hill Monastic Manuscript Library (St. John's University, Collegeville, Minn.) #39582 indicates that the book is now in Münster, Bistumsarchiv, CAG MS. 5.

Carthusians in Cologne between 1521 and 1538.[17] On the other hand, it is clear that the compiler of these *Collectaria* drew many excerpts from manuscript books. As a boy, Denys attended the abbey school at Sint-Truiden, located a few kilometers from the village of Rijkel where he was born. Not surprisingly, the abbey library came to possess manuscript copies of his writings. Among these was an autograph manuscript of Denys's *De reformatione claustralium*, or *Epistola scripta monachis Sancti Trudonis*, now lost; a fifteenth-century copy of the work from St. Trudo's survives, as do other fifteenth-century manuscripts from the abbey containing writings by Denys.[18]

Save one striking feature, the St. Trudo *Collectaria*, produced between the 1530s and the early 1570s, are medieval books, in their contents, organization, layout, rubrication, text-marking and script-types. These volumes are large and complex in their organization and variations. The group is constituted by five manuscripts now at the Bibliothèque de l'Université in Liège (MSS. 39C, 83C, 248C, 320A, 321A).[19] A sixth *Collectarium* (MS. 305A), according to librarians, has been missing for at least ten years. Another *Collectarium* from the abbey of St. Trudo, extraordinarily enough, is preserved in Paris at the Musée du Louvre (Département des Dessins, Collection Edmund de Rothchild MS. 1, n° I DR). Finally, a volume of documents preserved in Hasselt, Rijksarchief (Abdij Sint-Truiden 35; formerly Abdij Sint-Truiden Reg. Nr. 6681b) supplies futher evidence concerning the other books. It binds together *copiae* and documents pertinent to the abbey of St. Trudo, letters and literary excerpts. One document is dated 1475, but most range from 1531 to 1571. The

---

[17] On this edition, see Greven, *Die Kölner Kartause*, 50–85; Chaix, *Réforme et contre-réforme* 1: 211–43, 2: 444–507; Emery in CCM 121: 30–32.

[18] For *De reformatione claustralium*, see Emery in CCM 121: 239 n° 105. The text is contained in *Op. om.* 38: 209–42. A copy from St. Trudo's of this text is extant in Liège, Bibliothèque de l'Université, MS. 2736B, fols. 115r–151v. Other manuscripts from St. Trudo's containing works by Denys are Liège, BU, MSS. 54A, 292A, 358C. See Emery in CCM 121: 138–40, 184–85.

[19] Liège, BU, MSS. 320A and 321A are sixteenth-century *Collectaria* from St. Trudo's. These octavo manuscripts are surely related to the folio volumes, but not as immediately as the folio volumes are among themselves. The manuscripts do not contain texts by Denys, and I did not have the opportunity to examine them closely.

volume's most precious contents, from a literary perspective, are copies of many letters written by the Louvain humanist and theologian, Gerardus Moringus (d. 1556), perhaps in his own hand. Gerardus corresponded with Georgius Sarens, Abbot of St. Trudo (1533–1558), concerning the new edition of Denys's writings.[20] All but one of the *Collectaria* were produced and copied during Abbot Sarens's reign. Throughout the volume of documents preserved in Hasselt, a single writer—in margins, empty spaces and empty sides—wrote texts, drew pictures and diagrams and pasted in engravings. This same writer either annotated, filled in or copied all of the folio *Collectaria* from the abbey.

The St. Trudo books have a clear relation to text collections of the earlier Middle Ages. In a study of *florilegia* of classical authors, B. Munk Olsen finds five common characteristics that distinguish these collections from other research tools: (1) The collections extract from works judged worthy of authority; this is of special relevance to the St. Trudo group, for these books reveal in particular which fifteenth-century authors achieved authority in late medieval monastic circles; (2) The extracts are organized according to some scheme; (3) The compiler gives titles or sub-titles to the extracts, which indicate the contents or specify what is particularly relevant in them; (4) The compiler feels free to modify the texts in minor ways; (5) The compiler may compose prefaces and epilogues to the collections.[21] The St. Trudo books bear most of these marks.

Liège MS. 83C is dated 1549 and 1551 in two colophons; MS. 248C is dated 1550 and 1552 in two colophons. The manuscript in the Louvre is the latest in the group. Liège MS. 39C seems to be the earliest survivor among the folio volumes. The manuscript's colophon does not give a date. The collection's disposition, however, suggests that it is the earliest of the group and its watermarks yield the dates 1535–1545.[22] These dates are corroborated by evidence provided by chronicles contained in the manuscript.[23]

---

[20] Gerardus Moringus's letter to Abbot Georgius Sarens is printed in *Op. om.* 17: 15–20. On Gerardus's relations with Sarens, see De Vocht, *Monumenta humanistica*, 480–94, and also Emery, "Two More Copies," 5.

[21] Munk Olsen, "Les florilèges," 152–54.

[22] Piccard, *Buchstabe P. Abt. VII.* type 407 (Arnhem, 1535), and types 460–62 (Maastricht, Braunschweig, 1542–45).

[23] A chronicle of Roman pontiffs in MS. 39C ends (fol. 130v^b) with the name

Liège MS. 39C is a large paper folio volume (28.4 x 19.8 cm.) of 279 folios. The book has original foliation in rubricated Roman numerals (I–cclxi) beginning, after some front matter, with the *Collectarium* proper. The body of the text is written by one hand throughout, in a large, thick-stroked *textualis formata*, in two columns. In a few places, the same person who annotated or copied the other St. Trudo *Collectaria* has annotated the manuscript.

The *Collectarium* is divided into five books. The *Index sequentis collectarii* (fols. 4r^a–5v^b)[24] lists the topics and sub-topics of each book and indicates the folio numbers. The book headings in the index are rubricated, signed by black rounded paraphs and underlined in black ink. Alternately, the sub-topics for each book are written in black ink, signed by red rounded paraphs and underlined in red ink. This corresponds to the pattern in the body of the text, where the major headings are rubricated, signed by black paraphs and underlined in black ink, and the opening words of the entries, in black ink, are signed by red paraphs and underlined in red. The names of authors or the titles of books excerpted are rubricated; the larger extracts begin with three- or four-line, stylized red initials.

The first book of the *Collectarium* (fols. 8r^a–67v^b) treats the conscience (evil thoughts, temptations, sin in general), and then the capital vices, including sins of the tongue, and their remedies. These sections are followed by extracts on confession, penance, and servitude and liberty.

The main topics of the second book (fols. 69r^a–157v^b) are, in order: the life and Passion of Jesus Christ, beginning with a *Descriptio figure Jhesu Christi*; the Mass; the meaning of the word "Sacrament"; the gifts of the Holy Spirit; the mysteries of the life of the Virgin Mary; the ministry of angels; the feasts of the saints, constitut-

---

of Paulus III, but no entry for him is written. Paulus came to the office in 1534. The chronicle of Roman emperors ends (fol. 144r^a–v^a) with Carolus V, who came to reign in 1519. The chronicle of the bishops of Liège ends (fol. 149r^a) with an entry for Gerardus de Marka, who died in 1538, and then the names—with no entries—of Conradus de Brugis and Georgius ab Austria, who came to office in 1545. Finally, the chronicle of abbots of St. Trudo ends (fol. 157v^{a-b}) with Georgius Sarens. The entry states that he came to office in 1533. The original hand of the manuscript breaks off mid-entry; a second hand completes the entry, giving the date of Sarens' death in 1558.

[24] The last leaf of the index is mutilated.

ed largely by the section, *De diuersis sanctis secundum ordinem alphabetj*; a chronicle of the Roman pontiffs; a register of works of the fathers received by the Church, drawn mainly from Gelasius Papa; an almanac of the religious orders in the Church; a chronicle of the Roman emperors; a catalogue of the bishops of Liège; and finally, a chronicle of St. Trudo and his successors as abbot of the monastery.

The third book (fols. 159rᵃ–212vᵃ) treats the monastic life. It begins with a *Breuissima perfectionis formula* said to be "per quendam Sapientem edita," probably drawn from Henry Suso's *Horologium sapientiae*. Thereafter come sections concerning the service of God; exhortations to novices and monks; religious vows; obedience; the evangelical counsels; prayer and the recitation of the Hours; psalmody.

The fourth book (fols. 213rᵃ–236rᵃ) treats the virtues in general (love of neighbor and enemies); God's permission of evil and the tribulation of the good, the virtues of patience, humility and fear. The section entitled *De agro dominico* concerns the virtue of the Word of God, why God withdraws grace from men, those who lack consolation, the various signs of God's love and of one's own salvation and predestination. Finally, the section entitled *De multiplici tractione et vacatione* treats the reasons for withdrawing from the world and avoiding its temptations, on account of the defects of human nature, the fragility of the soul's union with the body, etc.

The fifth and last book (fols. 257rᵃ–264vᵇ) treats contempt of the world and the lovers of the world, followed by sections on the four last things: Death, Judgment, Hell and the punishment of the damned, Heaven and the joys and rewards of the blessed. This last section includes many *exempla*.

The order of the *Collectarium* traces an exhortatory movement from the purgation of vices through the mysteries of redemption to the particular requirements of the monastic life, concluding with a reinforcement of contempt of the world by meditation upon the last things. The exhortatory nature of the *Collectarium* is emphasized in later redactions.

The conventional medieval topics of this sixteenth-century collection are filled in with extracts from traditional medieval authorities. The extracts are generous, varying from a few lines to several columns. A few extracts are attributed to classical authors: Aristoteles, Galenus, Cato, Plinius, Seneca. Likewise there are a few extracts from the Scriptures. A large number of extracts are taken from patristic or pseudo-patristic authors: Cirillus, Basilius, Crisostomus, Eusebius, Theophilus,[25] Ambrosius, Augustinus, Hieronimus, Ciprianus, Gregorius, Isidorus, Prosper Aquitanus, Beda Venerabilis. As one might expect, the last of the Fathers, Bernard of Clairvaux (or pseudo-Bernard), is represented by many texts. Texts are also drawn from collections concerning the desert fathers (Abbas Macharius, Abbas Pastor, Ioannes Egiptus heremita, *Diuerse doctrine patrum antiquorum*, *In vitis patrum*), and, of course, from the *Regula* of Benedict.

Most impressive are the number and range of medieval authorities included: Ioannes Climacus, Rabanus Maurus, Theodolus (*De moribus*),[26] Anselmus, Hugo (de Sancto Victore), Richardus (de Sancto Victore), Guillermus Parisiensis, Guillibertus Tornacensis (O.F.M., d. 1270), Bonaventura, *Vita sancti Francisci*, Humbertus (de Romanis, O.P.), Vincentius (Bellovacensis, O.P.), Albertus Magnus, Thomas de Aquino, Iacobus de Voragine, O.P., Petrus Lemovicensis (d. 1304, *Liber de oculo morali*),[27] Nicolaus de Lira and Petrus de Natalibus (d. 1406). Especially numerous are extracts from the *Vita Christi* of the fourteenth-century Carthusian, Ludolphus (de Saxonia). Excerpts are also drawn from juridical works.[28]

Noteworthy are extracts from fifteenth-century authorities: Ioannes Gerson, Discipulus (Ioannes Herolt, O.P., d. 1468), Ioannes Cardinalis Turrecremata, Guilhemus de <Gouda, O.F.M.>,[29] Ioannes Tritemius, Godescalcus (Hollen, O.S.A.),[30] Ioannes Raulin

---

[25] This may be pseudo-Theophilus Antiochenus, *Commentaria in evangelia*. See Stegmüller, *Rep. bibl.* 2: 412 n° 2888.

[26] Bloomfield et al., *Incipits*, 43 n° 0334.

[27] See Bloomfield 475–76 n° 5532 (also n°s 0099, 1677, 2065), and Newhauser, "Der 'Tractatus moralis de oculo.'" The name in the manuscript is Petrus "Limoniensis."

[28] For example, *In decretis*, *In supplemento iuris*, and various *Casus papales* and *Casus episcopales*.

[29] The manuscript actually cites *Guilhelmus de Ganda de indumentis sacerdotalibus* (fol. 77r^b–v^b). The author must be Guillelmus de Gouda, fifteenth-century Franciscan, who wrote the treatise entitled *Expositio mysteriorum Missae et modus celebrandi*.

[30] The entries give only the first name, "Godscalcus." Godescalcus Hollen, O.S.A. (ca. 1411–81) wrote a huge collection of sermons entitled *Praeceptorium divinae legis* (many printed editions, 1481–1521), which is in effect a compendium

(1443–1514),[31] and Dionisius Rikel Cartusiensis. Only a few entries are drawn from sixteenth-century writers (Erasmus, Ioannes Adelphus Mulingus, Claudius Guillaudus Belliocensis).[32]

Many entries are from books that are anonymous in the manuscript: *Liber de apibus*, by Thomas Cantipratensis, O.P.; *Liber qui Summa de vitiis abbreviata dicitur*;[33] *Liber qui dicitur Virga directionis*; *Liber de quatuor nouissimorum* by Gerardus de Vliederhoven (14th c.); three works by the fifteenth-century Carthusian from Liège, Jacobus de Gruitrode, or attributed to him: *Liber qui Ortulus rosarum dicitur*, *Liber qui Lauacrum conscientie dicitur* and *Speculum anime peccatricis*;[34] and many passages from the huge encyclopedia for meditation and preaching, composed by Ioannes Mauburnus at the end of the fifteenth century, *Liber qui Rosetum dicitur*.[35] Many

---

of *moralia* for pastors. He also wrote special sermons *De novissimis* and *De oratione dominica*, as well as *Tractatus de septem sacramentis, de officio missae, de articulis fidei, de septem peccatis mortalibus, de novem peccatis alienis*. Another collection of sermons (printed 1517–20) includes a *Passionale, sive de Passione Christi*. All of these materials suit perfectly the *Collectarium*. See Zumkeller, "Hollen (Gottschalk)," and *Manuskripte*, 119–22 nᵒˢ 264–73.

[31] Jean Raulin (1443–1514), professor of theology at Paris and then Benedictine monk at Cluny. Raulin wrote two works the compiler probably used: *Collatio de perfecta religionis plantatione* (Paris: per magistrum Guidonem Mercatorem, 1499; Hain-Copinger 13702) and *Doctrinale mortis, seu opus de triplici morte, corporis, culpae et gehannae* (Paris: Berthold Rembolt for Jean Petit, 1518).

[32] For the humanist and printer (in Strassburg) Ioannes Adelphus Mulingus (Mülink), see Jöcher, *Allgemeines Gelehrten Lexicon* 1: 94; for Claudius Guillaudus Belliocensis (fl. 1540s), author of *Collationes in Matthaeum, Joannem, epistolas Pauli et reliquas Catholicas* (Paris, 1548), see Michael a S. Joseph, *Bibliographia critica* 2: 27.

[33] By Roger Sheepshead(?), abbreviated from Guillelmus Peraldus(?); Bloomfield 353 n° 4166. This is the text generally known as *Primo;* see Wenzel, "The Sources of Chaucer's Seven Deadly Sins."

[34] For Jacobus de Gruitrode, see Verjans, "Jacobus van Gruitrode"; Seynaeve, "Jacobus van Gruitrode"; Deschamps, "Middelnederlandse vertalingen"; Emery in CCM 121a: 445–565. Bloomfield nᵒˢ 0546, 1214, 3023 (pp. 62, 117, 260–61) names Thomas a Kempis as the author of *Hortulus rosarum*. The work in the manuscript, however, is probably by Jacobus de Gruitrode; see Deschamps, "De lange en de korte redactie." The evidence for Jacobus's authorship of *Lavacrum conscientiae sacerdotum* (Bloomfield 251 n° 2902) is given by Verjans, 468–69, and Seynaeve, 328–29. Petreius, *Bibliotheca Cartusiana*, 210, however, ascribes the *Lavacrum conscientiarum omnium sacerdotum* to the fifteenth-century Carthusian in Wittenburg, Ioannes Miskirchius. The *Speculum animae peccatricis* usually attributed to Jacobus may not be by him; see Emery in CCM 121a: 445–540.

[35] See Debongnie, *Jean Mombaer*. The *Rosetum* was composed ca. 1494–95 and printed at Paris in 1510.

excerpts are taken from an anonymous *Tractatus qui De professione monachorum dicitur*; a copy of this treatise survives in a manuscript from St. Trudo's, bound with Denys the Carthusian's *De reformatione claustralium* and a copy of a small text by Trudo of Gembloux, who was, we shall discover, the compiler of the *Collectarium*.[36] Finally, in the medieval fashion, several entries are attributed to *Quidam*.

If the format, topics and authorities of the *Collectarium* are medieval, another feature of the book is distinctly modern. Instead of illuminations, pasted on the versos opposite the beginning of each book and of other major sections are full-page engravings from printed books.[37] The later copies and redactions of the *Collectarium* contain many more engravings placed in the same positions, and the latest copy and redaction in the Louvre contains over fifty (which is why the Museum bought the book). Most of the engravings are accompanied by inscriptions on the pictures and around their bor-

---

[36] Liège, BU, MS. 2736B, fols. 32r^a–61r^a: "*Incipit tractatus de professione monachorum* Tractatus iste qui est de professione monachorum tres habet partes ... (32r^b).... *Incipit prologus* Cvm displiceat deo infidelis et stulta promissio Eccles. .v. promissio uera stulta sit cum promittens eam non intelligit ... (61r^a) ... qui autem requirunt dominum animaduertunt omnia (61r^b) Explicit tractatus cuiusdam sapientis de professione monachorum" [*litterae notabiliores*]. In manuscripts this treatise is variously attributed to Guillelmus de Lauduno, Guillelmus Peraldus, Guillelmus Pictaviensis, Hugo de Sancto Victore, Joannes Abbas and even Thomas de Aquino; see Hauréau, *Initia* 6: 256v–257r, and Schmeller and Meyer, *Schedarium* 2: 513a. Denys' *De reformatione claustralium* is copied in Liège MS. 39C, fols. 115r–151v. A short piece, "Summa pietatis et eruditionis Domino D. Trudoni Gemblacensi in Abbatia S. Benedicti" (late 16th–early 17th c. hand) is copied in fols. 177r–178r. The manuscripts are bound with printed texts: *Vita Sancti Trvdonis Confessoris apud Hasbanos*.... (Louvain: Apud Seruatium Zaffenum, 1540), fols. 2r–24r; *Specvlvm monachorvm a Dacranyo ordinis sancti Benedicti abbate conscriptum*.... (Louvain: Bartholomaeus Grauius, 1538), fols. 68r–95v; *Articvli orthodoxam religionem, sanctamque fidem respicientes, a sacrae theologiae professoribus Louaniensis universitatis editi*.... (Louvain: Chez Reynier Velpen et Iacques Bathen, 1545), fols. 96r–107v; *Doctissimi patris domini Petri Dorlandi de enormi proprietatis monachorum vicio dialogus cultissimus*.... (Louvain: Theodoricus Martinus Alostensis, 1530), fols. 155r–175v. Trudo of Gembloux, the compiler of the *Collectarium*, surely used texts now in this composite volume. He copied an excerpt *Ex speculo Dacriani abbatis* on an inserted sheet in Liège, BU, MS. 83C, fol. 167v^a–b. For the eighth-century Benedictine author of the *Speculum monachorum*, Dacrianus Abbas, see Michael a S. Joseph, *Bibliographia critica* 2: 111.

[37] Liège, BU, MS. 39C, front cover pastedown, fols. 7v, 68v, 131v, 134v, 149v, 158v, 212v (small), 236v, 265v.

ders, written by the hand evident in all of the books. Since some of the same engravings are pasted in different volumes, it is possible that the monks obtained spare sheets from the printers. I suspect rather that libraries in and around Liège own several sixteenth-century books with missing engravings.

The *Collectarium* in Liège MS. 39C also bears a fine full-page drawing on the last verso of the book (fol. 279v). The drawing was not made by the copyist, Jacobus Gommer. Around the death figure, drawn in grisaille in the center of the page, is a rubricated text, filling in the remaining writing-space, with an inscription, written in the ink of the text, forming a border around the picture and rubricated text. The same death figure accompanied by the same surrounding text is redrawn at the end of another copy of the *Collectarium* in Liège MS. 83C (fol. 418v).[38] Several drawings rendered in the same style are contained in the manuscript in the Louvre. These drawings enable an important identification. The hand of the texts accompanying the drawings is the distinct, spindly *bastarda libraria* of the writer who has also annotated or copied Liège MSS. 83C and 248C, the book of documents in Hasselt, and the manuscript in the Louvre. It is he, surely, who has cut, collected, pasted and inscribed the engravings in all of the books. The colophons in MS. 83C and in the manuscript in the Louvre identify this writer and adorner of books as Trudo of Gembloux, monk of St. Trudo.

The rubricated colophon at the end of Liège MS. 39C, copied by Jacobus Gommer, identifies Trudo as the original compiler of the *Collectarium*:

¶Collegit hunc librum frater Trudo Gemblacensis cenobita monasterij sancti Trudonis in hasbania. ¶Scripsit vero frater

---

[38] Liège, BU, MS. 39C, fol. 279v. The drawing depicts a death figure, a walking naked man with skeletal head and winding-cloth drapped over his shoulder. A balloon extending from his mouth contains the psalm verse: "Respice in me et miserere mei: quia vnicus et pauper sum ego. psal. xxiiii." Rubricated titles at the top center and bottom center of the page state: *Mors omnia steruit* and *Mors omnibus communis*. The picture is boxed by a running inscription; inside the frame, surrounding the figure, is a full page of rubricated text. In the drawing in MS. 83C, fol. 418v, the text surrounding the figure, filling the writing-space, has been written in the ink of the text, while the border inscription is rubricated. For other pictures drawn and redrawn by Trudo, see n. 74 below.

Jacobus Gommer eiusdem monasterij relligiosus sub domino
Georgio sarens abbate.   (Fol. 264v^b)

The names of the compiler, Trudo of Gembloux, the copyist, Jacobus Gommer, and the abbot of St. Trudo, Georgius Sarens, appear—
together or separately—in all the other surviving folio *Collectaria*
from the abbey. A fourth name appears in this book. A rubricated
inscription at the top of the otherwise blank folio 3r states: *Liber
monasterij Sancti Trudonis ad vsum fratris Joannis Metteroney*. As we
shall see, Jacobus Gommer also copied a later redaction of the *Collectarium*; having done so, he could let another brother use his first
copy.

At the end of the book, immediately before the colophon, are
two interesting notes to the reader:

> The readers of this book may draw from it, as an example of
> virtue, whatever they may find to be well said. Nor was it
> fitting, as Bernard says, for one person to say all things; so we
> may delight in collecting diverse writings from diverse writers,
> and we should give due thanks and praise to each one of them.
> Moreover, many things are contained here which are entrusted
> and left to the judgment of the reader.   (Fol. 264v^a)[39]

The second note is written in a slightly different script:

> We have added very little of our own, or nearly nothing at all.
> Low things, indeed, are exposed and crushed, as the very
> matter itself shows. Howsoever this may be, if something
> collected by us, which seems less than true to faith, will have
> been transmitted, let whoever might perceive the matter more
> correctly be free, by our good grace, to change or even obliter-
> ate what he has seen. Nothing is more our friend than truth
> itself. Let one do so according to the endowments given to
> him by the Lord, so that what we, according to our slight
> ability, have begun and fashioned, at one time or another may

---

[39] Liège, BU, MS. 39C, fol. 264v^a: "*Lectores librj huius in exemplum virtutis
trahant quicquid inuenerint bene dictum Neque *vt ait bernardus* ab vno omnia
dicere congruum erat. vt a diuersis diuersa colligere gratulemur. et debitas singulis
gratias referamus et laudes *Preterea mul*ta habentur que lectoris arbitrio credenda
relinquuntur.*"

be led back to the perfect and most high one. To the honor of him to whom we Christians ought to relate all things, truly the most good and greatest God, who lives sempiternally, the King of kings and Lord of lords.   (Fol. 264v^{a-b})[40]

The sense of these notes suggests that they were composed by the compiler. They allow users and copyists of the *Collectarium* to modify and improve the texts in the collection. The compiler himself took this opportunity twice more.

§

The *Collectarium* in Liège MS. 83C (28.0 x 20.0 cm., 421 fols.), now divided into two parts, contains 141 more folios than the earlier copy by Jacobus Gommer. The colophon at the end of the first part of the *Collectarium* (fol. 213r^b), comprising the original five books, indicates that Trudo of Gembloux collected and copied the text in 1549, under the Abbot Georgius Sarens.[41] The base script of the manuscript—a *bastarda libraria* with near looping on the ascenders—is larger, less compact and more thickly stroked than the *notula* employed by Trudo of Gembloux in other manuscripts. However, Trudo uses his more customary script in his many annotations to the book and on its many inserted leaves; a comparison between the two indicates that they are the same, except in scale.

Trudo's *Collectarium* of 1549 is an entirely new redaction of the one copied by Jacobus Gommer in the 1530s or early 1540s. In the first place, Trudo has reversed the first two books of the collection,

---

[40] Liège, BU, MS. 39C: "*De nostro* perpauca aut propemodum nulla adiecimus. Vulgaria quidem sunt obuia et protrita id quod res ipsa monstrat. Ut ut est si quid minus ad fidem veri a nobis collectum traditum fuerit. liberum sit *nostra bona gratia.* cuilibet rectius sentienti mutare que visa fuerint aut etiam obliterare Nichil enim nobis amicum magis ipsa veritate *Ffaciat* pro dotibus a domino sibi datis. vt id quod a nostra tenuitate inchoatum et informatum vtcumque fuerit. ad perfectum et summam perducatur. *Ad honore*m illius ad quem omnia nostra christiani conferre debemus. nimirum dej optimi maximi qui viuit sempiternus rex regum et dominus dominorum" (fol. 264v^{a-b}).

[41] Liège, BU, MS. 83C, fol. 213r^b: "Collegit et scripsit hunc librum frater trudo gemblacensis. cenobita monasterij sancti Trudonis in hasbania. sub dompno georgio sarens abbate. Anno nati christi XV^c xlix."

so that the book concerning Christ's life and Passion, the Mass and sacraments, the saints etc. (fols. 1r^a–51v^b) now precedes the book on conscience, the vices and their remedies etc. (fols. 52r^a–103r^b). I suspect that this reordering reflects a theological consideration: the remediation of the vices flows from the grace of Christ and the sacraments. The next three books, concerning monastic life, the virtues, contempt of the world and the four last things, follow the order of the earlier redaction (fols. 104r^a–155r^b, 156r^a–186r^b, 189r^a–233r^b).

Trudo retains the basic topical and sub-topical divisions of his earlier version, but he has added more sub-topics. For example, his treatment of the vices now not only embraces the capital sins, but their specific offshoots as well. The materials of the *Collectarium* are greatly expanded. In general, Trudo has retained his stock of authorities from the earlier version, but he has eliminated some texts and rearranged others. Moreover, he has added excerpts from many new authorities and texts not included in the first redaction. Thus, in the sections concerning the vices and virtues, the sacraments and liturgical feasts, he has pillaged much from the *Rationale diuinorum officiorum* and other writings by Guillelmus Durandus.[42] Concerning the saints, he has plundered texts from the *Cathalogus sanctorum* by Petrus de Natalibus and the *Breuiarium Romanum*. Other new authorities and works in book 1 include Cesarius (Arelatensis); Orosius; Timotheus Historiographus; the exempla collection *Ortulus anime*;[43] the *Catholicon* by Ioannes de Balbis Ianuensis, O.P.;[44] the *Fasciculus temporum* by Wernerus Rolevinck (15th c.); and a genealogy of Saints Benedict and Scholastica "Ex codice monasterij nostri." In book 2, Trudo adds new texts by Petrus Damianus; the *Dictionarius pauperum* (extracted from the *Distinctiones* of Nicolaus de Byard, fl. 1250s);[45] and from sermons of the Dominican preacher, Peregri-

---

[42] The *Rationale* is cited without the name of an author, but Durandus is cited by name for other entries. For Durandus's moral works, see Bloomfield 49, 201 n°s 0410, 2257.

[43] By Hartungus de Herwersleyben (Herbsleben), O.P. (14th c.); Bloomfield 514 n° 5959; Kaeppeli, *Scriptores* 2: 17 n° 1695.

[44] The author is not cited in the entries. Ioannes flourished in the second half of the thirteenth century; see Kaeppeli, *Scriptores* 2: 380–83 n° 2199.

[45] The author is not cited in the entries; see Stegmüller, *Rep. bibl.* 4: 18 n° 5695.

nus (de Oppeln).[46] Book 3 shows new entries from Valerius Maximus, Hilarius (Pictaviensis), Sigebertus Gemblacensis (11th c.), Petrus Comestor and Hugo de Floreto. In books 4–5 Trudo draws new excerpts from Gregorius Nazianzenus and the *Liber de viris illustribus ordinis cisterciensis*. Mainly in book 2 concerning the vices but also in books 3–5, Trudo inserts excerpts from the writings of the sixteenth-century Parisian theologian, Petrus Richardus.[47]

In the first redaction of the *Collectarium*, there are only three extracts from works by Denys the Carthusian.[48] In this second redaction, there are scores of texts excerpted from his writings, which are especially plentiful in the sections on the vices (book 2) and the virtues (book 4).[49] Moreover, in order to emphasize the exhortatory intent of the collection, Trudo ends each of the first four books with an *Exhortatio salutaris ad religiosos* drawn from Denys's writings.[50]

After he completed the copy of the revised five books of the *Collectarium* in 1549, Trudo continued to add extracts from his reading by way of inserted leaves, not much smaller than the original leaves and written in the same two-column format of his original text. Dates in various chronicles indicate that Trudo was still adding to, and working on, his 1549 copy more than twenty years later, at least until 1572.[51] Many of the new extracts are drawn from works

---

[46] Fl. 1305–27; see Kaeppeli, *Scriptores* 3: 211–12 n° 3194.

[47] Resident of the Collège d'Harcourt in Paris and author of *Confessionale, seu pastoralis decalogus [dialogus divinae legis], curatis necessario requisitus* (Paris, 1510); *Doctrinale sanctae ac providae vitae quatuor memoratu digne continens, scilicet mortem duplicem, poenus inferni et purgatorii, iudicium generale, beatitudinem aeternam....* (Paris: I. Badius Ascensius, 1519), and *Petri Richardi artium et sacre theologie professoris optime merite sermonum opus super epistolas et evangelia totius anni clarissimum....* (Paris: ab Joanne Faruo, 1518). The author should not be confused with the Parisian theologian of the same name noticed in Farge, *Biographical Registers*, 391–93 n° 416.

[48] Liège, BU, MS. 39C, fols. 29v^b–30r^a, 175v^b–176r^b, 261r^b–v^a.

[49] Denys is cited as Dionisius Rikel, a Rikel, Ryckel, Richelius.

[50] Liège, BU, MS. 83C, fols. 50r^b–51v^b, 102v^b–103r^b, 154v^a–155v^b, 187r^a–188r^b.

[51] These were moved to the second part (see below), where Trudo also inserted leaves. He usually fills in the chronicles, however, in empty spaces at the end. In the chronicle of the Roman pontiffs, the last original entry is Julius II, dated 1550 (fol. 220v^b). Additions in the *notula* script continue to Gregorius XIII, dated 1572 (fol. 221v^b). The additions to the chronicle of Roman emperors begin mid-entry for Carolus V and continue to Maximilianus, dated 1572 (fol. 236v^a–b). The chronicle of

of Denys the Carthusian.[52] The inserted leaves also reveal new authors and books in Trudo's library. The author copied most on the inserted leaves is Thomas a Campis.[53] Other inserted leaves contain many new excerpts from the authentic works of Bernard of Clairvaux,[54] excerpts from sermons by the sixteenth-century Franciscan Adam Sasbout Adelphensis (1516–1573),[55] from ·the *Tractatus de instructione iuuenum et nouitiorum* of Henricus de Coesueldia (O. Cart., 15th c.),[56] the *Liber reuelationum* of Sta. Birgitta,[57] and an anonyomus work, *Epistola scripta ad confessorem monialium.*[58]

Besides revising his original five-book *Collectarium*, Trudo added to it a second part, which he completed in 1551.[59] He moves the chronicles, which ended the book concerning the life and Passion of

---

bishops of Liège includes one more than the chronicle in MS. 39C, Robertus a Bergis (fol. 254r^a). The chronicle of the abbots of St. Trudo gives a long entry for the *Prior in throno*, Georgius Sarens (fol. 266r^a–v^b). Part of the entry (an *Epitaphium*) seems to have been added after Sarens's death in 1558. Georgius's successor is entered only by name (fol. 266v^b).

[52] Liège, BU, MS. 83C, fols. 31r^{a-b}, 41v^b, 47r^b–v^a—pasted slips over column, 62r^a–v^b, 70v^{a-b}, 98r^{a-b}, 152r^a–v^b.

[53] Liège, BU, MS. 83C, fols. 31r^b–v^b, 53r^a–v^b, 81r^a–v^b, 85r^a–v^b, 120r^a–v^b—*Vita boni monachi*, 124r^{a-b}—slip pasted over column, 125r^a–v^b, 198r^b–v^b.

[54] *De gradibus humilitatis, De persequtione sustinenda, De consideratione ad Eugenium, in homelia vndecima, in homelia quarta super euangelio Missus est* (Liège, BU, MS. 83C, fols. 70r^b–v^b, 73r^a–v^b, 141r^a–v^b, 160r^a–v^b, 168r^a–v^a).

[55] Liège, BU, MS. 83C, fols. 174r^a–v^b, 181r^a–v^b. An *Exhortatio ad religiosos* by Adam appears in the body of the text, just before Denys', at the end of book 1 (fols. 49r^a–50r^b). For the author, see Wadding, *Scriptores* 1: 115–17.

[56] Liège, BU, MS. 83C, fol. 114r^a–v^b.

[57] Liège, BU, MS. 83C, fol. 127r^a–v^b.

[58] Liège, BU, MS. 83C, fol. 70r^a–v^b. Denys wrote a treatise entitled *De reformatione monialium dialogus*, printed in *Op. om.* 38: 243–61. See Emery in CCM 121: 239 n° 106. Unusually, this work does not have a Prooemium, as do most of Denys' writings. Could this letter be the missing Prooemium?

[59] Interestingly, in the colophon Trudo calls his book a *Compendium*, but adds the title *Collectarium* above the line: "Compendium [*sup. lin.*: vel Collectarium] istud collegit et scripsit frater trudo gemblacensis cenobita in hasbania sub dompno georgio sarens abbate Anno nati christi XV^c .li." (fol. 406r^b). Just before the colophon, in rubricated letters, is the second note to the reader that appears in Jacobus Gommer's copy of the earlier redaction in MS. 39C. The first sentence of the note in MS. 83C is different; here Trudo also calls the book a *Compendium*, but adds the title *Collectarium* above the line: "Ea que in hoc compendio [*sup. lin.*: collectario] continentur de nostro ..." (fol. 406v^b).

Christ in his earlier redaction,[60] to the first section of the second part. To the original chronicles of the Roman pontiffs (MS. 83C, fols. 214r^b–221v^b), Roman emperors (fols. 223r^a–236v^b), bishops of Liége (fols. 249r^a–254r^b), and the abbots of St. Trudo (fols. 257r^a–266v^b), he adds new chronicles of the kings of France (fols. 240r^a–242v^b), the princes of Tongeren and dukes of Brabant (fols. 244r^a–247r^b), and a list of collegiate churches in the diocese of Liège (fol. 256r^a–b). He supplements his chronicle of the bishops of Liège with entries on the bishops of Utrecht and Tongeren.

Thereafter, Trudo compiles a complete medieval encyclopedia. To his original entries on the works of the Holy Fathers received by the Church, he now adds entries for the ancient philosophers, heretics and medical writers (fols. 274r^b–284v^b). Following in order are sections on astronomy (fols. 284v^b–288v^b); on the elements and physical features of the earth, and on times, liturgical feasts and the ages of history (fols. 288v^b–299v^b); on geography and places (fols. 299v^b–309r^a); a lapidary (fols. 309r^a–310r^a); a bestiary, encompassing waters and fishes (fols. 310r^a–314v^b), trees and herbs (fols. 340v^b–349v^b) besides mammals and birds (fols. 349v^b–370r^b); and a long section on man and the parts of his body and soul (fols. 314v^b–340v^b). The encyclopedia ends with grammatical aids: *Quedam nomina uel uocabula per alphabetum distincta* (fols. 371r^a–379v^a); *Littere numerales* (fols. 381r^a–383r^b); and *Quedam Adagia similia et colloquia* (fols. 384r^a–406r^b). Trudo's expanded redaction, like Vincent of Beauvais' *Speculum*, forms a *Collectarium doctrinale, morale, historiale et naturale.*[61]

For the encyclopedia in the second part, Trudo gives entries under the names of Dyascorides, Marcus Varro, Plinius, Constantinus medicus, Ysaac medicus, Petrus Blesensis (ca. 1155–ca. 1210), Michael de Hungaria (O.M., 15th c.), the humanist Beatus Rhenanus (1485–1547), and the sixteenth-century Professor of Theology at Paris, Martialis Masurier.[62] He draws extracts from many encyclope-

---

[60] Book 1 in Liège, BU, MS. 39C and book 2 in MS. 83C.

[61] *Doctrinale*: pt. 1, books 1 and end of book 5; *Morale*: pt. 1, books 2–4, and the beginning of book 5; *Historiale*: first sections of pt. 2; *Naturale*: last sections of pt. 2.

[62] Trudo cites "Martialis Masurier doctor theologus in *Tractatu de preparatione cordis.*" For Masurier (Mazurier), see Farge, *Biographical Registers*, 318–22 n° 339. The work Trudo cites was printed with the title *Doctrina cordis* (Paris: Pierre le Roy for Jean Petit, 1518).

dic works: Plutarchus, *De moralibus*; Sidonius, *Liber de naturis rerum*;[63] patristic hexaemeral literature (Ambrose, Basil); Isidore of Seville; the *Phisiologus*; Bartholomeus de Anglia, *De proprietatibus rerum*; the *Cronica Marburgensis*; and extensively from the writings of the Augustinian Hermit, Anthonius de Rampogelis (d. 1423).[64] And in each section, Trudo supplies abundant extracts from the writings of Denys the Carthusian, nearly forty altogether in the second part.[65] The last entry in the alphabetical register of *Colloquia*, ending the second part, is a discourse by Denys on the *Uerba sapientium* (fol. 406r[a-b]).

Perhaps as an afterthought, Trudo judged it best not to end his new redaction with materials concerning the worldly arts and sciences. Thus, he later[66] added another gathering containing a General Confession by Bernard of Clairvaux (fols. 407r[a]–409v[b]); a sermon on mortality attributed to Cyprian (fols. 411r[a]–412r[b]); extracts concerning death from Augustine, Chrysostom, Erasmus and anonymous letters (fol. 412r[b]–413v[b]); and a group of medieval texts, placed under the title-heading "Pious Exhortations for the contempt of the world."[67] Here too Denys the Carthusian speaks most of the last words (fols. 416v[b]–417v[b]).

---

[63] I have found no titles of Sidonius Apollonaris or pseudo-Sidonius that would seem to correspond to this title.

[64] Antonius Rampegolus de Ianua. See Bloomfield 125 n° 1312, and also n°s 0130, 1719, 4869 (pp. 25–26, 158, 411). The *Biblia aurea* or *Compendium Bibliae* and the *Compendium morale* are cited in Zumkeller, *Manuskripte*, 64–66 n°s 115–16.

[65] Liège, BU, MS. 83C, fols. 36r[a] (Tritemius' note on Denys' life, under the entry for Emperor Fredericus III), 235r[a]–v[b] (insert sheet, *In vita Dionisij Carthusianj*), 271r[a]–v[b] (insert sheet, "Dionisius ryckel in expositione capituli decimj sexti tertij librij Regum"), 274r[a], 278v[a-b], 282v[a-b], 283r[a-b], 284r[b]–v[b], 288v[b]–289r[b], 290r[a]–v[b], 291v[b]–293v[b], 295r[a] and 295v[b] (insert sheet), 301r[b]–v[a], 308r[a], 313r[b]–v[a], 315v[a-b], 317r[b]–v[a], 318r[a], 321r[a]–v[a], 322v[b]–323v[b], 324v[b], 330r[b], 331r[a-b], 331v[a]–333v[b], 334r[b], 336v[a-b], 341r[b]–v[b], 353v[b]–354v[a], 356v[a], 357v[b]–358r[a], 362v[a]–364v[b], 365r[a-b], 366v[b]–367r[a], 380r[b].

[66] How much later, one cannot know for sure. The new section, as I observe below, is ended by the drawing on fol. 418r. As usual, Trudo later filled in the remaining blank sides of the booklet with text. On fol. 418v[a-b], he remarks the visit of Emperor Phillip of Spain to Belgium in 1565.

[67] Liège, BU, MS. 83C: "GEns absque consilio ... ac nouissima prouiderent Deut. xxxix Et Salomon Fili mi audj disciplinam patris tui. ..." (fol. 414r[a]–v[b]); "CVm in medio laqueorum positi simus. ..." (fols. 414v[b]–415r[a]; Ps.-Augustinus, *Manuale*; Bloomfield 421 n° 4957); "UIdete quomodo caute ambuletis ... que sit voluntas Dei ephesios .v. Si debite vt oportet flebilem miserabilem atque damnabilem cursum seu statum mundj presentis temporis consideremus. ..." (fols. 415r[a]–

§

Jacobus Gommer copied Trudo of Gembloux's second redaction of his *Collectarium* in Liège, BU, MS. 248C (28.4 X 20.0 cm., 393 fols.).[68] Trudo and Jacobus worked in tandem. Trudo finished the first part of his second redaction in 1549; Jacobus finished his copy of this part in 1550.[69] Trudo completed the redaction of his new second part in 1551; Jacobus finished his copy of the second part in 1552.[70] Jacobus Gommer's copy of Trudo's new redaction of the *Collectarium* does not include, of course, the new materials Trudo subsequently inserted in his own book. An inscription at the end of the table of contents (fols. 56rᵃ–58rᵃ), which Jacobus prepared in this copy of the new redaction as he did in his copy of the earlier one, states that the book is "Ad usum fratris Jacobi gommer."

Jacobus'ss *textualis* script is less formed and angular than the one he wrote 10–15 years before. It becomes smaller in scale and more rapid as his copying progresses in the two parts. Otherwise, the manuscript presents a more difficult paleographical complication. After the first three lines of an entry in the encyclopedia of the

---

416rᵃ); "CVm anima nostra immortalis sit et propter splendorem intellectus omnj materiali natura sublimior. ..." (fols. 416rᵃ–416vᵇ). The sermon by Cyprian is entitled *De mortalitate*: "FRatres dilectissimj agnoscere se debet quj deo militat ..." (fols. 411rᵃ–412rᵇ).

[68] The copy of the two parts of the new *Collectarium* is contained in fols. 56rᵃ–386rᵇ of Liège, BU, MS. 248C. Fols. 387rᵃ–390vᵇ contain the general confession from Bernard of Clairvaux and extracts from Denys the Carthusian that Trudo put into the booklet he added to his own copy, but Gommer's text does not include the other materials found there. Instead, fols. 390vᵇ–393vᵇ of MS. 248C contain a collection of prayers. On the first part of this book, see below.

[69] Liège, BU, MS. 248C, fol. 224vᵃ: "Collegit hunc librum frater Trudo gemblacensis cenobita monasterij sancti Trudonis in hasbania. Scripsit vero frater Jacobus gommer. religiosus eiusdem monasterij. Sub domino Georgio Sarens abbate. Anno nati Christi XVᶜ.l. *Ffinis prime partis*."

[70] Liège, BU, MS. 248C, fol. 386rᵇ: "Collegit hunc librum frater Trudo gemblacensis cenobita monasterij sancti Trudonis in hasbania. Scripsit vero frater Jacobus gommer. religiosus eiusdem monasterij. Sub domino Georgio Sarens abbate. Anno nati Christi XVᶜ .Lij. *Finis secunde partis*." Immediately above this (fol. 386ᵃ⁻ᵇ) is the second reader's note as in Gommer's earlier copy and in Trudo's second redaction. It begins "Ea que in hoc compendio ..." As he did in his own copy, Trudo here corrects above the line: "vel collectario." The first reader's note, which Gommer placed before this one in his earlier copy, is now placed after the end of the Table of contents of the first part, on fol. 57vᵇ: "Lectores librj huius in exemplum virtutis. ..."

second part (fol. 294rᵃ, 1.40), the script changes to a distinctly modern, flowing bookhand. This hand continues for the remaining 100
folios of the book (to fol. 393vᵇ). The colophon to the second part,
stating that Jacobus Gommer is the copyist, is written in this script
(fol. 386rᵇ). The same phenomenon occurs in a separate manuscript
(fols. 1–55) that precedes the *Collectarium* in the bound volume. The
text here also begins in Jacobus Gommer's *textualis* hand, but the
script changes into the flowing modern bookhand in the middle of
the text of a prayer and continues to the end of the manuscript (fols.
16vᵇ, 1.31–53vᵃ).

It is possible that Jacobus suddenly stopped his copying and that
another writer took over. That late medieval copyists used different
scripts, however, is well-attested.[71] I think it is easier to trust the
colophon of the second part and to believe that the second script is
Jacobus Gommer's rapid writing than it is to believe that another
writer twice completed Jacobus'ss work and nevertheless ascribed 200
two-column folio sides of arduous copying to him.

As was his compulsive practice, Trudo of Gembloux annotated
Jacobus Gommer's new copy throughout, filling in the empty spaces
at the end of the books, supplying new texts, entering drawings, and
bringing the chronicles up-to-date from where Jacobus left off.[72]
Moreover, the manuscript attached to Jacobus Gommer's copy of the
Collectarium represents yet another collecting effort by Trudo of
Gembloux. The colophon at the end (fol. 53vᵃ), written by Trudo
himself, indicates that he collected the materials but was not their
copyist.[73] Trudo's new collection begins with a liturgical calandar
(fols. 2rᵃ–3vᵇ). The next section of the text (fols. 4rᵃ–30rᵇ) is a collec-

---

[71] See for example Doyle, "The Work"; Kruitwagen, "De schrijftmeester";
Lieftinck, "Pour une nomenclature," 24–28; Mynors, "A Fifteenth-Century Scribe";
Ouy, "Autographes calligraphiés"; Parkes, *English Cursive Bookhands*, 21–22, Pl. 21.

[72] For example, in Liège, BU, MS. 248C, fols. 232rᵃ–233vᵇ, 248rᵇ–vᵃ, 272vᵇ–273ᵃ,
respectively, Trudo brings the entries in the chronicle of Roman Pontiffs from
Julius III (dated 1550), where Jacobus finished, to Gregorius XIII (dated 1572); to
Jacobus's entry for the Emperor Carolus V, he adds entries for Ferdinandus and
Maximilianus (dated 1562); and to Jacobus's brief entry for Abbot Georgius Sarens
of St. Trudo, who died in 1558, he adds several *Epitaphia*.

[73] Liège, BU, MS. 248C, fol. 53vᵃ: "Collegit hec frater Trudo gemblacensis
natione cenobita monasterij sanctj Trudonis in hasbania Sub domino Georgio sarens
abbate."

tion of prayers and thanksgivings. A title-heading on the verso opposite the first page of the collection, written by Trudo of Gembloux, specifies the contents: "Obesecrationes Orationes Interpellationes et Gratiarum actiones de tempore et de sanctis secundum ordinem Kalendarij" (fol. 3v^b). Jacobus calls this section a *Dominicarium* (fol. 3v^b). A third section of the text (fol. 31r^a–46r^a), entitled *Festiloquium* (fol. 30r^b), contains the prayers, collects and antiphons for Saints' Days. A final section (fols. 48r^a–53v^a) contains liturgical formulae and prayers pertaining to monastic rites. With this compilation, Trudo returns the *Collectarium* to its liturgical origins.

§

Trudo did not wish to leave new materials he had gathered since completing the second redaction of his *Collectarium* dispersed in several books. His final redaction of the *Collectarium*, preserved in the Louvre, is a "beautiful" copy written in his own hand. Besides more humanist authors, into this final version he incorporated collections of prayers and texts and drawings he had already inserted into his own copy of his second redaction (Liège MS. 83C), or added to Jacobus Gommer's copy of this version (Liège MS. 248C), or found in the volume of abbey documents he annotated (Hasselt, Rijksarchief).[74] Most of all, he added to his final redaction texts

---

[74] Paris, Musée du Louvre, Dépt. des Dessins, Coll. Ed. de Rothschild, MS. 1, n° I DR. From materials inserted or added to his own copy of the *Collectarium* (Liège, BU, MS. 83C), Trudo incorporated into the Louvre manuscript extracts from sermons of Adam Sasbout Adelphensis and from the *Instructio iuuenum et nouitiorum* of Henricus de Coesueldia. Trudo added extracts from Carolus Fernandus (Prof. of Theology, Paris; d. 1496), *Speculum discipline*, to Jacobus Gommer's copy of the *Collectarium* (Liège, BU, MS. 248C, fols. 181v^a–b, 224v^b); these he incorporated into the Louvre manuscript. Also, he incorporated into the Louvre manuscript materials he found in Hasselt, Rijksarchief, Abdij Sint-Truiden 35, including the *Testamentum* of Jacobus Faber Stapulensis and extracts from the letters of Gerardus Moringus. See my discussion above, and the list of contents in the Louvre and Hasselt manuscripts presented in Kristeller, *Iter Italicum* 3: 131, 337. We already mentioned that a drawing of a death figure and surrounding text that Trudo made in Jacobus Gommer's copy of the first redaction he drew again in his own copy of the second redaction; see n. 38 above. Likewise, another death figure, standing in a coffin and holding the long arrow of death, which Trudo drew in MS. 83C, fol. 410v, he drew again in the Louvre manuscript, fol. 275v. Finally, in Jacobus Gommer's copy of the second redaction, Liège, BU, MS. 248C, fol. 389v,

from the works of Denys the Carthusian.[75] Trudo's last redaction
retains the original five-book structure of the *Collectarium* (fols.
13r^a–290r^b). He drops, however, the encyclopedia that made up the
second part of his second redaction. The second part is now constituted by a collection of prayers (fols. 291r^a–307r^b), seven psalms in
honor of the Virgin Mary (fols. 307v^b–309r^b), a litany for a good
death (fols. 309r^a–v^b), more psalms and prayers (fols. 310r^a–315v^b),
and a few final extracts (fols. 318r^a–326v^b), including a long text from
Denys the Carthusian (fols. 324v^a–325r^a).

The colophon in the manuscript does not give a date. Nor, for
the first time, does Trudo mention the abbot, Georgius Sarens.[76]
Thus it would seem that he made his final redaction after Abbot
Sarens's death in 1558. I think that he completed it around 1570,
after he had annotated and inserted all the new materials in the other
surviving copies of the *Collectaria*.[77]

With Trudo of Gembloux's final effort, the medieval way of
compiling and writing manuscript books came to an end at the abbey
of St. Trudo in Flemish Limburg. That Trudo continued to up-date,
revise and reduce into order the materials he read is not surprising:
this is the mind of the compiler. That he continued to supplement,
annotate and correct the copies made by Jacobus Gommer is more
intriguing. Here, I think, he expresses some propriety regarding his
text. Despite the notes permitting users to alter as piety might
require, Trudo perhaps came to see himself, not as a mere compiler,
but as an author, who had the privilege to control—as far as he was

---

Trudo made another full page drawing of a monk, nailed to a T cross, clasping a
flame in his right hand, holding a lantern in his left hand, and being stung by a
coiled serpent on his left side. The text surrounding the figure, however, is copied
by Jacobus Gommer. A rubric at the bottom reads: "Sex incumbant monacho
videlicet psaltere. legere. canere. orare. meditari. aliena peccata deflere." This same
figure, surrounded by rubricated text, with the same rubric at the bottom, appears
in the Louvre manuscript, fol. 158v.

[75] There are at least 60 generous extracts from Denys' writings in the Louvre
manuscript.

[76] Paris, Musée du Louvre, Dépt. des Dessins, Coll. Ed. de Rothschild, MS. 1,
n° I DR, fol. 290r^b: "Collegit hec et scripsit. frater Trudo gemblacensis natione.
cenobita monasterij sancti Trudonis in hasbania."

[77] It is tempting to think that the lost Liège, BU, MS. 305A might contain
Trudo's original first redaction of the *Collectarium*. The shelf-mark, however,
suggests a volume in small format, and one would expect a folio volume.

able—the transmission of his life-long learning. Whatever else, through the indefatigable efforts of Trudo of Gembloux the legacy of Denys the Carthusian's erudition, itself collected from hundreds of medieval books, was preserved, culled, and recollected 100 years after his death at the abbey where he began his lessons as a schoolboy. I think Denys would have approved of Trudo's collections from collections.

University of Notre Dame

D . L . D ' A V R A Y

Philosophy in Preaching:
The Case of a Franciscan
Based in Thirteenth-Century Florence
(Servasanto da Faenza)

ome of the historians who have done most for the study of medieval sermons, such as Siegfried Wenzel and Johannes Baptist Schneyer, have used the word "scholastic" to describe a tendency in thirteenth-century preaching.[1] An advantage of the term is that it draws attention to the formal structure of divisions and subdivisions which most mendicant sermons share with "hard-core" scholastic genres (Sentence commentaries, academic *Summae*) from the middle of the thirteenth century or a little before. The term also emphasizes the connection between preaching and academic schools, above all the university of Paris. A disadvantage of the term is that it makes it harder to focus on a most interesting development in later medieval preaching, viz., the appearance in model sermon collections of rigorous logical argument and explicit theological problem-solving, in passages borrowed from hard-core scholastic works like the *Summa theologica* of Thomas Aquinas. (There is indeed a history of the gradual penetration of Thomism into late medieval preaching to be written.) When the term scholastic is used in the loose and broad sense this development can be

---

[1] Wenzel, *Preachers, Poets*, 62. He is not entirely happy with the term, though he settles for it; I prefer a term which he himself suggested to me as a possibility: "artistic," which would capture both the connection with the technique of the *artes praedicandi* and the aesthetic character, which Wenzel has so successfully brought out, of this kind of preaching. In this connection one may add that the chapter in question, chap. 3 on "The Sermon as an Art Form," discusses and exemplifies one of the most fruitful and least explored approaches to medieval preaching. For Schneyer's use of the term "scholastic," see his *Geschichte der katholischen Predigt*, 131.

obscured, in that non-specialist readers may be encouraged to assume that it had already taken place in the thirteenth century. Whatever words we use—and it does not greatly matter so long as everyone is clear about the concepts behind them—it is important to chart the penetration of philosophy, logical argument and problem solving into preaching. Unsystematic soundings suggest to me that these phenomena were a normal part of printed model sermons in the later fifteenth century.[2] *Quaestiones* play a significant part in French vernacular sermons by Jean Gerson (1363–1429),[3] and it may be that the fourteenth century is the real period of transition. Scholastic influence in the tighter sense can certainly be observed in model sermons on the dead from the earlier fourteenth century:[4] Antoine Dondaine noticed it long ago in the collection by Giovanni di San Gimignano O.P.,[5] and the collection of Nicoluccio di Ascoli, another Dominican, includes passages like the following:

---

[2] To cite two examples from the Franciscan Roberto Caracciolo: (a) Proof that lust is a sin: "Secunda ratio dicit excessus. Nam secundum Tho. ii. ii q. c.liii, ideo luxuria peccatum est quia modum rationis excedit circa uenerea, in quibus ordo rationis est, ut causa procreande prolis et fornicationis euitande. *Uir habeat uxorem suam*, ut dicitur i. Cor. vii [2], *et mulier habeat uirum suum*. Omnis ergo actus qui non est secundum legem matrimonii circa uenerea deficit a ratione, ideo est peccatum." (*Opus quadragesimale* [I have used British Library IB 37022], unpaginated, chap. 1 of sermon 30, on the text *Hec est uoluntas dei* [1 Thess. 4.3]). See Aquinas, *Summa theologica*, 2a 2ae, q. 153, art. 3, Resp. (b) Problem solving: "Et sic patet sufficientia mandatorum. Sed statim est qui obiciat et dicat: Quod cum septem sint capitalia peccata, et non nisi de duobus fiat prohibitio, scilicet luxuria et auaritia, nihilque dicatur de superbia, de accidia, de gula, de inuidia et de iracundia, aut ergo ista non sunt peccata, aut regula preceptorum deficiet quia illa non prohibet. Respondet dominus Bon. quod omnia hec peccata prohibentur in preceptis decalogi implicite. Nam superbia prohibetur in adoratione dei, inuidia et ira in fuga homicidii, accidia in sanctificatione sabbati, et gula in detestatione luxurie. Luxuria autem et auaritia prohibentur explicite propter maiorem pronitatem quam ad illam omnes uniuersaliter habent. Et propter dicta asserit Bon. quod in omnibus preceptis quando deus explicite aliquid prohibet, implicite precipit eius contrarium, et quando aliquid explicite precipit, implicite prohibet eius contrarium" (ibid., near end of chap. 1 of sermon 3, on the text *Multi sunt uocati* [Matt. 20.16]). Cf. Bonaventura's commentary on Peter Lombard's Sentences: *Sententiarum*, lib. 3, dist. 37, art. 2, quaest. 1 (*Opera omnia*, 3:821–22, 824).

[3] Mourin, *Jean Gerson*, 341–42.

[4] I single out this genre only because I know it better than others of the period after 1300. In the remarks about the genre which follow, I summarize my "Sermons on the Dead."

[5] Dondaine, "La Vie et les oeuvres," 179–81.

Note that, according to the opinion of the doctors, no one merits eternal life *ex condigno*—and not only [do they not merit] so great a glory, but [not even] the smallest part [of what] the blessed have. And the reason is, according to Thomas, Ia IIae, final question,[6] that eternal life is a supernatural good exceeding human nature to so great a degree that the eye of man may [not] see it and the heart cannot raise itself up [to it]. Therefore, we cannot attain to these things by natural [powers] alone. Nor, even, does someone who is in a state of grace earn it *ex condigno*, as the same Thomas says in another article,[7] but only *ex congruo*....[8]

If we follow the same genre back into the thirteenth century, we find philosophical (and astrological) influence in sermons of Aldobrandino da Toscanella (who flourished in the later part of the century). Listing the different ways in which death consumes man, he says that it annihilates and destroys

natural things, namely beauty, strength, and bravery, and things of this kind. And they are called natural things because they are said to be given by nature, that is, by the power of the stars, which act by the power of the First Mover. For a (*or* the?) work of nature, according to the Philosopher, is a work of intelligence. Therefore whatever is in bodily things comes entirely from the stars. For [the stars] move them and impart their power to them. But on human souls they have no effect. For [human souls] are superior to the stars, and an active force must be superior to the thing on which it acts.[9]

---

[6] Thomas of Aquino, *Summa theologica* 1a 2ae, q. 114, art. 2, Resp.

[7] Ibid., 1a 2ae, q. 114, art. 3, Resp.

[8] "... nota quod secundum sententiam doctorum nullus meretur uitam eternam ex condigno, et non solum tantam gloriam, *sed* minimam partem que est in beatis, et ratio est, secundum Thomam Prima Secunde, q. ultima, quia uita eterna est bonum supernaturale excedens humanam naturam in tantum quod oculus hominis uideat et cor non ascendit. Ideo ad ipsa per pura naturalia attingere non possumus. Nec etiam existens in gratia meretur ex condigno, ut idem Thomas dicit in alio articulo, *sed* solum ex congruo" (Munich, Clm. 2981, fol. 45va), from a sermon on the text *Salomon in omni gloria* (Matt. 6.29). See Schneyer, *Repertorium*, 4:218, no. 157.

[9] "Item anicilando (fol. 189ra) et destruendo naturalia, scilicet pulcritudinem,

At this point the reader, noting that the last three examples are all from Dominican sermons, and perhaps unconsciously influenced by the fact that St. Francis is the most famous Franciscan and St. Thomas Aquinas the most famous Dominican, may be tempted to draw an antithesis between Dominican philosophical sophistication and Franciscan imaginative vividness in preaching. Such an antithesis has indeed been drawn in a recent study.[10] Three propositions, therefore, need to be clearly stated. First, explicit philosophical language and argument are not particularly prominent in thirteenth-century Dominican sermon collections; one cannot generalize from the case of an Aldobrandino da Toscanella or a Giordano da Pisa.[11] This proposition, by its nature (i.e., because it is negative) can only be verified by fairly wide reading in thirteenth-century mendicant sermon collections. Second, divisions and distinctions are the norm in Franciscan no less than in Dominican preaching in this period. One does not have to read so many thirteenth-century sermons to be convinced of this proposition, since random soundings will show that it is not easy to find exceptions.[12] The third proposition is that

---

fortitudinem et audacitatem, et huiusmodi. Et dicuntur naturalia quia dicuntur 'a natura data,' id est, uirtute stellarum, que uirtute primi motoris agunt quicquid agunt. Opus enim nature, secundum Philosophum, est opus intelligentie; unde quicquid est in corporalibus, totum est a stellis. Mouent enim ipsa, et suas uirtutes eis largiuntur. In animabus autem humanis nichil operantur. Sunt enim superiores stellis, et agens oportet esse superius patiente" (MS. Vatican, Ott. lat. 557, fols. 188vb–189ra), from a sermon on the text *Homo cum mortuus fuerit* (Job 14.10). See Schneyer, *Repertorium*, 1:246, no. 306.

[10] Lesnick, *Preaching in Medieval Florence*, especially chaps. 6 and 7. Though I do not agree with everything in this book, as will become apparent, I found it an extremely stimulating work which shows considerable ability.

[11] On Giordano's popularization of Aristotelian and Thomistic doctrine, see Delcorno, *Giordano da Pisa*, 183 and n. 6. Cf. also Grabmann, "Siger von Brabant," 187: "Ausser Remigio de' Girolami seien noch genannt . . . Giordano da Rivalto, der in seinen Predigten thomistische Gedanken weiten Kreisen vermittelte. . . .''

[12] Cf. Zafarana, "La Predicazione Francescana," 220: "Constatiamo l'assoluta, consolidata prevalenza del sermone tematico che fonda la sua struttura su divisioni o distinzioni impostate sul tema scritturale di partenza e ramificate in suddivisioni e suddistinzioni. . . .'' Lesnick, 136 and n. 9, says that "In his unedited *Sermones rusticani*, Berthold [of Regensburg, O.F.M.] avoided the scholastic divisions and distinctions. . . .'' But Zafarana, working on the sermons at first hand, says that Berthold uses and emphasizes the Old Testament historia, "assunta sovente come base per la *divisio* o *distinctio*" (228), and that he "evita il ramificarsi di suddivisioni-suddistinzioni,'' which is rather different. Everyone reading these well studied if

explicit philosophical language and argument can be found in at least one thirteenth-century Franciscan's sermons. It is perhaps not an accident that this Franciscan, Servasanto da Faenza,[13] is principally associated with Florence,[14] where there was a lay public with quite a high intellectual culture.[15] The milieu which produced Dante and Guido Cavalcanti[16] was not likely to be frightened by philosophical language. Servasanto's model sermons[17] are the only known basis for generalizations about Franciscan preaching at Florence in the thirteenth century.[18] However, it is safest to regard them as part of

---

unpublished sermons will know that Berthold uses divisions or distinctions constantly.

[13] On Servasanto da Faenza, see Oliger, "Servasanto da Faenza." On the sermons, see Balduinus ab Amsterdam, "Servasancti de Faenza." I have not been able to obtain the same author's articles in *Laurentianum* 6 (1965), 73–102, and *Laurentianum* 8 (1967), 108–37, cited in Schneyer, *Repertorium*, 5:376. See also Gamboso, "I Sermoni Festivi."

[14] On Servasanto's association with Florence, see Delcorno, *La Predicazione*, 34.

[15] Holmes, *Florence, Rome*, 72, 74–75.

[16] Ibid., 105, where Holmes describes Cavalcanti's poem "Donna me prega" as "written largely in the technical language of scholastic philosophy."

[17] For the value of model sermons as evidence and the related problem of audience, see D'Avray, *The Preaching of the Friars*, 104–31, where I tentatively argue that model sermon collections were intended mainly, but not only, for popular preaching. Lesnick shares the view that Latin model sermons tell us something about the popular preaching for which they must have been mainly used, since he argues from the evidence of Anthony of Padua's and Berthold of Regensburg's model sermons (Lesnick, 135–36, 140–41). It has been argued that the surviving sermons of Anthony of Padua go back before his entry into the Franciscan Order, to the time when he was a canon at Coimbra: Manselli, "Chi era Francesco d'Assisi," 1:356. On Berthold, see above, note 12. If the sermons of any Dominican preacher other than Giordano had been transmitted from the 13th or early 14th centuries in the vernacular, then there might be a stronger foundation for the theory that "the Franciscans' sermons, as they were actually delivered, were far less likely to be transcribed by avid listeners than were the Dominicans' sermons" (Lesnick, 141–42). As it is, one must either use sermons transmitted in Latin as a basis for comparisons between Dominican and Franciscan preaching in the period, or refrain from drawing comparisons (which seems unduly ascetic).

[18] I do not know of any other surviving sermons by Franciscan preachers based at Florence in the 13th or early 14th century. Lesnick uses the evidence of the Pseudo-Bonaventurean *Meditations on the Life of Christ* (see especially 143–71), but he himself says that this work was "directed in the first place to a poor Clare" (ibid., 144), and I would hesitate to use it as evidence for popular preaching as opposed to devotional reading. His actual analysis of the *Meditations* is perceptive and very interesting. Viewed as a contrast between two forms of thought (rather than between Franciscan and Dominican preaching), his book retains its value.

the history of thirteenth-century Franciscan preaching more generally, rather than as a chapter in a specifically Florentine story. While
it is entirely likely that some, even most, of the model sermons are
based on "live" sermons preached at Florence,[19] and though Servasanto doubtless hoped to supply material to Florentine confrères among
others, I know of nothing to associate them with a specifically Florentine context except Servasanto's long residence in the city.[20]

Servasanto's penchant for philosophical language can be illustrated
by an extended treatment of a particular sermon. I have chosen one
about nature and grace, on the text *Gratia dei sum id quod sum* (1
Corinthians 15.10).[21] Though I originally selected the sermon to
bring home in a concrete manner the points set out above, it turned
out on closer inspection to be an absorbing miniature synthesis, of
interest in its own right. The relevant parts will be translated *in
extenso*, so that readers may judge the questions at issue for themselves.

After the initial scriptural text, Servasanto begins with a philosophical distinction:

> *It is by the grace of God that I am what I am....* It is
> customary to distinguish between two kinds of Being [*esse*]:
> one natural, but the other moral. Or one which is called the
> "being of nature," the other the "being of grace." And one is
> called "first being," because it is the foundation of the other.
> The other, however, is called "second being," because it is the
> complement of the first. For the first being, which [*quod*] is
> the being of nature, is made perfect by a natural form. But the
> second being, which is moral being, the being of order, is
> made perfect by knowledge and by grace.

---

[19] Cf. Bataillon, "Approaches," 21: "If Servasanto of Faenza explains clearly
that, being too old to preach himself he writes models for his younger confrères,
these models are so personal that it is highly probable that they are in great part
sermons that he actually preached when younger." A caveat, however: Bataillon is
referring to another cycle of Servasanto's sermons (his reference, ibid., 32 n. 16, is
to MS. Assisi Comunale 520, fol. 99v, edited by Gamboso, 19—whereas I know
Servasanto mainly through Sunday sermons).

[20] I have read only a sample of Servasanto's sermons, so I cannot be categorical.

[21] The sermon is Schneyer, *Repertorium*, 5:382, no. 102. I have used MS. Troyes
1440, fols. 283ra–285vb (checked in places against BL MS. Harley 3221, fols. 205v–
207v).

Grace, however, (a) is taken sometimes in a general way, and is called grace, because it is given gratis; (b) sometimes it is taken in a particular sense, and then it is called grace because it renders the soul pleasing [*gratam*]. Therefore, grace taken in a general sense includes not only grace in the particular sense [*specialem gratiam*], but also nature itself. For it is an accepted truth that the being of nature itself, and all that we are able to do, and all knowing, and all willing of the good, and all doing, [all these] belong to us thanks to grace. For it was by grace that God made the world, that he divided it thus into a variety of parts, that he ordered it towards its final end; and, in short, whatever he does and did, whether by giving being or, in addition to that, well-being [*bene esse*], it is and was all by grace.

(*Gratia dei sum id quod sum*, prima Cor. xv. Consueuit distingui duplex esse: unum naturale, alterum uero morale. Uel unum quod dicitur esse nature, alterum esse gratie. Et unum dicitur esse primum, quia est alterius fundamentum. Alterum uero dicitur esse secundum, quia primi est complementum. Nam primum esse, quod est esse nature, perficitur naturali forma. Sed secundum esse, quod est esse moris et ordinis, perficitur scientia et gratia.

Gratia tamen accipitur aliquando genera/liter [fol. 283rb] et dicitur gratia quia gratis data; aliquando accipitur specialiter, et tunc gratia dicitur quia gratam reddit animam. Gratia ergo generaliter accepta includit non solum specialem gratiam, se*d* et ipsam naturam. Nam et ipsius nature esse,[22] et omne posse, et omne scire, et omne bonum uelle, et omne facere, constat ex gratia nobis esse. Gratia enim fuit quod deus mundum fecit, quod ipsum per partes uarias sic distinxit, quod in finem ultimum ordinauit; —et breuiter, quicquid facit et fecit, siue dando esse, siue[23] insuper bene esse, totum gratia est et fuit.[24])

This is not the sort of thing that readers of thirteenth-century sermons come across every day. It is followed by a division of the original text of the kind that one meets in any number of thirteenth-

---

[22] esse] est *MS.*
[23] dando esse siue] *corrected in MS. from* dando siue esse.
[24] MS. Troyes 1440, fol. 283ra–b.

century sermons.[25] It ends with the words: "as if St. Paul were saying: By myself I am nothing, by the grace of God I am,"[26] which is a cue for another cerebral passage:

> Therefore, the just, in a certain way, are; and that which they are, they are by the grace of God. The evil, however, even if in a certain sense [*secundum quid*] they "are," since, indeed, they "are" evil, nevertheless they cannot be said to "be" in a simple sense, because, through evilness, they have withdrawn from true being. For it is clear that a dead man is not a man, and it is no less clear that someone who has withdrawn from true life certainly does not live with true life. Therefore, every such person is seen to be [*existit*] dead. Therefore, that which he was, he ceases to be.

> (Iusti ergo aliquo modo sunt, et id quod sunt, a gratia dei sunt. Mali [fol. 283va] autem, et si secundum quid sunt, quia utique mali sunt, esse tamen simpliciter dici non possunt, quia a uero esse per malitiam recesserunt. Constat enim quod homo mortuus non est homo, et non minus constat quod qui a uera uita recessit, utique uera uita non uiuit. Mortuus ergo omnis talis existit. Ergo quod fuit, esse desiit.[27])

One notes the repetition of "Therefore" (*ergo*). Servasanto now brings the authority of Aristotle into play:

> For, also, Aristotle says in the *Meteors* that all that which does not do that thing for which it exists, ceases to be what it is. For since light was made for shining, if it should cease to shine, it certainly would not be light. Therefore, since man was made for the supreme Good, when he recedes from it, he ceases from truly being [*or*: truly he ceases from being]. Again, according to Aristotle, and to Boethius himself, and, what is

---

[25] In uerbo premisso notantur (*corr. from* notatur) maxime duo. Nam primo Apostolus diuinam exprimit largitatem siue gratie liberalitatem. Secundo ostendit humanam modicitatem. Ostenditur autem diuina liberalitas primo cum dicitur *gratia dei sum*. Secundo monstratur humana nichilitas siue modicitas cum additur: *id quod sum* (ibid., fol. 283rb).

[26] . . . quasi dicat Apostolus: Per me nichil sum, per dei gratiam sum (ibid.).

[27] MS. Troyes 1440, fol. 283rb–va.

more, to Augustine, being and good are fundamentally [*simpliciter*] interchangeable. Therefore, that which falls away from the good, equally withdraws from being. Therefore, as the evil lose goodness, they cease to be what they were, since, after they have turned to evil, they have also lost their human nature.

(Nam et in Methauris Philosophus dicit quod omne id quod non facit illud ad quod est, desinit esse quod est. Cum enim lux ad lucendum facta sit, si lucere desineret, utique lux non esset. Ergo cum homo ad summum bonum factus sit, cum ab illo recedit, uere esse desistit. Item secundum Philosophum, et ipsum Boetium,[28] et, quod maius est, Augustinum,[29] ens et bonum simpliciter conuertuntur. Ergo quod a bono deficit, pariter ab esse recedit. Ergo dum mali bonitatem perdunt, quod fuerant esse desistunt quia in malitiam uersi,[30] humanam quoque[31] amisere[32] naturam.[33])

The relevant passages in Aristotle's *Meteorologica* would seem to be Book 4.12, 389 b 31 and 390 a 10–13 (in the standard reference system), but Servasanto could have got the message at second hand from the anthology known as the *Auctoritates Aristotelis*.[34] The idea that being and good are interchangeable may not be Aristotelian at all,[35] though Servasanto may have felt that it was implied by the idea from the *Meteorologica* which he had referred to just before. As for Augustine, Servasanto may possibly have been thinking of *De doctrina Christiana*, book 1, chap. 32.[36] The influence of Boethius is indubitable. Servasanto may have had the little work on "How substances are good in virtue of their existence without being substantial goods"[37] in the back of his mind, but it looks as if he had a particular passage of

---

[28] Boetium] bonum *Troyes MS.*
[29] Augustinum] Augustin[us] *MS.*
[30] uersi] *om. MS.*
[31] quoque] utique *MS.* (cf. *Boethii Philosophiae Consolatio*, ed. Bieler, 71, line 45).
[32] amisere] *corr. in MS. from* admisere?
[33] MS. Troyes 1440, fol. 283va.
[34] *Les Auctoritates Aristotelis*, ed. Hamesse, 173, number 26.
[35] So I am informed by my colleague, Dr. Robert Sharples.
[36] *Sancti Aureli Augustini De doctrina Christiana*, ed. Green, 27.
[37] Boethius, *Quomodo substantiae.*

The Consolation of Philosophy before him as he wrote.[38]

The continuation of the same passage is Servasanto's source for the less philosophical material which follows, in which he argues that someone transformed by vices cannot be reckoned a human being.[39] The remainder of the sermon is less abstract and technical than the passages quoted; it is indeed a real sermon, not a piece of academic theology lost in the wrong genre. Nevertheless, the initial metaphysical reflections add resonance to the main part of the sermon, notably in the following two passages, which take on greater force when understood in connection with the passages quoted above than they would have on their own:

> (a) Job 27 (19): *The rich man when he shall sleep shall take nothing with him: he shall open his eyes and find nothing.* Therefore it is said in Acts. 9 (8) *that Saul, when his eyes were opened, saw nothing.* For how can something which does not exist be seen? Therefore, the disciples, at the Transfiguration of the Lord, having raised up their eyes, saw nothing but Jesus alone. Why? Because he alone truly *is.*

> (Iob xxvii[40] [19]: *Diues cum dormierit nichil secum affert: aperiet oculos suos et nichil inueniet.* Unde dicitur Act. ix [8] quod Saulus *apertis oculis nichil*[41] *uidebat.* Quomodo enim uideri potest quod non est. Unde discipuli in transfiguratione domini eleuatis oculis nichil uiderunt nisi solum Iesum. Quare? Quia ipse solus uere est.)[42]

> (b) For in these sins which are of the flesh alone men become entirely like brutes. And therefore, while they put on the nature of an animal, they are stripped of their own nature.

> (In hiis enim peccatis que solius carnis sunt, homines totaliter brutales fiunt. Et ideo dum brutalem naturam induunt, natura propria nudi fiunt.)[43]

---

[38] *Boethii Philosophiae Consolatio,* ed. Bieler, 71.
[39] Ibid., 71–72, and MS. Troyes 1440, fol. 283va–b.
[40] xxvii] xxviii *MS.*
[41] nichil *supplied in margin.*
[42] MS. Troyes 1440, fol. 385ra.
[43] Ibid.

This is not the only sermon in which Servasanto uses explicit philosophical argument,[44] but it is my impression from random soundings that the majority of his sermons are not held together by this kind of philosophical cement. Even so, it must be reiterated that it is easier to find material of this sort in Servasanto than in most of the other thirteenth-century mendicant preachers, whether Franciscan or Dominican, with which I am acquainted. Since virtually no mendicant sermons from the period have been transmitted in the vernacular (the corpus of Giordano's sermons, which almost fall within the period, being the one major exception known thus far), the hypercritical could argue that we are too far away from "live" mendicant preaching to say anything about it at all. If the models preachers worked from can tell us anything about sermons and scholastic philosophy, however, they point to a distinction between periods rather than religious orders. It is, indeed, possible that as the fourteenth century progressed, the influence of the Dominican order's official Thomism left its preachers an imprint of scholastic philosophy which marked them off from their Franciscan counterparts, but this has yet to be proved (and may not be true), since the manuscript sources have not been studied from this point of view. What we can say is that the Franciscan Servasanto da Faenza is in the vanguard of the invasion of preaching by philosophical argument, and that he knows how to integrate such argument into the sermon genre.

University College, London

---

[44] For an Aristotelian defence of marriage in another of Servasanto's sermons, see my article on "Some Franciscan Ideas."

DAVID ANDERSON

"Dominus Ludovicus" in the Sermons of Jacobus of Viterbo[1] (Arch. S. Pietro D. 213)

arly in the year 1300, Jacobus of Viterbo left his position as head of the Augustinian school of theology in Paris to take up similar responsibilities at the convent of St. Augustine in Naples, where, over the following two years, he completed his influential treatise on the Church, *De regimine Christiano*. It is usually assumed that both the move to Naples and the treatise written there are to be understood against a background of especially close relations between the papacy and Charles II of Anjou. *De regimine Christiano* is dedicated to Boniface VIII, and its strenuous arguments for a pre-eminent role of the Church in universal government helped define the Guelph political vision of both Charles II and his son and successor, Robert, who held their kingdom in southern Italy in fief directly from the pope and in despite of rival claims by the German emperor. The same channels of patronage are evident in Jacobus's subsequent appointments, for when the archbishoprics of Benevento and Naples became vacant—for various reasons the papacy had recently reserved the right of direct appointment to these sees and was selecting candidates in concert with the Angevin court rather than the local clergy—Boniface VIII installed him first in the one (on 3 Sept. 1302) and then in the other office (12 Dec. of the same year). Apparently it was in response to the pastoral duties of this position, which he was to keep until his death early in 1308, that Jacobus produced, among his very last works, a book of sermons, which though employing a less elaborate style than his discursive

---

[1] Vatican Library, MS. Archivio di San Pietro D.213.

writings, nevertheless show strong lines of continuity with his other
works, including a comfortable familiarity with the political aims of
the Angevin-Neapolitan court.[2]

Jacobus had not made his considerable reputation as a preacher
and this book of sermons, when he came to write it, was not designed as a collection of model works to be circulated in written
form. The single manuscript known to preserve them, now Vatican
Library MS. Archivio di San Pietro D.213, belongs instead to that
class of documents preserving sermons as they were prepared before
actual presentation at a particular time to a known audience. The
book is a well-laden vessel despite its smallish size (23 x 17 cm. and
126 fols.). Its leaves are covered by two dense columns of text, all in
the same hand, with some two hundred and twenty-five sermons,
sketches for sermons and *distinctiones*, each headed by a title. The
manuscript, which is missing some leaves at the beginning, has no
note of attribution in the original hand, only a *titulus* written on a
blank leaf (fol. 4) during the seventeenth century attributing the
sermones to Jacobus. In 1937, David Gutiérrez argued in favor of this
attribution on the basis of internal evidence, noting that the sermons
were written by a churchman of high rank in Naples, and that an
autobiographical reference in one of the occasional sermons is consistent with what we know of Jacobus's career. Gutiérrez went on to
suggest that the manuscript was an autograph, because its small,
semi-cursive script resembles that in a unique witness to another of
his works, an *Abbreviatio* of Aegidius's commentary on I *Sentences*.[3]

---

[2] *Jordani de Saxonia (. . .) Liber Vitasfratrum*, 459 n. 35: "Bonifatius VIII reservata
sibi provisione sedum episcopalium vacantium Beneventanae et Neapolitanae,
Jacobum Viterbiensem ad eas successive promovit, eodem anno 1302; ad Beneventa-
nam die 3 Septembris . . . ad Neapolitanam die 12 Decembris." He had been in
Naples from the time the Augustinians held their General Chapter in that city, in
mid-1300. Gutiérrez, "De vita"; in the separate edition, Gutiérrez, *De b. Jacobi
Viterbiensis O.E.S.A. vita*; and Mariani, *Chiesa e Stato*, 75–88. For the political background to Jacobus's writings, see Scholz, *Die Publizistik*, 129–52; and Mariani,
Chiesa e Stato, 151–74.

[3] For the manuscript, see Gutiérrez, "De vita," 297–98; Stornajolo, *Inventarium*,
2:162–65. In transcribing passages from the manuscript, I have silently expanded
abbreviations, regularized capitalization and introduced quotation marks for biblical
citations; the few other emendations or additions are indicated by brackets. The
autograph of Jacobus's *Abbreviatio* is Naples, BN MS. VII.C.52, concerning which
we now have the study of Giustiniani, "Il problema."

This promising identification was not pursued, and it was placed under something of a shadow by the attribution to Jacobus, in Schneyer's *Repertorium*, of only seven of the sermons contained in the manuscript.[4] Yet the evidence associating the manuscript with Jacobus is strong, as are the indications that this collection was written by the archbishop *via via* during his years in office. The crucial evidence lies in the organization of the book. Opening it reveals immediately the erasures and marginal additions, all in the same hand as the text, that indicate a working copy, while a closer examination of the contents yields a remarkably detailed chronology for their composition that places them precisely in the years of Jacobus's service in episcopal office.

The topics are those of sermons *dominicales* and *ad sanctos* arranged in a calendrical sequence through four yearly cycles and part of a fifth. A series of specific dates can be determined because various occasional sermons appear among the sermons *ad sanctos* and *dominicales*. As we shall see, these fix the liturgical cycles firmly between August, 1303 and November, 1307, leaving little room to doubt the works should be attributed to Jacobus, who served as archbishop during this very period of time. More important, this organization provides a remarkably precise instrument for dating the several parts of the codex, making it possible to correlate sermons that do not otherwise indicate the date or circumstance of their delivery with the public life of Naples during those years. They cast light in diverse and sometimes unexpected directions. For example, there are two funeral sermons from January, 1305, which tell us something about the New Year's tournaments of that year. The first concerns a *miles* named Philippo Minutolo, who died "in astiludio" (col. 132) and the second, which follows it in the codex, is simply headed "de quodam defuncto propter vulnus" (col. 133) and may have been adapted for more than one subject. Again three months later, Jacobus preaches expressly on a public event of special concern to the lords temporal, an expedition of the duke of Calabria into Tuscany.[5]

---

[4] Schneyer, *Repertorium*, 3:46–47. The *Repertorium* attributes to Jacobus: col. 1, "Cogitavi" (on St. Dominic); col. 49, "Nox precessit" (first Sunday of Advent); col. 50, "Joseph filius accrescens" (on Saint Andreas); col. 287, "Sicut in die" (first Sunday in Advent); col. 290, "Vocabis me" (on Saint Andreas); col. 393, "Hora est" (First Sunday in Advent); and col. 398, "Scitate" (First Sunday in Advent).

[5] Given his designation in the sermon as *miles* and the circumstances of his

The most interesting new prospect offered by the chronology of these sermons concerns Jacobus's two commemorative sermons on "Dominus" (and once, in an eloquent error of anticipation, "Beatus") Ludovicus, or Louis of Anjou, the second-born son of Charles II. For a short time in the mid-1290s Louis had been designated to inherit his father's Italian kingdom, after his one older brother—the Charles Martel so admired by Dante—was assigned the throne of Hungary in a carefully calculated division of the Angevin empire. But Louis made trouble for these dynastic projections by renouncing his worldly inheritance, over the period 1294–1296, in order to become a Franciscan friar. After he died, barely a year later, on 19 August 1297, there were calls for an investigation of sanctity, and these led relatively quickly to his canonization, which was proclaimed by Pope John XXII in 1317. Jacobus's sermons then, because they are datable to 1303 and 1304, claim an important place in the surviving literature on St. Louis of Toulouse. They are very early in the sequence of writings on the saint; they even antedate the papal inquest into Louis's sanctity, which, though petitioned for by Charles II as early as 1298 and 1300, was opened only in 1307.[6] We shall return to them later in this paper.

If the chronological sequence of the sermons provides us with a useful guide to the circumstances of their composition, it is the organization of the codex that gives us the key to the sermons' chronology. Our examination must therefore begin with the physical artifact.

The book has been rebound at least once; the current binding is

---

death, this Philippo Minutolo cannot be identified with Jacobus's predecessor of the same name, a canon of Salerno, later archbishop of that city (to 1298) and of Naples (1298–1301), who died 24 Oct. 1301 and whose tomb still dominates a chapel to the right of the altar in the duomo of Naples. Jacobus takes a decidedly benevolent view of the death of this Philippo Minutolo *miles*, in light of the papal sanctions against mortal tournaments and the role his own order of Augustinian Hermits was to play in protesting the Neapolitan tournaments a few decades later. For the dating of "In accessu ducis in Tusciam" (col. 149), see below, n. 6.

[6] Charles II's efforts to have an inquest opened are noted by Caggese, *Roberto d'Angiò*, 1:300, who cites Minieri-Riccio, *Saggio*, suppl. 2:1 n. 1, a document for 27 Jan. 1300. See also Caggese, 1:650, for evidence of similar requests as early as 1298. For the legal and institutional context of such requests, see Vauchez, *La sainteté*, 294ff., which notes the bull accepting the request that a *processus* be opened, issued by Clement V in 1307, and the inquest *de partibus* which took place in 1308.

seventeenth-century and includes a pair of guard leaves front and back. At present MS. Archivio di San Pietro D.213 begins with four leaves (two bifolia), of which the first three contain an index to the sermons and the fourth is blank, except for the *titulus* in a seventeenth-century hand, just mentioned: "Fratris Iacobi de Viterbio sermones." This small first quire was a late addition. The script of the index is markedly different from that in the rest of the book and much younger, probably of the sixteenth century. It is easy to distinguish from that in the eleven original quires, where we find a single hand using a semi-cursive script and making the erasures, cancellations and marginal additions that strongly suggest this is an author's working copy. The younger hand writing the index has also numbered the columns of text in the rest of the manuscript, providing some evidence for the accuracy of the sequence in which the old quires now stand. The numbering runs from columns 1 and 2 on the first recto of the second quire up to column 498 in the midst of the last quire. It was done at the same time the index was compiled, for the index gives a column number for each of the listed sermons. Evidently, by the time the index was compiled and the column numbers added, the book already lacked some leaves in front, for the text in the column numbered "1" begins in the midst of a sermon. But the original codex is complete and in order from this point on. It is composed of eleven fairly uniform quires, each with twelve leaves (six bifolia) except for the first, which has eight leaves, and the last, which has ten. Though it cannot be determined how many leaves or quires are lacking at the beginning, it is clear that none lack at the end of the book, for the last sermon in the manuscript ends on col. 498, well before the end of the last quire, where the remaining leaves have been ruled for text but are otherwise blank. Evidently the writer intended to continue the collection.

The material evidence that the manuscript is an autograph and preserves the original sequence of its quires (except for some loss at the beginning) goes a long way towards establishing the internal chronology. The sermons in the first original quire address topics from the liturgical calendar for early August: at the top of column one there is the end of a sermon on Saint Asprenus, which is followed on columns 1–9 by sermons on Saint Dominic, the Transfiguration, Saint Lawrence, Saint Clare and the Assumption of the Virgin. The calendrical cycle can then be traced through four more summers in which a similar sequence appears:

>   cols. 105–108 [beginning of second year] sermons on the
>   Transfiguration, Saint Lawrence and the Assumption
>   cols. 224–242 [beginning of the third year] sermons on the
>   Transfiguration, Saint Dominic, Saint Lawrence, Saint
>   Clare and the Assumption
>   cols. 366–373 [beginning of the fourth year] sermons on the
>   Transfiguration, Saint Lawrence and the Assumption
>   cols. 480–486 [beginning of the fifth year] sermons on the
>   Transfiguration, Saint Lawrence, Saint Clare and the
>   Assumption.

The sequence suggests that the whole collection could well have been written by Jacobus of Viterbo while he was archbishop of Naples. He was appointed to that post in December, 1302 and died early in 1308, serving in all just over five years. The four years and three months represented in this collection fit nicely into that span of time—even better if we consider the leaves (probably a single quire) now missing from the head of the manuscript. Setting the sermons against the chronology of Jacobus's episcopal service, it appears that he began composition sometime before August of 1303, probably several months earlier, and stopped about four and a half years later with a sermon for All Saints' Day, 1307, a few months before his death early in 1308.

There is, in fact, confirmation that these four liturgical cycles belong specifically to the period extending from early summer, 1303 to 1 November 1307. It appears in the handful of occasional sermons in the manuscript to which a date may be assigned. One of these, however, seems on first glance rather to contradict our chronology, so let us examine it first. It has the title "in morte Regine Ungarie sororis regis" (col. 27), which is disturbing because the death of a "queen of Hungary" in Naples must bring to mind Maria, the astute and influential wife of Charles II, who was the daughter of Stephan V of Hungary and who, after the death of her brother Ladislaus IV in 1290, assumed his title, referring to herself in official documents as "queen of Hungary, of Jerusalem and of Sicily." Any reference to Maria's death would put an attribution of the sermon to Jacobus beyond the range of possibility, for she died at the age of about seventy in 1323. Fortunately, however, the identity of the subject here changes on closer inspection of the sermon. The Maria of Hungary who died in 1323 was not a "sister of the king," at least not in the literal sense. But Charles II did have a sister who was—or more properly, some years before her death had been—queen of Hungary. This was Maria's youngest sister-in-law, Isabella of Anjou, whose life had run in counterpoint to Maria's own. Born ca. 1265, Isabella (or Elisabeth) was the last daughter of Charles I of Anjou.[7] She had been betrothed to Ladislaus, eldest son of Stephan V of Hungary, in the same treaty of 1270 that sent Stephan's daughter Maria to Naples to marry Charles, later Charles II and at the time duke of Calabria. Though she was too young for the marriage to be consummated, Isabella left her father's court and the warm Mediterranean landscape shortly after 1270, accompanied principally by two tutors, and took up residence at the Hungarian court. Her older husband, who would rule as Ladislaus IV ("the Cuman") from 1277 until he was assassinated in 1290, was much criticized in his time for a dissolute life in the company of his mother's people, the Cuman tribesmen, and for his marital infidelity. Among the many illustrative incidents the chroniclers liked to narrate was one from 1282 in which the barons of his realm locked up Ladislaus with Isabella in a fortress, so that, "away from his pagan concubines," he might provide an heir to the throne. And whatever credence one gives to such anecdotes, it is clear from the official fulminations of Pope Martin IV that Ladislaus IV imitated a different model of kingship than did the pious Angevins. Shortly after the murder of her husband Isabella returned to Naples, where records from the 1290s show her supported by and collaborating with her brother, now King

---

[7] Minieri-Riccio, *Genealogia*, 35–36 and 164, for the negotiations leading to the double marriage of 1270; cf. *Cambridge Medieval History*, 4:469–70. The marriage contract arranged by Stephan V of Hungary and Charles I of Anjou, which gave Charles's daughter Isabella to Stephan's son and Stephan's daughter Maria to Charles's son Charles, is badly misrepresented in one common reference work, K. and M. Uhlirz, *Handbuch*, 412–13. For Isabella's transfer to Hungary, see Minieri-Riccio, *Genealogia*, 107 and n. 196. In the company of Niccolaus, Archbishop of Trani, and Drogone de Beaumont, she set sail from Barletta in Sept. 1270, carrying with her her dowry of 200,000 silver marks. On Ladislaus's concubines, see e.g., Domanevszky, ed., *Chronici Hungarici*, 472–74, and for secondary literature, Mályusz, *Comentarii*, 506–9. For the episode of the castle, see Riccio, *De regibus*, 37. On the date of Isabella's death, see Minieri-Riccio, *Genealogia*, 119.

Charles II. She made at least one expedition back across the Adriatic, in 1299, but was then in Naples again by 1301, when she retired with a small community of religious women to Castel dell'Ovo to live under a Dominican rule. This was also the favored order of her brother. She died two years later, while Charles was staying with the *curia* in Rome, as we know from a letter he wrote there on 3 November 1303 to the representative of the Dominicans, requesting that all the provincials of the order have the friars say mass for the soul of "his sister, formerly the widowed queen of Hungary."

Isabella apparently died during the last days of October, 1303. Turning to MS. Archivio di San Pietro D.213, we find that Jacobus recorded his commemoration of "the king's sister, the queen of Hungary" between sermons for the feast of St. Luke and All Saints' Day in the first annual cycle, which is to say very late October, 1303. In its prologue it describes Isabella in a manner similar to the king's commemorative letter to the Dominicans. Its biblical text is "Regina autem ... domum convivii ingressa est. Daniel 5. [=5.10]," in which the word "regina" is said to be appropriate to the subject:

> "Regina autem" fuit pro statu, scilicet regina quia regis sponsa
> et regis filia. sed verum dicitur regina quia se ipsam bene rexit
> vel quia virtute egit.   (col. 27)

And if, in the design of the sermon, the subject's high status as queen "because she was spouse of a king and daughter of a king" serves only to introduce the theme of her higher nobility-in-virtue, "because she ruled herself well," this conventional development, too, would seem to match Charles's opinion of his sister and, indeed, what we can discover of Isabella's life and works.

The subjects of several other funeral sermons are easy to identify. After almost two yearly cycles have turned, there is a sermon "in morte domini Arciepiscopi Salernitani" (cols. 255–257), which appears between a commemoration of Saint Augustine and the feast of the Virgin's Nativity, or in early September. Although the name of the deceased is not given, and there were several archbishops of Salerno who died in office during the first decade of the fourteenth century, this sermon clearly regards Guillelmus *de Godonio*, a Provençal cleric associated with Robert of Anjou.[8] The sermon develops

---

[8] The letter of appointment from Boniface VIII, of 3 October 1298, refers to

the text "Pastor et agricola" in order to praise a man who served both church and state: "ut ista commemoratio intelligatur dirigi ad salernitanam ecclesiam vel potius ad totum regnum, quia mors huius domini preiudicialis est et dampnosa non solum illi ecclesie sed etiam toti regno" (col. 255), which describes Guillelmus but none of his successors. With his appointment in 1298 he immediately received permission to appoint a vicar, so that he might continue to serve the Angevin court, and although this and subsequent letters of proroga-tion say only that he was occupied in Robert's service (e.g., "pro negotiis Roberti, ducis Calabrie personaliter occupatus"[9]), the reason was undoubtedly his long involvement in Robert's campaigns to reconquer the island of Sicily. Guillelmus was to remain the elected, but not consecrated, and absentee archbishop until June of 1304. He died about a year later, on 4 September 1305, and the sermon was apparently delivered shortly thereafter.

Further confirmation appears promptly in the sermon "in morte domini Raymundi filii regis," written during the next month, just after the feast of the Nativity of the Virgin and before the feast of Saint Francis (col. 261). Although Raimundus was a common name in the Angevin dynasty from the time of Charles I's father-in-law, the Raymond-Berengar who was the fifth son of Maria of Hungary and Charles II, who held for a time the office of Grand Seneschal at the court in Naples, and who died on 10 October 1305, is the subject here.[10]

him as a "doctor decretorum," noted for his "literarum scientia," "elegantia morum" and "discretionis industria." See Crisci, *Il Cammino*, 1. Other letters call him "canonicus Caturcensis, capellanus pape, cancellarius Roberti ducis Calabrie," which suggests something of his earlier career. Cf. Ughelli, *Italia sacra*, 7: col. 428.

[9] *Les Registres de Boniface VIII*, ed. Digard et al., vol. 2, no. 3018, cited by Crisci. Guillelmus was, for example, resident in Catania with Robert of Anjou from mid-1299 to mid-1300. In June 1302 he was still holding special powers to lift excommunication in Sicily and in November of 1303 his consecration was again postponed because of his services to Robert of Anjou; see *Le Registre de Benoit XI*, ed. Grandjean, no. 212. He is mentioned in the chronicles of the Sicilian wars as well; Niccolò Speciale, for example, refers to him as "Guglielmo de Gudur, eletto Salernitano"; see the *Historia sicula*, bk. 5, chap. 19. It is a sign of the importance of ecclesiastical matters in this drawn-out conflict that Guillelmus was not conse-crated for almost two years after the peace of Caltabellota (24 Sept. 1302) and may have been in Sicily as late as January, 1304. For background on papal policy in the Sicilian wars, see Housley, *The Italian Crusades*, esp. chap. 4.

[10] Camera, *Elucubrazioni*, genealogical table 1. Cf. Monti, *La Dominazione*, 73–

Along with these sermons on the death of prominent figures associated with the royal court we find two others concerned with persons closely allied to Jacobus himself. The first is "in morte Bartholomei Vulcani," which appears on col. 121. By its position in the manuscript, this would seem to have been written sometime in September of 1304. Although we do not know precisely when Bartholomeus died, it was probably in late August or early September of that year. A record has been preserved of a royal document from 5 September 1304, confirming the will of "quondam Bartholomeus Bulcani de Neapolis" and noting that Fr. Jacobus, archbishop of Naples, had been among the witnesses to that will. It is, for our purposes, a double confirmation, because it provides an approximate date for Bartholomeus's death and also indicates there was a close friendship or other personal connection between him and Jacobus, of the sort that would explain why the author of these sermons should have preached at the funeral of this particular citizen of Naples, otherwise unknown and designated in the document and the sermon alike simply as *miles*.[11]

The second, "de mortuis pro magistro Bartholo" (col. 469), has already been noted by Gutiérrez (1937) as a good indication the sermons are those of Jacobus, for Magister Bartholus *de vallis Spoleti* succeeded him in his position at the Augustinian school in Paris in 1300 and succeeded him again as "lector principalis" in Naples in 1302, when Jacobus became archbishop.[12] What is known of Bartholus's death fits the chronological pattern also. The sermon comes late in the sequence, between the first and second Sunday of Pente-

---

79; and Caggese, 1:640, who cites a document of 4 April 1307 that refers to Raymond-Berengar as the "deceased brother of Robert of Anjou." In the sermon, which praises Raymond-Berengar's services to the state, Jacobus mentions his highest office, "Senescallus regni magnus" (col. 264). It is analyzed together with other funeral sermons on Neapolitan-Angevin princes in a forthcoming book by David D'Avray.

[11] In a document of 5 Sept. 1304, Charles II notes that "Fr. Jacobus," archbishop of Naples, and Fr. Mattheus of Aversa witnessed the will of "Bartholomeus bulcanus de Neapolis miles" and that their authoritative testimony ("qui praesentes fuerunt testamento quondam Bartholomaei Bulcani de Neapoli militis") is sufficient to establish the validity of that will even though its form is defective as regards certain legal formulas. Registrum Charles II, 1304-5, as printed in Cantera, *Documenti*, 20–22.

[12] Gutiérrez, "De vita," 298; *Jacobi de Viterbio, OESA, Disputatio*, ed. Ypma, vi.

cost, 1307, and we know that Bartholus was replaced as *lector princi-palis* in Naples in 1306.[13]

To sum up, there is one topic from 1303 (Isabella of Anjou); one from 1304 (Bartholomeus *Vulcani*); two from 1305 (the deaths of Guillelmus *de Godonio* and of Raymond-Berengar of Anjou); and one from 1307 (Magister Bartholus) that establish firm points of chrono-logical reference. All of them indicate that the four annual cycles of sermons were written sequentially during the years 1303–1307. This conclusion confirms the dating and attribution of the sermons, and something more as well, for once the sequence of these autograph sermons is fixed, their calendrical arrangement offers a remarkably precise index of the public events addressed by the archbishop during these years. That is, the codex provides us with dates for these public events. For example, published sources heretofore have indicated only that the church of San Pietro Martire was begun by Charles II in the mid-1290s. It is not known whether the construction was completed under Charles II or his successor Robert.[14] However, Jacobus's sermon for the dedication of the church appears on what is now column 14 of the archbishop's book, indicating a date between 19 and 25 August 1303. If the dedication ceremony took place at that time, the construction of the apse, at least, must have been completed by then. Another point of correspondence with public events is indicated by the date of the "supplicatio pro canonizatione alicuius ad summum pontificem," which appears on column 94, or mid-June in 1304. It has long been known that in 1305 the archbishop of Naples oversaw the collection of depositions concerning the sanctity of Celestine V, for whom a *processus canonizandi* had been opened that year. Since the contents of Jacobus's *supplicatio* also indicate that it concerns Celestine, there is good reason to believe that he was involved in the earlier petitioning that a *processus* be opened.[15] And

---

[13] "Antiquiores definitiones capitulorum generalium," 54: "ordinamus quod fr. Jacobus de Orto Magister, a festo trinitatis in antea ire possit et debeat ad studium de Neapoli, et loco fratris Bartholi in eodem studio maneat pro magistro."

[14] Traditional sources give conflicting accounts of the building of this church; see e.g., Caracciolo, *Napoli Sacra*, 454–55, who dates the founding to 1274. Archival sources show the purchase of land for the church occurred in the early 1290s and that the first stone was laid in 1294; see Venditti, "Urbanistica," 3:749–51 and 866, who follows the study of Cosenza, "La chiesa."

[15] D'Aloe, *Storia*, 481–83. Many of the depositions collected by Jacobus in 1306

again, the departure of the duke of Calabria for Tuscany that Jacobus
discusses in a sermon beginning on col. 149 can now be identified
specifically with the expedition undertaken by Robert of Anjou in
the spring of 1305. The position of the sermon in the codex matches
the dating to early March indicated by other sources. Robert left
Naples before the middle of that month, together with his wife
Sancia; they arrived in Florence around 22 April after a brief stay in
Perugia where the curia was meeting to elect a new pope.[16]

The most interesting implication of this precise chronology,
however, concerns the two sermons on Louis of Anjou. They appear
on cols. 12ff. and 110ff. and so must date to the years 1303 and 1304,
specifically to August 19 of those years.[17] They are the only memorial sermons—as distinct from funeral sermons on the one hand and
sermons *ad sanctos* on the other—in this collection, with the possible
exception of the "supplicatio pro canonizatione alicuius ad summum
pontificem" concerning Celestine V. That "supplicatio," as just
noted, can be understood in connection with attempts to make a case
for the canonization of the unworldly pope, who had made his
unique resignation in Naples and whose sanctity—to be recognized
officially in 1313—was promoted by the Angevin house. There is no
record mentioning Jacobus in connection with concurrent attempts
by the Angevins to open a *processus* concerning Louis, but the design
of his memorial sermons gives good reason to believe that he was
also asked to take part in that campaign. His high ecclesiastical rank
and his academic authority as a theorist of church government made
him an obvious choice in this instance.

The early date of these sermons on Louis of Anjou is then espe-

---

survive: see Seppelt, "Die Akten"; and Vauchez, 365–66. A nephew of Charles II,
Phillip the Fair of France, pressed successfully for the canonization in 1313; see
Vauchez, 91 and n. 52.

[16] For the expedition of the duke of Calabria, see Davidsohn, *Geschichte*, 3:293.

[17] This is the anniversary of Louis's death, which occurred on 19 August in
Marseille, and it is the day appointed in 1317 for his commemoration as a saint.
Before 1317, Robert of Anjou apparently celebrated his brother's memory in the
church of Santa Chiara in Naples on August 26th, but this cannot be the case here,
for Jacobus follows his first sermon on Louis of Anjou with a sermon on the
dedication of San Pietro Martire and then a sermon on St. Louis of France, whose
feast is celebrated on 25 August. See Caggese, 1:176, for the celebrations on 26
August; *Analecta Franciscana* 7:395–99, for the papal bull specifying 19 August; and
discussion in Saggese, "Miniature," 114 and nn. 8–10.

cially noteworthy because the later canonization would take place during the grave crisis in papal-Franciscan relations under John XXII. So strong were the pope's views and so fierce his campaign against his Franciscan opponents that one cannot reasonably avoid the assumption that he viewed the announcement of a new Franciscan saint as a matter of immediate significance. The official bull of canonization, *Sol oriens*, was published early in his pontificate, and the contemporary chronicler Ptolomeus of Lucca records that John XXII had taken a "personal interest" in the case, which had been prepared some years before and had not been approved by his predecessor.[18] Against this background, the emphasis one finds in written lives of the saint on themes of obedience and service to church administration might well be seen to reflect the direct influence of the pope. Such an emphasis is consistent with the position he would advance tenaciously in the following years during the debate over the meaning of evangelical poverty, the Franciscan rule and Franciscan obedience to papal authority.[19] The form of the saint's life must have seemed particularly significant in this regard, for a major focus of the "poverty" dispute was the definition of model lives—apostolic and Franciscan—as well as their imitation. A study by Edith Pasztor written in the 1950s showed convincingly that the narrative lives

---

[18] That John XXII took a personal interest in the *processus* concerning Louis is noted by the contemporary historian Ptolomeus of Lucca, a student of Thomas Aquinas later associated with the papal court in Avignon: Ptolomeus, *Historia*, col. 1211. The four new canonizations and the many requests denied under this pope suggest both the extent to which the papacy had centralized procedures for determining sanctity and the political considerations motivating this pope's decisions; Vauchez, 95ff.

[19] For the early lives, see *Analecta Franciscana* 7, which prints the *processus* of canonization (it had been discovered in 1909) and related documents. The earliest narrative lives include the outline used in the *processus* interrogations, the bull *Sol oriens* and the life by Johannes de Orta. On the common structure and pattern of emphasis in these works, see Pasztor, *Per la storia*, 58–59. An anonymous work similar to these was probably written in connection with the papal curia as well. Briefly mentioned by the editors of *Analecta Franciscana* 7, xliv, a draft of this work survives in two parts, evidently an autograph, in the miscellanies Paris, BN MS. 5376 and Vatican Library MS. Ottoboni lat. 2516. Excerpts from the Ottoboni manuscript were published as a supplement to the life of Johannes de Orta, in d'Alençon, 13: esp. 360 and 14: 21, 89. The portion in the Paris manuscript is transcribed in part in Heysse, "De vita S. Ludovici." It was written after 1317, because it contains an account of the canonization, but before 1343, because it refers to Robert of Anjou as king of Naples.

datable after 1317 all omitted or obscured biographical details that
must have circulated at least in Franciscan circles before the canonization. For example, although several Franciscan friars closely
associated with Louis, including Petrus *Scarrier* and Franciscus *Brun*,
who were once his tutors, also numbered among the disciples of
John Paul Olivi,[20] the lives of St. Louis, beginning with the summary in the bull of 1317, avoid any reference to Louis's opinions of
apostolic poverty or the eschatological ideas of Olivi and his followers. The question that may still be asked, however, is whether in
1317 John XXII acted more or less directly to shape the written lives
of Louis of Anjou or whether he accepted and authorized a model
that had been elaborated by others at some earlier time. Was his role
in this literary history that of censor or publisher?

One conclusion to be drawn from Pasztor's excellent study is that
a new reconstruction of the life of the young Angevin, based so far
as possible on materials antedating the canonization, would give us a
different and more radical figure. It is significant, then, that Jacobus's
sermons, despite their early date and their author's access to privileged information—he may have known Louis personally, and he
addressed an audience containing many people who had known him
well—do not do so. There are few concrete details here, the sermons
treating the form of Louis's life at a fairly high level of abstraction,
but they show clearly that there was a hagiographical tradition
behind the model life that was published at his canonization. What
Avignon promulgated in 1317, Naples had defined in its essential
outlines at least 15 years before.

The first commemorative sermon, to which Jacobus gave the title
"In anniversario domini Ludovici episcopi Tholosani," announces its
main argument immediately in its biblical text, "Probatus est in illo
et perfectus inventus est." There follows a tripartite, external division, not of the words in the verse but of the topic, in this case
"being proven perfect."

---

[20] Pasztor, 35–47, for analysis of the bull *Sol oriens* of 1317; 44–55, for the most
blatantly "corrected" life, that by Fra Paolino Veneto, included in his universal
chronicle, *Satyrica historia*. See also Bologna, *I pittori*, and Musto, "Queen Sancia of
Naples," 191. More cautious in construing the few signs that Louis was in sympa-
thy with Olivi and his followers is Paul, "Saint Louis d'Anjou," and idem, "Evangelisme."

Probatus est in illo et perfectus inventus est, et erit illi gloria
eterna Ecclesiasticus 31 [31.10]. verba ista possunt veraciter et
[?-]citer dici de domino ludovico, cuius felicis defunctionis
diem anniversarium observamus [. . .] circa quod sciendum est
quod hii qui promovendi sunt ad aliquem statum excellentio-
rem primo examinantur, secundo approbantur, tertio exaltan-
tur. in hunc modum [deus] animas promovens ad statum eter-
ne beatitudinis examinat, approbat et exaltat. et quia (quantum
homini iudicare fas est) dominus ludovicus velud electus et
predestinatus a deo promovendus erat ad statum beatitudinis,
ideo primo examinatus, secundo approbatus et ultimo exaltatus
est a deo. et hec tria notantur circa ipsum in verba proposita:
primo eius examinatio, secundo approbatio, tertio exaltatio.

(Col. 12)

The three headings, "testing, approval, and promotion," are then
elaborated with reference to Louis's life, which is described as a
progress through three states, that of layman, regular and finally
bishop. Since he is "proven" in each state, the exposition takes a neat
nine-part division, concluding with Louis's exaltation "ad statum
beatitudinis." The conclusion, which is implicit in the firmly progressive structure of the argument, is also anticipated at the end of
the introductory section, where Jacobus looks back two verses from
his chosen text to emphasize that "Dominus Ludovicus" should be
praised on the anniversary of his death for the "miracula" he worked
and has continued to work:

et bene conveniunt hec verba domino ludovico, si consideren-
tur que precedunt: "beatus," inquit, "dives qui inventus est
sine macula et qui post aurum non abiit, nec speravit in pecu-
nia et thesauris" [Ecclesiasticus 31.8]. "quis est hic?" potest
responderi: dominus ludovicus, et ideo laudabimus eum. fecit
enim mirabilia in vita sua, scilicet dum hic vixit miracula fecit
et nunc cum vivit in patria miracula facit. (col. 12)

A similar, tripartite division of his life with the consequent emphasis
on the last period as bishop (as well as, of course, the "miracula")
reappears in the life of Louis in the official *processus* documents and
in the subsequent writings that derive from them.

The second sermon, from 19 August 1304, is similar to the first in its structure. It develops the thesis that Louis was "blessed of the Lord," again with a tripartite external division. Jacobus gives it the title "In commemoratione domini l[udovici] filii domini regis Sicilie" (col. 110) and begins with the text "Ecce odor filii mei" from Genesis 27. These words are applied to Louis in two senses: first by referring the speaking voice to his earthly father, Charles II; then— and this yields the figure that Jacobus will pursue in his exposition— by taking the speaking voice with reference to his celestial father.

> *Ecce odor filii mei sicut odor agri, [cui benedixit Dominus] Genesis 27* [=27.27]. hec verba fuerunt patriarche ysaac de [corrected from "ad"] filio suo Jacob. sed possunt esse verba serenissimi domini nostri regis de [. . .] domino Ludovico, filio suo secundum carnem. tamen ad ampliorem eius commendationem dicam hec esse verba patris celestis, qui est universalis omnium pater, dicentis de domino ludovico *ecce odor*, etc.   (Col. 110)

This application reintroduces the theme of sanctity that was so prominent in the first sermon. Again the argument is structured by the three different states or conditions of life (*status*) Louis assumed: layman and prince, regular and bishop:

> fuit siquidem beatus Ludovicus dum hic vixit in triplici statu: primo in statu seculari, secundo in statu regulari, tertio in statu pastorali. et iuxta hunc triplicem statum ponitur triplex eius commendatio.

The direction of his argument in this second sermon, so clear in its theme and structure, is revealed in its verbal detail also. Jacobus had, throughout his first sermon, referred to Louis simply with the general title "Dominus." This is of course appropriate to the years 1303 and 1304 when Jacobus was preaching, though it is noteworthy that he chose not to refer to Louis as "frater." Now in 1304 his adoption of the text from Genesis gives him a thematic word in "Dominus benedixit" that allows him to use the suggestive adjective "beatus" in the paraphrase which opens the sermon. Louis is the "son" blessed of the Lord. And there is more. Jacobus apparently thought of applying "beatus" immediately as a title for Louis of Anjou, for at the beginning of the first section of his sermon, that on Louis's secular status, one finds the cancellation of "beatus" and reintroduction of "dominus":

prima eius commendatio est pro statu seculari, hec notatur cum dicitur [col. 111] *Ecce odor filii mei* circa quod sciendum, quod pater celestis beatum [canceled] dominum Ludovicum adhuc in statu seculari existentem, primo adoptavit in filium, secundo acceptavit ad meritum, tertio demonstravit in exemplum.

The trace of Jacobus's impulse and of his second thoughts in the autograph manuscript is eloquent, the more so because he has already used the same word in a different construction. Jacobus seems, in fact, to have chosen his text because it will allow him to use "benedictus" and "beatus" in reference to Louis of Anjou as he argues, in effect, that these close cousins to "sanctus" are appropriate in this context. Yet here he is backing away from "beatus" used in the more technical form of a title. To do so would be in perfect concert with Jacobus's argument, but he evidently feels that it is nevertheless improper. He was taking a part in the efforts to demonstrate that Louis should be recognized as a saint, but these efforts were only just beginning.

The special emphasis on episcopal office in both sermons cannot easily be explained with reference to Louis's biography, for he had a very short career as bishop of Toulouse. More significant perhaps are the indications that it has much in common with what Charles II intended for his son's career. These intentions shine in the king's acts throughout the mid-1290s, when it was becoming clear that Louis—then a hostage in captivity near Barcelona—would renounce his carnal lineage to join the Franciscan order. The witnesses for his *processus* consistently report that Charles II and Maria of Hungary first attempted to dissuade him from resigning his temporal rights and offices, and after failing to do so moved quickly to encourage a more conventional career within the church. Louis, the witnesses said, had also resisted this idea, and had finally accepted the miter with great reluctance, declaring his desire for a life as a simple Franciscan brother. He then served in that office very briefly, as is apparent from an outline of his movements from the time of his appointment until his death. Pope Boniface VIII asked Louis to be bishop of Toulouse at the end of December, 1296, shortly after the death of the previous bishop, Hugo Marcarius, which occurred on December 6; before that Louis had apparently been living his novitiate with a group of friars "extra Neapolim" and he refused to accept the bishopric until he had taken the rest of his vows as a Franciscan. This he did in Rome in late December, 1296. In the spring of 1297 he accompanied his father, Charles II, to Paris, along the way "showing pity to the poor during the cold winter" and in the summer he returned south, to Toulouse. But he did not stay there. In July, he was in Catalonia, to visit his sister Blanche and to help arrange peace between the king of Aragon, his brother-in-law, and the count of Foix. He again joined his father, now at Brignoles in Provence, where he fell ill and died on 19 August. He was entombed, according to his wishes, at the Franciscan church in Marseille.[21] He had been resident in Toulouse no more than a few months altogether, hardly long enough to demonstrate a model episcopal life, but long enough, perhaps, to exemplify the compromise between his own desires and those of his father for him.

It is then not surprising that the emphasis in Jacobus's sermons should recall Charles II. His responsibility for composing the sermons derived from his office as archbishop in Naples and his close relations with the royal court. Much as his treatise on the Church helped define the Guelph political view of Charles II, the two sermons on "Dominus Ludovicus" give shape to a commemoration of the king's deceased son that reflects Charles's particular views and interest. As far as we know, the sermons on "Dominus Ludovicus" had no written sources, but it is most probable that they had cross influences with the petitions of the Neapolitan court in favor of opening an official inquiry of sanctity. What emerged was a portrait of Louis at once consistent with Jacobus's own theories of church office, which he had recently elaborated in *De regimine Christiano*, and with the interests of his patron. Jacobus's focus does not fall on the figure of a young prince renouncing his temporal office to become a simple mendicant, although this is a common topic in contemporary Franciscan hagiography and even found a place later in John XXII's bull of canonization. Instead, the sermons give Louis's "third state" great prominence, subordinating the second state, the *status regularis*, to it. Within the progressive structure

---

[21] The documentary evidence for his career is reviewed in *Analecta Franciscana* 7, introduction, and by Pasztor, 2–11.

"lay-regular-bishop," the characteristically Franciscan themes of renunciation, simplicity and poverty are either ignored or subordinated to an older model of uncorrupted episcopal responsibility.

The sermon of 1303, for example, mentions poverty only in connection with Louis's unusual virtue in carrying out his temporal and ecclesiastical offices, first as a prince and later as bishop. Louis was tested by prosperity when he was a prince:

> liber tamen fuit ab hiis vitiis, quibus implicari solent multi divites, quorum unum est superbia, quia propter divitias alios despiciunt et se extollunt ... sed horum contraria dominus ludovicus habuit in statu sue prosperitatis. contra superbie vitium habuit virtutem profundissime humilitatis; contra vitium intemperantie habuit virtutem mitissime castitatis; contra vitium avaritie habuit virtutem amplissime largitatis, ut patet ex eius gestis. (Col. 13)

He was tested in a similar fashion when he held temporal power as a bishop, and again proved to be free from the vices common to holders of that office: while those in secular church offices tend to love pomp and ceremony, Louis loved poverty instead; he wasted no time on trivial speech with the rich and powerful, instead speaking at length with the humble and the poor; he detested delicacies, but chose asperity in food and clothing.

> dominus ludovicus quia bene gloriam et pompam contemptabat, laudes de se audire nolebat; ... ludovicus vilia officia fecit valenter et cum omnibus etiam pauperibus et vilibus personis longe conversabatur; ... ludovicus asperitatem vite eligebat in victu et vestitu. (Col. 13)

There really is no place for mendicancy here. The theme of poverty has been transferred to an older model of ecclesiastical perfection.

The figure of reforming bishop that Jacobus emphasizes in his sermons passed into the extensive new literature composed to commemorate Louis of Toulouse after his canonization in 1317.[22] His

---

[22] An analogous passage appears in *Sol oriens*: "unde factus jam Episcopus Tholosanus, per unum suum familiarem secretarium mandavit inquiri de suorum quantitate reddituum, quantumque sibi sufficeret pro moderatis expensis et rationabilibus faciendis, volens quod totum residuum in sustentandis pauperibus poneretur,

familiar identity among the saints developed from the same reconciliation of simplicity and poverty with the duties of secular office.
Narrative lives illustrating this ideal were written around the time of
the canonization; and in visual representations the new saint's characteristic iconography showed a young figure wearing a miter and
sandals, a saio under a rich episcopal cope.[23] The rapprochement
may be understood in terms of papal-Franciscan relations in and after
1317, for it is broadly consonant with the views of John XXII. And
without doubt the canonization of the young Angevin can be understood only against this particular background. But the composition
of a model life of St. Louis of Toulouse should be seen in a somewhat longer perspective. It had been shaped earlier and in different
circumstances. The two commemorative sermons by Jacobus of
Viterbo put us very near the beginning of that hagiographical tradition and perhaps at its source.

§

This paper has tried to identify some of the names appearing in the
sermons in MS. Archivio di San Pietro D.213, at first in order to
establish their authorship and chronology, and then to suggest the
sympathetic nature of Jacobus's relations with the court of Charles
II of Anjou. The two sermons analyzed in greater detail suggest a
collaboration extended to the court's sponsorship of candidates for
canonization. At the risk of provoking some annoyance by adding
yet another portrait to the list, I want to conclude with a glance at
one more contemporary Neapolitan career. This name does not
appear in Jacobus's sermons, but it has a place in the history of
writings on "Dominus Ludovicus." The name is Jacobus *Duèze*, later
Pope John XXII. In 1300, when Jacobus of Viterbo moved from
Paris to Naples, this contemporary of his from the Angevin lands in

---

quamquam praelatus tam magnus esset, ac filius tanti regis. . . . In hoc etiam Christi
imitatore vero humilitas vera fulsit."

    [23] The first example of this iconography is in Simone Martini's altarpiece,
commissioned by Robert of Anjou and now in the Capodimonte museum in
Naples. See Bologna, "Povertà," and idem, *I pittori*. For some later examples,
Bertaux, "Les saints"; Kleinschmidt, "St. Ludwig von Toulouse"; Kaftal, *Iconography*, s.v. "Louis of Toulouse."

Provence was "clericus et familiaris" in the household of Charles II. He was given a minor bishopric that year. In 1305, shortly after the second sermon had been written, *Duèze* was appointed a special counselor to Charles's son Robert. (One cannot fail to note the general similarity to the other learned bishop we have found attached to Robert's personal service, the Guillelmus *de Godonio* whose funeral sermon Jacobus of Viterbo preached that same year.) *Duèze* became Chancellor, first to Charles II in 1308, and then to Robert of Anjou; with Robert's support, he became bishop of Avignon in 1310. So the man who would issue *Sol oriens* had been a member of the same court circles that produced the two sermons on "Dominus Ludovicus" in 1303 and 1304. There can be no doubt that he was familiar with them and with much that went into their making. His career then tells us a good deal about the human agents behind the model life of Louis of Anjou that Jacobus proposed in those sermons as it, too, advanced from Naples to Avignon.

Universität Tübingen

KARL   REICHL

"No more ne willi wiked be": Religious Poetry in a Franciscan Manuscript (Digby 2)

On folio 15r of MS. Digby 2 in the Bodleian Library (SC 1603) one of the scribes of the manuscript copied a poem in which the speaker expresses his determination to be "no longer wicked." He is going to turn away from the snares of the world and devote his life to Christ by becoming a "frer menur," a Franciscan, and he will wear a knotted girdle from now on:[1]

> No more [ne][2] willi wiked be,
> Forsake ich wille þis worldis fe,
> þis wildis wedis,[3] þis folen gle.
> Ich wul be mild of chere,
> Of cnottis scal mi girdil be:
> Becomme[4] ich wil frere.
>
> Frer menur i wil me make

---

[1] Brown and Robbins, *Index*, no. 2293 [henceforth, *Index*]; q.v. also in Robbins and Cutler, *Supplement*; in *English Lyrics*, ed. Brown, 126. The three English poems of MS. Digby 2 were first edited by Furnivall, "Religious Poems," 309–12. In the following text, punctuation, word separation, and capitalization are editorial; abbreviations have been silently expanded.

[2] In the manuscript *ne* has been erased and is barely visible.

[3] This word can be read as *wedis* or *wodis*; in view of v. 5, *wedis* gives a better sense; *wildis* is taken by Brown and Bennett/Smithers as the genitive plural of nominalized *wilde*, meaning "of the wild (wanton) men"; see *English Lyrics*, 303 (s.v. *wildis*); *Early Middle English Verse and Prose*, ed. Bennett and Smithers, 606 (s.v. *wilde, wylde*).

[4] Brown and other editors print *becomen*, but the manuscript clearly reads *becōme*.

And lecherie i wille asake,
To Ihesu Crist ich wil me take
And serue in holi churche,
Al in mi ouris forto wake,
Goddis wille to wurche.

Wurche i wille þis workes gode
For him þat boyht us in þe rode.
From his side ran þe blode,
So dere he gan vs bie.
For sothe ic tel him mor þan wode
þat hantit licherie.

Immediately preceding this poem is a calendar (fols. 8r–13v), in which the feast of St. Francis is recorded for October 4 ("Natale beati Francisci, ordinis fratrum minorum fundatoris," fol. 12v). C. Brown interpreted the poem together with the entry for October 4 in the calendar as pointing to a Franciscan origin of the manuscript.[5] It has to be noted, however, that the same calendar also lists the feast of St. Dominic for August 5 ("Sancti Dominici confessoris, fundatoris fratrum predicatorum ordinis," fol. 11v), as well as that of St. Peter the Martyr, a member of the Dominican order, for April 29.[6] Among the philosophical treatises of the manuscript there is a *Summa predicamentorum* by a *frater* William of Montoriel, possibly a Franciscan from the north of Ireland.[7] There is also a treatise of sophisms whose author is probably Richard Fishacre, a Dominican teaching in Oxford (d. 1248) (see below, item [26]).[8] There can be

---

[5] "In addition to the express declaration in no. 66: 'Frer menur i wil me make,' we have the following note in the Kalendarium (Art. 6) under Oct. 4: 'Notate beati Francisci, ordinis Fratrum Minorum fundatoris,' " *English Lyrics*, xxvii. St. Francis died in 1226 and was canonized in 1228. The calendar also records under May 25 the feast of St. Urban and as commemoration: "Translacio beati Francisci, confessoris," fol. 10r. The translation of St. Francis' relics from the church of S. Giorgio, Assisi, to the New Basilica took place in 1230.

[6] "Sancti Petri Martyris de ordine predicatorum," fol. 9v. Petrus Martyr (or Peter of Verona) died in 1252 and was canonized in 1253. St. Dominic died in 1221 and was canonized in 1234.

[7] On William of Montoriel, see Lewry, "The Miscellaneous and the Anonymous."

[8] On Richard Fishacre, see Gilson, *History*, 354f., 702. He was the first Dominican to hold an Oxford degree in theology.

little doubt that this manuscript was compiled in Oxford, and it is more than likely that it can be associated with either the Grey or the Black Friars. Although it cannot be established beyond doubt that the manuscript was compiled in a Franciscan (rather than Dominican) house, the inclusion of the poem "No more ne willi wiked be" certainly speaks for Franciscans as compilers, and it is probably safe to assume that MS. Digby 2 was written in the Franciscan house of Oxford.

"No more ne willi wiked be" is not the only poem in this manuscript. There are two more poems in English, three in Latin, and one in French. They are all religious lyrics, some of them Passion poems. The English poems have been printed several times and have received some critical attention. The Passion poem in particular has been interpreted as expressing Franciscan spirituality and devotion, and it has also been discussed in the context of Franciscan influence on the development of the early Middle English religious lyric.[9] In view of the scarcity of early Middle English lyric poetry (virtually the whole corpus of the thirteenth- and early fourteenth-century religious and secular lyric is contained in C. Brown's *English Lyrics of the XIIIth Century*), we must rely for an appreciation of these poems not only on the texts themselves, but also on what evidence we can find of their place in contemporary literature and literary practice. Siegfried Wenzel has repeatedly shown how the use of lyrics in sermons can enlighten us concerning the medieval understanding of these lyrics and can help us avoid some of the pitfalls of applying the principles of modern criticism to medieval poetry.[10] In a similar way, the manuscript context can provide information on the milieu in which lyric poetry was cultivated, on the people interested in writing down lyrics and possibly on the use they made of the poetry transmitted. Since the work done by C. Brown and later R. H. Robbins on the manuscripts containing Middle English lyrics, our knowledge of manuscript provenance, manuscript affiliation, and manuscript composition has made some progress.[11] There can be no doubt that

---

[9] See in particular Jeffrey, *Early English Lyric*, 242ff. Compare also Kane, *Middle English Literature*, 137–38; Woolf, *English Religious Lyric*, 65–66; Wolpers, "Andachtsbild," 324–28; Bennett, *Poetry of the Passion*, 49.

[10] In particular in Wenzel, *Preachers, Poets*.

[11] Brown's introduction to *English Lyrics* (xi–xlii) is still worth reading, as is

a number of Middle English religious lyrics of the thirteenth and fourteenth century can be associated with friars, in particular with Franciscans, such as the translations of Latin hymns by William Herebert or the Commonplace Book compiled by John of Grimestone.[12] Nevertheless, many points remain unresolved, and the "Franciscan hypothesis," affirming the all-pervasive influence of Franciscan spirituality on the early Middle English religious lyric, is still as unproven as it was when it was first put forward by R. H. Robbins.[13]

Before looking at the English poems in the context of the other lyrics transmitted in MS. Digby 2, I will give a short summary of the manuscript contents. The manuscript comprises 152 folios and contains basically three types of texts: computational writings, philosophical treatises, and poetry.[14] It emerges from the dates given in some of the computational texts that the manuscript was compiled at the end of the thirteenth century (ca. 1280; see items [1] and [10]). The poems and most of the computational texts are found in the first part of the manuscript, the philosophical and logical texts are found on fols. 26r–94v and 122r–147r. Up to fol. 25v the manuscript contains the following items:

[1] fols. 1r–4r A computation of lunar eclipses from the year 1281 to 1300.

Robbins' classification of manuscripts containing lyrics in his edition of secular lyrics of the 14th and 15th centuries: *Secular Lyrics*, ed. Robbins, xvii–xxxiii. See also the classification in Wenzel, *Preachers, Poets*, 4–8. Robbins' manuscript classification of the late Middle English love lyric has been elaborated by Boffey in *Manuscripts of Courtly Love Lyrics*, 6–33.

[12] On William Herebert's lyrics see Gneuss, "William Hereberts Übersetzungen"; *Works of William Herebert*, ed. Reimer, 21–23 (use of poems in sermons), 111–38 (edition). On John of Grimestone, see *Descriptive Index*, ed. Wilson; Wenzel, *Preachers, Poets*, 101ff., 135ff.

[13] See especially Robbins, "The Authors"; for a more recent statement of this hypothesis, see Jeffrey, *Early English Lyric*. Some of the manuscripts listed and partially edited by Brown and Robbins have been studied subsequently. Digby 86 is no longer believed to belong to the group of "Friars' Miscellanies"; see Miller, "Early History"; Frankis, "Social Context," 183. For manuscript Trinity College Cambridge B.14.39 (323), see my edition and description, *Religiöse Dichtung*, especially 49–54. I would still classify this manuscript as a friars' miscellany, although definite proof for associating the manuscript with Franciscans rather than Dominicans cannot be adduced.

[14] See Macray, *Catalogi Codicum Manuscriptorum*, cols. 1–3.

Inc.: "Anno domini m° cc° 81."

Compare Thorndike-Kibre, col. 102: "Anno domini 1273 die Ianuarii super...."[15]

[2] fols. 4v–5r A Latin monodic song on the Virgin (with music).
Inc.: "In te concipitur."
Walther, 9123; Chevalier, 28134.[16]

[3] fol. 5r A Latin moralizing monodic song (with music).
Inc.: "In ecclesiis celi gloria."

[4] fol. 5v A Latin monodic song on the Passion (with music).
Inc.: "⌊A⌋ve purum vas argenti."

[5] fol. 6r An English poem on the Passion.
Inc.: "Hi sike al wan hi singe."
Index, 1365.

[6] fol. 6v An English poem on the Virgin.
Inc.: "Hayl mari, hic am sori."
Index, 1066.

[7] fol. 7r A list of the months, the number of days per month, the daytime and the nighttime hours.
Inc.: "Ianuarius habet dies 31."
Thorndike-Kibre, col. 653.

[8] fol. 7v A calculation of Easter.
Inc.: "Post martis nonas vbi sit noua luna requiras."

[9] fols. 8r–13v A calendar.

[10] fol. 14r A table for the calculation of Easter, from the year 1282 to 1300.
Inc.: "Anno gracie m° cc° lxxxij anno currente numero tunc per x inchoata est ista tabula per quam sciri potest indubitabiter dies septuagesime, quadragesime, pasce et bisextus."

[11] fol. 14v A drawing showing the points of the compass, etc.

[12] fol. 15r An English poem.
Inc.: "No more [ne] willi wiked be."
Index, 2293

[13] fol. 15v A French poem on the Virgin.
Inc.: "De ma dame du cel."

---

[15] Thorndike and Kibre, *Catalogue of Incipits* [henceforth, Thorndike-Kibre].
[16] Walther, *Initia carminum* [henceforth, Walther]; Chevalier, *Repertorium Hymnologicum*.

Sonet, 360.[17]

[14] fols. 16r–24v A Latin verse-computus with commentary.

Inc. (Commentary): "Per veterum sagacitatem compositus fuit kalendarii qui mira subtitilitate planetarum cursus et temporum distincciones considerabant."

Inc. (Computus): "Ter quinos domini quotiens potes aufer ab annis."

Walther, 19208.[18]

Thorndike-Kibre, col. 1033.

[15] fol. 24v Verses on the vigils for the feasts of saints.

Inc.: "Vigilias quinque nos docet Roma celebrare."

[16] fols. 25r–25v Notes on fasting and various computational verses and notes, followed by a table of months and signs of the zodiac.

Inc.: "Et primo ieiunamus in vere." (fol. 25r)

Inc.: "Po to, ligna cremo, de vite superflua demo."

Walther, 14374.

Inc.: "Bis senos menses tenet annus nomina quorum." (fol. 25v)

Walther, 2191.

On fol. 26r the philosophical and logical treatises begin. A detailed list of these texts is given by L. M. De Rijk.[19] The first group of texts is found on fols. 26r–94v. According to De Rijk, four philosophical texts can be distinguished:

[17] fols. 26r–67v Logical *summulae* (consisting of several parts).

Inc. (First part): "Cum sit nostra presens intencio ad artem dyalecticam."

Little, 61.[20]

[18] fols. 68r–79v A treatise on the *predicabilia*.

Inc.: "Cum cognicio quinque universalium."

---

[17] Sonet, *Répertoire*. The poem is also listed in Brayer, "Catalogue des textes," 41, no. 816.

[18] Walther gives Johannes de Garlandia as the possible author of the metrical computus and lists two 13th-c. manuscripts (but not Digby 2).

[19] See De Rijk, *Logica modernorum*, 2:56–59. Compare also Lewry, "The Miscellaneous and the Anonymous."

[20] Little, *Initia Operum* [henceforth, Little]; Little characterizes this work as "Anon. de logica" and lists only MS. Digby 24.

[19] fol. 79v Fragment of a will.

[20] fols. 80r–84v A commentary on Aristotle's *Categories* (fragmentary) (*Summa predicamentorum* by William de Montoriel).[21]

[21] fols. 85r–94v A commentary on Aristotle's *De Interpretatione* (fragmentary).

    Inc.: "In principio doctrine libri Peryermenias."

Between this and the next group of logical and philosophical treatises, beginning on fol. 122v, various computational texts are found:

[22] fols. 95r–110v A Latin verse-computus with commentary (fragmentary).[22]

    Inc. (Commentary): "*Gaudet,* etc.: Exposicio huius versus talis est."

    Inc. (Computus): "Gaudet sic iam lux martis phebus aprilis."

[23] fol. 111r A charm for staunching blood, in Latin, English, and French.

    Inc.: "Tres boni fratres."

[24] fol. 111v A charm against pain in the womb, in French.

    Inc.: "Notre dame seinte Mari."

[25] fols. 112r–121v A treatise on the quadrant.

    Inc.: "Post chilindri composicionem."

    Thorndike-Kibre, col. 1062.

On fol. 122r the second group of philosphical texts begins, consisting of a treatise on sophisms and Roger de Marston's philosophical text mentioned above:

[26] fols. 122r–140v A treatise of sophisms.[23]

---

[21] The first sixteen leaves from William de Montoriel's *Summa predicamentorum* are missing in MS. Digby 2 and are found in MS. Digby 24, fols. 1r–16v. See De Rijk, *Logica modernorum,* 2:59–60.

[22] This item consists possibly of several texts; see De Rijk, *Logica modernorum,* 2:58–59.

[23] See De Rijk, *Logica modernorum,* 2:59. As De Rijk points out, the treatise beginning on fol. 122r originally must have immediately followed fol. 111, as the first words of the treatise are found as catch-words at the bottom of fol. 111v. This treatise is also found in MS. Digby 24; for a detailed description, see De Rijk, *Logica modernorum,* 2:62–71. On Richard Fishacre as probable author, see De Rijk, *Logica modernorum,* 2:71–72.

Inc.: "Nulla est affirmacio in qua universale universaliter sump-
  tum predicatur."
Little, 153.
[27] fols. 141r–147v A physionomical treatise by Roger Bourth.
  Inc.: "De phisionomia inquirenda quedam continet necessaria et
  quedam utilia."
Little, 67.

Fols. 147v and 148v are empty; on fol. 148r there are seven discon-
nected lines (*probae pennae?*) from a logical text (beginning "Hec
exposicio"). The last four leaves of the manuscript contain:

[28] fols. 149r–150r Formulas for letters.
  Inc.: "Insinuacione presencium."
[29] fols. 151r–152v A grammatical treatise (fragmentary).
  Inc.: "Quid est littera."
Bursill-Hall, No. 188.77 (p. 174).[24]

The first English poem in the manuscript, "Hi sike al wan hi
singe" (item [5]), is a Passion poem.[25] It describes Christ on the
Cross in his agony, and the effect of his suffering and death on Mary,
but most of all on the speaker of the poem himself. The poem is a
meditative lyric, belonging to a group of Middle English poems on
the Passion in which the figure of Christ on the Cross evokes feelings of compassion and pity in the beholder, but also feelings of
repentance and contrition in sinful man. Many of these poems end,
as "Hi sike as wan hi singe," in a prayer for forgiveness and in an
invocation for Mary's intercession with her Son.[26] This poem is
also transmitted in MS. BL Harley 2253; of the two versions extant,
the one found in MS. Digby 2 is generally thought to be textually
superior.[27] In his edition of the Harley lyrics, K. Böddeker pointed
out that "Hi sike al wan hi singe" is both metrically and stylistically
so close to another Passion poem transmitted in the Harley manu-

---

[24] Bursill-Hall, *Census.* The same work, characterized as "Anon. De Grammatica" by Bursill-Hall, is found in a manuscript in Florence; see ibid., no. 91.8.1.
  [25] In *English Lyrics,* 122–24 (no. 64).
  [26] On the Middle English Passion lyrics, see Woolf, *English Religious Lyric,* 19–
66; Gray, *Themes and Images,* 122–45; see also above, n. 9.
  [27] *English Lyrics,* 216–17; compare also Wolpers, "Andachtsbild"; Hallwas,
"Two Versions." The Harley version is in *Harley Lyrics,* ed. Brook, 59–60.

script ("When y se blosmes springe"[28]) "that we must attribute both lyrics to one and the same poet."[29] Although a common authorship does not seem as convincing to us today as it did to Böddeker, it is nevertheless incontestable that the Digby poem is closely connected to other Middle English poems on the Passion and that it is by no means a unique example of this genre. "When y se blosmes springe" is in turn transmitted in another (otherwise unrelated) manuscript, BL Royal 2.F.viii, a fact which shows that this type of poetry enjoyed a certain popularity in medieval England.[30]

One of the three Latin songs in the Digby manuscript also belongs to the Easter cycle. It is a poem on Mary Magdalene, in the form of a dialogue between Mary Magdalene and the risen Christ. The poem precedes "Hi sike al wan hi singe" in the manuscript:[31]

[fol. 5v]
"[A]ve[32] purum vas argenti
     Decocta rubigine,
Christi custos monumenti
     Nati sine semine
     De Maria virgine.
Tibi primo se querenti
Necnon ad sepulcrum flenti
     Deitas in homine
     Pandit sub velamine.
     Flere desine!

---

[28] *Index,* no. 3963: *Harley Lyrics,* 54–55.

[29] Böddeker, ed., *Altenglische Dichtungen,* 210.

[30] MS. Royal 2.F.viii belonged to the Benedictine monastery of St. Albans; it contains a Latin psalter with commentary and many pencil annotations in the margins. The scribe of these notes wrote two English poems on the verso side of the first fly-leaf, one of them the Harley Passion poem, the other a Marian lyric ("On hire is al mi lif ilong," *Index,* no. 2687). The latter is also found in MSS. Cambridge, Trinity College B.14.39 (323); Oxford, Jesus College 29; and BL Cotton Caligula A.IX. On the Royal MS., see *Catalogue of the Royal and King's Collections,* ed. Warner and Gilson, 1:66–67; the Royal version of "When y se blosmes springe" is edited in *English Lyrics,* 120–22; for an edition of "On hire is al mi lif ilong," see Reichl, *Religiöse Dichtung,* 470–75.

[31] This poem is not listed in Walther. In the following edition, abbreviations have been silently expanded; punctuation and capitalization are editorial.

[32] MS *ve.* For help with the text of the Latin lyrics I am grateful to Dr. Neil Wright (Cambridge).

Pape, mulier, quid ploras!
　　Quem queris, quem musitas?
Cur hic iaces per tot horas?
　　Surge quid hic latitas!
　　Numquid hoc vult caritas
Quod in flendo sic laboras?
Hunc timorem mitte foras
　　Et tunc forte bonitas
　　Aderit et veritas
　　　　Quam tu flagitas.''

''Non me possum continere
　　Nec cessare debeo.
Semper volo Jhesum flere,
　　Nam amore langueo.
　　Heu, sublatum video
Qui solebat me docere.
Jhesu bone, miserere,
　　Facere quid debeo?
　　Nunc ut quondam soleo
　　　　Te non video.

Ortolane, si vidisti
　　Illum post quem musito?
Aut hunc si tu sustulisti,
　　Mihi, queso, dicito.
　　Gratu[m][33] currens concito,
Tollam vnde posuisti.
Sic me mestam refouisti,
　　Quem pro more solito
　　Vnguam more debito,
　　　　Nullum dubito.''

''O Maria, noli flere
　　Nec te plus affligere!
Resurrexi vivens vere,
　　Sed noli me tangere!

---

[33] MS *gratu.*

Ad patrem ascendere,
Nondum potes me videre.
Fides deest, illam quere,
  Et sic Petro dicere
  Quod me vides viuere.
    Vade propere!"

"Raboni, iam sunt exorta
  Vera nobis gaudia
Cum destructa mortis porta
  Viuis saluans omnia.
  Pro tua clemencia
Desolatos nos conforta
Et fac tandem ut absorta
  Fit mors in victoria,
  Tecum ut ecclesia
    Sit in gloria." Amen.

This poem takes its inspiration from the New Testament account of the Resurrection in St. John's Gospel (John 20.15–17). The dialogue of the biblical narrative, taken over almost verbatim, is slightly elaborated in the manner of a Passion play and embedded in a praise of Mary Magdalene (stanza I) and a prayer to Christ the Savior (stanza VI).[34] Both the first and the last stanza could also be spoken by the poet (or his persona), rather than by Christ and Mary Magdalene, respectively. Mary Magdalene's sorrow and disconsolate state of mind are very much in the foreground, evoking the tone of Passion poetry, even if the poem's theme is Christ's Resurrection. We find a similar mood in other Latin poems on the Resurrection. One of the poems ascribed to Philip the Chancellor (d. 1236 or 1237), for instance, shares with our song not only tone and mood, but also style and phraseology:[35]

O Maria, noli flere,
  iam non quaeras alium;
. . . .

---

[34] See the texts and discussion of "The Visit to the Sepulchre" in Young, *Drama of the Medieval Church*, 1:239ff.

[35] See Raby, *Christian-Latin Poetry*, 400.

> unde gemis, unde ploras?
> verum habes gaudium;
> latet in te, quod ignoras,
> doloris solacium;
> intus habes, quaeris foras
> languoris remedium.

Following "Hi sike al wan hi singe" in the manuscript is an English lyric on the Virgin [item 6]. It is a penitential poem, in which the speaker, miserably aware of his sins, addresses the Virgin and asks her to intercede for him with Christ. No other versions of this poem have been transmitted, although the images and motifs found in this lyric are common enough in Middle English Marian poetry.[36] There are two more poems on the Virgin in MS. Digby 2, one in Latin and one in French. The authorship of the Latin poem (item [2]) is uncertain; it has been attributed to both Alexander Nequam (1157–1217) and Henry of Avranches (d. after 1259).[37] In stanzas I to IV Mary is praised as the mother of God and a virgin free from original sin. The second half of the poem is devoted to Christ, who through his suffering and death on the cross has brought redemption and everlasting life to man (stanzas V to VIII). There is a similar shift from Mary to Christ in the French poem found on fol. 15v (item [13]). The poem consists of seven 10-line stanzas (stanza II is incomplete and has only 6 lines), rhyming a-b-a-b-c-c-b-c-c-b. The poem begins with the annunciation:[38]

> [fol. 15v]
> De ma dame du cel
> Chanteray un chant,

---

[36] Edited in *English Lyrics*, 124–25 (no. 65). On Marian lyrics in Middle English, compare Woolf, *English Religious Lyric*, 114–58.

[37] The poem is edited from MS. Digby 2 (with changes) in *Analecta hymnica*, ed. Blume and Dreves, 20:140 (no. 182); see also *Analecta hymnica*, ed. Blume and Dreves, 48:269–70 (no. 289). Compare also Raby, *Christian-Latin Poetry*, 383; Szövérffy, *Annalen der Hymnendichtung*, 2:182–83; Richard W. Hunt, *Schools and Cloister*, 55–56.

[38] The poem seems to be textually corrupt in several places and would need more linguistic attention for a critical edition than can be given in the present context. I am grateful to Prof. Christian Schmitt (Bonn) for looking at my translation. As with the other texts printed here from the manuscript, punctuation and capitalization are editorial; abbreviations have been silently expanded.

Ki Seynt Gabriel
Vynt e[n][39] saluont
5 E dit: Aue Mari,
Tu grace repleni
Conseueres tun enfont.
Fiz o rey, Messi,
Net mey ami.
10 Pussel eris, comant.

(About my lady from heaven / I will sing a song, / Whom St. Gabriel / Came greeting, / And [to whom] he said: Hail Mary, / Filled with grace, you / Will conceive your child. / A king's son, the Messiah, / Will be born to me as friend. / I decree that you will stay a virgin.)

The poem continues on the theme of God's omnipotence, manifesting itself in Mary's immaculate conception:

Cely ki cct et fet e put
Sanz dongere fere
Quonke ki il wet
30 Par une sul penser
Ben put en la pussel
Sa chambre munde e bel
Fer a sun woler.

(He who knows and does and is able / To do without difficulty / Whatever he wants / By a single thought / Could easily in the virgin / Make his clean and beautiful room / At his will.)

The last two stanzas describe man's redemption through Christ in terms of a peace-treaty, and the poem ends with a plea to Mary for help:

Deu vea en tere
Sun fiz tre bonment
Pur apeyser la gere
50 Ki Adam duta nent.
E sun fiz demeyne,

---

[39] MS *e* (Tironian note).

Vynt suffrir la peyn
Pur la puneys gent;
Hi iuni sa quarenteym.
55 Sa kot out teynt en greyn
Pur fer l'encordement.

(God sent to the world / His son very kindly / In order to bring peace to the war / Which Adam did not fear. / And he leads down his son, / He came to suffer pain / For later generations; / He fasted here for forty days. / His coat was dyed in red dye / To make the agreement.)

Ore est la pes fet,
Pur Deu le tenum nus,
Ki par male nus en geyt,
60 Li felun [e]⁴⁰ vius.
Querum le Marie
K'el nus seyt en ay
A sune fiz glorius,
Ki de mort en vie
65 Nus resussyt e gwy
En sun cel preciuse.

(Now the peace is made, / We have it because of God, / Who throws us away through evil, / The evildoers and malefactors. / Let us ask Mary / That she may be of help to us / With her glorious son, / Who raised us from death to life / And guides us / Into his precious heaven.)

Quite different from the other poems is the third Latin song (item [3]). It is a moralizing poem, in which the abuses found in the Church and in the life of its clerics are criticized:⁴¹

---

⁴⁰ MS *en*.

⁴¹ This poem is not listed in Walther. It is also found in the Dublin Troper; see the facsimile in Hesbert, ed., *Le Tropaire-Prosaire*, 187. I am grateful to Prof. John Stevens (Cambridge) for providing me with a copy of this page. As the text of the latter manuscript gives a better reading in a number of cases, I list the variants in the footnotes. As with the other texts printed here, abbreviations have been silently expanded; punctuation and capitalization are editorial.

[fol. 5r]
In ecclesiis celi gloria,
In solempniis vera gaudia,
In conviviis sint solacia
    Absque studiis.[42]
Et in clericis assint studia
    Spretis viciis.

Sed nunc video hiis contraria:
In superbiis est ecclesia,
In solempniis fit tristicia
    Absque gaudiis.
Et in clericis regnant vicia
    Spretis studiis.

In conuiuiis turpiloquium
Est et[43] crapula ciborum varium.
Nunc inebriat[44] quisque socium
    Cum preconiis.
Fit periurium, homicidium
    Cum luxuriis.

In ecclesiis fit detraccio
Lini et lane[45] dum fit questio,
De oue perdita non fit mencio
    In consiliis.
Sed ablacio, decimacio[46]
    Fit[47] cum preciis.

Inest clericis hec abusio,[48]
Inest maxima hec abieccio.[49]
Miles uacuus gestu vario

---

[42] Var. *tediis.*
[43] Var. *Inest.*
[44] Var. *inebriant.*
[45] Var. *latere.*
[46] Var. *et decimacio.*
[47] Var. *est.*
[48] Var. *abieccio.*
[49] Var. *abusio.*

Est cum falleris,[50]
Sic fit ystrio tanto [u]icio[51]
d[e] re[52] pauperis.

Apart from the English, French, and Latin lyrics of the first part of the manuscript, texts in English and French are also found on fol. 111r–v. Although the connection to the lyrics is tenuous (Christ's wounds are here a source of healing rather than devotion), the texts are interesting as a testimony of yet another aspect of religious sentiment, which was apparently quite important to the compilers of the manuscript:[53]

[fol. 111r]

Contra fluxum sanguinis

Tres boni fratres per vnam viam ambulabant et inuenit eos Dominus noster Jhesus Christus et dixit eis: "Tres boni fratres, quo itis?" Et illi dixerunt: "Domine, imus ad montem ad colligendum herbas pro uulneratis." Et dixit eis Dominus noster Jhesus Christus: "Tres boni fratres, uenite mecum et iurate mihi per crucificionem Christi et per lac Virginis Marie quod non in absconso dicatis necnon precium recipiatis. Ite ad montem et accipite[54] oleum oliue et lanam succidam ouis et ponite in plaga et dicite sic: 'Sicut Longinus miles lancea latus Domini nostri Jhesu Christi perforauit, non doluit, non diu sanguinauit, non rancliauit,[55] non putredinem fecit. Sic faciat Dominus de plaga ista: non doleat, non rancleat, nec putrescat, nec dolorem habeat. In nomine Patris. Pater noster ter'.''

---

[50] Var. *phaleris.*

[51] MS *oicio*; Var. *uicio.*

[52] MS *dare*; Var. *de re.*

[53] In the following texts abbreviations have been silently expanded, punctuation has been added and capitalization normalized. For a variant of the Latin text and the English poem, found in MSS. BL Additional 33996 and BL Harley 1600, see Heinrich, ed., *Medizinbuch,* 162–63. Compare also Gray, "Notes on Middle English Charms," 61–63.

[54] Manuscript corrected from *accipeite.*

[55] This is a Latinization of Middle English *ranclen,* "to fester, suppurate, swell," or Old French *rancler, räoncler* (the etymon of the Middle English word). See *Middle English Dictionary,* ed. Kurath et al., 8:139 (s.v. *ranclen*).

(Ad idem.) Vre louerd Crist was on erthe iwondid.
Sone hi[t]⁵⁶ was in heuene cud.
His wunde ne hoke⁵⁷, ne þis ne mote.
His ne swal, ne þis ne sal.

Crist and Seinte Marie be þi bote.
Pater noster. Trois fez.

(Ad idem.) Crist en croiz fu mis, la vint Longeus, de vne
lance le naufra ke sanc e eue en issi. A Crist cria merci e
il li fist. Ihesu Crist si vroyment cum wus le feitis ici, ansi
ueroymen esthonchez le sanc cesti. Al nun de le saint.⁵⁸
Pater noster, troiz fez la dites.

(Ad idem.) Veine tene tun sanc en teray,
Si cum Deu feit la lei.⁵⁹

[fol. 111v]

Noster Dame Seinte Mari fu malade de sa mariz et de son
ventre e de sa mere.⁶⁰ Si dist a son beu fiz: "Jo sui malade de
ma mere e de mun ventre et de ma mariz. Leuez vostre main
dester, Domine Deus, se me seingez⁶¹ le ventre, si benkes le
ventre, si ditis: 'In nomine Patris et Filii.'" Domine Deus, si
vroyment cum wus resutez char e sanc dedenz la Virgine
Marie, si vroyment el fu virge quant wus entratis en lui e ele
fust mere e virgine⁶² quant wus issutes de lui, si vroyment,
Domine Deus, warites ceste Noster Dame de mal e de enfirm-

---

⁵⁶ MS *hic.*

⁵⁷ Preterite of *āken,* "to ache"; see *Middle English Dictionary,* ed. Kurath et al.,
1:168 (s.v. *āken*).

⁵⁸ MS *sanit.*

⁵⁹ "Vein hold your blood in, pull [it] back,/ as God makes the law." The form
tene can be interpreted as *tiene,* the 3rd person singular subjunctive of *tenir,* or
possibly as the imperative of *tenir* (with inorganic final <e>); the latter fits better
into the construction of the sentence. The form *teray* I interpret as *trai* from *traire*
(again with an inorganic <e>). On inorganic letters in Anglo-Norman spelling, see
Pope, *From Latin to Modern French,* 461 (1238); on the reduction of /ie/ to /e/, see
ibid., 443 (1155).

⁶⁰ Both *mariz* and *mere* mean "uterus"; see *Altfranzösisches Wörterbuch,* ed.
Tobler and Lommatzsch, 5:col. 1203 (s.v. *marriz*) and 5:col. 1513 (s.v. *mere*).

⁶¹ MS *seigez.*

⁶² MS *ele fust mere e virgine* in the margin.

ete, Domine Deus, dont el sa pleint. Si leuez uoster main dester, Domine Deus, si seingez le ventre, si li benkes le ventre, si direz: "In nomine Patris. Pater noster. En la honurance de le Per, de le Fiz e de le Seint Epirit e de sa mort et de v plaies et en honurance de xl iors ki il iunat e de xii aposteles, numement en honurance de mon seinur Seint Andreu, Sein Johan, Sein Thomas, Seint Pere et Sein Liger."[63] Ki Deu e ma dame Seint Marie le alege e warisse de mal e de enfirmete. IXes repetitur hec particula. Domine Deus etc.

§

From this survey of texts and the short characterization of the poems and songs in the manuscript at least a general impression of the compilers and early readers of MS. Digby 2 can be gained. They were clerics, whose life revolved both around their studies and around their religious calling. As with all medieval clerics, the computation of the date for Easter and the establishment of the calendar with its feasts of saints were important concerns, which accounts for the presence of a certain number of such texts in the manuscript. The scribes and users of the manuscript were also more generally interested in astronomy (see item [25]) and in medical matters (items [23] and [24]), although in the latter case possibly more in the stories than in the charms themselves, as the charm against pain in the womb was obviously of little use to men. With its computational, astronomical, and pseudo-scientific texts, MS. Digby 2 can be compared with other "clerical" manuscripts which reveal similar interests and preoccupations.[64] The main focus of scribal activity was clearly on logic and philosophy. These texts (items [17], [18], [20], [21], [26]) reflect the intellectual climate of Oxford in the middle of the thirteenth century, when the teaching of the Aristotelian *Organon* became supplemented by the terministic logic of the "moderni."[65]

Although MS. Digby 2 is predominantly in Latin (scientific) prose, the poetry in the manuscript is by no means negligible. It is

---

[63] *Sein Liger* is St. Léger (Leodegar), bishop of Autun (d. 679).

[64] See, e.g., the contents of three manuscripts coming from two Benedictine monasteries, described in T. Hunt, "Deliciae Clericorum."

[65] See De Rijk, "Origins of the Theory," 161–73; De Libera, "Oxford and Paris Traditions," 174–87.

remarkable that three Latin poems were written down with their music, a fact which suggests professional musical skills in at least some of the scribes of the manuscript.[66] These songs also document that their scribes were familiar with the Latin song repertoire which was known in England in the first half of the thirteenth century. "In te concipitur" (item [2]) has come down to us in poetic anthologies, variously attributed to Alexander Nequam and Henry of Avranches, two poets and writers of the late twelfth/early thirteenth century; one of these anthologies is that which Matthew Paris (d. 1259) put together of the poems by Henry of Avranches.[67] The moralizing song "In ecclesiis celi gloria" is also contained in the Dublin Troper (compiled ca. 1360), where it is part of a group of Latin songs which circulated in thirteenth- and fourteenth-century England. Of these, one is a Latin lai on the flood, "Omnis caro peccaverat" (Walther, 13348); another, the Latin sequence "Angelus ad virginem" (Walther, 989), the song "hende Nicholas" of Chaucer's *Miller's Tale* sang at night.[68] "Angelus ad virginem" is also transmitted in MS. BL Arundel 248 (end of thirteenth/beginning of fourteenth c.), where the Latin text is accompanied by an English text ("Gabriel fram evene king"). This manuscript is one of the most precious sources of early Middle English songs, containing, apart from "Gabriel, fram evene-king," two poems on the Passion ("þe milde Lomb isprad o rode," "Iesu Cristes milde moder") and a moralizing poem ("Worldes blis ne last no throwe"), all with music.[69] There are, furthermore, a number of Latin and French religious songs in this important musical manuscript.[70]

---

[66] The three songs are written by three different hands.

[67] See Townsend and Rigg, "Medieval Latin Poetic Anthologies (V)," 379. See also n. 37 above.

[68] On the "Song of the Flood," see the discussion in Stevens, *Words and Music*, 144–55; on "Angelus ad virginem," see ibid., 444–46; Stevens, "Angelus ad virginem."

[69] The poems ("Gabriel, fram evene-king," *Index*, no. 888; "þe milde Lomb isprad o rode," ibid., no. 3432; "Iesu Cristes milde moder," ibid., no. 1697; "Worldes blis ne last no throwe," ibid., no. 4223) are edited in *English Lyrics*, 75–85; for an edition of their melodies, see *Medieval English Songs*, ed. Dobson and Harrison, 244–45 (no. 7, "Worldes blis"), 256–57 (no. 12, "Iesu Cristes"), 259–60 (no. 14, "þe milde Lomb"), 261–68 (no. 15, "Gabriel"); see also the textual and musical commentaries on nos. 7, 12, 14, and 15, ibid.

[70] There is no space here for a detailed analysis of the contents of MS. Arundel

From these manuscript affiliations, both of the Latin and of the Middle English poems, it can be deduced that the scribes of the Digby manuscript were well-versed in the lyrical production of their time. The Latin poems are part of the song repertoire of the thirteenth century extant in contemporary and later manuscripts (such as the Dublin Troper), while the Middle English poems, in particular "Hi sike al wan hi singe" (item [5]), belong to a cluster of early Middle English religious lyrics transmitted in a number of thirteenth-century and early fourteenth-century manuscripts.[71] Apart from "No more ne willi wiked be," none of these religious poems can be attributed with certainty to a Franciscan as author. It is true that the style and mood of many of these poems, in particular poems on the Passion such as "Hi sike al wan hi singe" of the Digby and Harley manuscripts or "Iesu Cristes milde moder" in the Arundel manuscript, might be characterized as Franciscan: the emotive appeal of the Latin sequence "Stabat iuxta Christi crucem," the model of "Iesu Cristes milde moder" and other Middle English *Stabat mater*-lyrics, is of a similar intensity as that of "Stabat mater dolorosa," the famous sequence commonly attributed to the Franciscan Jacopone da Todi (d. 1306).[72] What F. J. Raby said of "Stabat mater dolorosa," namely that it "grew out of the Franciscan devotion to the passion of Mary," can be said as well of "Hi sike al wan hi singe"—and its "companion piece" in the Harley manuscript, "When y se blosmes

---

248; see *Catalogue of Arundel Manuscripts*, 73–75; Hughes-Hughes, *Catalogue of Manuscript Music*, 1:157, 255, 424. See also Wooldridge, ed., *Early English Harmony*, plates 32 [fol. 153r], ("O labilis o flebilis," Walther, no. 12714), 33 [fol. 153v] ("Magdalene, laudes plene," Chevalier, 38770; "Flos pudicicie"/"Flur de uirginite," Walther, no. 66705), 34 [fol. 154r] ("Angelus ad virginem"/"Gabriel"; "þe milde Lomb"; "Worldes blis"), 35 [fol. 154v] ("Spei uena, melle plena"; "Iesu Cristes"), 36 [fol. 155r] ("Salue uirgo uirginum," Walther, no. 17182; "Reine pleine de ducur"; "Bien deust chanter ky eust leale amie," Sonet, 226). The last leaves of the manuscript contain the beginning of a Marian sequence ("Alleluia virga ferax Aaron"; fol. 200v) and a second sequence to the Virgin ("Risum facit dare"; fol. 201v).

[71] See the list in Reichl, *Religiöse Dichtung*, 108–9; see also n. 30 above.

[72] Jacopone's authorship is uncertain; see Raby, *Christian-Latin Poetry*, 437ff. The Latin sequence "Stabat iuxta Christi crucem" and the Middle English *Stabat mater*-poems are edited (with their melodies) in *Medieval English Songs*, 146–65, 251–57 (nos. 10–12).

springe."[73] There can be no doubt that the inspiration for many of these poems comes from a form of fervent and subjective religiosity which is particularly associated with Franciscan poetry.[74] On the other hand, neither this kind of religiosity nor this type of poetry was restricted to Franciscan circles. We have only to think of the poetry of John of Howden (d. 1275), in particular his *Philomena*, which later exerted such a strong influence on the English mystics of the fourteenth century, or of the many Middle English translations and imitations of Jean de Fécamp's "Candet nudatum pectus,"[75] The Franciscans were, like other clerics, both creators and propagators of religious poetry. MS. Digby 2 testifies to the importance accorded to religious songs and lyrics by the scribes and users of the manuscript, most probably belonging to the order of St. Francis. But the texts in the manuscript also reveal their "catholic" interests, by no means restricted to poetry pervaded by "Franciscan spirituality," however defined.[76] Their moral stance is clear: no more wickedness, no more lechery, no more vices, but more religious discipline and more attention to their studies ("Et in clericis assint studia / Spretis viciis," as it is said in item [3]). We can only hope that they carried out their good resolutions successfully.

Universität Bonn

---

[73] Raby, *Christian-Latin Poetry*, 437.

[74] See Raby, *Christian-Latin Poetry*, chap. 13 (415ff.); Moorman, *History of the Franciscan Order*, 256–77.

[75] On *Philomena*, see Raby, *Christian-Latin Poetry*, 389–95; Woolf, *English Religious Lyric*, 161–65; on the "Candet nudatum pectus," see Reichl, *Religiöse Dichtung*, 483–92; Copeland, "Middle English 'Candet'."

[76] Franciscan spirituality is difficult to define when it comes to showing its presence in particular texts. Compare the discussion in Jeffrey, *Early English Lyric*, 43–82.

RICHARD NEWHAUSER

"Strong it is to flitte"—
A Middle English Poem on Death
and Its Pastoral Context

he study of Middle English lyrics has greatly profited from recent philologically oriented scholarship which reads these texts not in anthologized form in modern surveys of medieval literature, but rather in the context of their manuscript surroundings as well as that of the prose works in the midst of which many of them have been transmitted. For the vast majority of Middle English religious lyrics, the latter context is most frequently defined by various forms of Latin pastoral literature: sermon texts, model sermon collections, preaching handbooks, treatises on vices and virtues, and the like. As Siegfried Wenzel, in particular, has clearly demonstrated, such works provide evidence for the function and significance perceived for these lyrics by the contemporary preachers and pastoral authors who composed or adopted them, and for their reception history.[1] Reading the lyrics in their pastoral contexts has also provided a necessary corrective to the interpretations of some Middle English poetry voiced by various types of modern or "historical" critics.[2] A few of the works which served as the context for Middle English poetry are known to have been composed by Franciscans who, along with the Dominicans who were active in England in the thirteenth and fourteenth century, eagerly used lyrics in pastoral and homiletic settings,[3] though these works

---

[1] Wenzel, *Preachers, Poets*, 3–20; idem, "Poets, Preachers."

[2] See, for example, Wenzel, "The Moor Maiden."

[3] Perhaps the prime example for this type of work, apparently written by a Franciscan, is *Fasciculus morum*, ed. and trans. Wenzel.

hardly amount to support for the contention that Franciscan spirituality was responsible in effect for the development of the early English religious lyric *per se*.[4] Because the universality of this claim is certainly untenable, one must examine each pastoral context individually before maintaining that it bears evidence of a connection with the Friars Minor. The brief treatise containing an unrecorded variant of a Middle English death lyric edited below from a manuscript in the Bodleian Library presents just such a case, for a close look at the text will reveal that it shows probable signs of having been composed in a Franciscan environment.

Oxford, Bodleian MS. Bodley 29[5] is a miscellany composed of two main vellum codices of the late thirteenth or early fourteenth century and containing now ii + 180 folios. Exactly how the manuscript made its way into the Bodleian collection is not known, but it was an early acquisition, for it is listed in a catalogue which was probably compiled in 1603–1604, within a year or two of the refounding of the library.[6] The present binding most likely stems from the same period, but the two main sections must have been united before this point, judging from the uniformity with which they have been sewn together beneath the binding. The name "J. Foxus" which occurs at the top of fol. 1r in a sixteenth-century hand may perhaps indicate that at one time the volume was in the possession of John Foxe (1516–1587), author of the popular Protestant martyrology *Acts and Monuments*, who studied in Oxford as a fellow of Magdalen College for a number of years (B.A. 1537, M.A. 1543). Though Foxe's interest in medieval scholarship centered on what he considered the precursors to the religious dissenters of his own day, during his early years in Oxford he also seems to have taken a historical interest in such orthodox theological texts as are found in the manuscript: his son, in any case, reported that as a student Foxe had "read over all that either the *Greek* or *Latine* Fathers had left in

---

[4] Cf. Jeffrey, *The Early English Lyric*; Robbins, "The Authors."

[5] See the description by Madan and Craster in *Summary Catalogue*, 2, 1:93, no. 1876.

[6] See the entry for MS. Bodley 29 in the list of manuscripts acquired by the library between 1600 and 1695 in Richard W. Hunt, *Summary Catalogue*, 1:90, no. 434. I am grateful to Dr. B. C. Barker-Benfield for supplying me with information on the manuscript's provenience.

their writings; the Schoolmen in their Disputations...."[7] Folios i
and ii, apparently remains from the original binding, are a fragment
of a thirteenth-century rent-roll of lands near Rouen,[8] though it is
not certain whether they should be seen in conjunction with the
macaronic use of Anglo-Norman phrases alongside Middle English
verse and prose in the fourteenth-century Latin text edited below.

That the early ownership of the manuscript may have involved
Franciscans is at least suggested by the major contents of both portions of the manuscript, a familiar type of friar "miscellany" (with
an emphasis on preaching aids) in which Middle English verse has
often been preserved.[9] In the first section one finds a copy, in a hand
of the early fourteenth century, of the *Summa abstinentiae*, generally
accepted as the work of Nicholaus de Byard, O.F.M., but attributed
in the *Summary Catalogue* to a "Gilbertus Minorita" (fols. 1r–127v;
capitula added later on fols. 128v and 179v);[10] and in the second
part, besides the brief treatise to be presented here, a copy (in a hand
of the late thirteenth or early fourteenth century) of a *Summa theologica*, or collection of distinctions, attributed by Bloomfield to the
same "Gilbertus Minorita" (fols. 129r–168v, with headings in the top
margins in a contemporary hand beginning with *De preceptis* on fol.
129r; corrected text supplied on fol. 174r–v, and chapter titles on fol.
173v),[11] as well as a version of the sermon themes on *Diaeta salutis*

---

[7] Simeon Foxe, "The Life," sig. B7v; quoted by Wooden, *John Foxe*, 1. On John
Foxe, see also Facey, "John Foxe"; *Dictionary of National Biography*, 7:581–90.

[8] Note, for instance, the mention on the verso side of fol. ii of *Sanctus dyonisius
in valle, Haguelon, Ribuef, Guerres*, etc.

[9] For a typology of manuscripts containing English verse in their relationship
to preaching, see Wenzel, *Preachers, Poets*, 4–7. For the affiliations of many of the
most important manuscripts containing Middle English religious verse, see Reichl,
Religiöse Dichtung; cf. also Brown, ed., *English Lyrics*, xx–xlii; idem, ed., *Religious
Lyrics of the XIVth Century*, xi–xxii.

[10] *Incipits*, ed. Bloomfield et al., no. 1841; Stegmüller, *Repertorium Biblicum*,
4:17–18, no. 5695; Pfander, "The Mediæval Friars," 24 and n. 2. The copy in
Bodley 29 is entitled *Manipulus morum* in a 15th-century hand at the top of fol. 1r.
There is an erroneous reference to MS. Bodley 29, "fol. 15va" (the manuscript is
written in single columns throughout!) in Schneyer, *Repertorium*, 7:274, no. 77
(S21).

[11] *Incipits*, 0787. It should be noted, however, that here, too, there is no attribution to "Gilbertus" in the manuscript. For an attribution of this text, under the
title *Distinctiones theologicæ*, to Gilbert the Great, abbot of Citeaux (d. ca. 1167), see
Dictionary of National Biography, 7:1193–94.

which frequently accompanied manuscript copies of that popular text (fols. 168v–173v).[12] It is obvious that beyond the clear association of Nicholas de Byard with the Gray Friars, the evidence just presented can perhaps be taken at most as suggestive, but certainly not proof, of the manuscript's Franciscan provenance. Moreover, regardless of the authorship of the *Summa abstinentiae*, both its transmission and that of the sermon themes on *Diaeta salutis* were broad enough to allow for the use of these texts in the early fourteenth century by readers (and preachers) other than Franciscans alone.[13] Even the association of the name "Gilbertus Minorita" with the manuscript and the texts it contains can hardly serve to place the codex incontestably in a Franciscan environment, for this association is based on mistaken attributions: the *Summa abstinentiae* is generally accepted as the work of another author, and the attribution to a "Gilbertus" of what appears to be the unique transmission of the *Summa theologica* in MS. Bodley 29 is not supported by a single mention of the name "Gilbertus" in the manuscript itself. In fact, one might add that the identity of "Gilbert" is altogether problematic: there is little bibliographic substantiation for the existence of a Franciscan named Gilbert in England in the late thirteenth or early fourteenth century who might come into question as the author of the *Summa abstinentiae* beyond the ambiguous evidence provided in connection with the copy of this work in Oxford, Bodleian Library MS. Bodley 542 (SC 2607).[14] The attribution of the *Summa abstinentiae* to "Gilbertus a

---

[12] *Incipits*, 0077, this manuscript not noted. See also the excellent study by Guyot, "La 'Dieta salutis,'" at 376. The name of "Gilbertus Minorita" was mistakenly connected with these folios, as well, in Bloomfield's first incipitarium: "A Preliminary List," 264, no. 12.

[13] Of the latter text, Owst, *Preaching*, 238 n. 3, noted that it was attributed to a Dominican, William of Mailli.

[14] *Summary Catalogue*, 2,1:449, no. 2607, item 1: "Summa sermonum que dicitur Summa abstinencie edita a quodam fratre Thoma [this last word marked for deletion] de ordine Minorum nomine Gilberto" (cf. also Owst, *Preaching*, 306 and n. 1). The *Summa abstinentiae* is clearly not the work of Gilbert of Tournai or Gilbert de la Porré, though it is possible the scribal reference here may be to the former. Madan and Craster appear not to have been entirely comfortable with the attribution of this text to a "Gilbert," for while their words are unequivocal in the description of MS. Bodley 29, the description of MS. Bodley 812, which also contains the *Summa abstinentiae*, only maintains that the work is "probably by Gilbertus a Minorite" (*Summary Catalogue*, 2,1:491, no. 2679, item 2), that for MS.

Minorite" by the authors of the *Summary Catalogue*, and then by Bloomfield and Owst, as well, seems to depend ultimately on the evidence of this manuscript. The fact that the *Summa theologica* occurs together with this treatise in MS. Bodley 29 apparently led Bloomfield to assume that it, too, may have been the work of "Gilbertus."[15] There is, in any case, nothing to be found on a Minorite author named "Gilbertus" in England in the late thirteenth or early fourteenth century in the exhaustive bibliographies of the *Collectanea Franciscana* and the *Bibliographia Franciscana*.[16] Thus, while the major contents leave one with the impression that MS. Bodley 29 is a friar's manuscript, they alone are not enough to prove the hypothesis of Franciscan ownership.

Indeed, were the major texts the only evidence of Franciscan provenance offered by the contents of the manuscript, one would be justifiably sceptical of identifying it altogether as the work of Gray

---

Bodley 45 reads only that "the author is believed to be Gilbertus a Minorite" (*Summary Catalogue*, 2,1:91, no. 1896), and the entry for MS. Bodley 400 notes merely that the text is "perhaps by Gilbertus a Minorite" (*Summary Catalogue*, 2,1:271, no. 2231, item 3). For other manuscript copies of the text, no attribution is given whatsoever: see, e.g., the variant in MS. Bodley 185 (*Summary Catalogue*, 2,1:205, no. 2087, item 2).

[15] See also the attributions of authorship which list "Gilbertus Minorita" in *Incipits*, 0078, 0143, 0178, and 4419. It should be noted that in all of these cases, as well, at least one copy of the text has been transmitted in a Bodleian manuscript which also contains a copy of the *Summa abstinentiae*, and this apparently led Bloomfield to list "Gilbert" among the possible authors of the texts. Thus, *Incipits*, 0078 is found together with the *Summa abstinentiae* in MS. Bodley 812 (SC 2679); with *Incipits*, 0143 in MS. Bodley 398 (SC 2087); with *Incipits*, 0178 in MS. Bodley 542 (SC 2607); and with *Incipits*, 4419 in MS. Bodley 400 (SC 2231). I have not been able to examine all the manuscripts involved in these entries, so my findings cannot be conclusive in this matter. The only other mention I have found of a "Gilbertus Minorita" by modern scholars is by Faes de Mottoni and Luna, 55, no. 6 (MS. Ottob. lat. 862, fols. 30rb–46va). However, the editors make it clear (see 56) that they are reproducing the attribution of *Incipits*, 0143. The text referred to by Schneyer, *Wegweiser*, 2 (mentioned in *Incipits*, 0078) may in fact not be the one Bloomfield gives at that point, but a different text altogether (which Schneyer lists as possibly the work of Hugh of St. Cher), but in any case Schneyer does not support Bloomfield's attribution of 0078 to "Gilbertus."

[16] Gilbertus de Dulwich, apparently a companion of Agnellus of Pisa, one of the first friars to come to England (during the lifetime of Francis of Assisi), appears to have flourished too early to come into question here. I would like to express my gratitude to Girard J. Etzkorn, of the Franciscan Institute at St. Bonaventure University, for his assistance in trying to trace "Gilbert the Minorite."

Friars. But the second half of the manuscript also contains numerous short tracts, sketches, and notes on theological matters added somewhat later in the fourteenth century, in one of which the English poem has its immediate context (fol. 178v), and the treatise containing these verses gives evidence that it, at least, was probably composed in a Franciscan environment, for this Latin text is an allegorical presentation of the physical characteristics and dress of what appears to be the Franciscan friar as *pugil domini contra diabolum*. There is nothing in the content of the treatise to reveal when it was composed, but its relatively rough appearance, among short notes and a page of pen trials at the end of the manuscript, may indicate that it was meant to be the scribe's personal "fair" copy of an earlier text: the marginal notation *alio* in the scribal hand at line 5 seems not to have been meant as a textual correction, but rather as the scribe's clear indication of what he had originally written unclearly in the text, or had unsuccessfully attempted to change to *alio* from his original *albo*, and the scribe has also taken the trouble to number in the left margin those items of appearance which are allegorized in the text. In any case, judging from the Anglicana features of the hand in which the tract was written[17] and the presence of Anglo-Norman in the text, as well, the date of composition of the treatise and of its recording in MS. Bodley 29 was probably no later than the mid-fourteenth century. This work demonstrates, then, that that part of the codex in which it is found was probably in Franciscan use in the first half of the fourteenth century, and viewed together with the major contents of this portion of the volume, it may make a Franciscan origin for this section, and perhaps for both parts of the manuscript as well, not altogether unlikely.

The allegoresis of ecclesiastical dress was, of course, not an invention of the Franciscans in the later Middle Ages. It had been used first, as a type of spiritual instruction, by the anchorites of the Egyptian desert at the very inception of monasticism in the late

---

[17] The hand is difficult to date because it is irregular and gives the impression of being either untrained or written hastily. Nevertheless, it shows no Secretary features and uses the **a** with a broad headstroke or two-compartment **a**, **d** with a looped ascender, "8"-shaped **g**, and **w** typical of Anglicana. An unusual feature of the hand is that with very few exceptions only long-**s** is used. For the features of Anglicana, see Parkes, *English Cursive Book Hands*, xiv–xvi and pl. 1–3.

fourth century, and it remained part of the cenobite's catechetical training throughout the medieval period.[18] Various aspects of pontifical, episcopal, and sacerdotal vestments were also frequently interpreted as having a mystical significance.[19] At the same time, another popular form of allegoresis developed in early Christian literature and flourished in the Middle Ages which enumerated the arms to be worn by the Christian in the spiritual battle against evil, based on the exhortation in Ephesians 6.10–17 (cited in the text edited below) to "put on all the armor which God provides, so that you may be able to stand firm against the devices of the devil."[20] Both the armament and its interpretation given in the passage addressed to the Ephesians (belt of truth, chain-mail of integrity, shoes of the gospel, shield of faith, helmet of salvation, sword of God's words) were eventually applied to (and supplemented by) the common elements which made up the armor worn by contemporary classes of knights. But the specific items in this expanded catalogue of arms were also extended to the spiritual battle to be fought with the *armatura Christi et sanctorum contra vitia*[21] by any Christian, for as one Middle English treatment of the theme puts it:

man and woman schulde gouernyn and chastysyn hys body as a good man of armys gouernyth & chastysith his hors, for, as Iob seith, al our lyuynge upon erde is kny3thod and fy3tynge a3enys þe fend, þe world and þe flesch.[22]

The author of the treatise edited below adopted and coalesced the form of both types of allegoresis for his own purposes: the details of

---

[18] For early monastic usage, see for example Evagrius Ponticus, *Traité Pratique*; and cf. also the early allegoresis by Jerome, *Epistolae*, 64 (PL 22:607–22).

[19] See Braun, *Die liturgische Gewandung*, 701–27; idem, *Die pontificalen Gewänder*.

[20] For the biblical background of the conception of life as a battle against spiritual enemies, see Job 7.1 and Ecclus. 2.1. The idea appears frequently in early Christian literature: cf. 2 Tim. 2.3–5. For an overview of this and medieval developments, see further Wang, *Der "Miles Christianus*," especially 21ff.

[21] Thus the title of the chapter devoted to spiritual warfare in Thomas Hemerken à Kempis, *Hospitale pauperum*, 16 (ed. Pohl, 228–30).

[22] *Dives and Pauper*, 10.5 (ed. Barnum, 304). See the similar treatments in "The Pore Caitif," ed. Brady, cxv–cxx, 138–50, 236–38; and the related text in *A Tretyse of Gostly Batayle*, ed. Horstman in *Yorkshire Writers*, 2:420–36. These treatises allegorize the knight's bridle, reins, saddle, and spurs.

dress he presents are obviously drawn from the habits of the friars, and they are allegorized as the armor of "spiritual knighthood." Thus, the "warrior" of the treatise is said to wear a russet tunic, on which blood spots are less obtrusive, just as he bears in mind the passion of Jesus and endures adversities patiently himself; he has a tonsure to avoid the same impairment of sight in battle witnessed in those whom harmful desires blind; and he carries a staff, as a sign of the cross, to check two of the devil's weapons: both the temptation and the despair of sin. The three couplets of English verse are to be written in the three corners of the friar's shield, that is to say, of his heart, as a reminder of death's imminence. The shape of this bit of armament appears to be less an imaginative analogy to the roughly triangular form of the human heart than it is a reflection of the actual shields worn by English knights, which became markedly less oblong and more clearly triangular in the course of the thirteenth and the early fourteenth century.[23] There is, of course, nothing unusual in the shield's use as a reminder of death in the poem and not, as in the model supplied by the Epistle to the Ephesians, as an emblem of faith. In general, the medieval allegoresis of all of the knight's weapons for spiritual combat allowed for much creativity in their interpretation.[24] But more specifically, the shield often appears as an important image in the *memorare novissima* theme in English pastoral literature of the later Middle Ages; indeed, a chapter in the *Fasciculus morum* devoted to the topic depicts death itself as a knight carrying a shield with four emblems to remind human beings of the imminence and finality of his coming, and the ultimate judgment awaiting all thereafter.[25]

One is, of course, justified in regarding the shield with some scepticism as a specifically Franciscan accoutrement. Whereas the tonsure, staff, bare feet, and a russet tunic[26] all correspond to details

---

[23] See the discussion of English knights' armament, and the illustrations of their shields, by Hartshorne, "Military Costume," 172ff., and figs. 146, 149, 151, and 152.

[24] Cf. Wang, 40ff., and specifically on the allegoresis of the shield, 65–75.

[25] *Fasciculus morum*, 1.13.125–41 (ed. Wenzel, 104).

[26] It seems that the color meant by the treatise is some darker shade of reddish brown, since blood spots will not stand out against it, though the exact quality of this color is not clear. The habits of English Franciscans are frequently spoken of in medieval documents as being made of russet cloth, but this designation also referred to a grayish color (hence, the title "Gray Friars"). See Moorman, *A*

of the appearance of the Friars Minor which must be allegorized into the armaments of the warrior, the shield is immediately appropriate for the allegoresis of the *miles Christianus* and cannot be correlated to anything in Franciscan dress. But this part of the sketch in MS. Bodley 29 is, in fact, a set-piece on *memoria mortis*, the permanent vehicle, as it were, for the three couplets of "Strong it is to flitte:" the only other version of the English verses known to exist in this brief form is contained in precisely the same immediate context, though the macro-structure into which the shield allegoresis has been placed is different from that in the Bodleian manuscript and is one which shows at least no obvious signs of Franciscan involvement. The poem is to be found in London, British Library MS. Harley 7322, a manuscript containing a preacher's notebook, of the second half of the fourteenth century, which has been shown to bear some relationship to the *Fasciculus morum*.[27] The Middle English verse is contained here in the draft of a sermon on the topic of the *remedium triplex contra luxuriam* (fol. 172r–v). The third cure for lust recommended by the preacher is the contemplation of what becomes of humanity after this life. The memory of the decay of the flesh is described here as the *optimum remedium contra peccatum illud*, and this corrective is made concrete in the image of the shield with its verse. In the wording of the manuscript (fol. 172v): "... nostre mortis memoria ... debet esse tibi pro scuto. ... In quo debent scribi tria, videlicet in quolibet angulo vnum verbum...." The English poem then follows, not integrated into the Latin text as in the Bodleian version, but written here as poetry, separated to the right of the Latin prose:

> Strong it hijs to flitte
> Fro worldes blisse to pitte.
> Strengore is to misse
> Heuene-riche blisse.

History, 359; Little, *Studies*, 59–60. Whatever the exact shade meant by the author of the treatise, it is clear that the friar's tunic is neither white nor black. As Moorman, 149, 185, points out, the Constitutions of Narbonne (1260) expressly forbade Franciscans to wear habits of these colors.

[27] Wenzel, *Verses in Sermons*, 116ff.; idem, *Preachers, Poets*, 258. The manuscript has been described by Herbert in *Catalogue of Romances*, 3:166–79.

Strengest is to wende
To pine witouten ende.[28]

The last two couplets have exchanged places here in comparison with the order in which they are found in MS. Bodley 29 (see the text edited below, lines 27–34). Where the friar's victory in spiritual warfare is to be emphasized, the poem ends with a reminder of heaven's bliss; where sin must be cured, the poem's audience is left with the warning of the pains of hell. Thus, while both configurations of this short death lyric may depend for their effect on the audience's fear of dying, the change in emphasis at the end of the poem differentiates the specific kind of fear each version of the lyric operates with: the Harleian text, in a sermon exhorting one to refrain from lust, makes typical use of a salutary "servile fear" which might lead someone to avoid sin because of a fear of retribution in hell, while the Bodleian lyric, meant for a context in which the battle against evil is waged by one who is already described as holy, calls for a response more closely akin to *timor filialis*, through which someone who loves God might fear to lose Him by succumbing to evil.[29] Whatever the difference in their emphasis, however, both English lyrics are clearly integral to the contexts in which they are found; neither poem is a translation or paraphrase of a section of Latin text which precedes it, nor can the function of the verses be reduced to that of a mnemonic tag alone.[30] In the context of the shield image in which they were transmitted, they serve as part of what might be called a verbal emblem, which has both a meditative and a rhetorical function. They are a concise, almost epigrammatic statement of the inexorable consequences of mortality, fixing the attention of their audience on the process of those consequences, on the rapidity with which the loss of the world can lead to hell or an exclusion from heaven, and all the more memorable for the reitera-

---

[28] Brown and Robbins, *Index*, no. 3219; q.v. also in Robbins and Cutler, *Supplement*. The poem was first printed in Furnivall, ed., *Political, Religious, and Love Poems*, 268.

[29] The two types of fear are discussed in the context of medieval death lyrics by Woolf, *English Religious Lyric*, 72ff. Cf. the much less differentiated presentation of fear in Pecheux, *Aspects*, 9–23.

[30] On the variety of functions fulfilled by Middle English verse in a pastoral context, see Wenzel, *Verses in Sermons*, 66ff.; idem, "The English Verses."

tive quality of the three-stress couplets in which they were composed and for the ease with which they can be visualized in their *loci* on the shield.[31] Rhetorically they provide emphatic substantiation of an appeal to the fear of death (as the Bodleian text puts it, they serve *ad roborandum istud scutum*) by tracing not only the progress to hell or the loss of heaven's bliss, but even more by effectively ordering that movement in a paradigm of grammatical comparison.

Because it represents a simplification of the comparative and superlative forms in that paradigm, the Harleian version appears to have been developed on the basis of the less regularized version preserved in MS. Bodley 29, but both configurations of "Strong it is to flitte" take as their starting point a striking couplet and its development in a thirteenth-century death lyric which inspired many variations to the end of the fifteenth century. This lyric reflects the custom of moving the corpse from the bed to the floor immediately after death, a journey of descent which continues when the corpse is placed in the grave. This downward movement is homiletically extended further from there, in the poetic imagination, by the descent into hell:

> If man him biðocte
> inderlike and ofte
> þu arde is te fore
> fro bedde to flore,
> uþ reuful is te flitte
> fro flore te pitte,
> fro pitte te pine
> ðat nevre sal fine,
> i þene non sinne
> sulde his herte winne.[32]

The *flitte / pitte* rhyme proved expressive enough of the corpse's

---

[31] For visual location as part of medieval mnemotechnics, see Carruthers, *The Book of Memory*; Yates, *The Art of Memory*, 50ff.

[32] Brown-Robbins, *Index*, no. 1422 (q.v. also Robbins-Cutler, *Supplement*); ed. Woolf, *English Religious Lyrics*, 78 (cf. also Silverstein, ed., *English Lyrics*, 21, no. 7; Kane, *Middle English Literature*, 122; Brown, *English Lyrics*, 19–20, no. 13, and variations printed on 173–75; T. Wright, ed., in Wright and Halliwell, *Reliquiæ antiquæ*, 1:235–36.

journey to be incorporated into a number of other related or derived English death lyrics in the Middle Ages, and the *memorare novissima* theme eventually was connected with that of the *proprietates mortis*.[33] In the fifteenth century, the rhyme was built into a lyric on the signs of death and the corpse's journey, with a supplemental direct warning to avoid sin, added to a copy of John Bromyard's *Summa predicantium*. In this lyric, after the corpse has been laid on the floor, the poet continues by apparently generalizing the experience of death (vv. 13–14):

> Thenne me shal forth fro hym flitte,
> Fro þe floor to þe putte.[34]

But the first step in a paradigmatic arrangement of this theme is represented in the first part of a lyric preserved in Cambridge, University Library MS. Gg.4.32, which may have been adopted from *Index* 4129:

> Sori is the fore
> Fram bedde to the flore,
> And werse is the flette
> Fram flore to the pette,
> And for senne thine
> From pette to the pine;
> Weilawei and wolawo!
> Thanne is joye al over-go.[35]

---

[33] For a variant, see Brown-Robbins, *Index*, no. 4129 (q.v. also Robbins-Cutler, *Supplement*), where the couplet appears as vv. 5–6 (ed. Brown, *English Lyrics*, 173–74; cf. also the corresponding verses in "Whosoo hym be thowght," ed. Murray, 36–37); for a previously unindexed copy of this verse in the Huntington Library, see Hanna, "The Index," 257–58, no. [A8]. On the traditions of the signs of death, see Robbins, "Signs of Death"; Gray, *Themes and Images*, 194.

[34] Ed. Fletcher, "A Death Lyric," 11–12. See Brown-Robbins, *Index*, nos. 4033 and 4047. Cf. also the version of this lyric in Wenzel, "Unrecorded Verses," 76, no. 85, where the couplet appears as: "þenne me schal him flut from þe flore to þe put." And see also the version in Brown, *English Lyrics*, 130, no. 71, without the *flitte / pitte* rhyme, though the key words occur at the end of vv. 15 and 19, respectively. On the sardonic tone of the latter lyric, see Bennett, *Middle English Literature*, 389; Tristram, *Figures of Life and Death*, 154; Gray, *Themes and Images*, 194.

[35] Brown-Robbins, *Index*, no. 3201 (q.v. also Robbins-Cutler, *Supplement*); ed. Halliwell in Wright and Halliwell, *Reliquiæ antiquæ*, 1:160. See Wenzel, *Preachers, Poets*, 198 n. 84.

The brief, three-couplet form of the death lyric develops this topic to its logical conclusion, as a way of giving direction to the audience's response to the specter of death. One can understand how the possibility of focusing so succinctly in a pastoral context on the loss of heaven's bliss or the pains of hell would have appealed to a Franciscan author, in view of his order's emphasis on preaching on the four topics of vices, virtues, punishment, and glory.[36] Yet one must also note that there is no necessary connection between the lyric in its many forms and the Franciscans in most of its manuscript appearances. The use of the lyric in MS. Bodley 29 may stand, then, as evidence for the varied utility of the couplets in the pastoral literature of medieval England, a use which probably included authors of the Franciscan Order.

APPENDIX

In the following I have silently expanded all Latin abbreviations (the expansion of vernacular abbreviations is indicated by italicization), but have otherwise reproduced the orthography found in the manuscript. The Middle English poem is edited here following modern conventions for indicating verses in poetry; in the manuscript it appears as part of the continuous text, without indentation. Editorial emendations are shown by < >, conjectural readings are found in [ ]. The numbering of the paragraphs in the left margin follows scribal practice. Capitalization and punctuation are my own. The *apparatus critici* give, first, notes on conjectures and emendations (keyed to superscript letters in the text) and, second, the identification of citations from Scripture (indicated by superscript numbers in the text). I am grateful to the Keeper of Western Manuscripts at the Bodleian Library for permission to publish the following edition and translation of this text.

---

[36] The topics are given in the order's second rule: *Regulae*, 2.9, (ed. in Francis of Assisi, *Opuscula*, 71). See also *Fasciculus morum*, 1.1.1–3 (ed. Wenzel, 32).

Oxford, Bodleian MS. Bodley 29, fol. 178v

1   Nota, quod pugil in pungna[a] rubeam induit tunicam, comam habet tonsam, scutum et baculum gerit et pedem caute regit. Sicut ergo pugil rubeam induit tunicam, sic et iste sanctus in anima passionem dominicam. Scitis enim, quod sanguis extractus minus apparet in rubeo quam in alio[b] colore. Ita est ex parte ista: si habeamus in mente, quantum Christus paciebatur pro nobis, nichil quasi apparebit, quicquid pati possumus pro eo.

2   E secundo se habuit ad modum pugillis habentis tonsuram in capite, quia omnia nociua deposuit in mente, de quo potest dici in figura illud Regum 14: Tondebat Absolon capillos capitis sui, quia grauabant eum.[1] Scitis enim, quod in pungna capilli superflui multum grauant, quia visum inpediunt. Ita spiritualiter in Psalmo: Comprehenderunt me iniquitates mei et non potui, ut viderem.[2] Multi enim excecati per varia desideria et nociua[3] videre non possunt vsure periculum, falsum iuramentum, nec reputa < n > t[c] peccatum decimas subtrahere, aliquos decipere, pauperes opprimere, sabatum violare et cetera. Et talia sunt, que inmergunt hominem in interitum et in perdicionem.[4]

3   Accipiamus pro scuto mortis memoriam, eo quod minuit et protegit ab omni periculo. Memorare nouissima et in eternum non peccabis,[5] dicit Ecclesiasticus. De isto scuto dicitur Trenis: Da eis, domine, scutum cordis,[6] scilicet mortis memoriam, et ad roborandum istud scutum pone in quolibet angulo vnum uerbum. Primum:

> Strong it is to flitte
> from werdles blisse to pitte.

In secundo angulo, secundum:

> Werse it is to wende
> to pyne witouten ende.

---

[a] pungna] *sic passim* MS
[b] alio] MS: alio (?) *vel* albo *emendatum in* alio (?); *in margine*: alio
[c] reputant] MS: reputat

In tercio angulo, tercium:

> But werst it is to misse
> of heuene-riche blisse.

4   Item accipe cum scuto baculum, id est crucis dominice signum. Iste ergo <est>[d] baculus, quem semper in manu habere debemus secundum illud in figura Dauid: Tulit baculum,[7] id est crucis dominice signum, et processit aduersus Philisteum.[8] Habeamus ergo istum baculum contra diabolum cum duobus cornibus, scilicet dileccione Dei et proximi siue spe et timore, ut contra peccati instigacionem opponatur cornu timoris, eo quod angelis peccantibus Deus non pepercit,[9] et contra desperacionem opponatur cornu spei, eo quod Deus sit misericors.[10]

5   Item in pungna respicitur ad pedes. Sic respicit diabolus affecciones hominum, ad quas magis inclinantur. Vnde in persona diaboli dicitur:[e] Considerat diligenter ubi sit pes eius.[11] Et secundum hoc per diuersos ictus, id est temptaciones diuersas, aggreditur genus humanum, nam si viderit hominem pronum ad iracundiam: Dunk get il sun entredeus, ut faciat discordiam, and dubbles þat dint entre sink, entre sis. Sed contra istud infortunium habemus remedium, si pretendere <possimus>[f] scutum, mortis memoriam, et ei aduertere ictum. If he se þi fot sinken in þe sond, hic est, si viderit affeccionem dispositam ad cordis duriciem terrena diligendo, dunk get il vn retret, eo quod suggerendo facit eum subtrahere elemosinas, oblaciones, decimas et cetera. Et quia senes [sunt m]agis[g] ponderosi quam iuuenes naturaliter, ideo pes eorum, id est affeccio, profundius [grau]etur[h] in sabulo. Ideo hostis antiquus ipsos aggreditur magis isto ictu quam [alio],[i] sed per scutum fidei possent euadere ictum secundum illud Apostoli:

---

[d] est] *om.* MS
[e] *post hoc verbum lacuna brevis invenitur in verbis*
[f] possimus] *om.* MS
[g] *ipsa verba sub macula sunt*
[h] *ipsum verbum sub macula est*
[i] *ipsum verbum sub macula est*

Sumentes scutum fidei.[12] Et nota de fide < ... >[j] quantum placet
< ... >.[k]

Notes to the Edition

1. V. 2 Reg. 14.26
2. Ps. 39.13
3. V. 1 Tim. 6.9
4. Ibid.
5. Ecclus. 7.40
6. Thren. 3.65
7. 1 Reg. 17.40
8. 1 Reg. 17.32
9. 2 Pet. 2.4
10. V. Ex. 22.27 et passim
11. 1 Reg. 23.22
12. Eph. 6.16

Translation

1   Observe that in combat the fighter is clothed in a russet
tunic, has cropped hair, bears a shield and a staff, and directs his
feet with caution. Thus, just as the warrior is clothed in a russet
tunic, so also, in his heart, is this holy man clothed in the Lord's
passion. For you know that blood drawn from the body is less
visible on a russet color than on any other one. This is true for us
in the same measure: if we keep in mind how much Christ suffered for us, whatever we can endure for him will seem to be
almost nothing.

2   Secondly, he has behaved like a warrior bearing the tonsure,
since he has gotten rid of everything harmful in his mind, this
man of whom the verse in 2 Samuel 14 may be said figurally:
"Absalom cut the hairs of his head since they were heavy on

---

[j] *ipsa verba legi non possunt*
[k] *ipsa verba legi non possunt*

him." For you know that in battle too much hair is a great inconvenience since it impedes the sight. Thus, in its spiritual sense, in the psalm: "My iniquities have overtaken me and I have not been able to see." For many who have been blinded by diverse ardent and harmful desires are not able to see the danger of usury, or of swearing false oaths, nor do they count it a sin to withhold tithes, to cheat others, to oppress the poor, to desecrate the sabbath, and so on. And these are the kinds of things which plunge a person into ruin and perdition.

3   Let us take up as a shield a remembrance of death because it limits the power of, and protects against, every danger. "Be mindful of your end and you will not sin for all time," says Ecclesiasticus. About this shield it is said in Lamentations: "Give them, Lord, a shield for the heart," that is to say, the remembrance of death, and to strengthen this shield place in every corner one verse. The first one: It is hard to move / From worldly bliss to the grave. In the second corner, the second one: It is worse to go / To misery without an end. In the third corner, the third one: But it is worst of all to be without / The bliss of the kingdom of heaven.

4   Likewise, take up the staff with the shield, that is the sign of the Lord's cross. Thus, this is the staff which we should always have in our hand according to the passage dealing with David as a *figura*: "Then he picked up his staff," that is, the sign of the Lord's cross, "and went out towards the Philistine." Thus, against the devil let us possess this staff with its two prongs on top, that is to say, the love of God and of one's neighbor, or hope and fear, so that against the incitement to sin he can be opposed by the prong of fear, because God did not spare the angels who sinned, and against despairing he can be opposed by the prong of hope, because God is merciful.

5   Likewise, in battle one looks at one's feet. In the same way, the devil pays attention to those inclinations to which people are chiefly drawn. For this reason it is said about the person of the devil: "He considers carefully where his foot is." And in accordance with this he assaults mankind with various blows, that is, various temptations, for if he sees someone who is prone to

wrath, then he hits out with his slashing blow (*entredeus*) in order to create discord, and he increases the force of the blow five and six times. But against this misfortune we have a remedy if we can hold the shield, the remembrance of death, in front of ourselves and direct the blow towards it. If he sees your foot sinking in the sand, that is, if he sees your inclination drawn towards hardness of the heart by the love of worldly things, then he hits out with his *retret*-blow, because by bringing this love to mind, he makes a person withhold alms, offerings, tithes, and so on. And since by nature old people weigh more than young ones, hence their foot, that is, their inclination, can be weighed down deeper in the sand. Hence, the ancient enemy assaults them more with this blow than with another, but they can avoid the blow by using the shield of faith, according to the word of Paul: "They take up the shield of faith." And observe about faith <...> how much it pleases <...>.

Trinity University, San Antonio

Siegfried Wenzel
List of Publications

BOOKS

The Sin of Sloth: Acedia in Medieval Thought and Literature. Chapel Hill: The University of North Carolina Press, 1967. Pp. xi, 269.

Verses in Sermons. "*Fasciculus Morum*" *and its Middle English Poems.* The Mediaeval Academy of America, Publication 87. Cambridge, Mass.: The Mediaeval Academy of America, 1978. Pp. x, 234.

Editor. *Medieval and Renaissance Studies. Proceedings of the Southeastern Institute of Medieval and Renaissance Studies, Summer 1975.* Chapel Hill: The University of North Carolina Press, 1978. Pp. viii, 133.

Co-editor with Larry D. Benson. *The Wisdom of Poetry. Essays in Early English Literature in Honor of Morton W. Bloomfield.* Medieval Institute Publications. Kalamazoo, Mich.: Western Michigan Univ. Press, 1982. Pp. 314.

Editor. *Summa virtutum de remediis anime.* The Chaucer Library. Athens, Ga.: The University of Georgia Press, 1984. Pp. ix, 373.

Preachers, Poets, and the Early English Lyric. Princeton, N.J.: Princeton Univ. Press, 1986. Pp. xii, 272.

Editor and translator. *Fasciculus Morum, a Fourteenth-Century Preacher's Handbook.* University Park: The Pennsylvania State Univ. Press, 1989. Pp. 756.

"*Monastic Preaching in the Age of Chaucer.*" The Morton W. Bloomfield Lectures on Medieval English Literature, vol. 3.

Kalamazoo, Mich.: Western Michigan Univ. Press, 1993. Pp. 29.

Macaronic Sermons: Bilingualism and Preaching in Late-Medieval England. Ann Arbor, Mich.: Univ. of Michigan Press, 1994

ARTICLES AND CONTRIBUTIONS

"A 'brincadeira' dos caboclos de Barra Velha," *Logos. Revista Cultural do Centro Academico da Faculdade de Filosofia da Universidade do Paraná* 7,16 (1952): 46–51.

"Petrarch's *Accidia*," *Studies in the Renaissance* 8 (1961): 36–48. Translated into German by Christiane Fisher. In *Petrarca*, edited by August Buck, 349–66. Wege der Forschung, vol. 353. Darmstadt: Wissenschaftliche Buchgesellschaft, 1976.

"Sloth in Middle English Devotional Literature," *Anglia* 79 (1962): 287–318.

"Ἀκηδία. Additions to Lampe's Patristic Greek Lexicon," *Vigiliae Christianae* 17 (1963): 173–76.

"Chaucer's Troilus of Book IV," *PMLA* 79 (1964): 542–47.

"Dante's Rationale for the Seven Deadly Sins (*Purgatorio* XVII)," *MLR* 60 (1965): 529–33.

"*Acedia*: 700–1200," *Traditio* 22 (1966): 73–102.

"The Three Enemies of Man," *Mediaeval Studies* 29 (1967): 47–66.

"The Seven Deadly Sins: Some Problems of Research," *Speculum* 43 (1968): 1–22.

"Two Notes on Chaucer and Grosseteste," *Notes and Queries* n.s. 17 (1970): 449–51.

"Robert Grosseteste's Treatise on Confession, 'Deus est,' " *Franciscan Studies* 30 (1970): 218–93.

"A Latin Miracle With Middle English Verses," *Neuphilologische Mitteilungen* 72 (1971): 77–85.

"The Source for the *Remedia* of the Parson's Tale," *Traditio* 27 (1971): 433–53.

"The Pilgrimage of Life as a Late Medieval Genre," *Mediaeval Studies* 35 (1973): 370–88.

"The Moor Maiden—A Contemporary View," *Speculum* 49 (1974): 69–74.

"The Source of Chaucer's Seven Deadly Sins," *Traditio* 30 (1974): 351–78.

"Unrecorded Middle-English Verses," *Anglia* 92 (1974): 55–78.

"The English Verses in the *Fasciculus morum*." In *Chaucer and Middle English Studies in Honour of Rossell Hope Robbins*, edited by Beryl Rowland, 230–48. London: George Allen and Unwin, 1974.

"The 'Gay' Carol and Exemplum," *Neuphilologische Mitteilungen* 77 (1976): 85–91.

"Chaucer and the Language of Contemporary Preaching," *Studies in Philology* 73 (1976): 138–61.

"Vices, Virtues, and Popular Preaching." In *Medieval and Renaissance Studies. Proceedings of the Southeastern Institute of Medieval and Renaissance Studies, Summer 1974*, edited by Dale B. J. Randall, 28–54. Durham, N.C.: Duke Univ. Press, 1976.

"*Mum and the Sothsegger*, lines 421–422," *English Language Notes* 14 (1976): 87–90.

"An Early Reference to a Corpus Christi Play," *Modern Philology* 74 (1977): 390–94.

"The Joyous Art of Preaching; or, the Preacher and the Fabliau," *Anglia* 97 (1979): 304–25.

"*St. Erkenwald* and the Uncorrupted Body," *Notes and Queries* n.s. 28 (1981): 13–14.

"Chaucer's Parson's Tale: 'Every Tales Strengthe.' " In *Europäische Lehrdichtung. Festschrift für Walter Naumann zum 70. Geburtstag*, edited by Hans Gerd Rötzer and Herbert Walz, 86–98. Darmstadt: Wissenschaftliche Buchgesellschaft, 1981.

"The Wisdom of the Fool." In *The Wisdom of Poetry. Essays in Early*

English Literature in Honor of Morton W. Bloomfield, edited by Larry D. Benson and Siegfried Wenzel, 225–40, 307–14. Kalamazoo, Mich.: Western Michigan Univ. Press, 1982.

"Pestilence and Middle English Literature: Friar John Grimestone's Poems on Death." In *The Black Death: The Impact of the Fourteenth-Century Plague*. Papers of the Eleventh Annual Conference of the Center for Medieval and Early Renaissance Studies, edited by Daniel Williman, 131–59. Medieval & Renaissance Texts & Studies, vol. 13. Binghamton, N.Y., 1982.

"Notes on the *Parson's Tale*," *The Chaucer Review* 16 (1982): 237–56.

"A New Occurrence of an English Poem from the Red Book of Ossory," *Notes and Queries* n.s. 30 (1983): 105–8.

"Medieval Sermons and the Study of Literature." In *Medieval and Pseudo-Medieval Literature*, edited by Piero Boitani and Anna Torti, 19–32. The J. A. W. Bennett Memorial Lectures, Perugia, 1982–83. Tübingen: Gunter Narr Verlag; Cambridge: D. S. Brewer, 1984.

"Poets, Preachers, and the Plight of Literary Critics," *Speculum* 60 (1985): 343–63.

Contributor, *The Riverside Chaucer*, 3rd edn., gen. ed., Larry D. Benson, 819, 954–65. Boston: Houghton Mifflin Co., 1986. [Explanatory notes on the Parson's Portrait (GP) and on Fragment X (ParsProl, ParsTale, Retr).]

"Medieval Sermons." In *A Companion to Piers Plowman*, edited by John A. Alford, 155–72. Berkeley: University of California Press, 1988.

"*Somer Game* and Sermon References to a Corpus Christi Play," *MP* 86 (1989): 274–83.

"Chaucer's Pardoner and His Relics," *Studies in the Age of Chaucer* 11 (1989): 37–41.

"Reflections on (New) Philology," *Speculum* 65 (1990): 11–18.

"The Continuing Life of William Peraldus's *Summa vitiorum*." In *Ad litteram. Authoritative Texts and Their Medieval Readers*, edited by Mark D. Jordan and Kent Emery, Jr., 135–63. Notre Dame

Conferences in Medieval Studies, 3. Notre Dame and London: Univ. of Notre Dame Press, 1992.

"The Middle English Lexicon: Help from the Pulpit." In *Words, Texts and Manuscripts: Studies in Anglo-Saxon Culture Presented to Helmut Gneuss on the Occasion of his Sixty-Fifth Birthday*, 467–76. Woodbridge: D.S. Brewer, 1992.

REVIEWS

Manning, Stephen, *Wisdom and Number. Toward a Critical Appraisal of the Middle English Religious Lyric* (Lincoln, Nebr., 1962), in *JEGP* 61 (1962): 911–13.

Lehnert, Martin, *Geoffrey Chaucer. Ausgewählte Canterbury Erzählungen, Englisch und Deutsch* (Halle, 1962), in *JEGP* 62 (1963): 680–83.

Clemen, Wolfgang, *Chaucers frühe Dichtung* (Göttingen, 1963), in *JEGP* 64 (1965): 165–66.

Benrath, Gustav Adolf, *Wyclifs Bibelkommentar* (Berlin, 1966), in *Speculum* 43 (1968): 121–23.

Mitchell, Jerome, *Thomas Hoccleve: A Study in Early Fifteenth-Century English Poetic* (Urbana, 1968), in *South Atlantic Quarterly* 67 (1968): 705–6.

Broomfield, F. (ed.), *Thomae de Chobham Summa Confessorum*, Analecta Mediaevalia Namurcensia, 25 (Louvain, 1968), in *Medium Aevum* 39 (1970): 53–56.

Koenig, V. Frederic (ed.), *Les Miracles de Nostre Dame par Gautier de Coinci*, vol. IV (Geneva, 1970), in *Medium Aevum* 41 (1972): 295.

Hempel, Wolfgang, *Übermuot diu alte: Der Superbia-Gedanke und seine Rolle in der deutschen Literatur des Mittelalters* (Bonn, 1970), in *Speculum* 48 (1973): 366–68.

Burrow, J. A., *Ricardian Poetry* (London, 1971), in *Medium Aevum* 42 (1973): 93–95.

Firth, J. J. Francis, C.S.B. (ed.), *Robert of Flamborough, Canon-Penitentiary of Saint-Victor at Paris: Liber poenitentialis* (Toronto,

1971), in *Medium Ævum* 43 (1974): 50–52.

Langland, William, *Piers Plowman. The Prologue and Passus I–VII of the B-Text as found in Bodleian MS. Laud Misc. 581*, ed. J. A. W. Bennett (Oxford, 1972), in *Speculum* 49 (1974): 745–46.

Rowland, Beryl, *Animals With Human Faces. A Guide to Animal Symbolism* (Knoxville, Tenn., 1973), in *Southern Folklore Quarterly* 38 (1974): 329–31.

Grayson, Janet, *Structure and Imagery in "Ancrene Wisse"* (Hanover, N.H., 1974), in *Medium Ævum* 45 (1976): 219–21.

Dobson, E. J., *Moralities on the Gospels* (Oxford, 1975), in *Speculum* 52 (1977): 648–52 (with Richard H. Rouse).

Pickering, O. S. (ed.), *The South English Nativity of Mary and Christ* (Heidelberg, 1975), in *Anglia* 95 (1977): 509–10.

Kristensson, G. (ed.), *John Mirk's "Instructions for Parish Priests"* (Lund, 1974), in *Speculum* 52 (1977): 705.

Hume, Kathryn, *"The Owl and the Nightingale." The Poem and Its Critics* (Toronto and Buffalo, 1975), in *Anglia* 96 (1978): 213–14.

Dobson, E. J. *The Origins of "Ancrene Wisse"* (Oxford, 1976), in *Speculum* 53 (1978): 354–56.

Tristram, Philippa, *Figures of Life and Death in Medieval English Literature* (New York, 1976), in *Speculum* 53 (1978): 638–40.

The Findern Manuscript (London, 1977), and *The Thornton Manuscript* (London, 1977), in *Speculum* 53 (1978): 804–5.

Greene, Richard Leighton (ed.), *The Early English Carols*, second edition (Oxford, 1977), in *Speculum* 54 (1979): 140–42.

Hudson, Anne (ed.), *Selections from English Wycliffite Writings* (Cambridge, 1978), in *N&Q* n.s. 26 (1979): 63–64.

Bloomfield, Morton W., et al. (eds.), *Incipits of Latin Works on the Virtues and Vices, 1100–1500* (Cambridge, Mass., 1979), in *Speculum* 55 (1980): 341–44.

Cambridge University Library MS Ff.2.38 (London, 1979), in *Speculum* 55 (1980): 406.

Besserman, Lawrence L., *The Legend of Job in the Middle Ages* (Cambridge, Mass., 1979), in *Speculum* 55 (1980): 523–24.

Thomson, David, *A Descriptive Catalogue of Middle English Grammatical Texts* (New York, 1979), in *Speculum* 55 (1980): 634–35.

Hamer, Richard (ed.), *Three Lives from the Gilte Legende* (Heidelberg, 1978), in *Anglia* 99 (1981): 513–14.

Kengen, J. H. L. (ed.) *Memoriale Credencium* (Nijmegen, 1979), in *Anglia* 99 (1981): 511–13.

Von Nolcken, Christina (ed.), *The Middle English Translation of the Rosarium Theologie* (Heidelberg, 1979), in *Anglia* 99 (1981): 510–11.

Danninger, Elisabeth, *Sieben politische Gedichte der HS. B.L. Harley 2253* (Würzburg, 1980), in *Anglia* 100 (1982): 177–78.

Friedman, John Block, *The Monstrous Races in Medieval Art and Literature* (Cambridge, Mass., 1981), in *JEGP* 81 (1982): 551–54.

Thomson, Williell R., *The Latin Writings of John Wyclif: An Annotated Catalog* (Toronto, 1983), in *Speculum* 60 (1985): 492–93.

Pearsall, Derek (ed.), *The Nun's Priest's Tale* (Norman, Okla., 1984), in *N&Q* n.s. 32 (1985): 95–97.

Hudson, Anne (ed.), *English Wycliffite Sermons*, vol. 1 (Oxford, 1983), in *N&Q* n.s. 32 (1985): 98–100.

Edwards, A. S. G. (ed.), *Middle English Prose. A Critical Guide to Major Authors and Genres* (New Brunswick, 1984), in *Anglia* 104 (1986): 478–81.

Gray, D. (ed.), *The Oxford Book of Late Medieval Verse and Prose* (Oxford, 1985), in *N&Q* n.s. 34 (1987): 64–65.

Hudson, Anne, *Lollards and Their Books* (London and Ronceverte, 1985), in *N&Q* n.s. 34 (1987): 258.

Kenny, A. (ed.), *Wyclif in His Time* (Oxford, 1986), in *N&Q* n.s. 35 (1988): 71–72.

Kohl, Stephan, *Das englische Spätmittelalter: Kulturelle Normen, Lebenspraxis, Texte* (Tübingen, 1986), in *Speculum* 63 (1988): 425–26.

Szittya, Penn R., *The Antifraternal Tradition in Medieval Literature* (Princeton, 1986), in *Anglia* 106 (1988): 492–95.

Reimer, Stephen R. (ed.), *The Works of William Herebert, OFM* (Toronto, 1987), in *SAC* 11 (1989): 279–83.

Spearing, A. C., *Readings in Medieval Poetry* (Cambridge, 1987), in *JEGP* 88 (1989): 390–91.

Gradon, P. (ed.), *English Wycliffite Sermons*, vol. 2 (Oxford, 1988), in *N&Q* 234 (1989): 370–71.

Clark, John P. H., and Cheryl Taylor (eds.), *Walter Hilton's Latin Writings*, 2 vols. (Salzburg, 1987), in *Speculum* 64 (1989): 969–71.

Ogilvie-Thomson, S. J. (ed.), *Richard Rolle: Prose and Verse, edited from MS Longleat 29 and related manuscripts* (Oxford, 1988), in *N&Q* n.s. 37 (1990): 73–74.

Minnis, A. J., and A. B. Scott (eds.), *Medieval Literary Theory and Criticism, c. 1100–c. 1375. The Commentary Tradition* (Oxford, 1988), in *Anglia* 108 (1990): 490–92.

Scase, Wendy, *"Piers Plowman" and the New Anticlericalism* (Cambridge, 1989), in *Yearbook of English Studies* 20 (1991): 326–27.

Iamartino, Giovanni (ed.), *Vizi capitali e pianetti in un sermone del Cinquecento inglese* (Milan, 1988), in *Speculum* 66 (1991): 174–75.

Hudson, Anne (ed.), *English Wycliffite Sermons*, vol. III (Oxford, 1990), in *N&Q* n.s. 38 (1991): 204–5.

Rubin, Miri, *Corpus Cristi: The Eucharist in Late Medieval Culture* (Cambridge, 1991), in *N&Q* n.s. 39 (1992): 212–13.

Griffiths, Jeremy, and Derek Pearsall (eds.), *Book Production and Publishing in Britain, 1375–1475* (Cambridge, 1989), in *MP* 90 (1992): 91–93.

Hagen, Susan K., *Allegorical Remembrance: A Study of "The Pilgrimage of the Life of Man" as a Medieval Treatise on Seeing and Remembering* (Athens, Ga., 1990), in *Speculum* 67 (1992): 421–23.

Machan, Tim William (ed.), *Medieval Literature: Texts and Interpretation*, Medieval & Renaissance Texts & Studies, vol. 79 (Binghamton, N.Y., 1991), in *Chaucer Yearbook* 1 (1992): 259–63.

Appendices

Manuscript References

Works Cited

Index

Manuscript References

Assisi, Comunale MS. 520: 268n

Cambridge, Gonville and Caius College MS. 217/232: 197

Cambridge, Gonville and Caius College MS. 328/715: 143n

Cambridge, Jesus College MS. 34: 153n

Cambridge, Pembroke College MS. 118: 153n

Cambridge, Pembroke College MS. 258: 153n

Cambridge, St. John's College MS. G.8: 182–83, 185–90

Cambridge, St. John's College Archives charter C 7.1: 155n

Cambridge, Trinity College MS. B.14.39 (323): 300n, 305n

Cambridge, University Library MS. Add. 710 (Dublin Troper): 310n, 315, 316, 368

Cambridge, University Library MS. Add. 3471: 154n

Cambridge, University Library MS. Dd.11.78: 315, 388

Cambridge, University Library MS. Gg.4.32: 330

Gaesdonk, Bibliothek des Collegium Augustinianum MS. 5 (now Münster, Bistumsarchiv, CAG MS. 5): 241n

Gloucester, Cathedral Library MS. 14: 153n

Hasselt, Rijksarchief, Abdij Sint-Truiden MS. 35 (formerly Abdij Sint-Truiden Reg. Nr. 6681 b): 242, 249, 259

Liège, Bibliothèque de l'Université MS. 39C: 242, 243–45, 248n, 249, 250n, 251n, 253n, 254n, 255n

Liège, Bibliothèque de l'Université MS. 54A: 242n

Liège, Bibliothèque de l'Université MS. 83C: 242, 243, 248n, 249, 251–57, 259, 260n

Liège, Bibliothèque de l'Université MS. 248C: 242, 243, 249, 257–59, 260n

Liège, Bibliothèque de l'Université MS. 292A: 242n

Liège, Bibliothèque de l'Université MS. 305A: 242, 260n

Liège, Bibliothèque de l'Université MS. 320A: 242

Liège, Bibliothèque de l'Université MS. 321A: 242

Liège, Bibliothèque de l'Université MS. 358C: 242n

Liège, Bibliothèque de l'Université MS. 2736B: 242n, 248n

Lincoln, Cathedral Church Add. charter no. 2194: 157n

Lincoln, Cathedral Church deed D&C Dij/77/2/6: 157n

London, British Library MS. Additional 33996: 312n

London, British Library MS. Additional MS. 41321: 195n

London, British Library MS. Arundel 248: 315, 316n

London, British Library MS. Cotton Caligula A.IX: 305n

London, British Library MS. Cotton Julius D.III: 5, 161–77

London, British Library MS. Cotton Titus D.V: 196

London, British Library MS. Harley 401: 200n, 364

London, British Library MS. Harley 1600: 312n

London, British Library MS. Harley 2253: 304

London, British Library MS. Harley 3221: 268n

London, British Library MS. Harley 7322: 327–28

London, British Library MS. Royal 2.F.VIII: 305

London, British Library MS. Royal 4.B.VIII: 155n

London, British Library MS. Royal 8.C.V: 158n

London, British Library MS. Royal 9.A.XIV.: 144n, 145, 147, 148,
    149n, 150n, 151, 152n, 153n

München, Bayerische Staatsbibliothek Clm. 2981: 265n

Naples, Biblioteca Nazionale MS. VII.C.52: 276n

Oxford, Bodleian Library MS. Bodley 29: 9, 320–24, 328–29, 331–33

Oxford, Bodleian Library MS. Bodley 45: 323n

Oxford, Bodleian Library MS. Bodley 185: 323n

Oxford, Bodleian Library MS. Bodley 398: 323n

Oxford, Bodleian Library MS. Bodley 400: 323n

Oxford, Bodleian Library MS. Bodley 542: 322, 323n

Oxford, Bodleian Library MS. Bodley 812: 322n, 323n

Oxford, Bodleian Library MS. Digby 2: 8, 297–317

Oxford, Bodleian Library MS. Digby 24: 303n

Oxford, Bodleian Library MS. Digby 86: 300n

Oxford, Bodleian Library MS. Douce 302: 181–82, 185–90

Oxford, Bodleian Library MS. Eng. Poet. a. 1 (Vernon MS.): 182n

Oxford, Bodleian Library MS. Eng th. c. 57: 185–90

Oxford, Bodleian Library MS. Laud misc. 19: 183, 185–90

Oxford, Bodleian Library MS. Laud misc. 99: 184, 185, 361

Oxford, Bodleian Library MS. Laud misc. 200: 195n, 196–97, 199n, 200n

Oxford, Bodleian Library MS. Laud misc. 345: 153n

Oxford, Bodleian Library MS. Rawlinson A.345: 153n

Oxford, Bodleian Library MS. Rawlinson Poet. 163: 12

Oxford, Jesus College MS. 29: 305n

Oxford, Jesus College MS. 39: 184, 185–90

Oxford, New College MS. 94: 156n

Oxford, University College MS. 123: 181, 185–90

Paris, Bibliothèque Mazarine MS. 985: 153n

Paris, Bibliothèque Nationale MS. 5376: 287n

Paris, Musée du Louvre, Département des Dessins, Collection Edmund de Rothchild MS. 1, no. I DR: 242, 243, 249, 259–60

Philadelphia, Rosenbach Foundation MS. 1083/80: 183n

Prague, National (olim University) Library MS. X. E. 9: 198

San Marino (CA), Huntington Library MS. 26.C.9 (Ellesmere MS.): 62n, 63, 64

San Marino (CA), Huntington Library MS. HM 19914: 145n, 153n, 154n

Shrewsbury, School MS. 7: 154

Troyes, Bibliothèque municipale MS. 1440: 268n, 269n, 270n, 272n

Vaticana, Biblioteca Apostolica MS. Archivio di San Pietro D.213: 8, 275–95

Vaticana, Biblioteca Apostolica MS. Ottob. lat. 557: 266n

Vaticana, Biblioteca Apostolica MS. Ottob. lat. 862: 323n

Vaticana, Biblioteca Apostolica MS. Ottob. lat. 2516: 287n

Vaticana, Biblioteca Apostolica MS. Palat. lat. 252: 121n

Works Cited

CCL = Corpus Christianorum. Series Latina.
CCM = Corpus Chritianorum Continuatio Medievalis.
CSEL = Corpus Scriptorum Ecclesiasticorum Latinorum.
EETS es = Early English Text Society. Extra Series.
EETS os = Early English Text Society. Original Series.
PG = Patrologiae Cursus Completus. Series Graeca.
PL = Patrologiae Cursus Completus. Series Latina.
RS = Rolls Series. Rerum Britannicarum Medii Aevi Scriptores.

Adams, Robert. "The Nature of Need in 'Piers Plowman' XX."
   Traditio 34 (1978): 273–301.
Alanus de Insulis [Alan of Lille]. *Anticlaudianus or The Good and
   Perfect Man*. Translated and edited by James J. Sheridan. Toronto:
   Pontifical Institute of Mediaeval Studies, 1973.
Albertano da Brescia. *De arte loquendi et tacendi*. Edited by Thor
   Sundby, in *Brunetto Latinos levnet og skrifter*. Copenhagen: Jacob
   Lunols, 1869.
Albertano da Brescia. *Liber consolationis et consilii*. Edited by Thor
   Sundby. London: Chaucer Society, 1873.
Alexander of Hales. *Doctoris irrefragabilis Alexandri de Hales (. . .)
   Summa theologica*. 4 vols. Quaracchi, 1924–48.
Alford, John A. "The Idea of Reason in *Piers Plowman*." In *Medieval
   English Studies Presented to George Kane*, edited by Edward Don-
   ald Kennedy, Ronald Waldron, and Joseph Wittig, 199–215.
   Woodbridge, Suffolk, and Wolfeboro, N.H.: D. S. Brewer, 1988.
Alford, John A. *Piers Plowman: A Glossary of Legal Diction*. Cam-
   bridge: D. S. Brewer, 1988.
Alford, John A. *Piers Plowman: A Guide to the Quotations*. Medieval
   & Renaissance Texts & Studies, vol. 77. Binghamton, N.Y., 1992.
Alford, John A. "The Role of the Quotations in *Piers Plowman*."
   Speculum 52 (1977): 80–99.
Aligheri, Dante. *Inferno*. Edited and translated by J. D. Sinclair. New
   York: Oxford Univ. Press, 1961.

Allen, Judson Boyce. *The Ethical Poetic of the Later Middle Ages.* Toronto: Univ. of Toronto Press, 1982.

Allen, Judson Boyce. "The Ironic Fruyt: Chauntecleer as Figura." *Speculum* 66 (1969): 25–35.

Allen, Judson Boyce. "Langland's Reading and Writing: *Detractor* and the Pardon Passus." *Speculum* 59 (1984): 342–62.

Altdeutsche Predigten und Gebete aus Handschriften. Edited by Wilhelm Wackernagel. Basel, 1876; repr. Darmstadt: Wissenschaftliche Buchgesellschaft, 1964.

Alter, Robert. *The Pleasures of Reading in an Ideological Age.* New York: Simon and Schuster, 1989.

Altfranzösisches Wörterbuch. Edited by A. Tobler and E. Lommatzsch. Vols. 1— . Berlin, Wiesbaden: Weidmann, 1925— .

Ambrose. *On The Duties of the Clergy.* In *The Nicene and Post-Nicene Fathers of the Christian Church*, 2nd series, vol. 10, translated by H. De Romestin et al., 1–89. Grand Rapids, MI: Eerdmans, 1969.

Analecta Franciscana. Vol. 7. Quaracchi, 1951.

Analecta Hymnica Medii Aevi. Edited by C. Blume and G. M. Dreves. 55 vols. Leipzig, 1886–1922.

Anderson, David. *Before the Knight's Tale: Imitation of Classical Epic in Boccaccio's Teseida.* Philadelphia: Univ. of Pennsylvania Press, 1988.

"Annales monasterii de Waverleia." In *Annales monastici.* Rolls Series 38. London: Longman, 1865.

Anselm of Canterbury. *De Veritate.* In *Truth, Freedom, and Evil: Three Philosophical Dialogues by Anselm of Canterbury,* edited and translated by Jasper Hopkins and Herbert Richardson, 91–120. New York: Harper, 1967.

"Antiquiores quae extant definitiones capitulorum generalium ordinis" (parts IX and X), *Analecta Augustiniana* 3 (1909): 53–59.

Aquinas, Thomas. *Divi Thomae Aquinatis (. . .) a Leone XIII P.M. (. . .) Summa theologica.* Editio altera Romana. 6 vols. Roma: Typographia Forzani et S., 1894–1923.

Aristotle. *Aristotelis Ars rhetorica.* Edited by R. Kassel. Berlin: de Gruyter, 1976.

Aristotle. *Ethica Nicomachea.* Translated by Robert Grosseteste. Edited by R.A. Gauthier. 3 vols. Aristoteles Latinus, vol. 26, 1–3. Leiden: Brill, Bruxelles: Desclee de Brouwer, 1972–74.

Aristotle. *Metaphysica.* Edited by W. D. Ross. Rev. ed. Oxford: Clarendon Press, 1953.

Arnold, Thomas, ed. *Select English Works of John Wyclif.* 3 vols. Oxford: Clarendon Press, 1869–71.

Aston, Margaret. *Lollards and Reformers: Images and Literacy in Late Medieval Religion.* London: Hambledon Press, 1984.

Audelay, John. *The Poems of John Audelay.* Edited by E. K. Whiting. EETS os 184. London: Oxford Univ. Press, 1931.

Auerbach, Erich. "Figura." In *Scenes from the Drama of European Literature*, 11–76. New York: Meridian Books, 1959.

Augustine of Hippo. *Confessiones.* Edited by Lucas Verheijen. CCL, vol. 27. Turnhout: Brepols, 1981.

Augustine of Hippo. *Contra Adimantum Manichaei discipulum.* PL 42:129–72.

Augustine of Hippo. *Contra mendacium ad consentium.* Edited by Joseph Zycha. CSEL, vol. 41. Wien, Prag: Tempsky; Leipzig: Freytag, 1900.

Augustine of Hippo. *De civitate Dei.* Edited by B. Dombart and A. Kalb. 2 vols. CCL, vol. 47–48. Turnhout: Brepols, 1955.

Augustine of Hippo. *De diversis quaestionibus octoginta tribus.* Edited by Almut Mutzenbecher. CCL, vol. 44A. Turnhout: Brepols, 1975.

Augustine of Hippo. *De doctrina Christiana.* Edited by Joseph Martin. CCL, vol. 32. Turnhout: Brepols, 1962.

Augustine of Hippo. *De vera religione.* Edited by K.-D. Daur. CCL, vol. 32. Turnhout: Brepols, 1962.

Augustine of Hippo. *Enarrationes in Psalmos.* Edited by E. Dekkers and J. Fraipont. 3 vols. CCL, vols. 38–40. Turnhout: Brepols, 1956.

Augustine of Hippo. *Epistolae.* Edited by A. Goldbacher. CSEL, vol. 44. Wien, Leipzig, 1904.

Augustine of Hippo. *In Ioannis evangelium tractatus CXXIV.* Edited by R. Willems. CCL, vol. 36. Turnhout: Brepols, 1954.

Augustine of Hippo. *On Christian Doctrine.* Trans. D. W. Robertson, Jr. The Library of Liberal Arts. Indianapolis: Bobbs-Merrill, 1958, repr. 1980.

Augustine of Hippo. *Sancti Aurelii Augustini De doctrina Christiana.* Edited by G. M. Green. CSEL, vol. 80. Wien: Hoelder-Pichler-Tempsky, 1963.

Augustine of Hippo. *Sancti Aurelii Augustini De sermone Domini in monte.* Edited by Almut Mutzenbecker. CCL 35. Turnhout: Brepols, 1957.

Auksi, Peter. "Wyclif's Sermons and the Plain Style." *Archiv für Reformationsgeschichte* 66 (1975): 5–23.

Balduinus ab Amsterdam. "Servasancti de Faenza, O. Min. Sermones Dominicales (cod. 1440, Troyes)." *Collectanea Franciscana* 37 (1967): 5–32.

Bale, John. *Scriptorum illustrium maioris Britannie (. . .) Catalogus.* Basel, 1557–59.

Barney, Stephen. "The Plowshare of the Tongue: The Progress of a Symbol from the Bible to *Piers Plowman.*" *Mediaeval Studies* 35 (1972): 261–93.

Bataillon, L. J. "Approaches to the Study of Medieval Sermons." *Leeds Studies in English,* new series 11 (1980): 19–35.

Bede, The Venerable. *Bedae Venerabilis Opera.* Edited by C. W. Jones. CCL 123B. Turnhout: Brepols, 1977.

Bede, The Venerable. *Ecclesiastical History of the English People.* Edited by Bertram Colgrave and R. A. B. Mynors. Oxford: Clarendon Press, 1969.

Benedict XI, Pope. *Le Registre de Benoit XI.* Edited by Charles Grandjean. Bibliothèque des Écoles françaises d'Athènes et de Rome, ser. 2, vol. 2. Paris, 1905.

Bennett, J. A. W. *Middle English Literature.* Edited and completed by Douglas Gray. Oxford: Clarendon Press, 1986, repr. 1990.

Bennett, J. A. W. *Poetry of the Passion. Studies in Twelve Centuries of English Verse.* Oxford: Clarendon Press; New York: Oxford Univ. Press, 1982.

Bennett, J. A. W. and G. V. Smithers, eds. *Early Middle English Verse and Prose.* With a Glossary by N. Davis. 2nd ed. Oxford: Clarendon Press, 1968.

Benson, Robert L. *The Bishop-Elect: A Study in Medieval Ecclesiastical Office.* Princeton: Princeton Univ. Press, 1968.

Bersuire, Pierre (Petrus Berchorius). *Metamorphosis Ouidiana Moraliter a Magistro Thoma Walleys (. . .) explanata.* Utrecht: Instituut voor Laat Latijn der Rijksuniversiteit, 1960–62.

Bertaux, E. "Les saints Louis dans l'art italien." *Revue des deux mondes* 158 (1900): 616–44.

Bestul, Thomas H. "Chaucer's Parson's Tale and the Late-Medieval Tradition of Religious Meditation." *Speculum* 64 (1989): 600–19.

Birney, Earle. *Essays on Chaucerian Irony*. Edited by Beryl Rowland. Toronto: Univ. of Toronto Press, 1985.

Blaise, Albert. *Dictionnaire Latin-Français des auteurs chrétiens*. Turnhout: Brepols, 1954.

Blake, Norman F. *The English Language in Medieval Literature*. Everyman's University Library. London: Dent, 1977.

Blodgett, James E. "William Thynne." In *Editing Chaucer: the Great Tradition*, edited by Paul Ruggiers, 35–52. Norman: Pilgrim Press, 1984.

Bloomfield, Morton W. "A Preliminary List of Incipits of Latin Works on the Virtues and Vices, Mainly of the Thirteenth, Fourteenth, and Fifteenth Centuries." *Traditio* 11 (1955): 259–379.

Bloomfield, Morton W. *The Seven Deadly Sins: An Introduction to the History of a Religious Concept with Special Reference to Medieval English Literature*. East Lansing: Michigan State College Press, 1952.

Blythe, Joan Heiges. "The Influence of Latin Manuals on Medieval Allegory: Deguileville's Presentation of Wrath." *Romania* 95 (1974): 256–93.

Blythe, Joan Heiges. "*Transitio* and Psychoallegoresis in *Piers Plowman*." In *Allegoresis: The Craft of Allegory in Medieval Literature*, edited by J. Stephen Russell, 133–55. New York: Garland, 1988.

Boccaccio, Giovanni. *Comedia della Ninfe Fiorentine (Ameto)*. Edited by Antonio Enzo Quaglio. Firenze: Sansoni, 1963.

Boccaccio, Giovanni. *Genealogie deorum gentilium*. Edited by V. Romano. Bari: G. Laterza, 1951.

Böddeker, Karl, ed. *Altenglische Dichtungen des MS. Harl. 2253, mit Grammatik und Glossar*. Berlin, 1878.

Bodleian Library. *Catalogus Codicum Manuscriptorum: Quarto Catalogues: II. Laudian Manuscripts by H. O. Coxe*. Revised by R. W. Hunt. Oxford, 1858–85, rev. ed. 1973.

Boethius. *Boethii Philosophiae consolatio*. Edited by L. Bieler. CCL, vol. 94. Turnhout: Brepols, 1957.

Boethius. *Quomodo substantiae in eo quod sint bonae sint cum non sint substantialia bona*. In *Boethius. The Theological Tractates*, edited and translated by H. F. Steward, E. K. Rand, and S. J. Tester, 38–51. Loeb Classical Library. London, Cambridge, Mass.: Harvard Univ. Press, 1973.

Boffey, Julia. *Manuscripts of English Courtly Love Lyrics in the Later Middle Ages*. Cambridge (U.K.), Dover, N.H.: D. S. Brewer, 1985.

Bologna, Ferdinando. *I pittori alla corte angioina di Napoli*. Saggi e studi di storia dell'arte. Rome: U. Bozzi, 1969.

Bologna, Ferdinando. "Povertà e umiltà: Il 'San Ludovico' di Simone Martini." *Studi Storici* 2 (1969): 231–59.

Bonaventura. *Commentary on Peter Lombard's Sentences*. Vol. 3 of *Opera Omnia*. Quaracchi, 1887.

Boniface VIII. *Les Registres de Boniface VIII*. Edited by Georges Digard, Maurice Faucon, and Antoine Thomas. 4 vols. Bibliothèque des Écoles françaises d'Athènes et de Rome, ser. 2, vol. 4. Paris, 1890.

The Book of Vices and Virtues. Edited by W. Nelson Francis. EETS os 217. London: Oxford Univ. Press, 1942; repr. 1968.

Borges, Jorge Luis. *Labyrinths*. Augmented edition. Edited by Donald A. Yates and James E. Irby. New York: New Directions, 1964.

Bori, Pier Cesare. *L'interpretazione infinita*. Bologna: Il Mulino, 1987.

Bowers, John M. *The Crisis of Will in Piers Plowman*. Washington, D.C.: The Catholic Univ. of America Press, 1986.

Boyle, Leonard E. "The Fourth Lateran Council and Manuals of Popular Theology." In *The Popular Literature of Medieval England*, edited by Thomas J. Heffernan, 30–43. Knoxville: Univ. of Tennessee Press, 1985.

Boyle, Leonard E. "The Inter-Conciliar Period 1179–1215 and the Beginnings of Pastoral Manuals." In *Miscellanea Rolando Bandinelli Papa Alessandro III*, edited by F. Liotta, 45–56. Siena: Accademia senese degli intronati, 1986.

Boyle, Leonard E. "Summae Confessorum." In *Les genres littéraires dans les sources théologiques et philosophique médiéval: Définition, critique, et exploitation*, 227–37. Publications de l'Institut d'Études Médiévales, 2ᵉ série, vol. 5. Louvain-la-Neuve: Institut d'Études Médiévales de l'Université Catholique de Louvain, 1982.

Brady, M. Teresa. "Lollard Sources of 'The Pore Caitif.'" *Traditio* 44 (1988): 389–418.

Braun, Joseph. *Die liturgische Gewandung im Occident und Orient nach Ursprung und Entwicklung, Verwendung und Symbolik*. Freiburg i. Br., 1907.

Braun, Joseph. *Die pontificalen Gewänder des Abendlandes nach ihrer geschichtlichen Entwicklung*. Stimmen aus Maria-Laach, Ergänzungsheft 73. Freiburg i. Br., 1898.

Brayer, E. "Catalogue des textes liturgiques et des petits genres religieux." In *Grundriß der romanischen Literaturen des Mittelalters 6: La littérature didactique, allégorique et satirique*, edited by H. R. Jauss et al., vol. 2, 19–53. Heidelberg: Winter, 1970.

Brook, G. L., ed. *The Harley Lyrics. The Middle English Lyrics of MS. Harley 2253*. 4th ed. Manchester: Manchester Univ. Press, 1968.

Brown, Carleton, ed. *English Lyrics of the XIIIth Century*. Oxford: Clarendon Press, 1932, repr. 1971.

Brown, Carleton, ed. *Religious Lyrics of the XIVth Century*. 2nd rev. ed. by G. V. Smithers. Oxford: Clarendon Press, 1957, repr. 1970.

Brown, Carleton and Rossell Hope Robbins. *The Index of Middle English Verse*. New York, 1943.

Burrow, J. A. *The Ages of Man: A Study in Medieval Writing and Thought*. Oxford: Clarendon, 1986.

Burrow, J. A. "Words, Works and Will: Theme and Structure in *Piers Plowman*." In *"Piers Plowman": Critical Approaches*, edited by S. S. Hussey, 111–24. London: Methuen, 1969.

Bursill-Hall, G. L. *A Census of Medieval Latin Grammatical Manuscripts*. Grammatica Speculativa, vol. 4. Stuttgart: Frommann-Holzboog, 1981.

Caggese, Romolo. *Roberto d'Angiò e i suoi tempi*. 2 vols. Florence, 1922–30.

Calendar of Patent Rolls of the Reign of Henry III, Vol. 2: A.D. 1225–1232. London, 1903.

Cambridge Medieval History. Edited by H. M. Gwatkin et al. 8 vols. Cambridge: Cambridge Univ. Press, 1911–36.

Camera, Matteo. *Elucubrazioni Storico-Diplomatiche su Giovanna I (...)*. Salerno, 1889.

Cannon, Christopher. "*Raptus* in the Chaumpaigne Release and a Newly Discovered Document Concerning the Life of Geoffrey Chaucer." *Speculum* 68 (1993): 74–94.

Cannon, H. L. "The Poor Priests: A Study in the Rise of English Lollardry." *Annual Report of the American Historical Association* 1 (1899): 451–82.

Cantera, Biagio, ed. *Documenti risguardanti il b. Giacomo di Viterbo*. Napoli: Accademia Reale delle Scienze, 1888.

Capes, William W. *Registrum Johannis Trefnant Episcopi Herefordensis, 1389–1404*. Canterbury and York Society, vol. 20. London, 1916.

Caracciolo, Cesare D'Engenio. *Napoli Sacra*. Naples, 1624.

Caracciolo, Roberto. *Opus Quadragesimale perutilissimum quod de penitentia dictum est*. Basle: Berthold Ruppel and Michael Wenssler, 1479[?].

Carruthers, Mary. *The Book of Memory: A Study of Memory in Medieval Culture*. Cambridge Studies in Medieval Literature, vol. 10. Cambridge: Cambridge Univ. Press, 1990.

Casagrande, Carla, and Silvana Vecchio. *I peccati della lingua: disciplina ed etica della parola nella cultura medievale*. Rome: Istituto della encyclopedia Italiana, 1987.

Catalogue of Manuscripts in the British Museum. New Series. Vol. I, Part 1: The Arundel Manuscripts. London, 1834.

Catalogue of the Western Manuscripts in the Old Royal and King's Collections, edited by George F. Warner and Julius P. Gilson. 4 vols. London: Trustees of the British Museum, 1921.

Catto, J. I. "John Wyclif and the Cult of the Eucharist." In *The Bible in the Medieval World. Essays in Memory of Beryl Smalley*, edited by Katherine Walsh and Diana Wood, 269–86. Studies in Church History, subsidia 4. Oxford: Blackwell, 1985.

Caxton, William. *Caxton's Aesop*. Edited by R. T. Lenaghan. Cambridge Mass.: Harvard Univ. Press, 1967.

Chaix, Gérald. *Réforme et contre-réforme catholiques: Recherches sur la Chartreuse de Cologne au XVIe siècle*. 3 vols. Analecta Cartusiana 80. Salzburg: Institut für Anglistik und Amerikanistik, 1981.

Chambers, R. W. "The Authorship of 'Piers Plowman.'" *Modern Language Review* 5 (1910): 1–32.

Chartularium Universitatis Parisiensis. Edited by H. Denifle and A. Chatelain. 2 vols. Paris, 1889.

Chastising of God's Children. Edited by E. Colledge and J. Bazire. Oxford: Blackwell, 1957.

Chaucer, Geoffrey. *The Minor Poems*, edited by G. B. Pace and A. David. *A Variorum Edition of the Works of Geoffrey Chaucer*, vol. 5. Norman, Okla.: Univ. of Oklahoma Press, 1982.

Chaucer, Geoffrey. *The Riverside Chaucer*. Edited by Larry D. Benson et al. 3rd ed. Boston: Houghton Mifflin, 1987.

Chaucer, Geoffrey. *The Works of Geoffrey Chaucer*. Edited by W. W. Skeat. 7 vols. Oxford: Clarendon Press, 1894–97.

Checchini, Aldo. "Un Giudice del Secolo Decimoterzo, Albertano da Brescia." *Imperiale Regio Istituto Veneto de Science, Lettere ed Arti* 14, 2 (1841): 5–77.

Cheney, C. R. *English Synodalia of the Thirteenth Century.* 2nd ed. London: Oxford Univ. Press, 1968.

Chenu, M.-D. *La Théologie comme science au XIIIe siècle.* 3rd rev. and augm. ed. Bibliothèque Thomiste, vol. 33. Paris: Librairie Philosophique J. Vrin, 1969.

Chenu, M.-D. *Towards Understanding St. Thomas.* Trans. A. M. Landry and D. Hughes. The Library of Living Catholic Thought. Chicago: Henry Regnery, 1964.

Chevalier, U. *Repertorium Hymnologicum.* 6 vols. Louvain, 1892–1920.

Chronica minora saec. IV, V, VI, VII. Edited by Th. Mommsen. MGH Auctores antiquissimi XIII. Berlin, 1898.

Cicero. *De Officiis.* Translated by Walter Miller. Loeb Classical Library. London: Heinemann, 1921.

Cigman, Gloria, ed. *Lollard Sermons.* EETS os 294. Oxford: Oxford Univ. Press, 1989.

Cigman, Gloria. "The Preacher as Performer: Lollard Sermons as Imaginative Discourse." *Journal of Literature and Theology* 2 (1988): 69–82.

Coleman, Janet. *Medieval Readers and Writers.* London: Hutchinson; New York: Columbia Univ. Press, 1981.

Collette, Carolyn. "Critical Approaches to the *Prioress's Tale* and the *Second Nun's Tale.*" In *Chaucer's Religious Tales,* edited by C. David Benson and Elizabeth Robertson, 95–107. Cambridge: D. S. Brewer, 1990.

Conciliorum œcumenicorum decreta. Edited by Josepho Alberigo et al. 3rd ed. Bologna: Istituto per le scienze religiose, 1973.

Copeland, R. "The Middle English 'Candet Nudatum Pectus' and Norms of Early Vernacular Translation Practice." *Leeds Studies in English* new series 15 (1984): 57–77.

Corpus Iuris Canonici. Edited by E. L. Richter, revised by E. Friedberg. 2 vols. 1879; repr. Graz: Akademische Druck- und Verlagsanstalt, 1955.

Cosenza, G. "La chiesa e il convento di S. Pietro Martire." *Napoli nobilissima* 8 (1899), 9 (1900).

Councils and Synods, with Other Documents Relating to the English Church, Vol. 2: A.D. 1205–1313. Edited by F.M. Powicke and C.R. Cheney. 2 vols. Oxford: Clarendon Press, 1964.

Courtenay, William J. *Schools and Scholars in Fourteenth-Century England.* Princeton: Princeton Univ. Press, 1987.

Coxe, Henry Octavius. *Catalogus Codicum Manuscriptorum qui in Collegiis Aulisque Oxoniensibus.* Vol. 1. Oxford, 1852.

Crisci, Generoso. *Il Cammino della Chiesa Salernitana nell'opera dei suoi vescovi (sec. v–xx).* Rome, Naples: Editrice Redenzione, 1976.

Curry, Walter C. *The Middle English Ideal of Personal Beauty as Found in the Metrical Romances, Chronicles, and Legends of the XIII, XIV and XV Centuries.* Baltimore: J. H. Furst, 1916.

Curtius, E. R. *European Literature and the Latin Middle Ages.* Translated by Willard R. Trask. Bollingen Series 36. New York: Pantheon, 1953.

D'Alençon, E. ["The Life of St. Louis of Toulouse by Johannes de Orta."] *Analecta Ord. Min. Capp.* 13 (1897): 338–51, 360–72; and 14 (1898): 16–22, 89–92.

D'Aloe, Stanislao. *Storia della Chiesa di Napoli, Provata con monumenti.* Naples, 1861.

D'Avray, David L. *The Preaching of the Friars. Sermons diffused from Paris before 1300.* Oxford: Clarendon Press; New York: Oxford Univ. Press, 1985.

D'Avray, David L. "Sermons on the Dead before 1350." *Studi Medievali,* 3a Serie, 31,1 (1990): 207–23.

D'Avray, David L. "Some Franciscan Ideas about the Body." *Archivum Franciscanum Historicum* 84 (1991): 393–63

Dahlberg, Charles. "Chaucer's Cock and Fox." *JEGP* 53 (1954): 277–90.

Davidsohn, Robert. *Geschichte von Florenz.* 4 vols. Berlin: Mittler, 1896–1927.

Davies, G. R. C. *Medieval Cartularies of Great Britain: A Short Catalogue.* London: Longmans, 1958.

Davies, Reginald T., ed. *Medieval English Lyrics.* London: Faber and Faber, 1963.

De Libera, A. "The Oxford and Paris Traditions in Logic." In *The Cambridge History of Later Medieval Philosophy,* edited by N. Kretzmann, A. Kenny, and J. Pinborg, 174–87. Cambridge: Cambridge Univ. Press, 1982.

De Lubac, Henri. *Exégèse médiévale.* 4 vols. Paris: Aubier, 1959–64.

De Rijk, Lambertus Marie. *Logica Modernorum: A Contribution to the History of Early Terminist Logic.* Wijsgerige teksten en studies, vol. 6. 2 vols. Assen: Van Gorcum, 1962–67.

De Rijk, Lambertus Marie. "The Origins of the Theory of the Properties of Terms." In *The Cambridge History of Later Medieval Philosophy*, edited by N. Kretzmann, A. Kenny, and J. Pinborg, 161– 73. Cambridge, New York: Cambridge Univ. Press, 1982.

De Vocht, Henry. *Monumenta Humanistica Lovaniensia. Texts and Studies about Louvain Humanists in the First Half of the XVIth Century: Erasmus-Vives-Dorpius-Clenardus-Goes-Moringus*. Louvain, 1934.

Deanesly, Margaret. *The Lollard Bible and Other Medieval Biblical Versions*. Cambridge: Cambridge Univ. Press, 1920.

Debongnie, Pierre. *Jean Mombaer de Bruxelles, Abbé de Livry: Ses écrits et ses réformes*. Louvain-Toulouse, 1927.

Deguileville, Guillaume de. *The Pilgrimage of the Lyf of the Manhode*. Vol. 1. Edited by Avril Henry. EETS os 288. London: Oxford Univ. Press, 1985.

Delcorno, Carlo. *Giordano da Pisa e l'Antica Predicazione Volgare*. Biblioteca di "Lettere" Italiane, vol. 14. Firenze: Leo S. Olschki, 1975.

Delcorno, Carlo. *La Predicazione nell' Età Comunale*. Scuola aperta. Lettere italiane, vol. 57. Florence: Sansoni, 1974.

Dempster, Germaine. "The Parson's Tale." In *Sources and Analogues of Chaucer's* Canterbury Tales, edited by W. F. Bryan and Germaine Dempster, 723–60. New York, 1941; repr. New York: Humanties Press, 1958.

Denys the Carthusian (Dionysius Cartusiensis). *Doctoris ecstatici D. Dionysii Cartusiani Opera omnia*. Cura et labore monachorum sacri ordinis Cartusiensis. 42 volumes in 44. Montreuil-sur-Mer, Tournai, Parkminster, 1896–1913, 1935.

Deschamps, Jan. "De lange en de korte redactie van het *Rosarium Jesu et Mariae* van de kartuizer Jacobus van Gruitrode en de Middelnederlandse vertaling van de korte redactie." In *Codex in Context: Studies over codicologie, kartuizergeschiedenis en laatmiddel-eeuws geestesleven aangeboden aan Prof. Dr. A. Gruijs*, edited by Chr. De Backer, A. J. Geurts and A. G. Weiler, 105–25. Nijmegen, 1985.

Deschamps, Jan. "Middelnederlandse vertalingen en bewerkingen van werken van de Kartuizer Jacobus van Gruitrode." In *Hulde-Album Dr. F. Van Vinckenroye*, 67–81. Hasselt, 1985.

A Devout Treatyse called the Tree & Twelve Frutes of the Holy Goost. Edited by J. J. Vaissier. Groningen: Wolters, 1960.

Dictionary of National Biography. Edited by Leslie Stephen and Sidney Lee. 24 vols. London, 1885–1901; repr. London: Oxford Univ. Press, 1937.

Dinshaw, Carolyn. *Chaucer's Sexual Poetics*. Madison: Univ. of Wisconsin Press, 1989.

Disce mori. Oxford, Bodleian Library MS. Laud Misc. 99.

Dives and Pauper. Vol. 1. Edited by Priscilla Heath Barnum. EETS os 275, 280. Oxford: Oxford Univ. Press, 1976–80.

Dobson, E. J. and F. L. Harrison, eds. *Medieval English Songs*. New York: Cambridge Univ. Press, 1979.

Domanevszky, Alexander, ed. *Chronici Hungarici composito saeculi XIV*. Scriptores Rerum Hungaricarum, vol. 1. Budapest, 1937.

Donaldson, E. Talbot. *Speaking of Chaucer*. New York: Norton, 1970.

Dondaine, Antoine. "Guillaume Peyrault, vie et oeuvres." *Archivum fratrum praedicatorum* 18 (1948): 162–236.

Dondaine, Antoine. "La Vie et les oeuvres de Jean de san Gimignano." *Archivum Fratrum Praedicatorum* 9 (1939): 128–83.

Donovan, Mortimer J. "The *moralite* of the Nun's Priest's Sermon." *JEGP* 52 (1953): 493–508.

Doyle, A. I. "Books Connected with the Vere Family and Barking Abbey." *Transactions of the Essex Archaeological Society* 25 (1959): 222–43.

Doyle, A. I. "Reflections of Some Manuscripts of Nicholas Love's *Myrrour of the Blessed Lyf of Jesu Christ*." *Leeds Studies in English* new series 14 (1983): 82–93.

Doyle, A. I. "The Shaping of the Vernon and Simeon Manuscripts." In *Studies in the Vernon Manuscript*, edited by D. Pearsall. Cambridge: D. S. Brewer; Rochester, NY: Boydell and Brewer, 1990.

Doyle, A. I. "The Work of a Late Fifteenth-Century English Scribe, William Ebesham." *Bulletin of the John Rylands Library* 39 (1956–57): 298–325.

Doyle, A. I., and M. B. Parkes. "The Production of Copies of the *Canterbury Tales* and the *Confessio Amantis* in the Early Fifteenth Century." In *Medieval Scribes, Manuscripts, and Libraries: Essays Presented to N. R. Ker*, edited by M. B. Parkes and Andrew G. Watson, 163–210. London: Scolar Press, 1978.

Drexel, Jeremias. *Orbis Phaethon: De universis viciis linguae*. Coloniae, 1631.

Dryden, John. *Poems and Fables*. Edited by J. Kinsley. London: Oxford Univ. Press, 1962.

Dunning, T. P. *Piers Plowman: An Interpretation of the A Text*. 1937; 2nd edition revised and edited by T. P. Dolan. Oxford: Clarendon Press, 1980.

The Durham Collectar. Edited by Alicia Corrêa. Henry Bradshaw Society 107. Woodbridge, Suffolk, and Rochester, N.Y.: Boydell and Brewer, 1992.

Edmund of Abingdon. *Speculum religiosorum and Speculum ecclesie*. Edited by Helen P. Forshaw. Auctores Britannici Medii Aevi, vol. 3. London: Oxford Univ. Press, 1973.

Edwards, A. S. G., ed. *Middle English Prose: A Critical Guide to Major Authors and Genres*. New Brunswick, N.J.: Rutgers Univ. Press, 1984.

Edwards, H. L. R. *Skelton: The Life and Times of an Early Tudor Poet*. London: Cape, 1949.

Emden, Alfred B. *A Biographical Register of the University of Cambridge to 1500*. Cambridge: Cambridge Univ. Press, 1963.

Emden, Alfred B. *A Biographical Register of the University of Oxford to A.D. 1500*. 3 vols. Oxford: Clarendon Press, 1957–59.

Emery, Kent, Jr. "Copyists, Text-Collectors and Authors in Some Late-Medieval Monastic Manuscripts." Forthcoming.

Emery, Kent, Jr. "Denys the Carthusian and the Doxography of Scholastic Theology." In *Ad litteram: Authoritative Texts and their Medieval Readers*, edited by Mark D. Jordan and Kent Emery, Jr., 327–59. Notre Dame, Ind.: Univ. of Notre Dame Press, 1992.

Emery, Kent, Jr. "Denys the Carthusian and the Invention of Preaching Materials." Forthcoming.

Emery, Kent, Jr. "Did Denys the Carthusian Also Read Henricus Bate?" *Bulletin de philosophie médiévale* 32 (1990): 196–206.

Emery, Kent, Jr. *Dionysii Cartusiensis Opera selecta. (Prolegomena) Bibliotheca manuscripta 1A-1B: Studia bibliographica*. CCM 121–121a. Turnhout: Brepols, 1991.

Emery, Kent, Jr. "Two More Copies of Henry of Ghent, *Summa*, and the Heuristic of Critical Editions (Henry of Ghent and Denys the Carthusian)." *Manuscripta* 36 (1992): 3–21.

Enkvist, Nils Erik. *Linguistic Stylistics*. Den Haag, Paris: Mouton, 1973.

Erasmus Roterdamus, Desiderius. *Opera Omnia*. Amsterdam: North-Holland, 1969–1974.

Evagrius Ponticus. *Traité Pratique, ou le Moine*. Edited by A. and C. Guillaumont. 2 vols. Sources Chrétiennes, vols. 170–71. Paris: Editions du Cerf, 1971.

Facey, Jane. "John Foxe and the Defence of the English Church." In *Protestantism and the National Church in Sixteenth Century England*, edited by P. Lake and M. Dowling, 162–92. London, New York: Croom Helm, 1987.

Faes de Mottoni, Barbara and Concetta Luna. *Aegidii Romani Opera omnia, vol. 1: Catalogo dei manoscritti (1–95), 1/1: Città del Vaticano*. Testi e Studi per il "Corpus Philosophorum Medii Aevi," vol. 5. Firenze: Olschki, 1987.

Farge, James K. *Biographical Registers of Paris Doctors of Theology, 1500–1536*. Subsidaria Mediaevalia 10. Toronto: Pontifical Institute of Mediaeval Studies, 1980.

Fasciculus morum. See Wenzel, Siegfried.

Fiala, Virgil, and Wolfgang Irtenkauf. "Versuch einer liturgischen Nomenklatur." In *Zur Katalogisierung mittelalterlicher und neuerer Handschriften*, edited by Clemens Köttelwesch (Zeitschrift für Bibliothekswesen und Bibliographie: Sonderheft), 105–37. Frankfurt am Main: Klostermann, 1963.

Fichte, Joerg O. *Erläuterungen*. In Geoffrey Chaucer, *Die Canterbury-Erzählungen: Mittelenglisch und Deutsch*. Trans. by Fritz Kemmler, annotations by Joerg O. Fichte. Vol. 3. Goldmann Klassiker mit Erläuterungen. Munich: Goldmann, 1989.

Fichte, Joerg O. "*Womanly Noblesse* and *To Rosemounde*: Point and Counterpoint of Chaucerian Love Lyrics." In *Reconstructing Chaucer: Selected Essays from the 1984 NCS Congress*, edited by Paul Strohm and Thomas J. Heffernan, 181–94. *Studies in the Age of Chaucer, Proceedings*, vol. 1. Knoxville, TN: New Chaucer Society, 1985.

Fitzralph, Richard. "Defensio curatorum." Trans. John Trevisa. In *Dialogus inter Militem et Clericum . . .*, edited by Aaron Jenkins Perry, 39–93. EETS os 167. Oxford: Oxford Univ. Press, 1925.

Fleming, John V. *The Roman de la Rose: A Study in Allegory and Iconography*. Princeton: Princeton Univ. Press, 1969.

Fletcher, Alan J. "A Death Lyric from the Summa Predicantium, MS. Oriel College 10." *Notes and Queries* 222 (1977): 11–12.

Floretum. In London, British Library MS. Harley 401.

Forshall, Josiah, and Frederic Madden, eds. *The Holy Bible, (. . .)*

Made from the Latin Vulgate by John Wycliffe and his Followers. 4 Vols. Oxford: Oxford Univ. Press, 1850.

Foxe, Simeon. "The Life of Mr. John Fox." In John Foxe. *Acts and Monuments (. . .)*. 3 vols. 9th ed. London, 1684.

Francis of Assisi. *Regulae*. In *Opuscula sancti patris Francisci Assisinensis*, vol. 71. Bibliotheca Franciscana Ascetica Medii Aevi, vol. 1. Quaracchi, 1904.

Frank, R. W., Jr. *Piers Plowman and the Scheme of Salvation*. Yale Studies in English 136. New Haven: Yale Univ. Press, 1957.

Frankis, J. "The Social Context of Vernacular Writing in Thirteenth Century England: the Evidence of the Manuscripts." In *Thirteenth Century England. I*, edited by P. R. Coss and S. D. Lloyd. Woodbridge, Suffolk: Boydell and Brewer, 1986.

Frost, William. "An Interpretation of Chaucer's Knight's Tale." *RES* 25 (1949): 290–304.

Furnivall, F. J., ed.. *Political, Religious, and Love Poems*. Rev. ed. EETS os 15. Oxford, 1903; repr. London: Oxford Univ. Press, 1965.

Furnivall, F. J. "Religious Poems from MS. Digby 2." *Archiv für das Studium der neueren Sprachen und Litteraturen* 97 (1896): 309–12.

Galbraith, V. H. "The Chronicle of Henry Knighton." In *Fritz Saxl 1890–1948: A Volume of Memorial Essays*, edited by D. J. Gordon, 136–48. London: Nelson, 1957.

Gamboso, V. "I Sermoni Festivi di Servasanto da Faenza nel codice 490 dell' Antoniana." *Il Santo* 13 (1973): 3–88.

Gerald of Wales (Giraldus Cambrensis). *Opera*. Edited by J. S. Brewer. 8 vols. Rolls Series 21. London: Longman, 1861–91.

Gerson, Jean. *Oeuvres complètes*. 10 volumes. Edited by P. Glorieux. Paris: Desclee, 1960–73.

Geus, Johannes. *Tractatus de viciis vocis*. Nurnberg, 1479.

Gibbs, M. and J. Lang. *Bishops and Reform 1215–1272*. London: Oxford Univ. Press, 1934.

Giles of Rome. *Commentarium b. Aegidii Romani in primum librum Magistri sententiarum*. Cordova, 1699.

Giles of Rome. *Commentarium in Canticum Canticorum*. In *Thomae Aquinatis Opera omnia*. Vol. 14. Parma, 1852–72.

Giles of Rome. *D. Aegidii Romani . . . de regimine principum libri iii*. Roma: apud Antonium Bladum, 1556.

Giles of Rome. *Rhetorica Aristotelis cum Egidii de Roma commentariis*. Venezia, 1515.

Gillespie, V. "Cura Pastoralis in Deserto." In *De Cella in Seculum: Religious and Secular Life and Devotion in Late Medieval England*, edited by M. G. Sargent, 161–81. Cambridge (U.K.), Wolfeboro, N.H.: D. S. Brewer, 1989.

Gilson, E. *History of Christian Philosophy in the Middle Ages*. New York: Random House, 1955.

Giustiniani, Pasquale. "Il problema delle idee in dio secondo Giacomo da Viterbo, OESA, con edizione della Distinzione 36 dell'Abbreviatio in I Sententiarum Aegidii Romani." *Analecta Augustiniana* 42 (1979): 285–345.

Glorieux, P. *Répertoire des maitres en théologie de Paris au XIIIe siècle*. 2 vols. Paris, 1938.

Glossa ordinaria. PL 113–14.

Gneuss, H. "William Hereberts Übersetzungen." *Anglia* 78 (1960): 169–92.

Goering, Joseph. *William de Montibus (c. 1140–1213): The Schools and the Literature of Pastoral Care*. Toronto: Pontifical Institute of Mediaeval Studies, 1992.

Goering, Joseph and Daniel S. Taylor. "The Summulae of Bishops Walter of Cantilupe (1240) and Peter Quinel (1287)." *Speculum* 67 (1992): 576–94.

Goldsmith, Margaret. *The Figure of Piers Plowman: The Image on the Coin*. Woodbridge, Suffolk: Boydell and Brewer, 1981.

Grabmann, M. "Siger von Brabant und Dante." Repr. in *Mittelalterliches Geistesleben. Abhandlungen zur Geschichte der Scholastik und Mystik*, vol. 3, 180–96. München: Max Hueber, 1956.

Gray, Douglas. "Notes on Some Middle English Charms." In *Chaucer and Middle English Studies in Honour of Rossell Hope Robbins*, edited by Beryl Rowland, 56–71. [Kent, Ohio]: Kent State Univ. Press, 1974.

Gray, Douglas. *Themes and Images in the Medieval English Religious Lyric*. London, Boston: Routledge & Kegan Paul, 1972.

Gray, Nick. "The Clemency of Cobblers: A Reading of 'Glutton's Confession' in *Piers Plowman*." *Leeds Studies in English*, new series 17 (1986): 61–75.

Gregory the Great. *Moralia in Job*. Edited by M. Adriaen. 3 vols. CCL 143–43B. Turnhout: Brepols, 1979–85.

Greven, Josef. *Die Kölner Kartause und die Anfang der katholischen Reform in Deutschland*. Katholisches Leben und Kämpfen im

Zeitalter Glaubensspaltung: Vereinsschriften der Gesellschaft zur Herausgabe des Corpus Catholicorum 6. Münster, 1934.

Griffin, Russell Morgan. *Chaucer's Lyrics*. Ann Arbor, 1984.

Grosseteste, Robert. *Templum Dei*. Edited by Joseph Goering and F. A. C. Mantello. Toronto Medieval Latin Texts, vol. 14. Toronto: Pontifical Institute of Mediaeval Studies, 1984.

Guigo II. *Lettre sur la vie contemplative, Douze méditations*. Edited by E. Colledge and J. Walsh. Sources Chrétiennes, vol. 163. Paris: Editions du Cerf, 1970.

Guindon, Roger. "Le 'De Sermone Domini in monte' de S. Augustin dans l'oeuvre de S. Thomas d'Aquin." *Revue de l'Université d'Ottawa: section spéciale* 28 (1958), *57-*85.

Gutiérrez, David. "De vita et scriptis beati Jacobi de Viterbio." *Analecta Augustiniana* 16 (1936-38): 216-24, 282-305, 358-81. Repr. as *De b. Jacobi Viterbiensis O.E.S.A. vita, operibus et doctrina theologica*. Città del Vaticano: Typis polyglottis, 1939.

Guyot, Bertrand-Georges. "La 'Dieta salutis' et Jean Rigaud." *Archivum Franciscanum Historicum* 82 (1989): 360-93.

Hackett, M. B. *The Original Statutes of Cambridge University: The Text and Its History*. Cambridge: Cambridge Univ. Press, 1970.

Hallwas, J. E. "The Two Versions of 'Hi Sike, Al Wan Hi Singe.'" *Neuphilologische Mitteilungen* 77 (1976): 360-64.

Halverson, John. "Aspects of Order in the *Knight's Tale*." *Studies in Philology* 57 (1960): 606-21.

Hamesse, Jacqueline, ed. *Les Auctoritates Aristotelis*. Philosophes Médiévaux, vol. 17. Louvain, Paris: Publications Universitaires, 1974.

Hamesse, Jacqueline. "Le vocabulaire des florilèges médiévaux." In *Méthodes et instruments du travail intellectuel au moyen âge*, edited by Olga Weijers (Études sur le vocabulaire du moyen âge 3), 209-30. Turnhout: Brepols, 1990.

Hanna, Ralph III. "*The Index of Middle English Verse* and Huntington Library Collections: A Checklist of Addenda." *Publications of the Bibliographical Society of America* 74 (1980): 235-58.

Hanna, Ralph III. "Will's Work." *New Historical Essays on Piers Plowman*. Edited by Kathryn Kerby-Fulton and Steven Justice. Forthcoming.

Hargreaves, Henry. "Wyclif's Prose." *Essays and Studies* n.s. 19 (1966): 1-17.

Hartshorne, A. "Military Costume." Revised by C. J. Foulkes. In *Mediaeval England*, edited by H. W. C. Davis, 170–93. Oxford: Clarendon Press, 1924.

Hauréau, B. *Initia operum scriptorum latinorum medii potissimum aevi ex codicibus manuscriptis et libris impressis alphabetice digessit.* 6 volumes. Turnhout: Brepols, 1974.

Haydon, Frank Scott, ed. *Eulogium historiarum.* 3 vols. Rolls Series 9. London: Longman, 1858–63.

Heawood, Edward. "Sources of Early English Paper Supply." *The Library* 4th ser. 10 (1929–30): 282–307, 427–54.

Heawood, Edward. *Watermarks, Mainly of the 17th and 18th Centuries.* Monumenta Chartae Papyraceae Historiam Illustrantia, vol. 1. Hilversum: Paper Publication Society, 1950.

Heinrich, F., ed. *Ein mittelenglisches Medizinbuch.* Halle, 1896.

Heltzel, Virgil B. *Fair Rosamond.* Northwestern University. Studies in the Humanities, vol. 16. Evanston: Northwestern Univ. Press, 1947.

Henderson, A. C. "Medieval Beasts and Modern Cages: The Making of Meaning in Fables and Bestiaries." *PMLA* 97 (1982): 40–49.

Henry of Ghent. *Henrici de Gandavo Quodlibet X.* Edited by Raymond Macken. Henrici de Gandavo Opera omnia, vol. 14. Leuven: Leuven Univ. Press, Leiden: Brill, 1981.

Henry of Ghent. *Magistri Henrici Goethals a Gandavo (. . .) Summa in tres partes praecipuas digesta.* Ferrara: apud Franciscum Succium, 1646.

Henry of Ghent. *Summae quaestionum ordinariarum (. . .) Henrici a Gandavo.* Paris: in aedibus J. Badii Ascensii, 1520; repr. St. Bonaventure, N.Y.: Franciscan Institute, 1953.

Henryson, Robert. *Poems.* Edited by C. Elliott. Oxford: Clarendon Press, 1974.

Herbert, J. A. *Catalogue of Romances in the Department of Manuscripts in the British Museum.* Vol. 3. London, 1910; repr. Bath: Pitmann Press, 1962.

Herebert, William. *The Works of William Herebert, OFM.* Edited by S. R. Reimer. Studies and Texts, vol. 81. Toronto: Pontifical Institute of Mediaeval Studies, 1987.

Hesbert, R. J., ed. *Le Tropaire-Prosaire de Dublin: MS Add. 710 de l'Université de Cambridge (vers 1360).* Monumenta Musicae Sacrae, vol. 4. Rouen: Imprimerie Rouennaise, 1970.

Heysse, Albanus. "De vita S. Ludovici ... in codicibus Paris 5376 et Ottob. lat. 2516." *Archivum Franciscanum Historicum* 40 (1947): 118–40.

Higden, Ranulf. *Polychronicon Ranulphi Higden, monachi Cestrensis.* Edited by Joseph Lumby. 9 vols. Rolls Series 41. London: Longman, 1865–86.

Hirsh, J. C. "A Fifteenth-Century Commentary on 'Ihesu for Thy Holy Name.' " *Notes and Queries* 215 (1970): 44–45.

Hodgson, P. "*Ignorancia Sacerdotum*: a Fifteenth-Century Discourse on the Lambeth Constitutions." *RES* 24 (1948): 1–11.

Hödl, Ludwig. "Articulus fidei: Eine begriffsgeschichtliche Arbeit." In *Einsicht und Glaube*, edited by J. Ratzinger and H. Fries, 358–76. Freiburg i. Br.: Herder, 1962.

The Holi Prophete Dauid seith. In *The Lollard Bible and Other Medieval Biblical Versions*, edited by Margaret Deanesly, 445–56. Cambridge: Cambridge Univ. Press, 1920.

Holmes, George. *Florence, Rome and the Origins of the Renaissance.* Oxford: Clarendon Press, 1986, repr. 1989.

Hook, Walter F. *Lives of the Archbishops of Canterbury.* London, 1865.

Housley, Norman. *The Italian Crusades.* Oxford: Clarendon Press, 1982.

Hövelmann, Gregor. "Gaesdonck MS 5: Eine unaufgeschnittene Handschrift des 15. Jahrhundert." *Antiquariat* 10 (1968): 217–22.

Howard, Donald. *The Idea of the Canterbury Tales.* Berkeley: Univ. of California Press, 1976.

Hudson, Anne. "A Chapter from Walter Hilton in Two Middle English Compilations." *Neophilologus* 52 (1968): 416–21.

Hudson, Anne. *Lollards and Their Books.* London, Ronceverte: The Hambledon Press, 1985.

Hudson, Anne. *The Premature Reformation: Wycliffite Texts and Lollard History.* Oxford: Clarendon Press; New York: Oxford Univ. Press, 1988.

Hudson, Anne, ed. *Selections from English Wycliffite Writings.* Cambridge, New York: Cambridge Univ. Press, 1978.

Hudson, Anne. "Wyclif and his followers: An Exhibition to mark the 600th anniversary of the death of John Wyclif." Bodleian Library Oxford. Oxford: Information Printing, 1984.

Hudson, Anne. "Wycliffite Prose." In *Middle English Prose: A Criti-*

cal Guide to Major Authors and Genres, edited by A. S. G. Edwards, 249–70. New Brunswick, N.J.: Rutgers Univ. Press, 1984.

Hudson, Anne, and Pamela Gradon, eds. *English Wycliffite Sermons*. Vols. 1–. Oxford: Clarendon Press, New York: Oxford Univ. Press, 1983–.

Hugh of St. Cher. *Opera omnia*. 8 vols. Lyons, 1668; Venice, 1732.

Hughes-Hughes, A. *Catalogue of Manuscript Music in the British Museum*. 3 vols. London, 1886–89.

Hunt, Richard W. "English Learning in the Late Twelfth Century." *Transactions of the Royal Historical Society* 4th ser. 19 (1936): 19–42.

Hunt, Richard W. "The Introductions to the Artes in the Twelfth Century." In *Studia mediaevalia in honorem admodum (...) Raymundi Josephi Martin Ordinis Praedicatorum (...) LXXum natalem diem agentis*, 85–112. Bruges: De Tempel, 1948.

Hunt, Richard W. *The Schools and the Cloister. The Life and Writings of Alexander Nequam (1157–1217)*. Edited and rev. by M. Gibson. Oxford: Clarendon Press; New York: Oxford Univ. Press, 1984.

Hunt, Richard W., ed. *A Summary Catalogue of Western Manuscripts in the Bodleian Library at Oxford*. Vol. 1. Oxford: Clarendon Press, 1953.

Hunt, T. "Deliciae Clericorum: Intellectual and Scientific Pursuits in Two Dorset Monasteries." *Medium Aevum* 56 (1987): 159–82.

H[unt], W[illiam]. "Grant, Richard." In *The Dictionary of National Biography*, 8:401.

Incipits of Latin Works on the Virtues and Vices, 1100–1500 A.D. Edited by Morton W. Bloomfield et al. Publications of the Mediaeval Academy of America, vol. 88. Cambridge, Mass.: The Mediaeval Academy of America, 1979.

Innocent III. *Lotharii Cardinalis (Innocentii III). De miseria humane conditionis*. Edited by Michele Maccarrone. Padua: Lucani, 1955.

Innocent III. *Sermo XI in die cinerum*. PL 217: 360–61.

Inventory of Church Goods temp. Edward III. Edited by Aelred Watkin. 2 vols. Norfolk Record Society 19. 1947.

Irving, Edward B., Jr. "The Nature of Christianity in *Beowulf*." *Anglo-Saxon England* 13 (1984): 7–21.

Irving, Edward B., Jr. *Rereading Beowulf*. Philadelphia: Univ. of Pennsylvania Press, 1989.

Isidore of Seville. *Etymologiarum ... Libri XX*. Edited by W. M.

Lindsay. Scriptorum classicorum bibliotheca Oxoniensis. Oxford: Clarendon Press, 1911.

Jacobi de Viterbio, OESA, Disputatio prima de quolibet. Edited by Eelcko Ypma. Cassiciacum, suppl. 1, vol. 1. Würzburg: Augustinus-Verlag, 1968.

Jacob's Well. Edited by Arthur Brandeis. EETS os 115. London: Kegan, Paul, 1900.

James, M. R. *A Descriptive Catalogue of the Manuscripts in the Library of Gonville and Caius College.* 2 vols. Cambridge, 1907.

James, M. R. *A Descriptive Catalogue of the Manuscripts in St. John's College, Cambridge.* Cambridge, 1913.

Jeffrey, David Lyle. "Chaucer and Wyclif: Biblical Hermeneutic and Literary Theory in the XIVth Century." In *Chaucer and Scriptural Tradition,* edited by David Lyle Jeffrey, 109–140. Ottawa: Univ. of Ottawa Press, 1984.

Jeffrey, David Lyle. *The Early English Lyric and Franciscan Spirituality.* Lincoln, Neb.: Univ. of Nebraska Press, 1975.

Jerome. *Epistolae.* PL 22: 325–1192.

Jöcher, Christian Gottlieb. *Allgemeines Gelehrten Lexicon.* 4 vols. Leipzig, 1750–51.

John le Neve. *Fasti ecclesiae Anglicanae, 1066–1300: III. Lincoln.* Edited by Diana E. Greenway. London: Institute of Historical Research, Univ. of London, 1977.

Johnson, Dudley R. "'Homicide' in the Parson's Tale," *PMLA* 57 (1942): 51–56.

Jolliffe, P. S. *A Checklist of Middle English Prose Writings of Spiritual Guidance.* Pontifical Institute of Mediaeval Studies, Subsidia Mediaevalia, vol. 2. Toronto: Pontifical Institute of Mediaeval Studies, 1974.

Jordani de Saxonia (...) Liber Vitasfratrum. Edited by Rudolph Arbesmann and Winfrid Huempfner. New York: Cosmopolitan Science and Arts Service, 1943.

Jusserand, J. J. "*Piers Plowman*: The Work of One or of Five." *Modern Philology* 6 (1909): 271–329.

Kaeppeli, Thomas, O.P. *Scriptores Ordinis Praedicatorum medii aevi.* 3 volumes to date. Rome, 1970—.

Kafka, Franz. *Parables and Paradoxes.* New York: Schocken, 1961.

Kaftal, George. *Iconography of the Saints in Italian Painting from its Beginnings to the Early XVIth Century.* 4 vols. Florence: Sansoni, 1952–85.

Kahn, Victoria. *Rhetoric, Prudence, and Skepticism in the Renaissance.* Ithaca: Cornell Univ. Press, 1985.

Kane, George. *Middle English Literature. A Critical Study of the Romances, the Religious Lyrics, Piers Plowman.* London: Methuen, 1951; repr. Westport, CT, 1979.

Kaske, R. E. " 'Ex vi transicionis' and its Passage in *Piers Plowman.*" *JEGP* 62 (1963): 32–60.

Kaske, R. E. *Medieval Christian Literary Imagery: A Guide to Interpretation.* Toronto: Univ. of Toronto Press, 1988.

Keen, Maurice. "Wyclif, the Bible, and Transubstantiation." In *Wyclif in his Times,* edited by Anthony Kenny, 1–16. Oxford: Clarendon Press, 1986.

Kellogg, Alfred L. "St. Augustine and the Parson's Tale." *Traditio* 8 (1952): 424–30.

Kemmler, Fritz. *"Exempla" in Context: A Historical and Critical Study of Robert Mannyng of Brunne's "Handlyng Synne."* Studies in English, vol. 6. Tübingen: Narr, 1984.

Kendall, Ritchie D. *The Drama of Dissent: The Radical Poetics of Nonconformity, 1380–1590.* Chapel Hill, London: Univ. of North Carolina Press, 1986.

Kenny, Anthony. "Realism and Determinism in the Early Wyclif." In *From Ockham to Wyclif,* edited by Anne Hudson and Michael Wilks, 165–77. *Studies in Church History,* subsidia 5. Oxford: Blackwell, 1987.

Kenny, Anthony. "The Realism of the *De Universalibus.*" In *Wyclif in his Times,* edited by Anthony Kenny, 17–29. Oxford: Clarendon Press; New York: Oxford Univ. Press, 1986.

Kenny, Anthony. *Wyclif.* Oxford, New York: Oxford Univ. Press, 1985.

Kenny, Anthony, ed. *Wyclif in his Times.* Oxford: Clarendon Press; New York: Oxford Univ. Press, 1986.

Ker, Neil R. *Medieval Libraries of Great Britain.* 2nd. ed. London: Offices of the Royal Historical Society, 1964; *Supplement to the Second Edition,* edited by Andrew G. Watson. London: Offices of the Royal Historical Society, 1987.

Kermode, Frank. *The Genesis of Secrecy.* Cambridge, Mass.: Harvard Univ. Press, 1979.

Kermode, Frank. "The Plain Sense of Things." In *An Appetite for Poetry,* 172–88. Cambridge, Mass.: Harvard Univ. Press, 1989.

Kirchberger, C. "The Homely Presence of Christ." *The Life of the Spirit* 4 (1949): 109–14.

Kirk, Elizabeth. *The Dream Thought of Piers Plowman.* New Haven: Yale Univ. Press, 1972.

Klaeber, Fr., ed. *Beowulf and the Fight at Finnsburg.* 3rd ed. New York: Heath, 1950.

Kleinschmidt, Beda. "St. Ludwig von Toulouse in der Kunst." *Archivum Franciscanum Historicum* 2 (1909): 197–215.

Knapp, Peggy Ann. *Chaucer and the Social Contest.* New York and London: Routledge, 1990.

Knapp, Peggy Ann. *The Style of John Wyclif's English Sermons.* Proprietatibus litterarum: Series practica, vol. 16. The Hague, Paris: Mouton, 1977.

Knighton, Henry. *Chronicon Henrici Knighton.* Edited by Joseph Rawson Lumby. 2 vols. Rolls Series 92. London: Her Majesty's Stationery Office, 1889–95; repr. London: Kraus, 1965.

Knowles, David, C. N. L. Brooke, and Vera C. M. London, eds. *The Heads of Religious Houses: England and Wales 940–1216.* Cambridge: Cambridge Univ. Press, 1972.

Köpf, U. *Die Anfänge der theologischen Wissenschaftstheorie im 13. Jahrhundert.* Beiträge zur historischen Theologie, vol. 49. Tübingen: Mohr, 1974.

Kristeller, Paul Oskar. *Iter Italicum. A Finding List of Incompletely Catalogued Humanistic Manuscripts of the Renaissance in Italian and Other Libraries.* 6 volumes (with separate index to volume 3). Leiden-London: Warburg Institute, 1963–92.

Kruitwagen, Bonaventura, O.F.M. "De schrijftmeester Herman Strepel (1447) en de schrijftsoorten van de Broeders van het Gemeene Leven en de Windersheimers." *Het Boek* 22 (1933–34): 209–30; 23 (1935–36): 1–54, 129–64.

La Fontaine, Jean de. *Fables.* Edited by V.-L. Saulnier. 2 vols. Bibliothèque de Cluny. Paris: Armand Colin, 1960.

Lambert, M. D. *Franciscan Poverty: The Doctrine of the Absolute Poverty of Christ and the Apostles in the Franciscan Order, 1210–1323.* London: SPCK, 1961.

Langland, William. *Piers Plowman: The Prologue and Passus I–VII of the B Text.* Edited by J. A. W. Bennett. Oxford: Clarendon Press, 1972.

Langland, William. *Piers the Ploughman.* Translated by J. F. Goodridge. Baltimore: Penguin, 1959.

Langland, William. *Piers Plowman: The A Version*. Edited by George Kane. London: Athlone, 1960.

Langland, William. *Piers Plowman: The B Version*. Edited by George Kane and E. Talbot Donaldson. London: Athlone, 1975.

Langland, William. *Piers Plowman: An Edition of the C-text*. Edited by Derek Pearsall. Berkeley: Univ. of California Press, 1978.

Langland, William. *The Vision of William Concerning Piers the Plowman in Three Parallel Texts*. Edited by Walter W. Skeat. 2 Vols. London: Oxford Univ. Press, 1886.

Lanham, Richard. *A Handlist of Rhetorical Terms*. Berkeley: Univ. of California Press, 1968.

The Lanterne of Liȝt. Edited by Lilian M. Swinburn. EETS os 151. London: Kegan Paul, 1917.

Latini, Brunetto. *Li Livres dou Tresor*. Edited by Francis J. Carmody. Berkeley: Univ. of California Press, 1948.

Lawton, David. "The Subject of *Piers Plowman*." *The Yearbook of Langland Studies* 1 (1987): 1–30.

Leff, Gordon. *Heresy in the Later Middle Ages*. 2 vols. Manchester: Manchester Univ. Press, New York: Barnes and Noble, 1967.

Leff, Gordon. "Ockham and Wyclif on the Eucharist." *Reading Medieval Studies* 2 (1976): 1–11.

Leff, Gordon. "Poverty and Prophecy." In *Heresy in the Later Middle Ages*, 1: 51–255. 2 vols. Manchester: Manchester Univ. Press, 1967.

Legge, D. "Toothache and Courtly Love." *French Studies* 4 (1950): 50–54.

Lehmann, Paul. *Mittelalterliche Büchertitel*. Sitzungsberichte der Bayerischen Akademie der Wissenschaften: Philosophisch-historische Klasse 1948. Munich: Verlag der Bayerischen Akademie der Wissenschaften, 1949.

Lesnick, Daniel R. *Preaching in Medieval Florence. The Social world of Franciscan and Dominican Spirituality*. Athens, Ga.: Univ. of Georgia Press, 1989.

Lewis, C. S. *The Allegory of Love*. Oxford: Oxford Univ. Press, 1936.

Lewry, Osmond. "The Miscellaneous and the Anonymous: William of Montoriel, Roger Bourth and the Bodleian MS. Digby 2." *Manuscripta* 24 (1980): 67–75.

Lewry, Osmond. "Robert Kilwardby's Writings on the Logica Vetus Studied with Regard to their Teaching and Method." D. Phil. diss., Oxford University, 1978.

Lieftinck, G. I. "Pour une nomenclature de l'écriture livresque de la période dit gothique: Essai s'appliquant spécialement aux manuscrits originaires des Pays-Bas médiévaux." In *Nomenclature des écritures du IXe au XVIe siècle* (Premier Colloque International de Paléographie Latine), 15–34. Paris, 1954.

Little, Andrew G. *Initia Operum Latinorum quae saeculis xiii, xiv, xv attribuuntur*. Manchester, 1904; repr. New York: Burt Franklin, 1958.

Little, Andrew G. *Studies in English Franciscan History*. Publications of the Univ. of Manchester, Historical Series 29. Manchester, 1917.

Long, R. J. "The Science of Theology according to Richard Fishacre: An Edition of the Prologue to his Commentary on the Sentences." *Mediaeval Studies* 34 (1972): 79–89.

Loserth, Johann. *Shirley's Catalogue of the Extant Latin Works of John Wyclif*. Wyclif Society. Oxford: Oxford Univ. Press, [1925].

Lottin, Odon. "La doctrine morale des mouvements premiers de l'appetit sensitif aux XIIe et XIIIe siècles." *Archives d'histoire doctrinale et littéraire du moyen âge* 6 (1931): 49–173.

Lottin, Odon. "Le traité d'Alain de Lille sur les vertus, les vices et les dons du Saint-Esprit." *Mediaeval Studies* 12 (1950): 20–56.

Lowes, John Livingston. "Chaucer and the Seven Deadly Sins." *PMLA* 30 (1915): 231–71.

Lydgate, John. *The Minor Poems of John Lydgate*. Edited by Henry MacCracken. 2 vols. EETS es 107; EETS os 192. Oxford: Oxford Univ. Press, 1911, 1934.

Lyndwood, William. *Provinciale, seu Constitutiones Angliae*. Oxford, 1679.

Macken, Raymond. *Bibliotheca manuscripta Henrici de Gandavo*. 2 vols. Henrici de Gandavo Opera omnia, vols. 1–2. Leuven: Leuven Univ. Press, and Leiden: Brill, 1979.

Macken, Raymond. "Les corrections d'Henri de Gand à sa Somme." *Recherches de théologie ancienne et médiévale* 44 (1977): 55–100.

Macken, Raymond. "Les corrections d'Henri de Gand à ses Quodlibets." *Recherches de théologie ancienne et médiévale* 40 (1973): 5–51.

Macken, Raymond, co-ordinator. *Henrici de Gandavo Opera omnia*. Vols. 1– . Leuven: Leuven Univ. Press, and Leiden: Brill, 1979– .

Macken, Raymond. "Les sources d'Henri de Gand." *Revue philosophique de Louvain* 76 (1978): 5–28.

Macken, Raymond. "La temporalité radicale de la creature selon Henri de Gand." *Recherches de théologie ancienne et médiévale* 38 (1971): 211–72.

Macken, Raymond. "La théorie de l'illumination divine dans la philosophie d'Henri de Gand." *Recherches de théologie ancienne et médiévale* 39 (1972): 82–112.

Macken, Raymond. "La volonté humaine, faculté plus élevée que l'intelligence selon Henri de Gand." *Recherches de théologie ancienne et médiévale* 42 (1975): 5–51.

Macray, W. D. *Catalogi codicum manuscriptorum Bibliothecae Bodleianæ, pars nona, codices a viro clarissimo Kenelm Digby, Eq. aur., anno 1634 donatos, complectens*. Oxford, 1883.

Mallard, William. "Clarity and Dilemma—the *Forty Sermons* of John Wyclif." In *Contemporary Reflections on the Medieval Christian Tradition: Essays in Honor of Ray C. Petry*, edited by George H. Shriver, 19–38. Durham, NC: Duke Univ. Press, 1974.

Mályusz, E. *Commentarii*. In Johannes de Thurocz, *Chronica Hungarorum*. Vol. 2. Budapest: Akadémiai Kiadó, 1988.

Manly, John M. "The Authorship of *Piers Plowman*, with a Terminal Note on the Lost Leaf." *Modern Philology* 7 (1909): 83–144.

Manly, John M. "The Lost Leaf of 'Piers the Plowman.'" *Modern Philology* 3 (1906): 359–66.

Manly, John M. "*Piers the Plowman* and its Sequence." In *The Cambridge History of English Literature, Volume II: The End of the Middle Ages*, edited by A. W. Ward and A. R. Waller, 1–42. Cambridge: Cambridge Univ. Press, 1908.

Manly, John M., and Edith Rickert. *The Text of the Canterbury Tales*. 8 vols. Chicago: Univ. of Chicago Press, 1940.

Mann, Jill. "The *Speculum Stultorum* and the *Nun's Priest's Tale*." *Chaucer Review* 9 (1975): 262–82.

Manning, S. "The Nun's Priest's Morality and the Medieval Attitude Towards Fables." *JEGP* 59 (1960): 403–16.

Manselli, R. "Chi era Francesco d'Assisi? Discorso Conclusivo." In *Francesco d'Assisi nella Storia. Secoli XIII–XV*. Atti del Primo Convegno di Studi per l'viii Centenario della Nascita di S. Francesco (1182–1982), edited by Servus Gieben, 1:349–59. 2 vols. Roma: Istituto Storico dei Cappuccini, 1983.

Map, Walter. *De Nugis Curialium: Courtiers' Trifles*. Edited and translated by M. R. James, revised by C. N. L. Brooke and R. A. B.

Mynors. Oxford: Clarendon Press, 1983.

Marcett, Mildred E. *Uhtred de Boldon, Friar William Jordan, and Piers Plowman.* New York: The Author, 1938.

Mariani, Ugo. *Chiesa e Stato nei teologi agostiniani del secolo XIV.* Uomini e dottrine, vol. 5. Rome: Edizioni di storia e letteratura, 1957.

Marie de France. *Fables.* Edited by A. Ewert and R. C. Johnston. Blackwell's French Texts. Oxford: Blackwell, 1942.

Marrone, Stephen P. *Truth and Scientific Knowledge in the Thought of Henry of Ghent.* Speculum Anniversary Monographs, vol. 11. Cambridge, Mass.: The Mediaeval Academy of America, 1985.

Matthew, F. D., ed. *The English Works of Wyclif Hitherto Unprinted.* EETS, os 74. 2d rev. ed. London: Kegan Paul, 1902.

Matthew, F. D., ed. "The Trial of Richard Wyche." *English Historical Review* 5 (1890): 530–44.

Maxwell-Lyte, H. C. and M. C. B. Dawes, eds. *The Register of Thomas Bekynton, Bishop of Bath and Wells 1443–1465.* 2 vols. Somerset Record Society, vol. 49. Frome, London: Butler & Tanner, 1934.

McCall, John P. *Chaucer Among the Gods: The Poetics of Classical Myth.* University Park and London: The Pennsylvania State Univ. Press, 1979.

McCormick, Sir William, and Janet E. Heseltine. *The Manuscripts of Chaucer's* Canterbury Tales: *A Critical Description of Their Contents.* Oxford, 1933.

McFarlane, K. B. *John Wycliffe and the Beginnings of English Nonconformity.* London: The English Universities Press, 1952; repr. 1966.

McIntosh, Angus. "Some Notes on the Text of the Middle English Poem *De Tribus Regibus Mortuis.*" *RES* new series 28 (1977): 385–92.

McIntosh, Angus et al. *A Linguistic Atlas of Late Medieval English.* 4 vols. Aberdeen: Aberdeen Univ. Press, 1986.

McLeod, W. "Alban and Amphibal: Some Extant Lives and a Lost Life." *Mediaeval Studies* 42 (1980): 407–30.

Mehl, Dieter. "Weltliche Lyrik im 13. und 14. Jahrhundert." In *Epochen der englischen Lyrik,* edited by Karl Heinz Göller. Düsseldorf: Bagel, 1970.

Michael a S. Joseph. *Bibliographia critica, sacra et prophana... et grandi operi: Adumbratum provectorum Lexicon, sive Idioma Sapientum inscripto, et jam praelo maturo, praemissa.* 4 volumes. Madrid, 1740–42.

Michael of Northgate. *Ayenbite of Inwit*. Edited by Richard Morris. EETS os 23. 1866; reissued, with corrections by Pamela Gradon. London: Oxford Univ. Press, 1965.

Middle English Dictionary. Edited by Hans Kurath et al. Vols. 1–. Ann Arbor: Univ. of Michigan Press, 1952–.

Middleton, Anne. "Two Infinites: Grammatical Metaphor in *Piers Plowman*." *ELH* 39 (1972): 169–88.

Miller, B. D. H. "The Early History of Bodleian MS. Digby 86." *Annuale Mediaevale* 4 (1963): 23–56.

Milton, John. *Complete Poems and Major Prose*. Edited by Merritt Hughes. New York: Odyssey, 1957.

Minieri-Riccio, Camillo. *Genealogia di Carlo I d'Angiò*. Naples, 1878.

Minieri-Riccio, Camillo. *Saggio di codice diplomatico*. Naples, 1878–80.

Minnis, A. J. "The *Accessus* Extended: Henry of Ghent on the Transmission and Reception of Theology." In *Ad Litteram: Authoritative Texts and their Medieval Readers*, edited by Mark D. Jordan and Kent Emery, Jr., 275–326. Notre Dame, Ind.: Univ. of Notre Dame Press, 1992.

Minnis, A. J. " 'Authorial Intention' and 'Literal Sense' in the Exegetical Theories of Richard Fitzralph and John Wyclif: An Essay in the Medieval History of Biblical Hermeneutics." *Proceedings of the Royal Irish Academy* 75, section C, no. 1. (1975): 1–31.

Minnis, A. J. "Chaucer and Comparative Literary Theory." In *New Perspectives in Chaucer Criticism*, edited by D. M. Rose, 53–69. Norman, Okla.: Pilgrim Books, 1981.

Minnis, A. J. *Chaucer and Pagan Antiquity*. Bury St Edmunds: D. S. Brewer, 1982.

Minnis, A. J. *Medieval Theory of Authorship: Scholastic Literary Attitudes in the Later Middle Ages*. 2nd ed. Aldershot: Scolar Press; Philadelphia: Univ. of Pennsylvania Press, 1988.

Minnis, A. J. and A. B. Scott. *Medieval Literary Theory and Criticism c.1100–c.1375: The Commentary Tradition*. Rev. ed. Oxford: Clarendon Press, 1991.

Monti, Gennaro Maria. *La Dominazione angioina in Piemonte*. Biblioteca della Società Storica Subalpina, vol. 116. Turin, 1930.

Moorman, John R. H. *A History of the Franciscan Order From Its Origins to the Year 1517*. Oxford: Clarendon Press, 1968; repr. Chicago: Univ. of Chicago Press, 1988.

Mourin, Louis. *Jean Gerson, predicateur français*. Rijksuniversiteit te Ghent. Werken uitg. door de Faculteit van de Wijsbegeerte en Letteren, vol. 113. Bruges: De Tempel, 1952.

Munk Olsen, Birger. "Les florilèges d'auteurs classiques." In *Les genres littéraires dans les sources théologiques et philosophiques médiévales. Définition, critique et exploitation* (Actes du Colloque international de Louvain-la-Neuve, 25–27 mai 1981), 151–64. Louvain-la-Neuve: Université catholique de Louvain, 1982.

Murphy, James J. *Renaissance Rhetoric: A Short-Title Catalogue of Works on Rhetorical Theory from the Beginning of Printing to AD 1700*. New York: Garland, 1981.

Murphy, James J. *Rhetoric in the Middle Ages: A History of Rhetorical Theory from Saint Augustine to the Renaissance*. Berkeley: Univ. of California Press, 1974.

Muscatine, Charles. *Chaucer and the French Tradition: A Study in Style and Meaning*. Berkeley: Univ. of California Press, 1957.

Muscatine, Charles. "The Locus of Action in Medieval Narrative." *Romance Philology* 17 (1963): 115–22.

Musto, Ronald. "Queen Sancia of Naples (1286–1345) and the Spiritual Franciscans." In *Women of the Medieval World: Essays in Honor of John H. Mundy*, edited by J. Kirchner and S. Wemple, 179–214. Oxford: Blackwell, 1985.

Mynors, R. A. B. "A Fifteenth-Century Scribe: T. Werken." *Transactions of the Cambridge Bibliographical Society* 1 (1949–53): 97–104.

A Myrour to Lewde Men and Wymmen: A Prose Version of the Speculum Vitae, *edited from B. L. MS Harley 45*. Edited by Venetia Nelson. Middle English Texts 14. Heidelberg: Winter, 1981.

Nash, P. W. "Giles of Rome and the Subject of Theology." *Mediaeval Studies* 18 (1956): 61–92.

Neckam, Alexander. *Corrogationes Novi Promethei*. Edited by L. S. Cropp. Ph.D. diss. University of Toronto, 1991.

Neckam, Alexander. *De naturis rerum*. Edited by Thomas Wright. Rolls Series 34. London: Longman, 1863.

Netter, Thomas, of Walden. *Doctrinale antiquitatum fidei Catholicae Ecclesiae*. Edited by F. Bonaventura Blanciotti. 3 vols. Venice, 1757–59; repr. Farnborough, Hants.: Gregg, 1967.

Newhauser, Richard. "Der 'Tractatus moralis de oculo' des Petrus von Limoges und seine *exempla*." In *Exempel und Exempel-samm-*

lungen, edited by Walter Haug and Burghart Wachinger, 95–136. Tübingen: Niemeyer, 1991.

Newhauser, Richard. *The Treatise on Vices and Virtues in Latin and the Vernacular*. Typologie des sources du moyen âge occidental, vol. 68. Turnhout: Brepols, 1993.

Noonan, John T., Jr. *Contraception, A History of Its Treament by the Catholic Theologians and Canonists*. Cambridge, Mass.: Harvard Univ. Press, 1965.

Oldham, J. Basil. *English Blind-stamped Bindings*. Cambridge: Cambridge Univ. Press, 1952.

Oliger, L. "Servasanto da Faenza O.F.M. e il suo 'Liber de Virtutibus et Vitiis.'" In *Miscellanea Francesco Ehrle*, 1, 148–89. Studi e Testi, vol. 37. Rome, 1924.

Orwell, George. *Animal Farm*. New York: Harcourt, Brace and World, 1954.

Osgood, Charles G., ed. *Boccaccio on Poetry*. Princeton: Princeton Univ. Press, 1930.

Ouy, Gilbert. "Autographes calligraphiés et scriptoria d'humanistes en France vers 1400." *Bulletin philologique et historique (jusqu'à 1610) du Comité des travaux historiques et scientifiques* 10 (1963): 891–98.

Owen, Charles A., Jr. "The Alternative Reading of the *Canterbury Tales*: Chaucer's Text and the Early Manuscripts." *PMLA* 97 (1982): 237–50.

Owen, Charles. A., Jr. "The Development of the *Canterbury Tales*." *JEGP* 57 (1958): 449–76.

Owen, Charles A., Jr. "Pre-1450 Manuscripts of the *Canterbury Tales*: Relationships and Significance (Part I)." *Chaucer Review* 23 (1988): 1–29.

Owst, G. R. *Literature and Pulpit in Medieval England*. 2nd ed. Oxford: Blackwell, 1966.

Owst, G. R. *Preaching in Medieval England*. Cambridge Studies in Medieval Life and Thought. Cambridge, 1926; repr. New York: Russell & Russell, 1965.

Parkes, M. B. *English Cursive Book Hands 1250–1500*. Oxford: Oxford Univ. Press, 1969; repr. London: Scolar Press, 1979.

Parkes, M. B. "The Influence of the Concepts of *Ordinatio* and *Compilatio* on the Development of the Book." In *Medieval Learning and Literature: Essays Presented to Richard William Hunt*, edited by J. J. G. Alexander and M. T. Gibson, 115–41. Oxford, 1976.

Pasztor, Edith. *Per la storia di san Ludovico d'Angiò (1274–1297)*. Roma: Istituto Storico Italiano per il Medio Evo, 1955.

Patrologiae Latinae Supplementum. Edited by A. Hamman, O.F.M. 5 vols. Paris, 1958–74.

Patterson, Lee. "Ambiguity and Interpretation: a Fifteenth-Century Reading of *Troilus and Criseyde*." *Speculum* 54 (1979): 287–329.

Patterson, Lee. *Negotiating the Past: The Historical Understanding of Medieval Literature*. Madison, London: Univ. of Wisconsin Press, 1987.

Patterson, Lee. " 'The Parson's Tale' and the Quitting of the 'Canterbury Tales.' " *Traditio* 34 (1978): 331–80.

Paul, J. "Evangelisme et Franciscanisme chez Louis d'Anjou." *Cahiers de Fanjeaux* 8 (Toulouse, 1973): 357–401.

Paul, J. "Saint Louis d'Anjou." *Cahiers de Fanjeaux* 7 (Toulouse, 1972): 59–90.

Paulmier-Foucart, Monique. "La compilation dans le *Speculum historiale* de Vincent de Beauvais: le cas Hugues de Fleury." In *L'historigraphie médiévale en Europe, Paris 29 mars-1er avril 1989*, edited by Jean-Philippe Genet, 51–66. Paris: Editions du Centre national de la recherche scientifique, 1991.

Paulmier-Foucart, Monique. "Ordre encyclopédique et organisation de la matière dans le *Speculum maius* de Vincent de Beauvais." In *L'encyclopédisme: Actes du Colloque de Caen, 12–16 janvier 1987*, edited by A. Becq, 201–26. Paris: Klincksieck, 1991.

Pecheux, Mary Christopher. *Aspects of the Treatment of Death in Middle English Poetry*. Ph.D. diss., Catholic Univ. of America, 1951.

Peraldus, Guilielmus. *Summa virtutum ac vitiorum*. 2 vols. Lugduni, 1668.

Petersen, Kate Oelzner. *The Sources of the Parson's Tale*. Radcliffe College Monographs 12. Boston, Mass.: Ginn, 1901, repr. New York: AMS, 1973.

Petreius, Theodorus. *Bibliotheca Cartusiana, sive Illustrium sacri Cartusiensis ordinis scriptorum catalogus*. Cologne: Antonius Hieratus, 1609; repr. Farnborough-Hants.: Gregg, 1968.

Pfander, H. G. "The Mediæval Friars and Some Alphabetical Reference-Books for Sermons." *Medium Ævum* 3,1 (1934): 19–29.

Piccard, Gerhard. *Die Wasserzeichenkartei Piccard im Hauptstaats-*

archiv Stuttgart (Veröffentlichen de staatlichen Archivverwaltung Baden-Würtemberg). 15 volumes in 22 to date. Stuttgart: Kohlhammer, 1961—.

Pierce the Ploughmans Crede. Edited by Walter W. Skeat. EETS os 30. London: Trübner, 1867.

Pitra, J. B., ed. *Spicilegium Solesmense.* 4 vols. Paris, 1852–58.

Pizzorno, P. Grimaldi. "Chauntecleer's Bad Latin: A Note on Decock-struction." Forthcoming in *Exemplaria.*

Plato. *Timaeus, a Calcidio translatus commentarioque instructus.* Edited by J. H. Waszink. Corpus Platonicum Medii Aevi. Plato latinus, vol. 4. London, Leiden: Brill, 1962.

Pollard, Alfred W., ed. "The Examination of Master William Thorpe." In *Fifteenth Century Prose and Verse*, edited by Alfred W. Pollard, 97–104. Westminster: Constable, 1903.

Pope, Mildred K. *From Latin to Modern French with Especial Consideration of Anglo-Norman. Phonology and Morphology.* 2nd ed. Manchester: Manchester Univ. Press, 1966.

"The Pore Caitif. Edited from MS. Harley 2336 With Introduction and Notes." Edited by Mary Teresa Brady. Ph.D. diss., Fordham Univ., 1954.

Prassel, Peter. *Das Theologieverständnis des Ägidius Romanus, O.E.S.A.* Europäische Hochschulschriften, ser. 23, vol. 201. Frankfurt/M.: Peter Lang, 1983.

Pseudo-Chrysostom. *In Evangelium Matthaei homiliae.* PG 56: 611–946.

Pseudo-Dionysius. *De Coelesti Hierarchia.* PG 3: 119–369.

Pseudo-Dionysius. *De Divinis Nominibus.* PG 3: 585–996.

Pseudo-Dionysius. *De Ecclesiastica Hierarchia.* PG 3: 369–584.

Ptolomeus of Lucca. *Historia ecclesiastica nova.* Edited by L. A. Muratori. *Scriptores rerum Italicarum*, vol. 11. Milan, 1727.

Quintilian. *Quintilian's Institutes of Oratory.* Trans. John Selby Watson. London: George Bell and Sons, 1907.

Raby, F. J. E. *A History of Christian-Latin Poetry From the Beginnings to the Close of the Middle Ages.* 2nd ed. Oxford: Clarendon Press, 1953.

Raimundus de Pennaforte. *Summa de Paenitentia.* Edited by Xaverio Ochoa and Aloisio Diez. Universa Bibliotheca Iuris, Instituto Iuridico Claretiano, volumen 1, tomus B. Rome, 1976.

Raymo, Robert R. "Works of Religious and Philosophical Instruction." In *A Manual of the Writings in Middle English 1050– 1500.* Vol. 7, edited by A. E. Hartung, 2255–2378, 2467–2582. New Haven, CT: Connecticut Academy of Arts and Sciences, 1986.

The Registrum antiquissimum of the Cathedral Church of Lincoln. Edited by C. W. Foster and Kathleen Major. 10 vols. Publications of the Lincoln Record Society, vols. 27, 29, 32, 34, 41, 42, 46, 51, 62, 67. Hereford: Hereford Times, 1958.

Reichl, Karl. *Religiöse Dichtung im englischen Hochmittelalter: Untersuchung und Edition der Handschrift B.14.39 des Trinity College in Cambridge.* Münchener Universitäts-Schriften, Texte und Untersuchungen zur Englischen Philologie, vol. 1. Munich: Fink, 1973.

Reiss, E. "Dusting Off the Cobwebs: A Look at Chaucer's Lyrics." *Chaucer Review* 1 (1968): 55–65.

Rhodes, J. "Sixteenth-Century Bed-Making." *S. Chad's College [Durham] Magazine* 36 (1978): 6–8.

Riccio, Michele. *De regibus Ungarie.* Basle, 1534.

Rickert, E. "A Leaf from a 14th Century Letter Book." *Modern Philology* 25 (1927): 249–55.

Rieger, Dietmar. "Die altprovenzalische Lyrik." In *Lyrik des Mittelalters.* Vol. 1, edited by Heinz Bergner, 197–390. Stuttgart: Reclam, 1983.

Riehle, Wolfgang. *The Middle English Mystics.* Translated by Bernard Strandring. London, Boston: Routledge and Kegan Paul, 1981.

Riverside Chaucer. See Chaucer, Geoffrey.

Robbins, Rossell Hope. "The Authors of the Middle English Religious Lyrics." *JEGP* 39 (1940): 230–38.

Robbins, Rossell Hope. "Chaucer's To Rosemounde." *Studies in the Literary Imagination* 4 (1971): 73–81.

Robbins, Rossell Hope, ed. *Secular Lyrics of the XIVth and XVth Centuries.* 2nd. ed. Oxford: Clarendon Press, 1955.

Robbins, Rossell Hope. "Signs of Death in Middle English." *Mediaeval Studies* 32 (1970): 282–98.

Robbins, Rossell Hope and John L. Cutler. *The Index of Middle English Verse. Supplement.* Lexington: Univ. of Kentucky Press, 1965.

Robertson, D. W., Jr. *A Preface to Chaucer.* Princeton: Princeton Univ. Press, 1962; repr. 1970.

Robertson, D. W., Jr. and Bernard Huppé. *Piers Plowman and Scriptural Tradition.* Princeton: Princeton Univ. Press, 1951.

Robson, J. A. *Wyclif and the Oxford Schools: The Relation of the "Summa de ente" to Scholastic Debates at Oxford in the Later Fourteenth Century*. Cambridge: Cambridge Univ. Press, 1961.

Rolle, Richard, of Hampole. *English Writings of Richard Rolle, Hermit of Hampole*. Edited by Hope Emily Allen. Oxford: Clarendon Press, 1931.

Römer, Franz. *Die handschriftliche Überlieferung der Werke des heiligen Augustinus*, Bd. II.1 *Grossbritannien und Irland: werkverzeichnis*. Vienna, 1972.

Roman de Renart (Branches I, II, III, IV, V, VIII, X, XV). Edited by Jean Dufournet (after E. Martin). Paris: Garnier-Flammarion, 1970.

Le Roman de Renart le Contrefait. Edited by Gaston Raynaud and Henri Lemaitre. Paris, 1914; repr. Geneva: Slatkine, 1975.

Roney, Lois. *Chaucer's Knight's Tale and Theories of Scholastic Psychology*. Tampa: Univ. of South Florida Press, 1990.

Rouse, Mary A. and Richard H. Rouse. "Florilegia of Patristic Texts." In *Les genres littéraires dans les sources théologiques et philosophiques médiévales. Définition, critique, exploitation* (Actes du Colloque international de Louvain-la-Neuve, 25–27 mai 1981), 165–80. Louvain-la-Neuve: Université catholique de Louvain, 1982.

Rouse, Richard H. and Mary A. Rouse. "Franciscans and Books: Lollard Accusation and Franciscan Response." *Studies in Church History*, subsidia 5 (1987): 364–84.

Rowland, Beryl. "Sermon and Penitential in the Parson's Tale and Their Effect on Style." *Florilegium* 9 (1987): 125–45.

Russell, George H. "The Poet as Reviser: The Metamorphosis of the Confession of the Seven Deadly Sins in *Piers Plowman*." In *Acts of Interpretation: The Text in its Contexts 700–1600. Essays in Medieval and Renaissance Literature in Honor of E. Talbot Donaldson*, edited by Mary J. Carruthers and Elizabeth D. Kirk, 53–65. Norman: Pilgrim Press, 1982.

Russell, Josiah Cox. *Dictionary of Writers of Thirteenth Century England*. Bulletin of the Institute of Historical Research, Special Supplement 3. London: Longman, 1936; repr. New York, 1971.

Saggese, Alessandra Perriccioli. "Miniature umbro-assisiati nella Napoli angioina: il Breviario I.B.20 della Biblioteca Nazionale." *Prospettiva* 53–56 (1988): 112–18.

Salter, H. E., ed. *Snappe's Formulary and Other Records*. Oxford: Clarendon Press, 1924.

Salter, Elizabeth, ed. *Chaucer: The Knight's Tale and the Clerk's Tale*. New York: Barron's, 1962.

Sayce, Olive. "Chaucer's 'Retractions': The Conclusion of the *Canterbury Tales* and Its Place in the Literary Tradition," *Medium Ævum* 40 (1971): 230–248.

Scase, Wendy. *Piers Plowman and the New Anticlericalism*. Cambridge: Cambridge Univ. Press, 1989.

Schmeller, A. G., and G. Meyer. *Schedarium initia amplectens praesertim ex codicibus Monacensibus Gottingensibus Bruxellensibus collecta*. 2 volumes (Appendix to Hauréau, *Initia operum scriptorum Latinorum Medii potissimum Aevi*). Turnhout: Brepols, 1974.

Schneider, Robert J. "Vincent of Beauvais' *Opus universale de statu principis*: A Reconstruction of its History and Contents." In *Vincent de Beauvais: Intentions et réceptions d'une oeuvre encyclopédique au Moyen Âge*, edited by Monique Paulmier-Foucart, Serge Lusignan, Alain Nadeau, 285–99. Montreal, 1990.

Schneyer, Johannes Baptist. *Geschichte der katholischen Predigt*. Freiburg i. Br.: Herder, 1969.

Schneyer, Johannes Baptist. *Repertorium der lateinischen Sermones des Mittelalters fuer die Zeit von 1150–1350*. 9 vols. Beiträge zur Geschichte der Philosophie und Theologie des Mittelalters, vol. 43. Münster: Aschendorff, 1969–80.

Schneyer, Johannes Baptist. *Wegweiser zu lateinischen Predigtreihen des Mittelalters*. Bayerische Akademie der Wissenschaften, Veröffentlichungen der Kommission für die Herausgabe ungedruckter Texte aus der mittelalterlichen Geisteswelt, vol. 1. Munich: Bayerische Akademie der Wissenschaften, 1965.

Scholz, Richard. *Die Publizistik zur Zeit Philipps des Schönen und Bonifaz' VIII*. Kirchenrechtliche Abhandlungen, vol. 6, Heft 8. Stuttgart: Enke, 1903.

Scott, A. B., Deirdre Baker, A. G. Rigg, "The Biblical Epigrams of Hildebert of Le Mans: A Critical Edition." *Mediaeval Studies* 47 (1985): 272–316

Scripta Leonis, Rufini, et Angeli, sociorum S. Francisci. Edited and translated by Rosalind B. Brooke. Oxford: Clarendon, 1970.

Sears, Elizabeth. *The Ages of Man: Medieval Interpretations of the Life Cycle*. Princeton: Princeton Univ. Press, 1986.

Seppelt, F. X. "Die Akten des Kanonisationsprozesses in dem Kodex zu Sulmona." In *Monumenta Coelestiniana*, 209–334. Paderborn, 1921.

Seynaeve, Koen. "Jacobus van Gruitrode." In *Historia et Spiritualitas Cartusiensis. Colloqui Quarti Internationalis Acta: Gandavi-Antverpiae-Brugis 16–19 Sept. 1982*, edited by Jan De Grauwe, 313–36. Destelbergen, 1983.

Shannon, Edgar Finley. *Chaucer and the Roman Poets*. New York, 1929; repr. 1964.

Shaw, Judith. "Corporeal and Spiritual Homicide, the Sin of Wrath, and the 'Parson's Tale.' " *Traditio* 38 (1982): 281–300.

Silverstein, Theodore, ed. *English Lyrics before 1500*. Evanston: Northwestern Univ. Press, 1971.

Sir Gawain and the Green Knight. Edited by J. R. R. Tolkien and E. V. Gordon. 2nd ed., edited by Norman Davis. Oxford: Clarendon Press, 1967.

Skelton, John. *Complete English Poems*. Edited by John Scattergood. New Haven: Yale Univ. Press, 1983.

Smalley, Beryl. "The Bible and Eternity: John Wyclif's Dilemma." *Journal of the Warburg and Courtauld Institutes* 27 (1964): 73–89.

Smalley, Beryl. *The Study of the Bible in the Middle Ages*. Notre Dame, Ind.: Univ. of Notre Dame Press, 1964.

Smith, Ben Jr. *Traditional Imagery of Charity in Piers Plowman*. The Hague: Mouton, 1966.

Sonet, J., S.J. *Répertoire d'Incipit de Prières en Ancien Français*. Société de Publications Romanes et Françaises, vol. 54. Geneva: E. Droz, 1956.

Speciale, Niccolò. *Historia sicula*. Edited by L.A. Muratori. Vol. 10 of *Scriptores rerum Italicarum*. Milan, 1723–51.

Speculum Christiani. Edited by Gustav Holmstedt. EETS os 182. London: Oxford Univ. Press, 1933.

Spencer, Helen L. "The Fortunes of a Lollard Sermon-Cycle in the Later Fifteenth Century." *Mediaeval Studies* 48 (1986): 352–96.

Statutes of the Realm. 9 vols. London: Eyre and Strahan, 1810–22; repr. London: Dawsons, 1963.

Stegmüller, Fridericus. *Repertorium Biblicum Medii Aevi*. 11 vols. Madrid: Consejo Superior de Investigaciones Cientificas, 1950–80; repr. 1989.

Stemmler, Theo. *Die englischen Liebesgedichte des Ms. Harl. 2253*. Diss., Universität Bonn. Bonn, 1962.

Stemmler, Theo. "My Fair Lady: Parody in 15th-Century English Lyrics." In *Medieval Studies Conference Aachen 1983*, edited by Wolf-Dietrich Bald and Horst Weinstock, 205–13. Bamberger Beiträge zur englischen Sprachwissenschaft, vol. 15. Frankfurt/M., New York: P. Lang, 1984.

Stemmler, Theo. "The Problem of Parody: Annot and John, for Example." In *Genres, Themes, and Images in English Literature*, edited by Piero Boitani and Anna Torti, 156–65. Tübingen: Narr, 1988.

Stemmler, Theo. Review of *Poets at Play: Irony and Parody in the Harley Lyrics*, by D. J. Ransom. *Studies in the Age of Chaucer* 8 (1986): 233–36.

Stevens, J. "Angelus ad virginem: The History of a Medieval Song." In *Medieval Studies for J. A. W. Bennett. Aetatis Suae LXX*, edited by P. L. Heyworth, 297–328. Oxford: Clarendon Press, 1981.

Stevens, J. *Words and Music in the Middle Ages. Song, Narrative, Dance and Drama, 1050–1350*. Cambridge Studies in Music. Cambridge, New York: Cambridge Univ. Press, 1986.

Stornajolo, Cosimo. *Inventarium codicum manuscriptorum latinorum archivii basilicae S. Petri in Vaticano*. Vol. 2. Città del Vaticano, 1968.

A Summary Catalogue of Western Manuscripts in the Bodleian Library at Oxford. 7 vols. Vols. 2–6, edited by Falconer Madan and H. H. E. Craster. Oxford: Clarendon Press, 1895–1953.

Szövérffy, Joseph. *Die Annalen der lateinischen Hymnendichtung. Ein Handbuch*. 2 vols. Die Lyrische Dichtung des Mittelalters. Berlin: E. Schmidt, 1964–65.

Tachau, Katherine H. *Vision and Certitude in the Age of Ockham: Optics, Epistemology and the Foundations of Semantics 1250–1345*. Studien und Texte zur Geistesgeschichte des Mittelalters, vol. 22. Leiden, New York: Brill, 1988.

Talbert, Ernest William, ed. "A Lollard Chronicle of the Papacy." *Journal of English and Germanic Philology* 41 (1942): 163–93.

Talbert, Ernest William and S. Harrison Thomson. "Wyclyf and His Followers." In *A Manual of the Writings in Middle English 1050–1500*. Volume 2, edited by J. Burke Severs, 517–33. Hamden, Conn.: Connecticut Academy of Arts and Sciences, 1970.

Tale of Beryn. Edited by F. J. Furnivall and W. G. Stone. EETS es 105. London, 1909.

Tatlock, J. S. P., and Arthur G. Kennedy. *A Concordance to the Complete Works of Geoffrey Chaucer and to the Romance of the Rose.* Washington, D.C., 1927.

Tavormina, M. Teresa. "*Piers Plowman* and the Liturgy of St. Lawrence: Composition and Revision in Langland's Poetry." *Studies in Philology* 84 (1987): 245–71.

Taxatio ecclesiastica Angliae et Walliae auctoritate P. Nicholai IV. Edited by T. Astle, S. Ayscough and J. Caley. London, 1802.

Textus Biblie cum Glossa ordinaria, Nicolai de Lyra Postilla, etc. 7 vols. Basel, 1506–8.

Théry, P. G. "An Unedited Text of Robert Grosseteste on the Subject-Nature of Theology." *Revue neoscolastique de philosophie* 36 (1934): 172–90.

Thomae de Chobham Summa confessorum. Edited by F. Broomfield. Analecta mediaevalia Namurcensia, vol. 25. Louvain: Editions Nauwelaerts, Paris: Beatrice Nauwelaerts, 1968.

Thomas Hemerken à Kempis. *Hospitale pauperum.* Edited by M. J. Pohl in *Thomae Hemerken a Kempis Opera omnia,* vol. 4. Freiburg i. Br., 1918.

Thomson, Williell R. *The Latin Writings of John Wyclyf: An Annotated Catalog.* Subsidia Mediaevalia, vol. 14. Toronto: Pontifical Institute of Mediaeval Studies, 1983.

Thorndike, L. and P. Kibre. *A Catalogue of Incipits of Mediaeval Scientific Writings in Latin.* Publications of the Mediaeval Academy of America, vol. 29. Rev. and augmented ed. Cambridge, Mass.: Mediaeval Academy of America, 1963.

Thynne, Francis. *Animadversions uppon the Annotacions and Corrections of Some Imperfections of Impressiones of Chaucer's Workes* (1598). Revised edition by F. J. Furnivall. EETS os 9. London: Trübner, 1875 (for 1865).

Townsend, D. and A. G. Rigg, "Medieval Latin Poetic Anthologies (V): Matthew Paris' Anthology of Henry of Avranches. (Cambridge, University Library MS. Dd.11.78)." *Mediaeval Studies* 49 (1987): 352–90.

A Tretyse of Gostly Batayle. In *Yorkshire Writers. Richard Rolle of Hampole and His Followers,* edited by C. Horstman, 2:420–36. New York: Macmillan, 1896.

Tristram, Philippa. *Figures of Life and Death in Medieval English Literature.* London: Elek, 1976.

Tyrwhitt, Thomas, ed. *The Canterbury Tales of Chaucer*. 2nd ed., 2 vols. Oxford: Clarendon Press, 1798.

Ughelli, Ferdinando. *Italia sacra*. 10 vols. Venezia, 1717–21.

Uhlirz, Karl and Mathilde. *Handbuch der Geschichte Oesterreich-Ungarns*. Vol. 1. 2nd rev. ed. by Mathilde Uhlirz. Graz: Hermann Boehlaus, 1963.

Vasta, Edward. "To Rosemounde: Chaucer's 'Gentil' Dramatic Monologue." In *Chaucerian Problems and Perspectives*, edited by Edward Vasta and Z. P. Thundy. Notre Dame, Ind.: Univ. of Notre Dame Press, 1979.

Vauchez, André. *La sainteté en occident aux derniers siècles du moyen âge*. Bibliothèque des Écoles françaises d'Athènes et de Rome, vol. 241. Rome: École Française de Rome, 1981.

Venditti, Arnaldo. "Urbanistica e architettura angioina." In *Storia di Napoli*, vol. 3. Naples: Edizioni scientifiche, 1969.

Verjans, Matthaeus, O.F.M.. "Jacobus van Gruitrode, Karthuizer (†1475)." *Ons Geestelijk Erf* 5 (1931): 435–69.

Vincent of Beauvais, *Speculum Historiale*. Vol. 4 of *Speculum Maius*. Graz: Akad. Druck-und Verlag, 1964–65.

von Nolcken, Christina, ed. *The Middle English Translation of the Rosarium theologie*. Middle English Texts, vol. 10. Heidelberg: Winter, 1979.

von Nolcken, Christina. "Notes on Lollard Citation of John Wyclif's Writings. *Journal of Theological Studies* new series 39 (1988): 411–37.

von Nolcken, Christina. "*Piers Plowman*, The Wycliffites, and *Pierce the Plowman's Creed*." *The Yearbook of Langland Studies* 2 (1988): 71–102.

von Nolcken, Christina. "An Unremarked Group of Wycliffite Sermons in Latin." *Modern Philology* 83 (1986): 233–49.

von Nolcken, Christina. "Wyclif in our Times: The Wyclif Sexcentenary, 1984." *The Yearbook of Langland Studies* 2 (1988): 143–54.

Vulgate Bible. Edited by Alberto Colunga and Laurentio Turrado. Madrid: Biblioteca de Autores Cristianos, 1965.

Wadding, Luke, O.F.M. *Scriptores Ordinis Minorum*. 3 volumes. Rome, 1906–21.

Wager, W. J. "'Fleshly Love' in Chaucer's *Troilus*." *Modern Language Review* 34 (1939): 62–66.

Walther, Hans. *Initia carminum ac versuum medii aevi posterioris latinorum*. Carmina medii aevi posterioris latina, vol. 1. 2nd ed. Göttingen: Vandenhoeck & Ruprecht, 1969.

Wang, Andreas. *Der "Miles Christianus" im 16. und 17. Jahrhundert und seine mittelalterliche Tradition*. Mikrokosmos, vol 1. Bern: Herbert Lang, Frankfurt/M.: Peter Lang, 1975.

Wenzel, Siegfried. "Chaucer's Parson's Tale 'Every Tales Strengthe.'" In *Europäische Lehrdichtung. Festschrift für Walter Naumann zum 70. Geburtstag*, edited by Hans Gerd Rötzer and Herbert Walz, 86–98. Darmstadt: Wissenschaftliche Buchgesellschaft, 1981.

Wenzel, Siegfried. "The English Verses in the *Fasciculus morum*." In *Chaucer and Middle English Studies in Honour of Rossell Hope Robbins*, edited by Beryl Rowland, 230–48. [Kent, Ohio]: Kent State Univ. Press, 1974.

Wenzel, Siegfried, ed. and trans. *Fasciculus morum: A Fourteenth-Century Preacher's Handbook*. University Park: Pennsylvania State Univ. Press, 1989.

Wenzel, Siegfried. "The Moor Maiden—A Contemporary View." *Speculum* 49 (1974): 69–74.

Wenzel, Siegfried. "Notes on the Parson's Tale." *Chaucer Review* 16 (1982): 237–56.

Wenzel, Siegfried. "Poets, Preachers, and the Plight of Literary Critics." *Speculum* 60 (1985): 343–63.

Wenzel, Siegfried. *Preachers, Poets and the Early English Lyric*. Princeton: Princeton Univ. Press, 1986.

Wenzel, Siegfried. "Robert Grosseteste's Treatise on Confession, *Deus est*." *Franciscan Studies* 30 (1970): 218–93.

Wenzel, Siegfried. *The Sin of Sloth: Acedia in Medieval Thought and Literature*. Chapel Hill: Univ. of North Carolina Press, 1967.

Wenzel, Siegfried. "The Source of Chaucer's Seven Deadly Sins." *Traditio* 30 (1974): 351–78.

Wenzel, Siegfried, ed. *Summa virtutum de remediis anime*. The Chaucer Library. Athens: Univ. of Georgia Press, 1984.

Wenzel, Siegfried. "The Three Enemies of Man." *Mediaeval Studies* 29 (1967): 47–66.

Wenzel, Siegfried. "Unrecorded Middle-English Verses." *Anglia* 92 (1974): 55–78.

Wenzel, Siegfried. *Verses in Sermons: "Fasciculus Morum" and its Middle English Poems*. The Mediaeval Academy of America Publication 87. Cambridge, Mass.: The Mediaeval Academy of America, 1978.

Wenzel, Siegfried. "Vices, Virtues, and Popular Preaching." In *Medieval and Renaissance Studies*, edited by Dale B. J. Randall, 28–54. Durham, N.C.: Duke Univ. Press, 1976.

"Whosoo hym be thowght." In *The Middle English Poem, Erthe upon Erthe*, edited by Hilda M.R. Murray, 36–37. EETS os 141. London: Oxford Univ. Press, 1911, repr. 1964.

Wilks, Michael. "*Reformatio Regni*: Wyclif and Hus as Leaders of Religious Protest Movements." *Studies in Church History* 9 (Oxford, 1972): 109–30.

Wilson, Edward. *A Descriptive Index of the English Lyrics in John of Grimestone's Preaching Book*. Medium Aevum Monographs, new series 2. Oxford: Blackwell, 1973.

Wimsatt, James I. "Guillaume de Machaut and Chaucer's Love Lyrics." *Medium Ævum* 47 (1978): 66–87.

Wolpers, Th. "Zum Andachtsbild in der mittelenglischen religiösen Lyrik." In *Chaucer und seine Zeit. Symposion für Walter F. Schirmer*, edited by A. Esch, 293–336. Buchreihe der Anglia, vol. 14. Tübingen: Niemeyer, 1968.

Wooden, Warren W. *John Foxe*. Twayne's English Authors Series, vol. 345. Boston: Twayne, 1983.

Wooldridge, H. E. and H. V. Hughes, eds. *Early English Harmony from the 10th to the 15th Century*. 2 vols. London: Quaritch, 1897–1913.

Woolf, Rosemary. *The English Religious Lyric in the Middle Ages*. Oxford: Clarendon Press, 1968.

Workman, Herbert B. *John Wyclif: A Study of the English Medieval Church*. 2 vols. Oxford: Clarendon Press, 1926.

Wright, T. and J. O. Halliwell, eds. *Reliquiæ antiquæ*. 2 vols. London: William Pickering, 1841–43; repr. New York, 1966.

Wurtele, Douglas. "The Penitence of Geoffrey Chaucer." *Viator* 11 (1980): 335–59.

Wyclif, Johannes. *Johann Wiclif's De veritate sacrae scripturae*, edited by Rudolf Buddensieg. 3 vols. Wyclif Society. London: Trübner, 1905–7.

Wyclif, Johannes. *John Wyclif's Polemical Works in Latin*. Edited by Rudolf Buddensieg. 2 vols. Wyclif Society. London: Trübner, 1883.

Wyclif, Johannes. *The Last Age of the Church*. Edited by James Henthorn Todd. Dublin: Univ. of Dublin Press, 1840.

Wyclif, Johannes. *Opera Minora*. Edited by Johann Loserth. Wyclif Society. London: C. K. Paul, 1913.

Wyclif, Johannes. *Tractatus de ecclesia*. Edited by Johann Loserth. Wyclif Society. London: Trübner, 1886.

Wyclif, Johannes. *Tractatus de universalibus*. Edited by Ivan J. Mueller and translated by Anthony Kenny. 2 vols. Oxford: Clarendon Press, 1985.

Yates, Frances A. *The Art of Memory*. Chicago: Univ. of Chicago Press, 1966, repr. 1984.

Yorkshire Writers: Richard Rolle of Hampole and his Followers. 2 vols. Edited by C. Horstman. London, 1895.

Young, Karl. *The Drama of the Medieval Church*. 2 vols. Oxford: Clarendon Press, 1933.

Yunck, John. "Satire." In *A Companion to Piers Plowman*, edited by John A. Alford, 135–54. Berkeley: Univ. of California Press, 1988.

Zafarana, Zelina. "La Predicazione Francescana." In *Da Gregorio VII a Bernardino da Siena. Saggi di Storia Medievale*, edited by O. Capitani et al. Quaderni del "Centro per il Collegamento degli Studi Medievali e Umanistici nell' Università di Perugia," vol. 17. Firenze: La Nuova Italia Editrice, 1987.

Zumkeller, Adolar. "Hollen (Gottschalk)." *Dictionnaire de spiritualité ascétique et mystique: Doctrine et histoire* 7 (Paris, 1969): 588–90.

Zumkeller, Adolar. *Manuskripte von Werken der Autoren des Augustiner-Eremitenordens in mitteleuropäischen Bibliotheken* (Cassiciacum 20). Würzburg: Augustinus, 1966.

Index

Abbey of the Holy Ghost, 179
Abelard, Peter, 122n
Abimelech, 38
Adam, 29, 30, 31, 34, 37, 111, 168, 170n, 172
Adams, Robert, 140
Aegidius Romanus. *See* Giles of Rome
Aesop, 36n, 38, 39
Ages of humankind, 255; four, 180; six, 5, 172–76; six, games of each, 165
Alanus de Insulis (Alain de Lille), *Anticlaudianus*, 64, 78, 122n
Alban, St.: monastic center, 184, 305n; verse life of, 162
Alberigo, Josepho, 153n
Albertano da Brescia, 124, 128, 130, 131, 133; *De arte loquendi et tacendi*, 4, 119, 121, 123; *Liber consolationis et consilii*, 123
Albertus Magnus, 246
Aldobrandino da Toscanella, 265, 266
Alexander of Hales, 231; *Summa theologica*, 231–34
Alexander of Stavensby (Bishop of Coventry), 146
Alexander the Great, 41, 42
Alford, John A., 4, 87, 96n, 97–117, 106n, 116n, 124–26
Aligheri, Dante, 27, 29, 30n, 32, 82, 96, 278; *Divine Comedy*, 64; *Inferno* XXXIII, 32
Alisaunder, 15

Allegoresis, 9; influence on Langland, 99; of Christian knight, 325–26; of ecclesiastical dress, 324–25; of Franciscan appearance (tunic, tonsure, staff, bare feet), 324–27; of shield, 9, 326–29. *See also* Exegesis, Interpretation
Allegory, 5, 35, 41; mystical and moral, 179; of bed, 179–90; of feast of wisdom, 99
Allen, Judson Boyce, 37n, 103, 119n, 120n, 124n, 125n
Allen, Hope Emily, 181n
Alter, Robert, 40n
Ambrose of Milan, 99, 100, 101, 102, 107n, 109, 117, 246, 256; *De officiis ministrorum*, 99–100, 102, 107n, 109
Anchoress, 183
Anderson, David, 8, 44n, 275–95
Angevin: court, 275–76, 283; empire, 278; model of kingship, 281
Anglo-Norman, 9, 321, 333
Anselm of Canterbury, 109n, 246
Anthony of Padua, 267n
Antichrist, 197, 204; bishops of, 196; church of, 204; clerks of, 196, 197n; sinful tongue users as heralds of, 140
Anticlaudianus. *See* Alanus de Insulis
Antiochenus, Pseudo-Theophilus, 246n
Antonius Rampegolus de Ianua, 256;

Biblia aurea, 256n; *Compendium morale,* 256n
Apostles' Creed, 135, 148
Aquinas, Thomas, 37, 37n, 209, 224n, 234n, 246, 248n, 264–66, 287n; *Summa theologica,* 224n, 263, 265
Aristotle, 39, 122, 214n, 225, 245, 265, 273n, 303; Aristotelianism, 209; Aristotelian prologue, 210; *Categories,* 303; *De interpretatione,* 303; *Metaphysica,* 214n; *Meteorologica,* 270–71; *Nicomachean Ethics,* 218, 225; *Organon,* 314; *Rhetorica,* 225; theory of causality, 235
Armstrong, Lawrin, 161n
Arnold, Thomas, 196, 203n
Articuli orthodoxam religionem, sanctamque fidem respicientes, 248n
Arundel, Archbishop, 181, 199
Asprenus, 279
Astle, T., 155n
Aston, Margaret, 192n, 200n
Astronomy, 28, 64, 314
Athenaeum, The, 12
Auctoritates Aristotelis, 271
Audelay, John, 181
Audience, medieval theories of, 192n
Auerbach, Erich, 37
Augustine of Hippo, 30, 68, 122, 143n, 161, 163n, 164, 185n, 197n, 223, 224, 228n, 233, 235, 246, 256, 271, 282; *Confessiones,* 217n; *Contra Adimantum,* 215n; *Contra mendacium,* 215, 216n; *De civitate Dei,* 173n, 216, 173n; *De diversis quaestionibus,* 215n; *De doctrina Christiana* 6, 123, 210, 215, 218–26, 230, 271; *De sermone Domini in monte,* 5, 163, 164n, 166n, 167n, 169n, 170; *De vera religione,* 215; *Enarrationes in Psalmos,* 216n; *Epistulae,* 224n; *In Ioannis Evangelium tractatus,* 228n, 234n
Augustinian: canons, 185, 241; convent (Naples), 275–76; friars, 185; hermits, 278; school of theology (Paris), 275, 284
Auksi, Peter, 194n

Ayenbite of Inwit. See Michael of Northgate
Ayscough, S., 155n

Baker, Deirdre, 162n
Balduinus ab Amsterdam, 267n
Bale, John, 154n, 155n
Baptism, 150–51
Barker-Benfield, B. C., 320n
Barking, Abbey, 183
Barney, Stephen, 96n, 120n
Barnum, Priscilla, 325n
Bartholomeus Anglicus, *De proprietatibus rerum,* 256
Bartholomeus Bulcani de Neapolis, 284
Bartholus, 285
Basil, 246, 256
Bataillon, L. J., 268n
Battle of Maldon, 46
Bazire, J., 184n
Becket, Thomas, verse life of, 162
Bede, the Venerable, 46, 75n, 108n, 165, 173, 246; *De temporum ratione,* 173n
Bekynton, Thomas, *Register,* 203n
Benedict of Nursia, 252; *Regula,* 246
Benedictine monasticism, 241, 314n
Benedict XI, Pope, 283n
Benevento, archbishopric of, 275
Bennett, J. A. W., 89, 192n, 299n, 330n
Bennett, J. A. W., and G. V. Smithers, 297n
Bennett, Nicholas, 157n
Benson, Robert L., 157n
Benson, Larry D., 79
Beowulf, 3, 43–59. See also Epic
Bernard of Clairvaux, 246, 250, 254, 256
Bersuire, Pierre (Petrus Berchorius), *Ovidius Moralizatus,* 38
Bertaux, E., 294n
Berthold of Regensburg, *Sermones rusticani,* 266n, 267n
Bestul, Thomas, 65n
Bible: **Genesis,** 26, 32; 27.27, 290; **Exodus** 22.27, 334n; **Judges** 9.7–

15, 38; **1 Samuel** 17.32, 334n; 17.40, 334n; **2 Samuel** 14.26, 334n; 23.22, 334n; **Judith** 8.6, 152; **Job** 7.1, 325n; 14.10, 266n; 27.19, 272; 31.31, 113; **Psalms** 6.7, 187; 13.1, 117n; 22, 116; 22.4, 116n, 117n; 22.5, 116; 39.13, 334n; 41.4, 116, 117n; 50.8, 89; 68.10, 36; 106.4, 111; 111.9, 115; **Proverbs** 9.1, 99, 100n; 9.2, 116; 11.22, 68; 11.26, 106; 22.10, 117n, 129; 23, 4, 99–116; 23.1, 100–101, 103, 116; 23.2, 107; 23.16, 107; 23.19–21, 109, 110, 112, 114; 23.23, 105–6; 23.26, 107; 23.31–32, 107; **Song of Songs** 1.15, 5, 179, 189; 4.2, 215n, 223; **Wisdom** 1.3, 187; 7.22, 231; 10.10, 111; **Ecclesiasticus**, 34; 2.1, 325n; 7.40, 334n; 10.15, 150; 11.9, 131n; 21, 122n; 31.8, 289; 31.10, 289; **Isaiah** 12.6, 190; **Lamentations** 3.65, 334n; **Daniel** 5.10, 282; **Hosea** 4.11, 113; **Matthew** 5.3, 197n; 5.45, 228; 6.9–17, 148; 6.25, 117n; 6.29, 265n; 7.6, 222, 227; 9.23–26, 170; 10.8, 105; 10.16, 197n; 10.22, 186; 11.29, 111; 13.47, 227–28; 20.16, 264; 23.13, 214, 216; 24.13, 186; 28.19–20, 227; **Luke** 7.12–16, 170; 9.59–60, 170; **John**, 26; 11.1–44, 170; 15.12, 111; 16.12, 230; 20.15–17, 307; **Acts** 9.8, 272; **Romans** 12.3, 225; 15.4, 36; **1 Corinthians** 1.17, 220; 3.1, 225; 7.2, 264n; 15.10, 8, 268; 15.14, 139; **2 Corinthians** 6.8, 197n; **Galatians** 5.15, 113; **Ephesians** 4.23, 107n; 5.3–5, 124n; 6.10–17, 325; 6.16, 334n; **Colossians** 3.8, 124n; 3.20, 111; **1 Thessalonians** 4.3, 264; 5.17, 186; 5.22, 187; **2 Thessalonians** 3.11, 136; **1 Timothy** 5.17, 143; 6.9, 334n; 6.10, 150; **2 Timothy** 2.3–5, 325n; **James** 1, 125; 2.1, 134; 2.26, 125; 3, 123, 125, 126, 133; 3.6, 4; 3.6–8, 120; **1 Peter** 4.8, 187; **2 Peter** 2.4, 334n; **1 John** 2.16, 150; 4.16, 111

Bible: God as *auctor* of, 214, 235; multiple mode of biblical discourse, 231–32, 234–35; unity of, 233
Bieler, L., 271n, 272n
Birgitta, St. (of Sweden), 182; *Liber revelationum*, 254
Birney, Earle, 11n
Bishops, 8, 158; and pastoral literature, 146; in *Piers Plowman*, 91; office of, 289–91, 293
Blaise, Albert, 109
Blake, Norman F., 11n, 19n
Blanche, sister of St. Louis of Anjou, 292
Blanciotti, Bonaventura, 200n
Blodgett, James E., 63n
Bloomfield, Morton, 120n, 153n, 246n, 247n, 252n, 256n, 321, 322n, 323
Blume, C., and Dreves, G. M., 308n
Blythe, Joan Heiges, 4, 119–42, 126n, 133, 139n
Boccaccio, Giovanni, 27, 33, 38, 51, 56; *Ameto*, 75–76, 78, 79n; *Genealogie Deorum Gentilium*, 38; *Il Teseida* 43, 44n
Boddeker, K., 304, 305
Boethius, 30, 43, 271; *De Musica*, 34; *Philosophiae Consolatio*, 271n, 272; *Quomodo substantiae*, 271n
Boffey, Julia, 300n
Boitani, Piero, 2, 3, 25–41
Bologna, Ferdinando, 288n, 294n
Bonaventure, 209, 246, 264n, 323n; *Vita sancti Francisci*, 246
Boniface VIII, Pope, 275, 276n, 282n, 283n, 288; *Liber Sextus*, 86n
Boniface IX, Pope, 199n
Book of Vices and Virtues, The, 84n, 86n, 89n, 179n, 183n
Borges, Jorge Luis, 25
Bori, Pier Cesare, 35
Bourth, Roger, 304
Bowers, John M., 120n
Boyle, Leonard E., 144n
Bradwardine, Thomas, 30, 37
Brady, M. Teresa, 198n, 201, 325n

Brady, Matthew, 45
Braun, Joseph, 325n
Brayer, E., 302n
Breviarium Romanum, 252
Brewse, Giles, 183
Brigit of Sweden, St. *See* Birgitta, St.
Brigittine friars, 185
Bromyard, John, *Summa predican-tium*, 330
Brook, G. L., 14n, 17n, 21n, 304n
Brooke, C. N. L., 155n
Broomfield, F., 143n
Brown, Carleton, 297n, 299, 321n, 330n
Brown, Carleton, and R. H. Robbins, 297, 300n, 328n, 330n
Brun, Franciscus, 288, 290
Buddensieg, Rudolf, 204n
Burrow, John, 165n, 205n
Bursill-Hall, G. L., 304
Byrhtnoth, 46

Caggese, Romolo, 278n, 284n, 286n
Cain, 46
Caley, J., 155n
Camera, Matteo, 283n
Cannon, H. L., 77n, 197n
Canon Law, 85–86, 89, 95, 197n, 185; doctrine of *donum Dei*, 106
Canonization, 8, 293–94; bull of, 287, 292; process of, 278, 285–91
Cantera, Biagio, 284n
Capes, William W., 199
Caracciolo, Roberto, 264, 285n; *Opus quadragesimale*, 264
Carolus Fernandus, *Speculum disci-pline*, 259n
Carolus V, 244n, 253n, 258n
Carruthers, Mary, 329n
Carthusians, 242
Casagrande, Carla, 120n
Cassian, John, 239
Catechesis, 5, 81–82; articles of faith, 146–48; beatitudes, 121, 146, 149; catechetical instruction, 145, 180; creed, 5, 139, 144, 146–47; daughters of God, 180; decalogue, 5, 136, 144, 146, 149, 180; evangelical

precepts, 144, 149; four last things, 245, 252; gifts of Holy Spirit, 121, 144, 146, 149, 244; the laity, 144–47, 150; last things, 149; Paternoster, 5, 144, 146, 148–49, 183; sacraments, 144–48, 149–50, 181, 244, 252; works of grace, 152; works of mercy, 5, 180; works of nature, 152. *See also* Virtues, Vices
Cato, 27, 126, 245
Catto, J. I., 203n
Cavalcanti, Guido, 267
Caxton, William, 36
Celestine V, Pope, 285, 286
Cervantes, Miguel de, *Don Quixote*, 25
Cesarius of Arles, 252
Chaix, Gerald, 242n
Chambers, R. W., 81, 87
Charles I of Anjou, 281–283, 291, 284n
Charles II of Anjou, 8, 275, 285, 292, 294, 295
Chastising of God's Children, 184, 185n, 201n
Chaucer, Thomas, 66
Chaucer, Geoffrey: attitude to abor-tion, contraception, and infanti-cide, 72–74, 77; biography, 61n, 67, 77–79; disgust for senile lech-ery, 75–77; disturbed response to sexuality, 69–78; familiarity with heroic tradition, 44; female sexu-ality (revulsion to), 68–69, 77; male sexual display (violent reac-tion to), 72, 77; relation to Chris-tianity, 44; trouble with interper-sonal relationships, 66; view of body as servant to sin, 68–69
Chaucer, Geoffrey, Works: *Boece*, 32; *Canterbury Tales*, 37, 49, 63–65, 79; *Clerk's Tale*, 32; *Envoy to Scogan*, 78, (image of rusting muse) 79; *Former Age*, 20n; *House of Fame*, 67; *Knight's Tale*, 3, 30, 32, 43–59; *Legend of Good Wom-en*, 19; *Man of Law's Tale*, 22n, 79 (endlink); *Melibee*, 32, 43, 65; *Mer-*

chant's Tale, 75–78, (relation to Parson's tale) 77–78; *Miller's Tale*, 315; *Monk's Tale*, 32, 65n; *Nun's Priest's Tale*, 2, 25–41; *Parson's Prologue*, 64–65, 77, 79; *Parson's Tale*, 3, 61–80, 164, (as personal penance) 65–77, (as separate composition) 62–65, (change of guide in) 64, (dramatic approach to) 61, (excremental imagery in) 69–71, 77, (gluttony in) 67, (image of "knitting up") 64, (incompatibility between prologue and tale) 65, (kissing in) 74–76, (lechery in) 74–78, (pride in) 71–72, (religious approach of) 61, (sins of the tongue in) 73, (sources of) 67–77, (specific cause of) 77, (species of penance in) 74, (stance on poetry in) 79, (wrath in) 72–73; *Retraction*, 37, 62–64, 66, 77, 79; *Retraction* as conclusion of treatise, 64, (as literary convention) 66n; *Romaunt of the Rose*, 16, 18, 22n, 32; *Second Nun's Tale*, 32; *Sir Topas*, 13; *Summoner's Tale*, 115; *To Rosemounde*, 2, 11–23; *Troilus and Criseyde*, 1, 20, 21, 30, 32, 33, 44, 184; *Wife of Bath's Tale*, 20, 57
Chaumpaigne, Cecily, 66, 77n
Checchini, Aldo, 123
Cheney, C. R., 146n
Chenu, M.-D., 210n, 226n
Chevalier, U., 301, 302
Chronicle: of kings of France, 255; of Roman emperors, 245, 255; of Roman pontiffs, 245, 255; of St. Trudo, 245, 255
Chronographical technique, 27
Chrysostom, John, 214, 216, 227, 246, 256
Cicero, 122–24, 234; *De officiis*, 99; *De oratore*, 123n
Cigman, Gloria, 195n, 200n
Clare, St., 279–80
Claudius Guillaudus (Belliocensis), 247; *Collationes in Matthaeum*, 247n

Clement V, Pope, 195, 278n
Clergy, 4; instruction for, 147; secular, 35; "new anticlericalism," 90
Clifford, Rosamond, 19
Coleman, Janet, 205n
Colledge, E., and J. Bazire, 184n, 201
Colledge, E., and J. Walsh, 182n
Collette, Carolyn, 206n
Compilation, methods of, 7, 237–41
Confession, 107, 151, 153n, 182, 244; as chamberlain, 179; as rumbling stomach, 108; in *Piers Plowman*, 81–83, 133–35; right to hear lay confession, 90
Conrad of Hirsau, 37–39; *Dialogue on the Authors*, 38
Conradus de Brugis, 244n
Constantinus medicus, 255
Contempt of the world, 245, 252, 256
Continuatio eulogii, 199n
Copeland, Rita, 317n
Correa, Alicia, 238
Cosenza, G., 285n
Council, Fourth Lateran, 5, 120, 153
Courtenay, William, 202n
Courtier, 162, 176
Coxe, Henry Octavius, 181, 184n
Crisci, Generoso, 283n
Cronica Marburgensis, 256
Cropp, L. S., 164n, 165n
Curry, W. C., 14, 15n, 17n
Curtius, E. R., 115
Cutler, John L., 297n. *See also* Robbins, Rossell Hope, and John L. Cutler
Cyprian of Carthage, 246, 256; *De mortalitate*, 256–57
Cyril, St. (Cirillus), 246

D'Aloe, Stanislao, 285n
D'Avray, D. L., 7, 263–73, 273n, 267n, 284n
Dacrianus Abbas, *Speculum monachorum*, 248n
Dahlberg, Charles, 35n
Damiani, Peter, 252
Dante. *See* Alighieri, Dante
Davidsohn, Robert, 286

Davies, G. R. C., 162
Davies, Reginald T., 11n, 15n
Davis, Norman, 15n
De Lubac, Henri, 25n
De motu et pena peccandi, 5, 161–77
De Rijk, L. M., 302, 303n, 314n
De Vocht, Henry, 243n
Deanesly, Margaret, 191, 198
Death, 47; as knight with shield, 326; domination of in epic, 45; fear of, 328–29; homicide, 30; moving corpse from bed to floor at, 329–30; of hero, 47; poetry on, 319–36; reminder of, 326–27; signs of, 330De Libera, A., 314n
Debongnie, Pierre, 247n
Deguileville, Guillaume de, 82, 96, 180; *Pilgrimage of the Lyf of the Manhode*, 179, 180n
Delcorno, Carlo, 267n
Dempster, Germaine, 164n
Denifle, H., and A. Chatelain, 158n
Denys the Carthusian, 7, 237–61; collecting methods, 240–41; *Commentary on Pseudo-Dionysius' De coelesti hierarchia*, 240; *Commentary on the Sentences*, 240; *De reformatione claustralium*, 242, 248; *De reformatione monialium dialogus*, 254n; *Epistola ad Cardinalem Nicolaum de Cusa (Monopanton)*, 240–41; *Epistola scripta monachis Sancti Trudonis*, 242; *Summa de vitiis et virtutibus*, 239
Deschamps, Jan, 247n
Deschamps, Eustache, 32
Destruction of Troy, 15
Devil, 162, 172, 177
Devotional prose, 183
Devout Treatyse, A, 180n
Diaeta salutis, sermon themes on, 321–22
Dictionarius pauperum, 252
Dido, 19
Dinshaw, Carolyn, 70n
Disce mori, 84n, 86n, 89n, 180, 183–85
Dismas, 86
Distinctiones monasticae, 116

Distinctiones theologicae, 321n
Diuerse doctrine patrum antiquorum, 246
Dives and Pauper, 325n
Divination, 152
Dobson, E. J., and F. L. Harrison, 315n
Domanevszky, Alexander, 281n
Dominic, St., 279; feast of, 298
Dominicans, 7, 103, 185, 209, 252, 264, 282, 298–300, 319; sermons of, 266, 267n, 273. *See also* Friars
Donaldson, E. Talbot, 62n, 98n
Dondaine, Antoine, 120n, 121n, 264
Donne, John, 20
Donovan, Mortimer J., 35n
Doyle, A. I., 5, 179–90, 183n, 258n
Doyle, A. I., and Malcolm Parkes, 63
Drama, exegetical, 4, 99
Dreams, 30, 34, 138
Drexel, Jeremias, *Orbis Phaethon: De universis viciis linguae*, 121
Drogone de Beaumont, 281n
Drunkenness, 112–14
Dryden, John, 26, 27, 29, 30, 39
Dufournet, Jean, 26n
Dunning, T. P., 114n
Durandus, William, *Rationale divinorum officiorum*, 252
Dyascorides, 255

Easter: calculation of, 301, 314; cycle, 305
Eco, Umberto, 33
Eden, Garden of, 31, 167–68
Edmund of Abingdon, *Speculum ecclesie*, 145n; *Speculum religiosorum*, 145n
Edward I, 87
Edward III, 87
Edwards, A. S. G., 61n
Elliott, C., 35n
Emden, Alfred B., 153n, 154n, 156n, 158n
Emery, Jr., Kent, 7, 237–61, 237n, 239n, 241n, 242n, 247n
Enemies of Humankind (world, flesh, devil), 125, 152, 183

Enkvist, Nils Erik, 206n
Epic, 3, 30; 43; 44n; 46, 130n, 139,
142; atmosphere, 43; beast, 35;
chaos in, 46–52; despair in, 55;
domination of death in, 45; exchange of services and wealth in
hall, 50; fratricide in, 46; kingship,
49–50; mock, 34; monster-gods of
disorder, 51; order, 51, 58; social
order, 46n; simile, 55; themes, 43;
theme of building, 46, 50–52, 58;
theme of destruction, 50, 52;
theme of mortality, 47; threat of
entropy, 3, 46; tragedy, 48, 58;
universe of, 44; violence, 48–51,
(contained by verbal constructions) 52–53, (converted into
game) 54–55, (in animal imagery)
54, (in early Germanic literature)
46–47; wall as limit, 46; warrior,
49. See also Heroic
Epistola scripta ad confessorem monialium, 254
Erasmus, Desiderius, 41, 247, 256;
Lingua, 121
Eriugena, John Scotus, 35
Errors of the laity, 151–52
Etzkorn, Girard J., 323n
Eucharist, 150–51, 181, 203n
Eusebius, 246
Evagrius Ponticus, Practicus, 325n
Eve, 31, 168
Ewert, A., and R. C. Johnston, 26n
Exegesis, 4, 7; allegorical, 3, 104, 116,
149, 224; anagogical, 25, 41; dramatic, 4, 99; fourfold, 25, 211–12;
individualizing discrimination, 7;
influence on Langland, 102; literal,
149, 224, 226; new "literalism,"
32, 33; non-literal, 41, 104; mystical, 226; of food, 107–8; rhetoric
in, 213–22, 233–34; scholastic, 224;
as script for Piers Plowman, 112–
14; scriptural, 6, 31, 32, 213, 222–
29, 233; scriptural, diversity of
interpretations in, 230–34; simplicity of form in, 232; traditional, 4;
tropological, 116, 138; Wycliffite,

195. See also Allegoresis, Interpretation
Ezekiel, 68

Faber, Jacobus (Stapulensis), Testa-
mentum, 259n
Faes de Mottoni, Barbara, 323n
Faith: instruction in, 146–47; milk of,
233, 234n
Fall (of humankind), 167–68
Fallacy, ironic, 2, 19
Farge, James K., 253n, 255n
Fasciculus morum, 2, 8, 84, 85n, 86n,
90, 94, 181, 320n, 326, 327, 331n,
336n. See also Wenzel, Siegfried
Fécamp, Jean de, "Candet nudatum
pectus," 317
Fein, Susanna, 182n
Fiala, Virgil, and Wolfgang Irtenkauf,
238n
Fichte, Joerg O., 12n, 14, 15, 17n, 19n
22, 35n
Fictionality, 2, 39, 40
"Firste Moevere," 58, 265
Fishacre, Richard, 298, 303n
Fitzralph, Richard, 90
Five Questions on Love, 199
Fleming, John V., 120n
Fletcher, Alan J., 330n
Floretum, 199, 200n, 201
Food: allegorization of, 103, 107–8; as
metaphor, 98–103; distinctio on,
100; meat, 107–8; of obedience,
112; Scripture as, 115–16, 233,
234n; sour loaf, 108, 133
Forshall, Josiah, and Frederic Mad-
den, 196, 198n, 199n, 201
Fortunes of Men, 58
Foster, C. W., and Kathleen Major,
157n
Foxe, John, 319, 321n; Acts and Monu-
ments, 320
Foxe, Simeon, 321n
Francesca da Rimini, 29
Francis of Assisi, St., 266, 317, 331n;
feast of, 298
Francis, Nelson, 179n, 183n
Franciscans, 7–9, 90, 103, 209, 254,

278, 291–92, 321–226; allegoresis of dress, 324–27; and book ownership, 88; buildings, 88; ideals of poverty, 8, 88, 287–88, 293; in Oxford, 8–9, 299; physical characteristics and dress, 9, 88; question of influence on religious poetry, 297–317, 319–20, 331; relations with papacy, 287; russet tunics of, 326, 327n; sermons of, 266–68, 273. See also Friars

Frank, Robert Worth, Jr., 97

Frankis, J., 300n

Fredericus III, 256n

Friars, 4, 35; dietary restrictions, 88; in Piers Plowman, 87–91, 95; miscellanies (manuscripts), 300, 321; pseudo-friars, 196; right to hear lay confession, 90. See also Dominicans, Franciscans

Frost, William, 51n

Furnivall, F. J., 297n, 328n

Furnivall, F. J., and W. G. Stone, 12n, 18n

"Galauntine," 20n

Galbraith, V. H., 194n

Galen, 245

Gamboso, V., 267n, 268n

Ganelon, 30, 37

Gelasius, Pope, 245

Genres, literary, 35n; 39; accessus, 210, 234; ballade, 11–13, 17, 22; bestiary, 255; breviary, 164; charm, 303; chanson de geste, 30; collectarium, 7, 237–61, (unified manuscript presentation) 237, 242, (unified rhetorical conception) 237–38; distinctio, 149, 276, 321, (influence on Langland) 99, (of food) 100; encyclopedia, 255, 260; exemplum, 26, 245; fable, 35, 38, 39, 40, 46, 79, (animal) 26, (apologue) 39; florilegium, 7, 238, 243; lapidary, 255; love-lyric, 12–22, 300n; manual (pastoral) 5, 8, 143, 146, (penitential) 120n, 121, (preaching) 144, 239, 247, 263n,

319; meditatio, 65n; parable, 39–40; romance, 29, 44n, 47; speculum sacerdotis, 152; saint's life, 162, 287–92; summa (moral) 239, (on vices) 121n, (on virtues) 121n; treatise (computational) 8–9, 300, 303, (grammatical) 304, (logical) 9, 302–3, 314, (on predicabilia) 302, (on priestly office) 144, (on quadrant) 303, (on sophisms) 298, 303, (on vices and virtues) 319 (philosophical) 8–9, 298, 300, 302–3, 314, (physionomical) 304, (rhetorical) 121, 123; verbal concordance (influence on Langland) 99. See also Allegory, Epic, Poetry, Sermon

Georgius ab Austria, 244n

Gerald of Wales (Giraldus Cambrensis), 84

Gerardus de Marka, 244n

Gerardus de Vliederhoven, Liber de quatuor nouissimorum, 247

Gerson, Jean, 238n, 240n, 246, 264; Collectorium super Magnificat, 238n; Monotesseron tetramonum, 240n

Geus, Johannes, Tractatus de viciis vocis, 121

Gibbs, M., and J. Lang, 158n

Gilbert de la Porré, 322n

Gilbert of Tournai, 322n

Gilbert the Great, 321n

Gilbert the Minorite, 321–23

Giles of Rome (Aegidius Romanus), 225, 234, 276; Commentarium in Canticum Canticorum, 234n; Commentarium in primum librum Sententiarum, 234n; De regimine principum, 225n; Rhetorica Aristotelis cum Egidii de Roma comentariis, 225n

Gilgamesh, 43

Gillespie, Vincent, 182n

Gilson, Etienne, 298n

Giordano da Pisa, 266, 267n, 273

Giovanni di San Gimignano, 264

Glorieux, P., 153n, 158n, 238n

Glossa ordinaria, 108n, 225, 227

Glossed Gospels, 198, 199
Gneuss, H., 300n
Godwin, 156n
Goering, Joseph, 4, 143–59, 143n, 145n, 147n, 148n, 151n, 154n, 161
Goering, Joseph, and Daniel S. Taylor, 146n
Goldsmith, Margaret, 114n
Gommer, Jacobus, 248, 251, 254n, 257–59
Good will, 101–2
Gordon, E. V., 15n
Gower, John, *Confessio Amantis*, 19; *Vox Clamantis*, 34
Grabmann, M., 266n
Gradon, Pamela, 195. *See also* Hudson, Anne, and Pamela Gradon
Grandjean, Charles, 283n
Gratian, *Decretum*, 85n, 86n
Gray, Douglas, 192n, 304n, 312n, 330n
Gray, Nick, 108
Green, G. M., 271n
Gregorius Nazianzenus, 253
Gregory I, Pope, 164n, 170n, 197n, 246; *Moralia in Job*, 164, 217n
Gregory XIII, Pope, 253n
Greven, Josef, 242n
Grosseteste, Robert, 146, 149n, 218n; *Dictum*, 199n; *Templum Dei*, 145, 148n, 149n
Guelphs, 275, 292
Guigo II, *Scala claustralium*, 182
Guillelmus de Godonio, 282–83, 285, 295
Guillelmus de Gouda, *Expositio mysteriorum Missae et modus celebrandi*, 246n
Guillelmus de Lauduno, 248n
Guillermus Parisiensis, 246
Guindon, Roger, 163n
Gutiérrez, David, 276, 284

Hackett, M. B., 154n
Hallwas, J. E., 304n
Halverson, John, 46
Hamesse, Jacqueline, 238n, 271n
Handwriting: anglicana, 324; anglicana formata, 180, 182; anglicana bastard, 182n; bastarda libraria, 249, 251; modern bookhand, 258; notula script, 253; secretary, 184; semi-cursive, 279; textualis formata, 244, 257–58
Hanna, Ralph, III, 3, 81–96, 330n
Hargreaves, Henry, 194n
Hartshorne, A., 326n
Hartung, Albert, 3, 61–80
Hartungus de Herwersleyben, *Ortulus anime*, 252
Hasdrubal, 34
Hauréau, B., 248n
Haydon, Frank Scott, 199n
Heawood, Edward, 183n
Hector, 21
Heinrich, F., 312n
Hell: harrowing of, 139; descent to, 329; pains of, 331
Heltzel, Virgil B., 19n
Henderson, A. C., 35n
Henricus de Coesueldia, *Tractatus de instructione iuuenum et nouitiorum*, 254, 259n
Henry, Avril, 180n
Henry II, 19
Henry III, 157, 158
Henry of Avranches, 308, 315
Henry of Ghent, 6, 209–35; as ideological synthesizer, 209; *Quodlibeta*, 209n, 230n; *Summa quaestionum ordinariarum*, 6, 210–35
Henryson, Robert, *Morall Fabillis of Esope the Phrygian*, 35
Herbert, J. A., 327n
Herebert, William, *Hymns*, 300
Heretics, 105, 203, 225, 228, 255
Hero, 47; comes to terms with limits, 46; confrontation with danger and death, 46; death of, 47; staves off chaos, 46
Heroic, 3; brutality, 55; effort, 46; pathos, 55; resistance, 49; savior, 47; society (Germanic) 50; talents, 48; tradition, 44; tragedy, 58; world, 43–59; values, 44. *See also* Epic
Herolt, John, 246

Heysse, Albanus, 287n
Higden, Ranulph, *Polychronicon*, 157
Hildebert of Le Mans, *Biblical Epigrams*, 162–64n
Hilton, Walter, *Scale of Perfection*, 183
Hirsh, J. C., 183n
Hoccleve, Thomas, *Regiment of Princes*, 183n
Hodgson, P., 185n
Hödl, Ludwig, 147n
Holi Prophete Dauid seith, The, 191
Hollen, Gottschalk, 246n, 247n; *Passionale*, 247n; *Praeceptorium divinae legis*, 246n
Holmstedt, Gustav, 182n
Homer, 44; *Iliad*, 45, 56
Honorius III, Pope, 158
Hook, Walter F., 156n, 157n
Hordern, William, 184n
Horstman, Carl, 179n, 325n
Housley, Norman, 283n
Hovelmann, Gregor, 241n
Howard, Donald, 62n
Hubert de Burgh, 157
Hudson, Anne, 191–200n
Hudson, Anne, and Pamela Gradon, 195n
Hugh of St. Cher, 103–17, 135, 136, 179, 323n; *Opera omnia in universum Vetus et Novus Testamentum*, 103, 105–7, 109–17; *via recta* in, 109–12
Hugh of St. Victor, 179, 246, 248n
Hughes-Hughes, A., 316n
Hugo de Floreto, 253
Humbert of Romans, 246
Hungary, 278; Queen of, 280–82
Hunt, R. W., 143n, 234n, 308n, 320n
Hunt, T., 314n
Hunt, William, 156, 158n
Huppé, Bernard, and D. W. Robertson, Jr., 98n, 114n
Huss, John, 33
Hypallage, rhetorical figure of, 107
Hypocrite, 105, 115, 117, 121, 128–29, 137, 141, 205

Ignorancia sacerdotum, 146, 148n, 180,

184. *See also* Pecham, John
Imagery: animal, 54, (bear) 54, (boar) 54, (bull) 54, (cat) 124, (dog) 75, 222–23, 227–28, (dragon) 52, (eagle) 54, 67, (fish) 21, 227, (fly) 176, (gryphon) 54, (horse) 126, (hound) 54, 74, (leopard) 54, (lion) 54, (monster) 45, 47, 49–50, (pig) 69, (pike) 20, (rat) 124–25, (raven) 54, (sheep) 223, (snake) 107, 168, 176, (sow) 71, (steer) 54, (swine) 68, 227–28, (wolf) 54, (worm) 20, 176; bread of penitence, 116n; excremental, 69–71, 77; "knitting up," 64; milk of faith, 233, 234n; rusting muse, 79; ship, 169; soul (as bed) 179, (as garden) 179; tree of patience, 137. *See also* Food, Similitudes
Innocent III, Pope, 163, 172; *De miseria humane conditionis*, 5, 164, 165, 173n
Interpretation, 40; allegorical, 4, 25, 35; historical perspective in, 2; humanism in, 38; literal, 3, 25–41; moral, 25; perverse, 226; plain sense, 40–41; Robertsonianism, 2, 31. *See also* Allegoresis, Exegesis
Irving, Edward B., Jr., 3, 43–59
Isabella of Anjou, 281, 282, 285
Isabelle, wife of Richard II, 18
Isidore of Seville, 37, 38, 165, 173, 174n, 246, 256; *Etymologiae*, 173n

Jacob's Well, 84n, 85n, 86, 89
Jacobus de Gruitrode, *Lavacrum conscientie*, 247; *Ortulus rosarum*, 247; *Speculum anime peccatricis*, 247
Jacobus de Voragine, 246
Jacobus of Viterbo, 8, 275–95; *Abbreviatio* of Aegidius's commentary on *I Sentences*, 276; as Archbishop, 277, 280, 284, 292; political background, 276n; *De regimine Christiano*, 275, 292
Jacopone da Todi, "Stabat mater dolorosa," 316
James, M. R., 143n

Jean de Meun, 120n. See also *Roman de la Rose*
Jeffrey, David Lyle, 192n, 299n, 317n, 320n
Jerome, 112, 246; *Epistolae*, 325n
Jesus (Christ), 8, 31, 37, 39, 40, 86, 196, 206, 251, 252, 255, 297
Jocher, Christian Gottlieb, 247n
Johannes Abbas, 248n
Johannes Climacus, 246
Johannes de Balbis, *Catholicon*, 252
Johannes de Orta, 287n
Johannes Egiptus, 246
Johannes Mauburnus, *Rosetum*, 247
Johannes Miskirchius, 247n
Johannes Tritemius, 246
John le Neve, 156n, 158n
John of Garland, 302n
John of Grimestone, *Commonplace Book*, 300
John of Howden, *Philomena*, 317
John XXII, Pope (Jacobus Duéze), 8, 278, 287, 288, 292, 294, 295; canonization of Louis of Anjou, involvement in, 288; *Constitutiones Clementinae*, 86n
Johnson, Dudley R., 73n
Jolliffe, P. S., 180n
Jones, C. W., 173n
Jordan, William, 99n
Jordan of Saxony, *Liber Vitasfratrum*, 276n
Judas Iscariot, 30
Judges, 106
Julius III, Pope, 258n
Jusserand, J. J., 81, 83
Justice, Steven, 83n

Kaeppeli, Thomas, 252n, 253n
Kafka, Franz, 41
Kaftal, George, 294n
Kahn, Victoria, 122n
Kane, George, 98n, 299n, 329n
Kane, George, and E. T. Donaldson, 119n, 128n
Kaske, R. E., 103, 114n, 133
Keats, John, 25
Keen, Maurice, 203n

Kellogg, Alfred, 143n
Kemmler, Fritz, 143n, 145n, 152n, 155n
Kempis, Thomas a. *See* Thomas Hemerken à Kempis
Kendall, Ritchie D., 194n
Kenny, Anthony, 201n, 202n, 204n
Ker, Neil, 161n
Kerby-Fulton, Kathryn, 83n
Kermode, Frank, 40, 41n
Kilwardby, Robert, 234n
Kinsley, J., 27n
Kirchberger, C., 183n
Kirk, Elizabeth, 98
Klaeber, F., 48n
Knapp, Peggy Ann, 194n, 199n
Knighthood: English, 326n; spiritual, 326
Knighton, Henry, 193–94, 196–97, 206
Knowles, David, 155n
Kopf, U., 210n
Kristeller, Paul, 259n
Kruitwagen, Bonaventure, 258n
Kurath, Hans, 312n, 313n

La Fontaine, Jean de, *Fables*, 39, 40
Ladislaus IV, 280, 281
Lai de l'Ombre, 21
Lambert, M. D., 88
Lancelot, 3, 29, 36, 37, 40
Langland, William: influence of biblical commentary on, 99; influence of penitential tradition on, 119; interest in narrative economy, 87; on lawyers, judges, physicians, teachers, 106; relation to catechetic material, 82, 87; view of confession, 3, 90–95
Langland, William, *Piers Plowman*: 3–4, 81–142; Anima, 135–39, (and curious knowledge) 136; authorship controversy, 81, 83; avarice, 128, 137, 141; banquet, 4, 97–117, 133, (source of) 97–117, (metaphor of food in) 98–103; Book (personfication), 139; book of James, influence on, 125–42; canon law

in, 85–86, 89, 95, 106; charity, 134–35, 137–38; Clergy, 4, 97–98, 102, 105–10, 113, 130; Conscience, 97–98, 101, 108, 113–14, 126, 134, 139–42; contemplation, 95; contrition, 141; corrupt penance, 89; Couetyse, 81–96, (compared with prostitute) 85, (despair in) 94, 95n, (failure to repent of) 91–93, (terror of) 94; detractor, 120n; doubling in, 3, 90–95; Do-well, 105, 110, 117, 129, 132–34, (as knowledge in action) 97, (meaning of) 97–102; Envy, 93n, 141; False, 83n; Flattery, 141; friar(s), 87–91, 95–96, 97–105, 108–17, 124, 126, 129, 132–33, 136; 3euan-3elde-a-3eyn, 3, 83–87, 91–93, 96; Glutton, 127; Good Samaritan, 138; grace, 142; grammatical metaphor in, 109–10; Hawkyn, 133–34; Holy Church, 120, 125, 127, 130, 137; Imaginatif, 116, 131–32, 135; influence of glossed Bible on, 117; Liar, 125–27; lawyers, 125; lay penance, 91; love, 110–13, 120, 126, 137; loyalty, 131; Meed, 83n, 125–28; minstrels, 124, 126, 134; moral geometry in, 109; Moses, 138; national stereotypes in, 83, 95; Need, 140–41; pardon, 128; pardoner, 119, 124, 126; Patience, 98–102, 105, 108–17, 133–34, (tree of) 137, (poverty of) 105, (as representative of *via recta*) 111; penance in, 125–27, 134; Piers, 128, 138; pilgrim(s), 125, 133; problem of confession, 81–96; priest, 89–91, 95–96, 128; prostitute, 85–89, 91; quotations in, 124; Reason, 126–28, 130–31; Repentance, 85–96, 128; restitution, 92–94, 128; revisions in, 82, 85, 87, 90, 91, 92, 94–96; rhetoric in, 123, 131, 137–40; Robert the robber (or ruyflare), 3, 81–96; Robin the Ribaudour, 128; Sloth, 81–83, 124, 127, 133, 141; Scripture, 120, 130–31; spiritual inertia in, 92–94; Study, 120, 130–32; Thought, 129; Truth, 127, 128n, 129; Unity, 119, 126, 140–41; Waryn, 83n; Will, 88, 96n, 97–100, 104, 108–9, 112, 125, 128–41; Wisdom, 83n; Wit, 129–30; Wrath, 81, 90; Z-text, 120n

Langton, Stephen, 157
Lanham, Richard, 107n
Lanterne of Li3t, 196, 197
Latini, Brunetto, *Li Livres dou Tresor*, 121
Laurence of Stanfield, 154
Laurent, Frère, *Somme le Roi*, 84n, 86, 179
Lawler, Traugott, 61n, 96n
Lawrence, St., 279, 280; vigil mass of, 115
Lawton, David, 95
Lawyers, 106
Learning. *See* Wisdom . . . worldly
Lectus floridus, 5, 179–90
Leff, Gordon, 88, 201n, 202, 203n
Léger of Autun, 314n
Legge, Dominica, 21
Lehmann, Paul, 238n, 240n
Lenaghan, R. T., 36n
Lesnick, Daniel R., 266n
Lewis, C. S., 11
Lewry, Osmund, 234n, 298n, 302n
Liberal Arts, 131
Libri Extravagantium, 86n
Liddell, Mark, 71n
Liège: bishops of, 255; collegiate churches of, 255
Lincoln, schools of, 156. *See also* Richard of Wetheringsett
Little, Andrew G., 302n, 327n
Liturgy: books, 237; calendar, 258; cycles, 280; feasts, 252, 255
Loer, Dirk, 241
"Lollard Chronicle of the Papacy, A," 195
Lollards. *See* Wycliffites
Lollius, 33
London, Vera C. M., 155n
Long, R. J., 210n
Loserth, Johann, 198, 199n, 204n

Lottin, Odon, 122n, 163n
Louis of Anjou: Bishop of Toulouse, 289–91; canonization of, 286–94; Franciscan involvement with, 288–94; iconography of, 294; "model" life of, 287–90, (emphasis on episcopal office in) 291–93, (suppression of Franciscan themes in) 293; Pope John XXII on, 288, 292
Love, Nicholas, *Mirror of the Life of Christ*, 181
Love: compared to toothache, 21; courtly, 18, 34; in *Piers Plowman*, 110–13; of God, 245
Lover, 47; and fish, 21; as love's thrall, 22; as pike, 20; as meek, obedient, 18; of world, 245; sleepless, 19–20. *See also* Genres: love-lyric
Ludolphus (de Saxonia), *Vita Christi*, 246
Lumby, Joseph Rawon, 193
Luna, Concetta, 323n
Lydgate, John, 19
Lyndwood, William, *Provinciale*, 86n, 185

MacCracken, Henry, 19n
Macharius, 246
Machaut, Guillaume de, *Tout ensement com le monde enlumine*, 13
Macken, Raymond, 209n, 210n, 230n
Macray, W. D., 300n
Madan, Falconer, and H. H. E. Craster, 320n, 322n
Magisterium, 33
Mallard, William, 194n
Malory, Thomas, 48
Malyusz, E., 281n
Manipulus morum, 321n
Manly, John M., 62, 81–83
Manly, John M., and Edith Rickert, 62n
Mann, Jill, 34n
Manning, Stephen, 36n
Manselli, R., 267n
Mantello, F. A. C., 145n, 148n

Map, Walter, 84
"Mapamonde," 13–14
Marcarius, Hugo, 288
Marcett, Mildred E., 99n
Maria of Hungary, wife of Charles II, 280, 288
Mariani, Ugo, 276n
Marie de France, 57; *Del cok e del gulpil*, 26
Marriage, 151
Marrone, Stephen P., 209n
Marston, Roger de, 303
Martel, Charles, 278
Martin IV, Pope, 281
Martini, Simone, 294n
Mary (Magdalene), 8; poem on, 305–7
Mary (Virgin), 31, 244, 260; monodic song on, 301; poetry on, 301, 307–10, 316
Mass, treatment of, 244, 251
Masters (*magistri artium*), 103–6, 209
Masurier, Martialis, 255
Matthew, F. D., 192, 197n, 198n, 200, 207
Maximian, *Elegiae*, 175n
Maximilianus, 253n
Maxwell-Lyte, H. C., and M. C. B. Dawes, 203n
McCall, John P., 44n
McCormick, William, and Janet E. Heseltine, 63n
McFarlane, K. B., 201n
McIntosh, Angus, 181n, 183n
McLeod, W., 162n
McLuhan, Marshall, 235
Mehl, Dieter, 11n
Memory, 166, 238–40, 329n
Michael a S. Joseph, 247n
Michael de Hungaria, 255
Michael of Northgate, *Ayenbite of Inwit*, 84n, 86n, 89n, 179n
Middle English, dialects: Buckinghamshire, 181; Nottinghamshire, 183; Shropshire, 182n; Staffordshire, 182n
Middle English Dictionary, 89n, 312n, 313n
Middleton, Anne, 96n, 110n

Miles, 277, 278n, 284; *Miles Christ-ianus,* 327
Miller, B. D. H., 300n
Milton, John, 130n, 140
Minieri-Riccio, Camillo, 278n, 281n
Minnis, A. J., 6, 36, 36n, 44n, 192n, 209–35, 211n, 214n, 224n, 234n, 235n
Minnis, A. J., and A. B. Scott, 32n, 37n, 211n, 224n, 225n 232n, 234n
Minutolo, Philippo, 277, 278n
Miroir du monde, 84n, 86
Mirror of Simple Souls, The, 179
Mirror of the Life of Christ. See Love, Nicholas
Monastic life, 245, 252; of desert fathers, 246, 324–25
Monti, Gennaro Maria, 283n
Moorman, John R. H., 326n, 327n
Moral lesson, 26, 34–35, 39–41
Morignus, Gerardus, 243n, 259n
Morris, Richard, 179n
Morte Arthure (alliterative), 44
Motu et pena peccandi, De, 5, 161–77
Mulingus, Joannes Adelphus, 247
Munk Olsen, Birger, 243
Murray, Hilda M. R., 330n
Muscatine, Charles, 51n, 82
Music. *See* Poetry
Mutzenbecker, Almut, 163n
Mynors, R. A. B., 258n
Myrour to Lewde Men and Wymmen, A, 84n, 86, 89n

Naples: archbishopric of, 275, 280, 284, 292; court in, 276
Nash, P. W., 210n
Neckam, Alexander, 165, 170n, 175n, 308, 315; *Corrogationes novi Pro-methei,* 164n, 165; *De naturis rerum,* 164n
Neoplatonism, 209
Nero, 34, 37
Netter, Thomas, 193n; *Doctrinale,* 200n
Newhauser, Richard, 8, 9, 120n, 246n, 319–36
Niccolaus, Archbishop of Trani, 281n

Nicholas of Cusa, 240
Nicholaus de Byard, *Distinctiones,* 252; *Summa abstinentiae,* 321–23
Nicolaus de Lira, 246
Nicoluccio di Ascoli, 264
Nominalism, 202, 206
Noonan, John T., 73n, 74n
Nuns, 183–84

Ockham, William of, 203n
Odysseus, 45
Oldham, J. Basil, 181n
Oliger, L., 267n
Olivi, John Paul, eschatology of, 288
Olsen. *See* Munk Olsen, Birger
Onomatopoeia, 12
Originalia, 239
Ormulum, 179
Orosius, 252
Orwell, George, *Animal Farm,* 42n
Ouy, Gilbert, 258n
Ovid, 44n
Owen, Dorothy, 159
Owen, Charles A., Jr., 62
Owst, G. R., 70n, 72n, 86, 322n, 323
Oxford: book market, 143; Francis-cans, 299
Oxford English Dictionary, 180n

Pace, G. R., and A. David, 12n
Paganism, 44; immortal gods of, 45
Paleography. *See* Handwriting
Paris, Matthew, 315
Paris, University of, 209n, 263
Parkes, Malcolm, 63n, 258n, 324n. *See also* Doyle, A. I., and Malcolm Parkes
Parody, 2, 11–22, 27–28, 108; in Mid-dle English literature, 19n; op-posed to exaggeration and incon-gruity, 22
Passion (of Jesus), 244, 251; English poem on, 301, 304–7, 315–16; monodic song on, 301; play, 307
Pastoral instruction, 5, 8, 143, 145, 146, 184; reform of, 144
Pasztor, Edith, 287, 288, 292n
Patterson, Lee, 61n, 77n, 120n, 184n, 191n

Paul, J., 288n
Paul, St., Cathedral of, 183
Paul the Apostle, 2, 35, 36, 40, 207, 225, 238, 241, 270
Paulmier-Foucart, Monique, 239n
Paulus III, Pope, 244n
Pearsall, Derek, 83, 87, 89
Peasant, 162, 176–77
Peasants' Revolt (1381), 34
Pecham, John, 184; Lambeth Constitutions, 146, 148n. See also *Ignorantia sacerdotum*
Pecock, Reginald, 193n
Penitence, 3, 64, 65, 107, 151–52, 244; and abstinence, 6; allegory of, 100; bread of, 116n; as chamberer, 180; conflict with learning, 4–5, 117; and contrition, 68; friars' abuse of, 88; and good works, 6; as indigestion, 108; individual, 3; as remedy for prideful learning, 106; and tears, 6
Pennaforte, Raymund of, 3, 68, 69, 72–74, 76, 164n
Peraldus, Guilielmus, 3, 68n, 71–72, 74n, 82, 119–138, 141–42, 247n, 248n; *Summa de vitiis et virtutibus*, 4, 119–22
Peregrinus (de Oppeln), *Sermones*, 252–53
Peter, Epistle of, 68
Peter of Verona, 298n
Peter the Martyr, 298
Petersen, Kate O., 68n, 73n, 164n
Petrarch, Francis, 33
Petreius, Theodorus, 247n
Petrus Blesensis, 255
Petrus Comestor, 253
Petrus de Herenthals, *Collectarius super librum Psalmorum*, 238n
Petrus de Natalibus, 246; *Cathalogus sanctorum* 252
Petrus Dorlandus, *Dialogus de enormi proprietatis monachorum vicio*, 248n
Petrus Lemovicensis, *Liber do oculo morali*, 246
Petrus Lombard, 264n; *Sententiae*, 7,

164n, 210, 239–40
Petrus Richardus, *Confessionale*, 253n; *Doctrinale sanctae ac providae vitae*, 253n; *Sermonus opus*, 253n
Pfander, Homer G., 321n
Philip of Eye, 157
Philip of Spain, 256n
Philip the Chancellor, 307
Philip the Fair of France, 286n
Philology, 1, 9, 25, 319
Philosophy, 30; and preaching, 263–74
Physicians, 106
Physiologus, 34, 256
Piccard, Gerhard, 243n
Pictaviensis, Guillelmus, 248n
Pierce the Plowman's Crede, 205
Pierre de Saint Cloud, 26
Piers Plowman. See Langland, William
Pietro Martire, St., dedication of church of, 285
Pitra, J. B., 116n
Pizzorno, P. Grimaldi, 32n
Plato, *Phaedo* 39; *Timaeus*, 218
Pliny, 245, 255; *Naturalis Historia*, 173n
Plutarch, *De moralibus*, 256
Poetry, incipits: "Albani celebrem celo terrisque triumphum," 162; "Alleluia virga ferax Aaron," 316n; "Angelus ad virginem," 315, 316n; "Ave purum vas argenti," 301, 305–7; "Bien deust chanter ky eust leale amie," 316n; "Bis senos menses tenet annus nomina quorum," 302; "Candet nudatum pectus," 317; "De ma dame du cel," 302, 308–10; "Est nemus unde loquar," 162; "Et primo ieiunamus in vere," 302; "Exposito iam proposito," 161–77; "Flos pudicie," 316n; "Flur de uirginite," 316n; "Gabriel fram evene king," 315, 316n; "Gaudet sic iam lux martis phebus aprilis," 303; "Hayl mari hic am sori," 301; "Hi sike al wan hi singe," 301, 304, 316, 317; "Hic ardent seraphim," 162; "Hic exempla

satis uobis scribam nouitatis,"
162; "In ecclesiis celi gloria," 301,
311–12, 315; "In te concipitur,"
301, 315; "Jesu Cristes milde
moder," 315–16; "Magdalene,
laudes plene," 316n; "Mens in
parte cupit," 162; "No more ne
willi wiked be," 297–98, 301, 316;
"O labilis o flebilis," 316n; "O
Maria, noli flere," 307–8; "Omnis
caro peccaverat," 315; "Po to,
ligna cremo, de vite superflua
demo," 302; "Quasi coruus
crocito," 162; "Reine pleine de
ducur," 316n; "Risum facit dare,"
316n; "Salue uirgo uirginum,"
316n; "Spei uena, melle plena,"
316n; "Stabat iuxta Christi
crucem," 316; "Stabat mater
dolorosa," 316; "Strong it is to
flitte," 319–36; "Ter quinos domini quotiens potes aufer ab annis,"
302; "The milde Lomb isprad o
rode," 315, 316n; "Ure louerd
Crist was on erthe iwondid," 313;
"Vigilias quinque nos docet Roma
celebrare," 302; "When y se
blosmes springe," 305, 317;
"Whosoo hym be thowght,"
330n; "Worldes blis ne last no
throwe," 315, 316n

Poetry: anthology of, 162, 315; dialogue between Mary Magdalene
and Jesus, 8, 305; Franciscan
influence on, 299–300; Goliardic,
162; Harley lyrics, 16, 20, 304; in
sermons, 299, 300n, 319, 321n;
Latin, 8, 161–78, 297–318; manuscript context of, 299, 300n, 319,
321n; Marian lyric, 305n, 308n,
316n; Middle English, 8–9, 297–
301, 304–5, 315–17, 319–21, 327–
33; Middle English *Stabat mater*,
316; mnemonic tag, 328; and
modern criticism, 299, 319; moral
poem on abuses in the Church, 8,
310–12, 315; of the passion, 8,
299, 304–7, 315–16; of the resur-

rection, 307; on death, 9, 319–36;
Old French, 8, 299, 308, 316; Old
Provençal, 22; penitential pieces
addressed to the Virgin, 8, 308;
reception history, 319; religious,
8–9, 161–78, 297–317, 319–36;
song repertoire of 13th century,
316–17; songs with music, 301,
315; verbal emblem, 328. *See also*
Genres: ballade, love-lyric

Pollard, Alfred W., 192, 195, 203n,
205

Polton, Thomas, *Register*, 203n

Pope, Mildred K., 313n

Porete, Margaret, 179

Pore Caitif, The, 198n, 325n

Postquam. See *Summa virtutum de
remediis anime*

Poverty: evangelical, 287; Franciscan
ideals of, 8, 88, 287–88, 293; and
Patience in *Piers Plowman*, 105

Powicke, F. M., and C. R. Cheney,
146n

Preacher, 103, 150; false, 196, 206;
Jacobus of Viterbo as, 275–95;
notebook of, 327; true, 193, 197,
206; wicked, 136–37

Preaching, 7, 70, 152, 227–30; for
laity, 148; philosophical influences
on, 7, 263–73; research tools for,
144, 239–41, 247, 263n, 321; scholastic, 263–64, (divisions and distinctions in) 266, 267n, 268, 270,
288. *See also* Sermon

Predestination, 30

Priam, 34, 37

Priests: pastoral literature for, 143–45,
148, 150, 152, 184; priests and
penitence in *Piers Plowman*, 89–
91; right to hear lay confession,
90; true and false, 196–97, 207

Primo (treatise on vices), 3, 69, 71, 247n

Priscillianus Abilensis, *Collectario de
diversis sententiis*, 238n

Professione monachorum, De, 248

Prosper Aquitanus, 246

Prostitute, tithing of according to canon law, 85–87

Pseudo-Augustine, 256n
Pseudo-Bernard, 246
Pseudo-Bonaventure, *Meditations on the Life of Christ*, 267n
Pseudo-Chrysostom, *In Evangelium Matthei homiliae*, 214n, 216n, 228n
Pseudo-Dionysius, *De coelesti hierarchia*, 216n, 240; *De divinis nominibus*, 216n; *De ecclesiastica hierarchia*, 216n
Pseudo-Sidonius, 256n
Pseudo-Theophilus of Antioch, *Commentaria in Evangelia*, 246n
Ptolomeus of Lucca, *Historia*, 287
Purvey, John, 198n
Pynson, Thomas, 63n

Quinel, Peter, 146
Quoniam (treatise on vices), 3, 71, 75

Rabanus Maurus, 238, 246; *Collectarium de santorum patrum opusculis*, 238n
Raby, F. J. E., 307n, 308n, 316, 317n
Raisings from dead by Jesus, 163–64, 170–71
Ralph of Dunstable, 162
Ransom, Daniel, 19n
Raulin, Jean, *Collatio de perfecta religionis plantatione*, 247n; *Doctrinale mortis*, 247n
Raymo, Robert, 180n, 183n, 185n
Raymond-Berengar, son of Maria of Hungary, 283–85
Raynaud, Gaston, and Henri Lemaitre, 26n
Regulae (Franciscan), 331n
Reichl, Karl, 8, 9, 297–317, 316n, 317n, 321n
Reimer, S. R., 300n
Reiss, E., 12n–14, 21
Renart Le Contrefait, Branch VI, 26
Rhenanus, Blessed, 255
Rhetoric, 6, 210, 213–22, 233–34, 238–39
Rhodes, J., 183n
Richard I, 37
Richard II, 87, 199n
Richard le Grant (alias Weathershed).

See Richard of Wetheringsett
Richard of Dove, 157
Richard of Leicester, 5, 154, 155, 158
Richard of St. Victor, 246
Richard of Wetheringsett, 5, 143–59; Archbishop of Canterbury, 155–59; Chancellor of Cambridge University, 154–55; Chancellor of Lincoln Cathedral, 155–59; Rector of Wetheringsett church, 157–59; *Summa "Qui bene presunt,"* 4, 5, 143–59
Richard the Lionhearted, 34
Rickert, Edith, 18. *See also* Manly, John M., and Edith Rickert
Rieger, Dietmar, 22
Riehle, Wolfgang, 179
Rigg, A. G., 5, 161–77, 162n
Robbins, Rossell Hope, 15n, 18, 19n, 22n, 299, 300, 330n. *See also* Brown, Carleton, and R. H. Robbins
Robbins, Rossell Hope, and J. L. Cutler, 328n, 329n
Robert of Anjou, 275, 282, 284n, 285, 286, 287n, 294n, 295
Robertson, D. W., Jr., 31, 164n, 222n, 223n
Robertson, D. W., Jr., and Bernard Huppé, 98n, 114n
Robertus a Bergis, 254n
Robinson, F. N., 79
Robson, J. A., 201n, 204n
Roger of Weseham, 146
Rolevinck, Wernerus, *Fasciculus temporum*, 252
Rolle, Richard (hermit of Hampole), *Form of Living*, 181
Roman de la Rose (Guillaume de Lorris), 16, 18, 21
Roman de Renart, Branch II (Pierre de Saint Cloud), 26
Romer, Franz, 164n
Roney, Lois, 51n
Rouse, Mary A., and Richard H. Rouse, 88, 238n
Rowland, Beryl, 70n
Rudolphus, *Miracula sanctorum*, 238n

Ruffus, Maurice (le Rus), 154–55
Russell, George, 82
Russell, Josiah Cox, 153n
Rypon, Robert, 70n, 71

Saggese, Alessandra Perriccioli, 286n
Salerno, archbishops of, 282–83
Salter, Elizabeth, 51n
Salter, H. E., 199
Sarens, Georgius, 243n, 244n, 250, 251, 254n, 257n, 260
Sasbout, Adam (Adelphensis), *Sermones*, 254, 259
Satire, 130n
Sayce, Olive, 66n
Scarrier, Petrus, 288
Scase, Wendy, 90
Scattergood, John, 183n
Schmeller, A. G., and G. Meyer, 248n
Schmitt, Christian, 308n
Schneider, Robert J., 239n
Schneyer, Johannes Baptist, 263, 265–268n, 277, 321n, 323n
Scholastica, St., 252
Scholz, Richard, 276n
Scott, A. B., 162n
Scripta Leonis, 88
Scrope, Jane, 183
Sears, Elizabeth, 165n
Seasons, debate between, 162
Self-will, 162, 176–77
Semiramis, 21
Seneca, 68, 122, 123, 245
Senses, five, 163n, 166, 180
Seppelt, F. X., 286
Sermon, 5–9, 71, 121, 127, 179, 247n, 252, 254, 256–57, 263–73, 275–95; audience, 192; commemorative, 288–90, 292, 294; for Ash Wednesday, 163; funeral, 277, 282–86, 295; memorial, 286; model collections, 7, 263–64, 267–68, 273, 319, (in popular preaching) 267n; on nature and grace, 268–73; presentation copies (autograph manuscript), 276–95; sequences, 239; vernacular, 264, 273; Wycliffite, 192, 197, 199, (vernacular cycle)

195n, 202–3
Servansanto da Faenza, 7, 263–73
Seynaeve, Koen, 247n
Shannon, Edgar Finley, 44n
Sharples, Robert, 271n
Shaw, Judith, 73n
Sheepshead, Roger, *Summa de vitiis abbreviata*. See *Primo*
Sheridan, James, 122n
"Short Glosses" (Wycliffite), 201
Shrewsbury, 205
Sidonius Apollonaris, *Liber de naturis rerum*, 256
Sigebertus Gemblacensis, 253
Siger von Brabant, 266n
Silverstein, Theodore, 329n
Similitudes: confession (as chamberlain) 179, (as rumbling stomach) 108; death as knight with shield, 326; evangelical preaching as fish net, 227–28; in pastoral instruction, 147, 149; in teaching, 215, 223; Holy Spirit as fire and water, 149; lover as pike, 20; lover's pain as toothache, 21; meekness as pillow, 179; Penitence (as chamberer) 180, (as indigestion) 108; saints as teeth of church, 223; seven vices as seven chains, 165; sins as thralldom, 68; tongue (as fire) 120, 142, (as pen of Holy Spirit) 129, 132, (as unruly beast) 135. *See also* Food, Imagery
Sin(s), 5; adultery in the heart, 163; as thralldom, 68; causes of, 165; consequences of, 161, 171, (external sorrows) 172–77, (internal languor) 171–72; malice in speech, 163n; of omission or commission, 150–51, 181; of speech, 167n, 168–69; of thought, word, deed, 146, 150–51, 181; original, 164, 172; process of (suggestion, delight, consent), 161, 163–64, 166–69; psychology of, 85; three degrees of, 163. *See also* Tongue, Vices, Virtues
Sinclair, J. D., 30n

Sinon, 30
Sir Gawain and the Green Knight, 15, 54
Skeat, Walter W., 12, 13, 14n, 17, 128n
Skelton, John, *Philip Sparrow,* 183
Skirlawe, Bishop, 195
Slyght, Dorothe, 184
Smalley, Beryl, 32, 204n
Smith, Ben H., 11n
Smyth, *Greek Grammar,* 107n
Snappe's Formulary, 199
Socrates, 39
Soldier, 162, 171, 176–77
Solinus, *Collectanea,* 173n
Sonet, J. S. J., 302n
Song of Roland, 46, 55
Source study, criteria of (density, rarity, context, utility), 115–17
Spade, Paul Vincent, 202n
Speciale, Niccoló, *Historia sicula,* 283n
Speculum Christiani, 183
Speght, Thomas, 62
Spencer, Helen, 191n
Sphinx, riddle of, 175
Statius, *Thebaid,* 43
Stegmüller, Fridericus, 238n, 246n, 252n, 321n
Stemmler, Theo, 2, 11–23, 15n, 17n, 19n
Stephan V of Hungary, 280–81
Sterne, Lawrence, 30
Stevens, John, 310n, 315n
Stevens, Wallace, 40
Stow, John, 62
Straw, Jack, 34, 36
Style: high, 29; sacred stylistics, 6, 210–22; scriptural, 216–17, (obscurity of) 222–23
Summa theologica, 321–23
Summa virtutum de remediis anime, 3, 67, 179. *See also Postquam, Primo*
Sundby, Thor, 119n, 123n
Suso, Henry, 179; *Horologium sapientiae,* 245
Swinburn, Lilian M., 196
Syon Abbey, 182–84; prayer beads, 183

Szoverffy, Joseph, 308n

"Taas," 45, 49
Tachau, Katherine H., 209n
Talbert, Ernest W., 194n–95
Tale of Beryn, 12, 17, 18
Tatlock, J. S. P., and Arthur G. Kennedy, 71n
Tavormina, M. Theresa, 115n
Taylor, Daniel S., and Joseph Goering, 146n
"Temenos," 46n
Theodolus, *De moribus,* 246
Theology, 210, 320; affective or speculative, 234; doctrinal controversies in thirteenth century, 209; elegance and wisdom in, 220–22, 233; four causes of, 211; its audience, 210–19, 229, (carnal Christians in) 227–30, (diverse capacity of) 222–35, (heretics in) 225, 228–29, (spiritual men in) 230, (uneducated listeners in) 224–29, (women in) 228; and knowledge, 211, 214–15; origins of, 235; polysemy of, 232–34, 240; science of, 210, 214n, 230–32; style in (clear) 218–19, 224, (eloquent) 217, 219, (obscure) 215–17, (ornate) 213–14, 218, 221, (profound) 224, (simple) 213–17, 229; teacher of, 211, 216–17, 221, 232–33
Theophilus (Pseudo-Theophilus Antiochenus), 246
Thomas Cantipratensis, *Liber de apibus,* 247
Thomas Hemerken à Kempis, 325n, 247n, 254; *Hospitale pauperum,* 325n
Thomas of Chobham, *Summa confessorum,* 143, 149
Thomson, Williell R., 194n, 198n
Thorndike, L., and Pearl Kibre, 301–3
Thorpe, William, 191, 203n, 205, 207; "The Examination," 195
Thynne, Francis, 62, 63
Timotheus Historiographus, 252
Tithing, 152; of prostitute, 85–86; of usurer, 85–86, 89

Tobler, Adolf, and Erhard Lommatzsch, 313n
Todd, James Henthorn, 192n
Tolkien, J. R. R., 15n
Tongeren: bishops of, 255; princes of, 255
Tongue: as fire, 120, 142; as pen of Holy Spirit, 129, 132; as unruly beast, 135; evil progeny, 121–22; evil speaking, 123–24; guarding, 121; sins of, 4, 73, 82, 119–42, 244, (blasphemy) 135, 141, (mendacium) 124–26, 140–41, (multiloquium) 124, (otiosa verba) 132, 134, (peccati defensio) 127, 141, (peccatum bilinguium) 121, 128–29, 137, 141, (turpiloquium) 130, 134, 142, (remedies for) 122; wicked, 121. See also Sin(s)
Toothache, compared to lover's pain, 21
Tornacensis, Guillibertus, 246
Tournai, 209n
Tournaments, in preaching, 277–78n
Townsend, D., and A. G. Rigg, 315n
Tractatus de oblacione iugis sacrificii, 195–96
Trajan, 131
Translation, 40; literal, 32, 33; of Latin hymns, 300
Tretyse of Gostly Batayle, A, 325n
Tristram, Philippa, 39, 40, 330n
Troy, destruction of, 14
Trudo, St.: Benedictine abbey of, 237–61; chronicle of, 245
Trudo of Gembloux, 7; Collectarium, 241–61, (colophons in) 249–51, 258, (death figure drawing in) 249, (redactions of) 252–61, (sources of) 245–48, 252–56, 259; compiler and author, 259–61; use of engravings, 7, 248–49
Turrecremata, John (Cardinal), 246
Twelve Conclusions, 199
Typology, biblical, 3, 36
Tyrwhitt, Thomas, 63

Ubi sunt tradition, 58

Ughelli, Ferdinando, 283n
Uhlirz, M., 281n
Underwood, Malcolm, 155n
Urban, St., 298n
Urban, Pope, 195
Utrecht, bishops of, 255

Vaissier, J. J., 180n
Varro, Marcus, 255
Vasta, Edward, 16n
Vauchez, André, 278n, 286
Vecchio, Silvano, 120n
Venditti, Arnaldo, 285n
Veneto, Paolino, Satyrica historia, 288n
Verjans, Matthaeus, 247n
Via recta, 109–12; humility, obedience, and charity in Piers Plowman, 110–14
Vices, 3, 4, 244–45, 252–53, 272, 293; avarice, 81–96, 84n, 85, 125, 137, 141, 150, 205, (theft as part of) 84n, 85n, 86–87, (trades as dependent on) 86; envy, 52, 93n, 104, 127, 141, 205; gluttony, 67, 115, 117, 127, 132, 205; lechery, 141, 205, 264, 327–28; pride, 71–72, 136, 150, 205, 215, 219, 225, 228; seven capital, 5, 82, 121, 127, 133, 136, 140, 144, 146, 149–50, 162, 244, 252, 264n, (as seven chains) 165, (numerical analysis of) 150, (remedies for) 149, 244, 252; sloth, 81–83, 124, 127, 133, 141; threefold (1 John 2.16), 150; usury, 85; wrath, 72–73, 81, 90, 127. See also Enemies of Humankind, Sin(s), Tongue, Virtues
Vincent of Beauvais, 239n, 246; Speculum Historiale, 173n, 255
Vinsauf, Geoffrey of, 30, 34
Virga directionis, 247
Virgil, Aeneid, 33, 44
Viris illustribus ordinis Cisterciensis, Liber de, 253
Virtues, 4, 245, 252–53; cardinal, 5, 121–22, 141, 144, 180; charity, 110–14, 134–35, 137–38, 226;

courage, 48; devotion, 48; fear, 245; hope, 138; humility, 106, 110–14, 225, 245; justice, 162; kindness, 101, (liberality and good will constituents of) 101; loyalty, 48; meekness, as pillow on bed of conscience, 179; moderation, 225; obedience, 110–14, 245, 287; obedience as food, 112; patience, 98, 108–17, 245; prudence, 4, (as remedy against sins of the tongue) 122–25, 128, 130, 133–42, (three degrees of) 122n; seven, 146, 149; theological, 5, 121, 139, 144, 180. *See also* Sin(s), Vices

Virtutibus imitandis, De, 162

Vita sancti Francisci, 246

Vita sancti Trudonis confessoris apud Hasbanos, 248n

Vitae patrum, 246

von Nolcken, Christina, 6, 191–208, 193n, 194n, 195n, 197n, 199, 201, 203n, 205n

Wackernagel, Wilhelm, 179

Wager, W. J., 184n

Walter of Cantilupe (Bishop of Worcester), 146

Walther, Hans, 161n, 301, 302, 305n, 310n, 315, 316n

Wanderer, The, 58

Wang, Andreas, 325n, 326n

Warner, George F., and Julius P. Gilson, 155n, 305n

Watson, Andrew G., 161n

Weathershed, Richard. *See* Richard of Wetheringsett

Welsh, national stereotype of, 83–84

Wenzel, Siegfried, 1–10, 61n, 64–65, 67n–69n, 75n, 76n, 81, 82, 84n, 121n, 143, 146n, 148n, 152n, 179, 263, 299, 319, 321n, 330n, 331n; *The Sin of Sloth*, 95, 120n, 124n, 143n; *Verses in Sermons*, 182n, 327n, 328n

Whiting, E. K., 181n

Wilks, Michael, 207n

William de Montibus, 154n, 156n,

158; *Errorum eliminatio*, 151; *Numerale*, 147

William of Mailli, 322n

William of Montoriel, *Summa predicamentorum*, 298, 303

William of Paris, 246

William of St. Amour, 98n

Wilson, Edward, 300n

Wimsatt, James, 13n

Windesheim Congregation, 241

Wireker, Nigel, *Burnellus* or *Speculum stultorum*, 34

Wisdom: feast of, 99, 100, 116; proverbial, 29; relationship to eloquence, 6; worldly, 102–8, 117; prideful, 106

Wolpers, Th., 299, 304n

Women, 30–31, 33; and worms, 20; as passive sufferers, 56–57; "conseils" of, 30, 56, 57, 68, 69

Wooden, Warren, 321n

Wooldridge, H. E., and H. V. Hughes, 316n

Woolf, Rosemary, 299n, 304n, 308n, 317n, 328n

Workman, Herbert, 197n

Wounds of Jesus, as source of healing, 312

Wright, Neil, 305n

Wright, Thomas, and J. O. Halliwell, 329n

Wurtele, Douglas, 62n

Wyche, Richard, "The Trial," 195, 200

Wyclif, John, 6, 33, 192n, 193, 201–7; *De amore sive ad Quinque quaestiones*, 199n; *Glossed Gospels*, 196, 198–99; *Opus imperfectum in Matthaeum*, 197n; *Tractatus de ecclesia*, 204n; *Tractatus de universalibus*, 202n; *Twelve Conclusions*, 199; *De ve octuplici*, 204n; *De veritate sacre scripture*, 204n

Wycliffites, 6, 191–208; Bible, 180n, 204, (commentaries on) 199, (translation of) 191, 195, 198–99; discussion of church, 203–4; realism of, 202–6; resolution for, 206–

7; secrecy of, 201; teachers, 191;
texts, 191–208, (anonymity of)
198n, 201n, (erasure of information in, 201n, (generalization in)
195–206, (group audience for)
200–203, 206, (group work on)
199–200, (opinions in) 194, (overall mode) 194, (presentation of self
in) 198–99, (sameness of) 6, 191–
208, (vocabulary of, 194, 198, 200;
value of unity for, 206–7

Yates, Frances, 329n
"Yeres3iues," 106
Young, Karl, 307n
Ypma, Eelcko, 284n
Ysaac medicus, 255
Yunck, John, 106n

Zacour, Norman, 155n
Zafarana, Zelina, 266n
Zoroaster, 173
Zumkeller, Adolar, 247n, 256n

Richard G. Newhauser, Associate Professor of English at Trinity University, San Antonio, Texas, has held research grants from Fulbright, The National Endowment for the Humanities, and Deutsche Forschungsgemeinschaft. He has published on Gawain in *Studies in Philology*, and on Petrus von Limoges in *Exempel und Exempelsammlungen* (Tübingen). A book, *The Treatise on Vices and Virtues in Latin and the Vernacular* is forthcoming by Turnhout, Belgium.

John A. Alford, Professor of English at Michigan State University, has held fellowships with Guggenheim, The National Endowwment for the Humanities. and the California Humanities Institute. Among his books are: *English Romanticism: Preludes and Postludes*, (ed.) (Colleagues Press, 1993); *Piers Plowman: A Guide to the Quotations*, Medieval & Renaissance Texts & Studies, vol. 77 (Binghamton, 1992); *Piers Plowman: A Glossary of Legal Diction* (Boydell and Brewer, 1988); *A Companion to Piers Plowman*, ed. (Berkeley, 1988); *Literature and Law in the Middle Ages: A Bibliography of Scholarship* (with Dennis P. Seniff), (Garland, 1984); as well as numerous articles in *PMLA, Speculum, Medium Aevum, Modern Philology, Modern Language Quarterly, Chaucer Review.*

ꝯRTS

ꝰEꝺIEVAL & ꝶENAISSANCE TEXTS & STUꝺIES
is the publishing program of the
Center for Medieval and Early Renaissance Studies
at the State University of New York at Binghamton.

ꝯRTS emphasizes books that are needed —
texts, translations, and major research tools.

ꝯRTS aims to publish the highest quality scholarship
in attractive and durable format at modest cost.